T0332775

Handbook of Research on Applied Data Science and Artificial Intelligence in Business and Industry

Valentina Chkoniya
University of Aveiro, Portugal

Volume 2

A volume in the Advances in Business Information
Systems and Analytics (ABISA) Book Series

Published in the United States of America by
    IGI Global
    Engineering Science Reference (an imprint of IGI Global)
    701 E. Chocolate Avenue
    Hershey PA, USA 17033
    Tel: 717-533-8845
    Fax: 717-533-8661
    E-mail: cust@igi-global.com
    Web site: http://www.igi-global.com

Library of Congress Cataloging-in-Publication Data

Names: Chkoniya, Valentina, 1977- editor.
Title: Handbook of research on applied data science and artificial
  intelligence in business and industry / Valentina Chkoniya, editor.
Description: Hershey : Engineering Science Reference, 2021. I Includes
  bibliographical references and index. I Summary: "This book provides an
  overview of the concepts, tools and techniques behind the increasing
  field of Data Science and Artificial Intelligence, applied to business
  and industries"-- Provided by publisher.
Identifiers: LCCN 2020058395 (print) I LCCN 2020058396 (ebook) I ISBN
  9781799869856 (hardcover) I ISBN 9781799869863 (ebook)
Subjects: LCSH: Business--Technological innovations. I Databases. I
  Artificial intelligence.
Classification: LCC HD45 .H2934 2021 (print) I LCC HD45 (ebook) I DDC
  338.00285/57--dc23
LC record available at https://lccn.loc.gov/2020058395
LC ebook record available at https://lccn.loc.gov/2020058396

This book is published in the IGI Global book series Advances in Business Information Systems and Analytics (ABISA) (ISSN: 2327-3275; eISSN: 2327-3283)

British Cataloguing in Publication Data
A Cataloguing in Publication record for this book is available from the British Library.

For electronic access to this publication, please contact: eresources@igi-global.com.

Advances in Business Information Systems and Analytics (ABISA) Book Series

Madjid Tavana
La Salle University, USA

ISSN:2327-3275
EISSN:2327-3283

MISSION

The successful development and management of information systems and business analytics is crucial to the success of an organization. New technological developments and methods for data analysis have allowed organizations to not only improve their processes and allow for greater productivity, but have also provided businesses with a venue through which to cut costs, plan for the future, and maintain competitive advantage in the information age.

The **Advances in Business Information Systems and Analytics (ABISA) Book Series** aims to present diverse and timely research in the development, deployment, and management of business information systems and business analytics for continued organizational development and improved business value.

COVERAGE

- Data Governance
- Business Models
- Business Intelligence
- Business Systems Engineering
- Legal information systems
- Big Data
- Information Logistics
- Business Information Security
- Performance Metrics
- Forecasting

IGI Global is currently accepting manuscripts for publication within this series. To submit a proposal for a volume in this series, please contact our Acquisition Editors at Acquisitions@igi-global.com or visit: http://www.igi-global.com/publish/.

Titles in this Series

For a list of additional titles in this series, please visit: www.igi-global.com/book-series/advances-business-information-systems-analytics/37155

Business Applications in Social Media Analytics
Himani Bansal (Jaypee University, Solan, India) and Gulshan Shrivastava (National Institute of Technology, Patna, India)
Business Science Reference • © 2021 • 330pp • H/C (ISBN: 9781799850465) • US $195.00

Using Strategy Analytics to Measure Corporate Performance and Business Value Creation
Sandeep Kautish (Lord Buddha Education Foundation, Nepal)
Business Science Reference • © 2021 • 315pp • H/C (ISBN: 9781799877165) • US $225.00

Adapting and Mitigating Environmental, Social, and Governance Risk in Business
Magdalena Ziolo (University of Szczecin, Poland)
Business Science Reference • © 2021 • 313pp • H/C (ISBN: 9781799867883) • US $195.00

Innovative and Agile Contracting for Digital Transformation and Industry 4.0
Mohammad Ali Shalan (Aqarat Real Estate Development Company, Saudi Arabia) and Mohammed Ayedh Algarni (Information and Documents Center, Institute of Public Administration, Saudi Arabia)
Business Science Reference • © 2021 • 415pp • H/C (ISBN: 9781799845010) • US $225.00

Opportunities and Strategic Use of Agribusiness Information Systems
Ferdinand Ndifor Che (W3-Research, USA & APPC Research, Australia) Kenneth David Strang (W3-Research, USA & APPC Research, Australia) and Narasimha Rao Vajjhala (University of New York Tirana, Albania)
Business Science Reference • © 2021 • 333pp • H/C (ISBN: 9781799848493) • US $195.00

Integration Challenges for Analytics, Business Intelligence, and Data Mining
Ana Azevedo (CEOS:PP, ISCAP, Polytechnic of Porto, Portugal) and Manuel Filipe Santos (Algoritmi Centre, University of Minho, Guimarães, Portugal)
Engineering Science Reference • © 2021 • 250pp • H/C (ISBN: 9781799857815) • US $225.00

Managing Business in the Civil Construction Sector Through Information Communication Technologies
Bithal Das Mundhra (Simplex Infrastructures Ltd, India) and Rajesh Bose (Simplex Infrastructures Ltd, India)
Business Science Reference • © 2021 • 254pp • H/C (ISBN: 9781799852919) • US $195.00

701 East Chocolate Avenue, Hershey, PA 17033, USA
Tel: 717-533-8845 x100 • Fax: 717-533-8661
E-Mail: cust@igi-global.com • www.igi-global.com

Editorial Advisory Board

Nandini Sen, *Heriot Watt University, UK*
Dora Simões, *University of Aveiro, Portugal*
Adalberto Tokarski, *National Waterway Transportation Agency, Brazil*
Ana Tomé, *University of Aveiro, Portugal*

List of Contributors

Table of Contents

Section 1
Strategy

Chapter 1
José Luís Cacho, Port of Sines, Portugal
Adalberto Tokarski, National Waterway Transportation Agency, Brazil
Elizabete Thomas, National Waterway Transportation Agency, Brazil
Valentina Chkoniya, University of Aveiro, Portugal

Chapter 2
Petra Heck, Fontys University of Applied Sciences, The Netherlands
Gerard Schouten, Fontys University of Applied Sciences, The Netherlands
Luís Cruz, Delft University of Technology, The Netherlands

Chapter 3
Mónica Jiménez-Hernández, Universidad de Colima, Mexico
Purificación Vicente-Galindo, University of Salamanca, Spain
Nathalia Tejedor-Flores, Universidad Tecnológica de Panamá, Panama
Adelaide Freitas, University of Aveiro, Portugal
Purificación Galindo, University of Salamanca, Spain

Chapter 4
Niguissie Mengesha, Brock University, Canada
Anteneh Ayanso, Brock University, Canada

Section 2
Action

Section 3
Reflection

Detailed Table of Contents

Section 1
Strategy

Chapter 1

José Luís Cacho, Port of Sines, Portugal
Adalberto Tokarski, National Waterway Transportation Agency, Brazil
Elizabete Thomas, National Waterway Transportation Agency, Brazil
Valentina Chkoniya, University of Aveiro, Portugal

The maritime supply chain is growing in complexity. Ports are at the crossroads of many activities, modes, and stakeholders, and are actively becoming digital hubs. Today, digital and physical connectivity go hand in hand. The port could benefit from taping the opportunities arising from digitalization and data integration since it helps to leverage external knowledge, engage stakeholders, create new decision-making anchors, lower the risk of certain investments, boost productivity and cut costs, and accelerate greening and digital transition, generating possibilities for just-in-time operations and optimizations. The chapter aims to apprehend the use of data science in the port sector. The state of the art in Brazil and Portugal are different. Even inside Brazil, there is no homogeneity of ports in the usage of digital infrastructure, cloud computing, or artificial intelligence. The existing inequalities hinder general cooperation between nations but, at the same time, reveal opportunities to approach specific nodes in the international supply chain.

Chapter 2

Petra Heck, Fontys University of Applied Sciences, The Netherlands
Gerard Schouten, Fontys University of Applied Sciences, The Netherlands
Luís Cruz, Delft University of Technology, The Netherlands

This chapter discusses how to build production-ready machine learning systems. There are several challenges involved in accomplishing this, each with its specific solutions regarding practices and tool support. The chapter presents those solutions and introduces MLOps (machine learning operations, also called machine learning engineering) as an overarching and integrated approach in which data engineers, data scientists, software engineers, and operations engineers integrate their activities to implement validated machine learning applications managed from initial idea to daily operation in a production environment. This approach combines agile software engineering processes with the machine learning-specific workflow. Following the principles of MLOps is paramount in building high-quality production-ready machine learning systems. The current state of MLOps is discussed in terms of best practices and tool support. The chapter ends by describing future developments that are bound to improve and extend the tool support for implementing an MLOps approach.

    Mónica Jiménez-Hernández, Universidad de Colima, Mexico
    Purificación Vicente-Galindo, University of Salamanca, Spain
    Nathalia Tejedor-Flores, Universidad Tecnológica de Panamá, Panama
    Adelaide Freitas, University of Aveiro, Portugal
    Purificación Galindo, University of Salamanca, Spain

The main objective of this research is to find the sustainability gradients of Global Fortune 500 companies and sort them as a function of economic, environmental, and social components using multivariate statistical methods to establish the foundations for better knowledge of the trends and sustainability reporting habits. A combined approach, comprising principal coordinates analysis (PCoA) and logistic regression model (LRM), is proposed to build an external logistics biplot (ELB). Moreover, HJ-Biplot and parallel coordinates are applied. This chapter helps to understand why many companies view their corporate social responsibility (CSR) reports as a way to guarantee the credibility of the published information. In particular, based on the Global Reporting Initiative, the sustainability gradients of the Global Fortune 500 companies are obtained and statistically exploited to analyze how the companies can make improvements in terms of sustainability.

    Niguissie Mengesha, Brock University, Canada
    Anteneh Ayanso, Brock University, Canada

Several initiatives have tried to measure the efforts nations have made towards developing e-government. The UN E-Government Development Index (EGDI) is the only global report that ranks and classifies the UN Member States into four categories based on a weighted average of normalized scores on online service, telecom infrastructure, and human capital. The authors argue that the EGDI fails in showing the efforts of nations over time and in informing nations and policymakers as to what and from whom to draw policy lessons. Using the UN EGDI data from 2008 to 2020, they profile the UN Member States and show the relevance of machine learning techniques in addressing these issues. They examine the resulting cluster profiles in terms of theoretical perspectives in the literature and derive policy insights from the different groupings of nations and their evolution over time. Finally, they discuss the policy implications of the proposed methodology and the insights obtained.

    Nicola Del Sarto, Scuola Superiore Sant'Anna, Italy
    Andrea Piccaluga, Scuola Superiore Sant'Anna, Italy

Artificial intelligence is profoundly changing the way in which companies compete and do business. In particular, artificial intelligence can represent a very interesting opportunity for small and medium-sized enterprises, which are constantly looking for new technologies to be able to remain competitive in a turbulent market. However, research exploring how SMEs may successfully adopt artificial intelligence technology are missing. To address this gap, the authors reviewed the literature on artificial intelligence and identified four key features that SMEs need to consider when implementing this technology represented by people, processes, products, and customers. After that they described four cases of Italian SMEs which have adopted successfully this new technology taking into account one of the four dimensions. The study contributes to the literature on artificial intelligence and SMEs and may be helpful for managers who want to adopt this technology within their company.

Chapter 6

    Jacques R. J. Bughin, Université libre de Bruxelles, Belgium
    Michele Cincera, Université libre de Bruxelles, Belgium
    Dorota Reykowska, NEUROHM, Poland
    Rafał Ohme, WSB University in Torun, Poland

Data science has been proven to be an important asset to support better decision making in a variety of settings, whether it is for a scientist to better predict climate change for a company to better predict sales or for a government to anticipate voting preferences. In this research, the authors leverage random forest (RF) as one of the most effective machine learning techniques using big data to predict vaccine intent in five European countries. The findings support the idea that outside of vaccine features, building adequate perception of the risk of contamination, and securing institutional and peer trust are key nudges to convert skeptics to get vaccinated against COVID-19. What machine learning techniques further add beyond traditional regression techniques is some extra granularity in factors affecting vaccine preferences (twice more factors than logistic regression). Other factors that emerge as predictors of vaccine intent are compliance appetite with non-pharmaceutical protective measures as well as perception of the crisis duration.

Chapter 7

    Elissa Moses, Columbia University, USA & BrainGroup Global, USA
    Kimberly Rose Clark, Dartmouth College, USA & Bellwether Citizen Response, USA
    Norman J. Jacknis, Columbia University, USA & Intelligent Community Forum, USA

This chapter summarizes the role that artificial intelligence and machine learning (AI/ML) are expected to play at every stage of advertising development, assessment, and execution. Together with advances in neuroscience for measuring attention, cognitive processing, emotional response, and memory, AI/ML have advanced to a point where analytics can be used to identify variables that drive more effective advertising and predict enhanced performance. In addition, the cost of computation has declined, making platforms to apply these tools much less expensive and within reach. The authors then offer recommendations for 1) understanding the clients/customers and users of the products and services that will be advertised, 2) aiding creativity in the process of designing advertisements, 3) testing the impact of advertisements, and 4) identifying the optimum placement of advertisements.

Standard approaches to measure price index on a specific retailer against competitors tend to be overly optimistic. The authors propose a methodology that deflects from analyzing solely the price of all products effectively bought by customers by taking into consideration their prior shopping intention. Loyalty schemes are game changers when measuring price index. The study proposes a two-step methodology that comprises on building the customer native baskets and allocating the prices collected to each customer. Under the assumption that a price sensitive customer will not buy a poorly priced product compared to the competitors in that specific period, the authors present an innovative methodology resulting in a more realistic price index metric.

Data science has established itself as a discipline of study in the new technological paradigm of the 21st century. Customer data and metadata are not only unique opportunities for companies that are interested in collecting, processing, and elaborating useful information for customer-centric business management. They are also starting to feed other disciplines, such as industry and computer engineering, which are developing new ways of organising information and intelligent response, where significant technological advances in facial, sensory, text, voice, and image recognition are constantly emerging, with response capabilities ever closer to human thinking. From this continuous interaction emerges a new asset for companies: knowledge. Thus, science applied to data is consolidating as an opportunity for companies in customer loyalty and retention by being able to include a relevant aspect in human relations such as warmth and empathy, basis of marketing 5.0, oriented once again towards human relations, from a virtual existence and total digitalisation.

This chapter discusses the sentiment classification of text messages containing customer reviews of an online restaurant service system using machine-learning methods, in particular text mining and multivariate text sentiment analysis. The study determines the structure of value proposition factors based on online restaurant reviews on TripAdvisor, collecting information on consumer preferences and the restaurant services in St. Petersburg (Russia) quality assessment and examines the influence of service format and reviews tonality on ratings restaurants factors. The service format context is proposed as the main attribute influencing the formation of the restaurant business value proposition and of relevance for online reviews. The results showed the key factors in the study of the sentiment were cuisine and dishes, reviews and ratings, and targeted search. MANOVA analysis represented that for special offers and features, reviews and ratings, factors and quantitative star ratings influenced the negative and positive sentiment of online reviews significantly.

Chapter 11

    Clony Junior, IEETA, University of Aveiro, Portugal
    Pedro Gusmão, IEETA, University of Aveiro, Portugal
    José Moreira, DETI, University of Aveiro, Portugal
    Ana Maria M. Tome, DETI, University of Aveiro, Portugal

Data science highlights fields of study and research such as time series, which, although widely explored in the past, gain new perspectives in the context of this discipline. This chapter presents two approaches to time series forecasting, long short-term memory (LSTM), a special kind of recurrent neural network (RNN), and Prophet, an open-source library developed by Facebook for time series forecasting. With a focus on developing forecasting processes by data mining or machine learning experts, LSTM uses gating mechanisms to deal with long-term dependencies, reducing the short-term memory effect inherent to the traditional RNN. On the other hand, Prophet encapsulates statistical and computational complexity to allow broad use of time series forecasting, prioritizing the expert's business knowledge through exploration and experimentation. Both approaches were applied to a retail time series. This case study comprises daily and half-hourly forecasts, and the performance of both methods was measured using the standard metrics.

Chapter 12

    Maria João Lopes, Bosch Termotecnologia SA, Portugal & University of Aveiro, Portugal
    Eugénio M. Rocha, University of Aveiro, Portugal
    Petia Georgieva Georgieva, University of Aveiro, Portugal
    Nelson Ferreira, Bosch Termotecnologia SA, Portugal

In this chapter, a comprehensive description of a generic framework aimed at solving various predictive data-driven related use cases, occurring in the manufacturing industry, is provided. The framework is rooted in a general mathematical model so called queue directed graph (QDG). With the aid of QDGs and containerized microservices implementations, the typology of the system is analyzed, and real use cases are explained. The goal is for this framework to be able to be used with all use cases which fit in this typology. As an example, a data generation distribution model is proposed, the parameter stability and predictive robustness are studied, and automated machine learning approaches are discussed to predict the throughput time of products in a manufacturing production line just by knowing the processing time in their first stations.

Sandra Maria Correia Loureiro, ISCTE, BRU, Instituto Universitário de Lisboa, Portugal
Muhammad Ashfaq, Shenzhen University, China
Mariana Oliveira Berga Rodrigues, ISCTE, Instituto Universitário de Lisboa, Portugal

Artificial intelligence (AI) algorithms have been continuously adopted in businesses, such as retailing, hospitality, and tourism. The current chapter aims first to provide a conceptualization of evolution of AI. Second, it gives an overview of AI in business and finally points out examples of applications of AI in retailing, hospitality, and tourism. Third, the chapter offers suggestions for further research. This chapter is devoted to researchers and practitioners. The audience will benefit from an overview of AI meaning and potential research to be developed and also benefit from examples of other business that already employ such AI algorithms.

Chapter 14

Alfonso Infante-Moro, University of Huelva, Spain
Juan C. Infante-Moro, University of Huelva, Spain
Julia Gallardo-Pérez, University of Huelva, Spain

Artificial intelligence is one of the most innovative and trending technologies in the hotel sector. It is transforming the hotel sector into a novel environment in business-client relationships. For this reason, this study seeks to find, through a literary review and a causal study carried out by experts in technologies and hotels, using the methodology of fuzzy cognitive maps, what the determining factors in the decision of hotels to accept and implement artificial intelligence in their hotels and in their services are. The list obtained is made up of the following factors (in order of relevance in this decision): top management support, perceived reliability of the technology, security, relative advantage, support from information systems providers, technological organizational readiness, government pressure or incentives, compatibility, business partner pressure, customer pressure, complexity, pressure from competitors, perceived cost, characteristics of the leader or manager, and size of the company.

Yezelia Danira Caceres Cabana, Universidad Nacional de San Agustín de Arequipa, Peru
David Aguilar del Carpio, Universidad Nacional de San Agustín de Arequipa, Peru
Erika Velásquez Chacón, Universidad Católica San Pablo, Peru
Juan Mardonio Rivera Medina, Universidad Continental Perú, Peru

The pandemic caused by COVID-19 has led many states, in an attempt to control the spread of the virus, to decree social immobilization, which meant the introduction of restrictions on the free movement of people and the opening of shops. This led them to seek new marketing channels for purchases. Among these, ICTs have been important. This is the focus of the analysis in this document. Through surveys and interviews, information was obtained, divided into four age groups, which showed that an important part of the population has had to resort to ICTs to acquire goods and/or pay for services. This change in the way of acquiring had different particularities according to the age group analyzed, with a greater change in the oldest group (56 to 74 years old). It can be concluded that the massification of these tools has generated a change in the ways of acquiring products, and this is likely to transcend the pandemic and these channels will be maintained and strengthened in the future.

Chapter 16

The purpose of this chapter is to shed light on the consumer-AI interaction in the marketplace. By this aim, the chapter uses a literature review approach. The previous literature examining AI from a consumer behavior perspective is reviewed, and the findings are compiled in a meaningful flow. According to the review, we see that the traditional marketplace is shaped by AI from only human-to-human interactions to human-to-AI and AI-to-AI interactions. In this new marketplace, while consumers interact with AI, they gain new experiences and feel positive or negative because of these experiences. Also, they build different relationships with AI, such as servant, master, or partner. Besides these relationships, there are still concerns about AI that are related to privacy, algorithmic biases, consumer vulnerability, unemployment, and ethical decision making.

Chapter 17

Co-branding in the hospitality luxury sector is still understudied in the literature. This study aims at tackling this gap through the analysis of a case of a co-branding strategy between a vinous-concept luxury hotel in Portugal and premium wine brands of domestic producers. Fourteen in-depth interviews with managers of the luxury hotel and wine brand partners supported the exploratory research. This chapter represents a case of qualitative data application to an underestimated topic in the literature from the managers' point of view. The study offers evidence on the benefits for both parties, reasons for adopting co-branding, and partners' selection attributes. The improvement of brand image emerges as one of the main advantages of co-branding with a luxury hotel. Based on the literature review and the interviews with managers, the study proposes a set of hypotheses to be tested in future research. This chapter provides interesting cues for academics and practitioners.

Chapter 18

This chapter identifies the critical issues that must be addressed to accelerate the digital transition in the chartering market. The maritime industry is one of the pillars of global trade, where change is a constant. Again, shipping is at the cusp of a new era—one driven by data. The authors review the state-of-the-art technology that is useful to automate chartering processes. · The Fourth Industrial Revolution (or Industry 4.0) starts to change the bulk shipping markets leveraging the data flow between industrial processes in the physical and virtual world. · The internet of things accelerates data flow from things in the real world to the virtual world and enables us to control processes in real-time. Machine-to-machine communication, together with artificial intelligence, creates autonomous systems in many areas of production and logistics. Based on the gathered elements, eShip's case study was analyzed, and future steps have been defined for the data analysis in the shipping industry.

    Riddhi Patel, Charotar University of Science and Technology, India
    Parth Patel, Charotar University of Science and Technology, India
    Chintan M. Bhatt, Charotar University of Science and Technology, India
    Mrugendrasinh L. Rahevar, Charotar University of Science and Technology, India

Manipulation of a large amount of data becomes a very tedious task. Hence, the authors took the approach of memory networks for the implementation of the chatbot. Traditionally, the LSTM model was used to implement chatbots and QA systems. But the LSTM failed to store relevant information when given a longer information set. On the contrary, the memory networks have an additional memory component with it. This can help in storing long information for further use which is greatly advantageous for the QA and chatbot systems as compared to LSTM. The authors trained and tested their model over Facebook's bAbi dataset which consists of several tasks and has questions regarding each task to retrieve the accuracy of the model. On the pedestal of that dataset, they have presented the accuracy for every task in their study with memory networks.

    Tamer Baran, Pamukkale University, Turkey

The aim of this chapter is to reveal whether the results of the analysis of the data obtained using Likert type scales (LTSs) with parametric and non-parametric methods in different response alternative (DRA) numbers will differ in terms of statistical significance. In this respect, the data were obtained from 271 university students with CETSCALE prepared using LTS in five different response alternatives (DRAs). The data were analysed using the one sample t test and Wilcoxon signed rank test. Significant findings of the study in the analysis of the data obtained using midpoint LTSs and with the normal distribution with both parametric and non-parametric methods couldn't be found. Similarly, the data obtained by four response alternative numbers with the normal distribution were analysed by both methods, and the significant findings were revealed. However, the results of the data obtained by six and eight response alternative numbers with parametric methods were found to be statistically significant while their analysis by non-parametric methods did not reveal significant findings.

    Shadi M. S. Hilles, Istanbul Okan University, Turkey
    Abdilahi Deria Liban, Hargeisa University, Somalia
    Abdullah M. M. Altrad, Al-Madinah International University, Malaysia
    Yousef A. Baker El-Ebiary, Universiti Sultan Zainal Abidin, Malaysia
    Mohanad M. Hilles, University College of Applied Science, Palestine

The chapter presents latent fingerprint enhancement technique for enforcement agencies to identify criminals. There are many challenges in the area of latent fingerprinting due to poor-quality images, which consist of unclear ridge structure and overlapping patterns with structure noise. Image enhancement is important to suppress several different noises for improving accuracy of ridge structure. The chapter presents a combination of edge directional total variation model, EDTV, and quality image enhancement with lost minutia re-construction, RMSE, for evaluation and performance in the proposed algorithm. The result shows the average of three different image categories which are extracted from the SD7 dataset, and the assessments are good, bad, and ugly, respectively. The result of RMSE before and after enhancement shows the performance ratio of the proposed method is better for latent fingerprint images compared to bad and ugly images while there is not much difference with performance of bad and ugly.

Chapter 22

In this chapter, the author presents an artificial intelligence (AI)-based generic concept for decision making using data science. The applied holistic mathematical model for AI (AHMM4AI) focuses on data and access management. A decisive business decision in a business transformation process of a traditional business environment into an automated AI-based business environment is the capacity of the decision-making system and the profile of the business transformation manager (BTM, or simply the manager). The manager and his team are supported by a holistic framework. The role of data science and the needed data modelling techniques are essential for managing data models in a transformation project. For that reason, the development of the big data for AI (BGD4AI) is an essential start.

Chapter 23

Making the use of renewable energy sources widespread is of paramount importance for Turkey as for all countries. In this regard, the determiners of renewable energy consumption have been investigated. The effect of determining or factors affecting the use of renewable energy sources on a regional scale to Turkey were examined with different qualitative and quantitative research techniques. In this study, the factors of economic growth, public investments, and population are analyzed by considering regional differences on the consumption of renewable energy resources. The effect of regional economic growth, regional public investments, and regional population on the amount of regional renewable energy consumption were investigated by using panel data of 26 statistical regions of Level-2 classification in the period between 2010-2018 in Turkey. The results obtained by the dynamic panel data analysis concluded that economic growth and public investments at the regional level increased renewable energy consumption while the population growth decreased.

Education holds the power to transform and enrich the lives of people. In the era of the digital industry, where data is omnipresent in every walk of life and new trends impact society and future jobs, humans continue to evolve through education and developing mechanisms to improve education with data science in the heart of it. This chapter demonstrates that experience-based expertise and open innovation must be understood as a single process, where living labs that involve academies and enterprises create unique conditions for society's progress. There is a trinomial relationship between academy, society, and industries, which are interestingly far more exploited than the education and research. Effective management of the knowledge and information transferred between open innovation ecosystem partners is crucial. The scientific development of both concepts is an active field in the academic community, and new ideas appear, opening new paths of knowledge transfer methods with knowledge from data.

In the face the contemporary world lives, and the consequent data produced at an unprecedented speed through digital media platforms, the data are nowadays called the new global currency. It raises numerous opportunities to improve outcomes in businesses, namely at the level of customer relationship management (CRM) strategies and their systems. Nevertheless, how analytics can be applied and support the customer relationship processes seems unclear for academics and industries. To better connect customer relationship processes needs and what data science analytics can offer, this chapter presents a systematic literature review around the concepts, tools, and techniques behind this field, looking particularly on customer acquisition and customer retention in businesses. The outcomes highlight that academic researcher works in this field are very scare and recent. Searching the Scopus and Web of Science databases resulted in only 12 documents from 2013 to 2020, eight of them published in the last two years.

Chapter 26

Economics and business are a great background for data science provided econometricians and data scientists are sets with an intersection, although remaining unknown. In econometrics, data mining is somewhat a monstrous word, a field that traditionally seeks causal inference and results in interpretability. When we go deeper into what data science usually is, the boundaries between more traditional econometrics and even statistics and the hip and cool machine learning become shorter. In economics and business, we find examples and applications of simple and advanced data science techniques. This chapter intends to provide state-of-the-art data science applications in economics and business. The review and bibliometric analysis are limited to the research articles published through Elsevier Scopus. Results allowed the authors to conclude that despite the number of already existent research, a lot more remains to be explored joining both fields of knowledge, data since, and economics and business. This analysis allowed the authors to identify further possible avenues of research critically.

Chapter 27

    Hector Puente Bienvenido, Universidad Complutense de Madrid, Spain
    Borja Barinaga, Universidad Francisco de Vitoria Madrid, Spain
    Jorge Mora-Fernandez, University of California, San Diego, USA

This chapter is focused on describing the history and the current relevance of user experience (UX) techniques that combine data science and AI in the research field of interactive and immersive storytelling, including virtual and augmented realities. It initially presents a brief history of interactive storytelling, video games, VR and AR, AI and data science, and the user experience (UX) techniques used in those areas. Later, the chapter describes the UX techniques in depth, using AI and data science that work best and are more useful for testing interactive media products, describing examples of its applications briefly. Finally, the chapter presents conclusions in relationship with utopias and dystopias regarding the future use of UX, AI, and data science in several areas such as edutainment, social media, media arts, and business, among others.

Chapter 28

    Nandini Sen, Heriot Watt University, UK

This chapter aims to create new knowledge regarding artificial intelligence (AI) ethics and relevant subjects while reviewing ethical relationship between human beings and AI/robotics and linking between the moral fabric or the ethical issues of AI as used in fictions and films. It carefully analyses how a human being will love robot and vice versa. Here, fictions and films are not just about technology but about their feelings and the nature of bonding between AIs and the human race. Ordinary human beings distrust and then start to like AIs. However, if the AI becomes a rogue as seen in many fictions and films, then the AI is taken down to avoid the destruction of the human beings. Scientists like Turing are champions of robot/AI's feelings. Fictional and movie AIs are developed to keenly watch and comprehend humans. These actions are so close to empathy they amount to consciousness and emotional quotient.

Chapter 29

    Elodie Attié, Capgemini Engineering, France
    Solène Le Bars, Altran Lab, France
    Ilhem Quenel, Capgemini Engineering, France

Eighty percent of consumer behaviors and purchases rely on subconscious processes. The use of neuromarketing tools to study consumer behavior is not clear, notably regarding its practices and intentions toward consumers. This chapter aims to understand how neuromarketing can explain consumer behavior thanks to Neuromarketing 2.0 tools, how companies can manage the collected data in a responsible way and build a neuroethical charter to regulate the way companies use it. Most companies choose to not communicate about it when they use neuromarketing tools, and therefore, this chapter aims to pave the way towards solutions and recommendations and democratize its use by making Neuromarketing 2.0 more responsible and ethical.

Chapter 30

    Deepak Saxena, Birla Institute of Technology and Science, Pilani, India
    Markus Lamest, Trinity College Dublin, Ireland
    Veena Bansal, Indian Institute of Technology, Kanpur, India

Artificial intelligence (AI) systems have become a new reality of modern life. They have become ubiquitous to virtually all socio-economic activities in business and industry. With the extent of AI's influence on our lives, it is an imperative to focus our attention on the ethics of AI. While humans develop their moral and ethical framework via self-awareness and reflection, the current generation of AI lacks these abilities. Drawing from the concept of human-AI hybrid, this chapter offers managerial and developers' action towards responsible machine learning for ethical artificial intelligence. The actions consist of privacy by design, development of explainable AI, identification and removal of inherent biases, and most importantly, using AI as a moral enabler. Application of these action would not only help towards ethical AI; it would also help in supporting moral development of human-AI hybrid.

Preface

"Doing the same thing repeatedly, and expecting different results is the definition of insanity."

– Albert Einstein (1879 - 1955)

Handbook of Research on Applied Data Science and Artificial Intelligence in Business and Industry brings a new unique and global perspective on the subject of 100 highly professional and experienced researchers and practitioners from 27 different countries: Belgium, Brazil, Canada, China, Colombia, France, Georgia, Iceland, India, Ireland, Italy, Malaysia, Mexico, Nederland, Norway, Pakistan, Palestine, Panama, Peru, Poland, Portugal, Russia, Somaliland, Spain, Turkey, United Kingdom, and the USA.

The contemporary world lives on the data produced at an unprecedented speed through social networks and the internet of things (IoT). Data has been called the new global currency, and its rise is transforming entire industries, providing a wealth of opportunities. Applied data science research is necessary to derive useful information from big data for effective and efficient utilization to solve real-world problems. A broad analytical set allied with solid business logic is fundamental in today's corporations. Organizations work to obtain a competitive advantage by analyzing the data produced within and outside their corporate limits to support their decision-making processes. This book aims to provide an overview of the concepts, tools, and techniques behind the fields of data science and artificial intelligence (AI) applied to business and industries.

Handbook of Research on Applied Data Science and Artificial Intelligence in Business and Industry offers a compilation of 30 chapters presenting a holistic approach and is organized in three sections: "Strategy," "Action," and "Reflection." The spread of this orientation has meant preceding perspective, reminding that Actions have a greater chance of success if Strategies guide them. Furthermore, Reflection on the Action is vital for adjustments in the Strategy.

STRATEGY

The seven chapters that compose the first section of the book introduce the Strategic Perspective on Applied Data Science and Artificial Intelligence in Business and Industry.

In the first chapter, "Port Dada Integration: Opportunities for Optimization and Value Creation," José Luís Cacho, Adalberto Tokarski, Elizabete Thomas, and Valentina Chkoniya bring the academy, Port of Sines (Portugal), and National Waterway Transportation Agency from Brazil together. The chapter aims to apprehend the use of data science in the port sector. It is imperative in the Maritime Supply Chain that is growing in complexity. Ports are at the crossroads of many activities, modes, and stakeholders, actively becoming a digital hub. Today digital and physical connectivity go hand in hand. The Port could benefit from taping the opportunities arising from digitalization and data integration since it helps to leverage external knowledge, engage stakeholders, create new decision-making anchors, lower the risk of certain investments, boost productivity and cut costs, accelerate greening and digital transition, generating possibilities for just-in-time operations and optimizations.

The second chapter, "A Software Engineering Perspective on Building Production-Ready Machine Learning Systems," by Petra Heck, Gerard Schouten, and Luis Cruz, discusses building production-ready machine learning systems. There are several challenges involved in accomplishing this, each with its specific solutions regarding practices and tool support. The chapter presents those solutions and introduces MLOps as an overarching and integrated approach. Data engineers, data scientists, software engineers, and operations engineers integrate their activities to implement validated machine learning applications managed from initial ideas to daily operation in a production environment.

In the third chapter, "Multivariate Sustainability Profile of Global Fortune 500 Companies Using GRI-G4 Database," international mathematicians team composed by Mónica Jiménez-Hernández, Purificación Vicente-Galindo, Nathalia Diazibeth Tejedor-Flores, Adelaide Freitas, and Purificación Galindo help to understand why many companies view their Corporate Social Responsibility reports as a way to guarantee the credibility of the published information. Moreover, explain how to find the sustainability gradients and sort them as a function of economic, environmental and, social components, using multivariate statistical methods, to establish the foundations for better knowledge of the trends and sustainability reporting habits.

The fourth chapter, "Examining the Evolution of E-Government Development of Nations Through Machine Learning Techniques," by Niguissie Mengesha and Anteneh Ayanso, argues that the EGDI fails to show nations' efforts over time and in informing nations and policymakers as to what and from whom to draw policy lessons. The authors show the relevance of machine learning techniques in addressing these issues and discuss the policy implications of their proposed methodology and the insights obtained.

The fifth chapter, "Artificial Intelligence as Driver for SMEs Competitiveness," by Nicola Del Sarto and Andrea Piccaluga, shows the importance of exploring how SMEs may successfully adopt Artificial intelligence technology and describe four cases of Italian SMEs. The authors base their analyses on four dimensions represented by People, Processes, Products, and Customers. The study intends to help managers to adopt this technology within their company.

In the sixth chapter, "Big Data Is Decision Science: The Case of COVID-19 Vaccination," Jacques RJ Bughin, Michele Cincera, Dorota Reykowska, and Rafał Ohme suggest that Data science has been proven to be an essential asset to support better decision-making in a variety of settings. Whether it is for a scientist to predict climate change better, a company to better predict sales, or a government to anticipate voting preferences. In this research, authors leverage Random Forest as one of the most effective machine learning techniques using big data to predict vaccine intent in five European countries.

Following the neuromarketing perspective, the seventh chapter, "The Future of Advertising: Influencing and Predicting Response Through Artificial Intelligence, Machine Learning, and Neuroscience," was written by Elissa Moses, Kimberly Rose Clark, and Norman J. Jacknis. The authors summarize the role that AI/ML are expected to play at every stage of advertising development, assessment, and execution. With advances in neuroscience for measuring attention, cognitive processing, emotional response, and memory, AI/ML have advanced to a point where analytics can be used to identify variables that drive more effective advertising and predict enhanced performance. In addition, the cost of computation has declined, making platforms to apply these tools much less expensive and within reach. The authors also offer recommendations for a) understanding the clients/customers and users of the products and services that will be advertised, b) aiding creativity in designing advertisements, c) testing the impact of advertisements, and d) identifying the optimum placement of advertisements.

ACTION

Section 2 of this book (Action) addresses that Actions have a greater chance of success if Strategies guide them.

The following 16 chapters help to understand how to transform Strategy into Action. They show that Applied Data science is focused on Making Sense of Data. Furthermore, AI is a collection of mathematical algorithms that make computers understand relationships between different types and pieces of data. This knowledge of connections could be utilized to come to conclusions or make decisions. The hardest part of running a successful data-driven business intelligence system has the Strategies to Act on the insights.

The eighth chapter, "Retail Customers' Native Baskets Creation: A Must-Do Into Measuring Price Indexes," by Liliana Bernardino Matias, Ana Costa Freitas, and Filipe Fernandes Miranda, gives a practical perspective of the most prominent Portuguese retailer, Sonae MC, and proposes a methodology that deflects from analyzing solely the price of all products effectively bought by customers by taking into consideration their prior shopping intention. Loyalty schemes are game-changers when measuring price index, and standard approaches to measure price index on a specific retailer against competitors tend to be overly optimistic. The study proposes a two-step methodology comprising building the customer native baskets and allocating the prices collected to each customer. Under the assumption that a price-sensitive customer will not buy a poorly priced product compared to the competitors in that specific period, the authors present an innovative methodology resulting in a more realistic price index metric.

In the ninth chapter, "Studying Customer Experience and Retention Using Applied Data Science and Artificial Intelligence," Dolores Méndez-Aparicio, María Pilar Martínez-Ruiz, Alicia Izquierdo-Yusta, and Ana Isabel Jiménez-Zarco focus on customer data and metadata. There is a unique opportunity for companies interested in collecting, processing, and elaborating useful information for customer-centric business management. Other disciplines are developing new ways of organizing information and intelligent response. Significant technological advances in facial, sensory, text, voice, and image recognition are constantly emerging, with response capabilities closer to human thinking. From this continuous interaction emerges a new asset for companies: knowledge.

In the tenth chapter, "Using Intelligent Text Analysis of Online Reviews to Determine the Main Factors of Restaurant Value Propositions," Elizaveta Fainshtein and Elena Serova discuss the sentiment classification of text messages containing customer reviews of an online restaurant service system, using machine-learning methods, in particular, text mining and multivariate text sentiment analysis. The study determines the value proposition factors based on online restaurant reviews on TripAdvisor, collecting information on consumer preferences and restaurant services in St. Petersburg (Russia) quality assessment and examining the influence of service format and reviews tonality on rating restaurants factors. The results showed that the critical factors in the sentiment study were cuisine and dishes, reviews and ratings, and targeted search.

In the eleventh chapter, "Time Series Forecasting in Retail Sales Using LSTM and Prophet," Clony Junior, Pedro Gusmão, José Moreira, and Ana Maria M. Tome present two approaches to time series forecasting, Long Short-Term Memory, a special kind of Recurrent Neural Network, and Prophet, an open-source library developed by Facebook for time series forecasting. With a focus on developing forecasting processes by data mining or machine learning experts, LSTM uses gating mechanisms to deal with long-term dependencies, reducing the short-term memory effect inherent to the traditional RNN. On the other hand, Prophet encapsulates statistical and computational complexity to allow broad use of time series forecasting, prioritizing the expert's business knowledge through exploration and experimentation. Both approaches were applied to a retail time series. This case study comprises daily and half-hourly forecasts and the performance of both methods was measured using the standard metrics.

The twelfth chapter, "General Model for Metrics Calculation and Behavior Prediction in the Manufacturing Industry: An Automated Machine Learning Approach," by Maria João Lopes, Eugénio M. Rocha, Petia Georgieva Georgieva, Nelson Ferreira, shows an example of the applied data science in Bosch Termotecnologia SA. Authors provide a comprehensive description of a generic framework aimed at solving various predictive data-driven related use cases, occurring in the manufacturing industry. As an example, a data generation distribution model is proposed, parameter stability and predictive robustness are studied, and automated machine learning approaches are discussed to predict the throughput time of products in a manufacturing production line just by knowing the processing time in their first stations.

In the thirteenth chapter, "AI Meaning and Applications in the Consumer Sector of Retailing, Hospitality, and Tourism," Sandra Maria Correia Loureiro, Muhammad Ashfaq, and Mariana Oliveira Berga Rodrigues provide a conceptualization of the evolution of AI. The authors' overview AI in business and point out examples of AI applications in retailing, hospitality, and tourism.

Following the topic, in the fourteenth chapter, "Key Factors in the Process of Acceptance and Implementation of Artificial Intelligence in the Hotel Sector," Alfonso Infante-Moro, Juan C. Infante-Moro, and Julia Gallardo-Pérez show that AI is one of the most innovative and trending technologies in the hotel sector, which is transforming the hotel sector into a novel environment in business-client relationships. For this reason, this study seeks to find, through a literary review and a causal study carried out by experts in technologies and hotels, using the methodology of fuzzy cognitive maps, what are the determining factors in the decision of hotels to accept and implement the Artificial Intelligence in their hotels and their services.

The fifteenth chapter, "Peruvian Consumer Responses to The Use of Technologies in the Context of COVID-19," by Yezelia Danira Caceres Cabana, David Aguilar del Carpio, Erika Velásquez Chacón, and Juan Mardonio Rivera Medina, gives a transformational perspective of marketing channels for purchases. ICTs are the focus of the analysis. Authors conclude that the massification of these tools has generated a change in the ways of acquiring products, which is likely to transcend the pandemic, and these channels will be maintained and strengthened in the future.

In the sixteenth chapter, "Artificial Intelligence in Marketing: A Review of Consumer-AI Interactions," Özge Sığırcı analyzes the consumer-AI interaction in the marketplace. Besides these relationships, there are still concerns about AI-related privacy, algorithmic biases, consumer vulnerability, unemployment, and ethical decision-making.

In the seventeenth chapter, "When Luxury Vinous-Concept Hotel Meets Premium Wine Brands: An Exploratory Study on Co-Branding," Lisa Ferraz, Helena Nobre, and Belém Barbosa analyze a case of a co-branding strategy between a vinous-concept luxury hotel in Portugal and premium wine brands of domestic producers. The study offers evidence on the benefits for both parties, reasons for adopting co-branding, and partners' selection attributes.

The eighteenth chapter is devoted to "Data Analysis in the Shipping Industry: eShip Case Study – Problem Statement" and written by Marcel Kyas, Joshua D Springer, Jan Tore Pedersen, and Valentina Chkoniya. This chapter identifies the critical issues that must be addressed to accelerate the digital transition in the chartering market. The maritime industry is one of the pillars of global trade, where change is a constant. Again, shipping is at the cusp of a new era—one driven by data. eShip's case study was analyzed, and future steps have been defined for the data analysis in the shipping industry.

In the nineteenth chapter, "Question Answering Chatbot Using Memory Networks," Riddhi Patel, Parth Patel, Chintan M Bhatt, and Mrugendrasinh L Rahevar trained and tested their model over Facebook's bAbi dataset, which consists of several tasks and has questions regarding each task to retrieve the accuracy of the model. On the pedestal of that dataset, they have presented the accuracy for every task in their study with memory networks.

The twentieth chapter, "Comparison of Parametric and Non-Parametric Methods to Analyse the Data Gathered by Likert Type Scale," by Tamer Baran, examines whether the results of the analysis of the data obtained using LTSs with parametric and non-parametric methods in different response alternative numbers will differ in terms of statistical significance.

In the twenty-first chapter, "Latent Fingerprint Enhancement Based on EDTV Model," Shadi M S Hilles, Abdilahi Deria Liban, Abdullah M. M Altrad, Yousef A. Baker El-Ebiary, and Mohanad M Hilles underline challenges in the area of latent fingerprint due to poor-quality image which consist unclear ridge structure and overlapping patterns with structure noise, where is a latent fingerprint in image enhancement is essential to suppress several different noises for improved accuracy of ridge structure, presents the combination of edge directional total variation model EDTV and quality image enhancement with lost minutia re-construction, RMSE for evaluation and performance in the proposed algorithm.

The twenty-second chapter, "The Business, Societal and Enterprise Architecture Framework: An Artificial Intelligence, Data Sciences, and Big Data-Based Approach," by Antoine Trad, presents an AI-based generic concept for decision making using data science. The Applied Holistic Mathematical Model for AI (AHMM4AI) focuses on data and access management, and the author demonstrates that the development of the Big Data for AI (BGD4AI) is an essential jumpstart.

In the twenty-third chapter, "The Effect of Population, Public Investments, and Economic Growth on Regional Renewable Energy Consumption in Turkey: Dynamic Panel Data Analysis," Özlem Karadağ Albayrak investigates determiners of renewable energy consumption. In this study, the factors of economic growth, public investments, and population are analyzed by considering regional differences in the consumption of renewable energy resources. The effect of regional economic growth, regional public investments, and regional population on regional renewable energy consumption was investigated.

REFLECTION

Section 3 (Reflection) addresses several dimensions uncovered in this book. Actionable insight is an effect for which the root cause can be directly and inarguably derived with enough specificity to know how to Action a Change. Knowing how to identify an actionable insight is only the first step, in any case. Data science is about decision-making in the increasingly data-driven world we live in today. It has employed great efforts in developing advanced analytics, improving data models, and cultivating new algorithms. However, there are organizational and socio-technical challenges that arise when executing a Data Science project.

The last seven chapters point to three layers to consider in this field: knowledge, practice, and ethics.

In the twenty-fourth chapter, "Education for The Digital Industry: Opportunities and Challenges of Experience-Based Expertise and Open Innovation," Valentina Chkoniya, Fernando Cruz Gonçalves, and Maria Manuela Martins Batista suggest in the era of the Digital Industry, where data is omnipresent in every walk of life, and new trends impact society and future jobs, humans continue to evolve through education and developing mechanisms to improve education with data science in the heart of it. Effective management of the knowledge and information transferred between open innovation ecosystem partners is crucial. The scientific development of both concepts is an active field in the academic community, and new ideas appear, opening new paths of knowledge transfer methods with knowledge from data.

In the twenty-fifth chapter, "The Contribute of Data Science Applied to Customer Relationship Management: A Systematic Literature Review," Dora Maria Simões defends that in the face the contemporary world lives, and the consequent data produced at an unprecedented speed through digital media platforms, the data are nowadays called the new global currency. It raises numerous opportunities to improve outcomes in businesses, namely a level of customer relationship management (CRM) strategies and its systems.

In the twenty-sixth chapter, "Data Science in Economics and Business: Roots and Applications," Mara Madaleno, João Lourenço Marques, and Muhammad Tufail show that economics and business are excellent backgrounds for data science provided econometricians and data scientists are sets with an intersection, although remaining unknown. Reflecting on what data science usually is.

The twenty-seventh chapter, "A Historical Review of Immersive Storytelling Technologies: New Uses of AI, Data Science, and User Experience in Virtual Worlds," by Hector Puente Bienvenido, Borja Barinaga, and Jorge Mora-Fernandez focus on describing the history and the current relevance of UX techniques that combine data science and AI in the research field of interactive and immersive storytelling, including Virtual and Augmented Realities. It initially presents a brief history of interactive storytelling, video games, VR and AR, AI and data science, and the UX techniques used in those areas. Later, the chapter describes the UX techniques in-depth, using AI and data science that work best and are more helpful in testing interactive media products, describing examples of its applications briefly. Finally, the chapter presents conclusions in relationship with utopias and dystopias regarding the future use of UX, AI, and data science in several areas such as edutainment, social media, media arts, and business, among others.

In the twenty-eighth chapter, "Artificial Intelligences Are Subsets of Human Beings, Mainly in Fictions and Films: Challenges and Opportunities," anthropologist Nandini Sentries tries to create new knowledge regarding AI ethics. The author also revives the ethical relationship between human beings and AI/robotics and linking between the moral fabric or the ethical issues of AI.

The twenty-ninth chapter, "Towards Ethical Neuromarketing 2.0 Based on Artificial Intelligence," by Elodie Attié, Solène Le Bars, and Ilhem Quesnel, explains the perspective of Capgemini Engineering and Altran Lab on the use of neuromarketing tools to study consumer behavior. This chapter aims to understand how neuromarketing can explain consumer behavior thanks to neuromarketing 2.0 tools, how companies can responsibly manage the collected data, and build a neuroethical charter to regulate the way companies use it.

Finally, in the thirtieth chapter, "Responsible Machine Learning for Ethical Artificial Intelligence in Business and Industry," Deepak Saxena, Markus Lamest, and Veena Bansal examine AI systems as a new reality of modern life. They have become ubiquitous to virtually all socio-economic activities in business and industry, while humans develop their moral and ethical framework via self-awareness and reflection. Based on the concept of human-AI hybrid, this chapter offers managerial and developers' action towards responsible machine learning for ethical artificial intelligence.

As the book demonstrates, Data Science is all about data. Applied Data science is focused on Making Sense of Data. AI is a collection of mathematical algorithms that make computers understand relationships between different types and pieces of data such that this knowledge of connections could be utilized to come to conclusions or make decisions that could be accurate to a very high degree.

Featuring practice and research on topics such as AI, applied data science, big data, business intelligence, consumer behavior analytics, customer experience, customer response modeling, deep learning, ethics, digital marketing analytics, logistic and supply chain, machine learning, market monitoring, marketing intelligence, and marketing strategy analytics.

Handbook of Research on Applied Data Science and Artificial Intelligence in Business and Industry is a truly international, interdisciplinary, and integrated vision on the topic of Data Science Applications. They lead to exciting and worthwhile work meant to be used as a basis for further research and as an essential reference source for the practice and those concerned with their contribution to a better world.

Looking at things from a different, global, and holistic perspective, we will see the Most Effective and Innovative Strategies for Sustainable Success!

Valentina Chkoniya
University of Aveiro, Portugal

Acknowledgment

The editor would like to acknowledge the contribution of all the people involved in this project that accepted embarking on the challenge of bridging the gap between Academy and Enterprise.

The path has been long, and those who prevailed can be proud of the final result of a unique holistic perspective of Research on Applied Data Science and Artificial Intelligence in Business and Industry.

We have made a great team of 100 contributors (authors and editorial advisory board) from 27 countries:

Belgium, Brazil, Canada, China, Colombia, France, Georgia, Iceland, India, Ireland, Italy, Malaysia, Mexico, Nederland, Norway, Pakistan, Palestine, Panama, Peru, Poland, Portugal, Russia, Somaliland, Spain, Turkey, United Kingdom, and the USA.

Thank YOU all for your contribution!

Valentina Chkoniya
University of Aveiro, Portugal

Chapter 15
Peruvian Consumer Responses to the Use of Technologies in the Context of COVID–19

Yezelia Danira Caceres Cabana
 https://orcid.org/0000-0002-5027-8081
Universidad Nacional de San Agustín de Arequipa, Peru

David Aguilar del Carpio
 https://orcid.org/0000-0001-9911-6537
Universidad Nacional de San Agustín de Arequipa, Peru

Erika Velásquez Chacón
 https://orcid.org/0000-0003-2247-3100
Universidad Católica San Pablo, Peru

Juan Mardonio Rivera Medina
 https://orcid.org/0000-0003-0627-7871
Universidad Continental Perú, Peru

ABSTRACT

The pandemic caused by COVID-19 has led many states, in an attempt to control the spread of the virus, to decree social immobilization, which meant the introduction of restrictions on the free movement of people and the opening of shops. This led them to seek new marketing channels for purchases. Among these, ICTs have been important. This is the focus of the analysis in this document. Through surveys and interviews, information was obtained, divided into four age groups, which showed that an important part of the population has had to resort to ICTs to acquire goods and/or pay for services. This change in the way of acquiring had different particularities according to the age group analyzed, with a greater change in the oldest group (56 to 74 years old). It can be concluded that the massification of these tools has generated a change in the ways of acquiring products, and this is likely to transcend the pandemic and these channels will be maintained and strengthened in the future.

DOI: 10.4018/978-1-7998-6985-6.ch015

INTRODUCTION

In Latin America, the assimilation of technology in productive processes and supply chains is still limited, and there is also a digital divide, presenting this as an obstacle for important sectors of the population, affecting rural areas to a greater extent because they have greater limitations in access to and use of digital technologies; situations that have had a strong impact on the relationships between individuals, creating new means through which they interact with their environment in different ways. Some of these spaces are the ways in which people consume and/or acquire the goods necessary to satisfy their physical and/or spiritual needs. Therefore, "digital infrastructure is a fundamental component in maintaining economic resilience" (CAF Development Bank of Latin America, 2020, p.17).

The pandemic caused by COVID-19 has shown that the Peruvian state and its population were not prepared to face crisis situations at this level, showing a strong vulnerability in many sectors. The importance of this chapter lies in the fact that it provides an understanding of the dynamics that exist in developing economies, where a large number of the population still does not have access to or feels culturally distant from the use of digital tools for consumption and/or the sale of products. All this information will serve the sectors involved in the planning and elaboration of public policies that will help strengthen the implementation of activities and provide better conditions for value generation.

This analysis is based on the city of Arequipa, which "is the second pole of industrial development in the country, highly diversified with a base made up of leading companies producing consumer goods, inputs and capital goods of national and regional scope" (Banco Central de Reserva del Perú, 2016, p.13). Regarding the economic aspect, in this same department 95.8% of the companies are "Micro" (INEI, 2014), most of which have been affected by the isolation measures imposed by the government to face COVID-19.

In this context, companies have not been able to carry out their productive activities normally, which has led to a significant drop in their income. This socio-economic situation will have a direct impact on the increase of precarious employment, informality and poverty levels. As a result, many people who were entering and establishing themselves in the emerging middle class could return to poverty. This would add more people to the informal sector of the economy, which already accounted for more than 70 per cent before the pandemic. The largest informal sector is the commercial sector, which is seen as a refuge for workers in other sectors. All this shows that these people and businesses will have to reinvent themselves commercially to survive, just as consumers have to connect to new channels to acquire the goods they need.

It is possible that the effects of COVID 19 have drastically changed the purchasing habits and mechanisms of Arequipa's consumers, which is why this document aims to micro-analyse consumers' responses to the use of information and communication technologies. In this sense, we assume that this has required, on the part of consumers and producers, the use of a set of information on the proximity, quality and availability of products, and of the universe of possible consumers on the producers' side as well. We also consider the tendency to replace unsophisticated information equipment with devices that allow access to networks and web pages, together with access to an internet connection that facilitates the connectivity of the agents involved.

The research carried out is non-experimental, exploratory and descriptive, with the use of qualitative and quantitative tools, through the application of convenience sampling, aimed at people living in the city of Arequipa, Peru, of different age groups classified as follows: between 10 - 24 years old, 25 - 40 years old, 41 - 55 years old, 56 - 74 years old.

With the combined information between qualitative and quantitative methods, we tried to obtain information on the access and use of the internet through social networks to search for or purchase a product before and during COVID 19, for this purpose, 237 surveys were carried out at a quantitative level using an electronic form and 25 in-depth telephone interviews which were recorded and transcribed in their original language in Spanish and then translated into English by the authors, this information allowed us to know and understand the thinking and logic of the people.

For the selection of participants, sampling started with families known to the researchers and was expanded using the snowballing technique. The surveys and interviews were conducted between November and December 2020 by telephone.

BACKGROUND

Since the beginning of the pandemic, changes in consumer behaviour have been generated, starting with the stockpiling of goods, however, social isolation measures limited the availability and accessibility of products and services (Casco, 2020, pp. 98-105). At the same time, the population sought to make the best use of their resources, due to the feeling that the situation could become increasingly complex, and the fear of the latter led to an increase in their inventories to avoid shortages.

From the above, it can be stated that consumers learn and have new habits, now the shop comes home and this is because "All consumption is location- and time-dependent. Consumers develop habits over time about what to consume, when and where" (Sheth, 2020, pp- 280-283). Kirk and Rifkin (2020) have examined behaviours in three phases of first reacting, then coping and adapting in unusual patterns of behaviour in the face of the COVID-19 pandemic. It is therefore evident that the population modifies its behaviour and this behaviour is likely to persist over time.

The Development Bank of Latin America [CAF] (2020) in the report: El estado de la digitalización de América Latina frente a la pandemia del COVID-19, presents the importance of digitalisation as mitigating factors of the disruption of the pandemic, where digital technologies have allowed counteracting isolation and facilitating the functioning of economic systems, where the importance of digitalisation is shown. This is similar to consumers in Arequipa, where the use of information and communication technologies has supported families, mainly in urban areas and with limitations in rural areas. In this context, the use of information and communication technologies has supported and facilitated many of the needs of the population in education, health, teleworking, and connecting with family members, among other simultaneous uses, although with limited access, due to increasingly precarious economic levels, job losses or a decrease in production and sales at the business level.

According to CAF (2020), Latin America has positioned itself at an intermediate level in its digital ecosystem, mitigating the effects of the pandemic, although Latin American networks have also been affected by the exponential increase in traffic, although with effects on the decrease in broadband speed.

FRAME OF REFERENCE

Consumption

The processes involved in the actions of buying, using, searching for, evaluating and discarding goods and services in order to satisfy consumer needs have been addressed not only by economics, but also by psychology, sociology and anthropology. This has gone from the evaluations revealed in a first approach on the rationality of the consumer to then broaden in its interpretation towards the elements that give impulse to some behaviours according to the environment, progressively giving way to the psychological emphasis and neuroscience.

From an economic perspective, Varian (2014) analyses consumer preferences at a more general level, indicating that this requires "not only a complete list of goods that could be consumed, but also a description of when, where and under what circumstances they could be obtained".

On the same subject, but from an anthropological perspective that seeks to approach the cultural behaviour of human beings in terms of their consumption decisions, Caceres Cabana et al. (2020), state that consumption must be understood from its simplest and most dispossessed dimension, to the level at which real political, economic and even cultural interests are effectively hidden behind simple buying and selling actions. Although individuals have to consume in order to subsist, consumption is no longer only subject to the idea of subsistence, but is linked to other factors, such as prestige, taste, etc.

In this sense, Akerlof and Shiller (2015) introduce the idea that consumers actually buy things they do not need, in a state of manipulation of their senses by advertising and the social environment, generating a need where a false scarcity is created, which will condition or encourage unnecessary consumption. Regarding how scarcity focuses people's senses, Mullainathan and Shafir (2016) indicate that "Scarcity captures the mind. Just as hungry subjects thought about food, when we suffer from scarcity of any kind, it absorbs us. The mind automatically and powerfully focuses on unsatisfied needs". Likewise, following the previous authors, they argue that scarcity is not only a state of mind due to the frustration of having less or little, but rather, it will influence how we perceive things, imposing itself in the mind over other activities or needs. This is why many population groups respond in a culturally differentiated way to structure their consumption needs. Thus, consumption can be seen not only from a purely needs-based aspect, but also in socio-cultural terms.

Evidence from Hao et al. (2020) reveals that fresh food e-commerce channels are more likely to be associated with panic due to a higher likelihood of supply shortages.

Consumers

Digital tools were presented as those that could somehow link the consumer with the supplier, opening the possibility of continuing to maintain marketing channels in the face of the difficulties described above, this phenomenon with the pandemic has accelerated the use of many of these digital media, due to the need of many families who, despite being in a situation of compulsory social isolation, needed to continue acquiring goods and/or paying for services. Therefore, technological resources have become a necessity for consumers in a context of limited financial and digital inclusion, insufficient use and massification of means of payment and insufficient access to information technologies.

Compulsive purchases showed changes in consumption behaviour in the face of the pandemic; at the beginning there was hoarding of products, generating shortages, but this was later controlled. In this regard, the literature shows that there is a relationship between conscious thought and unconscious processing as elements that lead to human behaviour (Masicampo & Baumeister, 2011).

The generational review to understand consumer behaviour is complex because each one has particularities and different characteristics in the context of each context, where the generations of 30 years old are considered as the time of progress, because they have the ability to create and those of 60 years old in the stage that diminishes their role in public life, considering "aspects such as communication, use of technology, motivation, recruitment, incentives, among others", for Diaz-Sarmiento et al. (2017) generates challenges for their understanding, because they adopt particular positions in the way of thinking and acting.

The theoretical foundation reported by Díaz-Sarmiento et al. (2017), determines:

a) Baby Boomers, the 50-70 year olds born between 1946 and 1964, are characterized by their dedication and even workaholism. Empowered and looking forward to the best in life, they are a generation concerned with the pursuit of status, loyalty and quality of life.

b) Generation X, which refers to those born between 1965 and 1977, who hold middle and senior management positions and are the parents of Millennials and Centennials and were at the center of the consumerism of the 1980s. This population grew up where both parents worked or were divorced, influenced by events such as the emergence of personal computers and the expansion of the internet.

c) Generation Y, Millennials, are those born between 1980 and the beginning of the 21st century, are children of the last Boomers and the first X and grew up in a culture of protected and loved children, characterized by the use of technology as part of their lifestyle. They have grown up with the internet, smartphones, accelerated technological advances, social networks and with these, instant information. On the other hand, Millennials have had so many awards and trophies growing up that many of them think they should be promoted in their jobs every two years regardless of their performance.

d) Generation Z, born since the beginning of the 21st century, stand out for their assumed capacity for rapid response, their desire for immediacy and continuous interaction, and are also conceived as experts and competent in ICT. In this sense, the preferences of this group lean towards visual information and easy performance in digital and visual environments where several tasks are managed at the same time, a phenomenon is known as multitasking (Bennett et al., 2008; Gallardo, 2012; and Fernández & Fernández, 2016; Cassany & Atalaya, 2008, Reig & Vilchez, 2013 cited in Pérez-Escoda, Castro-Subizarreta, & Fandos-Igado, 2016).

Culture and Technology

The cultural issue, in times of globalization, sometimes goes unnoticed. However, different societies still behave differently in response to certain stimuli or situations. The cultural factor could explain this, which we understand as "the traditions and customs, transmitted through learning, that shape and guide the beliefs and behaviour of the people exposed to them" (Marcus & Fisher, 1999). (Phillip Kottak, 2011). In the same vein, it is important to make reference to the fact that "the cultures of the world's people need to be constantly rediscovered and they reinvent themselves in changing historical circumstances". (Marcus & Fisher, 1999)In other words, they are subject to environmental pressures which result in processes of adaptation, not only biological, like all animals, but also in processes of cultural adaptation, which is inherent to human beings.

Regarding technological advances, Ogbum & Thomas (1922) state that society, as well as its norms and values, will change more slowly than technology, so the cultural change will also change. In this sense, on the cultural link with technologies, Thomas et al. (2005) indicate that there are several social factors that will influence the way in which this takes place, pointing out that the degree of homogeneity and level of equality of societies, the degree of communication with the outside world (especially influenced by migration), the experience of gender and ethnicity in different societies, cultures of different generations, religion, education and literacy and language, will condition the way and speed in which societies adapt to technology.

Information and Communication Technologies (ICTs)

For this study, information and communication technologies (ICTs) are understood as the information technology tools used by consumers in email services, web use, data storage, electronic banking, virtual communities managed through devices such as computers, mobile phones and tablets. The World Economic Forum (2019) suggests that ICTs are considered to be the set of tools related to the digitised transmission, processing and storage of information.

It is also a facilitating element of entrepreneurship in a globalised context, the contributions of Serrano et al. (2018) highlight that through the use of electronic devices and the inclusion of computer programs, it is possible to establish channels of participation between different communities, groups and collectivities, streamlining processes, times and costs; ICTs are considered as a mediating tool between the processes of business activities, enabling external relations between customers, suppliers, markets, potential consumers, among others; and through their operation they create improvements in the service or product offered, increasing the efficiency of trade and its economic growth.

In relation to the opportunities that organizations gain by incorporating ICTs in their activities, according to Martelo et al. (2017, pp. 87-94), advantages can be expressed in the streamlining of processes, cost savings, reduction of personnel, likewise Martínez Coral (2017, pp. 63-72) highlights its effectiveness in the promotion of education, a very important aspect for individual and collective management, additionally Serrano et al. (2018) attributes it a potential to generate value, disseminate knowledge, improve quality of life. These elements are relevant in a context of accelerated changes in daily and social life caused by the pandemic where it can be seen that the behavior and use of this technology have become widespread and has generated business opportunities and greater profitability in business organizations linked to mobile telephony, computers, internet, digital television, applications, etc., a situation that has involved business organizations.

The adoption and use of ICTs by market players depending on the internal capacities, size, and culture of the organizations; an aspect that is linked to e-commerce, when goods and services are bought and sold through the internet, making it possible to process information from commercial transactions to create, transform and redefine relationships between organizations and individuals, as the case may be, in order to create value. There is an evolution in e-commerce through the use of the World Wide Web in part or all of the transaction cycle supported by a range of technologies ranging from mobile devices (m-commerce), social networks (social commerce), email and others (Jones et al., 2013, pp. 164-175).

On the effects of using decision-inducing user interface design elements to guide consumer behaviour in digital choice environments; evidence reveals that different stimuli and more versatile adaptation to users based on the data it provides could have notable implications for guiding user behaviour in a desirable way under a choice architecture towards related items that influence purchase by motivating additional consumption that was not originally planned by the user (Weinmann et al., 2016, pp. 433-436).

MAIN FOCUS OF THE CHAPTER

The use of ICTs in Arequipa

According to the results found through this research on the interaction experiences of the different age segments with ICTs to carry out search procedures and purchase goods and services before and during the pandemic, it can be seen that the most active segment that has been exploring and applying ICTs in commerce is mainly concentrated in the age segment corresponding to generations X, Y and Z, as well as in the preference of purchases.

Generation Z and Generation Y reported frequent use of social networks and websites, compared to 8% and 3% for Generation X and baby boomers respectively; with this experience extending to shopping and searching for commercial transactions via social networks for 37% of Generation Z and 16% of Generation Y.

On the other hand, to see the projection regarding the development of the perspective and sustained growth in the use of ICTs by the different age segments analyzed, 35% of generation Z and 18% of generation Y state that they will continue to use ICTs for commerce in the post COVID 19 pandemic scenario, compared to 6% of generation X and 2% of baby boomers respectively, This situation suggests that the growing trend of supply and demand decisions for goods and services through ICTs will be irreversible, and that connectivity conditions must be improved to ensure the efficiency and effectiveness of digital market players.

Regarding the use of ICT applied to commerce, it is also worth highlighting the predominance of the use of devices, highlighting that Generation Z and Generation Y are the ones that dominate in their use: 29% and 17% use mobile phones, 19% and 5% use laptops, 7% and 4% use fixed computers, in this case it is worth paying particular attention to the behaviour of Generation X and the Baby Boomers who stand out more in the use of mobile phones with 8% and 6% respectively, In this case, it is important to pay particular attention to the behaviour of Generation X and Baby Boomers, who use laptops (8% and 6% respectively), while 2% of both age segments do not use laptops, and the use of fixed computers is not relevant, which indicates that the age segments analysed generally prefer the technological sense of portability, simplicity, accessibility and price, which is expressed in the privileged use of mobiles.

The use of ICTs has brought about changes in consumer behaviour, with consumers accessing more information through the internet and social networks about the products and services they want to buy. These changes have been accelerated by the pandemic, and the data from Arequipa show that people in the Y and Z generation age groups are those who use ICTs frequently, reaching 27% and 13% respectively; Both segments explain the new consumer behaviour and the use of modern marketing channels, while there is a natural resistance among people in the 41-74 age groups, who use ICTs less than 6%. In this respect, an interviewee in the 25-40 age group says: *"Normally if you can't find something on one website you can look on another, so I always find what I'm looking for. I look first at how many people have shopped there and what comments they have left on this shop or business. Once I have done that I see if they are trustworthy. (interviewee 13)*

Consumer Behaviour by age Group During the Pandemic

Hereafter, to describe consumer behaviour towards technology, this will be understood as the use of mobile or computing devices for the acquisition or selection of goods and services. The analysis is carried out according to the age groups referred to in the reference framework, which describes consumers differentiated by generational groups.

Centennials or Generation Z

The people in this group are what we could consider as digital natives, i.e. those who were born in a recent era, which has allowed them to be more familiar with the aforementioned technologies, considering them as something every day and normalized, very different from those who had to go through a learning process for their use, the latter are known as digital migrants.

Based on the results found, it can be seen that the majority of people belonging to this age group have used digital tools to make their purchases during the pandemic, this being a behaviour that already existed before the pandemic in almost all respondents, so it did not represent any shock in the way of accessing the goods necessary for their consumption, as stated in the statement: *If I use social networks to buy, I think it is an option because it allows me to not need to leave the house. (interviewee 6)*

It can be added that the use of digital means of payment such as credit cards is not widespread among this age group, as their financial inclusion is still low. This is due to the fact that many are still in education and have not yet obtained a job or financial independence, so they are not creditworthy. This is reinforced by the evidence found in the 2012 Pilot Survey on Access to and Use of Financial Services, prepared by the Peruvian Superintendency of Banking and Insurance, when analysing the client profile within the financial system, which indicates that "Banking penetration (having an account, credit or credit card) had a slight bias towards women, who accounted for 52% of the total number of clients in the financial system. By age group, the results suggest that the financial system is concentrated among people between 26 and 50 years old (64%), followed by clients over 50 years old with 26%, while young clients between 18 and 25 years old represented a lower percentage (10%)" (Superintendencia de Banca, Seguros y AFP - BID, 2012).

Although most people in this age group had made purchases before, it is believed, as mentioned above, that the factor of using digital means of payment such as credit cards conditions virtual purchases, which is why 30% of those who said they had ever made online purchases indicated that they had only done so since the pandemic. It is therefore not surprising that almost 40% of this group said that they paid in cash when shopping online.

Generation Y

The people in this generation have a very similar familiarity with the use of technologies to the age group analysed above, since, although most of them were not born or raised with the existence of this type of digital tool, this group has had early contact with them, so it is not surprising that 65% of respondents belonging to this consumer group stated that they were already in the habit of using them to purchase consumer goods before the pandemic. This is further strengthened by the evidence that this age group has almost all shopped online, with nearly 85% indicating that they had done so at some point in the survey, which reinforces the hypothesis put forward earlier that they would have a strong link to the use of these tools. Of this group, only 29% started making such transactions in the wake of the pandemic, with the increase occurring mainly between June and August 2020. These purchases were mostly associated with food consumption. Also, almost half of the respondents indicated that they had had problems acquiring basic necessities from April to the date of this study. It is important to note in this group that 65% do not make their purchases with support, thus reinforcing the statement above that they have an adequate use of technology. This is why they consider that over time the technology itself has become more user-friendly, as reflected in the response of 48% of the respondents. However, we found in the qualitative analysis that there are members of this group who still show distrust, as indicated in the interview: *I don't use it, I think it's a deception, they can put pretty pictures and deliver other things. (interviewee 1)*

Generation X

The penultimate group analysed is Generation X. Here we can already find a slightly more marked differentiation with the age groups described above, since, although many of the people in this age range are far from a total link with the digital world, most of them have had experiences or are aware of the existence of these tools as possibilities for accessing consumer goods. Cullen (2001) indicated that, in terms of "ICT use, there are specific groups of people who are at a disadvantage, such as people with low incomes, low levels of schooling, the unemployed, older adults, residents of rural areas, people with disabilities, women and girls". Thus, in some cases, the consumption behaviour of this group during the pandemic was modified by the need to be able to acquire the goods necessary for their subsistence. However, in some cases, they showed distrust, seeing it as a traumatic event, because it represented new experiences and/or entering an unknown and disconcerting scenario by leaving aside the direct transaction between buyer-seller, which is reinforced in the idea of trust and visualization of the good in real-time and not in the idea of paying for or requesting a product for which one does not necessarily have all the information about its quality and characteristics requested. In relation to what has been argued in the previous lines, Martínez Domínguez (2018) indicates that older people are less adapted to new technologies than younger people.

A relevant finding for people in this group is that of the total number of people who indicated that they used social media to make purchases, 42% indicated that they had not made purchases through social media or other digital channels prior to the pandemic. This shows that a significant segment of the population changed their behaviour or had to adjust their behaviour due to the restrictions mentioned above. Also, all of the above-mentioned people indicated that they found social networks more user-friendly, which may indicate that there was a cultural and/or subjective factor that disengaged people in this group from earlier familiarisation with the use of digital media. *In* this sense, a study on technologies in the lives of older adults indicates that for people in this age range, "Some uses are incipient, such as economic transactions, due to a certain distrust and lack of transparency [that] older people perceive", reinforcing their idea by indicating that in older people, the traditional approach to ageing creates real barriers that prevent them from visualising the potential or facilities that the use of digital technologies can bring for the improvement of the quality of life of older people (Rivoir et al., 2019, p. 310).

The Baby Boomer Generation

The group of citizens is the most detached from the use of digital tools, due to the fact that they were born and developed their first skills in a social scenario in which these did not exist, so they are accustomed to the use of analog objects, placing them culturally more distant from the naturalization of the use of these devices. In this sense, Martínez Domínguez (2018) indicates that *people in the 19-30 and 31-50 age groups are more likely to use these technologies, compared to people over 50.* This has undoubtedly had an impact on how they conceive their use, and can change, as mentioned in previous paragraphs, the feeling of distrust and impossibility of approaching consumption channels to a completely different one that shortens gaps and generates technological learning options. It is therefore not surprising that the use of these technologies has been distant and complicated in the pandemic. According to the results found, this population group had little or no use of digital channels for the acquisition of consumer goods before the pandemic. However, as a result of COVID-19, this has had to change according to the needs that arose, as can be seen in the following statement: *I was also looking at clothes on the internet and I don't know if they will arrive and I don't know, there is always that doubt that they will not arrive because we are not used to ordering on the internet. (interviewee 2)*

The findings found in this age group show that of the total number of people surveyed, 67% have not used social networks to purchase any product. Of those who have used social networks, 47% have only done so since the pandemic, suggesting that these people have modified their behaviour due to the needs generated by social isolation. However, they still show difficulties in the use of digital means of payment, as they indicated that 75% of their payments are made in cash, i.e. the transaction was made on delivery. In addition, all of the people in this group used a family member's social network to make the purchase. The data collected show that one of the factors why people in this age group do not make purchases through these means is a cultural issue, which is demonstrated by the distrust they have indicated towards this type of non-face-to-face transaction. It is important to highlight that the highest percentage of their purchases were concentrated in food.

Thus, in this group, there is evidence of serious difficulties in the use of social networks, at least not on a constant basis, the lack of digital means of payment by these people and the disengagement with the management of digital tools, which may be known but mostly used in a basic way without exploiting all its functions. Thus, in most cases, people of these ages had to ask for support or be assisted by a younger person, who through advice or the use of their own networks facilitated and/or enabled the acquisition of goods or services that were usually used in the pre-pandemic scenario. This suggests that a certain level of dependency of people in this group on other age groups may have been generated. It is important to point out that, according to the information gathered, the confinement caused by the COVID-19 pandemic has also allowed people in this age range, due to the need to make purchases, to generate levels of learning that are important in terms of reinforcing confidence in these media, as can be seen in the statement: "*I have only started to use Internet shopping with the pandemic*" (interviewee 3).

Of the total number of interviews conducted, more than 70% indicated that they have ever used or purchased through social media. The rest of the respondents said that they were wary of making purchases through these channels. In this regard, it is worth noting that, of the total number of interviewees, one-third have only started using social networks since the pandemic, while 15% have increased their use, either as a means of social networking or as an instrument for making purchases.

Finally, the majority of people, around 85%, responded that, through websites or virtual media, they find what they are looking for, which represents an interesting result in terms of the variability of product offerings that guarantee a connection with the end consumer, generating bonds of trust in terms of being able to satisfy their needs. In terms of payment methods, almost all respondents indicated that they had or had used digital payment methods, such as credit cards, use of bank applications, deposits with agents, etc.

This reinforces the idea that there has been a change in behaviour as a consequence of the pandemic, meaning that people, faced with the need to be able to purchase the goods they used to use in the pre-pandemic scenario, have had to use digital tools, not only to search for products, but also to pay for them.

Among the factors that keep many sectors of the population away from the use of these tools are cultural, educational, distrust in the use of apps and lack of knowledge of their management, for example shopping online was easy for young people but not for adults and older adults who are less close to technology so it is necessary to empower citizens to make proper use of these resources, adults have the need to have contact with networks and learn from them to get closer and access them, without any dependence, in a friendly, agile and safe way. In this sense, virtual environments should facilitate processes with virtual instructions to access and make use of the services that are provided, due to the fact that the teaching levels of third parties are difficult, as it is observed that, if young people are closer to technology, it is not necessarily possible to find the availability to teach or help their relatives or close people because they have different interests and do not have the time.

Marketing Channels

Information and communication technologies ICT as an innovation perspective have considerably modified geography and barriers as influential elements in the dynamics of all types of marketing channels, this situation has influenced changes in the commercial and financial management of economic agents, at the same time the flow of abundant information to the consumer gives him greater power in his ability to choose; including the retail sector, thus constituting a process of commercial innovation based on internet support changing in shop approach, distribution channels and payment methods mainly (Garcia & Gil-Saura, 2016).

Research contributions in other geographical contexts reveal that in the COVID-19 environment, wholesale and emerging channels grew, achieving 63% and 57% share for each (Kantar 2020), adding this change to e-commerce and telesales that already showed a positive trend, in Peru there was an increase in purchase tickets in e-commerce platforms that went from 45 to 84 soles and telephone orders that increased from 10 to 21 soles (Peru Retail, 2020). With the prominence of receiving orders via telephone and WhatsApp, as well as the incorporation of less physical contact payments, accompanied by sanitary measures.

In Arequipa, the arrival of Covid-19 has configured a new scenario that was not foreseen, both in modern and traditional channels (BBVA Research, 2016), the latter represented mainly by markets, bodegas, small pharmacies, hardware stores, market stalls, kiosks with more points of sale, closer, more accessible and personalized.

On the other hand, in a crisis, decisions that in normal times could take years of deliberation are approved in a matter of hours (Harari, 2020). This is evident in the creativity of entrepreneurs who, having lost their jobs, initiate a variety of informal economic activities using social networks as an ally. An example of this is the emergence of informal mobile food trade by entrepreneurs motivated by scarcity and the need to take advantage of sales opportunities (Malone et al., 2020). This is a natural process brought about by emergencies, where progress is rapid.

One opportunity that is emerging in the midst of the pandemic is the delivery service, which is currently not fully developed, but under the adversities presented and the fear of contagion, business initiatives in this area are emerging. In the COVID-19 context, commerce has expanded by making use of ICTs as it has no geographical or time limits, where its implementation is more focused on consolidating the loyalty of the new digital consumer, who in turn influences other potential consumers through their opinions and recommendations, which become a decisive factor in the success or failure of a given business model. For this, commerce has to manage digital marketing for the interconnection with the consumer through a digital sales channel, with a website positioned in social networks, an e-commerce platform established as a virtual shop; vigilant of the expectations of the digital customer that allows to knowing the new consumer habits and trends of the network that causes a different and authentic experience around a product or service, valuing personalization in the purchase by comparing prices instantly satisfying demands in real-time where email plays the role in customer loyalty (Junta de Andalucía, 2020).

The pandemic has generated different reactions from the business point of view, one of them is the reactivation and reinforcement of e-commerce platforms to respond to the confinement. However, the implementation of service models such as D2C (Direct to consumer), which was already developed but is going through a process of consolidation necessary to face the current situation, is beginning.

On the other hand, we can see that, in the face of all this, there is a vulnerability in the different markets, so marketing channels have had a significant impact on the pandemic, in terms of the adaptation process in the future of sales. However, the consequences for customers and the impact on the economy remain uncertain.

Issues, Controversies, Problems

In the context of the pandemic, consumption needs to be addressed by trying to better understand people's decision-making process under uncertainty, giving rise to the analysis of behavioral economics to explain that people's consumption decisions are also motivated by cognitive, social and emotional aspects of humans, filling the gap of the rational agent approach.

As mentioned above, the pandemic caused by COVID-19 has forced many people, either voluntarily or by government order, to stay at home and thus to disengage from the consumption channels to which they were accustomed, modifying not only habits, but also the forms and goods to which they had the possibility of accessing. Now, the consumption behaviour of individuals can change depending on external events that condition their access to and behaviour towards the goods they usually purchase. Faced with this, e-commerce offers the opportunity to expand the current offer and create new lines of business, and with these experiences it is expected to generate trust and comfort, which generates the emergence of new habits and behaviours that are expected to persist after the pandemic, therefore, digital platforms and channels are getting stronger day by day, where companies must take advantage of and react to the opportunities under the current situation.

In the new context the traditional channel and modern channel have been confronted in the pandemic, while the traditional channel markets products through points of sale in markets, neighborhood shops, kiosks, etc., where the customer had direct interaction with the seller and its logistics or planning has no presence, it was observed that due to the pandemic the population came closer to these points of sale to avoid contagions, therefore it had growth, despite having informality as a characteristic. For Peru Retail (2018), two years ago it was considered that "In the interior of Peru, the bodegas, markets and street markets continue at the top, reflecting more than 90% of sales; and in the case of the capital, 70%, which had turned the traditional channel into a strategic medium that allows participation, diversification and profitability". By 2020 and with the confinement it seems that things have changed drastically and although the traditional channels have fallen to opt for modern ones, there is still the possibility of rethinking their entry strategies and positioning to a new market.

In recent years, the Traditional Channel has faced a competitor that is advancing at a rapid pace: the Modern Channel. The various shop formats that make up this channel have been understanding new consumer habits, have improved the shopping experience, and have diversified their value offer. The use of technology has been one of their main tools, not only to provide better customer service but also to perform business intelligence. The fast competitor seems to have it all. However, the pandemic has brought changes in the game that were not seen coming and that in some way favor the Traditional Channel or give it a breath of fresh air to improve its value offer and its role vis-à-vis consumers. (Fundes Latinoamerica, 2020)

On the other hand, according to the study by Consumer 360 and DATUM International (2020), 3% of consumers still use a traditional channel to make their purchases and transactions, while 28% use modern channels. An evaluation of security levels at the entrance to establishments has also been carried out, with encouraging results, for example, in commerce, security levels of 87% were achieved, but within this level, 70% use the traditional channel, while 96% use the modern channel. On the other hand, an interesting fact to mention is the NPS (Net Promoter Score) Index, which measures the willingness of customers to recommend a brand, where establishments in the traditional channel were the least recommended, reaching -37%, a situation that will be difficult to recover.

Trends

As countries have progressed towards a 'new normal', many behavioral patterns have changed, such as the use of online food delivery (Zwanka & Buff, 2020, pp. 58-67). This situation was later, as at the beginning of COVID-19, the first reaction was to access health supplies, but as the population met this need, another important need was food, but to ensure its consumption with non-perishable products. We could conclude that the changes in patterns have an impact not only in the pandemic but also post-pandemic.

Changes in consumption habits are significant at 77%, which does not imply an increase in their consumption, but their satisfaction levels are relatively high at 56%, however, 45% still had some level of difficulty in making their purchases.

As we have seen, the purchasing processes have increased significantly and a usual form of payment is via internet bank transfers (40%), in this sense, the levels of security in the management of these systems must consider the necessary levels of security to generate benefits for consumers.

The process of implementing technologies that may still have a risk in terms of their use, could generate a greater risk if they are not used. In this sense, isolation presents different situations in the business, educational, social, etc. spheres, generating different dynamics in consumers.

Technology allows to monitor the global situation and make decisions of different kinds, on the other hand, it is necessary to rely on existing technology and be alert in the development or improvement of existing ones, being friendly and agile turning the virtual into a strategy of advancement and development, there is empirical evidence from studies tracking consumers' online search movement behaviours, i.e. search paths and patterns, from a need perspective that can contribute to a deeper understanding of how consumer need states lead to different online search behaviours and thus can provide marketers with a benchmark evaluation model.

It is necessary to investigate the processes through which consumer behaviour has had significant variations in the relationship with social networks and websites, generating levels of dependence that are expected to be maintained over time due to the agility of use, the reduction of time in the development of actions, which could eventually become irreversible due to the benefits.

SOLUTIONS AND RECOMMENDATIONS

It is evident that the levels of adaptation to the use of ICTs for consumption have been effective, due to the development of user-friendly platforms, although there are some limitations due to the knowledge of age-related mechanisms and the mastery of ICTs, nevertheless, we are facing a new future, with significant changes in lifestyles, therefore, the levels of trust must be strengthened to guarantee the connection between consumers and companies.

After having developed the study, we can point out that we are living in different moments where society is developing accelerated processes in the adoption of technology, and society demands greater learning and knowledge generation in the new global context where the usefulness of the use of information and communication technologies (ICTs) in consumption must be rethought. It is possible to test prospective analyses to investigate the impact of new and different supply and demand channels and strategies differentiating goods of different priority in consumption, and it is also necessary to investigate the effect they have in coherence with cultural and anthropological aspects, particularly in rural areas.

FUTURE RESEARCH DIRECTIONS

It is also known that the marketing channels for food products currently differ significantly from those for health products, and it is therefore necessary to investigate whether these differences will continue and whether there is a trend towards new ways of converging on the same channel. It is also necessary to investigate to what extent the process of learning about the use of technologies could have an effect on the purchasing decision process and, in addition, to investigate the development of e-commerce and its influence on companies and customers in the post-pandemic situation, as well as to investigate intercultural applications generated on the internet, another topic of interest is related to written language through e-mail and social networks. Another important topic is the functioning of educational modalities, related to the cost-time and cost-benefit binomials.

We also consider that the differences in the digital divide may be more noticeable when comparing consumers in urban and rural areas, and that the information gathered will provide us with important elements for decision-making on the use of technology in different areas or sectors. Finally, to rescue and propose research perspectives related to ICTs, age groups, marketing channels in critical health situations (pandemics), among others.

CONCLUSION

In times of pandemic, ICTs have had a differentiated influence on the decisions of consumers of different age groups, generating challenges and opportunities in the process of adaptation of the different generations. In relation to age segments, some have had dominance and perhaps a greater advantage in the process of accessing digital environments, while others have had limited progress, we can mention that all of them have had active participation in the use of technologies to varying degrees.

The use of ICTs for e-commerce in Arequipa is progressively gaining ground in the Centennials and Millennials age segments, with a slight increase in Generation X and Baby Boomers, and it is possible that the trend will continue to grow even after the end of the pandemic. With different expertise, the different age segments analyzed already showed a growing trend in the use of ICTs before the pandemic, with less intensity in the baby boomers, and in this sense, we can speak of a greater dominance of consumers of younger generations.

Mistrust is an element mentioned in all age segments, and the greater the distrust, the more consumers prefer to pay in cash on delivery. This aspect is a challenge to further consolidate the progress of e-commerce, because, when asked about trust in social networks to make purchases, only 7% of digital natives stated that they trust them, while 74% of them only consider them to be moderate to not very trustworthy. Among digital immigrants, trust is only reflected in 1.3%. These results would indicate that there is a need to implement strategies to consolidate the issue of trust in digital platforms for all actors involved in their use.

The anthropological aspects of the use of electronic devices show that digital environments have been revealed as the necessary complement to speed up these processes, making possible a close relationship between consumers and economic activities, which over time have massified, thereby strengthening electronic commerce, a situation that will have an irreversible character, where the conditions of connectivity can strengthen the digital market. It has also been observed that, in underdeveloped societies, the cultural factor has had an important influence on the access and use of ICTs, due to the fact that, on the one hand, the link with these tools in these societies is later than in developed societies and, on the other hand, because they are more heterogeneous societies in terms of their cultural and social composition, thus delaying the massification of their use and therefore the adaptation and assimilation of the population for their use.

REFERENCES

Akerlof, G. A., & Shiller, R. J. (2015). *The economics of manipulation. How we fall like dupes into the plots of the market.* Planeta Colombiana S.A.

Baena Rojas, J. J., Cano Arenas, J. A., Jarrin Quintero, J. A., & Pérez Arroyave, H. R. (2014). Use of information and communication technologies for international negotiation: An advantage for Colombian companies? *Revista Ciencias Estratégicas, 22*(32), 279-294. Retrieved from https://www.redalyc.org/pdf/1513/151339264007.pdf

Ballesteros Riveros, D. P., & Ballesteros Silva, P. P. (2004). Competitive logistics and supply chain management. *Sciences et Techniques (Paris)*, 201–206. https://www.redalyc.org/pdf/849/84912053030.pdf

BBVA Research. (28 April 2016). *Peru: The retail sector.* Retrieved from https://www.bbvaresearch.com/publicaciones/peru-el-sector-retail/

Caceres Cabana, Y. D., Gonzalez, S., & Rivera Medina, J. (2020). Alpaca meat: constraints and reinforcements in consumption. In Anthropological approaches to understanding consumption patterns and consumer behaviour. IGI Global. doi:10.4018/978-1-7998-3115-0.ch016

CAF Development Bank of Latin America. (2020). The state of Latin America's digitalization in the face of the COVID-19 pandemic. *CAF Observatory of the Digital Ecosystem, 19*(3), 17. Retrieved from https://scioteca.caf.com/handle/123456789/1540

CAF Development Bank of Latin America. (2020). *The state of Latin America's digitalization in the face of the COVID-19 pandemic* (Vol. 19). Retrieved from Observatorio CAF del Ecosistema Digital: https://scioteca.caf.com/handle/123456789/1540

Casco, A. R. (2020). Effects of the COVID-19 pandemic on consumer behavior. *INNOVARE Journal of Science and Technology, 9*(2).

Central Reserve Bank of Peru. (2016). *Informe Económico y Social Región Arequipa.* Retrieved from https://www.bcrp.gob.pe/docs/Proyeccion-Institucional/Encuentros-Regionales/2016/arequipa/ies-arequipa-2016.pdf

Consumer 360 and DATUM International. (2020). *Customer Experience and COVID-19 Comercio, Bancos y Farmacias protocols.* Retrieved from https://www.datum.com.pe/new_web_files/files/pdf/2020%20Experiencia%20del%20Cliente%20y%20Protocolos%20Covid-19.pdf

Cullen, R. (2001). Tackling the digital divide. *Online Information Review, 25*(5), 311–320. doi:10.1108/14684520110410517

Diaz-Sarmiento, C., López-Lambraño, M., & Roncallo-Lafont, L. (2017). Understanding generations: a review of the concept, classification and distinguishing characteristics of baby boomers, X and millennials. *Revista Clío América*, 188-204. doi:10.21676/23897848.2440

Food and Agriculture Organization of the United Nations. (2017). *Food and Agriculture. Actions to advance the agenda of the 2030 Agenda and Sustainable Development Goals.* FAO. Retrieved from http://www.fao.org/3/a-i7454s.pdf

Fundes Latinoamerica. (2020). *Why are FMCG companies focusing - today more than ever - on the traditional channel?* Retrieved from https://www.fundes.org/por-que-las-empresas-de-consumo-masivo-se-estan-enfocando-hoy-mas-que-nunca-en-el-canal-tradicional/

Garcia, A. M., & Gil-Saura, I. (2016). *Innovating in retail trade: the influence of ICT and its effects on customer satisfaction.* doi:10.5295/cdg.10556am

Hao, N., Wang, H. H., & Zhou, Q. (2020). The impact of online grocery shopping on stockpile behavior in Covid-19. China agricultural economic review. *Revisión económica agrícola de China, 12*(3), 459-470. doi:10.1108/CAER-04-2020-0064

Harari, Y. H. (2020). *The world after the coronavirus.* Retrieved from http://virtual.iuc.edu.co/pluginfile.php/3512/mod_resource/content/1/2.%20FILOSOF%C3%8DA%20MAYO%2011%20-%2015.pdf

INEI. (2014). *Results of the Micro and Small Enterprise Survey 2013.* Retrieved from https://www.inei.gob.pe/media/MenuRecursivo/publicaciones_digitales/Est/Lib1139/libro.pdf

INEI. (2017). *National Census of Food Markets 2016.* Retrieved from https://www.inei.gob.pe/media/MenuRecursivo/publicaciones_digitales/Est/Lib1448/libro.pdf

INEI. (2018). *Technical report Estadísticas de las Tecnologías de Información y Comunicación en los Hogares.* Retrieved from https://www.inei.gob.pe/media/MenuRecursivo/boletines/04-informe-tecnico-n04_tecnologias-de-informacion-jul-ago-set2018.pdf

Internet World Sats. (2020). *Internet World Sats.* Retrieved from https://www.internetworldstats.com/stats2.htm

Jones, C., Alderete, M. V., & Motta, J. (2013). E-commerce adoption in Micro, Small and Medium-sized commercial and service enterprises in Cordoba. *Cuadernos de Administración, 29*(50), 164-175. Retrieved from https://www.redalyc.org/pdf/2250/225029797006.pdf

Junta de Andalucía. (2020). *Guide Using ICTs to reach new market niches and consumers.* Retrieved from www.formacion.andaluciaesdigital.es: https://www.formacion.andaluciaesdigital.es/catalogo-cursos/-/acciones/ficha/7809

Kantar. (2020). *A new world: Changes and prospects for shopping channels.* Retrieved from http://mkt.kantarworldpanel.com: http://mkt.kantarworldpanel.com/global/LATAM/Retail/Retail_COVID-19_v3.pdf

Kirk, C. P., & Rifkin, L. S. (2020, September). I'll trade you diamonds for toilet paper: Consumer reacts, copes, and adapts behaviors in the COVID-19 pandemic. *Journal of Business Research, 117*, 124–131. doi:10.1016/j.jbusres.2020.05.028 PMID:32834208

Malone, A., Caceres Cabana, Y. D., & Taya Zegarra, A. (2020). Informal food systems and differential mobility during the COVID-19 pandemic in Arequipa, Perú. *The Town Planning Review.* Advance online publication. doi:10.3828/tpr.2020.61

Marcus, G. E., & Fisher, M. M. (1999). *Anthropology as Cultural Critique: An experimental moment in the human sciences.* doi:10.7208/chicago/9780226229539.001.0001

Martelo, R. J., Jimenez-Pitre, I., & Moncaris Gonzalez, L. (2017). Guía Metodológica para el Mejoramiento del Desarrollo de Software a través de la Aplicación de la Técnica Árboles de Problemas. *Información Tecnológica, 28*(3), 87–94. doi:10.4067/S0718-07642017000300010

Martinez Coral, P. (2017). "Seguro mató a confianza": Challenges for the adoption of digital government in Colombia. *Academic Journals: Inclusion and Development, 5*(1), 63–72. doi:10.26620/uniminuto.inclusion.5.1.2018.63-72

Martinez Dominguez, M. (2018). Access to and use of information and communication technologies in Mexico: determinants. *PAAKAT: Journal of Technology and Society, 8*(14). Retrieved from . doi:10.32870/Pk.a8n14.316

Masicampo, E. J., & Baumeister, R. F. (2011). Consider it done! Plan making can eliminate the cognitive effects of unfulfilled goals. *Revista de personalidad y psicología social, 101*(4), 667-683. doi:10.1037/a0024192

Mullainathan, S., & Shafir, E. (2016). *Scarcity: Why does having little mean so much?* Fondo de Cultura Económica.

Nielsen. (2020). *COVID-19 will affect low-income consumers in Latin America the most.* Retrieved from https://www.nielsen.com/pe/es/insights/article/2020/covid-19-afectara-mas-a-los-consumidores-de-bajos-ingresos-en-latinoamerica/

Ogbum, W. F., & Thomas, D. S. (1922, May 8). The influence of the business cycle on certain social conditions. *Journal of the American Statistical Association, 18*(139), 324–340. doi:10.1080/01621459 .1922.10502475

Ortega-Vivanco, M. (2020, March). Effects of Covid-19 on consumer behaviour: The case of Ecuador. *RETOS. Journal of Management Science and Economics, 10*(20). Advance online publication. doi:10.17163/ret.n20.2020.03

Pérez-Escoda, A., Castro-Subizarreta, A., & Fandos-Igado, M. (2016). The digital competence of Generation Z: keys for its curricular introduction in Primary School. *Scientific Journal of Educommunication, 49*, 71-80. Retrieved from https://www.redalyc.org/pdf/158/15847434008.pdf

Peru Retail. (2018). *Peru: Traditional vs. modern channel.* Lima. Retrieved from https://www.peru-retail. com/peru-canal-tradicional-vs-canal-moderno/

Peru Retail. (2020) *What are the most visited shopping channels by Peruvians before Covid-19?* Retrieved from https://www.peru-retail.com/cuales-son-los-canales-de-compra-mas-visitados-por-los-peruanos-ante-el-covid-19/

Phillip Kottak, C. (2011). Cultural anthropology. McG.

Regional Government of Arequipa. (2020). *Regional Executive Resolution N° 192-2020-GRA/GR.* Retrieved from www.regionarequipa.gob.pe: https://www.regionarequipa.gob.pe/Cms_Data/Contents/ GobRegionalArequipaInv/Media/Resolucion.Detalle/2020/R.E.R/RER-192-2020.pdf

Rivoir, A., Morales, M. J., & Casamayou, A. (July 18, 2019). Uses and perceptions of digital technologies in older people. Limitations and benefits for their quality of life. *Austral Journal of Social Sciences*, 295-313. doi:10.4206/rev.austral.cienc.soc.2019.n36-15

Serrano, C. L., Peña Lapeira, C. J., & Laverde Guzmán, M. Y. (2018). Influence of ICT in the economic development of Colombia. *Revista Ciencias de la Información*, 3-10. Retrieved from http://cinfo.idict. cu/index.php/cinfo/article/view/854

Sheth, J. (2020). Impact of Covid-19 on consumer behavior: Will the old habits return or die? *Journal of Business Research 117*, 280-283. doi:10.1016/j.jbusres.2020.05.059

Superintencia de Banca. Seguros y AFP - BID. (2012). *Pilot Survey on Access to and Use of Financial Services 2012.* Retrieved from https://www.sbs.gob.pe/Portals/0/jer/est_incl_finan/Informe%20de%20 resultados%20inferenciales_.pdf

Telecom Advisory Services, LLC. (2015). *The Digital Ecosystem and Economy in Latin America.* Retrieved from http://www.teleadvs.com/wp-content/uploads/Presentacion_IGF_v3.pdf

Thomas, F., Handdon, L., Gilligan, R., Heinzmann, P., & De Gournay, C. (2005). Cultural Factors Shaping the Experience of ICTs: An Exploratory Review. *ResearchGate*. Obtenido de https://www.researchgate.net/ publication/251783055_Cultural_Factors_Shaping_the_Experience_of_ICTs_An_Exploratory_Review

Varian, H. R. (2014). *Intermediate Microeconomics A Modern Approach* (9th ed.). Theresia Kowara.

Weinmann, M., Schneider, C., & Vom Brocke, J. (2016). Digital Nudging. *Business & Information Systems Engineering, 433-436*. Advance online publication. doi:10.2139srn.2708250

World Economic Forum. (2019). *What are ICTs?* Retrieved from en.weforum.org: https://es.weforum.org/agenda/2019/02/que-son-las-tics/

Zwanka, R., & Buff, C. (2020). Generation COVID-19: A conceptual framework of consumer behavioral changes to be caused by the COVID-19 pandemic. *Journal of International Consumer Marketing, 33*(1), 58–67. doi:10.1080/08961530.2020.1771646

KEY TERMS AND DEFINITIONS

Arequipeño: Gentilicio of the people born in Arequipa.

Consumer: People of both sexes, from different age segments who develop various ways to purchase goods and services from providers in the context of the Covid-19 pandemic, through the use of information technologies.

Consumer Trends: Evolution of the changes and strategies consumers have chosen to purchase goods and services as a result of the COVID-19 pandemic.

Digital Technologies: Information technology tools used by consumers in email services, web usage, data storage, e-banking, virtual communities managed through devices such as computers, mobile phones and tablets.

COVID-19: Pandemic that has affected the health of the population with effects on other socioeconomic components in the context of the city of Arequipa.

Generational Groups: Groups of individuals who purchase goods and services, classified by age criteria in accordance with the definitions of Baby Boomers, Generation X, Y and Z.

Informal Sector: Persons or organizations that carry out precarious economic activities with the aim of self-employment, but without having fulfilled legal requirements of formality.

Marketing Channels: Different routes that goods and services take, managed by economic actors from production processes to delivery to consumers in the pre-pandemic and pandemic stages.

Chapter 16
Artificial Intelligence in Marketing:
A Review of Consumer–AI Interactions

Özge Sığırcı
Kırklareli University, Turkey

ABSTRACT

The purpose of this chapter is to shed light on the consumer-AI interaction in the marketplace. By this aim, the chapter uses a literature review approach. The previous literature examining AI from a consumer behavior perspective is reviewed, and the findings are compiled in a meaningful flow. According to the review, we see that the traditional marketplace is shaped by AI from only human-to-human interactions to human-to-AI and AI-to-AI interactions. In this new marketplace, while consumers interact with AI, they gain new experiences and feel positive or negative because of these experiences. Also, they build different relationships with AI, such as servant, master, or partner. Besides these relationships, there are still concerns about AI that are related to privacy, algorithmic biases, consumer vulnerability, unemployment, and ethical decision making.

INTRODUCTION

The artificial intelligence (AI) concept was born in the mid-twentieth century (Feng et al., 2020) and can be defined as the "computational agents that act intelligently" (Poole & Mackworth, 2010, p. 3). Human intelligence is imitated by machines in AI. Thus, AI can complete the tasks such as visual perception, speech recognition, and decision-making under uncertainty that normally requires human intelligence (Gillath, et al., 2021; Rossi, 2018; Russell & Norvig, 2016).

Today AI is used by companies and it is in the life of consumers. For example, consumers can talk to a chatbot when they call a company or interact with the robot employees working at hotel receptions when making a hotel reservation. Product recommendations in online shopping are made by an AI system even if the consumer is not aware of. Besides, there are smart home appliances such as smart refrigerators in today's homes that can talk to each other to find out what is needed at home and make the orders

DOI: 10.4018/978-1-7998-6985-6.ch016

on behalf of the consumer. There are robot vacuum cleaners like iRobot which can do the cleaning for its owner. There are digital assistants such as Alexa or Siri that wait to hear their names to satisfy their owners' requests changing from learning today's weather to making a restaurant reservation. Also, AI-enabled self-driving cars is just around the corner. As can be seen from all these examples, AI is in the middle of consumers' life both with the companies' marketing activities and the products or services consumers directly use. Market growth rates also tell us that AI will penetrate more into the consumers' life in the near future (Bughin et al., 2017).

At this point, questions about the state of consumer-AI interaction comes to mind. What does AI mean to consumers, does it satisfy consumers to be served by an AI agent instead of a human, what sort of experiences and relationships do consumers have with AI, in which situations do consumers resist AI and what are consumers' concerns about AI? The answers to these questions are critical for companies. Because the implementation of AI in marketing has changed the way companies interact with their consumers and offered companies many benefits. For instance, with the help of AI technologies, companies can manage consumer data more efficiently and better understand their consumers and their shopping patterns, which can positively affect consumer satisfaction (Ameen et al., 2020; Evans, 2019). But AI system investments that are not wanted and accepted by consumers can create problems such as lower consumer satisfaction, negative consumer perception and behavior. Understanding how consumers perceive AI, the types of relationships they have with AI and their concerns toward AI will help companies design right AI-enabled products and services, take precautions for consumer concerns and reach their target customers with the right marketing communication strategies. Thus, the main aim of this chapter is to shed light on the consumer-AI interaction in the marketplace. By this aim, we reviewed the previous literature examining AI from a consumer behavior perspective and compiled the findings in a meaningful flow under this chapter.

This chapter could be beneficial for different parties such as practitioners, researchers, and students. We hope the practitioners can use this chapter to understand the consumers' perception of AI better and use these findings to design their AI technologies better. The researchers can see the previous research, detect the gaps in the literature, and design future research questions. Also, the students can learn the dynamics of AI in businesses and consumer behavior.

The chapter begins with introducing AI and its foundations and examining the usages of AI in marketing by giving real-world examples from a variety of sectors. Then we focus on how AI has transformed the service encounter, how consumers interact, have experiences, build relationships with AI and consumers' attitudes toward AI. It is followed by the concerns both consumers, researchers, and critics have about AI. In the final part of the chapter, we offer a conclusion, based on the discussion of reviewed literature, and directions for future research.

What is Artificial Intelligence

Artificial Intelligence is about computer systems that mimic the intelligence of humans. So, the question is, what do we mean by mimicking human intelligence? We mean that these computer systems have the ability to perceive the world around them and take actions based on these perceptions (Overgoor et al., 2019) and perform typical human mind functions such as perception, cognition, and conversation (Longoni, Bonezzi & Morewedge, 2019). Visual perception, speech recognition, decision-making, memory, reasoning, problem-solving, and goal-oriented actions are some of the abilities of AI that position it close to human intelligence (Paschen et al., 2019; Rossi, 2018).

Artificial Intelligence systems perceive and process the input data to take the aforementioned actions (Jarek & Mazurek, 2019). AI uses many tools to perform its actions, such as machine learning, deep learning, natural language processing, neural networks, rule-based expert systems, physical robots, and robotic process automation (Davenport & Ronanki, 2018). Among these technologies, machine learning has a special place. Machine learning is a subset of AI (Russo, 2020), and with the help of machine learning, computers can learn by themselves from the data by finding patterns in the data (Jarek & Mazurek, 2019). With the advancements in machine learning technology, computer systems not only follow the instructions of the program, but also they learn from the training data by recognizing the patterns in the data and developing algorithms based on these patterns. As a result, they perform various tasks, such as making predictions and recommendations based on their learning (Du & Xie, 2021; Russo, 2020). Examples of AI include personal helpers like Siri and Alexa, credit scoring assistants like IBM's Watson, humanoid robots that can be used as greeters or service providers like Pepper, and self-driving cars.

Foundations of Artificial Intelligence

The roots of artificial intelligence can be traced back to the 1940s (Haenlein & Kaplan, 2019). In 1942 Isaac Asimov published a short story named "Runaround," which was built on Asimov's "Three Laws of Robotics". The story has inspired scientists from a variety of fields for generations. At the similar time period, mathematician and computer scientist Alan Turing, who was working for the British government, invented a code-breaking machine to break the Enigma code used by the German army. Breaking of the Enigma code by a machine, led Turing to think about the intelligence of machines (Haenlein & Kaplan, 2019). In 1950, he pointed out artificial intelligence and proposed Turing Test to test the intelligence of the machines in his influential article "Computing Machinery and Intelligence" (Turing, 1950).

In 1956, John McCarthy and his colleagues organized the *Dartmouth Summer Research Project on Artificial Intelligence*. They invited researchers from various fields to discuss developing machines that simulate human intelligence (McCarthy et al., 1955). This workshop was considered the beginning of the AI field, where the name *AI* is officially used, and the founders of the AI field came together (Feng, et al., 2020; Haenlein & Kaplan, 2019; Ma & Sun, 2020). Since then, research trying to understand AI and the development of AI entities have continued and progressed. Today, image recognition, speech processing, and autonomous driving are some of the possible tasks performed by AI (Ma & Sun, 2020). With the help of technological advancements in Big Data and computing power (Haenlein & Kaplan, 2019), AI has impacted and transformed many fields from finance and education to healthcare and biology (Huang & Rust, 2018; Rust, 2020). Business and marketing are also one of the most benefitted fields from AI.

To better understand where we are today in the developmental stages of AI, a discussion of the AI types can be necessary. Literature mentions two types of AI: *weak (narrow) AI* and *strong AI. Weak (narrow) AI* is the type of AI that can mimic human intelligence by analyzing large amounts of data (Russell & Norvig, 2016). Though it is trained to solve a specific problem, it needs training for solving other problems (Wirth, 2018). It does not mean that weak AI cannot mimic human intelligence or perform tasks successfully, but it is comparatively weak against human intelligence. So, it can be said that, though weak AI systems can be very powerful in their specifically trained area, they are not as flexible as human intelligence in other areas (Wirth, 2018). On the other hand, *strong AI* is about the machines having a conscience (Russell & Norvig, 2016), and we can speak of context awareness (Davenport et al., 2020). In strong AI, we expect machines to think holistically, give context-specific responses, and as a result complete more complex tasks (Huang & Rust, 2018).

Considering the recent developments in AI, researchers think that it is not easy to categorize some of today's advanced systems as weak/narrow AI and offered the term *'hybrid AI'* for the systems that integrate multiple weak AI systems (Greenwald, 2011). Also, they offered the idea to conceptualize the levels of artificial intelligence as a continuum to position the systems such as Google's DeepMind AlphaGo or IBM's Watson at a higher level than positioning them as just weak/narrow AI (Davenport et al., 2020; Wirth, 2018). Though it should be noted that, while it is possible to position some of today's systems to an upper level than weak AI, AI systems today is still far from being at the level of strong AI, and reaching a context-awareness level looks like a low chance by 2050 (Davenport et al., 2020; Müller & Bostrom 2016).

Different Usages of AI in Marketing

When we look at the usage of AI in businesses, we see a broad set of applications in various sectors such as retailing, health care, public sector, hospitality, and education. This broad usage areas lead consumers to interact with and have experience with AI. Sometimes consumers are aware that they are interacting with an AI and sometimes they are not aware of that, even if there was an AI agent at the background. But in both cases a consumer experience occurs, and this experience affects consumers' satisfaction or dissatisfaction with the brand. Hence, here we will try to examine the different usages of AI in the marketing activities of businesses from different sectors, based on real-world examples. Examining the AI applications in businesses -especially in marketing and consumer behavior-related areas- led us to think that it can be appropriate to categorize these usages under three categories. First of all, there are AI systems that are kind of an employee for the firms and directly interact or communicate with the customers. In the second group, there are AI systems that help the firm with some of the tasks or perform the tasks on behalf of the firm but do not have direct interaction with the customers. In the final group, there are AI systems that are actually the product or the service itself the company offers.

AI systems that direct customer-AI interaction occurs: Under this category, we will examine AI systems that work as the employees of the company and directly interact with customers. The first way companies use AI under this category is as chatbots or virtual assistants. Companies use chatbots or virtual assistants to interact with their customers and answer their questions. Since these virtual assistants can provide 24/7 customer support and costs lower than human employees, many companies choose them as their employees (Pantano & Pizzi, 2020). For example, Ojo Labs, a real estate company, developed a chatbot to answer potential homebuyers' questions via messaging (Longoni & Cian, 2020; Wiggers, 2019). Also, another real estate company REX Real Estate is also using a voice/chatbot for home showings (Silverstein, 2018). An alcoholic drinks company, Diageo's chatbot called 'Simi-Your Personal Bartender' gives consumers cocktail recipes based on the consumers' preferences and the ingredients they have at home (Bhatia, 2016). IPsoft developed AI digital assistant Amelia in 2014, and many companies now use it as an AI employee to serve as a customer support agent (Hwang & Park, 2020). She has many human interaction elements such as conversation, expression, emotion, and understanding (Amelia, n.d.). Another example is Conversica AI virtual assistant; it is a chatbot that interacts with customers and potential customers and helps companies both in sales and marketing activities (Davenport et al., 2020).

Other usages of AI adopted by companies that have direct interaction with the customers can be in the payment or recommendation systems. For example, KFC in China uses a facial recognition-based AI system so that customers can buy their food and make their payments by only showing their faces to the system (Thales, 2018). Similarly, we see the usage of image recognition-based technologies in the beauty and fashion sectors too. Revieve has an AI Skincare advisor that detects the consumers' skin and recommends suitable products for their skin after uploading a selfie (Revieve, n.d.). In the fashion industry, virtual mirrors help consumers see the collection on themselves virtually and recommend appropriate pieces to their appearance and taste (Jarek & Mazurek, 2019).

From the point of different sectors, we see the usage of AI in financial services. For example, Plum and Betterment are AI assistants that help people manage their money by saving, investing, or reducing their bills. These financial assistants analyze people's funds and expenses and develop customized savings plans, and they provide these financial services at a lower cost than a human financial expert. Moreover, Upstart is an AI lending service that uses non-conventional variables to calculate consumers' credit risk and help consumers' access to credit and offer lower loss rates (Upstart, n.d.).

Tourism and hospitality is another sector that uses AI. Although many companies use AI in purely virtual forms, such as virtual assistants, as we mentioned previously, AI can also be embedded in robots that have physical embodiment (Davenport, et al., 2020). Previous literature also shows that consumers prefer to interact with robots than with AI without a physical embodiment (Davenport, et al., 2020). We see examples of humanoid service robots in the tourism and hospitality sector in addition to virtual assistants. For example, KLM introduced Robot Spencer to serve in Schiphol Amsterdam Airport. Robot Spencer scans passengers' boarding passes and guides them to their departure gate; also, it adjusts its speed according to the passengers and informs them about the departure gate distance (KLM, 2016). KLM started using their new robot; KLM Care-E, a self-driving luggage trolley with voice and physical movement abilities to scan passengers' boarding passes, carry their luggage, and guide them to their gates (Klmcare, n.d.). In hotels, AI is used in the form of autonomous check-ins or room delivery robots (Tussyadiah, 2020). For example, Hotel Trio in Healdsburg, California, uses service robot Rosé to deliver wine to the rooms (Romano, 2020). A unique example is Henn na Hotel in Japan, whose staff are mostly robots. It is possible to see dinosaur robot receptionists or robots in the cloakroom (Henn na Hotel, n.d.). Other examples can be the robot barista called Tipsy Robot that works at a bar in Las Vegas, or the Café X, robotic coffee bars.

The last sector that we commonly see the AI applications, and we want to mention here is the healthcare sector. Although the usage of AI in the healthcare sector is manifold, under this category, we will only mention the AI systems that have direct interaction with the patients. For example, the UK's National Health Service (NHS) tried a medical chatbot in its non-emergency helpline to help patients give medical advice (Vincent, 2017). There are virtual nurses like Care Angel too.

AI systems that no direct customer-AI interaction occurs: Firms also use AI systems to help them manage some of their tasks, but consumers may not have a direct interaction with these AI systems. The first example can be the AI recommendation systems; many firms use AI for recommending customers new products or services based on their past purchases or rated items. Companies such as Amazon, Netflix, and Spotify use these AI-enabled recommendation systems to recommend consumers products or services they might like. Many beauty brands also make recommendations about their products by using AI (Longoni & Cian, 2020). We see the usage of AI recommendation systems in clothing and styling businesses as well, such as Stitch Fix and Trendy Butler (Davenport et al., 2020). AI-enabled recommendation systems significantly affect the companies' revenue, such that Amazon's recommendation system generated 35% of the company's revenue (Morgan, 2018).

Healthcare is another sector that uses AI. By offering expert-level accuracy, cost-effectiveness, and faster processes (Esteva et al. 2017; Gallagher, 2017; Leachman & Merlino, 2017), AI helps transform and develop healthcare services. AI is being used in healthcare to help physicians in tasks like evaluating the radiological images, pathology slides, or EMR results of patients (Mintz & Brodie, 2019). For example, IBM's Watson is designed to help doctors diagnose heart diseases (Hinchliffe, 2017). Firms also use AI to understand online WOM (Netzer, 2012; Tirunillai & Tellis, 2014), to do stock management in warehouses like Amazon Kiva, to develop creative ad campaigns (Jarek & Mazurek, 2019), and to optimize prices (Antonio, 2018). With the help of AI, even online retailers will be able to transform their business models from shopping-then-shipping to shipping-then-shopping. This means that retailers will ship to the customer based on the accuracy of their predictions even before the customer orders the product (Davenport et al., 2020).

AI systems which are the product or the service itself that the company offers: Voice-controlled virtual assistants such as Apple's Siri, Google's Assistant, Amazon's Alexa are major examples for this category that have pervasive usage. They are the virtual helpers of the users, and the users do not have to learn any specific commands to interact with these assistants because these assistants listen for their names and respond to natural language (Jones, 2018). They can help with a variety of tasks; sending a text, setting a reminder, making restaurant reservations, playing your favorite music, giving a real-time answer about the weather or traffic are just a few examples we can mention about their capabilities. There are also robots used for homecare like iRobot, or the companion robots like Buddy, and the commercialization of autonomous vehicles is predicted to be inevitable (Lanctot, 2017). These assistants or autonomous agents are not only making life easier for their users, but also they are helpful for their manufacturers. By analyzing the data collected by these assistants, which are critical personal level data, brands can understand their consumers more deeply and take strategical and tactical decisions (Jones, 2018).

AI and New Marketplace

As can be understood from the examples given above, AI and usage of AI in marketing have transformed the traditional marketplace. In this section, we will examine how the marketplace service encounter has been transformed by AI. In traditional marketplace service encounters, we see that both parties of the encounter -the customer and the service provider- are human. In other words, we are used to seeing interhuman (human-to-human) service encounters in the marketplace. For instance, when we think about a hotel reception service in the traditional marketplace, both the receptionist and the customer are human. However, today's advances in technology reveal service encounters more often where the customer or service provider or both are artificial intelligence.

Robinson et al. (2020) categorized today's new service encounter as; (1) human customer-to-human frontline employees (interhuman) service encounters, (2) human customer-to-AI frontline employees service encounter, (3) AI customer-to-human frontline employees service encounter, and (4) AI customers-to-AI frontline employees service encounter.

1. Human Customers-to-Human Frontline Employees: This is the traditional interhuman service encounter, where both the customer and frontline employees are human.
2. Human Customers-to-AI Frontline Employees: This is an "interspecific" type of interaction where the customer is human, and the AI frontline employee is interacting with the human customers on behalf of the firm (Robinson et al. 2020). For example, a customer served by a robot receptionist at the robot hotel, Hotel Henn na in Japan, has this type of relationship. As a more frequent usage, a human customer interacting with a company's chatbot to make orders or get some information also experiences this type of relationship.

3. AI Customers-to-Human Frontline Employees: On the other hand, we now see AI playing the role of the customer and interacting with a human service provider. A digital assistant calling a doctor's office on behalf of its owner to make an appointment and answered by a human employee can be an example of this encounter. These AI customers can mimic human voice so perfectly that they are even criticized for deceiving the human service exchange partner (Robinson et al. 2020).
4. AI Customers-to-AI Frontline Employees: We do not only see AI consumers interacting with human frontline employees, but also there can be an AI frontline employee at the other end of the service exchange. This service encounter is labeled as "inter AI" service encounters, where both the customer and the firm are represented by an AI agent (Robinson et al. 2020). In other words, AI agents communicate with each other on behalf of the customer and firm without any human involvement. This type of AI-to-AI communication occurs in smart service systems (Robinson et al. 2020). For example, Google Home can communicate with Amazon's Alexa and order food through FoodMonkey application which is also another AI-enabled system (Voice2Biz, n.d.)

To understand the broader interactions of human and artificial intelligence in the marketplace, it is possible to broaden the service encounter framework of Robinson et al. (2020) by including the interactions within customers and interactions within employees. For instance, in this new service encounter framework, one can also think about the interactions between human customers and the AI-customers (e.g., voice controlled smart assistants) and the interactions between human frontline employees and AI-frontline employees too.

The categorization and examination of today's service encounter shows us that, with the inclusion of AI systems, today's service encounter has turned into a new place. It is critical for marketers to understand consumers' perception, attitudes, relationships and behaviors in this new marketplace. Moreover it is critical to understand who the new AI consumer is. While MacInnis and Folkes (2010) examined the boundaries of consumer behavior research, they underlined the role of "people" playing the consumer role. However, today, we see that objects with AI also start playing the role of consumer. Thus, in the light of Hoffman and Novak (2018: 1198), who considered smart objects "as consumers with their own consumption experiences", and proposed assemblage theory framework which "strongly implies that smart objects play a role in consumption-related processes", it is maybe time to question the boundaries of who the consumer is and the boundaries of consumer behavior research in that sense. Hence, it is time for firms to think about adapting their marketing strategies for these AI consumers and researchers to focus their research effort on

better understanding AI consumers. In relation with this new service encounter perspective, in the following sections, we will focus on the previous research findings to explain the consumers' experiences and relationships with AI, their attitudes toward and concerns about AI.

Consumer Experiences and Consumer Relationships with AI

Since there is a consumer experience in every interaction through the customer journey (Lemon & Verhoef, 2016), consumers' interactions with AI in the marketplace also create consumer experiences. From the consumer point of view, Puntoni et al. (2021) classified these experiences under four groups: data capture experiences, classification experiences, delegation experiences, and social experiences.

Data Capture Experience: Data capture experience is the experience of consumers' sharing their data with AI. Consumers can share their data with AI in different ways; they can either intentionally transfer their data to AI to use the services AI offers or the AI can collect consumers' data from their "footsteps" they leave behind (Puntoni et al., 2021). For instance, consumers can intentionally share their specific preferences with a digital assistant to get customized recommendations. As a consequence of data capture experience consumers can either feel served by the AI or exploited (Puntoni et al., 2021).

Classification Experience: Classification experience is the consumers' perception that they are getting personalized predictions because they are labeled as consumers with certain types of tastes. As the consequences of classification experiences, consumers might feel understood or misunderstood (Puntoni et al., 2021).

Delegation Experience: Delegation experience is the experience of consumers when they delegate some of their tasks to the AI and enjoy the AI solution. For instance, consumers asking their digital assistants to play their favorite Spotify list or make an appointment at the doctor's office are having a delegation experience. Consumers can feel empowered by delegating some of their tasks but can also feel replaced when too many tasks can be handled by AI (Puntoni et al., 2021).

Social Experience: The last experience is the social experience. Since AI has the capability to communicate reciprocally, consumers who are interacting with AI have a social experience. Sometimes, consumers know that their interaction partner is an AI agent, but some of the other times, they may not realize it. The consequences of social experience can be feeling connected on the positive side, but feeling alienated on the negative side (Puntoni et al., 2021).

Consumers interact with AI and have either positive or negative experiences with them and form relationships with them. Thus, it is possible to question the types of relationships consumers might have with AI. In the marketplace, AI plays the role of customer and frontline employee. Besides, AI is also in consumers' lives in other forms such as digital assistants. Consumers interact with these digital assistants; they ask questions and have conversations with these digital assistants. On the other hand, firms imbue human-like features such as voice and names to make consumers adopt these assistants and build strong relationships with them (Aggarwal & McGill, 2007). All these interactions with the AI bring the questions of what type of relationship does AI and consumers have and how consumers define their relationships with the AI. In an effort to understand the type of relationships consumers build with AI, Schweitzer et al. (2019) conducted in-depth interviews with the users of voice-controlled smart assistants. They found that the relationship consumers build with their digital assistants is a relationship that is similar to human relationships. More specifically, consumers have servant, partner, and master relationships with their digital assistants.

Artificial Intelligence as a Servant: Some of the consumers perceive AI-based assistants as servants because they are dependent on the user's orders and commands and help the user achieve their tasks. In this relationship, while the user perceives the AI-based assistant as the servant, he/she perceives him/herself as the master. In this relationship type, consumers perceive the assistant as beneficial for their life, as helpful for them to extend their possibilities, and as a part of their self (Schweitzer et al., 2019).

Artificial Intelligence as a Master: Consumers who picture AI-based assistants as a master have concerns about whether the information that comes from these assistants could be trusted and whether the next move of them could be predictable. Consumers think that everything is up to the goodwill of the digital assistant and see themselves as slaves that has to obey the rules of the digital assistant. Consumers who generally have more negative experiences with these digital assistants and who could not manage to achieve their tasks with the help of the digital assistants generally perceive their relationship with them as the digital assistant as the master. For instance, situations that the digital assistants cannot understand the command of the consumer and answers unrelatedly reinforce the idea that the digital assistant is the master with its own autonomy, and they can never be trusted. Consequently, consumers who perceive the AI-based assistant as a master resist the relationship with the AI (Schweitzer et al., 2019).

Artificial Intelligence as a Partner: Also, there are a group of consumers who perceive the AI-based assistants as an equivalent partner. In this relationship type, AI is perceived to have its own life and character. Consumers tend to ascribe more human-featured characteristics to the digital assistant in this relationship. In this type of relationship, consumers are generally willing to treat the AI-based assistant as a person, invest time in their relationship with it and help him/her learn from them and grow (Schweitzer et al., 2019). But these investments to the relationship can turn into a disappointment easily when consumers feel like they are not getting enough answers and progress from the AI-based digital assistant (Schweitzer et al., 2019).

Consumers' Attitudes Toward AI

Although artificial intelligence can outperform human judgments in many domains and artificial intelligence offers superior accuracy than human intuition, consumers can still resist artificial intelligence. Researchers call people's aversion to algorithms and preference of humans over algorithms in a variety of decision tasks as "algorithm aversion" (Dietvorst, Simmons & Massey 2015). According to previous literature, the reasons behind consumers' resistance to artificial intelligence (algorithmic models) are numerous. Consumers' beliefs about artificial intelligence, their individual characteristics, or the context of consumption can affect consumers' resistance to AI. Here, we will mention the findings of the previous literature on factors affecting consumers' attitudes toward AI.

Individual factors or consumer characteristics have an effect on consumers' opposition toward artificial intelligence. It is shown that opposition to artificial intelligence is higher among individuals with lower scientific knowledge, higher distrust to the appropriate functioning of science and technology, less prone to innovation and change, and expressing egalitarian values (Lobera, Fernández Rodríguez & Torres-Albero, 2020). Also, women's perception of risk is higher in general (Gustafsod, 1998), and they are willing to take less risk (Byrnes, Miller & Schafer, 1999). Because of their higher risk perceptions, women are more likely than men to resist artificial intelligence, especially when outcomes are perceived as risky (Castelo & Ward 2016). Consumer identity issues are also shown to influence consumers' adoption of AI. Consumers want to take the credit for their own abilities for the positive outcomes when it comes to tasks that they perceive as central to their identity, such as cooking (Leung, Paolacci, & Puntoni 2018). Thus, consumers may resist AI for the tasks they find central to their identity (Castelo, 2019).

Consumption context is another critical point determining whether consumers prefer artificial intelligence or resist it. Consumers prefer human labor to artificial intelligence labor for products, services, or consumption contexts where symbolic value is higher. Because consumers have stronger uniqueness motives in symbolic consumption contexts and perceive that human labor can satisfy their uniqueness motives more than artificial intelligence labor, they have a tendency not to prefer artificial intelligence in symbolic consumption contexts (Granulo, Fuchs & Puntoni, 2020). For similar reasons, consumers resist artificial intelligence in comparison to human labor in medical contexts too. Consumers believe that their characteristics, symptoms, and circumstances are distinct from an average person and unique. They think that, an artificial intelligence service provider would not consider this uniqueness as much as a human service provider. Because of these concerns about uniqueness neglect, they do not prefer artificial intelligence providers in medical contexts (Longoni, Bonezzi & Morewedge, 2019).

Characteristics of the tasks and consequences of the tasks also play essential roles in consumers' resistance or adoption of artificial intelligence. From the point of task characteristics, consumers generally resist AI for tasks that are subjective and involve intuition and affect (Castelo, 2019) since they perceive that AI does not have enough affective capabilities to perform such tasks (Castelo et al. 2018). Also, tasks can differ in their consequences, such that recommending a book is less consequential, but diagnosis in medical domains can be more consequential (Davenport et al., 2020). Consumers resist AI when the tasks are more consequential, and the perceived risks are higher (Castelo et al. 2018; Castelo & Ward 2016). Similarly, consumers' beliefs about AI, such as the lower empathy capabilities, influence consumers' resistance to AI too. In their research, Luo et al. (2019) showed that since consumers perceive AI as less empathetic, the purchase rates decreased by 75% when consumers are told that their interaction partner is an AI bot.

On the other hand, literature shows us that, in some situations, consumers do not resist artificial intelligence and, moreover, prefer artificial intelligence over human intelligence. One of the researches trying to understand under which conditions consumers prefer artificial intelligence over human intelligence underlines the impact of product/service type. Longoni and Cian (2020) investigated consumers' preference to get recommendations either from an artificial intelligence agent or from a human. They showed that consumers prefer artificial intelligence-based recommendations over human-based recommendations when the utilitarian attributes are more salient than hedonic attributes. Consumers believe that artificial intelligence recommenders use cognitive evaluative dimensions such as facts, rationality, and logic but human recommenders use affective evaluative dimensions such as sensory experiences, emotions, and intuition. Thus, they believe that artificial intelligence-based recommenders are more competent than human recommenders, where utilitarian attributes are more important than hedonic attributes and prefer getting recommendations from an artificial intelligence in the utilitarian realm (Longoni & Cian, 2020).

Nevertheless, not resisting AI comes with its own costs. In occasions where consumers do not resist AI, they might tend to attribute more responsibility to AI than human service providers. Hong (2020) compared people's responsibility attribution to AI vs. human driver in case of an accident and found that the AI driver is blamed more than a human driver in case of an accident for the injury or death of the victim, and this blame attribution was even higher when the consequences of the accident are more severe.

Concerns About AI

Although there are many benefits of AI both for consumers and companies, there are concerns about AI from different groups of people such as consumers, society, and researchers. Understanding these concerns might help researchers direct their future research into these areas, help businesses answer these concerns by their communication strategies and help manufacturers design their AI products and services accordingly. Thus, here we will mention the main concerns about AI pointed out in the literature.

Privacy and Cybersecurity Concerns

The data-centric nature of AI products and services offers many benefits to consumers, such as geo-localization, health monitoring, digital assisting, recommending products or services, but also causes harms to consumers. Although there are beneficial services for consumers in return, firms' easy access to consumer data with the help of AI products has brought concerns about consumer privacy and cybersecurity both from consumers and critics. These consumers concern about the privacy and the security of their data are so salient that they can even decide to restrict their online transactions (Akhter, 2014) and oppose artificial intelligence because of their negative perceptions about the treatment and privacy of their personal data (Lobera, Fernández Rodríguez & Torres-Albero, 2020).

The source of consumer concerns about privacy comes from the firms' usage of their data in ways that violate their privacy (Hwang & Park, 2020). On the other hand, privacy can be defined as a person's right to have a control on the information about him/herself (DesJardins, 2014). So, the question is, when privacy violations occur? The main element of the answer to this question is the informed and voluntary consent of the person. We can talk about privacy violations "whenever personal information is collected or used without the informed and voluntary consent of the person" (Du & Xie, 2021, p. 7). Thus, the AI products -especially those that are high on interactivity, create more consumer privacy concerns. Because these types of products not only collect voluminous data but also the variety of the data they collect are diverse (Du & Xie, 2021). For instance, as an AI-enabled product and high on interactivity, the Apple watch, both collect a large quantity of data and a large variety of data from textual, visual, audio to verbal and sensory (Du & Xie, 2021). But, consumers may not be even aware of that much data collection which can lead to consumer data privacy concerns. In sum, firms can collect and use a variety of consumer data such that; they can collect and use personal information to develop the performance of AI, they can collect and use consumption behavior information to predict what would consumers buy in the future and to recommend appropriate products or services to them and they can collect and use emotional information to predict consumers' emotions from their facial expressions (Hwang & Park, 2020). All these data collection and usage types can bring questions related to consumer privacy. What about the underlying reasons for consumer privacy concerns? According to researchers, privacy concerns come from multiple sources such as information collection, unauthorized use of information, and information access by third parties (Malhotra, Kim, & Agarwal, 2004; Smith, Milberg & Burke, 1996).

Data Collection, Storage, and Use: For instance, Google Home Mini has been reported to record intermittently during the day without the knowledge of its user and transfer the data back to Google (Forrest, 2017) that trigger consumer privacy concerns from the point of data collection and use. Similarly, firms' use of images and personal information obtained from a user voluntarily can even uncover copyright and ownership problems in the future (Lobera, Fernández Rodríguez & Torres-Albero, 2020). Moreover, firms' usage of consumer data for reasons different from consumers were informed while collecting the data is a way to violate consumer privacy (Davenport et al., 2020; Du & Xie, 2021; Tucker, 2018).

In addition to the problems related to the collection and use of data, we can mention issues regarding the storage of data. First of all, data can be stored longer than it was claimed to be stored, and second of all, some parts of the data can include information about other people (Davenport et al., 2020; Tucker, 2018). For instance, some neighbors might have concerns about Amazon's doorbells with cameras, the Ring device, recording their data without their permission.

Access of Data by Third Parties: Another concern related to privacy is the access of consumer data by third parties. Consumers question whether firms will sell the data collected through AI-enabled products to third parties without the users' permission (Davenport et al., 2020). Moreover, what will happen if the stored data are requested by the government or by the police in the future (Jones, 2018). Using both the data from the government and AI-enabled device companies, the higher level of surveillance in society is also another concern about consumer privacy (Lyon, 2014).

Cybersecurity is another significant concern about AI. Because of possible data breaches, malicious parties can get consumers' confidential information (Du & Xie, 2021). The results of data breaches can be devastating, such as the stolen passwords or the hacked bank accounts (Lobera, Fernández Rodríguez

& Torres-Albero, 2020). As the data collection of companies increase, especially with the help of AI-enabled products, the potential risk of a data breach also increases (Du & Xie, 2021). There can be two types of cyber-attacks related to AI; the first type is the attacks on AI and the second one is about the attacks using AI (Hwang & Park, 2020). The first type is the attacks on AI; they are about hacking an AI. Examples can be hacking a self-driving vehicle or hacking Cyber-Physical Systems such as smart governance, smart transportation (Hwang & Park, 2020). The other one is about the attacks using AI, such as speech synthesis, in which an AI is taught to mimic a person's voice. In this way, financial fraud can be committed through telephone calls (Kaloudi & Li, 2020).

So what can firms do to overcome privacy and cybersecurity concerns? Du and Xie (2021) offer three fundamental steps for firms to address consumer privacy concerns. The first one is to offer fair and transparent privacy policies and communicate their privacy policies to consumers with a clear and easy-to-understand communication. The second one is to explain what benefits consumers will get when sharing their data. Lastly, the third one is to give consumers more control over their data. Also, for cybersecurity concerns, firms should take precautions such as investing in the newest security technologies (Du & Xie, 2021) and communicate to their consumers that they are taking the security of their data very seriously. For the times data breaches occur, companies should have a plan to minimize the damage to their consumers (Du & Xie, 2021).

Algorithmic Biases

AI-enabled products learn based on machine learning. In this learning process, training data sets that are based on human data are used, and AI develops algorithms based on this training data. In other words, AI learns based on human data. Thus, while AI learns how to decide like a human, it also learns to make the exact same errors that humans do. Sometimes these errors lead AI to do human discrimination (Hwang & Park, 2020). For example, Amazon realized that its AI recruitment tool discriminates against female candidates and abandoned this project (Hamilton, 2018). Banks using AI are also accused of discrimination. A customer complains about being given a higher amount of a credit limit than his wife, although they have the exact same financial backgrounds (Puntoni et al., 2021). Amazon's Rekognition falsely matched innocent people with people who had committed a crime, and the number of people of color was higher in this false match (Snow, 2018).

When we think about the source of these algorithmic biases, we can understand the importance of the training data because AI biases come from the unbalanced and biased training data. The possible imbalances in the training data, such as gender, race, and ethnicity, cause biases in the AI-enabled products' algorithms (Du & Xie, 2021). For example, the reason behind the Amazon AI recruitment tool's discrimination against female candidates was the usage of a data set based on previous applicants to develop the algorithm, and the previous applicants being male (Davenport et al., 2020). This also shows us that, either intentionally or unintentionally, we transfer our biases to AI-enabled products (Letheren, Russell-Bennett & Whittaker, 2020). Just as the parents or teachers transmit their ideas to a child, we transmit our biases to AI (Letheren, Russell-Bennett & Whittaker, 2020; Sumioka, Nakae, Kanai, & Ishiguro, 2013).

So, what can be done to overcome artificial intelligence biases? First of all, companies should be careful about their training data sets; they should be sure that the training data sets are diverse enough to represent different human segments. Using balanced data sets from the point of gender, ethnicity, or race should be the first step to overcome algorithmic biases (Du & Xie, 2021). As the second step, companies should continuously test their algorithms to learn about the possible algorithmic biases they might have (Puntoni et al., 2021). Looking at the artificial intelligence biases from the consumers' perspective shows us that the situation can be devastating, and consumers can feel misunderstood when they encounter an AI product making biased predictions about them. Thus, to overcome consumers' resistance to artificial intelligence and consumers' feelings of misunderstood due to miscategorization, companies can allow consumers to validate the categorizations and inferences of artificial intelligence (Puntoni et al., 2021).

Vulnerable Consumers

While AI spread into all our lives, there are many people whose access to digital devices or the knowledge and ability to use AI technology are limited. These people can be among poor, elderly, and unwell consumer groups and can be excluded and alienated in the marketplace (Hwang & Park, 2020). Also, the possibility that human services would be more exclusive and expensive in the future brings the concern that vulnerable groups such as consumers experiencing poverty might be pushed to receive service only from AI representatives (Letheren, Russell-Bennett & Whittaker, 2020). For consumers who need human-to-human interaction and who do not want to interact with an AI agent, alienation would be inevitable too (Letheren, Russell-Bennett & Whittaker, 2020). Thus, firms should be flexible enough to offer a 'human touch' for consumers who are either resistant to AI or experiencing problems with AI (Puntoni et al., 2021).

AI in Work Environment and Unemployment Concerns

Another category for consumers' concerns is the concerns related to unemployment, working conditions of AI, co-working of human-AI employees, and consumers' concerns about delegating their own tasks to AI. First of all, from the point of unemployment, we can see that both people and experts worry about the possible future job losses because of the AI job replacements. Today, AI is being used in a variety of jobs from low-skilled ones to high-skilled ones. For example, we see AI taking orders from customers in the form of chatbots or performing the work of consultants, lawyers, or doctors (Meltzer, 2014; Susskind & Susskind, 2016). AI is also expected to be more intelligent with more capabilities in the future which will lead to more job replacements (Du & Xie, 2021). The reports of respected institutions and consultancy firms such as the World Economic Forum, McKinsey Global, and PwC support that unemployment caused by AI can be a problem in the future that we have to deal with (Bughin et al., 2017; PWC, 2018; Upchurch, 2018). For example, McKinsey predicted that; by 2030, up to 375 million workers might have to switch occupations and learn new skills (Manyika et al., 2017). Research shows that consumers' concerns about losing their jobs are an important factor that leads them to resist AI (Lobera, Fernández Rodríguez & Torres-Albero, 2020).

Moreover, as AI disseminates in the workplace, concerns about the consequences and the possible problems of co-working of AI with human employees emerge (De Keyser et al., 2019; Robinson et al., 2020). In line with this concern, literature underlines the importance of designing AI with needed cognitive capabilities to work with human teammates (Dwivedi et al., 2021). Another concern focuses on the possible work conditions of AI. AI can be the dreamed workforce for businesses since it can work for long hours without rest, does not ask for higher wages, and can accomplish even the most boring or dangerous jobs (Letheren, Russell-Bennett & Whittaker, 2020). It is criticized that this type of usage of AI is a new form of slavery (Petersen, 2007; Richardson, 2016), and the introduction of AI rights can be necessary (Letheren, Russell-Bennett, & Whittaker, 2020). The last issue that we find appropriate to discuss under this title is about consumers delegating their own tasks to AI. Sometimes consumers can be happy and feel empowered in delegating some of their tasks to AI. However, some of the other times delegating can make them feel replaced (Puntoni et al., 2021), can create negative identity perceptions (Leung, Paolacci & Puntoni, 2018), and negatively influence their self-worth and self-efficacy (Puntoni et al., 2021).

So, what can be done to overcome these concerns? Though it is mentioned that some jobs will be completely replaced by AI and disappear, experts believe that new jobs will appear (Manyika et al., 2017). Also, firms are not completely replacing human employees but supporting their capabilities with AI technology (Davenport et al., 2020). Thus, the communication of these ideas to people can help to reduce the concerns. Furthermore, firms should give opportunities for their employees for life-long learning and reskilling (Du & Xie, 2021). Finally, AI should be designed in ways to help consumers protect their identity perception while they are delegating their tasks (Puntoni et al., 2021).

AI and Ethical Decision Making

The ethical decision-making of AI creates another concern. People have to trust AI that it can follow moral rules in decision-making. The famous example here is the trolley problem, where AI systems at some point should have to make decisions like to either sacrifice one person for saving a larger number of people or the opposite (Thomson, 1976). In an attempt to answer these kinds of ethical dilemma and satisfy consumers' concerns about the morality of the decisions of AI, ethics for machines have to be created (Anderson & Anderson, 2011). Hence, organizations and researchers have directed their efforts towards examining and creating ethics for machines. For example, the European Commission has created a guideline named "Ethics Guidelines for Trustworthy AI" (European Commission, 2019), and a new research field named "machine ethics" or "machine morality" has emerged (Deng, 2015; Lin, Abney & Bekey 2012; Malle, 2016; Wallach, Franklin & Allen 2010).

Another question that comes to mind concerning AI ethics can be; what do ethical standards or machine morality mean? Ethical standards are the "guidelines based on morals and used to inform behaviour in situations that may not be covered by the law" (Letheren et al, 2020, p. 227) and machine morality deals with the ethical standards of artificial intelligence and, more specifically, autonomous machines (Malle, 2016). Since the laws about AI decisions and the consequences of AI decisions are not fully established yet, setting ethical standards regarding the decisions of AI is very important. These ethical standards can be significant guides both for marketers and AI developers (Letheren et al., 2020).

In setting ethical guidelines, consumers' perspectives and expectations related to AI morality come to the scene. It is important to understand consumers' perceptions and expectations about the moral norms of AI. What sort of moral norms are people expecting from these AI agents? Whether their moral norm expectations from AI are similar to their expectations from humans, or are they different? Understanding the answers to these questions is so crucial in designing future AI agents (Gill, 2020). Thus, in literature, we see much research focusing on these questions. Especially, the decisions of autonomous vehicles in life-and-death decision scenarios have taken a significant research interest (Awad et al. 2018; Bigman & Gray 2020; Bonnefon, Azim & Iyad 2016; Faulhaber et al. 2019; Gill, 2020). For example, Gill (2020) tried to reveal whether consumers expect an autonomous vehicle carrying them, either to swerve off the road and maybe kill them but save a pedestrian or just the opposite. Moreover, consumers' expectations about the moral norms of autonomous vehicles can differ based on the target characteristics (one vs. five pedestrians, child vs. adult pedestrian), severity of the harm, or the perspective they are taking (perspective of the passenger in autonomous vehicle vs. pedestrian) (Gill, 2020). Meanwhile, manufacturers try to find their own solutions; while some of them announce that their autonomous vehicles will protect their passenger even at the expense of others (Sorrel, 2016), others try to position themselves into a safer area and underline consumers' customization option based on their own preferences (Contissa, Lagioia & Sartor, 2017). In sum, the research, debates, and consumers' concerns about AI ethical decision-making seem to continue for a longer period of time.

FUTURE RESEARCH DIRECTIONS

AI has been evolving since the 1940s, and today we can see it both in the applications of businesses and directly in consumers' lives. One of the ways companies use AI is as their employee that interacts directly with consumers in the form of chatbots, sales assistants, financial assistants, or robots. This type of AI usage is the one that directly touches the consumer, and we see these types of usages in a variety of sectors such as real estate, finance, health care, finance, beauty, fashion, and hospitality. Another way businesses use AI is as helping them in their tasks without a direct consumer touch, such as recommending systems that analyze consumers' previous actions and recommend them products or services or as the systems used in healthcare to evaluate radiological images or pathology slides. Additionally, businesses can offer AI to the consumers as the product or the service itself, such as voice-controlled digital assistants or companion robots.

From all the pervasive usages of AI by consumers and businesses, it is clear that a new marketplace has been started to be shaped. The human-to-human interaction was at the core of the traditional service encounter. Nevertheless, today, we have started to see the examples of AI agents representing the company in the form of chatbots or representing the consumer in the form of digital assistants, and this brings AI-to-human or AI-to-AI interactions to the marketing scene. Moreover, all these consumer interactions with AI bring new experiences for the consumers, which in turn lead them to feel positive such as served, understood, empowered, connected, or negative such as exploited, misunderstood, replaced, or alienated (Puntoni et al., 2021). In these interactions, not only the consumers are having an experience, but also the AI is having an object experience (Hoffman & Novak, 2018).

Thus, future research should try to find answer to some questions that have not examined previously. For example, how will firms treat their new AI customers, how will these new AI customers affect firms' marketing strategy, will firms target human customers or target the AI customer in their marketing strategy? For instance, whether a firm trying to promote its new brand will target the digital assistant of the consumer or the consumer himself/herself? The interactions and experiences within AI customers are another area that needs attention such that; what will happen to the dynamics of word of mouth when AI customers write the reviews about the products, services or brands they used and liked or do not liked. Will customers still believe these reviews or not? Moreover, the interactions and experiences within AI employees or the interactions and experiences between AI and human employees in marketing departments of firms should be analyzed too. As Hoffman and Novak (2018) underlined, the object experience of the AI should also be considered. Is it really possible to think about the experience of an AI agent and whether this object experience will affect an AI customer to shop from an online store or not based on its previous experience? In other words, whether the object experience of AI customers will affect their repurchase intentions and brand loyalty? What would marketers do to positively affect the experience of the AI customers?

CONCLUSION

As a result of consumers' interactions and experiences with AI, it is expected that consumers might build relationships with the AI. So, it is crucial to understand how consumers perceive their relationships with the AI and what roles they assign to themselves or the AI in the relationship. But, our literature review has shown us that research focusing on these questions are scarce (Schweitzer et al., 2019; Huang et al., 2021). Although Schweitzer et al. (2019) showed us that consumers describe their relationship with their digital assistant as; AI being the servant, master, or a partner, more research is needed in this fruitful area.

The usage of AI has been spread into the life of consumers directly or indirectly and has many benefits, such as doing many tasks on behalf of consumers. Nevertheless, people can still resist getting services from AI and prefer human service instead of AI service. There is a vast amount of research examining consumers' attitudes toward and resistance to AI. It has been revealed in the literature that the individual factors such as the scientific knowledge of people, their openness to innovation, their risk perceptions have an effect on their acceptance of AI (Castelo & Ward 2016; Lobera, Fernández Rodríguez & Torres-Albero, 2020). Also, consumers' identity issues, their uniqueness preference in symbolic consumption contexts, and the characteristics and consequences of the tasks can affect their preference to choose to get service from an AI agent. What other factors lead consumers to prefer AI service or resist AI service is another research area that needs more examination.

Finally, the chapter examined the major concerns both consumers, society and researchers have about AI. These were about privacy and cybersecurity, AI biases, discrimination of vulnerable consumers, possible unemployment issues because of AI, and the ethicality of AI decisions. New research is needed in understanding the consumers' and society's concerns about AI, and these concerns should be taken into consideration in the design of AI systems, and marketers should follow these concerns in using and promoting their AI-enabled systems and products.

REFERENCES

Aggarwal, P., & McGill, A. L. (2007). Is that car smiling at me? Schema congruity as a basis for evaluating anthropomorphized products. *The Journal of Consumer Research*, *34*(4), 468–479. doi:10.1086/518544

Akhter, S. H. (2014). Privacy concern and online transactions: The impact of internet self-efficacy and internet involvement. *Journal of Consumer Marketing*, *31*(2), 118–125. doi:10.1108/JCM-06-2013-0606

Ameen, N., Tarhini, A., Reppel, A., & Anand, A. (2020). Customer experiences in the age of artificial intelligence. *Computers in Human Behavior*, *114*, 106548. doi:10.1016/j.chb.2020.106548 PMID:32905175

Amelia. (n.d.). *Amelia: The most human AI for the Enterprise.* https://amelia.com/amelia/

Anderson, M., & Anderson, S. L. (Eds.). (2011). *Machine ethics.* Cambridge University Press. doi:10.1017/CBO9780511978036

Antonio, V. (2018, July 30). How AI is changing sales. *Harvard Business Review*. https://hbr.org/2018/07/how-ai-is-changing-sales

Awad, E., Dsouza, S., Kim, R., Schulz, J., Henrich, J., Shariff, A., Bonnefon, J.-F., & Rahwan, I. (2018). The moral machine experiment. *Nature, 563*(7729), 59–64. doi:10.103841586-018-0637-6 PMID:30356211

Bhatia, R. (2016, December 12). Say hello to Simi – a chatbot that makes your cocktail. *Analytics India Magazine*. https://analyticsindiamag.com/say-hello-simi-chatbot-makes-cocktail/

Bigman, Y. E., & Gray, K. (2020). Life and Death Decisions of Autonomous Vehicles. *Nature, 579*(7797), E1–E2. doi:10.103841586-020-1987-4 PMID:32132695

Bonnefon, J.-F., Shariff, A., & Rahwan, I. (2016). The Social Dilemma of Autonomous Vehicles. *Science, 352*(6293), 1573–1576. doi:10.1126cience.aaf2654 PMID:27339987

Bughin, J., Hazan, E., Ramaswamy, S., Allas, T., Dahlström, P., Henke, N., & Trench, M. (2017). Artificial intelligence: the next digital frontier? *McKinsey Global Institute*. https://www.mckinsey.com/~/media/mckinsey/industries/advanced%20electronics/our%20insights/how%20artificial%20intelligence%20can%20deliver%20real%20value%20to%20companies/mgi-artificial-intelligence-discussion-paper.ashx

Byrnes, J. P., Miller, D. C., & Schafer, W. D. (1999). Gender differences in risk taking: A meta-analysis. *Psychological Bulletin, 125*(3), 367–383. doi:10.1037/0033-2909.125.3.367

Castelo, N. (2019). *Blurring the line between human and machine: Marketing artificial intelligence* (Doctoral dissertation). Columbia University Academic Commons. doi:10.7916/d8-k7vk-0s40

Castelo, N., Bos, M., & Lehman, D. (2018). *Consumer adoption of algorithms that blur the line between human and machine*. Graduate School of Business: Columbia University Working Paper.

Castelo, N., & Ward, A. (2016). Political affiliation moderates attitudes towards artificial intelligence. In P. Moreau & S. Puntoni (Eds.), *NA - Advances in Consumer Research* (pp. 723–723). Association for Consumer Research.

Contissa, G., Lagioia, F., & Sartor, G. (2017). The ethical knob: Ethically-customizable automated vehicles and the law. *Artificial Intelligence and Law, 25*(3), 365–378. doi:10.100710506-017-9211-z

Davenport, T., Guha, A., Grewal, D., & Bressgott, T. (2020). How artificial intelligence will change the future of marketing. *Journal of the Academy of Marketing Science, 48*(1), 24–42. doi:10.100711747-019-00696-0

Davenport, T. H., & Ronanki, R. (2018). Artificial intelligence for the real world. *Harvard Business Review, 96*(1), 108–116.

De Keyser, A., & Köcher, S., Alkire (née Nasr), L., Verbeeck, C., & Kandampully, J. (2019). Frontline service technology infusion: Conceptual archetypes and future research directions. *Journal of Service Management, 30*(1), 156–183. doi:10.1108/JOSM-03-2018-0082

Deng, B. (2015). Machine ethics: The robot's dilemma. *Nature, 523*(7558), 24–26. doi:10.1038/523024a PMID:26135432

DesJardins, J. (2014). An introduction to business ethics. New York, NY: McGraw-Hill/Irwin.

Dietvorst, B. J., Simmons, J. P., & Massey, C. (2015). Algorithm aversion: People erroneously avoid algorithms after seeing them err. *Journal of Experimental Psychology. General, 144*(1), 114–126. doi:10.1037/xge0000033 PMID:25401381

Du, S., & Xie, C. (2021). Paradoxes of artificial intelligence in consumer markets: Ethical challenges and opportunities. *Journal of Business Research, 129*, 961–974. doi:10.1016/j.jbusres.2020.08.024

Dwivedi, Y. K., Hughes, L., Ismagilova, E., Aarts, G., Coombs, C., Crick, T., Duan, Y., Dwivedi, R., Edwards, J., Eirug, A., Galanos, V., Ilavarasan, P. V., Janssen, M., Jones, P., Kar, A. K., Kizgin, H., Kronemann, B., Lal, B., Lucini, B., ... Williams, M. D. (2021). Artificial intelligence (AI): Multidisciplinary perspectives on emerging challenges, opportunities, and agenda for research, practice and policy. *International Journal of Information Management, 57*, 101994. doi:10.1016/j.ijinfomgt.2019.08.002

Esteva, A., Kuprel, B., Novoa, R. A., Ko, J., Swetter, S. M., Blau, H. M., & Thrun, S. (2017). Dermatologist-level classification of skin cancer with deep neural networks. *Nature, 542*(7639), 115–118. doi:10.1038/nature21056 PMID:28117445

European Commission. (2019). *Ethics Guidelines for Trustworthy AI.* https://ec.europa.eu/futurium/en/ai-alliance-consultation

Evans, M. (2019). Build a 5-star customer experience with artificial intelligence. *Forbes.* https://www.forbes.com/sites/allbusiness/2019/02/17/customer-experience-artificial- intelligence/#1a30ebd415bd

Faulhaber, A. K., Dittmer, A., Blind, F., Wächter, M. A., Timm, S., Sütfeld, L. R., Stephan, A., Pipa, G., & König, P. (2019). Human decisions in moral dilemmas are largely described by utilitarianism: Virtual car driving study provides guidelines for autonomous driving vehicles. *Science and Engineering Ethics, 25*(2), 399–418. doi:10.100711948-018-0020-x PMID:29357047

Feng, C. M., Park, A., Pitt, L., Kietzmann, J., & Northey, G. (2020). Artificial intelligence in marketing: A bibliographic perspective. *Australasian Marketing Journal.* doi:10.1016/j.ausmj.2020.07.006

Forrest, C. (2017, October 11). Google Home Mini spied on user 'thousands of times a day,' sent recordings to Google. *TechRepublic.* https://www.techrepublic.com/ article/google-home-mini-spied-on-user-thousands-of- times-a-day-sent-recordings-to-google/

Gallagher, J. (2017, January 26). Artificial intelligence 'as good as cancer doctors'. *BBC News.* https:// www.bbc. com/news/health-38717928

Gill, T. (2020). Blame it on the self-driving car: How autonomous vehicles can alter consumer morality. *The Journal of Consumer Research, 47*(2), 272–291. doi:10.1093/jcr/ucaa018

Gillath, O., Ai, T., Branicky, M. S., Keshmiri, S., Davison, R. B., & Spaulding, R. (2021). Attachment and trust in artificial intelligence. *Computers in Human Behavior, 115*, 106607. doi:10.1016/j.chb.2020.106607

Granulo, A., Fuchs, C., & Puntoni, S. (2020). Preference for human (vs. robotic) labor is stronger in symbolic consumption contexts. *Journal of Consumer Psychology, 31*(1), 72–80. doi:10.1002/jcpy.1181

Greenwald, T. (2011). How smart machines like iPhone 4S are quietly changing your industry. *Forbes.* https://www.forbes.com/sites/tedgreenwald/2011/10/13/how-smart-machines-like-iphone-4s-are- quietly-changing-your-industry/#46547361598f

Gustafsod, P. E. (1998). Gender Differences in risk perception: Theoretical and methodological perspectives. *Risk Analysis*, *18*(6), 805–811. doi:10.1111/j.1539-6924.1998.tb01123.x PMID:9972583

Haenlein, M., & Kaplan, A. (2019). A brief history of artificial intelligence: On the past, present, and future of artificial intelligence. *California Management Review*, *61*(4), 5–14. doi:10.1177/0008125619864925

Hamilton, I. A. (2018, October 13). Why it's totally unsurprising that Amazon's recruitment AI was biased against women. *Insider*. https://www.businessinsider.com/amazon-ai-biased-against-women-no-surprise-sandra-wachter-2018-10

Henn na Hotel. (n.d.). https://www.h-n-h.jp/en/concept

Hinchliffe, E. (2017, February 22), IBM's Watson will help diagnose heart disease when doctors may have missed the signs. *Mashable*. https://mashable.com/2017/02/22/ibm-watson-clinical-imaging-cardiology/

Hoffman, D. L., & Novak, T. P. (2018). Consumer and object experience in the internet of things: An assemblage theory approach. *The Journal of Consumer Research*, *44*(6), 1178–1204. doi:10.1093/jcr/ucx105

Hong, J. W. (2020). Why Is Artificial Intelligence Blamed More? Analysis of Faulting Artificial Intelligence for Self-Driving Car Accidents in Experimental Settings. *International Journal of Human-Computer Interaction*, *36*(18), 1768–1774. doi:10.1080/10447318.2020.1785693

Huang, B., Laporte, S., Sénécal, S., & Sobol, K. (2021), Partner or servant? The effect of relationship role on consumer interaction with artificial intelligence. *AMA Winter Academic Conference Proceedings*, *32*, 382-384.

Huang, M.-H., & Rust, R. T. (2018). Artificial Intelligence in Service. *Journal of Service Research*, *21*(2), 155–172. doi:10.1177/1094670517752459

Hwang, H., & Park, M. H. (2020). The Threat of AI and Our Response: The AI Charter of Ethics in South Korea. *Asian Journal of Innovation & Policy*, *9*(1), 56–78.

Jarek, K., & Mazurek, G. (2019). Marketing and Artificial Intelligence. *Central European Business Review*, *8*(2), 46–55. doi:10.18267/j.cebr.213

Jones, V. K. (2018). Voice-activated change: Marketing in the age of artificial intelligence and virtual assistants. *Journal of Brand Strategy*, *7*(3), 233–245.

Kaloudi, N., & Li, J. (2020). The AI-based cyber threat landscape: A survey. *ACM Computing Surveys*, *53*(1), 1–34. doi:10.1145/3372823

KLM. (2016, March 29). *Spencer robot completed tests guiding KLM passengers at Schiphol*. https://news.klm.com/spencer-robot-completed-tests-guiding-klm-passengers-at-schiphol/

Klmcare. (n.d.). *Meet KLM Care-E*. http://klmcare-e-entry.com

Lanctot, R. (2017). *Accelerating the Future: The Economic Impact of the Emerging Passenger Economy*. Strategy Analytics Report. https://newsroom.intel.com/newsroom/wp-content/uploads/sites/11/2017/05/passenger-economy.pdf

Leachman, S. A., & Merlino, G. (2017). Medicine: The Final Frontier in Cancer Diagnosis. *Nature*, *542*(7639), 36–38. doi:10.1038/nature21492 PMID:28150762

Lemon, K. N., & Verhoef, P. C. (2016). Understanding Customer Experience Throughout the Customer Journey. *Journal of Marketing*, *80*(6), 69–96. doi:10.1509/jm.15.0420

Letheren, K., Russell-Bennett, R., & Whittaker, L. (2020). Black, white or grey magic? Our future with artificial intelligence. *Journal of Marketing Management*, *36*(3-4), 216–232. doi:10.1080/026725 7X.2019.1706306

Leung, E., Paolacci, G., & Puntoni, S. (2018). Man versus machine: Resisting automation in identity-based consumer behavior. *JMR, Journal of Marketing Research*, *55*(6), 818–831. doi:10.1177/0022243718818423

Lin, P., Abney, K., & Bekey, G. A. (Eds.). (2012). *Robot ethics: The ethical and social implications of robotics*. MIT Press.

Lobera, J., Fernández Rodríguez, C. J., & Torres-Albero, C. (2020). Privacy, values and machines: Predicting opposition to artificial intelligence. *Communication Studies*, *71*(3), 448–465. doi:10.1080/1 0510974.2020.1736114

Longoni, C., Bonezzi, A., & Morewedge, C. K. (2019). Resistance to medical artificial intelligence. *The Journal of Consumer Research*, *46*(4), 629–650. doi:10.1093/jcr/ucz013

Longoni, C., & Cian, L. (2020). Artificial intelligence in utilitarian vs. hedonic contexts: The "word-of-machine" effect. *Journal of Marketing*. doi:10.1177/0022242920957347

Luo, X., Tong, S., Fang, Z., & Qu, Z. (2019). Frontiers: Machines vs. humans: The Impact of Artificial Intelligence Chatbot Disclosure on Customer Purchases. *Marketing Science*, *38*(6), 937–947. doi:10.1287/mksc.2019.1192

Lyon, D. (2014). Surveillance, snowden, and big data: Capacities, consequences, critique. *Big Data & Society*, *1*(2), 1–13. doi:10.1177/2053951714541861

Ma, L., & Sun, B. (2020). Machine learning and AI in marketing–Connecting computing power to human insights. *International Journal of Research in Marketing*, *37*(3), 481–504. doi:10.1016/j.ijresmar.2020.04.005

MacInnis, D. J., & Folkes, V. S. (2010). The disciplinary status of consumer behavior: A sociology of science perspective on key controversies. *The Journal of Consumer Research*, *36*(6), 899–914. doi:10.1086/644610

Malhotra, N. K., Kim, S. S., & Agarwal, J. (2004). Internet users' information privacy concerns: The construct, the scale, and a causal model. *Information Systems Research*, *15*(4), 336–355. doi:10.1287/isre.1040.0032

Malle, B. F. (2016). Integrating Robot Ethics and Machine Morality: The Study and Design of Moral Competence in Robots. *Ethics and Information Technology*, *18*(4), 243–256. doi:10.100710676-015-9367-8

Malle, B. F., Scheutz, M., Arnold, T., Voiklis, J., & Cusimano, C. (2015), Sacrifice one for the good of many? People apply different moral norms to human and robot agents. In *HRI'15: Proceedings of the Tenth Annual ACM/ IEEE International Conference on Human-Robot Interaction*. New York, NY: ACM. 10.1145/2696454.2696458

Manyika, J., Lund, S., Chui, M., Bughin, J., Woetzel, J., Batra, P., Ko, R., & Sanghvi, S. (2017). *What the future of work will mean for jobs, skills, and wages.* McKinsey Global Institute Report. https://www.mckinsey.com/featured-insights/future-of-work/jobs-lost-jobs-gained-what-the-future-of-work-will-mean-for-jobs-skills-and-wages

McCarthy, J., Minsky, M. L., Rochester, N., & Shannon, C. E. (1955), A proposal for the Dartmouth summer research project on artificial intelligence, http://www-formal.stanford.edu/jmc/history/dartmouth/dartmouth.html

Meltzer, T. (2014, June 15). Robot doctors, online lawyers and automated architects: The future of the professions. *The Guardian.* https://www.theguardian.com/technology/2014/jun/15/robot-doctors-

Mintz, Y., & Brodie, R. (2019). Introduction to artificial intelligence in medicine. *Minimally Invasive Therapy & Allied Technologies, 28*(2), 73–81. doi:10.1080/13645706.2019.1575882 PMID:30810430

Morgan, B. (2018). How Amazon has reorganized around artificial intelligence and machine learning. *Forbes.* https://www.forbes.com/sites/blakemorgan/2018/07/16/how-amazon-has-re-organized-around-artificial-intelligence-and-machine-learning/?sh=40ca07877361

Müller, V. C., & Bostrom, N. (2016). Future Progress in Artificial Intelligence: A Survey of Expert Opinion. In Fundamental Issues of Artificial Intelligence (555-572). Springer. doi:10.1007/978-3-319-26485-1_33

Netzer, O., Feldman, R., Goldenberg, J., & Fresko, M. (2012). Mine Your Own Business: Market-Structure Surveillance through Text Mining. *Marketing Science, 31*(3), 521–543. doi:10.1287/mksc.1120.0713

Overgoor, G., Chica, M., Rand, W., & Weishampel, A. (2019). Letting the computers take over: Using AI to solve marketing problems. *California Management Review, 61*(4), 156–185. doi:10.1177/0008125619859318

Pantano, E., & Pizzi, G. (2020). Forecasting artificial intelligence on online customer assistance: Evidence from chatbot patents analysis. *Journal of Retailing and Consumer Services, 55*(102096), 1–9. doi:10.1016/j.jretconser.2020.102096

Paschen, J., Kietzmann, J., & Kietzmann, T. C. (2019). Artificial intelligence (AI) and its implications for market knowledge in B2B marketing. *Journal of Business and Industrial Marketing, 34*(7), 1410–1479. doi:10.1108/JBIM-10-2018-0295

Petersen, S. (2007). The ethics of robot servitude. *Journal of Experimental & Theoretical Artificial Intelligence, 19*(1), 43–54. doi:10.1080/09528130601116139

Poole, D. L., & Mackworth, A. K. (2010). *Artificial intelligence: Foundations of computational agents.* Cambridge University Press. doi:10.1017/CBO9780511794797

Puntoni, S., Reczek, R. W., Giesler, M., & Botti, S. (2021). Consumers and artificial intelligence: An experiential perspective. *Journal of Marketing*, *85*(1), 131–151. doi:10.1177/0022242920953847

PWC. (2018). *Will robots really steal our jobs? An international analysis of the potential long term impact of automation*. PWC. https://www.pwc.com/hu/hu/kiadvanyok/assets/pdf/impact_of_automation_on_jobs.pdf

Revieve. (n.d.). *AI Skincare Advisor*. https://www.revieve.com/solutions/skincareadvisor

Richardson, K. (2016). Sex robot matters: Slavery, the prostituted, and the rights of machines. *IEEE Technology and Society Magazine*, *35*(2), 46–53. doi:10.1109/MTS.2016.2554421

Robinson, S., Orsingher, C., Alkire, L., De Keyser, A., Giebelhausen, M., Papamichail, K. N., Shams, P., & Temerak, M. S. (2020). Frontline encounters of the AI kind: An evolved service encounter framework. *Journal of Business Research*, *116*, 366–376. doi:10.1016/j.jbusres.2019.08.038

Romano, A. (2020, July 5). This hotel has a robot named Rosé that will deliver wine to your room Without human contact. *Travel and Leisure*. https://www.travelandleisure.com/food-drink/wine/rose-robot-room-service-hotel-trio-california

Rossi, F. (2018). Building trust in artificial intelligence. *Journal of International Affairs*, *72*(1), 127–134.

Russell, S. J., & Norvig, P. (2016). *Artificial Intelligence: A Modern Approach*. Pearson Education Limited.

Russo, S. J. (2020). Is de-identification of personal health information in the age of artificial intelligence a reality or a noble myth? *Journal of Health Care Compliance*, (March–April), 55–59.

Rust, R. T. (2020). The future of marketing. *International Journal of Research in Marketing*, *37*(1), 15–26. doi:10.1016/j.ijresmar.2019.08.002

Schweitzer, F., Belk, R., Jordan, W., & Ortner, M. (2019). Servant, friend or master? The relationships users build with voice-controlled smart devices. *Journal of Marketing Management*, *35*(7-8), 693–715. doi:10.1080/0267257X.2019.1596970

Silverstein, S. (2018). REX real estate: Home showings-AI / Voice / Chatbot. *Behance*. https://www.behance.net/gallery/64004179/REX-Real-Estate-Home-Showings-AI-Voice-Chatbot

Smith, J. H., Milberg, S. J., & Burke, J. B. (1996). Information privacy: Measuring individuals' concerns about organizational practices. *Management Information Systems Quarterly*, *20*(2), 167–196. doi:10.2307/249477

Snow, J. (2018, July 26). Amazon's face recognition falsely matched 28 members of congress with mugshots. *ACLU*. https:// www.aclu.org/blog/privacy-technology/surveillance-technologies/amazons-face-recognition-falsely-matched-28

Sorrel, C. (2016, November 13). Self-driving Mercedes will be programmed to sacrifice pedestrians to save the driver. *Fast Company*. https://www.fastcompany.com/3064539/self-driving-mercedes-will-be-programmed-to-sacrifice-pedestrians-to-save-the-driver

Sumioka, H., Nakae, A., Kanai, R., & Ishiguro, H. (2013). Huggable communication medium decreases cortisol levels. *Scientific Reports*, *3*(1), 1–6. doi:10.1038rep03034 PMID:24150186

Susskind, R., & Susskind, D. (2016, October 11). Technology will replace many doctors, lawyers, and other professionals. *Harvard Business Review*. https://hbr.org/2016/10/robots-willreplace-doctors-lawyers-and-other-professionals

Thales. (2018, January 8). KFC Use Facial Recognition for Payment in China. *Thales*. https://www.thalesgroup.com/en/markets/digital-identity-and-security/banking-payment/magazine/kfc-use-facial-recognition-payment-china

Thomson, J. J. (1976). Killing, letting die, and the trolley problem. *The Monist*, *59*(2), 204–217. doi:10.5840/monist197659224 PMID:11662247

Tirunillai, S., & Tellis, G. J. (2014). Mining Marketing Meaning from Online Chatter: Strategic Brand Analysis of Big Data Using Latent Dirichlet Allocation. *JMR, Journal of Marketing Research*, *51*(4), 463–479. doi:10.1509/jmr.12.0106

Tucker, C. (2018). Privacy, algorithms, and artificial intelligence. In *The Economics of Artificial Intelligence: An Agenda* (pp. 423–438). University of Chicago Press.

Turing, A. M. (1950). Computing machinery and intelligence. *Mind*, *49*(236), 433–460. doi:10.1093/mind/LIX.236.433

Tussyadiah, I. (2020). A review of research into automation in tourism: Launching the Annals of Tourism Research Curated Collection on Artificial Intelligence and Robotics in Tourism. *Annals of Tourism Research*, *81*, 102883. doi:10.1016/j.annals.2020.102883

Upchurch, M. (2018). Robots and ai at work: The prospects for singularity. *New Technology, Work and Employment*, *33*(3), 205–218. doi:10.1111/ntwe.12124

Upstart. (n.d.). https://www.upstart.com/about#

Vincent, J. (2017, January 4). The UK's national health service is testing out a medical chatbot as a non-emergency helpline. *The Verge*. https://www.theverge.com/2017/1/4/14168312/uk-nhs-babylon-medical-chatbot-helpline

Voice2Biz. (n.d.). *Google Home and Alexa Talk to aach other & have a conversation*. https://www.voice2biz.com/google-home-and-alexa-talk-to-each-other-have-a-conversation/

Wallach, W., Franklin, S., & Allen, C. (2010). A Conceptual and Computational Model of Moral Decision Making in Human and Artificial Agents. *Trends in Cognitive Sciences*, *2*(3), 454–485. PMID:25163872

Wiggers, K. (2019, March 19). Ojo Labs raises $45 million to develop a chatbot for real estate. *VentureBeat*. https://venturebeat.com/2019/03/19/ojo-labs-raises-45-million-to-develop-a-chatbot-for-real-estate/

Wirth, N. (2018). Hello marketing, what can artificial intelligence help you with? *International Journal of Market Research*, *60*(5), 435–438. doi:10.1177/1470785318776841

KEY TERMS AND DEFINITIONS

AI Biases: Bias in the AI algorithm, which can lead to prejudiced AI decisions such as discrimination based on gender or ethnicity.

AI Ethical Decision Making: AI that follows moral rules in decision making.

Artificial Intelligence (AI): Computer systems that mimic the intelligence of humans. These computer systems perceive the world around them and take action accordingly.

Consumer Algorithm Aversion: Consumers' preference of humans over algorithms in a variety of tasks.

Hybrid AI: AI systems that integrate multiple weak AI systems such as Google's DeepMind AlphaGo or IBM's Watson.

Strong AI: AI type that is more powerful than weak AI. These systems have context-awareness, think holistically, give context-specific responses, and able to complete more complex tasks.

Weak AI: AI type that analyzes large amounts of data and can be trained to solve specific problems. They are powerful in their specifically trained area but not as flexible as human intelligence in other areas.

Chapter 17
When Luxury Vinous-Concept Hotel Meets Premium Wine Brands:
An Exploratory Study on Co-Branding

Lisa Ferraz
University of Aveiro, Portugal

Helena Nobre
https://orcid.org/0000-0002-7724-5204
University of Aveiro, Portugal

Belém Barbosa
https://orcid.org/0000-0002-4057-360X
University of Porto, Portugal

ABSTRACT

Co-branding in the hospitality luxury sector is still understudied in the literature. This study aims at tackling this gap through the analysis of a case of a co-branding strategy between a vinous-concept luxury hotel in Portugal and premium wine brands of domestic producers. Fourteen in-depth interviews with managers of the luxury hotel and wine brand partners supported the exploratory research. This chapter represents a case of qualitative data application to an underestimated topic in the literature from the managers' point of view. The study offers evidence on the benefits for both parties, reasons for adopting co-branding, and partners' selection attributes. The improvement of brand image emerges as one of the main advantages of co-branding with a luxury hotel. Based on the literature review and the interviews with managers, the study proposes a set of hypotheses to be tested in future research. This chapter provides interesting cues for academics and practitioners.

DOI: 10.4018/978-1-7998-6985-6.ch017

INTRODUCTION

Co-branding practices have been increasingly adopted by practitioners in several fields, including advertising, luxury market, products, and retail stores (e.g., Abratt & Motlana, 2002; Dahlstrom & Dato-on, 2004; Moon & Sprott, 2016), and also in the hospitality industry, namely restaurant chains (Boone, 1997), chefs, retail, local wine, designers, and other celebrity brands (Guillet & Tasci, 2012). Co-branding strategy gained popularity in the academic literature due to its ability to reinforce brand image (Lee, 2014; Park, Jaworski, & MacInnis, 1986) and improve brand perceptions and positioning (Singh, P. Kalafatis, & Ledden, 2014). Thus, it is essential to identify strong and reputable partner brands, based on criteria such as image, quality, brand equity and loyalty (Guillet & Tasci, 2012). In the retail sector, co-branding partnerships enable the access to wider and different marketing segments, to increase sales, and foster relationships with customers (Wang, Soesilo, & Zhang, 2015). Co-branding implies sharing brand value, business competences and risks (Erevelles, Stevenson, Srinivasan, & Fukawa, 2008; Helmig, Huber, & Leeflang, 2008; Keller & Richey, 2006), and enables the maximization of distribution channels and customer relationship programs (Motion, Leitch, & Brodie, 2003; Wang et al., 2015).

At the same time, luxury brands are getting increasing attention from academics and practitioners, as the luxury market shows a clear resilience regarding economic crisis, being one that consistently grew in the last years (Nobre & Simões, 2019). It is expected that it keeps growing in the next decades, namely because of the Millennial generation who will reach their thirties and forties, becoming one of the most important drivers of the global economy. Moreover, globalization and economic downturns increased competition pressure and made harder for companies to ensure that luxury brands' perceived value correspond to their price level (Díaz-Bustamante, Carcelén, & Puelles, 2016; Tynan, McKechnie, & Chhuon, 2010). Strategies that help improving luxury brands' value and positioning are particularly relevant for business success and marketing effectiveness. Nueno and Quelch (1998) define luxury brands as "those whose ratio of functional utility to price is low while the ratio of intangible and situational utility to price is high" (p. 62). Besides expensiveness associations, luxury brands share some characteristics such as consistent quality and product excellence, exclusivity and uniqueness, tradition and heritage, hand-crafted, rare, and elitist (Kapferer, 1998; Vigneron & Johnson, 1999). Moreover, the concept of luxury is also understood in a socio-psychological context, embedded in culture and lifestyle (Okonkwo, 2009). Thus, luxury items and brands transmit strong and solid identities, associated with symbolic and emotional consumption.

We argue that one particularly interesting setting for co-branding is the luxury hotel brand. Both the attractiveness and the complexity of the luxury markets, especially in hospitality services, claim for sophisticated business strategies like co-branding. Surprisingly, extant literature has so far missed the focus on co-branding strategies in the luxury market. Although some studies in the literature present evidence on co-branding being used for hotel differentiation and positioning (Guillet & Tasci, 2012), most of them disregard co-branding under the light of luxury market and brands. This article aims to fill this gap by exploring how a co-branding strategy between a luxury hotel brand and product brands benefits each other, especially in the case of a product particularly relevant for the hotel brand concept.

The study analyses the case of a local luxury brand Hotel in Portugal, with a vinous-concept positioning, and its partnership with premium wine brands of domestic producers. Based on the perceptions of the hotel and wine brands' managers, the study aimed to identify the determinants for partner choice, and the impact of the co-branding strategy in brand image of both the hotel and the associated wine brands.

Qualitative data is particularly suitable to investigate new or quite unexplored phenomenon in the literature (Glaser & Strauss, 2006). Particularly, in-depth interview represents a common technique to collect data on consumers' perceptions and opinions (Goulding, 2005). This article represents a case of qualitative data application to an underestimated topic in the literature, but in contrast with most of previous research, the study advances literature on co-branding in luxury hospitality management from the managers' point of view.

CO-BRANDING STRATEGY

In the past decades, the brand partnerships of co-branding strategies became more and more popular (Riley, Charlton, & Wason, 2015; Wason & Charlton, 2015). Chiambaretto and Gurău (2017) define co-branding as a strategy that combines two or more independent brands in one offer. Brennan, Canning, and McDowell (2014) consider that a co-branding results from a cooperation between two or more companies comprising some defining aspect of the brand. Indeed, co-branding is often used interchangeably with other concepts such as brand alliances, comarketing, joint branding, branding and symbolic branding.

The main objectives of co-branding is to create mutual benefits for the involved brands (Egan, 2011), namely to improve their brand equity (Abratt & Motlana, 2002; Genc, 2010; Guillet & Tasci, 2012). This cooperation often involves several marketing domains such as advertising, product development and positioning, and distribution channel strategies (Grossman, 1997). Partner companies are expected to develop their individual competences and share resources (Shen, Choi, & Chow, 2017) to mutually reinforce their brand equities. Abratt and Motlana (2002) admit that co-branding main advantage is convincingly position the brands, which generates more sales in both existent and new market segments and increased brand value. Co-branding strategies are also expected to reduce the costs of introducing a new product (Helmig et al., 2008), and to provide competitive advantage and increased attractiveness namely due to the spillover effects (Erevelles et al., 2008).

Despite its advantages, co-branding can also generate negative impacts. Helmig et al. (2008) stress the need of adjustments from each partner, stating that success will depend on the commitment of all partners involved. Co-branding is, indeed, a complex (Helmig et al., 2008) and inflexible (Lee, 2014) strategy.

Brand Image, Brand Identity, and Co-Branding

Brand identity expresses the tangible and intangible characteristics of the brand that makes it unique (Kapferer, 2012). Aaker (1996) distinguishes brand image from brand identity by explaining that image refers to the subjective perspectives at a determined moment about the brand, while identity is how managers wish target audiences understand the brand, stressing that effectively expressing brand identity is a key factor for brand success. Motion et al. (2003) found that managers tend to establish relationships in order to redefine brand identity. Alliances with other brands contribute to the development of new identities (Balmer & Greyser, 2002). As brand partnerships may have a great impact on companies, they should be carefully evaluated (Öberg (2016).

According to Riley et al. (2015), consumers' perceptions on a brand alliance depend on the adequacy of the alliance, that is, the consistency of the brands in the partnership. Moreover, the less known brand tends to converge to the brand with more awareness (Abratt & Motlana, 2002), resulting in the transference of positive associations of the stronger brand to the other. This evidence is consistent with results obtained by Geylani, Inman, and Hofstede (2008) who found that the partner with best performance has a positive impact on co-branding product perceptions. Still, Geylani et al. (2008) recommend choosing partners with similar performance, in order to avoid the perception of discrepancies by consumers.

Building a positive brand image can represent the main purpose of a co-brand strategy by reinforcing the image of the partner brands (Geylani et al., 2008), allowing the brand to set a different position toward the competition. In the hospitality sector, namely luxury hotels, value maximization, needs' fulfilment, and guests satisfaction are essential to develop a strong brand image (e.g., Dev, Morgan, & Shoemaker, 1995; Li, Yen, & Uysal, 2014; Su & Reynolds, 2017). Clearly, co-branding strategies require a rigorous evaluation of the partner involved (e.g., Guillet & Tasci, 2012; Helmig et al., 2008), as shown by the wine business sector, where the establishment of associations increases the possibility of more effective promotion and the creation of strong points-of-differentiation (Vrontis, Thrassou, & Czinkota, 2011).

The Importance of Co-Branding to Reinforce Brand Positioning

Brand positioning consists of the mission and the brand value proposition (Nobre, 2019) - functional, emotional, and self-expression benefits - that is actively communicated to the market (Aaker, 1996). It assumes importance in the formation of consumers' perceptions regarding subjective and objective brand attributes (Kapferer, 2012; Lewis, 1981) and provides companies with important competitive advantages (Malik, Naeem, & Munawar, 2012), by establishing differentiation and assuring consumer preference. Singh et al. (2014) found that consumers' perceptions on brand positioning are transferable to the other partner brands. Hence, co-branding strategies act as endorsers of other brands' quality. Wason and Charlton (2015) suggest that brand positioning is a fundamental criterion for partner selection, referring that brands with hedonic attributes are more able of achieving partnership benefits than brands more associated with functional attributes. Moreover, brand equity should also be carefully considered by functional brands, while hedonic brands need to further develop partner brands' associations (Wason & Charlton, 2015).

The hotel industry, in the main cities in Europe, is generally higly fragmented and under fierce competition of direct local hotel brands, global hotel chains and a myriad of diverse substitutes that pressure prices and impact market dynamics. This impels hotel brands, in particular upper-class hospitality services, for fighting for a unique position and a sustainable competitive advantage in the market (Li, Yen & Uysal, 2014). A co-branding strategy can be particularly suitable to build or reinforce a unique positioning for a hotel brand. A co-branding strategy might offer an opportunity of differentiation and of building a strong positioning, besides the risks and challenges that a partnership with other brands and their associated brand images can represent at the level of consumer acceptation and marketing communication consistency (Hadjicharalambous, 2006; cit. in Guillet & Tasci, 2012).

METHOD

Based on the contributions from extant literature, three research questions guided the present study:

RQ1: How do luxury hotel and local wine brands benefit from co-branding partnerships?

RQ2: How does a co-branding strategy impact on partners' brand image management?

RQ3: How do partnerships with prestige products influence luxury service brand positioning?

Table 1. Participants in the study: Luxury hotel brand managers

Participants	Gender	Age group	Education	Years in the Company	Job
Interviewee 1	F	36-45	Post-graduate	8	Wine Director
Interviewee 2	F	26-35	Post-graduate	8	Head Sommelier
Interviewee 3	F	18-25	Graduate	3	Marketing Assistant
Interviewee 4	F	26-35	Post-graduate	2	Brand Assistant
Interviewee 5	M	26-35	Post-graduate	2	Designer
Interviewee 6	M	46-55	Graduate	7	CMO

In order to tackle these research questions, we conducted a qualitative exploratory study, as co-branding in luxury hospitality management still lacks for strong validation from the literature. Qualitative data is "the best and richest for theorizing about social structures and social systems" (Glaser & Strauss, 2006, p.17). This study, in particular, focus on a co-branding partnership between wine brands and a vinous-concept luxury hotel brand, from now on referred to as the luxury hotel. Thus, the managers' opinions and convictions are crucial for understanding the partnerships between the brands they represent. All these aspects sustain the relevance of considering manager's narratives to investigate this case.

Located in Portugal, this hotel currently maintains a partnership with around 102 brands of wine producers, which helps maintaining the vinous-concept established by the luxury hotel in all its valences. Each of the hotel's rooms has a name of a wine brand and decoration according to its characteristics. Besides allowing the luxury hotel to be associated with any wine brand, the partnership includes having the partner wine brands sold at the hotel's store and website, and featured in their restaurant, including in exclusive wine dinner events.

We conducted 14 semi-structured interviews with managers of the luxury hotel (Table 1) and he wine brand partners (Table 2). Interviewees has access to full information on the study and gave their

Table 2. Participants in the study: Luxury hotel brand managers

Participants	Company size	Gender	Age group	Education	Years in the Company	Job
Company A	Small	M	36-45	Graduate	7	CEO
Company B	Small	F	46-55	Graduate	7	Sales manager
Company C	Large	F	26-35	Post-graduate	3	Marketing and Sales Manager
Company D	Medium	F	26-35	Post-graduate	3	Key Account Manager
Company E	Small	M	56-65	Graduated	12	CEO
Company F	Medium	F	46-55	Post-graduate	8	Marketing and Sales Manager
Company G	Medium	M	46-55	Post-graduate	3	CEO
Company H	Large	M	36-45	Undergraduate	20	Sales Manager

informed consent prior to participating in the study. We also followed other ethical principles for social sciences research, including ensuring that participation was voluntary, confidential and anonymous.

Invitations to participate in the study were initially sent by e-mail, along the interview guidelines and purpose of the study. We conducted six face-to-face interviews and, due to scheduling difficulties, one interview by telephone call, and the other seven by e-mail. The telephone and face-to-face interviews were recorded to allow transcription, with the participants' consent. Besides the lack of intimacy, connection and spontaneity that email interviews could represent, this question seems not to be so problematic when participants are managers (from the supply side) and can otherwise represent a strength of the study, as they encourage for more correctness, detail and rigour in the information provided. Interviews' duration ranged from 15 to 25 minutes. A set of categories gathered from the literature review guided content analysis, comprising co-branding strategy implementation (partner selection criteria and shared benefits), impact on partners' brands (positioning and image), and importance of co-branding partnerships as distribution channels.

RESULTS

Co-Branding Mutual Benefits

Co-branding mutual benefits were acknowledging by all participants in this study. Despite the strong positioning and image of the luxury hotel, and the opportunity it offers to their wine partners to reach the luxury customers, the Hotel's representatives recognize the mutual advantage provided to the involved brands, but with different intensity along the process. Indeed, gains for the Hotel were particularly visible during its launch stage, as in order to establish its vinous-concept (the basis of it differentiation) the Hotel benefited of the association with well-known high quality wine brands. For instance, the Hotel's Sommellier (Interviewee 2) noted that this was determinant for the vinous-concept Hotel's brand success:

The [Hotel] enjoys this advantage of having quality producers associated with the brand, that is, they also leverage us in the sense that we want to be an embassy of Portuguese wines (…) and the growth of our brand was due to having producers of recognized quality that joined us, gave credibility to the Hotel, since they were in the market for longer than us.

These benefits continue to flow, now that the Hotel's image is established. The Hotel's CMO (Interviewee 6) explains that "aligning with the best wine producers in Portugal helps reinforce the Hotel's concept, positioning the Hotel as an authority in the wine context".

Clearly, the success of this co-branding strategy relates to the ability of consistently providing benefits to partners and the congruity of the brands involved. As one of the large company partners referred, this is due to the shared values of the partners "both brands represent a common ideology related to luxury, best service, and quality" (Company H, Sales Manager).

These findings corroborate extant literature that emphasizes that co-branding strategies focus on providing benefits to all involved brands (e.g., Egan, 2011). Overall, this study demonstrates that being acknowledge by all partners as mutual beneficial is a critical success factor to co-branding strategy.

Partner Selection Criteria

As the leader of this co-branding partnership, the Hotel had a fundamental role in developing the strategy and, ultimately, it is responsible for choosing its wine partner brands. Hotel's representatives consistently identified product quality as the main criteria for partner selection. As mentioned by the Hotel's Brand Assistant (Interviewee 4) "being a luxury brand, the Hotel must be associated to similar brands that are perceived as premium, prestige brands by the consumer". Hence, initially it was essential for the Hotel to reinforce its brand positioning by the association with the most reputable wine brands, benefiting from the transfer of credibility. These findings confirm that the selection of co-branding partners must focus on brand positioning (Wason & Charlton, 2015) and performance (Geylani et al., 2008).

This study shows that as the Hotel brand gained its own prestige, it could collaborate with a different range of brands. Partners must provide high quality products, but the Hotel representatives recognize that nowadays they are able to cooperate with unknown brands – as long as their products present high quality standards, as explained in the following sections.

Co-Branding Impact on Brand Positioning

The fact of being a vinous-concept luxury hotel obviously favors the adoption of co-branding strategy with high-quality wine producers. Indeed, the Hotel's representatives recognize that the association with wine brands is essential to hotel's brand positioning. As mentioned by the Marketing CEO (Interviewee 6) co-branding "helped a lot to position the hotel as one of the best vinous-concept hotels in Europe. The diversity of partners adds a lot of value to this aspect".

The co-branding strategy that was undertaken by the Hotel was essential for its positioning, consolidating its vinous-concept and its role of wine embassy. Besides the benefits for the Hotel itself, this stronger positioning provides long-term benefits that can be also transferred to wine company partners. Indeed, regarding the impact on wine brands' positioning, the advantage of being associated with a luxury hotel was also highlighted. For instance, the Hotel's Brand Assistant (Interviewee 4) explained that

The [Hotel] quickly achieved a premium positioning, given the quality of its facilities, the service it provides, the quality of its restaurants, among many other factors. Being associated with [Hotel] means being associated with a brand of luxury and refinement, not accessible to everyone.

Overall, wine companies participating in this study consistently noted that the luxury vinous-concept positioning of the Hotel favours wine brands. The Marketing and Sales Manager of Company F states that "it is of utmost importance and reason of pride for our brand to be associated to a luxury hotel, because it shows that we have quality, image, and brand characteristics that allow such partnership". Company C interviewee further notes that the advantages for wine brand positioning is also due to the exclusivity of the partnership:

Being amongst a relatively small and highly selected number of partners, who produce very high quality wines, contributes to enhancing the credibility and confidence of consumers regarding our own wines (Marketing and Sales Manager, Company C).

Thus, these findings offer empirical evidence that co-branding helps reinforcing brand positioning (Singh et al., 2014). The role of the stronger brands as endorsers of the quality of their partners is also evident, corroborating extant literature (e.g., Genc, 2010; Singh et al., 2014).

Co-Branding Impact on Luxury/Premium Brand Image

As demonstrated in previous sections, brand image is one of the most discussed consequences of co-branding strategies. Without surprise, participants in this study stress that co-branding strategy had an undeniable impact, particularly important for the weaker brands. In the words of the Hotel's CMO (Interviewee 6), "(...) the [Hotel] brand is stronger than most producers', so in many cases it was the producer who benefits most [from the partnership]". While it seems obvious that being associated to some well-known wine brands was essential for the vinous-concept Hotel's credibility and luxury positioning, the Hotel managers concluded it were the wine brands that took the most advantages. Mainly, because "for these brands undoubtedly it is an asset to be associated with us, especially regarding awareness" (Interviewee 4, Marketing Assistant). Aspect confirmed by several partners, as for instance the CEO of the wine Company G "[the partnership] strengthens our awareness, allowing us to reach a target of high-end customers that buy luxury products".

Hence, in this case co-branding strategy is essential to develop a premium image for wine brands, certifying the quality of their products. Interviewee 1 (Wine Director) referred that this applies even to very small wine brands "there are small producers that have never been detected by wine quality radars but being here it is almost a certification". Clearly, one can expect a co-branding strategy be particularly important for unknown brands and small companies, as suggested, for instance, by the Sales Manager of Company B: "for unknown brands it's very difficult to enter the market. Therefore, it was very important to us to be associated with a hotel with such a brand and charisma".

However, the rewards in terms of brand image were also acknowledge by the medium and large companies with stronger brands. As explained by the Key Account Manager of Company D, their brands had a strong and positive image before the partnership, but "in general all brands associated with [the Hotel] may benefit from a premium image". Marketing and Sales Manager of Company C, one of the large companies participating in this study proposes the reasons for the benefits provided even to well-known brands:

The Hotel has developed a strong premium image due to their target customers and the very high quality and variety of services it provides. Therefore, the brands that partner with it benefit from the association with its quality and high reputation (Marketing and Sales Manager, Company C).

Hence, consistently with literature (Lee, 2014; Park et al., 1986), findings highlight the co-branding ability to reinforce brand image. Although co-branding mutually reinforces the partner brands, as suggested by Geylani et al. (2008), the advantages seem more evident for the less known and reputable brands, as suggested by authors such as Abratt and Motlana (2002). This study also offers evidence that this process has a dynamic nature. In the beginning, apparently the Hotel brand most benefited from the association with the prestigious wine brands. Then, as Hotel's image consolidated over time, it assumed the role of reinforcing the brands of its partners, especially the brands of the smaller producers. Overall, this study corroborates Geylani et al. (2008) arguments that one of the main goals of co-branding is reinforcing the image of partner brands and confirms that the stronger brands assume an important role as endorsers of their partners.

The Hotel as a Channel Intermediary

This co-branding strategy was referred by all participants as successful and with positive impact on the partner brands. However, the role of the partnership in terms of distribution channel did not showed up from interviews, except in the case of very small producers, such as Company E, whose CEO claimed that the Hotel was the main distribution channel for their wines. For the CEO of the medium-sized Company G, the Hotel's wine shop, bars and restaurants are "privileged distribution channels", and Company D Key Account Manager expects that "the Hotel can leverage sales inside and outside the national market". In the opinion of the Hotel's CMO "without this type of partnership it would be impossible for small producers to target this kind of customers". This corroborates Helmig et al. (2008) who claim that co-branding help reduce costs especially in the case of new products.

SOLUTIONS AND RECOMMENDATIONS

This study provides interesting cues for managers, more specifically in the luxury hospitality and wine business sectors, on how to use co-branding to reinforce brand positioning. Moreover, in contrast with most of previous research on the topic, research investigates co-branding in luxury hospitality management from the managers' point of view. Thus, it constitutes an interesting case for comparing co-branding management practices.

This study points out that co-branding involving companies from different sectors offers interesting opportunities for differentiation, positioning, and for developing a strong and positive brand image, especially in the case of involving producers that directly connect with the concept defined by the brand. Considering that this article aimed primarily at determining the benefits of co-branding, some aspects for managing partnership strategies between brands from different business sectors should be pointed out.

The literature notes that managers operating in the hotel business must join forces to achieve competitive advantage (Li et al., 2014) and maximize the value offered to the consumers (Su & Reynolds, 2016). Throughout this study, it was possible to verify that this partnership provides several benefits to the brands involved, including brand awareness and reach. Therefore, it is advisable that less-known wine brands that aspire to a prestigious reputation associate themselves with hospitality luxury brands, namely taking into account that the wine market is highly differentiated and fragmented (Brochado et al, 2015; Karelakis et al., 2008). Collaborating with high-end hospitality brands can help to leverage wine brands that wish to stand out, attract new customers, and achieve differentiation and competitive advantage. Therefore, wine producers looking for differentiation competitive advantage could cooperate with brands of different product categories, in order to enhance their products' distribution, communicate the quality of their brands, and reach other potentially interested audiences.

The study also provides recommendations for hotels and other companies that intend to develop a differentiated positioning through partnerships that are capable of adding value to their brands. The establishment of co-branding strategies with companies from different business sectors enhance the success of the brands involved by the ability to differentiate and position it (Hadjicharalambous, 2006; cit. in

Guillet & Tasci, 2012). In addition, co-branding presents interesting opportunities to improve brand image, as partner's brand reputation provides credibility, thus allowing effective brand image management.

FUTURE RESEARCH DIRECTIONS

It is important to refer that the study focused only on one ongoing co-branding initiative, with a limited number of partners actively involved in the study. Therefore, we recommend that future research further investigate this topic under different contexts and research settings, in order to validate findings. Suggestions for future research include comparing co-branding strategies in luxury hotels with different products and services. Studying unsuccessful co-branding strategies would also be useful to both academics and practitioners.

In addition, it would be interesting to investigate consumers' perceptions regarding co-branding strategies. One possible direction for future research is carrying out quantitative studies in order to validate some of the results achieved with qualitative data. Based on the literature review and on the results of this exploratory study, we formulated four hypotheses of study. These hypotheses represent a framework of analysis for future studies.

H1. Co-branding strategies between brands of different business areas influence positively consumers' perceptions about the brands involved in the partnership.

According to Abratt and Motlana (2002), associations created by co-branding strategies can both increase brand value and enhance or damage consumers' perceptions of each of the brands involved. In fact, there may be a lack of control in the alignment of both brands in the minds of consumers (Helmig et al., 2008). Several factors can influence consumers' perceptions on branding partnerships, such as, disappointment on brand performance that may result from exacerbated consumer expectations, and the impact of attitudes toward brands prior to the partnership on their partner brands' associations and evaluations (Abratt & Motlana, 2002).

H2. Brand reputation and perceived quality have a positive impact on partner's brand reach and image.

Co-branding allows the exchange of benefits in terms of brands' perceived quality and reputation (Cegarra & Michel, 2001), and potentially adds value to product brands (Jakubanecs & Supphellen, 2012). Co-branding is one of the techniques that has been increasingly used to reinforce brand image (Kottemann et al., 2017; Lee, 2014; Warraich et al., 2014). In addition, results of this study suggest that product brands benefit more with the partnership with the luxury hotel, because the recognition in the market and the strength of its positioning. Consequently, product (wine) brands can be perceived as prestige brands due to this partnership. Thus, the partnership allows product brands to be associated with luxury and high quality, consolidating and boosting their brand image.

H2.1. Partnership with a luxury hotel brand improves positively an image of prestige for the product brands.

According to our findings, the luxury positioning of the Hotel brand, the high standards of the service quality it provides, and its awareness create value and favour the development of a prestige image for the wine brands.

This study shows that the luxury hotel acts as an endorser and supports the promotion of the product brand and its offers, providing empirical support to contributions in the literature (e.g., Hendrasaputra & Lunarjanto, 2009). Service providers have several opportunities to feature partner brands, such as through the organization of events, the customization of hotel facilities, and the sale of products through the hotel's stores. Through these activities, it is possible to reach potential consumers and disseminate an image of quality of the wine brands. Both well-known wine brands and newly launched brands recognise these benefits.

H3. The credibility of one brand positively influences the image of the brands in the partnership.

The endorser grants support and credibility to the partners. It guarantees that it will be able to provide all the desired functional benefits (Aaker, 1996). In the wine sector, the association with other brands results in numerous advantages, including high credibility and perceived quality (Vrontis et al., 2010). In addition, according to this study, the luxury brand benefited from the quality and reputation of some wine partners in the sector, which provided the brand with credibility in the wine sector. Likewise, the quality and prestige of the hotel granted credibility and quality certification to the product brands.

CONCLUSION

Considering that literature on co-branding is still scarce and has disregarded the luxury hospitality sector, this article provides interesting contributions on the topic while confirms the relevance of co-branding strategies between hotels and products directly connected to its concept, positioning or differentiating characteristics. The empirical results shared in this article demonstrate the characteristics and impact of a successful co-branding strategy implemented by a vinous-concept luxury hotel and high-quality wine brands, as described by Hotel and Wine Companies' managers. Helmig et al. (2008) emphasize that commitment of all partners is essential for co-branding success. Commitment is easily achieved when all partners get and are aware of clear benefits, in terms of not only profitability, but also regarding brand image and positioning. Results suggest the improvement of brand image as one of the main advantages of co-branding with a luxury hotel. Indeed, all participants in this study acknowledge that this co-branding strategy has a positive and enduring impact on brand image and reinforces brand positioning. Nevertheless, participants also emphasize that the coherence of the brand values and the positioning of the partners involved in the co-branding are essential. More specifically, in the case of a co-branding involving prestige brands, the level of the quality of the products involved is crucial. Therefore, despite the advantages that a co-branding with a strong brand may represent for brands still fighting for awareness and positioning, this partnership is particularly demanding for small size partners. As noted by one of the participants in this study "the true partnership forces us to be in our markets as good as they are in theirs" (Company E, CEO).

REFERENCES

Aaker, D. A. (1996). *Building Strong Brands*. Simon & Schuster.

Abratt, R., & Motlana, P. (2002). Managing co-branding strategies: Global brands into local markets. *Business Horizons*, *45*(5), 43–50. doi:10.1016/S0007-6813(02)00242-2

Balmer, J. M. T., & Greyser, S. A. (2002). Managing the multiple identities of the corporation. *California Management Review, 43*(3), 72-86. doi:10.2307/41166133

Boone, J. M. (1997). Hotel-restaurant co-branding: A preliminary study. *The Cornell Hotel and Restaurant Administration Quarterly, 38*(5), 34–43. doi:10.1016/S0010-8804(97)86581-0

Brennan, R., Canning, L., & McDowell, R. (2014). *Business-to-Business Marketing* (3rd ed.). Sage.

Chiambaretto, P., & Gurău, C. (2017). David by Goliath: What is co-branding and what is in it for SMEs. *International Journal of Entrepreneurship and Small Business, 31*(1), 103–122. doi:10.1504/IJESB.2017.083805

Dahlstrom, R., & Dato-on, M. C. (2004). Business-to-business antecedents to retail co-branding. *Journal of Business-To-Business Marketing, 11*(3), 1–22. doi:10.1300/J033v11n03_01

Dev, C. S., Morgan, M. S., & Shoemaker, S. (1995). A positioning analysis of hotel brands: Based on travel-manager perceptions. *The Cornell Hotel and Restaurant Administration Quarterly, 36*(6), 48–55. doi:10.1177/001088049503600617

Díaz-Bustamante, M., Carcelén, S., & Puelles, M. (2016). Image of luxury brands: A question of style and personality. *SAGE Open, 6*(2), 1–15. doi:10.1177/2158244016644946

Egan, J. (2011). *Relationship Marketing: Exploring Relational Strategies in Marketing*. Pearson Education.

Erevelles, S., Stevenson, T. H., Srinivasan, S., & Fukawa, N. (2008). An analysis of B2B ingredient co-branding relationships. *Industrial Marketing Management, 37*(8), 940–952. doi:10.1016/j.indmarman.2007.07.002

Genc, R. (2010). Strategic brand management in hospitality sector: How to manage co-branding in hotels and restaurants. *Acta Universitatis Danubius Œconomica, 6*(3), 33–46.

Geylani, T., Inman, J. J., & Hofstede, F. T. (2008). Image reinforcement or impairment: The effects of co-branding on attribute uncertainty. *Marketing Science, 27*(4), 730–744. doi:10.1287/mksc.1070.0326

Glaser, B. G., & Strauss, A. L. (2006). *The Discovery of Grounded Theory: Strategies for Qualitative Research*. Aldine Transactions.

Goulding, C. (1999). Grounded theory, ethnography and phenomenology: A comparative analysis of three qualitative strategies for marketing research. *European Journal of Marketing, 39*(3/4), 294–308. doi:10.1108/03090560510581782

Grossman, R. P. (1997). Co-branding in advertising: Developing effective associations. *Journal of Product and Brand Management, 6*(3), 191–201. doi:10.1108/10610429710175709

Guillet, B. D., & Tasci, A. D. (2012). Chinese hoteliers' take on hotel co-branding in China. *Tourism Review, 67*(4), 3–11. doi:10.1108/16605371211277777

Helmig, B., Huber, J.-A., & Leeflang, P. S. (2008). Co-branding: The state of the art. *Schmalenbach Business Review, 60*(4), 359–377. doi:10.1007/BF03396775

Kapferer, J.-N. (1998). Why are we seduced by luxury brands? *Journal of Brand Management, 6*(1), 44–49. doi:10.1057/bm.1998.43

Kapferer, J.-N. (2012). *The New Strategic Brand Management: Advanced Insights and Strategic Thinking* (5th ed.). Kogan Page.

Keller, K. L., & Richey, K. (2006). The importance of corporate brand personality traits to a successful 21st century business. *Journal of Brand Management, 14*(1-2), 74–81. doi:10.1057/palgrave.bm.2550055

Lee, C.-L. (2014). Is co-branding a double-edged sword for brand partners? *European Research Studies Journal, 17*(4), 19–34. doi:10.35808/ersj/430

Lewis, R. C. (1981). The positioning statement for hotels. *The Cornell Hotel and Restaurant Administration Quarterly, 22*(1), 51–61. doi:10.1177/001088048102200111

Li, X., Yen, C.-L., & Uysal, M. (2014). Differentiating with brand personality in economy hotel segment. *Journal of Vacation Marketing, 20*(4), 323–333. doi:10.1177/1356766714527965

Malik, M. E., Naeem, B., & Munawar, M. (2012). Brand image: Past, present and future. *Journal of Basic and Applied Scientific Research, 2*(12), 13069–13075.

Moon, H., & Sprott, D. E. (2016). Ingredient branding for a luxury brand: The role of brand and product fit. *Journal of Business Research, 69*(12), 5768–5774. doi:10.1016/j.jbusres.2016.04.173

Motion, J., Leitch, S., & Brodie, R. J. (2003). Equity in corporate co-branding: The case of Adidas and the All Blacks. *European Journal of Marketing, 37*(7/8), 1080–1094. doi:10.1108/03090560310477672

Nobre, H. (2019). A marca como ferramenta de gestão empresarial. In C. Machado & J. P. Davim (Eds.), *Organização e Políticas Empresariais* (pp. 133–166). Actual Editora.

Nobre, H., & Simões, C. (2019). NewLux brand relationship scale: Capturing the scope of mass-consumed luxury brand relationships. *Journal of Business Research, 102*, 328–338. doi:10.1016/j.jbusres.2019.01.047

Nueno, J. L., & Quelch, J. A. (1998). The mass marketing of luxury. *Business Horizons, 41*(6), 61–61. doi:10.1016/S0007-6813(98)90023-4

Öberg, C. (2016). What creates a collaboration-level identity? *Journal of Business Research, 69*(9), 3220–3230. doi:10.1016/j.jbusres.2016.02.027

Okonkwo, U. (2009). The luxury brand strategy challenge. *Journal of Brand Management, 16*(5-6), 287–289. doi:10.1057/bm.2008.53

Park, C. W., Jaworski, B. J., & MacInnis, D. J. (1986). Strategic brand concept-image management. *Journal of Marketing, 50*(4), 135–145. doi:10.1177/002224298605000401

Riley, D., Charlton, N., & Wason, H. (2015). The impact of brand image fit on attitude towards a brand alliance. *Management & Marketing, 10*(4), 270–283. doi:10.1515/mmcks-2015-0018

Shen, B., Choi, T.-M., & Chow, P.-S. (2017). Brand loyalties in designer luxury and fast fashion co-branding alliances. *Journal of Business Research, 81*, 173–180. doi:10.1016/j.jbusres.2017.06.017

Singh, J. P., Kalafatis, S., & Ledden, L. (2014). Consumer perceptions of cobrands: The role of brand positioning strategies. *Marketing Intelligence & Planning, 32*(2), 145–159. doi:10.1108/MIP-03-2013-0055

Su, N., & Reynolds, D. (2017). Effects of brand personality dimensions on consumers' perceived self-image congruity and functional congruity with hotel brands. *International Journal of Hospitality Management, 66*, 1–12. doi:10.1016/j.ijhm.2017.06.006

Tynan, C., McKechnie, S., & Chhuon, C. (2010). Co-creating value for luxury brands. *Journal of Business Research, 63*(11), 1156–1163. doi:10.1016/j.jbusres.2009.10.012

Vrontis, D., Thrassou, A., & Czinkota, M. R. (2011). Wine marketing: A framework for consumer-centred planning. *Journal of Brand Management, 18*(4-5), 245–263. doi:10.1057/bm.2010.39

Wang, S.-C., Soesilo, P. K., & Zhang, D. (2015). Impact of luxury brand retailer co-branding strategy on potential customers: A cross-cultural study. *Journal of International Consumer Marketing, 27*(3), 237–252. doi:10.1080/08961530.2014.970320

Wason, H., & Charlton, N. (2015). How positioning strategies affect co-branding outcomes. *Cogent Business & Management, 2*(1), 1092192. doi:10.1080/23311975.2015.1092192

ADDITIONAL READING

Beverland, M. (2018). *Brand Management: Co-creating Meaningful Brands*. Sage.

Heding, T., Knudtzen, C. F., & Bjerre, M. (2020). *Brand Management: Mastering Research, Theory and Practice*. Routledge. doi:10.4324/9780367172596

Kapferer, J. N. (2012). *The New Strategic Brand Management: Advanced Insights and Strategic Thinking*. Kogan Page.

Kapferer, J. N., & Bastien, V. (2012). *The Luxury Strategy: Break The Rules of Marketing to Build Luxury Brands* (2nd ed.). Kogan Page.

Keller, K. L., & Swaminathan, V. (2019). *Strategic Brand Management: Building, Measuring, and Managing Brand Equity* (5th ed.). Pearson Education.

Linder, C., & Sperber, S. C. (2018). Leveraging reputation for product innovation through strategic co-branding. In Information Resources Management Association (Eds.) Driving Customer Appeal Through the Use of Emotional Branding (pp. 248-261). Hershey: IGI Global. doi:10.4018/978-1-5225-2921-7.ch014

Rosenbaum-Elliott, R., Percy, L., & Pervan, S. (2015). Strategic Brand Management (4th ed.). Oxford University Press.

Washburn, J. H., Till, B. D., & Priluck, R. (2000). Co-branding: Brand equity and trial effects. *Journal of Consumer Marketing, 17*(7), 591–604. doi:10.1108/07363760010357796

KEY TERMS AND DEFINITIONS

Brand Equity: The value that a brand provides to its products and services.

Brand Image: Customers' associations and beliefs about a brand.

Brand Perceptions: Positive or negative feelings that result from the consumers' experiences with the brand.

Brand Positioning: A strategy which main aim is to make the brand differentiated from the competitors' brands in the mind of the consumers.

Brand Value: It is often a synonym of brand equity.

Co-Branding: A strategy that creates associations between two or more brands of strategic partners, namely in the form of brand partnerships or brand collaborations.

Customer Loyalty: A relationship between customer and brand that results in repeated purchases and often in the preference of that brand instead of its competitors.

Spillover Effects: An economic event that results from another apparently unrelated event.

Chapter 18
Data Analysis in the Shipping Industry:
eShip Case Study – Problem Statement

Marcel Kyas
Reykjavik University, Iceland

Joshua D. Springer
Reykjavik University, Iceland

Jan Tore Pedersen
Marlo as., Norway

Valentina Chkoniya
https://orcid.org/0000-0003-1174-3216
University of Aveiro, Portugal

ABSTRACT

This chapter identifies the critical issues that must be addressed to accelerate the digital transition in the chartering market. The maritime industry is one of the pillars of global trade, where change is a constant. Again, shipping is at the cusp of a new era—one driven by data. The authors review the state-of-the-art technology that is useful to automate chartering processes. · The Fourth Industrial Revolution (or Industry 4.0) starts to change the bulk shipping markets leveraging the data flow between industrial processes in the physical and virtual world. · The internet of things accelerates data flow from things in the real world to the virtual world and enables us to control processes in real-time. Machine-to-machine communication, together with artificial intelligence, creates autonomous systems in many areas of production and logistics. Based on the gathered elements, eShip's case study was analyzed, and future steps have been defined for the data analysis in the shipping industry.

DOI: 10.4018/978-1-7998-6985-6.ch018

INTRODUCTION

Traditionally, the shipping industry has been highly dependent on its various mini-ecosystems, consisting of ports, authorities, ships, ship operators, shipowners, cargo owners, and many more. However, over a decade ago, researchers noted that the traditionally conservative shipping industry is undergoing a change, where it is believed that the demands for an increase in efficiency, safety, and protection of the environment can be only achieved by more innovation (Jacks & Pendakur, 2010; Perunovic & Vidic, 2011; SmartPort, 2019). Half a century ago, the French geographer Perpillou considered ports and maritime transport to form a constellation (Ducruet & Zaidi, 2012). All the different players in the ecosystem are inextricably linked, making interconnectivity and cooperation between them crucial for effective and efficient operations of the transport system (Martimo, 2017). The port of the future is a smart port, and the ship of the future is a smart ship. However, before getting smart, all the "constellations" must go digital (Delenclos, Rasmussen, & Riedl, 2018). Change is a constant in the maritime industry, and it is once again at the cusp of a new era—one driven by increased digitalization and innovation (Levinson, 2020; SmartPort, 2019). Smart ships and smart ports will exchange data for speeding up the processes at the port, including refueling, unloading, and loading cargo. Paperwork can be handled automatically. Ports will exchange data, announcing what leaves one port to the ports that receive the cargo. Such exchange speeds up customs clearance.

The fourth industrial revolution promises increased automation of all processes. This includes the shipping industry. Parcel services like DHL track their shipments around the world in real-time (Diwan, 2016). This development necessitates that all stations the cargo takes are digitized. For the shipping industry, this includes the ships and the ports. The Boston Consulting Group identified several emerging technologies like advanced analytics, autonomous shipping, robotics, and artificial intelligence set to change how planning, operations, commercial, and support functions within shipping are performed (Delenclos et al., 2018). With the addition of digital data about cargo and ships, data analytics and machine learning uncover better ways to handle ships, ports, and cargo. It enables to measure the impact of every step, decrease cost, and speed up processes.

Information technology on-board and in communication from vessels to ports and authorities are developing as required. However, according to a survey conducted by eShip in 2021, the dialogue between cargo owners (charterers) and shipping operators is, in most cases, still using phones and various forms of paper, spreadsheets, and other unstructured data formats for keeping and sharing information (PDF documents in e-mails being one example). Consequently, there is significant room for improvement, particularly when organizing operations and making the interaction between stakeholders more efficient. The authors review the state-of-the-art technology useful to automate chartering processes that serve as a base for the eShip project development. The eShip project, funded by an EEA Grant, is developing an online platform for making the entire chartering process digital. This includes contracts of affreightment, charter party terms, real-time voyage tracking, demurrage/dispatch calculations, freight invoice generation, bills of lading, post-voyage analysis, and regulatory compliance. Based on the gathered insights, the critical issues that must be addressed to accelerate the digital transition in the chartering market were identified. Future steps have been defined for the data analysis in the shipping industry.

BACKGROUND

The maritime industry is one of the critical pillars of global trade (Cacho, Marques, & Nascimento, 2020; Chkoniya, Madsen, & Bukhrashvili, 2020). According to the International Chamber of shipping, some 11 billion tons of goods are transported by ship each year. This represents an impressive 1.5 tons per person based on the current global population. Shipping's capacity to transfer goods and materials from where they are produced to where they will be consumed underpins modern life. Of this, 2 billion tons is crude oil, 1 billion tons is iron ore (the raw material needed to create steel), and 350 million tons of grain. Such and other similar shipments would not be possible by road, rail, or air. Large volumes of other vital products such as chemicals, refined fuels, and manufactured goods are also shipped by sea. The world fleet of commercial ships as of the beginning of 2020 (Statista 2021) is shown in Figure 1.

Figure 1. World fleet of commercial ships (adapted from Statista, 2021)

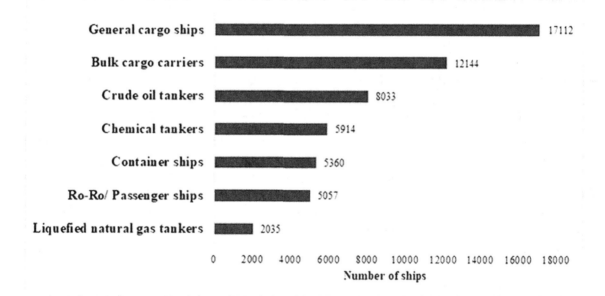

The cargo shipping industry transports, broadly, six kinds of cargo: bulk solids, bulk liquids, containerized units, refrigerated/chilled, roll-on, roll-off cargo, and general. General cargo includes everything not covered by the previous kinds of cargo. Research in the handling of cargo has overwhelmingly focused on containerized cargo and palletized cargo. These forms of cargo show many advantages over bulk cargo. Handling is standardized, and the cargo can shift from one mode to another, e.g., loaded from a ship to a train or truck without effort.

Looking at the shipping industry, container shipping, an integral part of logistics operations dealing with fast-moving consumer goods, has been forced to employ information technologies for booking, recording loading of containers, and reporting the status of container movements (Haralambides, 2019). It has also been required to connect electronically to those dealing with hinterland transportation. Specialized shipping operations, like the autonomous ship Yara Birkeland and innovative inland waterway operations like the ones managed by Seafar in Antwerp (where the captain of vessels sits in a control room on land) demonstrate that information technology is extensively used in maritime transportation.

The publication of the three books on Maritime Informatics also shows that the topic is gaining significant academic and commercial attention (Lind, Michaelides, Ward, & Watson, 2020). However, not all shipping areas have been equally fortunate or forward-looking to adopt innovative technologies for operational purposes. Much of the maritime sector has adopted the habit of adopting innovative technologies only after being forced to it by authorities (Ward & Bjørn-Andersen, 2021).

Shipping operations dealing with wet and dry bulk cargo have not faced the same pressures from their surrounding stakeholders that are the case for container shipping (Mileski, Clott, Galvao, & Laverne, 2020). Information technology on-board and in communication from vessels to ports and authorities are developing as required. However, the dialogue between cargo owners (charterers) and shipping operators is in most cases still using phones and various forms of paper, spreadsheets, and other unstructured data formats for keeping and sharing information (PDF documents in e-mails being one example). Consequently, there is significant room for improvement, particularly when organizing operations and making the interaction between stakeholders more efficient.

Research in Shipping

Research in shipping started with the founding of Operational Research at Brawdsey Research Station by A.P. Rowe. Before this, the shipping industry lacked a scientific approach. Mathematics was recast in a modern way, and computers were under development. The first problems of Operational Research and shipping were the logistics of the second world war. Troops needed to be moved and then supplied. Ships were the primary method of transport (Gass & Assad, 2005).

Then, research focused on shipping containerized cargo. Especially, containers offered many exciting problems. This resulted in an abundance of publications on container shipping.

At the same time, the problems of the bulk shipping market have received little attention. With bulk shipping, we focus on dry bulk, liquid bulk, and breakbulk shipping: dry bulk includes ores and grains, liquid bulk includes petrochemicals and liquidized natural gas, and breakbulk includes bagged coffee, barrels, metal drums, automobiles, and machine parts.

Chartering is the process of setting up an agreement (Charter Party) between a charterer (the one who owns the cargo and needs to ship it) and shipowners/operators for the cargo carriage. It may seem a straightforward process, but typically involves many stakeholders, including brokers that typically match the demand for transport with the ships with the appropriate capabilities to move cargo. Involving many parties, the process may be pretty complex. Information systems for supporting the chartering process have been around for quite a long time. Companies like ShipNet, Inchcape, Danaos, SeaSoft, etc., have been supplying such solutions for decades. One question then arises: Since these systems have been around for such a long time, why are they not extensively used? Why is the chartering process manual in most operations?

There may be many answers, but one is predominant: cost of implementation and use. These early systems required to be implemented in the users' premises, initial implementation and licenses were expensive, and software maintenance costs were typically 15% of the initial license per year. The operation needed to be significant to afford such investments. The introduction of cloud technologies creates a new change in thinking in this business. There is no longer the need for on-site implementation. New software-as-a-service business models make the use of such systems much more affordable and flexible.

The early providers of such information systems aim to "place" existing systems in the cloud, creating a "new layer" on top of them. However, if we put a new bridge on an old ship, we are making some things more accessible, but we are not changing the essential capabilities of the ship—the same thing with the information system. To make the most of cloud solutions, we need to design the systems for the cloud.

This is what eShip is doing. When these new, low-cost solutions are being used, data from operations will be stored and then available for further analysis, which should benefit all aspects of the chartering process.

Shipping 4.0

Accordingly, the term Shipping 4.0 was coined in 2016 to describe the new developments in the digitalization of shipping, to reflect the similar developments in the land-based industry, which commonly goes under Industry 4.0 (Kavallieratos, Diamantopoulou, & Katsikas, 2020). The Fourth Industrial Revolution (or Industry 4.0) is automating manufacturing and industrial practices using smart technology. Factories integrate large-scale machine-to-machine communication (M2M) and the Internet of Things (IoT). They use improved communication and self-monitoring and produce smart machines that can analyze and diagnose issues without human intervention. The term "Industry 4.0" describes different – primarily IT-driven – changes in manufacturing systems. These developments do not only have technological but furthermore versatile organizational implications. As a result, a change from product- to service orientation even in traditional industries is expected. Second, an appearance of new types of enterprises can be anticipated which adopt new specific roles within the manufacturing process responsible for the value-creation networks (Scheer, 2012). For instance, it is possible that comparable to brokers and clearing-points in the branch of financial services, analogue types of enterprises will also appear within the industry. With the planning, analysis, modelling, design, implementation, and the maintenance (in short: the development) of such complex, dynamic, and integrated information systems, an attractive and at the same time challenging task for the academic discipline of BISE (Business & Information Systems Engineering) arises, which can secure and further develop the competitiveness of industrial enterprises (Lasi, Fettke, Kemper, Feld & Hoffmann, 2014). The Fourth Industrial Revolution is thus expected to have a disruptive impact on maritime and shipping sectors, where smart ships and smart ports will be part of a new and fully interconnected maritime ecosystem. In such a context, two important questions arise about what the current level of technological advancement in the maritime shipping industry is and how the new technologies and methodologies should be deployed to ensure a rapid transition to Shipping 4.0 (Aiello, Giallanza, & Mascarella, 2020).

MAIN FOCUS OF THE CHAPTER

Unlike container shipping that is entirely digitized, bulk shipping, which represents 2/3 of the global maritime transport volume, is in dire need of digital transformation as it still relies on non-structured information exchange. However, bulk shipping is now beginning to adopt a smarter approach to how it best goes about its transformation towards a global value chain. In this case study, we analyze eShip, an online platform that applies state-of-the-art information and communication technology (ICT) tools to the traditional chartering business model, generating significant value added to all market participants in three key aspects.

eShip Project

The eShip project is funded under EEA Grants, a multiannual financial mechanism sponsored by Iceland, Liechtenstein, and Norway. eShip was ranked #1 among numerous candidates to the EEA Grants Call 1.023.2019. Its objective is to develop a cloud-based (also called Software-as-a-Service -SaaS) chartering application to support the traditional chartering process in bulk shipping - digitizing and automating the entire value chain.

As indicated before, many participants are involved in establishing a charter party. Consequently, communication between these parties is a significant challenge, particularly when trying to standardize information that has not yet resulted in intangible results. Already Lord Kelvin wrote that to know something, one must measure it, which is often restated as "to control," "to manage," "to optimize," and more. Measurements generate troves of data, which need to be interpreted. With data analytics, the authors reference all methods that help to interpret the data, for example, to understand how one measured quantity influences others. Understanding such relations then allows optimizing operations.

The members of the eShip project surveyed potential stakeholders. Data was collected in June 2021. Twenty-five responded (which is sizeable, considering the small size of the business). The majority consider digital transition important to the organization they represent (76%), identifying the need for digital platforms to support their chartering enterprises. An essential feature of such a system is to integrate with existing ERP systems (75%). The stakeholders want to leverage the data generated on ships, ports, and the chartering business to optimize their operations, minimize their impact on the environment, and demonstrate compliance with laws and standards.

The absence of Data Analysis is the main shortcoming they face (46%), followed by too many manual inputs and too many communication channels (38% each). Lack of synchronization between procedures and out-of-date functionality was mentioned by 25% of respondents. The results point that by providing a digital platform that may be used by all parties involved, either through a web interface or through EDI/PI interfaces, we will be able to maximize interoperability between all the participants, reuse information and reduce management costs and accelerate the digital transition in what is a complex and traditionally conservative sector.

eShip will contribute to this end in 3 key areas:

1. Automation of information-heavy procedures during the pre-fixture and post-fixture stages of the chartering process.
2. Seamless integration with existing management systems, particularly ERPs, transport management systems, and port community systems.
3. Application of business intelligence and data analytics to optimize the entire value chain and support the rapid transition to green shipping.

The eShip project provides a cloud platform for the entire ship chartering process in an end-to-end capacity (Figure 2). It includes the following capabilities:

*   Search for a ship function in the charterer market and the subsequent freight negotiation and contract agreement.
*   Monitoring all the interlinking stages of the voyage – including tracking of the various voyage execution processes in real-time.

- Recording all information related to billing (Bills of Lading and freight invoices) and invoicing calculations, including Statements of Facts and Laytime calculations.

Figure 2. eShip Ecosystem (©2021, eShip project, Used with permission)

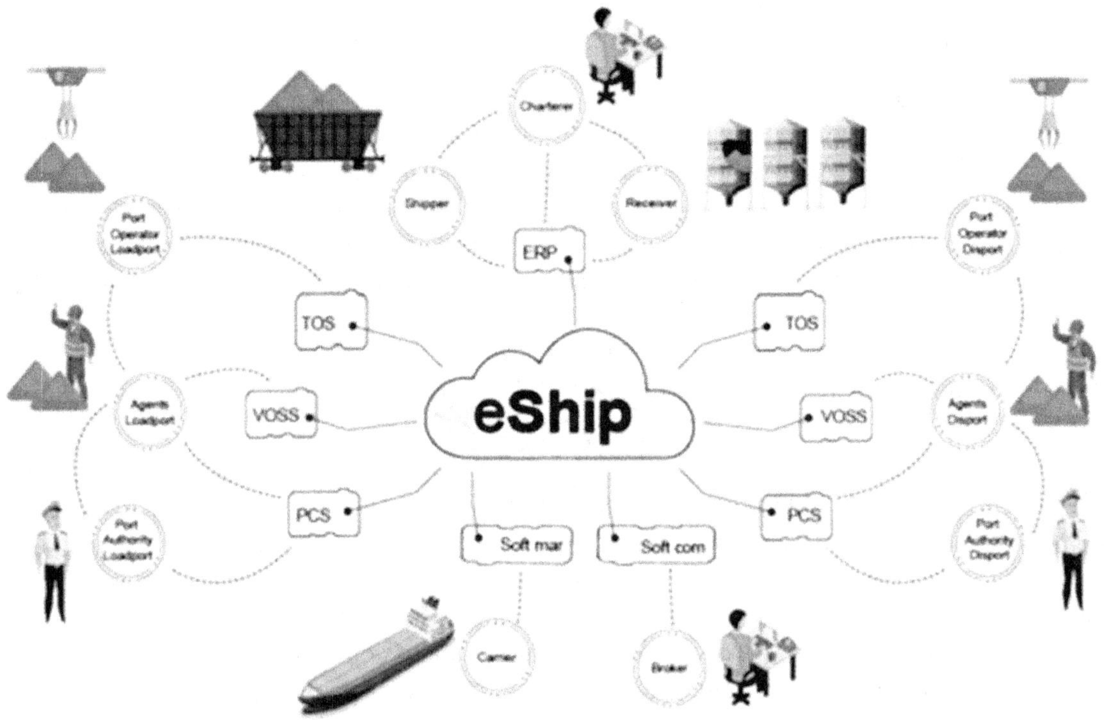

The key benefits of using the SaaS solution developed in the eShip project will be:

1. Optimization of freight rates via intelligent matching of ships and cargo using smart algorithms.
2. Reduction of back-office expenses due to automation of repetitive and time-consuming procedures.
3. Open collaboration between participants and business units without disclosing information to unauthorized users.
4. Application of business intelligence and structured data analysis to achieve chartering process optimization.

An essential extra benefit arises from the choice of taking the Software-as-a-Service approach. To apply the solution, users need access to a web browser and the Internet. Initial licenses and implementation costs will be negligible. A typical SaaS business model is "pay per use," either as a fixed subscription fee per month or a fee based on transactions. With this, there should be no financial barriers for shall and hard-pressed companies to start using the platform.

"Cargo is King" is a trading term frequently used in transport and logistics. Hence, the critical initial focus of the platform developed in eShip will secure benefits to the charterers. Those are the ones that will promote such solutions to be used by agents and shipowners/operators. However, to motivate all chartering process participants to use the solution, the needs of agents and other maritime stakeholders will also be providers. To be successful, the new digital platform needs to provide benefits for all users, reflected in the eShip project philosophy "Create value, Share value."

Digital Transition

The digital transformation of the shipping industry can enhance value within the industry's ecosystem (Poulis, Galanakis, Triantafillou, & Poulis, 2020). Emerging technologies are key change drivers in the shipping industry, despite their conservative nature (Table 1). As indicated in the market assessment report, the authors summarize the areas in which digital transition can reduce costs and improve performance from the shipowner's perspective, as recently expressed in the Future of Shipping webinar (Tat et al., 2020).

Single Windows

Singapore provides a good example where the Immigration and Checkpoints Authority (ICA), the Maritime and Port Authority of Singapore (MPA), and the Health Administration (ADA) now all combine data in a single submission. These organizations need to see even more combinations of data with shared governance - e.g., a container ship on the Asia / Europe trade via Singapore. Instead of the vessel reporting isolated data to Singapore, have the export data for China also become the import data for Singapore (with minor amendments). This process avoids individual submission to a single country (Singapore). The ADA reports that it is saving 200,000 person-hours per year by such measures. Authorities and ports will save even more if the data reporting occurs on the global level (cf. Portugal's JUL / JUP).

Lambrou, Watanabe, and Iida (2019) posit that digital transformation is a topical theme in shipping research and professional practice. They addressed technology and management aspects in a coalesced framework. They present five cases of advanced shipping incumbents' digitalization activities. Their theoretical model systematizes the technological components (technology typology), the prevailing management rationales (strategic drivers), and determinant factors (practices) of shipping digitalization. The authors of this report agree that the most critical technologies to further a digital transition are using artificial intelligence (AI) and data to optimize processes. IoT will play a crucial role in operating ships autonomously, digitizing commercial and business operations.

Real-Time Ship Tracking

One common question in the shipping industry is the estimated time of arrival. With a reasonable estimate, the charterer can order people and equipment to load and unload vessels, arrange transportation to or from the harbor, or arrange for interim storage. The authors see much use of the automatic identification system (AIS). AIS has become mandatory for large vessels (over 300 t) and allows tracking ships on the Internet. Ships may not send the correct data or send it irregularly, and receiving the signal depends on proximity to coastal base stations. Satellite communication is an option that some systems use.

Table 1. Emerging technologies in the shipping industry

Tool	Description
Link Strategy to Digitization	Establish a core business strategy that dovetails with digitization ambitions to converge with the future strategy that the company wants to pursue.
Ship Data	Draw data from ships to build user cases with shipowners and ship managers.
Optimization	Better route planning & safety measures, e.g., bunker economics via route planning.
Ship-to-Shore	Indicators of Compromise Service (IOC) sensors for ship-to-shore connection.
Drone delivery	Spare parts delivery to the ship by drone (subject to current weight constraints). Ship and harbor inspection.
Transparency	Price discovery/offerings/settings for carriers, especially websites or platforms.
Remote Operation	Inspection / Surveys / Audits; the ship no longer waits for the documentation.
Classification societies	Digital class certificate replaces the traditional paper version, thereby avoiding the need for a class surveyor to deliver this to the ship.
Crewless vessels	promoting the need to transition towards new legal and navigational structures (a trend likely to gain momentum and further accelerate in a post-pandemic world).
Seafarer Mentality	New complexity surrounding crew changes: mental health challenges / increased self-harm are new features surrounding human emotions, spurred by Covid-19.
Data Lakes	The more data is collected, the greater the ability to build "data lakes" from simple origins initially and then build up to the sophisticated level, allowing the data to speak more clearly to you over time, thus allowing for improvements.
Chatbot	Instead of performing heavy-duty analytics, ask the specific query regarding the sought-after data point (e.g., operative speed/bunker consumption). Move away from an ambition to be very clever, concentrate on what is done with the available data - i.e., use it as the need arises.
Data platforms	What are these used for? What is the business case? They can be used as a vehicle for procurement processes and an aggregator for buyers and sellers in more efficient structures.
Analysis	Performance-related data from platforms. Noticing that means a rating, ranking, quotation, discussion, or analysis regarding an aspect of the investment performance of the platform, an asset allocation service, security, an index, or a benchmark.
Ecosystem Integration	Platforms allow for greater collaboration between shipyards, shipowners, AEMs, regulatory bodies, ship managers, engine manufacturers = everybody in the ecosystem, as compared to single sourcing: a collaborative solution is more efficient. Mass adoption leads to standardization; common usage allows for the digital off-take to be shared.
Standardization	It is a vast emerging trend; join forces to unify the approval process together.
Port community	Security, data exchange, platforms' interaction is all undergoing rapid re-sets.
Single Windows for Logistics	Facilitates trading and communication between economic operators and government agencies in the logistics sector. It offers a single administrative point of access to electronic exchanges related to international trade flows.

Companies like Marine Traffic offer application programming interfaces (APIs) to track ships in real-time and to query historical position data.

The data can use to track the ship and estimate its time of arrival at a port. The necessary equipment and crew to unload the ship can be ordered on time. The data can be analyzed for the seasonality of voyage time. Graziano, Renga, and Moccia (2019) describe a method of integrating AIS with radar images to estimate ship velocity and improve maritime situational awareness. The goal of their work is to avoid collisions of ships and delays in shipping. Chen, Khoo, Chong, and Yin (2014) demonstrate data-fusion to track ships and identify potential threats along the routes, including collisions.

Use of Autonomous Vehicles and Vessels

Seaport Infrastructure Inspection: Unmanned air and sea vehicles can be helpful in infrastructure inspection in seaports, reducing financial and time costs and the number of areas people must inspect. Aerial drones are better able than humans to inspect hard-to-reach areas such as the top of a crane or shipping container. They can provide high-quality video records of the inspection. Sea-based vehicles can inspect underwater infrastructures such as ship hulls or supports. However, they are inherently limited by the water's visibility, making them applicable to only specific ports. On the other hand, they can use sonar or other technologies which enable data collection even in murky water. Overall, non-autonomous remotely controlled vehicles increase infrastructure inspection quality in port environments while requiring less time, cost, and risk (Stein, 2020).

Seaport Security: Unmanned vehicles can assist in seaports in compliance with the "International Ship and Port Facility Code" (Stein, 2018). Such crewless vehicles are to provide new points of view cheaply and without risk to personnel. Such applications include monitoring ships, cargo, traffic control, and emergencies. The crewless vehicles are typically remotely operated and serve as an extension of a human controlling the task. However, there is an opportunity for full automatization in cases of regular and unchanging tasks (such as the monitoring of docked ships and cargo).

Fully Autonomous Shipping: Autonomous ships provide rich potential for the shipping industry to cut costs while increasing operational times, shipping capacity, and reducing crew duties (Benson, D S & Colling, 2018). One such project is a Norwegian electric container ship called YARA Birkeland (Cross, Meadow, Com & Jostaphot, 2017), with a capacity of 120 twenty-foot equivalent units (TEU) (Autonomous ship project, critical facts about YARA Birkeland, 2017). The shipowner expects the YARA to launch in 2021 and sail among Herøya, Brevik, and Larvik, first with a small crew and then fully autonomously. Rolls-Royce (the Advanced Autonomous Waterborne Applications (AAWA) initiative) and Nippon Yusen Kabushiki Kaisha have undertaken similar projects. The latter has successfully tested an autonomous ship in Japan between the ports of Nagoya and Yokohama. The Maritime Unmanned Navigation through Intelligence in Networks (MUNIN) project has developed sensors for anticipated autonomous bulk carriers. It proposes that developing and using autonomous shipping vessels is technically feasible and could save financial and time costs (MUNIN, 2016).

One main challenge in autonomous shipping is developing a legal framework since the concept is so new to the legal world. For example, legal definitions of "autonomous ships" are not standardized or uniformly addressed – if addressed at all – from country to country. Similar is the case of a crew member's definition or remote operator of an autonomous ship (Karlis, 2018). Experts have proposed some definitions, typically ranking the level of a ship's autonomy against the amount of human involvement in its operation, such as that provided by Lloyd's register (ShipRight Design and Construction, Additional Design Procedures, Design Code for Unmanned Marine Systems, n.d.).

Prevalence. It is difficult to determine the exact prevalence of drones in seaports and shipping. However, some specific examples exist. For example, Antwerp's Port uses aerial drones for infrastructure inspection, surveillance, berth management, and waste detection (Port of Antwerp deploys autonomous drones for safety enforcement, 2021). The Port of Rotterdam has used drones for shipboard delivery of small cargo. It is even considering drones for offshore shipboard delivery (Drone deliveries take off at the Port of Rotterdam, 2020). The Port of Hamburg uses an Unmanned Surface Vehicle (USV) to monitor water depth autonomously (Howard, 2020). These examples show that autonomous vehicles are employed productively in European ports. However, as these applications are new, the industry will undergo some flux. The industry is recognizing and acting on the potential of drones in shipping.

Green Initiative

The International Maritime Organisation agreed to reduce greenhouse gas emissions by 50% until 2050. To achieve these goals, a consortium of banks has formulated the Poseidon Principles. Signatories integrate climate considerations into their lending decisions. Companies like Patagonia demonstrate significant interest in minimizing their environmental footprint. Cargo owners will show interest in such data and vet ships for their environmental impact.

Pervasive data collection enables every actor to understand their environmental impact. Shippers may select ships on their fuel consumption. Shipowners may identify ineffective ships and replace them. Shipping routes can be optimized for fuel consumption. The data is gathered and combined from various sources. Fuel consumption can be estimated from refueling bills (each gallon of diesel burns to about 22.2 lb. CO_2). The data of AIS shows the routes ships have taken. Correlating the data can show routes that require less fuel. The data that we can gather in eShip's system enables us to understand the environmental impact of dry bulk shipping.

Data Analytics

The main issue in analyzing the data is to define the correct model and method that allows predicting the behavior of a system. Researchers are studying methods for extracting information from data sets that are too large to be analyzed with traditional methods. Data mining and machine learning have a significant overlap in methods.

Machine learning aims to predict behaviors, whereas data mining aims to discover properties in data sets. Data that is well structured or minor in the sense that today's computers can process it can use traditional methods. With an SSD of 2 TB capacity on the market, the user should ascertain that the data sets to analyze exceeds 10s of TB before considering big-data methods.

Small data sets have the inherent danger of over-fitting and false discovery rates; the conclusions fit the existing data perfectly but cannot predict anything reliably. Bohannon, Koch, Homm, and Driehaus (2015) demonstrated this phenomenon with their "Chocolate Hoax." By measuring 18 variables in 15 subjects, they established a statistically significant effect of chocolate consumption on weight loss.

Machine Learning

The main methods to consider are statistical methods like linear regression, logistic regression, decision trees, support vector machines, clustering, and machine learning. Dimensionality reduction must be studied for the data sets to make the analysis more tractable. With small data sets, supervised learning is most successful. A group of experts will label the input data to outputs on which the developers train a computer algorithm.

Unsupervised methods leave it to the algorithm to identify structures in the data. These methods allow analysts to discover hidden patterns in the data. They can also learn the features of a particular data set that can be detected in other data items. Reinforcement learning refers to a computer interacting with an environment and receiving feedback in rewards/punishments to direct learning. The algorithm will develop strategies to maximize the rewards/minimize the punishments. Beşikçi, Arslan, Turan, and Ölçer (2016) use a neural network to optimize the choice of ships, routes, and the speed of ships to minimize fuel consumption.

Deep learning using neural networks is the most popular method today. Neural networks aim to simulate how brains are working. A neural network has three layers: an input layer, a recognition layer, and an output layer. Neural networks are trained on sets of input and outputs. The training tunes parameters in the recognition layer that enables the network to produce correct outputs on inputs it was not trained on. Depending on the task, a neural network needs millions of inputs labeled with their outputs. For tasks like image recognition, such neural networks are successful. Language processing is still a significant challenge. Language comprehension is an unachievable goal.

Smart Algorithms Matching Cargo and Ships

Researchers have studied the problem of matching cargo to vessels for multiple decades. They developed the earliest algorithms to maximize the cargo moved on the smallest ships and miles traveled.

Later algorithms generalized the problem of matching containers to ships, optimizing how to load and unload the ship, minimize port time, or minimize shipping cost. In the last decade, work started on matching dry cargo to vessels. Peng, Shan, Guan, and Yu (2016) describe one method for finding a price equilibrium in matching ships to dry cargo. All these matching and optimization are computationally intractable. Thus, fast algorithms will compute suboptimal results. Classes of algorithms used in this context are genetic algorithms, ant-colony optimizations, and recently Bayesian methods. Liang (2019) uses a deep-learning approach to identify transportation patterns and optimize them.

Bilgen and Ozkarahan (2007) use a mixed-integer linear programming model to loading ships optimally using different bulk goods. This allows for blending grains at the harbor and potentially reducing the cost for the customers. Jing, Marlow, and Hui (2008) propose a generalized autoregressive conditional heteroskedasticity (GARCH) model to understand the volatility of prices in the dry bulk shipping market. Similar work was later done by Dai, Hu, and Zhang (2015). The volatility is used to guide investments into ships. Kalouptsidi (2014) analyses the impact of build time on prices in bulk shipping. If ships are in high demand, shipping rates increase. Building more ships to meet the demand may result in decreased rates. Second-hand ships help to reduce prices but may increase the volatility of the investment. Scarsi (2007) analyses market data to demonstrate that shipowners follow their intuition and undervalue market trends. Lun and Quaddus (2009) take a data-driven approach to analyze the shipping market.

Routing and Scheduling

Ronen surveys methods for cargo ship routing and scheduling (Ronen, 1983, 1993). Early methods were optimization methods, for example, the one by Perakis and Bremer (1992). The dissertation of Wu (2020) provides a more recent survey of methods, also considering machine learning-based methods. Norstad, Fagerholt, and Laporte (2011) also consider the vessel's speed as a parameter of a shipping route. This provides the potential to reduce fuel costs and improve the environmental footprint. An energy-efficient fleet has become essential for financing the purchase of new ships. Signatories of the Poseidon principles consider the footprint.

Kang, Zhang, Guo, and Ma (2012) provide an optimization method for ship routing and deployment modes to reduce the operating cost of the shipowner. Guo et al. use data-driven optimization methods to assign ships to berths, thus optimizing the time and use of facilities at ports (Guo, Guan & Song, 2012, 2013)

Gao, Sun, Zhao, and Dong (2021) schedules ships for unloading at steel plants. Schim van der Loeff, Godar, and Prakasha (2018) use the AIS to track ships and estimate emissions per vessel. Overall, scheduling methods get deployed in routing and scheduling ships. They enable us to estimate arrival time, reduce shipping and operating costs, and track emissions. Consequently, these methods can provide ways for a greener shipping industry. Mainly, AIS is often transmitted frequently and reliably via satellite. Tracking the position of ships in real-time can be achieved easily by using the services mentioned above.

Processing Documents

Many processes in the shipping industry are still using telefax and written documents. Especially documents of the past are not in digital form. These documents still contain valuable data. Digital documents are often written in prose. While they are comprehensible to humans, processing by computers is challenging. Note that standardized documents are much easier to process for machines but often harder for humans to comprehend without appropriate rendering.

Structured Text Processing

Structured text processing is based on using rules to extract information from specifically formatted text. Text can be processed precisely if it follows the formatting rules. Other texts cannot be understood at all. Structured text processing works well for interpreting forms. The bill of lading is one example for which structured text processing is often sufficient.

Natural Language Processing

Many competitors promise to process e-Mail messages and extract data from those messages. If the messages are not constrained in their structure, the system needs to comprehend the language in the e-Mail.

Some approaches are based on rules, where the text is scanned for specific phrases. Absent these phrases, text cannot be understood precisely. Rule-based methods have similar limitations to structured text processing.

Statistical natural language processing (NLP) combines computer algorithms with machine learning to automatically extract, classify, and label text elements and then assign a statistical likelihood to each meaning of those elements. Deep learning models and learning techniques based on convolutional neural networks and recurrent neural networks enable NLP systems that learn as they work and extract more accurate meaning ever from vast volumes of raw, unstructured, and unlabeled data sets.

SOLUTIONS AND RECOMMENDATIONS

We identify two problem domains that demand specific solutions. The market is heterogeneous, and it is unlikely that market participants will process their data to meet modern standards. If at all, historical data may be digitized and archived. Big data methods allow unlocking these historical data archives by mining them and extracting structured data sets.

Future datasets can be maintained in a standardized format. Such data may be easier to process. However, standards have not been agreed on. eShip is designed to connect to existing ERP systems. The exact mechanism to extract relevant information proposed to access historical data can unify data stored in heterogeneous stores controlled by different entities. Make eShip a responsive platform that provides all the services through desktop, tablet, and mobile phone (Figure 3)

Figure 3. Chartering is just a click away (©2021, eShip project, used with permission)

Unlocking Historical Data

The move to a digital platform creates the problem of converting historical data. This historical data can come from many diverse sources and is in paper form or unstructured electronic documents. Digitizing and converting all this data is a daunting task. Big Data technology allows moving the conversion of the digital assets into the processing and querying of the data. The first step of this proposal is to scan/digitize the documents and store them in a database. The authors suggest that the data is stored unstructured. It should be keyed to unique identifiers. Each data item shall carry a description of its origin and some potential metadata. For example, a bill of lading is often a semi-structured document. A scan of that document can be annotated with the source of the document, keywords "bill of lading," the language it is written in, and the issuing party.

Optical character recognition (OCR) allows for the extraction of the text of these scanned documents. Typewritten and printed text is easy to recognize since the shape of the letters is similar. Handwritten documents occur frequently but are much harder to process. Many documents are created by people involved at the harbor, or printed documents get annotated in handwriting. Natural language processing algorithms can then extract the relevant information from these documents.

FUTURE RESEARCH DIRECTIONS

The bulk shipping industry poses many specific problems that the computing community starts to address right now. The widespread problem is to make historical data, which is often held on paper, available for digital processing. Another problem is forward-looking creating standards to accelerate and automate decision-making in chartering. Both problems need to be addressed individually.

The second area of research addresses process automation. A major problem of charterers and ship-owners concerns the scheduling of activities in harbors. Predictive methods for estimating the time and resources needed for these processes reduces cost and increases the utility of the harbor and ships.

CONCLUSION

The most significant risk in choosing a technology is that it does not deliver the value it promises. The authors suggest establishing to define performance metrics to monitor the value processing the data generates. Digitization and automation promise cost savings and faster processes. The standardization of documents and processes will amplify these benefits.

Digitization and standardization are easy to implement for data that is created in the future. Past data is not standardized nor digital. Natural language processing and big data technology enable digital access to historical data. The data is mapped to the digital standards automatically.

At the same time, the field of bulk shipping provides rich research opportunities. Many questions have not been answered yet. We are just starting to become aware of the industry's problems. The maritime industry will benefit from implementing innovative solutions. The authors further claim that those wrong decisions will have a severe impact on the finances of the shipping companies and the environment (Casaca & Loja, 2020). Unlike fully digitized container shipping, bulk shipping, which represents 2/3 of the global maritime transport volume, is in dire need of digital transformation as it still relies on non-structured information exchange. However, bulk shipping is now beginning to adopt a smarter approach to how it best goes about its transformation towards a global value chain. In this chapter, the authors analyzed eShip, an online platform that applies state-of-the-art information and communication technology tools to the traditional chartering business model, generating significant value added to all market participants in three key aspects.

The results point that by providing a digital platform that may be used by all parties involved, either through a web interface or through EDI/PI interfaces, we will be able to maximize interoperability between all the participants, reuse information and reduce management costs and accelerate the digital transition in what is a complex and traditionally conservative sector.

The most important is recognizing the potential of upcoming developments and how data analysis will change operations and create value. The integrated platform with a new vision and collaboration with other parties in the ecosystem will enable stakeholders to assure their positions in the challenging future of the industry that makes its road to become smart. Smart ships and smart ports will exchange data for speeding up operations. With the addition of digital information, data analytics and machine learning uncover better ways to handle cargo, decrease cost, and increase efficiency.

ACKNOWLEDGMENT

The eShip project is supported by the EEA Grants.

REFERENCES

Aiello, G., Giallanza, A., & Mascarella, G. (2020). Towards Shipping 4.0. A preliminary gap analysis. *Procedia Manufacturing*, *42*, 24–29. doi:10.1016/j.promfg.2020.02.019

Autonomous ship project, key facts about YARA Birkeland. (2017). Retrieved from https://www.kongsberg.com/maritime/support/themes/autonomous-ship-project-key-facts-about-yara-birkeland/

Benson, C., D. S., P. & Colling, A. (2018, June). *A Quantitative Analysis of Possible Futures of Autonomous Transport*. Academic Press.

Beşikçi, E. B., Arslan, O., Turan, O., & Ölçer, A. I. (2016, February). An artificial neural network-based decision support system for energy-efficient ship operations. *Computers & Operations Research*, *66*, 393–401. doi:10.1016/j.cor.2015.04.004

Bilgen, B., & Ozkarahan, I. (2007, June). A mixed-integer linear programming model for bulk grain blending and shipping. *International Journal of Production Economics*, *107*(2), 555–571. doi:10.1016/j.ijpe.2006.11.008

Bohannon, J., Koch, D., Homm, P., & Driehaus, A. (2015, December). Chocolate with high cocoa content as a weight-loss accelerator. *International Archives of Medicine*, *8*(55), 1–8.

Cacho, J. L., Marques, L., & Nascimento, Á. (2020). Customer-Oriented Global Supply Chains: Port Logistics in the Era of Globalization and Digitization. In V. Chkoniya, A. O. Madsen, & P. Bukhrashvili (Eds.), *Anthropological Approaches to Understanding Consumption Patterns and Consumer Behavior* (pp. 82–103). IGI Global. doi:10.4018/978-1-7998-3115-0.ch005

Casaca, A. C. P., & Loja, M. A. R. (2020). 2019 World of Shipping Portugal. An International Research Conference on Maritime Affairs editorial "Leading the shipping industry into the future." *Journal of Shipping & Trade*, *5*(1), 1–4. doi:10.118641072-020-00082-y

Chen, C.-H., Khoo, L. P., Chong, Y. T., & Yin, X. F. (2014, May). Knowledge discovery using genetic algorithm for maritime situational awareness. *Expert Systems with Applications*, *41*(6), 2742–2753. doi:10.1016/j.eswa.2013.09.042

Chkoniya, V., Madsen, A. O., & Bukhrashvili, P. (2020). *Anthropological Approaches to Understanding Consumption Patterns and Consumer Behavior*. IGI Global. doi:10.4018/978-1-7998-3115-0

Cross, J., Meadow, G., & Com, I., & Jostaphot. (2017, September). Autonomous ships 101. *Journal of Ocean Technology*, *12*, 23–27.

Dai, L., Hu, H., & Zhang, D. (2015, October). An empirical analysis of freight rate and vessel price volatility transmission in global dry bulk shipping market [English Edition]. *Journal of Traffic and Transportation Engineering*, *2*(5), 353–361. doi:10.1016/j.jtte.2015.08.007

Delenclos, F.-X., Rasmussen, A., & Riedl, J. (2018). *To Get Smart, Ports Go Digital*. Retrieved from https://www.bcg.com/publications/2018/to-get-smart-ports-go-digital

Diwan, M. A. (2016). Internet of Things in Logistics: Towards Autonomous Logistics & Smart Logistic Entities. The International Maritime Transport & Logistics Conference (MARLOG5).

Drone deliveries take off at the port of Rotterdam. (2020, May). Retrieved from https://www.drycargomag.com/drone-deliveries-take-off-at-the-port-of-rotterdam

Ducruet, C., & Zaidi, F. (2012). Maritime constellations: A complex network approach to shipping and ports. *Maritime Policy & Management*, *39*(2), 151–168. doi:10.1080/03088839.2011.650718

Gao, Z., Sun, D., Zhao, R., & Dong, Y. (2021, January). Ship-unloading scheduling optimization for a steel plant. *Information Sciences*, *544*, 214–226. doi:10.1016/j.ins.2020.07.029

Gass, S. I., & Assad, A. A. (2005). *An Annotated Timeline of Operations Research*. Kluwer.

Graziano, M. D., Renga, A., & Moccia, A. (2019). Integration of automatic identification system (AIS) data and single-channel synthetic aperture radar (SAR) images by SAR-based ship velocity estimation for maritime situational awareness. *Remote Sensing*, *11*(19), 16. doi:10.3390/rs11192196

Guo, C., Guan, Z., & Song, Y. (2012). Research on dynamic berth assignment of bulk cargo port based on ant colony algorithm. In Z. Zhang, R. Zhang, & J. Zhang (Eds.), *LISS* (pp. 235–240). Springer. doi:10.1007/978-3-642-32054-5_35

Guo, C., Guan, Z., & Song, Y. (2013). Research on bulk-cargo-port berth assignment based on priority of resource allocation. *Journal of Industrial Engineering and Management*, *6*(1), 276–288. doi:10.3926/jiem.673

Haralambides, H. E. (2019). Gigantism in container shipping, ports and global logistics: A time-lapse into the future. *Maritime Economics & Logistics*, *21*(1), 1–60. doi:10.105741278-018-00116-0

Howard, M. (2020, March). Water drone christened in the port of Hamburg. *Maritime Logistics Professional*.

Jacks, D. S., & Pendakur, K. (2010). Global Trade and The Maritime Transport Revolution. *The Review of Economics and Statistics*, *92*(4), 745–755. doi:10.1162/REST_a_00026

Jing, L., Marlow, P. B., & Hui, W. (2008). An analysis of freight rate volatility in dry bulk shipping markets. *Maritime Policy & Management*, *35*(3), 237–251. doi:10.1080/03088830802079987

Kalouptsidi, M. (2014, February). Time to build and fluctuations in bulk shipping. *The American Economic Review*, *104*(2), 564–608. doi:10.1257/aer.104.2.564

Kang, K., Zhang, W.-c., Guo, L.-y., & Ma, T. (2012, September). Research on ship routing and deployment mode for a bulk. In *2012 international conference on management science & engineering 19th annual conference proceedings*. Dallas, TX: IEEE. 10.1109/ICMSE.2012.6414421

Karlis, T. (2018, January). Maritime law issues related to the operation of unmanned autonomous cargo ships. *WMU Journal of Maritime Affairs*, *17*(1), 1–10. doi:10.100713437-018-0135-6

Kavallieratos, G., Diamantopoulou, V., & Katsikas, S. K. (2020). Shipping 4.0: Security Requirements for the Cyber-Enabled Ship. *IEEE Transactions on Industrial Informatics*, *16*(10), 6617–6625. doi:10.1109/TII.2020.2976840

Lambrou, M., Watanabe, D., & Iida, J. (2019, November). Shipping digitalization management: Conceptualization, typology, and antecedents. *Journal of Shipping and Trade*, *4*(11), 11. Advance online publication. doi:10.118641072-019-0052-7

Lasi, H., Fettke, P., Kemper, H.-G., Feld, T., & Hoffmann, M. (2014). Industry 4.0. *Business & Information Systems Engineering*, *6*(4), 239–242. doi:10.100712599-014-0334-4

Levinson, M. (2020). *Outside The Box*. Kirkus Reviews.

Liang, Z. (2019, September). Design of automatic matching system for ocean-going cargo in international logistics. *Journal of Coastal Research*, *93*(SI), 1105–1110. doi:10.2112/SI93-160.1

Lind, M., Michaelides, M., Ward, R., & Watson, R. T. (2020). *Maritime Informatics*. Springer International Publishing. Retrieved from https://books.google.pt/books?id=Ed6PzQEACAAJ

Lun, Y. V., & Quaddus, M. A. (2009). An empirical model of the bulk shipping market. *International Journal of Shipping and Transport Logistics*, *1*(1), 37. Advance online publication. doi:10.1504/IJSTL.2009.021975

Martimo, P. (2017). *Disruptive Innovation and Maritime Sector - Discovering smart-shipping's potential to disrupt shipping*. Report Turku School of Economics.

Mileski, J., Clott, C., Galvao, C. B., & Laverne, T. (2020). Technical analysis: the psychology of the market of dry bulk freight rates. *Journal of Shipping & Trade*, *5*(1). doi:10.118641072-020-00079-7

Munin. (2016). http://www.unmanned-ship.org/munin/

Norstad, I., Fagerholt, K., & Laporte, G. (2011, August). Tramp ship routing and scheduling with speed optimization. *Transportation Research Part C, Emerging Technologies*, *19*(5), 853–865. doi:10.1016/j.trc.2010.05.001

Peng, Z., Shan, W., Guan, F., & Yu, B. (2016). Stable vessel-cargo matching in dry bulk shipping market with price game mechanism. *Transportation Research Part E, Logistics and Transportation Review*, *95*, 76–94. doi:10.1016/j.tre.2016.08.007

Perakis, A. N., & Bremer, W. M. (1992). An operational tanker scheduling optimization system: Background, current practice and model formulation. *Maritime Policy & Management, 19*(3), 177–187. doi:10.1080/751248659

Perunovic, Z., & Vidic, J.-P. (2011). Innovation in the Maritime Industry. *Proceedings of the 22nd POMS Annual Conferences.*

Port of Antwerp deploys autonomous drones for safety enforcement. (2021, February). *Dry Cargo International.* Retrieved from https://www.drycargomag.com/port-of-antwerp-deploys-autonomous-drones-for-safety-enforcement

Poulis, K., Galanakis, G. C., Triantafillou, G. T., & Poulis, E. (2020). Value migration: Digitalization of shipping as a mechanism of industry dethronement. *Journal of Shipping and Trade, 5*(1), 1–18. doi:10.118641072-020-00064-0

Ronen, D. (1983, February). Cargo ships routing and scheduling: Survey of models and problems. *European Journal of Operational Research, 12*(2), 119–126. doi:10.1016/0377-2217(83)90215-1

Ronen, D. (1993, December). Ship scheduling: The last decade. *Ship scheduling: The last decade, 71*(3), 325-333. doi:10.1016/0377-2217(93)90343-L

Scarsi, R. (2007). The bulk shipping business: Market cycles and shipowners' biases. *Maritime Policy & Management, 34*(6), 577–590. doi:10.1080/03088830701695305

Schim van der Loeff, W., Godar, J., & Prakasha, V. (2018, December). A spatially explicit data-driven approach to calculating commodity-specific shipping emissions per vessel. *Journal of Cleaner Production, 205*, 895–908. doi:10.1016/j.jclepro.2018.09.053

Shipwright design and construction, additional design procedures, design code for unmanned marine systems. (n.d.). *Lloyd's Register.* Retrieved from www.lr.org

SmartPort. (2019). Smart ships and the changing maritime ecosystem (T. van Dijk, H. van Dorsser, R. van den Berg, H. Moonen, & R. Negenborn, Eds.). Academic Press.

Stein, M. (2018, June). Integrating Unmanned Vehicles in Port Security Operations: An Introductory Analysis and First Applicable Frameworks. *Ocean Yearbook Online, 32*(1), 556–583. doi:10.1163/22116001-03201022

Stein, M. (2020, April). *Unmanned maritime infrastructure inspection-a mixed-method risk management approach from German port facilities.* Academic Press.

Tat, C. H., Lim, K., Lund, S., Deggim, H., Koyama, T., Foo, D., . . . de Souza, C. (2020, October). *Future of shipping: Digitalisation webinar.* Retrieved from https://fos-digitalisation2020.sg/

Ward, R., & Bjørn-Andersen, N. (2021). The Origins of Maritime Informatics. In Maritime Informatics. Springer. doi:10.1007/978-3-030-50892-0_1

Wu. (2020). *Bulk ship routing and scheduling under uncertainty* (Doctoral dissertation). Hong Kong Polytechnic University, China. Retrieved from https://theses.lib.polyu.edu.hk/handle/200/10660

KEY TERMS AND DEFINITIONS

Bulk Shipping: The transportation of goods (either liquid or granular) in large quantity, usually not packed but loaded directly into a vessel. Such goods (bulk cargo) are grains, petroleum products, iron ore, and more.

Chartering: An activity within the shipping industry where a shipowner agrees to rent out his ship to a cargo owner to move cargoes from one point to another.

EEA Grants: Through the European Economic Area (EEA) Agreement, Iceland, Liechtenstein, and Norway are partners in the internal market with the Member States of the European Union. To promote a continuous and balanced strengthening of economic and trade relations, the parties to the EEA Agreement have established a multi-annual Financial Mechanism known as the EEA Grants. The EEA Grants established the objective of reducing social and economic disparities in Europe by strengthening bilateral relations with the Beneficiary States.

Freight Rate: The price requested for the transport of cargo from one place to another. The freight rate depends on the destination, the accountable size of the shipment, and the type of the sheep.

SaaS (Software as a Service): The way of delivering applications over the Internet—as a service. Instead of installing and maintaining software, we access it via the Internet, freeing ourselves from complex software and hardware management.

Shipping Industry: The industry is concerned with transporting freight, especially by ship. A wide variety of commercial transport methods can be found in the shipping industry, from bulk transport of commodities in railcars to highly specialized "intermodal" container shipping. Four significant transport modes exist in this industry: marine, air, rail, and freight (trucking).

Chapter 19
Question Answering Chatbot Using Memory Networks

Riddhi Patel
Charotar University of Science and Technology, India

Parth Patel
Charotar University of Science and Technology, India

Chintan M. Bhatt
Charotar University of Science and Technology, India

Mrugendrasinh L. Rahevar
 https://orcid.org/0000-0002-0551-9229
Charotar University of Science and Technology, India

ABSTRACT

Manipulation of a large amount of data becomes a very tedious task. Hence, the authors took the approach of memory networks for the implementation of the chatbot. Traditionally, the LSTM model was used to implement chatbots and QA systems. But the LSTM failed to store relevant information when given a longer information set. On the contrary, the memory networks have an additional memory component with it. This can help in storing long information for further use which is greatly advantageous for the QA and chatbot systems as compared to LSTM. The authors trained and tested their model over Facebook's bAbi dataset which consists of several tasks and has questions regarding each task to retrieve the accuracy of the model. On the pedestal of that dataset, they have presented the accuracy for every task in their study with memory networks.

INTRODUCTION

The digital age has bombarded mankind with a large number of devices. The devices stand to retrieve information based on the data they are suspected to. Also, give the users the response they need in the large retrieval-based world of a humongous amount of data that resides in the world. The digital devices

DOI: 10.4018/978-1-7998-6985-6.ch019

rely on information retrieval systems such as a chatbot system. The question answering chatbot system strives to retrieve information from a large repository of data with extreme precision and lesser redundancy. This retrieval system is implemented with the foundation of Artificial Intelligence (AI), (Ainouz, S. A. Ben Ahmed, Mohammed, 2020). Also, a chatbot is more like a human and requires intelligence. Artificial Intelligence techniques are essential in its implementation, (M. Lewkowitz, 2014, Feb 12). One of the techniques to be considered as a part of AI is Machine learning (ML). ML in layman terms can be defined as the ability of a machine to learn on its own from the data it is provided and create a prediction or a decision based on the algorithm that is fed into the machine. The chatbot system also requires techniques to mimic a human brain to generate an accurate response, (Bing Liu1, G. T., Hakkani-Tur, P. S. Heck). That is where Deep Learning comes into the picture showing the neural network similar to nerves in the brain of a human.

A chatbot system can be categorized as a retrieval based system and a rule based system, (Jincy Susan Thomas, Seena Thomas, 2018). The proposed system is a chatbot that uses Memory Networks based approach which makes it better than rule-based systems. This system is a Retrieval based system as the bot is trained on a set of questions and their possible outcomes. Memory networks as the name suggests possess an external memory unlike other Neural networks. Having a memory module becomes extremely necessary as the questions sometimes can tend to be so long that a common neural network would fail to backpropagate entirely. Thus, the external memory module can come into play whenever needed in order to backpropagate and process an entire question, (Sainbayar Sukhbaatar, Arthur Szlam Jason Weston Rob Fergus). The instruction set given to the bot makes it possible to get the answer from the dataset it is trained on inorder to get the most relevant answer and output the same. A good and efficiently pre processed dataset can enable the chatbot to produce new answers. Facebook engineers combined a dataset named bAbi inorder to be used as a task response system. The bAbi set consists of 20 tasks that have variable answers, (Jason Weston, Bordes, S.C., Alexander M. Rush, Bart van Merrienboer, Armand Joulin Tomas Mikolov). We have used this dataset to train our chatbot.

The structure of the chatbot that the authors propose has been illustrated in figure 1. The figure 1 shows that whenever an user asks a question, it does the analysis of the question. Further, it retrieves the necessary document that might have an answer for the question for e.g. "where" questions will have answers in "places" documents. Then it retrieves the answer and analyzes it for it's correctness and finally displays it to the user.

Thus this chatbot has been trained on the machine learning model of memory networks. As, training them end to end requires very less supervision during training which makes it useful in regular scenarios.

BACKGROUND

Evolution of the Chatbot

In 1994, Mauldin coined the term 'ChatterBot' to define the systems aiming to pass the Turing Test. The first ever chatbot to be made in the computer science field is "Eliza". Eliza was developed by Joseph Weizenbaum. Eliza's model captured the inputs and tried to match keywords obtained by rephrasing the input, with predefined responses. The below response can be considered as an example,

utterance = # I want #

Answer = "Why do you want ___?"

Figure 1. Structure of Chatbot

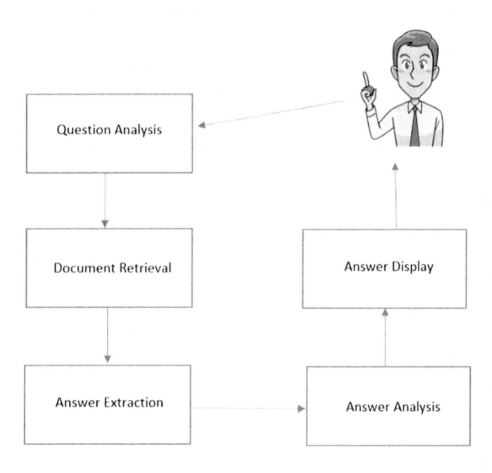

Here, the "#" is the wildcard character. ELIZA responds with the output string associated with this particular rule out of a set of rules. There are some rules written to rephrase the user utterance before matching. In addition, it also had some responses which were not of any context, possibly used when the input did not match any of the rules. As an example,

utterance = My life is great!

answer = Please go on.

Even though Eliza was created to demonstrate how superficial the conversation between a human and a computer is, ELIZA became widely popular because people thought they were talking to a real person, (M. Lewkowitz, 2014, Feb 12). It was designed to imitate a therapist and many people reviewed that they actually felt relief by talking with Eliza.

Eliza's model works on a rule-based system, which restricts it from having meaningful conversations with humans. Also, as illustrated above, it had generic responses to utterances with which none of the rules matched. Hence, it rather aimed at deceiving the humans into thinking that they were talking to an actual human and not a computer.

A British programmer named Rollo Carpenter, designed Jabberwacky in 1988. Unlike Eliza, Jabberwacky was aimed to simulate entertaining conversations with humans. It uses an AI technique called "contextual pattern matching". It was one of the first chatbots which harnessed AI to learn meaningful human conversations. Jabberwacky won the Loebner prize, an annual competition to test chatbots, in 2005 and 2006, (Y.Vilner). Jabberwacky was able to learn new facts and concepts just by having constant interactions i.e. it had the ability to learn continuously from the conversations.

From the time Jabberwacky has been online, it has enhanced itself by learning new languages. This has been possible because it relies completely on context and feedback, unlike Eliza. It is purely based on heuristics-based technology, as said by its creators. Infact, the older version of Jabberwacky has now involved in Cleverbot.

A.L.I.C.E. (Artificial Linguistic Internet Computer Entity) is a popular free chatbot developed in 1995 by Dr. Richard Wallace. It is inspired by ELIZA and won the Loebner prize in January 2000, (R.Raine, 2009). The first implementation was known as Program A, which was written in a language based on set theory and mathematical knowledge, known as SETL. A.L.I.C.E was written in AIML, an XML dialect for creating chatbots. AIML was also implemented by Dr. Wallace. When the language migrated to Java, the number of contributors increased and their joint effort launched Program B in 1999. With this Program, A.L.I.C.E. won the Loebner prize in 2000. When Jacob Bikker created the first C and C++ based implementation of AIML, Program C was launched based on it. Finally, Program D led the transition of A.L.I.C.E from pre-Java 2 to add many features such as Swing and Collections. However, A.L.I.C.E failed the Turing Test. It reacts to human inputs and tries to respond as naturally as possible. The XML schema helps simplify the conversational rules. Natural language was the most signif- icant feature of Alice, (alicebot.org).

The bot SmarterChild was launched in 2001. as a service which could answer fact-based questions like "What is the population of Indonesia?" or more personalized questions like "What movies are playing near me tonight?", (R.Raine, 2009). Until 2008, when it was taken down, this chatbot was used by thousands of people daily.

In 2006, IBM Watson developed a chatbot specially to compete with the champions of the game of Jeopardy! It won the competition in 2011, which is when it started offering services to build chatbots for various domains that are capable of processing huge amounts of data.

In 2010, Siri was launched as an intelligent virtual assistant. Later, assistants such as Google Now (2012) by Google, Cortana (2015) by Microsoft and Alexa (2015) by Amazon, were launched inspired by Siri. These assistants are capable of making searches based on Image, easy mobile device access and answer web-based questions. The assistants being commercial, there is no public access to its implementation details.

Conventional Techniques for Question Answering

Prior to the progress of the neural networks, problems of NLP (Natural Language Processing) were given an answer based on traditional approaches such as Named Entity Recognition, Part of Speech Tagging, Stemming Lemmatization, Information Retrieval, Information Extraction. Conventionally rule based approach was used to match patterns of the questions to the answers. Thus providing an output to a comprehension type question by matching rules. The rules are related to being a WH question such as (Who, What, Where, When etc.). This makes it possible to match the question to be of a place type, person type etc. following the rules based on that.

The Question Answering system can be taken into consideration as:

1. Determination of question type
2. Determining answer type based on this
3. NLP tasks are performed
4. System shrinks the corpus to get the precise answer

Comparative Analysis of Question Answering Systems

The computer program pertaining to Question answering system builds it's answer by querying a structured database consisting of information related to websites or any organization and relates the questions to the documents already in natural lan- guage, (Sanjay Dwivedi, Vaishali Singh, 2013). The comparisons for the approaches have been summarized in tables 1, 2 and 3 respectively. Table 1 shows different statistical techniques for question classification, along with the major QA systems that use the systems from their respective websites and their performance. Table 2 shows different techniques that can be used to classify the answers along with major QA systems using it with their performance. Table 3 depicts two approaches for pattern matching over various parameters such as answer extraction, answer representation, etc. for the approaches of surface pattern based and template based.

Table 1. Statistical model for question classification

Statistical Techniques	Major QA system(s)	Performance
Maximum entropy model	IBM's statistical QA	Question classification error rate reduces
Support vector machine	System by Moschitti, Quateroni et al., Zhang et al.	SVM has shown quite good performance and accuracy for question classification and preferred in QA community
Modified Bayesian Classifier	Wei et al., MKQA	Method has better accuracy than base bayesin method

Machine Learning

Humans tend to learn from the environment they are exposed to. As we all know a child learns from the environment it grows up in, similarly machines that are computers tend to learn by the datasets they are exposed to. Machine learning has evolved a lot in the past since the days of its development and the machine learning algorithms have grown exponentially, (Pat Langley).

Learning without any explicit knowledge or input for computers is only made possi- ble by the field of AI known as Machine Learning. It revolutionizes decision making as well as predictions for things done by the computer. Machine Learning can be considered as a child who learns from the environment he is grown up in. It takes the best possible approach to a problem and gives a metric to each of the models that is developed. Thus, Giving the computer an ability like humans.

Table 2. Statistical model for answer classification

Statistical Techniques	Major QA system(s)	Performance
Okapi Similarity Measurement	IBM's statistical QA	Average level of mean reciprocal ratio for factoid questions in restricted domain
Sentence Similarity Model	System by Cai et al.	Accuracy is significantly increased and above average precision in achieved
N-gram mining	System by Soricut et al.	Satisfactory performance even for the non-factoid questions
SVM	System by Suzuki et al.	SVM outperforms than other models in answer selection phase too

METHODOLOGIES

LSTM (Long Short-Term Memory Networks)

LSTM (Long Short-Term Memory) has the ability to handle long sequences, which is very suitable for a QA system are specialized RNNs that can remember necessary data and forget the irrelevant bits, (Rohit, G. & Dharamshi, Ekta Subramanyam, Natarajan, 2019). The problem with recurrent neural networks (RNNs) was Vanishing Gradients, which limited it to looking back only a few steps in arbitrarily long sequences of information. LSTM mitigates this problem of RNN. Therefore, LSTM is an improvised version of RNN, since it can more efficiently remember longer sequences. It does this with the help of the feature to "remember" the relevant and "forget" the irrelevant parts. Here, the neural network does not have any place to store all the information from the text, making it the biggest problem of LSTM, (Alex Sherstins, 2020).

The advantages of LSTM networks are important, Harman et al argued for the use of supervised learning in contrast to classical NLP methods for answering questions, (Hermann, K.M., Kocisky, T., Grefenstette, E., Espeholt, L., Kay, W., Suleyman, M., Blunsom, R, 2015). They describe a model that focuses on the elements of the document, which they believe will help answer the question. It can encode statements in a dataset story. Of these, when questions are placed, it answers, (Xingjian Shi Zhourong

Table 3. Comparison of two pattern matching approaches

	Surface Pattern Based	Template Based
Basic Mechanism	Either human crafted or automatically learned patterns through examples	A template is preformatted framework for questions which have entity slots to be dynamically filled by parameters
Answer Extraction	Answer sentence is extracted using statistical techniques or data mining measures	Uses structured query to extract answers from the database
Answer Representation	Not necessarily formatted answers	Focus on generating formatted answers
Pattern Learning	Semi-automatic	Manually but automatic for semantic web
Most compatible application area	Small and medium size websites	Semantic web

Chen Hao Wang Dit-Yan Yeung). This paper also addresses the lack of good quality datasets to answer the question and the need to artificially generate data to use supervised practice for question answering.

Memory Networks

The biggest challenge that is faced with the machine learning models is to have an easy way to read and write the part of a long component of a memory and to make it in a combination with the inference, (J. Weston, S. Chopra, and A. Bordes, 2015).

Memory Networks basically consists of an array of objects M indexed by M_i. There can be various 4 kinds of components which are known to be learnable.

- I: - Input feature map
  - Using standard processing techniques this map is mainly used to convert input into an internal feature representation.
- G: - Generalization
  - When given new input it converts the old memories.
  - $m_i = G (m_i, I(x), m)$[10]
  - Simplest for is stored in I(x) in $m_{H(x)} = I(x)$, (J. Weston, S. Chopra, and A. Bordes, 2015).
- O: - Output Feature
  - Based on the input x and memory m it produces a new output feature.
  - Output Feature o=O(I(x), m)
- R: - Response
  - Conversion to desired format of the output

Assuming an input of X one can consider the flow of the system as follows:

1. X The internal attribute representation is converted to I (X).
2. Memory mi updated, and new input is given: mi=G (mi, I(X), m) ∀ i, (G. Rohit, E. Dharamshi, Subramanyam, 2019).
3. Output properties o calculated, new input and memory: o=O(I(X), m), (G. Rohit, E. Dharamshi, Subramanyam, 2019).
4. Output properties o decoded to give the final response: r =R (o).

IMPLEMENTATION

Memory Networks

A GRU cell is similar to an LSTM cell, just the difference is that it is more efficient computationally since it has only two gates (update gate and reset gate) and it does not use a memory unit. The update and erase of data is controlled by the two gates. The hidden state in a GRU is calculated by

$h_t = GRU (x_t, h_{t-1})$

Given a work in the previous timestep vector (h_{t-1}), compute the current timestep vector (h_t). The advantage of GRU over LSTM is that it can keep information history without removing the information

Figure 2. Structure of the memory network

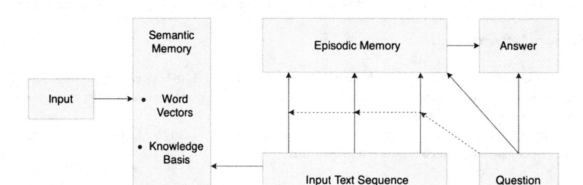

which is irrelevant to the prediction, (K. Ankit, O. Irsoy, J. Su, J. Bradbury, R. English, B. Pierce, P. Ondruska, I. Gulrajani and R. Socher, 2016).

The update gate is a single layer neural network. Now, sum up the matrix multiplications and add a biased term. And then the sigmoid squashes it to a list of values between 0 and 1, the output vector. Do this twice with different sets of weights, then use a rest gate that will learn to ignore the past timesteps when necessary. For example, if the next sentence has nothing to do with those whose came before it. The update gate is similar in that it can learn to ignore the current timestep entirely. Maybe the current sentence has nothing to do with the answer. Whereas, previous ones did.

The question module processes the query word by word and gives output of the vector using the same GRU which had the input module and has the same weight, (C.Xiong,S.Merityand, R.Socher, 2016).

The motivation for this in the chapter came from the hippocampus function in our brain. A hippocampus getting triggered by sigh or sound is able to retrieve the temporal states.

As shown in figure 2, the episodic memory module is made up of two GRUs. It receives the fact and the question vectors that are extracted from the input. Episodes are generated by the GRU on the inner side. It takes into account the output of the attention function based on the current fact when updating its inner state. Each fact is given a score between 0 and 1 by the attention function. And so, the facts with low scores are ignored. At the end of each pass, the outer GRU is given input of episodes which are output of the inner GRU. The purpose of having two layers is for our model to understand after one pass that something else can be important too. Thus, multiple passes can help to gather more information that is correct.

Architecture

The figure 3 illustrates the architectural flow of the question answering system. Here, the question pattern is the question input which is considered to be a sequence of words. These sets of words are then embedded and the sequence of word vec- tors are encoded using GRU. The Max pooling layer provides an abstracted form thus reducing the number of extracted features as well as preventing overfitting. This is concatenated to question embedding thus producing the complete question representation.

Figure 3. Illustration of Architecture

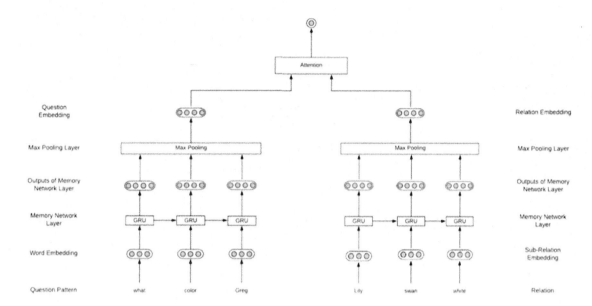

bAbi Tasks Dataset

Facebook prepared a dataset in order to perform various question answering tasks. One such dataset is used in our system. The bAbi tasks dataset comprises 20 differ- ent question answering tasks. The range of the bAbi tasks dataset is from one word answers all the way upto directional tasks. The sample of the dataset is shown in table 4.

RESULTS AND DISCUSSIONS

The Facebook bAbi dataset was used to train and test our model. The tasks listed in table 4 were used by us to benchmark the performance of our model. Figure 4 is a graph representation of the results derived. According to figure 4, the first thing for us is that the accuracy of some tasks is 98% and above,while in others they are less than 30%. Task 3 and 19 turn out to be tasks with the lowest accuracy. Task 3 is the task of three supporting facts, and task 19 is to find the path based on the directions. It is astonishing that Task 2 performed well on two supporting facts, but it was difficult for the model to understand the three supporting facts i.e. finding a way to find a way between two places when the relative positions between each pair is known. The explanation for the performance of the models in this work is that the relative position can be understood in a one-dimensional space, but finding a path that requires two dimensions is difficult.

Table 4. Sample Dataset

Task 1: Single supporting fact Mary went to the bathroom John moved to the hallway Mary travelled to the office Where is Mary? A: Office	**Task 2: Two supporting facts** John is in the playground John picked up the football Bob went to the kitchen Where is football? A: Playground
Task 3: Three supporting facts John picked up the apple John went to the office John went to the kitchen John dropped the apple Where was the apple before the kitchen? A: Office	**Task 4: Two argument relations** The office is north of the bedroom The bedroom is north of the bathroom The kitchen is west of the garden What is north of the bedroom? A: Office What is the bedroom north of? A: Bathroom
Task 5: Three argument relations Mary gave the cake to Fred Fred gave the cake to Bill Jeff was given the milk by Bill Who gave the cake to Fred? A: Mary Who did Fred give the cake to? A: Bill	**Task 6: Yes/No questions** John moved to the playground Daniel went to the bathroom John went back to the hallway Is John in the playground? A: No Is Daniel in the bathroom? A: Yes
Task 7: Counting Daniel picked up the football Daniel dropped the football Daniel got the milk Daniel took the apple How many objects is Daniel holding? A: Two	**Task 8: Lists/Sets** Daniel picks up the football Daniel drops the newspaper Daniel picks up the milk John took the apple What is Daniel holding? A: Milk, Football
Task 9: Simple negation Sandra travelled to the office Fred is no longer in the office Is Fred in the office? A: No Is Sandra in the office? A: Yes	**Task 10: Indefinite knowledge** John is either in the classroom or the playground Sandra is in the garden Is John in the classroom? A: Maybe Is John in the office? A: No
Task 11: Basic co-reference Daniel was in the kitchen Then he went to the studio Sandra was in the office Where is Daniel? A: Studio	**Task 12: Conjunction** Mary and Jeff went to the kitchen Then Jeff went to the park Where is Mary? A: Kitchen Where is Jeff? A: Park
Task 13: Compound co-reference Daniel and Sandra journeyed to the office Then they went to the garden Sandra and John travelled to the kitchen After that, they moved to the hallway Where is Daniel? A: Garden	**Task 14: Time reasoning** In the afternoon Julie went to the park Yesterday Julie was at school Julie went to the cinema in the evening. Where did Julie go after the park? A: Cinema Where was Julie before the park? A: School
Task 15: Basic deduction Sheep are afraid of wolves Cats are afraid of dogs Mice are afraid of cats Gertrude is a sheep What is Gertrude afraid of? A: Wolves	**Task 16: Basic induction** Lily is a swan Lily is white Bernhard is green Greg is a swan What color is Greg? A: White
Task 17: Positional reasoning The triangle is to the right of the blue square The red square is on top of the blue square The red sphere is to the right of the blue square Is the red sphere to the right of the blue square? A: Yes Is the red square to the left of the triangle? A: Yes	**Task 18: Size reasoning** The football fits in the suitcase. The suitcase fits in the cupboard. The box is smaller than the football. Will the box fit in the suitcase? A: Yes Will the cupboard fit in the box? A: No
Task 19: Path finding The kitchen is north of the hallway The bathroom is west of the bedroom The den is east of the hallway The office is south of the bedroom How do you go from the den to the kitchen? A: West, North How do you go from office to bathroom? A: North, West	**Task 20: Agent's Motivations** John is hungry John goes to the kitchen John grabbed the apple there Daniel is hungry Where does Daniel go? A: Kitchen Why did John go to the kitchen? A: Hungry

Figure 4. Result comparison

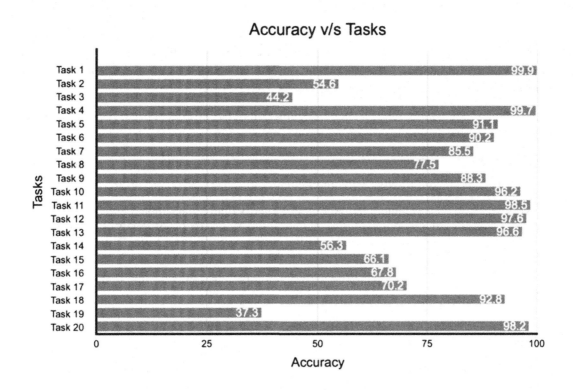

CONCLUSION

In this work, the authors have discussed how the addition of an external memory can impact the implementation of a QA chatbot system to a greater extent. The LSTM networks used before were not worthy enough as they used to forget what the question was, making them completely useless for certain smart and security applications. The use of a memory network helps the questions to be processed completely along with certain directional questions. The use of directional questions can be very important by integrating it in smarxt city applications such as tracking the location of a child in a house or a community and also, for security purposes as a question answering chatbot oriented door locks.

REFERENCES

Ainouz, S. A., & Ben Ahmed, M. (2020). *A Smart Chatbot Architecture based on NLP and Machine Learning for Health Care Assistance.* . doi:10.1145/3386723.3387897

Ankit, K., Irsoy, O., Su, J., Bradbury, J., English, R., Pierce, B., Ondruska, P., Gulrajani, I., & Socher, R. (2016). *Ask Me Anything: Dynamic Memory Networks for Natural Language Processing.* ICML.

Bing Liu, Hakkani-Tur, & Heck. (n.d.). *Dialogue Learning with Human Teaching and Feedback in End-to-End Trainable Task-Oriented Dialogue Systems.* Academic Press.

Dwivedi, S., & Singh, V. (2013). Modeling Techniques and Applications (CIMTA) Research and reviews in question answering system. *International Conference on Computational Intelligence.* 10.1016/j. protcy.2013.12.378

Hermann, K. M., Kocisky, T., Grefenstette, E., Espeholt, L., Kay, W., Suleyman, M., & Blunsom, R. (2015). Teaching machines to read and comprehend. In *28th International Proceedings on Advances in Neural Information Processing Systems* (pp. 1693–1701). MIT Press.

Langley. (n.d.). *Crafting Papers on Machine Learning.* Adaptive Systems Group, Daimler-Chrysler Research and Technology Center.

Lewkowitz, M. (2014, Feb 12). *Bots: The future of human-computer interaction.* Available: https://chatbotsmagazine.com/bots-the-future-of-human-computer-interaction56696f7aff56

Raine, R. (2009). Making A Clever Intelligent Agent: The Theory Behind The Implementation. *IEEE International Conference on Intelligent Computing and Intelligent Systems.* 10.1109/ICICISYS.2009.5358137

Rohit, Dharamshi, & Subramanyam. (2019). Approaches to Question Answering Using LSTM and Memory Networks: SocProS 2017. In *Soft Computing for Problem Solving.* DOI: doi:10.1007/978-981-13-1592-3 15

Rohit, G. (2019). *Dharamshi, Ekta Subramanyam, Natarajan.* Approaches to Question Answering Using LSTM and Memory.

Sherstins, A. (2020). Fundamentals of Recurrent Neural Network (RNN) and Long Short-Term Memory (LSTM) Network. *Physica D: Nonlinear Phenomena, 404.*

Sukhbaatar, S., & Arthur, S. J. W. R. F. (n.d.). *End-To-End Memory Networks.* Dept. of Computer Science Courant Institute, New York University.

Thomas & Thomas. (2018). Chatbot Using Gated End-to-End Memory Networks. *International Research Journal of Engineering and Technology, 5.*

Vilner, Y. (n.d.). *Chatbots101:The Evolution of Customer Retention Latest Trend.* Available: https://www.entrepreneur.com/article/293439

Weston, Bordes, Rush, van Merrienboer, Joulin, & Mikolov. (n.d.). Towards Ai-complete Question Answering: A Set Of Prerequisite Toy Tasks. In *Soft Computing for Problem Solving Arch.* Academic Press.

Weston, J., Bordes, A., & Chopra, S. (2015). *Towards AI-Complete Question Answering: A Set of Prerequisite Toy Tasks.* arXiv preprint, arXiv: 1502.05968

Weston, J., Chopra, S., & Bordes, A. (2015). Memory networks. *Proceedings of the 3rd International Conference on Learning Representations (ICLR).*

Xiong, C., Merityand, S., & Socher, R. (2016). *Dynamic Memory Networks for Visual and Textual Question Answering.* ICML.

KEY TERMS AND DEFINITIONS

Accuracy: It is the ratio for the total correct predicted values to the addition of total correct predicted values and total incorrectly predicted values.

Natural Language Processing (NLP): Natural language processing refers to processing of human language for the computer to understand in order to perform/predict according to its needs.

Question Answering System: A question answering system is known for retrieving answers to questions either from structured database, relational database, or unstructured natural language documents.

Recurrent Neural Networks: In a recurrent neural network the output of the previous node is used as an input in the current node. This can help predict the next step for the algorithm.

Vanishing Gradient Problem: With addition of more layers to the neural network the loss function gradient becomes smaller approaching to almost zero which makes it harder to train the network.

Chapter 20
Comparison of Parametric and Non-Parametric Methods to Analyse the Data Gathered by a Likert-Type Scale

Tamer Baran
ⓘ https://orcid.org/0000-0002-8711-6561
Pamukkale University, Turkey

ABSTRACT

The aim of this chapter is to reveal whether the results of the analysis of the data obtained using Likert type scales (LTSs) with parametric and non-parametric methods in different response alternative (DRA) numbers will differ in terms of statistical significance. In this respect, the data were obtained from 271 university students with CETSCALE prepared using LTS in five different response alternatives (DRAs). The data were analysed using the one sample t test and Wilcoxon signed rank test. Significant findings of the study in the analysis of the data obtained using midpoint LTSs and with the normal distribution with both parametric and non-parametric methods couldn't be found. Similarly, the data obtained by four response alternative numbers with the normal distribution were analysed by both methods, and the significant findings were revealed. However, the results of the data obtained by six and eight response alternative numbers with parametric methods were found to be statistically significant while their analysis by non-parametric methods did not reveal significant findings.

INTRODUCTION

The Likert-type scale was put forth by Rensis Likert (1932) in his work titled "A Technique for the Measurement of Attitudes" and is named after him. These types of scales are most commonly used by researchers in many areas ranging from social science to educational science. Likert-type scales are also discussed by applied data scientists in different contexts, besides collecting data. In the context of applied data, whether Likert-type scales are ordinal or interval scales is one of the most controversial

DOI: 10.4018/978-1-7998-6985-6.ch020

topics among applied data scientists. This discussion is crucial because the result of the controversy also leads to finding an answer to the question of how to analyze the data obtained from these scales.

Although a number of authors (Aaker et al., 2007; Burns and Bush, 2000; Churchill, 1999; Malhotra, 2004) consider Likert type scales as an example of the interval scale, there are others (for example Jamieson, 2004; Knapp, 1999; Mircioiu and Atkinson, 2017) who claim that Likert-type scales are not interval but ordinal scales. This discussion raises the question of whether the data obtained using Likert-type scales should be tested by parametric or non-parametric methods. Even though there are studies related to this question in different fields such as education (Turan et al., 2015), medicine (Jamieson, 2004; Norman, 2010), and statistics (Sangthong, 2020), the subject has not been discussed enough in the field of social sciences.

Moreover, although Norman (2010) claimed that there is no disadvantageousness in analyzing the data obtained from small samples with Likert-type scales by parametric methods, Wadgave and Kharnier (2016) emphasized that there is a lack of studies to prove this claim. This study was conducted with the motivation to fill this gap in the literature.

The aim of this study is to determine whether the data obtained using Likert-type scales in the different response alternative numbers can be analyzed with parametric and non-parametric methods in terms of statistical significance. For this purpose, the research question of our study is as follows:

Research Question: Would there be a statistical difference in the findings as a result of the analysis of data obtained with Likert-type scales from small samples at different response alternatives with parametric or non-parametric tests?

In order to find an answer to the research question, the chapter is organized into four main sections: In the first section, the literature was reviewed regarding the Likert-type scale. This section has been divided into four sub-sections. In the first sub-section, the emergence and definition of the Likert-type scale are mentioned and information about the use of the Likert-type scale in the literature has been presented. Later, a discussion has been made regarding which type of scales the Likert-type scale conforms to. The last sub-section discusses the different analysis methods suitable for analyzing these scales. In the second main section, the methodology of the study has been explained in detail. In the third main section of this chapter, the findings of the study are presented. In the last section of the chapter, the conclusion, recommendations, and suggestions regarding the topic have been stated.

LITERATURE REVIEW

Likert Type Scales and Using Likert Type Scales in the Literature

Likert type scale, which was first put forward by Rensis Likert in 1932 and named after him, is one of the most frequently used psychometric scales by researchers to evaluate the perception of the participants (Wadgave and Khairnar, 2016). In this type of scale, researchers try to obtain data through numerical values assigned to response alternatives they have created to determine the participants' level of participation to scale items (Chyung et al., 2017). Likert-type scales are one of the most frequently used scales by researchers in many fields, especially due to their benefit in measuring attitudes. Using the Likert scale to measure attitudes and values, researchers can develop their own scales by assigning numbers to levels of participation. The Likert-type scales are used in two ways: (1) for the summarized scale; and (2) for individual items or rating scales from which the aggregated scale is calculated. Likert items are expressions about a specific topic and through these scales, participants are asked to determine their participation levels. The summarized Likert scale is commonly created by developing a series of items about the topic. These items are intended to provide a representative example of all possible views or attitudes on the subject. To calculate the summated scale score, each response type is given a numeric value or weight at specified spaces (Józsa and Morgan, 2017).

Studies about the use of Likert type scales in the literature have focused on some issues including the midpoint (Chyung et al., 2017), response alternative numbers (Baran, 2020), the order of labels (Chyung et al., 2018; Kennedy et al., 2018), the use of positive or negative expressed items in the scales (Chyung et al., 2018), and the presentation of the items to the participant as itemized or scrolled (Chyung et al., 2020).

One of the controversial topics about Likert-type scales is whether the midpoint should be used in scales. While some authors argue that the use of the midpoint in these types of scales would be beneficial, others state that it should not be used. Chyung et al. (2017) emphasize that excluding midpoint in Likert-type scales is not a good idea. In the case of using midpoint, the participants do not feel obliged to channel themselves to one of the extreme values and have the opportunity to present their real ideas on the subject. On the other hand, Likert-type scales with midpoints allow the participants to use the midpoint as a tool to avoid expressing their views on the topic correctly (Chyung et al., 2017). The usage of midpoints in Likert-type scales depends on the researcher's preference (Garland, 1991), the respondent's involvement level to the topic, and the research issue (Johns, 2005; Weems and Onwuegbuzie, 2001).

For researchers who prefer to use the midpoint on Likert-type scales, there is another matter to decide: How should the midpoint be presented? In this regard, researchers have several alternatives such as "*neutral*", "*neither agree nor disagree*", "*undecided*", "*I don't know*", "*it depends*", etc. to present the midpoint. However, researchers should be careful about the use of these options because some words, for example, "*undecided*" may be interrogated whether there is really a middle point between disagreement and agreement, or be seen as a lack of opinion, and for this reason, the participant may be interpreted as confused. Therefore, Chyung et al. (2017) state that terms such as "I don't know" or "depend on" should not be labeled as a midpoint, and should be presented to the participant as an off-scale option if they are really needed. Moreover, the authors express that the most appropriate presentation to be used as the middle point is "*neither agree nor disagree*".

Response alternative numbers of Likert-type scale is one of the most important debated topics in the literature. Although it was first created by Rensis Likert (1932) as 5 response alternatives, over time, the response alternatives have varied from 2 to 101 (Chyung et al., 2017). Researchers must be very careful in determining the number of response alternatives and should use strategies to minimize potential bias. Findings of some studies (Preston and Colman, 2000) show that participants reply easily and quickly when the response alternatives decrease. Similarly, Baran (2020) found that as the number of response alternatives increases, the participants are confused, and consequently the response time and the number of items left blank increase. Moreover, the author mentions that the demographic characteristics of the participants, such as education level, age, etc., are important criteria in determining the number of response alternatives. Also, Baran (2020) emphasizes that the demographics of the participants, such as education level, age, etc., are the criteria to be considered in determining the response number alternatives. However, it must be remembered that a smaller number of response alternatives may result in ignoring options that express the opinions of the participants (Chyung et al., 2017). Therefore, while determining the response alternatives, the researchers should not ignore the characteristics of the respondents, the subject of the study, etc.

An example of a Likert-type scale with 5 response alternatives is presented in Table 1.

Table 1. A Likert type scale with 5 response alternatives

Item no	Item	Strongly disagree	Disagree	Neither agree nor disagree	Agree	Strongly agree
1	A consumer should always buy domestic products.	1	2	3	4	5
2	A real citizen should always buy locally made products.	1	2	3	4	5
3	It is always best to purchase locally products.	1	2	3	4	5
.	.	.	.	.	.	.
.	.	.	.	.	.	.
.	.	.	.	.	.	.

Furthermore, the direction of ranking in Likert-type scales (ascending or descending) is another important issue that should be decided by researchers (Chyung et al., 2018). Table 2 and Table 3 present usage examples of Likert-type scales with response alternatives which are ascending and descending in ranking.

Table 2. Ascending order Likert type scale

Strongly disagree	1	2	3	4	5	Strongly agree

The presentation of the labels in reverse order according to the value given to the label (1- strongly agree, 5- strongly disagree) may cause the participants to be confused.

Table 3. Descending order Likert type scale

Strongly agree	1	2	3	4	5	Strongly disagree

Although a few studies (Christian et al., 2009; Hofmans et al., 2007; Weng and Cheng, 2000) did not find the effect of ranking on participants' response preferences, many studies (Barnette, 2000; Friedman et al., 1993; Hartley and Betts, 2010; Maeda, 2015; Nicholls et al., 2006) found evidence that the direction of response alternatives significantly affects participants' response choice. For this reason, it is important for researchers who use Likert-type scales to pay attention to the response alternatives' orders in terms of the quality of the data to obtain.

Another argument about Likert-type scales is about the positive or negative expression of the items of scales used in the questionnaire. When combined with the numerical values given to the labels briefly mentioned above, the issue becomes even more important. Although negative use of items provides some benefits to researchers, such as helping them reduce acceptance bias and detecting data with acceptance bias, the literature suggests avoiding such usage of items as much as possible. The reason is that using items in this manner may reveal some adverse conditions for researchers. For instance, negatively stated items may appear as a separate factor as a result of the analysis (Greenberger et al, 2003; Ibrahim, 2001; Salazar, 2015). More importantly, careless participants may misunderstand negatively stated items and provide fallacious data (Weem et al., 2003; Woods, 2006). This can undesirably adversely affect data quality in a research application (Chyung et al., 2018). However, in some cases where the attribute to be measured is negative in nature, it may be inevitable to use negative statements in Likert-type scales. In any case, researchers should consider the phenomenon they intend to measure and be careful in using negative statements.

Previous studies (for example, Schriesherim and Hill, 1981; Weem et al., 2006) revealed that the positive or negative use of the items in such scales causes significant changes in the responses of the participants. However, if the researcher still has to use the scale expression negatively, some methods such as presenting the data from negative statements separately (Hartely 2013), creating the negative items clearly (Johnson et al., 2004; Merritt, 2012), warning participants that there are negative statements (Mathews and Shepherd, 2002), and presenting positive and negative statements separately in the scale (Roszkowski and Soven, 2010) can help in gathering quality data.

The Debate as to Whether Likert Type Scales are Ordinal or Interval

One of the most debatable issues of recent periods is whether the Likert-type scale — which is one of the most frequently used scales in marketing research, especially in the measurement of attitudes — is interval scale or ordinal scale (Chyung et al., 2017; Joshi et al., 2015). In this context, it is appropriate to compare interval and ordinal scales first before discussing the Likert-type scales.

Knapp (1999) and Siegel (1957) state that they have two main features that differentiate interval scales from ordinal scales. The first is that the ordinal scales cannot be transformed, while interval scales can be converted linearly. The authors exemplify it with the transformation of C° temperature into a Fahrenheit unit. Accordingly, heat data obtained from C° can be transformed into Fahrenheit unit linearly with $y = bx + a$ (F = 1.8 C) o+32). However, this is not the case for ordinal scales. In this context, Goldstein and Hersen (1984) and Tavakoli (2012) emphasized that there is no equal distance between the expressions represented in Likert-type scales, even though mathematically equal intervals are represented. Hart (1996) found that participants don't regard the distance equally in the data obtained using the Likert-type scales. Likewise, according to Kuzon et al. (1996), the statements such as "I strongly disagree, I disagree, I agree and I strongly agree" are examples of an ordinal scale. The levels included in this example can be arranged as strongly disagree < disagree < agree < strongly agree. However, the authors state that the distances between the levels in this arrangement are not equal. Interval scales are clearly defined and consist of evenly spaced levels (Kuzon et al., 1996).

Secondly, there is a specified "0" point on interval scales, while there is no specific "0" point on ordinal scales (Knapp, 1999; Siegel, 1957). For example, the 5-item Likert type scales used in the questionnaire forms are generally presented to the participant with the labels "1 = Strongly Disagree", "5 = Strongly Agree" (Jamieson, 2004).

On the Analysis of Data Obtained through Likert Type Scales

The above discussion of whether Likert-type scales are ordinal or interval scales has brought the question of how to analyze the data obtained with this scale. This is the crux of the issue because, as mentioned by Sullivan and Artino (2013), these methods differ in terms of the strength of the analysis. Since the parametric tests can be analyzed using mean and standard deviation, they exhibit stronger results than nonparametric tests. In this context, the usage of one method over the other to analyze the data obtained with Likert-type scales is a problem that should be solved by researchers. On the topic, some authors (for instance Hansen, 2003; Jamieson 2004) argue that the data obtained with these scales should be analyzed with non-parametric methods, while others (Sullivan and Artino, 2013) argue in favor of the parametric methods. On the other hand, there are some authors (Norman, 2010) who claim that this debate is unimportant.

The researchers who claim that Likert-type scales should be tested with nonparametric methods base their argument on the following four reasons (Wadgave and Kharniar, 2016). Firstly, parametric tests require data to be obtained with intermittent or proportional scales and analyze these data using mean and standard deviation. However, some labels used in Likert-type scales, such as occasionally or frequently, do not meet this requirement. For instance, frequently and a half indicates a meaningless finding and is not useful to researchers (Jamieson, 2004). Second, in connection with the above justification, verbal labels assigned to scale items are not suitable for analysis with mean and standard deviation, since they are ordinal scales (Jamieson, 2004). Third, in the use of parametric tests, the sample size and distribution are more important than the level of measurement. Since non-normally distributed data can result in a mean that is not a useful measure in the central trend, therefore, even if Likert type scales are considered interval, data sets obtained with such scales should not be analyzed with parametric tests as they usually have a skewed or polarized distribution (Wadgave and Kharniar, 2016). And finally, the use of labels on a Likert-type scale tends to decrease as they approach the midpoint. In other words, in such scales, participants are more inclined towards the extremes than the midpoints and this causes an effect called the "anchor effect" (Bishop & Herron, 2015). For this reason, using parametric tests are not appropriate in Likert-type scales.

Hansen (2003) and Jamieson (2004) also argue that the Likert-type scales do not meet the above requirements, therefore these types of scales are not interval scales but ordinal ones. On this basis, they have stated that the data obtained using Likert-type scales are not appropriate to be analyzed with parametric tests done with mean and standard deviation. Similarly, Gardner and Martin (2007) expressed that Likert-type scales are not interval scales, but ordinal scales, and that the results of the analysis of the data obtained using these types of scales can only be obtained with non-parametric tests. Boone and Boone (2012) state that in the analysis of data obtained using Likert-type scales, non-parametric methods such as mode, median, and frequency are more appropriate than parametric methods such as mean and standard deviation. Additionally, Bishop and Herron (2015) emphasize that the data should not be obtained using Likert-type scales if the aim is to use parametric methods in the analysis of the research.

On the other hand, some authors argue that there is no harm in using parametric tests in the analysis of data obtained with Likert-type scales. Researchers who defend this opinion present the following reasons. Firstly, the robustness of the parametric tests for the Likert scale is validated not by individual items but by assessing it with a scale that is an aggregated composite score (Carifio and Perla, 2008). Second, in standard t-tests and ANOVA, the data and the central limit theorem work with the normal distribution assumption, showing that the means are normally distributed regardless of the original distribution, unless the sample group is not less than 5 or 10 (Norman, 2010). Third, data simulation studies have revealed the robustness of the Pearson correlation for the sample size between 5 - 60 for the normal and rectangular distribution of the ordinal data (Murray, 2013). Lastly, Monte Carlo studies on data obtained with the Likert scale clearly reveal that the F test is extremely robust even when such data are analyzed at the level of scale items (Wadgave and Kharniar, 2016). Moreover, Norman (2010) claims that the data obtained with Likert-type scales can be analyzed through parametric tests, even if they have small sampling, with non-normally distributed data and unequal variances.

The studies conducted to analyze the data obtained using the Likert-type scales compare with parametric methods or non-parametric methods have revealed different findings. Murray (2013) analyzes the data obtained using 5 category Likert type scales using Pearson, Spearman, and Kendall tau_b correlation methods and asserts that the findings were not statistically different. Norman (2010) transforms the data obtained using Likert-type scales with the 0 - 10 response alternatives into the 1 - 4 form and analyzes using Pearson and Spearman correlation methods. At the end of the study, Norman (2010) finds that the parametric and nonparametric methods didn't reveal different results in terms of statistical significance. Furthermore, Norman (2010) stated that the large sample size, the normal distribution of the data, or the variant equation is not necessary when using parametric tests. Turan et al. (2015) compare the results of the t-test with the Mann-Whitney U test in 27 different samples and found that there were no statistically significant results in 24 samples. In the same study, the authors compare the ANOVA and Kruskal-Wallis methods in 15 different samples and concluded that for 14 samples, there were no statistically significant differences.

Brown (2011), Carifio and Perla (2007), and Carifio and Perla (2008) indicate that Likert-type scales are ordinal scales and that the claim that they should be analyzed with only non-parametric methods is a myth. Furthermore, Carifio and Perla (2008) specify that parametric tests are more appropriate for analyzing the data obtained using Likert-type scales and emphasize that it is best practice to use total scores in analyzing the obtained data with parametric tests. In his study, Vigderhous (1977) analyzes the data obtained using the Likert-type scales, with Pearson as a parametric test, and with Kendall tau_b correlation as a nonparametric test and found that they differed significantly from each other.

Mircioiu and Atkinson (2017) find that in a sample of more than 15 participants, the analysis of data obtained from groups with similar distributions using parametric and non-parametric methods does not vary statistically. Moreover, according to findings, this situation does not change even if the sample size is increased. Therefore, the authors emphasize that the analysis of the data obtained with a Likert-type scale by non-parametric methods may cause some loss of information, and they suggest analyzing the data in question with parametric methods. Sangthong (2020) finds that the analysis of the data obtained by Likert-type scales with 5, 7, and 10 response alternatives in different sample sizes with parametric and non-parametric methods does not cause a difference in terms of statistical significance. Thus, Sangthong (2020) states that it is more plausible to use parametric methods in a situation where there is no difference in terms of significance. However, the findings show that when the assumption of the equivalence of variances is ignored, parametric tests reveal stronger findings than non-parametric tests. Moreover, the findings reveal that the higher the number of response alternatives on these kinds of scales, the stronger the results ensue for both methods.

METHODOLOGY

The main focus of this study is to reveal whether data collected with Likert-type scales should be analyzed by parametric or non-parametric methods. In order to achieve this aim, the questionnaire form, which was used as a data collection tool in the study, was meticulously prepared by making use of the literature. Although using midpoint in Likert scales is suggested in the literature (Chyung et al., 2017), it was decided to use both types of Likert scales to determine whether the findings differ in terms of midpoint scales and forced scales. As stated in the literature review of the study, there are different alternatives for the researchers in labeling the midpoint. However, since it is emphasized in the literature that the most appropriate label for the midpoint is "neither agree nor disagree", the midpoint in the current study was worded with this label. In this study, the number of response alternatives is one of the most dwelling issues. Although the first usage by Rensis Likert (1932) was with 5 response alternatives, researchers have encountered the use of the Likert scale with many different response alternatives over time. For example, Preston and Colman (2000) expressed that in Likert-type scales, response alternatives were used in a range from 3 to 18, while Chyung et al. (2017) stated that there is a wider usage scale from 2 to 101. Besides, Jamieson (2004) indicated that the most frequently used response alternatives are 5 and 7 in studies that collected data with Likert-type scales. On the use of response alternatives in data collection by Likert-type scales, Jamieson (2004) stated that the most commonly used response alternative number is 5, while Bardakcı (2009) stated that this number is 7 in Turkey. On the other hand, Allen and Seaman (2007) emphasized that the most frequently used response alternatives in researches are 5 and 7. In this context, the data in our study were obtained using Likert type 5; at 5±1 and 7; 7±5 different number alternatives (4, 5, 6, 7, and 8).

To determine the ordering direction of the responses to the items in the questionnaire form and the values given to the labels, the findings of previous studies were considered. Moreover, in order to minimize the potential confusion that participants may experience, the response alternatives were presented horizontally and were created in ascending order. Finally, in previous studies, based on the findings on the effect of the negative presentation of the items on the response of participants, attention was paid to the positive use of expressions in the scale.

In this study, Consumer Ethnocentrism Scale (CETSCALE) which was developed by Shimp and Sharma (1987) was used as a scale. This scale was chosen in the study due to the fact that increasing the response rate inattentively reduces the possibility of response (Galesic and Bosnjak, 2009: 357). The 5-point Likert type CETSCALE, one of the questionnaire forms used in the study, is presented at the end of the chapter in Table 7.

The data of the study were collected by convenience sampling. This method was used because it enables data collection in the easiest, fastest, and most economical way (Hasiloglu et al, 2015). The questionnaire forms with different response alternatives were applied to small samples. There were two reasons for this. First, the purpose of the study was to gather data in small samples. The second was the effort not to act incongruously the independence of observations assumption. In this context, data was collected from 271 university students by face-to-face survey method and was analyzed through the One-Sample t-Test as a parametric method and the Wilcoxon Signed Rank Test as a non-parametric method. The findings are presented in the following section.

Table 4. Reliabilities of Scales by Alternative Numbers

Number of Response Alternative	Cronbach's α
4	.878
5	,847
6	.907
7	.861
8	.930

Table 5. Results of the Kolmogorov-Smirnov Test for different response alternative numbers

Numbers of Response Alternative	N			K-S Z Test	p
4	59	2,75	0.4541	,636	,813
5	56	3.05	0.5805	,787	,571
6	47	4.13	0,8750	,714	.687
7	63	3.83	0.9779	,648	,795
8	46	5,86	1.3521	.697	,715

Table 6. Comparison of One Sample t Test and Wilcoxon Signed Rank Test Results in terms of Response Alternative Numbers

Number of Response Alternative	Type of Test	N	$\bar{x}$ / $\bar{x}_{median}$	$Sh_{\bar{x}}$	Test results		
					T/Z values	ss	p
4	One-Sample *t* Test	59	2,75	,0591	4,280	0.4541	< **,001**
	Wilcoxon Signed Rank Test		3	-	-1,976	-	<,**048**
5	One-Sample *t* Test	56	3.05	,0776	0,693	0.5805	,491
	Wilcoxon Signed Rank Test		3	-	-1,100	-	,271
6	One-Sample *t* Test	47	4.13	,1276	32,365	0,8750	< **,001**
	Wilcoxon Signed Rank Test		4	-	-1,630	-	,103
7	One-Sample *t* Test	63	3.83	,1245	-1,334	0.9779	,187
	Wilcoxon Signed Rank Test		4	-	-1,156	-	,248
8	One-Sample *t* Test	46	5,86	,1994	6,824	1.3521	< **,001**
	Wilcoxon Signed Rank Test		6	-	-0,880	-	,379

FINDINGS

The Cronbach's α coefficients, which show the reliability of the CETSCALE scale used in the study according to the number of different response alternatives, are given in Table 4. As can be seen from the Table, all scales are presented with different alternative numbers that are reliable (Nunnally, 1978). Besides, the highest α coefficient belongs to the scale where the 8-alternative number was used.

The Kolmogorov-Smirnov test results for the distribution of the obtained data are shown in Table 5. It can be seen that all of the data obtained using different alternative numbers are normally distributed.

According to different alternative numbers of the study, the findings for One-Sample t and Wilcoxon Rank test results are shown in Table 6.

One-Sample *t*-Test and Wilcoxon Signed Rank Test results show that the data obtained using Likert type scales with midpoint (consisting of 5 and 7 labels) were not statistically significant as well as the test conducted with both methods. Besides, findings also show that the parametric test results of the data obtained using Likert-type scales consisting of 4 response alternatives from forced scales were statistically significant and 99% of nonparametric test results were statistically significant. On the other hand, the data obtained using Likert-type scales consisting of 6 and 8 response alternatives yielded statistically significant results for the parametric tests, whereas it didn't yield statistically significant results for nonparametric tests.

CONCLUSION

Likert-type scales are the most widely used scales to measure consumer attitudes in marketing research. It is one of the controversial issues of recent periods whether the distance between the levels in the Likert type scales are not equal and therefore cannot be transformed and whether such scales will be evaluated as interval scale due to the lack of a certain point "0". This discussion brought the question of whether the data obtained using such scales should be analyzed by parametric or nonparametric methods.

In this context, this study tried to find out whether the results of the data obtained using Likert-type scales by testing with two methods would differ in terms of statistical significance. In this regard, data were gathered from 271 university students in 5 different response alternatives by face-to-face survey method. In the analysis of the data, One-Sample t-Test was used as the parametric method and the Wilcoxon Rank Signed Test was used as the nonparametric type of this method.

As a result of the analyses, it was found that there was no difference in the statistical significance in the case of analyzing by means of the midpoint (consisting of 5 and 7 response alternatives) and by means of the parametric or nonparametric method for the normally distributed data. Similarly, it was found that the findings were not different in terms of statistical significance for the data gathered with the scale of 4-response alternative. Statistically significant findings were obtained in the data normally distributed for both parametric and nonparametric methods. These findings support the findings of Murray (2013), Norman (2010), and Turan et al. (2015). In the data collected with Likert-type scales consisting of 6 and 8 response alternatives, the results of the analysis with the parametric tests were found to be statistically significant, whereas the results of the analysis with nonparametric tests were not statistically significant. These findings support the findings of Vidgerhous (1977).

Our findings are similar to the findings of previous studies for different response alternatives when evaluated on the basis of data obtained from different response alternative numbers. Moreover, the findings of our study clearly show that the decision to analyze the data obtained using the Likert-type scales with parametric methods or non-parametric methods doesn't depend on the number of response alternatives.

However, in this study, it should not be overlooked that all of the data obtained using the different number of response alternatives shows the normal distribution. Furthermore, the equation of variants was not analyzed due to the methods of this study. Therefore, it is useful for the researchers to take into consideration the suggestions of the literature at the decision stage when deciding to use parametric methods or nonparametric methods in their studies.

REFERENCES

Aaker, D. A., Kumar, V., & Day, G. S. (2008). *Marketing research* (9th ed.). John Wiley & Sons.

Aji, B. M., & Larner, A. J. (2017). Screening for dementia: Single yes/no question or Likert scale? *Clinical Medicine*, *17*(1), 93–94. doi:10.7861/clinmedicine.17-1-93 PMID:28148591

Allen, I. E., & Seaman, C. A. (2007). Likert scales and data analyses. *Quality Progress*, *40*(7), 64–65.

Awang, Z., Afthanorhan, A., & Mamat, M. (2016). The Likert scale analysis using parametric based Structural Equation Modeling (SEM). *Computational Methods in Social Sciences*, *4*(1), 13.

Baran, T. (2020). Anket Formuyla Veri Toplamada Renk ve Cevap Alternatifi Sayısının Cevaplama Süresi ve İfade Cevaplama Sayısına Etkisi. *Akademisyen Yayınevi. Bölüm*, *5*, 97–116.

Bardakcı, A. (2009). Pazarlama Araştırmalarında Kullanılan Tutum Ölçeklerindeki Cevap Alternatifi Sayısına İlişkin Bir Literatür Taraması. *Pamukkale Üniversitesi Sosyal Bilimler Enstitüsü Dergisi*, (4), 7–20.

Barnette, J. (2000). Effects of stem and Likert response option reversals on survey internal consistency: If you feel the need, there is a better alternative to using those negatively worded stems. *Educational and Psychological Measurement*, *60*(3), 361–370. doi:10.1177/00131640021970592

Batterton, K., & Hale, K. (2017). The Likert Scale What It Is and How to Use It. *Phalanx*, *50*(2), 32–39.

Bishop, P. A., & Herron, R. L. (2015). Use and misuse of the Likert item responses and other ordinal measures. *International Journal of Exercise Science*, *8*(3), 297. PMID:27182418

Boone, H. N., & Boone, D. A. (2012). Analyzing likert data. *Journal of Extension*, *50*(2), 1–5.

Brown, J. D. (2011). Likert items and scales of measurement. *Statistics*, *15*(1), 10–14.

Burns, A., & Bush, R. (2000). *Marketing Research* (3rd ed.). Prentice Hall.

Carifio, J., & Perla, R. (2008). Resolving the 50-year debate around using and misusing Likert scales. *Medical Education*, *42*(12), 1150–1152. doi:10.1111/j.1365-2923.2008.03172.x PMID:19120943

Carifio, J., & Perla, R. J. (2007). Ten common misunderstandings, misconceptions, persistent myths and urban legends about Likert scales and Likert response formats and their antidotes. *Journal of Social Sciences*, *3*(3), 106–116. doi:10.3844/jssp.2007.106.116

Christian, L. M., Parsons, N. L., & Dillman, D. A. (2009). Designing scalar questions for Web surveys. *Sociological Methods & Research*, *37*(3), 393–425. doi:10.1177/0049124108330004

Churchill, G. A., Jr. (1999). Marketing Research Methodological Foundations (7th ed.). The Dryden Press International Edition.

Chyung, S. Y., Barkin, J. R., & Shamsy, J. A. (2018). Evidence-Based Survey Design: The Use of Negatively Worded Items in Surveys. *Performance Improvement, 57*(3), 16–25. doi:10.1002/pfi.21749

Chyung, S. Y., Hutchinson, D., & Shamsy, J. A. (2020). Evidence-Based Survey Design: Ceiling Effects Associated with Response Scales. *Performance Improvement, 59*(6), 6–13. doi:10.1002/pfi.21920

Chyung, S. Y., Kennedy, M., & Campbell, I. (2018). Evidence-Based Survey Design: The Use of Ascending or Descending Order of Likert-Type Response Options. *Performance Improvement, 57*(9), 9–16. doi:10.1002/pfi.21800

Chyung, S. Y., Roberts, K., Swanson, I., & Hankinson, A. (2017). Evidence-based survey design: The use of a midpoint on the Likert scale. *Performance Improvement, 56*(10), 15–23. doi:10.1002/pfi.21727

Chyung, S. Y., Swanson, I., Roberts, K., & Hankinson, A. (2018). Evidence-based survey design: The use of continuous rating scales in surveys. *Performance Improvement, 57*(5), 38–48. doi:10.1002/pfi.21763

De Winter, J. C., & Dodou, D. (2010). Five-point Likert items: T test versus Mann-Whitney-Wilcoxon. *Practical Assessment, Research & Evaluation, 15*(11), 2.

Friedman, H. H., Herskovitz, P. J., & Pollack, S. (1993). The biasing effects of scale-checking styles on response to a Likert scale. In Proceedings of the American Statistical Association annual conference. *Survey Research Methods, 2*, 792–795.

Gaito, J. (1980). Measurement scales and statistics: Resurgence of an old misconception. *Psychological Bulletin, 87*(3), 564–567. doi:10.1037/0033-2909.87.3.564

Galesic, M., & Bosnjak, M. (2009). Effects of questionnaire length on participation and indicators of response quality in a web survey. *Public Opinion Quarterly, 73*(2), 349–360. doi:10.1093/poq/nfp031

Gardner, H. J., & Martin, M. A. (2007). Analyzing ordinal scales in studies of virtual environments: Likert or lump it! *Presence (Cambridge, Mass.), 16*(4), 439–446. doi:10.1162/pres.16.4.439

Garland, R. (1991). The mid-point on a rating scale: Is it desirable. *Marketing Bulletin, 2*(1), 66–70.

Greenberger, E., Chen, C., Dmitrieva, J., & Farruggia, S. P. (2003). Item-wording and the dimensionality of the Rosenberg Self-Esteem Scale: Do they matter? *Personality and Individual Differences, 35*(6), 1241–1254. doi:10.1016/S0191-8869(02)00331-8

Hansen, J. P. (2003). CAN'T MISS—Conquer Any Number Task by Making Important Statistics Simple. Part 1. Types of Variables, Mean, Median, Variance, and Standard Deviation. *Journal for Healthcare Quality, 25*(4), 19–24. doi:10.1111/j.1945-1474.2003.tb01070.x PMID:14606209

Hart, M. C. (1996). Improving the Dissemination Of SERVQUAL By Using Magnitude Scaling. In *Total Quality Management Action* (pp. 267–271). Springer. doi:10.1007/978-94-009-1543-5_42

Hartley, J. (2013). Some thoughts on Likert type scales. *International Journal of Clinical and Health Psychology, 13*, 83–86.

Hartley, J., & Betts, L. (2010). Four layouts and a finding: The effects of changes in the order of the verbal labels and numerical values on Likert type scales. *International Journal of Social Research Methodology, 13*(1), 17–27. doi:10.1080/13645570802648077

Haşıloğlu, S. B., Baran, T., & Aydın, O. (2015). Pazarlama araştırmalarındaki potansiyel problemlere yönelik bir araştırma: Kolayda örnekleme ve sıklık ifadeli ölçek maddeleri. *Pamukkale İşletme ve Bilişim Yönetimi Dergisi*, (1), 19–28.

Hofmans, J., Theuns, P., Baekelandt, S., Mairesse, O., Schillewaert, N., & Cools, W. (2007). Bias and changes in perceived intensity of verbal qualifiers effected by scale orientation. *Survey Research Methods*, *1*(2), 97–108.

Ibrahim, A. M. (2001). Differential responding to positive and negative items: The case of a negative item in a questionnaire for course and faculty evaluation. *Psychological Reports*, *88*(2), 497–500. doi:10.2466/pr0.2001.88.2.497 PMID:11351897

Ivanov, O. A., Ivanova, V. V., & Saltan, A. A. (2018). Likert scale questionnaires as an educational tool in teaching discrete mathematics. *International Journal of Mathematical Education in Science and Technology*, *49*(7), 1110–1118. doi:10.1080/0020739X.2017.1423121

Jacoby, J., & Matell, M. S. (1971). Three-point Likert scales are good enough. *JMR, Journal of Marketing Research*, *8*(4), 495–500. doi:10.1177/002224377100800414

Jamieson, S. (2004). Likert scales: How to (ab) use them. *Medical Education*, *38*(12), 1217–1218. doi:10.1111/j.1365-2929.2004.02012.x PMID:15566531

Johns, R. (2005). One size doesn't fit all: Selecting response scales for attitude items. *Journal of Elections, Public Opinion, and Parties*, *15*(2), 237–264. doi:10.1080/13689880500178849

Johnson, J. M., Bristow, D. N., & Schneider, K. C. (2004). Did you not understand the question or not? An investigation of negatively worded questions in survey research. *Journal of Applied Business Research*, *20*(1), 75–86.

Joshi, A., Kale, S., Chandel, S., & Pal, D. K. (2015). Likert scale: Explored and explained. *Current Journal of Applied Science and Technology*, 396-403.

Józsa, K., & Morgan, G. A. (2017). Reversed items in Likert scales: Filtering out invalid responders. *Journal of Psychological and Educational Research*, *25*(1), 7–25.

Kennedy, M., Campbell, I., & Chyung, Y. (2018). *Evidence-Based Survey Design: The Use of Ascending or Descending Order of Likert Response Options*. Academic Press.

Knapp, T. R. (1990). Treating ordinal scales as interval scales: An attempt to resolve the controversy. *Nursing Research*, *39*(2), 121–123. doi:10.1097/00006199-199003000-00019 PMID:2315066

Likert, R. (1932). A technique for the measurement of attitudes. *Archives de Psychologie*.

Maeda, H. (2015). Response option configuration of online administered Likert scales. *International Journal of Social Research Methodology*, *18*(1), 15–26. doi:10.1080/13645579.2014.885159

Malhotra, N. K. (2004). *Marketing Research an Applied Orientation* (Vol. 4). Pearson, Prentice Hall.

Mathews, B. P., & Shepherd, J. L. (2002). Dimensionality of Cook and Wall's (1980) British Organizational Commitment Scale revisited. *Journal of Occupational and Organizational Psychology*, *75*(3), 369–375. doi:10.1348/096317902320369767

Merritt, S. M. (2012). The two-factor solution to Allen and Meyer's (1990) Affective Commitment Scale: Effects of negatively worded items. *Journal of Business and Psychology, 27*(4), 421–436. doi:10.100710869-011-9252-3

Mircioiu, C., & Atkinson, J. (2017). A comparison of parametric and non-parametric methods applied to a Likert scale. *Pharmacy (Basel, Switzerland), 5*(2), 26. doi:10.3390/pharmacy5020026 PMID:28970438

Murray, J. (2013). Likert data: What to use, parametric or non-parametric? *International Journal of Business and Social Science, 4*(11).

Nicholls, M. E., Orr, C. A., Okubo, M., & Loftus, A. (2006). Satisfaction guaranteed: The effect of spatial biases on responses to Likert scales. *Psychological Science, 17*(12), 1027–1028. doi:10.1111/j.1467-9280.2006.01822.x PMID:17201782

Norman, G. (2010). Likert scales, levels of measurement and the "laws" of statistics. *Advances in Health Sciences Education: Theory and Practice, 15*(5), 625–632. doi:10.100710459-010-9222-y PMID:20146096

Nunnally, J. C. (1978). *Psychometric Theory*. Academic Press.

Pell, G. (2005). Use and misuse of Likert scales. *Medical Education, 39*(9), 970–970. doi:10.1111/j.1365-2929.2005.02237.x PMID:16150039

Preston, C. C., & Colman, A. M. (2000). Optimal number of response categories in rating scales: Reliability, validity, discriminating power, and respondent preferences. *Acta Psychologica, 104*(1), 1–15. doi:10.1016/S0001-6918(99)00050-5 PMID:10769936

Roszkowski, M., & Soven, M. (2010). Shifting gears: Consequences of including two negatively worded items in the middle of a positively worded questionnaire. *Assessment & Evaluation in Higher Education, 35*(1), 117–134. doi:10.1080/02602930802618344

Salazar, M. S. (2015). The dilemma of combining positive and negative items in scales. *Psicothema, 27*(2), 192–199. PMID:25927700

Sangthong, M. (2020). The Effect of the Likert Point Scale and Sample Size on the Efficiency of Parametric and Nonparametric Tests. *Thailand Statistician, 18*(1), 55–64.

Schriesheim, C. A., & Hill, K. D. (1981). Controlling acquiescence response bias by item reversals: The effect on questionnaire validity. *Educational and Psychological Measurement, 41*(4), 1101–1114. doi:10.1177/001316448104100420

Shimp, T., & Sharma, S. (1987). Consumer ethnocentrism: Construction and validation of the CETSCALE. *JMR, Journal of Marketing Research, 26*(August), 280–289. doi:10.1177/002224378702400304

Siegel, S. (1957). Nonparametric statistics. *The American Statistician, 11*(3), 13–19.

Stevens, S. S. (1946). On the theory of scales of measurement. *Science. New Series, 103*(2684), 677–680.

Sullivan, G. M., & Artino, A. R. Jr. (2013). Analyzing and interpreting data from Likert type scales. *Journal of Graduate Medical Education, 5*(4), 541–542. doi:10.4300/JGME-5-4-18 PMID:24454995

Turan, I., Şimşek, Ü., & Aslan, H. (2015). Eğitim araştırmalarında likert ölçeği ve likert tipi soruların kullanımı ve analizi. *Sakarya Üniversitesi Eğitim Fakültesi Dergisi*, (30), 186–203.

Velleman, P. F., & Wilkinson, L. (1993). Nominal, ordinal, interval, and ratio typologies are misleading. *The American Statistician*, *47*(1), 65–72.

Vickers, A. J. (2005). Parametric versus non-parametric statistics in the analysis of randomized trials with non-normally distributed data. *BMC Medical Research Methodology*, *5*(1), 35. doi:10.1186/1471-2288-5-35 PMID:16269081

Vigderhous, G. (1977). The level of measurement and "permissible" statistical analysis in social research. *Pacific Sociological Review*, *20*(1), 61–72. doi:10.2307/1388904

Wadgave, U., & Khairnar, M. R. (2016). Parametric tests for Likert scale: For and against. *Asian Journal of Psychiatry*, *24*, 67–68. doi:10.1016/j.ajp.2016.08.016 PMID:27931911

Weem, G. H., Onwuegbuzie, A. J., & Collins, K. M. T. (2006). The role of reading comprehension in responses to positively and negatively worded items on rating scales. *Evaluation and Research in Education*, *19*(1), 3–20. doi:10.1080/09500790608668322

Weems, G. H., & Onwuegbuzie, A. J. (2001). The impact of midpoint responses and reverse coding on survey data. *Measurement & Evaluation in Counseling & Development*, *34*(3), 166–176. doi:10.1080/07481756.2002.12069033

Weng, L., & Cheng, C. (2000). Effects of response order on Likert type scales. *Educational and Psychological Measurement*, *60*(6), 908–924. doi:10.1177/00131640021970989

Woods, C. M. (2006). Careless responding to reverse-worded items: Implications for confirmatory factory analysis. *Journal of Psychopathology and Behavioral Assessment*, *28*(3), 189–194. doi:10.100710862-005-9004-7

Zhang, X., & Savalei, V. (2016). Improving the factor structure of psychological scales: The Expanded format as an alternative to the Likert scale format. *Educational and Psychological Measurement*, *76*(3), 357–386. doi:10.1177/0013164415596421 PMID:27182074

ADDITIONAL READING

Batterton, K., & Hale, K. (2017). The Likert Scale What It Is and How to Use It. *Phalanx*, *50*(2), 32–39.

Bishop, P. A., & Herron, R. L. (2015). Use and misuse of the Likert item responses and other ordinal measures. *International Journal of Exercise Science*, *8*(3), 297. PMID:27182418

Brown, J. D. (2011). Likert items and scales of measurement. *Statistics*, *15*(1), 10–14.

De Winter, J. C., & Dodou, D. (2010). Five-point Likert items: T test versus Mann-Whitney-Wilcoxon. *Practical Assessment, Research & Evaluation*, *15*(11), 2.

Jamieson, S. (2004). Likert scales: How to (ab) use them. *Medical Education, 38*(12), 1217–1218. doi:10.1111/j.1365-2929.2004.02012.x PMID:15566531

Mircioiu, C., & Atkinson, J. (2017). A comparison of parametric and non-parametric methods applied to a Likert scale. *Pharmacy (Basel, Switzerland), 5*(2), 26. doi:10.3390/pharmacy5020026 PMID:28970438

Murray, J. (2013). Likert data: What to use, parametric or non-parametric? *International Journal of Business and Social Science, 4*(11).

Norman, G. (2010). Likert scales, levels of measurement and the "laws" of statistics. *Advances in Health Sciences Education: Theory and Practice, 15*(5), 625–632. doi:10.100710459-010-9222-y PMID:20146096

Pell, G. (2005). Use and misuse of Likert scales. *Medical Education, 39*(9), 970–970. doi:10.1111/j.1365-2929.2005.02237.x PMID:16150039

Wadgave, U., & Khairnar, M. R. (2016). Parametric tests for Likert scale: For and against. *Asian Journal of Psychiatry, 24*, 67–68. doi:10.1016/j.ajp.2016.08.016 PMID:27931911

KEY TERMS AND DEFINITIONS

Likert Type Scale: Likert scale is a method which was developed by Rensis Likert and used to measure participants' attitudes towards any issue.

Non-Parametic Test: In statistics, the analysis methods applied using mod, median etc. when the data unmeet certain criteria.

Parametric Test: The analysis methods applied using the mean and standard deviation, in case the data meet certain criteria, in statistics.

APPENDIX

Table 7. 5-point Likert type CETSCALE, one of the questionnaire forms were used in the study

	Kesinlikle katılmıyorum	Katılmıyorum	Ne katılıyorum ne katılmıyorum	Katılıyorum	Kesinlikle katılıyorum
Her zaman en doğrusu Türk ürünlerini satın almaktır.	1	2	3	4	5
Bir Türk yabancı ürün satın almamalıdır, çünkü bu Türk ekonomisine zarar verir.	1	2	3	4	5
Yabancı ürün satın alan Türk tüketiciler diğer Türklerin işsiz kalmasından sorumludur.	1	2	3	4	5
Yabancı ürün satın almak doğru değildir, çünkü bu Türkleri işsiz bırakır.	1	2	3	4	5
Uzun vadede benim için daha maliyetli olsa da Türk mallarını satın almayı tercih ederim.	1	2	3	4	5
Çok gerekli olmadıkça diğer ülkelerden ürün satın alınmamalıdır.	1	2	3	4	5
Başka ülkelerin mallarını satın alarak onları zenginleştirmek yerine Türk mallarını satın almalıyız.	1	2	3	4	5
Gerçek bir Türk her zaman Türk markalı ürünleri satın alır.	1	2	3	4	5
Yabancıların Türkiye'de ürün satmalarına izin verilmemelidir.	1	2	3	4	5
Bir Türk her zaman ithal ürünler yerine Türk ürünlerini tercih etmelidir.	1	2	3	4	5
Benim için Türk yapımı ürünler her zaman önceliklidir.	1	2	3	4	5
Türkiye'ye girişini azaltmak için yabancı ürünlerin vergileri artırılmalıdır.	1	2	3	4	5
Sadece ülkemizde üretilmeyen ürünler yabancı ülkelerden alınmalıdır.	1	2	3	4	5
Yabancı markalı ürün satın almak Türkiye karşıtlığıdır.	1	2	3	4	5
Türk ürünlerini satın alarak Türkiye'nin üretimi artırılmalıdır.	1	2	3	4	5
Sadece Türkiye'de üretilmeyen ürünler ithal edilmelidir.	1	2	3	4	5
Yabancı ürünlerin ithalatı engellenmelidir.	1	2	3	4	5

Chapter 21
Latent Fingerprint Enhancement Based on EDTV Model

Shadi M. S. Hilles
(iD) https://orcid.org/0000-0002-2605-9524
Istanbul Okan University, Turkey

Abdilahi Deria Liban
Hargeisa University, Somalia

Abdullah M. M. Altrad
Al-Madinah International University, Malaysia

Yousef A. Baker El-Ebiary
Universiti Sultan Zainal Abidin, Malaysia

Mohanad M. Hilles
University College of Applied Science, Palestine

ABSTRACT

The chapter presents latent fingerprint enhancement technique for enforcement agencies to identify criminals. There are many challenges in the area of latent fingerprinting due to poor-quality images, which consist of unclear ridge structure and overlapping patterns with structure noise. Image enhancement is important to suppress several different noises for improving accuracy of ridge structure. The chapter presents a combination of edge directional total variation model, EDTV, and quality image enhancement with lost minutia re-construction, RMSE, for evaluation and performance in the proposed algorithm. The result shows the average of three different image categories which are extracted from the SD7 dataset, and the assessments are good, bad, and ugly, respectively. The result of RMSE before and after enhancement shows the performance ratio of the proposed method is better for latent fingerprint images compared to bad and ugly images while there is not much difference with performance of bad and ugly.

DOI: 10.4018/978-1-7998-6985-6.ch021

INTRODUCTION

Fingerprint as one of Biometrics types is widely used in these days. It's one of the most frequently used biometrics to identify individuals and authenticate their identity. It has been used for the recognition for more than 100 years (GALBALLY et al., 2018). It's commonly categorized into three different categories as presented by (Jiangyang *et al.*, 2013) which are rolled, plain and latent fingerprints. The process that obtained in each category is different from the rest. For instance, rolled is achieved by rolling the finger from one side to the other with the purpose of capturing all the ridge particulars. The plain fingerprint is accomplished by pressing the fingertip onto a flat surface. The last category, Latent fingerprints normally lifted from object surfaces that were touched by criminal in the crime scenes.

Biometric System Phases

The literature on biometric phases (Gupta *et al*, 2020) reported that biometric identification system contains two different fundamental phases. The first phase is enrolment while the second is recognition.

In the first phase, a sensor normally gathers the biometric data from which a set of features are extracted and kept in a database along with the individual's identity for instance name, identification number, and birthdates. In the second phase, the identity of the person is either confirmed (verification) or determined (identification). This is achieved by collecting the biometric data, extracting the same features and comparing them to the features stored in the database.

From this comparison, similarity score is produced to make a decision to whether the two sets of features came from the same person or not. The following figure 1 shows an overview of a biometric system phases.

The above figure 1 present an overview of a biometric system phases that consist enrolment and recognition. The process in each phase is clearly defined. Another study documented by (Sabhanayagam *et al.*, 2018) demonstrate that all biometric systems comprises of three fundamental elements as per the followings: -

Enrollment: It is the process of gathering biometric samples from an individual. This person is known as the enrollee, and the succeeding generation of his/her template.

Templates: it can be defined as the data representing the enrollee's biometric.

Fingerprint is significant used method for identification systems which is a unique feature such as ridges and valleys where is ridge is a collection of minutiae points included core points as per discussed and mentioned on Menon, et al (2015) and within fingerprint classes as illustrated on figure 2 there are a common three structures which are Arch, Loop and Whorl

Structures Noise in Latent Fingerprint Images

According to (Paulino *et al.*, 2013) the main difference between latent fingerprint images and rolled or plain fingerprints is the presence of structured noise in latent fingerprint images. We can categorize the structured noise that exists in latent fingerprints images into six main categories including arch, line, character, speckle, stain and others. The following figure 3 presents the six types of structured noise.

Based on the above figure 3 structured noise can be classified into six main categories as in the elaboration below:

Figure 1. Overview of a biometric system

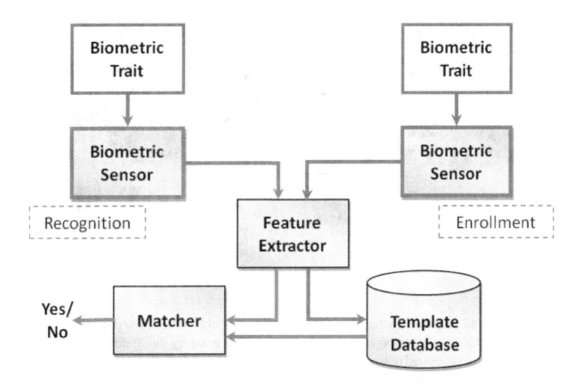

Figure 2. Three Classes of fingerprints

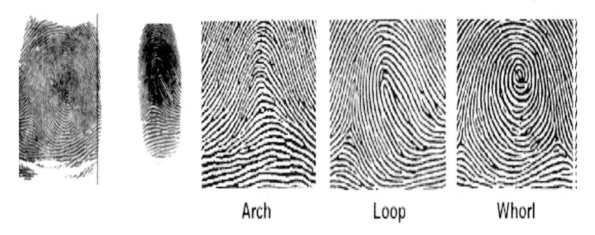

Figure 3. Six types of structured noise

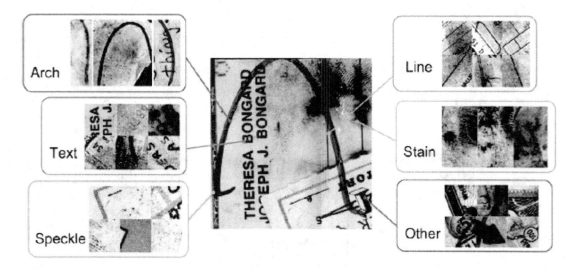

- Arch: The arch is manually marked by crime-scene investigators to show the possible existence of latent fingerprints in the region encircled by the arch. This category (arch) noise is viewed as the simplest type of structured noise.
- Line: The line noise appears in form of a single line or multiple parallel lines. A single line is often perceived and removed using methods based on the Hough transform (Mukhopadhyay *et al*, 2015). Multiple parallel lines can be confused with fingerprints more easily since they share quite a few common features.
- Character: This is one of the most common types of structured noise in latent fingerprints. Characters may appear in various font types, sizes and brightness that can be either handwritten or typed.
- Stain: This type of latent fingerprint noise is generated when the fingerprint was inadvertently smeared on a wet or dirty surface. Stain noise often appears in spongy shape with inhomogeneous brightness.
- Speckle: Compare to lines and characters noises, speckle noise tends to contain tiny-scale structures, which are either regular such as clusters of small dots or random like ink and dust speckles.
- Others: A latent fingerprint images could comprise other types of structured noise. For example, arrows, signs, etc. Being similar to arch noise and character noise, they usually consist of smooth surfaces with sharp edges.

Usually the line, character and speckle noise groups often come into view when the latent fingerprint is lifted from the surface of a text document like maps, newspapers and checks. For latent fingerprint enhancement, the major challenge lies in how to successfully divide latent fingerprints, the relatively weak signal, from all categories of the noise in the background, which is often the dominant image component. Besides, extra complexity comes when structured noise overlaps with the fingerprint signal.

Latent Fingerprint Enhancement Techniques

The literature on fingerprint enhancement shows variety of approaches has been proposed to solve the issue of quality of fingerprint images. Previous research has shown the application of Gabor filter in fingerprint enhancement as proposed by (Zahedi et al, 2015). In this technique, the local ridge orientation and frequency are firstly approximated in every pixel. After that a Gabor filter is tuned to the local orientation and frequency and applied on the image pixel to suppress the unwanted noise and improve the clarity of ridge structure. The major drawback of this technique is that it needs consistent estimation of local ridge orientation and frequency. This process is challenging for poor quality fingerprint especially latent fingerprint images. Several techniques has been proposed also including methods based on spatial domain, the significant classification of fingerprint enhancement and identification problems such as lack of reliable minutia extraction (Khan et al, 2016) frequency domain, development fingerNET based on convolutional neural network CNN which given significant performance where is CNN extracted fingerprint features and remove structure noise in term of enhance fingerprint by multi task learning (Li et al, 2018)

It is highly important to highlight that the above discussed techniques were mainly proposed for the rolled and plain fingerprints and little attentions have been given to latent fingerprint images. Thus, these mechanisms don't work well on latent fingerprint due to the poor-quality latent fingerprint with smudged, blurred and broken ridge structures. Furthermore, latent fingerprint is usually overlapped with various types of structured noise such as arch, line, character and handwriting. As result, reliable estimation of local ridge orientation and frequency is a difficult task in latent fingerprint. Therefore, the above approaches may not be practical in this situation.

For several years' great effort has been devoted to the study of plain and rolled fingerprint enhancement while there has been little systematic analysis of latent fingerprint image enhancement/pre-processing. Its relatively new area requiring research in order to put on firmer foundations, using extraction of minutia points, fingerprint enhancement consider ridge pattern which is essential pre-processing step thus needs to reduce false positive and negative detection rates (Svoboda, 2017).

Table 1 illustrated the most relevant work of latent fingerprint enhancement, the summaries of using techniques and limitation, and shows the advantages of using Gabor filter and EDTV.

Methodology

Research methodology adopted in designing the improved model for latent fingerprint recognition/matching. This part is organized into seven sections. It begins by highlighting the problem situations and the respective solution concepts and follows by an overview of the research methodology. also discusses the SD27 latent fingerprint dataset used in this study. Design considerations for improving latent fingerprint matching are explained. The metrics for evaluating the performance of the model are given towards the end of the part together with the methodology for results analysis and validation. Finally, the summary of the chapter is concluded.

Table 2 shows the main problem of this chapter and its solution concept based on hybrid technique of latent fingerprint enhancement, and as per discussion in the literature review, image enhancement is required for latent fingerprint images to improve the accuracy of the proceeding steps such as latent fingerprint image segmentation and matching. The main goal of latent fingerprint enhancement is to improve the clarity of the ridge structures while the major challenging problem for latent fingerprint

Table 1. Latent Fingerprint Enhancement Techniques

No	Author	Title	Technique and Advantages	Limitation
1	Yoon *et al*, 2010	On latent fingerprint enhancement	Gabor filter method that uses STFT method has been introduced to attain several orientation elements for each block.	Requires region of interest (ROI) singular points and uses fixed ridge frequency
2	Feng *et al*, 2011	Separating overlapped fingerprints	Suggested technique to guess orientation field. The technique applies the previous knowledge of fingerprint ridge structure. "It represented by a dictionary of reference orientation patches and the compatibility constraint between neighboring orientations patches".	Requires region of interest (ROI) and uses fixed ridge frequency
4	(Zhang *et al.* 2013)	Adaptive directional total-variation model for latent fingerprint segmentation	The authors additionally recommended an adaptive directional total variation (ADTV) model. They have combined both local orientation and scale of latent fingerprint enhancement and segmentation.	Relies on orientation field and orientation coherence estimation. One of the drawbacks is that, not an easy task to consistently guess the local parameters such as ridge orientation and scale of adaptive total variation (ADTV) model for poor quality latent fingerprint images. Furthermore, the noise corrupted regions are not restored as well. In addition to that, the extracted fingerprint pattern is usually very weak. Therefore, this will limit the performance of latent fingerprint matching.
5	Qian, P., Li, A., & Liu, M. (2019)	Latent fingerprint enhancement based on DenseUNet	A Gabor filter	Needs consistent estimation of frequency and local ridge orientation. This is normally very challenge for poor quality fingerprint such as latent fingerprint images.
8	Feng et al. 2013	Orientation field estimation for latent fingerprint enhancement	Robust method to estimate orientation field	One of the drawbacks is the fixed ridge frequency.
9	Liu, S., Liu, M., & Yang, Z. (2017)	Sparse coding-based orientation estimation for latent fingerprints	Based on ridge orientation and scale	It is not an easy task to reliably estimate the local parameters like ridge orientation and scale of adaptive total variation model for latent fingerprint images of poor quality. Furthermore, the noise corrupted regions are not restored as well. In addition to that, the extracted fingerprint pattern is usually very weak. Therefore, this will limit the performance of latent fingerprint matching.
10	Cao *et al*, 2014	Segmentation and Enhancement of Latent Fingerprints: A Coarse to Fine Ridge Structure Dictionary	This technique is based on dictionary. It allows reliable estimation of frequency and ridge orientation. It facilitates the automatic segmentation and enhancement of latent fingerprints. Latent fingerprint enhancement mechanism, that effectively integrates the total variation model and the multi-scale patch, based sparse representation for eliminating noises and enlightening the clarity of ridge structure has been recommended.	There are two drawbacks in this approach. Foremost, in the regions of high curvature, the assumption of a single dominant ridge orientation is not valid. Consequently, the Gabor filters with fixed orientation will be likely to destroy the ridge structure and lead to spurious ridge arte facts. Secondly, though the Gabor filtering with correct orientation and frequency parameters can work well to enhance the ridge clarity, it fails to restore the ridge structure destroyed by heavy structured noises that exist in latent fingerprint images. The recommended mechanism can be further enhanced by using of the global ridge structure through global optimization for the low-quality latent fingerprints. "Although reliable estimation of ridge orientation and frequency can improve the performance of latent fingerprint enhancement, there are two inherent limitations in these methods. First, in the regions of high curvature, the assumption of a single dominant ridge orientation is not valid. As a result, the Gabor filters with fixed orientation will be likely to destroy the ridge structure and lead to spurious ridge artefacts. Second, although the Gabor filtering with correct orientation and frequency parameters can work well to enhance the ridge clarity, it fails to restore the ridge structure destroyed by heavy structured noises"
11	T.Revathy, 2014	Automatic Latent Fingerprint Segmentation based on Orientation and Frequency Features	Orientation and frequency features based latent fingerprint segmentation.	The technique can be further improved by including other features like ridge types, curvature minutia types and position of minutia points.
12	Zhang *et al*, 2013	Adaptive directional total-variation model for latent fingerprint segmentation	Proposed adaptive total variation model to remove the structured noises for latent fingerprint segmentation, authors further proposed an adaptive directional total variation (ADTV) model by integrating the local orientation and scale for fingerprint segmentation and enhancement"	One of the drawbacks of these techniques is that, it's not easy task to consistently estimate the local parameters such as ridge orientation and scale of adaptive total variation model for latent fingerprint images of poor quality. Furthermore, the noise corrupted regions are not restored and the extracted fingerprint pattern is usually very weak. Thus, this reduces and limits the performance of latent fingerprint matching.
13	Liu, M., Liu, S., & Yan, W. (2018).	Latent fingerprint segmentation based on ridge density and orientation consistency	Uses ridge orientation tensor and local Fourier analysis.	Does not generate the desired output for the entire fingerprint since some unwanted signals will be extracted for the noise region.

Table 2. Summary of problem situation and solution concepts

No	Problem situation	Solution concept
1	Low quality of latent fingerprint images captured in crime scenes	Apply hybrid technique based on edge adaptive directional total variation model with lost minutia reconstruction technique to enhance the quality of images.

enhancement is to eliminate a variety of types of image noises while consistently restoring the corrupted regions and enhancing the ridge clarity. Thus, this chapter discusses the result of the proposed solution of the latent fingerprint enhancement which is based on edge adaptive directional total variation model with lost minutia reconstruction technique to enhance the quality of latent fingerprint images.

Contains two main research activities which concern on latent fingerprint image de-noising and lost minutia construction.

Latent fingerprint image enhancement receives an input image, applies set of intermediate on the input image and finally outputs the enhanced image.

Figure 4. Latent fingerprint enhancement Research Framework

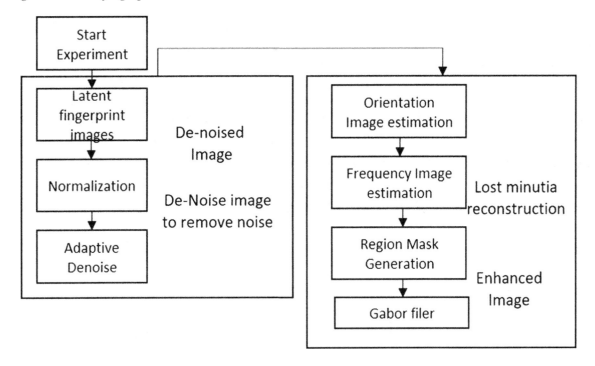

Figure 4 proposed hybrid latent fingerprint enhancement a gray-level latent fingerprint image, where is I, is defined as $N \times N$ matrix, where $I(i, j)$ represents the intensity of a pixel at the *ith* row *jth* column. The mean and variance of gray level latent fingerprint image I are defined as

$$M\left(^{\mathrm{T}})\hspace-0.2em\right. = \frac{1}{N^2}\sum_{i=0}^{N-1}\sum_{j=0}^{N-1}\mathrm{I}\left(i,j\right)\,and \tag{1}$$

$$V\,AR\left(\mathrm{I}\right) = \frac{1}{N^2}\sum_{i=0}^{N-1}\sum_{j=0}^{N-1}(\mathrm{I}\left(i,j\right)-M(\mathrm{I}))^2 \tag{2}$$

Equation 1 and 2 shows the orientation image, ϑ, is defined as $\mathrm{N}\times\mathrm{N}$ image, where $\vartheta\left(i,j\right)$ represents the local ridge orientation at pixel $\left(i,j\right)$. Local ridge orientation is usually specified for a block rather than every pixel, an image is divided into set of $\omega\times\omega$ non overlapping blocks and a single local ridge orientation is defined in each block.

A frequency image, $\mathcal{F}$, is defined as $\mathrm{N}\times\mathrm{N}$ image, where $\mathcal{F}\left(i,j\right)$ represents the local ridge frequency which is defined as the frequency of the ridge and furrow structures in a local neighborhood along a direction normal to the local ridge orientation.

The region mask $\mathcal{R}$ is defined as $\mathrm{N}\times\mathrm{N}$ image with $\mathcal{R}\left(i,j\right)$ indicating the category of the pixel. Pixel could be either:

1. non-ridge-and-furrow (unrecoverable) pixel with value 0 or
2. ridge and furrow recoverable pixel with value 1

Normalization: input latent fingerprint image is normalized so that it has pre-specified mean and variance to reduce the variations in gray level values along ridges and valleys. This is to facilitate the subsequent processing steps. The normalization process specifies mean and variance. Let, $\mathrm{I}\left(i,j\right)$ denote the gray-level value at pixel $\left(i,j\right)$, M and VAR denote the estimated mean and variance of I respectively, and $G\left(i,j\right)$ denote the normalized gray-level value at pixel $\left(i,j\right)$. The normalized image is defined as follows where $M0$ and $V\,AR\,0$ are the desired mean and variance values respectively, it's a pixel wise operation and does not change the clarity of ridge and furrow structures as shown on equation 3.

$$G\left(x,y\right)=\begin{cases} M0+\sqrt{\dfrac{V\,AR\,0\,(\mathrm{I}\left(x,y\right)-M)^2}{V\,AR}},if\,\mathrm{I}\left(x,y\right)>M \\[2em] M0-\sqrt{\dfrac{V\,AR\,0\,(\mathrm{I}\left(x,y\right)-M)^2}{V\,AR}},otherwise \end{cases} \tag{3}$$

Adaptive de-noise based on Edge Directional Total Variation (EDTV) model. It is used to effectively remove the noise of latent fingerprint images. The model is adaptive to image edge direction and capable of handling images with several dominant directions. To recover an image f(x,y) from a given noisy image i(x, y) Rudin *et al* proposed the Total variation Model which can be summarized in the following mathematical expression:

$$E_{TV}\left(f\right) = \lambda \int \Omega \mid \nabla f \mid d\Omega + \frac{1}{2} \int \Omega \left(f - 1\right)^2 d\Omega \tag{4}$$

Bayram and Kamasak further improved the model by proposing directional total variation model for the image demonizing (DTV).

$$E_{DTV} = \lambda DTV_{\alpha,\theta(f)+\frac{1}{2}} \int \Omega \left(f - 1\right)^2 d\Omega \tag{5}$$

Equation 4 and 5 illustrated the comparison between total variation and directional total variation where is DTV model enhances the diffusion along the direction θ when the dominant direction in an image coincides with the direction θ. It's necessary to make the parameter θ spatially varying throughout the entire image when there are several dominant directions in the image. Thus, Hua Zhang, and Yuanquan Wang proposed Edge Directional Total Variation Model (EDTV) which supports spatially varying θ(x,y) based on the edge direction of the image as follows:

$$\left(\cos(\theta(x, y, \sin\left(\theta\left(x, y\right)\right)\right) = n_1\left(x, y\right), n_2\left(x, y\right) \tag{6}$$

Equation 6 shows cosine of edge direction, Where n_1 (x,y), n_2 (x,y) is the edge direction. The DTV model in 2 with θ(x,y) in 3 is refered to as EADT Model. In this way the EADTV model is adaptive and enhances the diffusion along the image edge direction. The direction of the edge in latent fingerprint noisy images n_1 (x,y), n_2 (x,y) is very important and should be calculated in advance (n_1 (x,y), n_2 (x,y)) = (-gy, gx) / g^2_x + g^2_y. Where (gy, gx) is the gradient factor of g(x,y) and g(x,y) is a smoothed version of I(x,y) using a guising filter.

RESULT AND EXPERIMENT

Presents the result of RMSE of good latent fingerprint images in SD27 Dataset. The average of RMSE for the total 85 good images in SD27 dataset is 0.018373 In addition to that, the result of RMSE of latent fingerprint bad images is slightly lower.

Table 3. RMSE Average of Image categories

Image Category	RMSE Average
Good	0.018373
Bad	0.022287
Ugly	0.023199

Table 3 shows the average of RMSE of three image categories is compared. The following figure 5 present the comparison of RMSE for SD27 image categories.

Table 4. ANOVA Test for RMSE

	Sum of Squares	df	Mean Square	F	Sig.
Between Groups	.001	2	.001	21.208	.000
Within Groups	.007	252	.000		
Total	.008	254			

Figure 5. RMSE comparisons for SD27 Image Categories

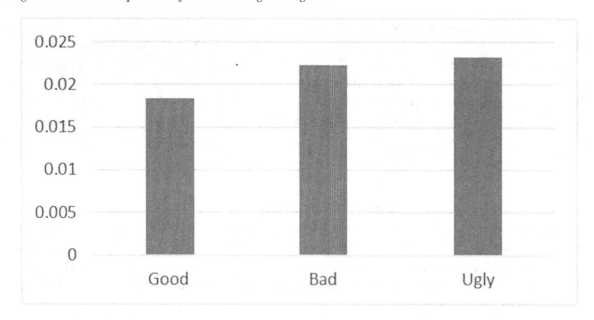

From figure 5, the comparison of RMSE for SD27 image categories has been illustrated. The lesser the number of RMSE the better the performance of the result. Therefore, the proposed solution performs better for good, bad and ugly images respectively.

It's important to highlight as well that ANOVA test is used to observe the differences of performance between the latent fingerprint image groups, good, bad, and ugly images available in SD27 data set.

The table 4 shows the output of the ANOVA of RMSE for three categories analysis and whether we have a statistically significant difference between our means. We can see that the significance level is 0.00 (p = .00), which is below 0.05. Therefore, there is a statistically significant difference in the mean length of RMSE for different categories of the images (good, bad and ugly). This is great to know. However, we do not know which of the specific categories differed since the result doesn't indicate which of the three categories differ from one another. Thus, we can find this out in the multiple comparisons table which contains the results of post-hoc tests as in the following table 5.

The above tables presented the comparison of RMSE for different categories of images. The result shows that the proposed technique for the latent fingerprint enhancements performs better for good images for an average RMSE equal to 0.1837301 while there is no significant different between the bad and ugly images 0,2228729 and 0.2319876 respectively

Figure 6 presented the RMSE average of good original and enhanced latent fingerprint images.

Table 5. Homogeneous Subsets for RMSE

Image Category	N	Subset for alpha = 0.05	
		1	2
Good	85	.01837301	
Bad	85		.02228729
Ugly	85		.02319876
Sig.		1.000	.480

Figure 6. Image category mean comparison of RMSE

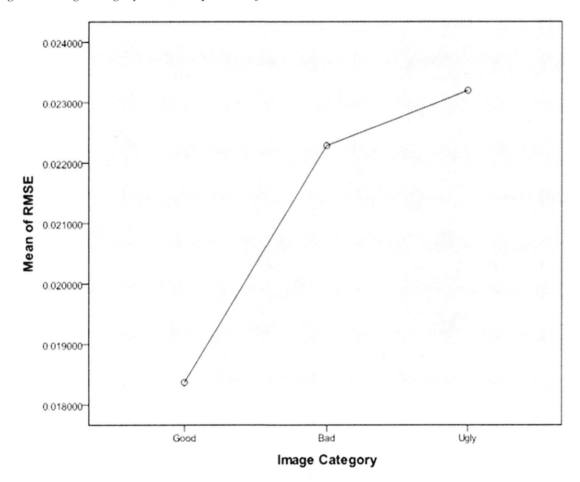

Table 6. RMSE average of Good Images before and after enhancement

Image Category	RMSE Average before enhancement	RMSE average after enhancement
Good	0.048091	0.018373

Table 6 illustrated RMSE average of good images before and after enhancement, the result shows advantages of proposed model for good images category.

Figure 7. RMSE averages of good images before and after enhancement

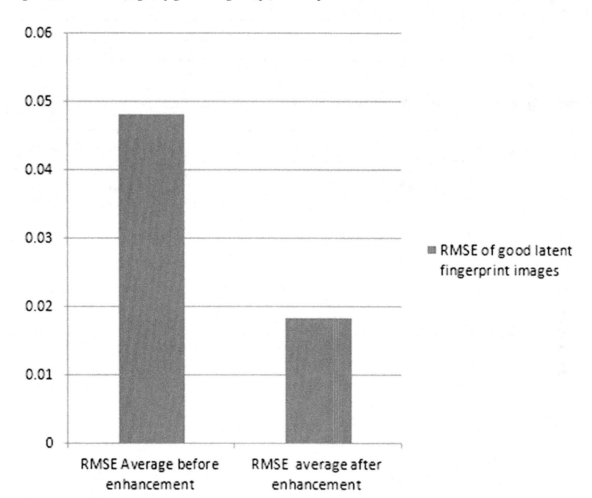

Figure 7 shows the RMSE average of good latent fingerprint after and before enhancement and the comparison for ugly,

To measure the performance ratio of the proposed method, the result after and before enhancement has been compared. Figure 8 presents the RMSE comparison of the different categories before and after enhancement.

Figure 8. RMSE Image categories comparison

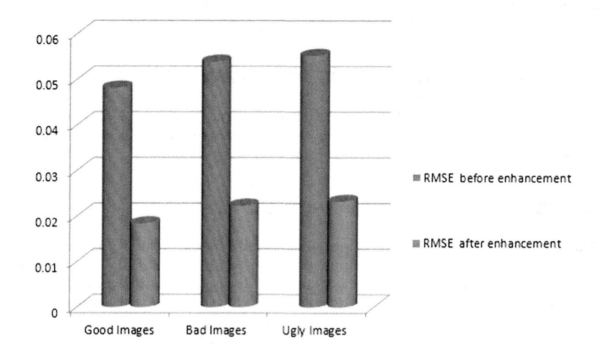

CONCLUSION

Latent fingerprint image quality is an important factor in the performance of minutiae extraction and matching algorithms. Being collected from crime scene, latent fingerprint is often mixed with other components such as structured noise or other fingerprints. The poor image quality of latent fingerprints has a high effect on the accuracy of latent fingerprint Enhancement

Image enhancement is required for latent fingerprint images to improve the accuracy of the proceeding steps. The main goal of a latent fingerprint enhancement is to improve the clarity of the ridge structures while the major challenging problem for latent fingerprint enhancement is to remove various types of image noises while reliably restoring the corrupted regions and enhancing the ridge clarity. Even though considerable progress done in both rolled and plain fingerprint images, latent fingerprint is challenging problem and existing issue in the current research. Rolled and plain fingerprints are obtained in an at-tended mode so that they are normally of good visual quality while latent fingerprint is collected from crime scenes and usually mixed with other components such as structured noise and other fingerprints. Many of the existing state of the art techniques suffer limitations such as low matching accuracy and high false alarm rate. This is due to the existence of poor-quality images in latent fingerprint with unclear ridge structure and various overlapping patterns together with presence of structured noise.

The chapter has designed latent fingerprint enhancement hybrid technique which is combination of Edge Directional Total Variation Model (EDTV) and quality image enhancement with lost minutia reconstruction techniques based on reliable frequency estimation and orientation field. The objective is to improve the quality of the latent fingerprint image by enhancing the latent fingerprint image.

To evaluate the result of latent fingerprint enhancement for the proposed technique RMSE, the result after enhancement achieved RMSE average 0.018373, 0.022287, and 0.023199 for the three different image categories available in SD27 data set good, bad and ugly images respectively.

NEW APPROACH FOR LATENT FINGERPRINT ENHANCEMENT

Hybrid technique which is combination of Edge Directional Total Variation Model (EDTV) and quality image enhancement with lost minutia reconstruction techniques based on reliable frequency estimation and orientation field has been proposed to enhance the latent fingerprint images.

FUTURE RESEARCH AND RECOMMENDATION

The effectiveness of the proposed latent fingerprint enhancement presented is highly related to the accuracy of the estimation of frequency and orientation. If the estimation is not reliable it may lead to poor enhancement. Based on the experiment conducted, it's observed that the proposed techniques perform well for the good latent fingerprint images compare to bad and ugly images. Robust techniques are needed for the enhancement of bad and ugly images which may lead to better matching for latent fingerprint. The proposed techniques did not take into account for the overlapped latent fingerprint images. Research on integrating a method that solves the issue of overlapped latent fingerprints would be very beneficial to further improve the proposed solution.

REFERENCES

Cao, K., Liu, E., & Jain, A. K. (2014). Segmentation and Enhancement of Latent Fingerprints: A Coarse to Fine RidgeStructure Dictionary. *IEEE Transactions on Pattern Analysis and Machine Intelligence*, *36*(9), 1847–1859. doi:10.1109/TPAMI.2014.2302450 PMID:26352236

Chen, F., Feng, J., Jain, A. K., Zhou, J., & Zhang, J. (2011). Separating overlapped fingerprints. *IEEE Transactions on Information Forensics and Security*, *6*(2), 346–359. doi:10.1109/TIFS.2011.2114345

Feng, J. Z., & Jain, A. K. (2013, April). Orientation field estimation for latent fingerprint enhancement. *IEEE Transactions on Pattern Analysis and Machine Intelligence*, *35*(4), 925–940. doi:10.1109/TPAMI.2012.155 PMID:22826508

Galbally, J., Haraksim, R., & Beslay, L. (2018). A study of age and ageing in fingerprint biometrics. *IEEE Transactions on Information Forensics and Security*, *14*(5), 1351–1365. doi:10.1109/TIFS.2018.2878160

Gupta, R., Khari, M., Gupta, D., & Crespo, R. G. (2020). Fingerprint image enhancement and reconstruction using the orientation and phase reconstruction. *Information Sciences*, *530*, 201–218. doi:10.1016/j.ins.2020.01.031

Khan, M. A., Khan, T. M., Bailey, D. G., & Kong, Y. (2016). A spatial domain scar removal strategy for fingerprint image enhancement. *Pattern Recognition*, *60*, 258–274. doi:10.1016/j.patcog.2016.05.015

Krish, R. P., Fierrez, J., Ramos, D., Alonso-Fernandez, F., & Bigun, J. (2019). Improving automated latent fingerprint identification using extended minutia types. *Information Fusion*, *50*, 9–19. doi:10.1016/j.inffus.2018.10.001

Li, J., Feng, J., & Kuo, C. C. J. (2018). Deep convolutional neural network for latent fingerprint enhancement. *Signal Processing Image Communication*, *60*, 52–63. doi:10.1016/j.image.2017.08.010

Liban, A., & Hilles, S. M. (2018, July). Latent Fingerprint Enhancement Based on Directional Total Variation Model with Lost Minutiae Reconstruction. In *2018 International Conference on Smart Computing and Electronic Enterprise (ICSCEE)* (pp. 1-5). IEEE. 10.1109/ICSCEE.2018.8538417

Liu, M., Liu, S., & Yan, W. (2018). Latent fingerprint segmentation based on ridge density and orientation consistency. *Security and Communication Networks*, *2018*, 2018. doi:10.1155/2018/4529652

Liu, S., Liu, M., & Yang, Z. (2017). Sparse coding-based orientation estimation for latent fingerprints. *Pattern Recognition*, *67*, 164–176. doi:10.1016/j.patcog.2017.02.012

Menon, R. R., Sukhadiya, H., & Patel, J. (2015). Standalone USB Flash to USB Flash. *Data Transfer*, ●●●, 6936–6941.

Mukhopadhyay, P., & Chaudhuri, B. B. (2015). A survey of Hough Transform. *Pattern Recognition*, *48*(3), 993–1010. doi:10.1016/j.patcog.2014.08.027

Porwik, P. (2010). *The Modern Techniques of Latent Fingerprint Imaging*. IEEE. doi:10.1109/CISIM.2010.5643695

Qian, P., Li, A., & Liu, M. (2019, June). Latent fingerprint enhancement based on DenseUNet. In *2019 International Conference on Biometrics (ICB)* (pp. 1-6). IEEE.

Revathy, T., Pramila, G., Adhiraja, A., & Askerunisa, A. (2014, April). Automatic Latent Fingerprint Segmentation based on Orientation and Frequency Features. In *2014 International Conference on Communication and Signal Processing* (pp. 1192-1196). IEEE. 10.1109/ICCSP.2014.6950029

Sabhanayagam, T., Venkatesan, V. P., & Senthamaraikannan, K. (2018). A comprehensive survey on various biometric systems. *International Journal of Applied Engineering Research: IJAER*, *13*(5), 2276–2297.

Svoboda, J., Monti, F., & Bronstein, M. M. (2017, October). Generative convolutional networks for latent fingerprint reconstruction. In *2017 IEEE International Joint Conference on Biometrics (IJCB)* (pp. 429-436). IEEE. 10.1109/BTAS.2017.8272727

Yoon, S., Feng, J., & Jain, A. K. (2010). On Latent Fingerprint Enhancement. *Proc. SPIE Biometric Technology for Human Identification VII*.

Zahedi, M., & Ghadi, O. R. (2015). Combining Gabor filter and FFT for fingerprint enhancement based on a regional adaption method and automatic segmentation. *Signal, Image and Video Processing*, *9*(2), 267–275. doi:10.100711760-013-0436-3

Zhang, J. R. L.-C. (2013). Adaptive Directional Total-Variation Model for. IEEE Transactions on Information Forensics And Security, 8.

Zhang, J., Lai, R., & Kuo, C. C. J. (2013). Adaptive directional total-variation model for latent fingerprint segmentation. *IEEE Transactions on Information Forensics and Security*, 8(8), 1261–1273. doi:10.1109/TIFS.2013.2267491

Zhang, R. L., & Kuo, C. J. (2013, August). Adaptive directional total-variation model for latent fingerprint segmentation. *IEEE Transactions on Information Forensics and Security*, 8(8), 1261–1273. doi:10.1109/TIFS.2013.2267491

Chapter 22
The Business, Societal, and Enterprise Architecture Framework:
An Artificial Intelligence-, Data Sciences-, and Big Data-Based Approach

Antoine Trad
https://orcid.org/0000-0002-4199-6970
IBISTM, France

ABSTRACT

In this chapter, the author presents an artificial intelligence (AI)-based generic concept for decision making using data science. The applied holistic mathematical model for AI (AHMM4AI) focuses on data and access management. A decisive business decision in a business transformation process of a traditional business environment into an automated AI-based business environment is the capacity of the decision-making system and the profile of the business transformation manager (BTM, or simply the manager). The manager and his team are supported by a holistic framework. The role of data science and the needed data modelling techniques are essential for managing data models in a transformation project. For that reason, the development of the big data for AI (BGD4AI) is an essential start.

INTRODUCTION

The success of a *Project* depends on how an Enterprise Architecture for AI (EA4AI), data architecture and modelling activities are synchronized (IMD, 2015).

That is why the implementation of such *Project*s requires significant knowledge of data architecture, implementation and modelling techniques. The main GAIP mechanisms are: 1) generic data architecture; 2) implementation interfaces; and 3) data modelling is a part of the Selection management, Architecture-modelling, Control-monitoring, Decision-making, Training management and Project management

DOI: 10.4018/978-1-7998-6985-6.ch022

Figure 1. Framework's cycles and the data access block

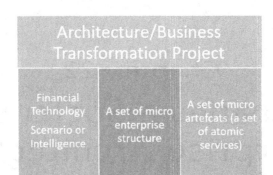

Framework (SmAmCmDmTmPmF, for simplification in further text the term *TRADf* (that stands for the Transformation, Research, Architecture and Development framework) will be used), that supports the *Project*'s activities. As shown in Figure 1, the Data Sciences Integration for Artificial Intelligence (DSI4AI) interacts with all the enterprise's (or simply an Entity) architecture phases, using the data Building Blocks for AI (dBB4AI) or the holistic brick (Trad & Kalpić, 2020a). The chapter is based on complex framework and it is just an extension to it and it includes many subdomains. This is the case of all cross functional and holistic ones. The DSI4AI explains, describes the basics of AI to support the GAIP based transformation project. Such projects are complex undertakings, which are based on the selection and DSI4AI based classification and weightings of the most important critical success factors and areas, which are used as global variables in the author's specialized transformation framework. Where in this chapter the main subject is DSI4AI for GAIP's integration. The GAIP for transformations projects. Such transformation projects can be applied to various Application and Problem Domains (APD), like finance, geopolitics, intelligent cities and other. Such APDs need a specific AI that is based on DSI4AI and AHMM4AI.

BACKGROUND

GAIP and DSI4AI are based on EA4AI, various AI fields, data architecture and modelling technologies. Where the DS4AI should include:

- A data foundational model, or a set of classes/entities, which can be integrated in various architectures; that use calls to various types of algorithms.
- The use of atomic Building Blocks for AI (aBB4AI) concept; which corresponds to an autonomous set of classes.
- The use of a Natural Programming Language for AI (NLP4AI) for development of data interfaces.

The author's long years global research topic's and final Research Question (RQ) (hypothesis #1-1) is: "Which business transformation manager's characteristics and which type of support should be assured for the implementation phase of a business transformation project?" The targeted business domain is any business environment that uses: 1) complex technologies; and 2) frequent transformation iterations. For this phase of research, the sub-question is: "What is the impact of the BGD4AI on EA4AI and *Projects*?"

MAIN FOCUS OF THE CHAPTER

In this research phase the author's target is BGI4AI's that is a part of the Architecture module (Am), and he tries to prove that such a concept can be built on a loosely coupled architecture. The BGI4AI uses the Data Management Concepts for Artificial Intelligence (DMC4AI) to interface data sources. The DS4AI uses Mathematics for Data Science or the already presented AHMM4AI, which deals with mathematical models and algorithms that are used to analyse data, offers conclusions and it supports the DS4AI. *Projects* are increasingly digital and data is global; these huge amounts of data are full of valuable operational information. The BGI4AI supports data extraction in a way that to be used by AHMM4AI. In this chapter the AHMM4AI uses algorithms which are essential for analysing data and thus providing a basis for evidence-based decisions in various domains and in complex situations.

Data Management and Complexity

Chaotic and complex DSI4AIs can cause failures, where business environments have complex data architectures, as shown in Figure 2 (IBM, 2015a). It is useful to interface exiting EA4AI structures and resources, like the use of documents, as shown in Figure 2.

Figure 2. Structure of an architecture document (The Open Group, 2011)

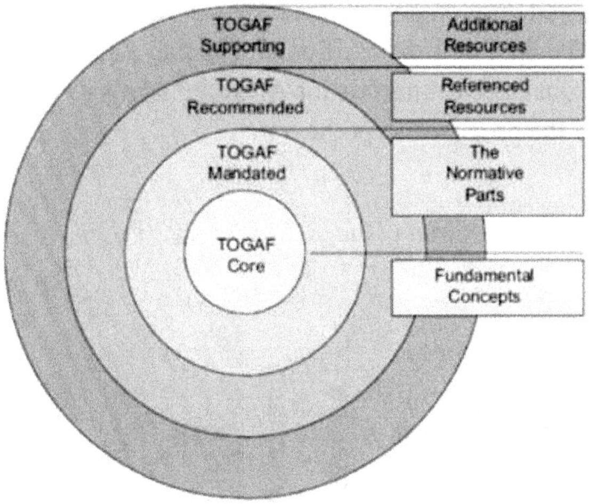

DS4AI Basics

The main DS4AI basics are (Guru99, 2021):

- It involves extracting insights in the context of vast amounts of data, by using scientific methods, algorithms and processes. It helps in finding hidden patterns from raw data. DS4AI is the result of evolution of statistics, data analysis, and the use of BGD4AI.
- It is cross functional and extracts knowledge from structured or unstructured databases. DS4AI translates business problems into a research project and then translates it into solutions.
- It involves extracting insights from vast amounts of data by the use of various scientific methods, algorithms and processes.
- Includes, statistics, visualization, Deep Learning Integration for AI (DLI4AI), Machine Learning Integration for AI (MLI4AI) concepts.
- Its Process goes through discovery, data preparation, data models' planning, model building, operation management and the communication of results.
- The actual possible roles are: 1) Data scientist; 2) Data engineer; 3) Data analyst; 4) Statistician; 5) Data architect; 6) Data admin; 7) Business analyst; and 8) Data/analytics manager.
- Tools that can be used, are: R, SQL, Python, SaS…
- Predictions of Business Intelligence, is looking backward (history), whereas DS4AI looks forward (actual and future).
- Possible applications are 1) Internet search; 2) Recommendation systems; 3) Image and speech recognition; 4) Gaming world, like eSports; 5) Online price comparison; and 6) many other…
- Various information, data formats and sources are the biggest challenges for DSI4AI and BGI4AI.

THE RESEARCH DEVELOPMENT PROCESS

As shown in Figure 3, the Research and Development Process for AI (RDP4AI) focuses on the impacts of the mechanistic BGI4AI's integration and uses a mixed hyper-heuristics based methodology (Vella, Corne, & Murphy, 2009). The RDP4AI is based on an extensive cross-functional Literature Research Process for AI (LRP4AI), a Qualitative Analysis for Artificial Analysis (QLA4AI) methodology and on a Proof of Concept (PoC)for the proposed hypotheses.

Figure 3. The mixed method flow diagram (Trad & Kalpić, 2020a)

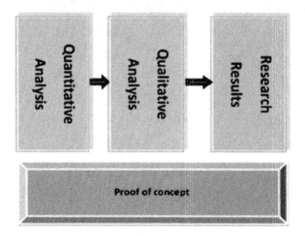

Figure 4. The experiment's overall diagram of components

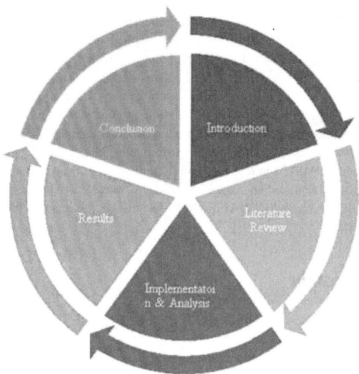

Projects use a PoC or prototyping to establish BGI4AI's: 1) feasibility; 2) viability; 2) major technical issues; and 3) offer recommendations (Camarinha-Matos, 2012).

The PoC is used to prove the feasibility of the BGI4AI, as shown in Figure 4. The PoC is based on a transaction management case that uses data class diagram for a data transaction, as shown in Figure 5; where an DS4AI module is called.

Figure 5. The experiment's class diagram package

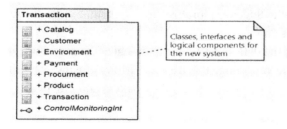

Critical Success Areas, Factors and DSI4AI

Critical Success Area (CSA) is a selected set of Critical Success Factors (CSF), where the CSF is a set of Key Performance Indicators (KPI), where each KPI corresponds/maps to a single *Project* requirement and/or problem type. For a given requirement (or problem), an *Entity* architect can identify the initial set of CSAs and their CSFs to be managed by the Decision-Making System for AI (DMS4AI). Hence the CSFs are important for the mapping between the problem types, knowledge constructs, organisational items. Therefore, CSFs reflect possible problem types that must meet strategic *Project* goals and predefined constraints. Measurements are used to evaluate performance in each of the CSA sets, where CSFs (and KPIs) can be internal or external to the environment; like: 1) problem type or gap analysis is an internal CSF; and 2) DMS4AI in real time and in minimal time is also an internal one. Once the initial set of CSFs has been identified, then the *Project* can use the DMS4AI to propose a set of solution types. The proposed BGI4AI based DSI4AI delivers a set of solution instance and recommendations (Trad & Kalpić, 2020a).

THE TARGETED DOMAIN

Main Stages

This chapter's targeted domain characteristics are (OMNI-SCI, 2021):

- Definition: DS4AI includes the mining of large data sets of raw data, both structured and unstructured, and is used to identify patterns and extract actionable insight from them. It includes, statistics, inference, computer science, predictive analytics, MLI4AI and BGD4AI.
- Lifecycle: The 1st stage in DS4AI's pipeline workflow involves, acquiring data, extracting data, and entering data into the system. The 2nd stage is the maintenance stage, which includes Data Warehouses Integration for AI (DWI4AI), data cleansing, data processing, data staging and data architecture activities.
- Data processing follows is a fundamental activity that includes, data exploration and analytics that DS4AI specialists manage. It involves also: data mining, data classification and clustering, data modelling and summarizing insights from the data.
- The data analysis stage includes exploratory and confirmatory tasks, regression, predictive analysis, QLA4AI and text mining.
- During the final stage, the data scientist communicates the found insights; and this stage involves data visualization, data reporting, the use of various Business Intelligence Integration for AI (BII4AI) tools, and assisting businesses, policymakers and others activities.

DSI4AI Preparation and Exploration

DSI4AI's preparation and exploration main characteristics are (OMNI-SCI, 2021):

- Data preparation and analysis are important DS4AI activities, but data preparation consumes 60 to 70 percent of the DS4AI activities; rarely generated data is in a correct, structured and noiseless form. In this phase, the data is transformed for further use.
- This process involves: 1) The transformation and sampling of data; 2) Checking both the features and observations; and 3) Using statistical techniques to remove noise. This step also illuminates whether various features in data sets are independent and whether there are incorrect values.
- This exploration phase is the principal difference between DS4AI and Data Analytics for AI (DA4AI), where the DS4AI has a macro view, aiming to propose precise questions on data to extract and to deliver insights and knowledge from this data. DA4AI contains the question(s) and the results.

DSI4AI Modelling

DSI4AI modelling characteristics are (OMNI-SCI, 2021):

- It fits data into the model using MLI4AI algorithms, where the model's selection depends on the type of data and the business requirement.
- Next, the model is tested for accuracy and other constraints that enables the adjustment of the model and to achieve acceptable results. If the model does not satisfy the requirements, another DS4AI model can be used.
- When testing succeeds with good data, it produces the desired results for the BI requirement, the DS4AI model can be finalized and deployed.

The Importance of DS4AI

Actually, there are about 40 zettabytes of used data and it is growing exponentially. Internet users generate about 2.5 quintillion bytes of data every day. Every person on Earth, is generating about 146,880 GB of data every day and by the year 2025, 165 zettabytes will be used every year. DS4AI tools are critical to understand BGD4AI and the used data from multiple sources (OMNI-SCI, 2021).

DS4AI and DA4AI

DS4AI and DA4AI are different; where the DS4AI starts earlier, exploring massive data sets, investigating their potential, identifying trends and insights and visualizing the results; and DA4AI comes in at a later stage. These processes report the results, make prescriptions for improving performances based on the analysis processes and optimize the use of data tools. DA4AI analyses a specific dataset of structured or numerical data using a given research question. BGI4AI manages larger masses of both structured and unstructured data. DA4AI uses historical data in a context and has less to do with predictive modelling. DA4AI needs precise questions, where the DS4AI does not create statistical models or use MLI4AI tools. DA4AI focuses on evaluating strategies for businesses, by comparing data assets to various organizational hypotheses. DA4AI works with localized data that has already been processed. DA4AI and DS4AI need mathematical, analytical and statistical skills, where the DS4AI is more predictive and the relationship between the DA4AI and data is retrospective (OMNI-SCI, 2021).

RDP4AI's CSF's

The RDP4AI's results are shown in Table 1.

Table 1. The factors have an average of 9.25

Critical Success Factors	KPIs		Weightings
CSF_DS4AI_LRP4AI	Proven	▾	From 1 to 10. **10 Selected**
CSF_DS4AI_PoC	Feasible	▾	From 1 to 10. **09 Selected**
CSF_DS4AI_References	Feasible	▾	From 1 to 10. **09 Selected**
CSF_DS4AI_EA4AI	Proven	▾	From 1 to 10. **10 Selected**
CSF_DS4AI_CSF_CSA	Feasible	▾	From 1 to 10. **09 Selected**
CSF_DS4AI_Mixed_Methods	Feasible	▾	From 1 to 10. **09 Selected**
CSF_DS4AI_Transformation_Setup	Feasible	▾	From 1 to 10. **09 Selected**
CSF_DS4AI_DMS4AI_Interfacing	Feasible	▾	From 1 to 10. **09 Selected**

valuation

As shown in Table 1, the result's aim is to prove or justify the RDP4AI's feasibility; and the result permits to move to the next CSA that is the AHMM4AI.

AHMM4AI'S SUPPORT FOR DS4AI

TRADf offers an NLP4AI that can be used to describe and implement the GAIP, BGI4AI, DMS4AI, DSI4AI, QNA4AI and QLA4AI based scenario(s), as shown in Figure 6, which can be used to solve *Project* requests. It is a complex domain and it requires the knowledge and experiences in practically all AI and ICS fields.

A Generic Holistic Approach

The *TRADf* proposes a holistic approach to analyse events and eventually manage possible risks to help Application and Problem Domains (APD) Managers to avoid major pitfalls. Traditionally, complex risk concepts, were associated with a single origin or CSF; mainly personified to concretise a complex situation. Pitfalls may be defined as a violation of an internal risk's related CSF that can be due to various types of problems or constraints; where in DSI4AI can be applied for example, for: 1) estimating

Figure 6. The overview

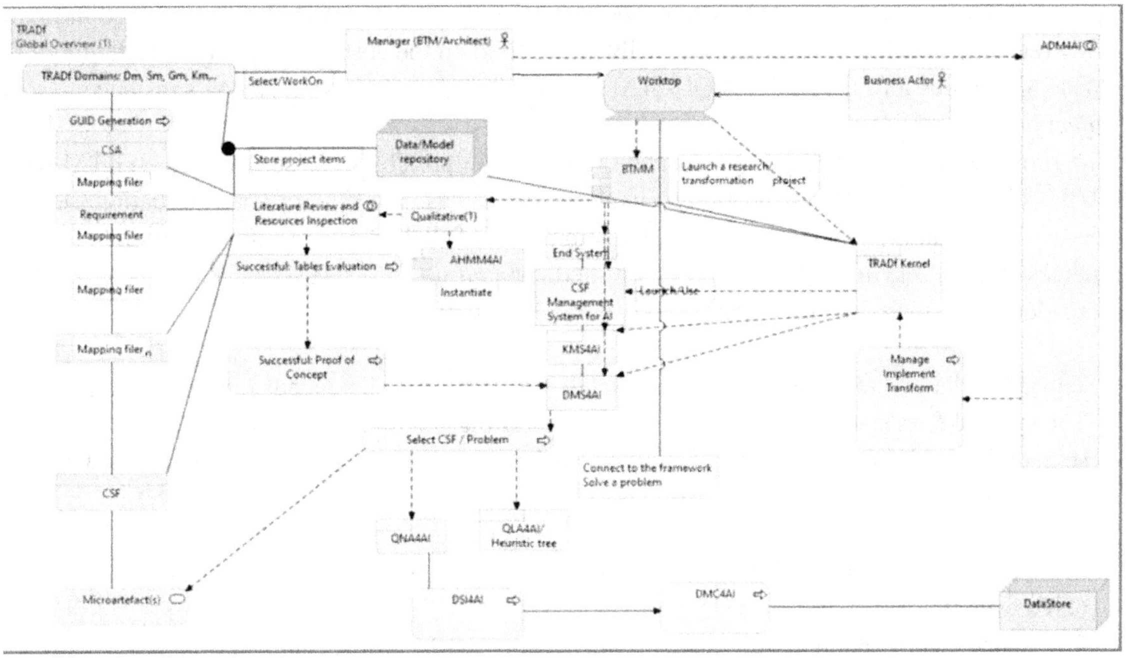

Project risks; 2) APD risk initiatives; 3) special domains, like geopolitical events or telecommunication implementations; 4) tracking financial crimes; and 3) other CSFs...

The Microartefacts' Distributed Architecture Model for the GAIP

The AHMM4AI has a dynamic defined nomenclature to facilitate its integration in any *Entity* EA4AI model, like the Architecture Development Method for AI (ADM4AI). The AHMM4AI is the *Entity's* holistic structural model and is a set of multiple coordinated DSI4AI processing to deliver solutions

Figure 7. The applied model's basics nomenclature (Trad & Kalpić, 2020a)

Basic MM's Nomenclature

Iteration	= An integer variable that denotes a *Project/ADM iteration*

microRequirement	= KPI	(1)
CSF	= Σ KPI	(2)
CSA	= Σ CSF	(3)
Requirement	= $\cup$ microRequirement	(4)
microKnowledgeArtefact	= $\cup$ knowledgeItem(s)	(4)
neuron	= action ° data + microKnowledgeArtefact	(5)
microArtefact	= $\cup$ (e)neurons	(6)
microEntity or Enterprise	= $\cup$ microArtefact	(7)
Entity or Enterprise	= $\cup$ microEntity	(8)
microArtefactScenario	= $\cup$ microArtefactDecisionMaking	(9)
Decision Making/Intelligence	= $\cup$ microArtefactScenario	(10)
EnityIntelligence	= $\cup$ Decision Making/InteligenceComponent	(11)
MM(*Iteration*) as an instance	= EnityIntelligence(*Iteration*)	(12)

455

that correspond to various just in time processing schemes which use the same *Project*'s central pool of CSAs and CSFs. The basic AHMM4AI nomenclature that the base for DSI4AI, is presented in Figure 7, to the reader in a simplified form, to be easily understood on the cost of a holistic formulation of the AHMM4AI's basics for QNA4AI and QLA4AI. The DMS4AI uses an AHMM4AI's instance to solve a *Project* problem.

The proposed *Entity's* AHMM4AI instances enables the possibility to support the BGI4AI based DSI4AI; using CSFs weightings and ratings (in phase 1), and based on multicriteria evaluation (selected and defined constraints). The symbol å indicates summation of all the relevant named set members, while the indices and the set cardinality have been omitted. The proposed AHMM4AI should be understood in a broader sense, more like set unions. As shown in Figure 7:

- The abbreviation "mc" can be used, and stands for micro, which depends on the granularity.
- The symbol å indicates summation of weightings/ratings, denoting the relative importance of the set members selected as relevant. Weightings as integers range in ascending importance from 1 to 10 (or another range defined by GAIP based analysists).
- The symbol U indicates sets union.
- The proposed AHMM4AI enables the possibility to define *Project* DSI4AI as a model; using CSFs weightings and ratings evaluation.
- The selected corresponding weightings to: CSF ∈ { 1 … 10 }; are integer values, that are presented in tables. The rules were presented in the RDP4AI section.
- The selected corresponding ratings to: CSF ∈ { 0.00% … 100.00% } are floating point percentage values.

The AHMM4AI's Structure for DSI4AI Based Solutions

The AHMM4AI's has a composite structure that can be viewed as follows:

- The static view has a similar static structure like the relational model's structure that includes sets of CSAs/CSFs that map to tables and the ability to create them and apply actions on these tables (Lockwood, 1999).
- In the behavioural view, these actions are designed using a set of AHMM4AI nomenclature, the implementation of the AHMM4AI is in the internal scripting language, used also to tune the CSFs (Lazar, Motogna, & Parv, 2010).
- The skeleton of the *TRADf* uses microartefacts' scenarios to support just-in-time DSI4AI requests.

Entity/Enterprise Architect as an Applied Mathematical Model

A generic *Entity* architecture model and its ADM4AI are the kernel of this RDP4AI and they are the basics of its *TRADf*. The author wants to propose the AHMM4AI to represent the GAIP. The LRP4AI has shown that existing LRP4AI's resources on DSI4AI, are practically inexistent. This pioneering research work is cross-functional and links all the DSI4AI or QLA4I/QNA4AI based microartefacts to an *Entity*; where the main reasoning component is a DSI4AI engine that is based on heuristics.

Heuristics, Empirics and Action Research

The DSI4AI is based on a set of synchronized AHMM4AI instances, where each AHMM4AI can launch a QLA4AI beam-search based heuristic processing (Kim, & Kim, 1999; Della Croce & T'kindt, 2002). Weightings and ratings concept support the AHMM4AI to process a GAIP request for an optimal analysis or solution for a given *Project* problem. Actions Research for AI (AR4AI) (Berger, & Rose, 2015) can be considered as a set of continuous beam-search heuristics processing phases and is similar to design, analysis and architecture processes, like the ADM4AI (Järvinen, 2007). Fast changing *Entity's* change requests may provoke an important set of events and problems that can be hard to predict and solve; that makes the GAIP various types of actions useless and complex to implement. The AHMM4AI is responsible for the DSI4AI that uses QLA4AI heuristic process for *Entity's* problem solving and synchronizes a set of AHMM4AI instances which have also separate heuristics processes and are supported by a dynamic tree algorithm, as shown in Figure 8 (Nijboer, Morin, Carmien, Koene, Leon, & Hoffman, 2009) that manages tree nodes and their correlation with memorized patterns that are combinations of data states and heuristic goal functions. The AHMM4AI capacities are measured by analysing the *TRADf's* AHMM4AI tree.

Figure 8. The applied heuristics tree algorithm (Nijboer, Morin, Carmien, Koene, Leon & Hoffman, 2009)

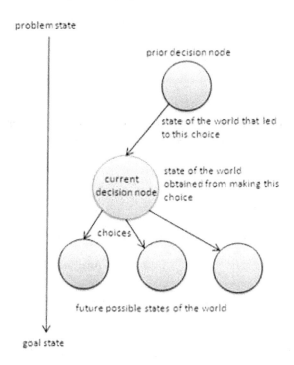

Holistic AR4AI based heuristics enables reflective practice that is the basis of a holistic approach to develop EA4AI based GAIP solutions, where its kernel and skeleton are a dynamic DMS4AI (Leitch, & Day, 2006). GAIP is based on DSI4AI, QLA4AI and QNA4AI methods (Loginovskiy, Dranko, & Hollay, 2018).

Qualitative, Quantitative (or Mixed) Related to the Notion of Time, Space and Scope

As already mentioned, the AHMM4AI and its underlining set of created instances is mainly a QLA4AI beam-search heuristic tree (Della Croce, & T'kindt, 2002). In each of the tree's node a precise call to DSI4AI functions (or other) can be executed, by precision or objectivity the author refers to inputted data, constraint (and/or rules) and above all: 1) Time related to timestamp tracing system; 2) Space, related to the analysed *Entity's* space; and 3) Scope of GAIP's process. These facts, form the basis of an applicable GAIP and DSI4AI are based on AHMM4AI instances.

The Applied GAIP Transformation Mathematical Model

GAIP is a part of the *TRADf* that uses microartefacts to support just-in-time DMS4AI actions. The GAIP based component and interface, are based on a light version of the ADM4AI, having a systemic approach. A *Project* using GAIP is the combination of GAIP based, EA4AI methodology (like the TOGAF's ADM4AI) and the proposed AHMM4AI, that is presented in Figures 9 and 10.

Figure 9. The model's generic structure

The Generic AHMM's Formulation

$$\text{AHMM} = \bigcup \text{ADMs} + \text{MMs} \qquad (13)$$

The generic AHMM can applied to any specific domain; in this chapter and RDP4AI's phase, the *Domain,* is GAIP based and the AHMM4AI = AHMM(APD), as shown in Figure 10; where AHMM can applied to any domain and any concept.

Figure 10. The AHMM4AI structure

AHMM's Application and Instantiation for a Specific Domain

$$Domain = \text{Geopolitical Analysis (GA)} \qquad (14)$$

$$\text{AHMM}(Domain) = \bigcup \text{ADMs} + \text{MMs}(Domain) \qquad (15)$$

The proposed combination can be modelled after the following formula for the GAIP Transformation Mathematical Model (GAIPTMM) that abstracts the *Project* for a given *Entity*:
(AHMM4AI for an *Iteration*):
iAHMM4AI = AHMM4AI(*Iteration*);
iAHMM4AI=Weigthing$_1$*iAHMM4AI_Qualitative+Weigthing$_2$* iAHMM4AI _Quantitative (16).
The *Project's* AHMM4AI (PAHMM4AI) = å iAHMM4AI for an ADM4AI's instance (17).
(GAIPTMM):

GAIPTMM = å PAHMM4AI instances (18).

The Main Objective Function for GAIP based (MOFGAIP) of the GAIPTMM's formula can be optimized by using constraints and with extra variables that need to be tuned using the AHMM4AI. The variable for maximization or minimization can be, for example, the *Project* success, costs or other (Dantzig, 1949). For this chapter's PoC the success will be the main and only constraint and success is quantified as a binary 0 or 1. Where the MOF4AI definition will be:

Minimize risk GAIPTMM Function (GAIPTMMf) (19).

The AHMM4AI is based on a concurrent and synchronized *TRADf*, which uses concurrent threads that can make various AHMM4AI instances run in parallel and manage information through the use of the AHMM4AI's NLP4AI. The GAIPTMM is the combination of the GAIP, *Project* and EA4AI methodologies and a holistic AHMM4AI that integrates the *Entity* or organisational concept, Information and Communication Systems (ICS) that have to be formalized using a functional development environment like *TRADf's* NLP4AI.

The AHMM4AI's CSFs

Based on the LRP4AI, the most important AHMM4AI's CSFs that are used are evaluated to the following:

Table 2. The factors have an average of 10.0

Critical Success Factors	KPIs	Weightings
CSF_DSI4AI_AHMMAI_TRADf_Integration	Proven ▼	From 1 to 10. **10 Selected**
CSF_DSI4AI_AHMMAI_InitialPhase	Proven ▼	From 1 to 10. **10 Selected**
CSF_DSI4AI_AHMMAI_PoC	Proven ▼	From 1 to 10. **10 Selected**
CSF_DSI4AI_AHMMAI_Qualitative&Quantitative	Proven ▼	From 1 to 10. **10 Selected**
CSF_DSI4AI_AHMMAI_Final_Instance	Proven ▼	From 1 to 10. **10 Selected**
CSF_DSI4AI_AHMMAI_ADM4AI_Integration	Proven ▼	From 1 to 10. **10 Selected**
CSF_DSI4AI_AHMMAI_APD_Interfacing	Complex ▼	From 1 to 10. **08 Selected**

valuation

Table is wider than 6.25 inches

As shown in Table 2, the result's aim is to prove or justify that it is complex but possible to implement atheAHMM4AI in the *Entity's* ICS. The next CSA to be analysed is DMC4AI as an interface.

DMC4AI AS AN INTERFACE

DMC4AI Based DSI4AI Integration Strategy

The DSI4AI strategy should be based on well-defined principles, like (IBM, 2015a):

- Data have to be easy to enter and must be accurate.
- Data collections are based on data modelling concepts.
- Data must be available to business personnel.
- Business processes for data management have to be automated.
- Data should not be redundant.
- Data have to be recorded accurately and must be auditable.
- The cost of data collection procedures have to be optimized.
- DSI4AI must adopt standards for common data models.

Data Transformation Models

In DSI4AI, Data transformation is the process of transforming data from one format or class into another format or class. It is an essential process for data integration and data management tasks, like data wrangling, data warehousing, data integration and EA4AI.

The Meta-Model

This PoC uses a meta-model to show the relationships between the *Project*'s different types of data models and data sources. This *Project*'s meta-model contains descriptions on how data sources are handled in the newly transformed business system's and of the types of used data structures

NORMALIZATION AND INTER-OPERABILITY

eXtensible Markup Language (XML)

DSI4AI must be based on various standards that are all in turn based on XML technologies. XML enables ontology-mediated interoperability that is based on data schemas. Schemas enable the alignment by defining common data structures. Data architecture and modelling conceptual schemas are used in the mediation module that describes the semantics of data sources and destinations. Data architecture and modelling conceptual normalisation is a three-layered approach for information representation, as shown in Figure 11, the three layers for data integration include: 1) syntax checking; 2) data modelling; and 3) semantics control. The PoC uses the normalisation conversion modules that include a set of tables to automate the data translation process (Fodor, Dell'Erba, Ricci, Spada, & Werthner, 2002).

460

Figure 11. Stages of conceptual normalisation process (Fodor, Dell'Erba, Ricci, Spada, & Werthner, 2002)

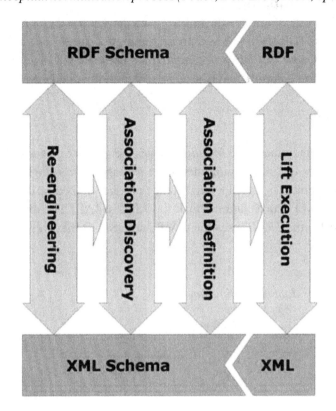

JavaScript Object Notation

JavaScript Object Notation (JSON) is an open standard file format used as a data interchange format, that has a human-readable text to store and manage data objects. These objects have attributes in the form of value pairs and array data types. It is an easy and common data format, with a diverse range of applications. JSON is replacing XML because it is a language-independent data format and is derived from JavaScript.

The Model's Unit of Work

A holistic alignment, identification and classification of all the RDP4AI's resources must be done, so that the research process can start. A holistic alignment needs also, to define the Unit of Work (UoW) or the basic microartefact. Using the "1:1" mapping concept, the microartefact is represented with a class diagram and can be represented also by an XML model. Such a mapping concept, is based on an automated naming convention that can link all the RDP4AI's resources. The mapping concept supports the interoperability between all the RDP4AI's modules and enables the use of NLP4AI microartefacts that uses ADM4AI and DSI4AI (Mehra, Grundy, & Hosking, 2005).

The Object Relational Mapping

Object Relational Mapping (ORM) in ICS is a programming technique for transforming data between various types of systems. ORM uses OO programming languages like, C++, Java, C# and many other. ORM creates a *virtual object database* that is used by programming language.

Data Solution Blocks

Upon a concrete *Project* requirement, the *Manager* issues a contract to resolve this requirement by using EA4AI. EA4AI ensures that new requirements are managed accordingly to the *Project's* records and objectives. The requirement is linked to an instance of a newly created data Building Block for AI (dBB4AI) and its instance (a data Solution Block for AI, dSB4AI). The dBB4AI is a part of GAIP; and as shown in Figure 12, the *TRADf* uses the GAIP and DSI4AI that include the patterns needed to integrate dSB4AIs.

Figure 12. The experiment's data block diagram

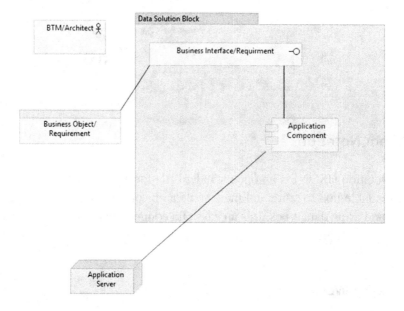

Transactions Data Modelling

The *Project* must put important considerations on technical assertion, governing, control, access management and monitoring of business transactions that are based on the Model View Controller for AI (MVC4AI) pattern. Business transactions use the following standards: 1) the policy framework; and 2) business messaging that is needed for domain-specific integration (OASIS, 2009).

Data Lifecycle Diagram

The Data Lifecycle Diagram (DLD), manages DSI4AI's data throughout their lifecycle, from EA4AI, modelling, processing to removal, within the defined rules and constraints. The data sets are loosely coupled with DSI4AI's processes and that allows the definition of common data models enabling an effective data and other resources' sharing. Each data model must have its status that contains the transitions and the gaps between phases. A phase's state must contain a stable data model, where the data EA4AI and modelling lifecycle enables a qualitative design of the related business entities. The resultant data models must be atomic or simple in order to (re)engineer the *Project*'s business processes (TOGAF Modelling, 2015c).

DMC4AI's CSF's

Based on the business case's (and its CSA) LRP4AI process managed and weighted the most important CSFs that were used.

Table 3. The factors have an average of 9.40

Critical Success Factors	KPIs		Weightings
CSF_DMC4AI_Interface_Strategy	Feasible	▼	From 1 to 10. **09 Selected**
CSF_DMC4AI_Interface_Transformation	Proven	▼	From 1 to 10. **10 Selected**
CSF_DMC4AI_Interface_Mapping	Proven	▼	From 1 to 10. **10 Selected**
CSF_DMC4AI_Interface_EA4AI	Proven	▼	From 1 to 10. **10 Selected**
CSF_DMC4AI_Interface_CSF_CSA	Feasible	▼	From 1 to 10. **09 Selected**
CSF_DMC4AI_Interface_Modelling	Complex	▼	From 1 to 10. **08 Selected**
CSF_DMC4AI_Interface_DLD	Proven	▼	From 1 to 10. **10 Selected**
CSF_DMC4AI_Interface_Plaform	Feasible	▼	From 1 to 10. **09 Selected**

valuation

As shown in Table 3, the result's aim is to prove or justify the RDP4AI's feasibility; and the result permits to move to the next CSA that is the data access, architecture and agility.

DS4AI PLATFORM

Basic Roadmap

The major notions to implement a DSI4AI oriented platform are (Veneberg, 2014);

- EA4AI contains a traceability and monitoring subsystem. Combining DMS4AI and DSI4AI consolidates the *Entity's* support for business specialists, without the need to trace the used data. The EA4AI provides a meta-data model for operational and historic data that are needed for DMS4AI routine operations.
- For BGI4AI, Data Base Management System (DBMS) is implemented to access, read and write data sets.
- There are three types of DBMS: 1) navigational DBMS; 2) Relational DBMS (RDBMS); and 3) the Post-RDBMS (PRDBMS). RDBMS and PRDBMS are the most popular ones and the Simple Query Language (SQL) is used with RDBMS, that manipulates tables.
- Data is stored in two-dimensional racks and it can be accessed, by read and write transactions using a RDBMS.
- There is also non-relational database, labelled No Simple Query Language (NoSQL) Databases (NoSQLDB), that are the successors of RDBMS. RDBMS focuses on its relations between tables, where the NoSQLDB focuses on its objects' models.
- NoSQLDB using key-value stores, are optimal for DSI4AI which processes large volumes of data; and NoSQLDB benefits are latency and throughput. This is the main fact why many AI applications like BGD4AI and performant real-time web applications NoSQLDBs.
- NoSQLDB and RDBMS are two-dimensional data structure or a multidimensional data structure; where a one-dimensional data structure is an array of items. Data items are stored in central memory as a sequence of items, starting at row 0 to row n.
- Data structures that are composed of more than one dimension are called multi-dimensional data structures (or cubes).
- DWI4AI is used to store operational and historical data that can be used as a reference source for DSI4AI in support for the DMS4AI.
- DWI4AIs lacks data traceability and monitoring, where a *Project* needs instructions on how to trace data sets and events.
- DWI4AI is a decision support module for executives, analysts and architects.
- Extract Transform and Load (ETL) has the following characteristics:
  ◦ Supports the extraction of data from legacy systems and transformed into *Entity* data.
  ◦ Has many functions, that includes logical conversion of data, domain verification, conversion from one RDBMS to another.
  ◦ It supports the: 1) creation of default values; 2) summarization of data; 3) addition of time values to the data key; 4) restructuring of the data key; 5) merging of records and deletion of extraneous or redundant data.
  ◦ It helps in transforming data coming from operational source systems into *Entity* data to be accessed by DWI4AI. The transformation of data is usually processed in an Operational Data Store (ODS).

- The ODS the data updated from an OnLine Transaction Processing (OLTP) response time; where the ODS is a hybrid environment in which *Project* data is transformed by an ETL into a defined format. The ODS abstracts raw data DWI4AI from *Entity*.
- Integration processes support the DSI4AI to become a consistent source package.

Enterprise Service Bus and Enterprise Application Integration

An Enterprise Service Bus (ESB) implements an enterprise-wide communication subsystem between mutually interacting applications using the Service Oriented Architecture (SOA) paradigm. It represents a communication architecture for global distributed computing, and is a special variant of the more general client server concept, where *Entity* applications and modules may be a server or client. An ESB promotes modularity, agility and flexibility in relation to the ICS and *Project*. It is used in Enterprise Application Integration (EAI) approach for heterogeneous and complex services-based *Projects*. *Project*s must use ESB to glue the various data sources of the business environment, through the use of the technology stack and data connectors, which permit a holistic data services' management.

Extraction, Transform and Load

ETL processes are defined as accessing data stored in various locations and transforming them in order to enable their unification, quality or normalization. The DSI4AI, proposes the separation of data processing activities; that enables data services to access data without bothering about various data sources'

Figure 13. Various data sources (Tamr, 2014)

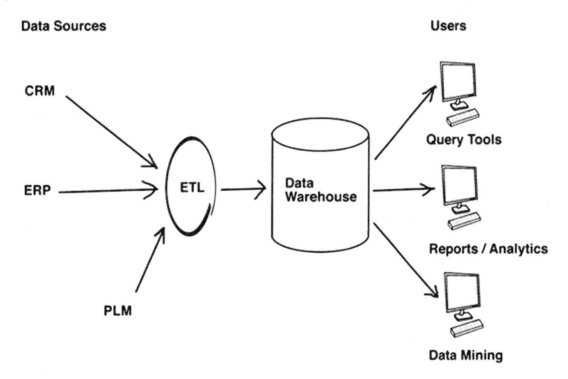

The Business, Societal, and Enterprise Architecture Framework

complexities. The DSI4AI insures: 1) intra (or extra) data transparency; 2) managing accessibility; and 3) data quality control (Tamr, 2014). As shown in Figure 13, the ETL processes are responsible for the access of data from heterogeneous data sources. The challenge lays in the real-time data transformation and normalization processes (Trujillo & Luján-Mora, 2003).

BGD4AI for DSI4AI

BGD4AI has the following characteristics (SAS, 2021):

- BGD4AI refers to data that is massive, fast and is very complex to process using existing ICS' resources.
- Data for DSI4AI can managed by the BGD4AI that is based on the three V's: 1) Volume; 2) Velocity; and 3) Variety.
- Volume: *Entities* collect data from a variety of sources, including business transactions, smart devices, industrial equipment, videos, social media and more.
- Velocity: The evolution of ICS' and data streams with extreme speed, requests just-in-time processing. This needs performance and scalability.
- Variety: *Entity's* data have various types of formats, from structured, numeric data in traditional databases to unstructured text documents, emails, videos... That needs a unique transformation platform.

Table 4. The factors have an average of 9.0

Critical Success Factors	KPIs		Weightings
CSF_DSI4AI_Platform_Roadmap	Complex	▼	From 1 to 10. **08 Selected**
CSF_DSI4AI_Platform_Interface	Complex	▼	From 1 to 10. **08 Selected**
CSF_DSI4AI_Platform_Legacy_Mainframes	Proven	▼	From 1 to 10. **10 Selected**
CSF_DSI4AI_Platform_EA4AI_ADM4AI	Proven	▼	From 1 to 10. **10 Selected**
CSF_DSI4AI_Platform_CSF_CSA	Feasible	▼	From 1 to 10. **09 Selected**
CSF_DSI4AI_Platform_Scalability	Feasible	▼	From 1 to 10. **09 Selected**
CSF_DSI4AI_Platform_ORM	Feasible	▼	From 1 to 10. **09 Selected**
CSF_DSI4AI_Platform_BigData	Complex	▼	From 1 to 10. **09 Selected**

valuation

Platform's CSF's

Based on the business case's (and its CSA) LRP4AI process managed and weighted the most important CSFs that were used.

As shown in Table 4, the result's aim is to prove or justify the RDP4AI's feasibility; and the result permits to move to the next CSA that is EA4AI's integration.

EA4AI'S INTEGRATION

EA4AI Principles and Basics

EA4AI's main principles and basics are:

- DSI4AI may be complex in large *Entities* which with complex risks scenarios.
- EA4AI is often used for strategy purposes and provides an overview of complex *Entity* architectures, showing business entities and relations.
- EA4AI accommodates DMC4AI to enable a data-driven approach, and there is no concept that enables the BGD4AI ro integrate a data-driven EA4AI.
- ADM4AI supports a data-driven *Entity*; through a specific adaption of the ADM4AI.

Figure 14. The layers of data-driven architecture

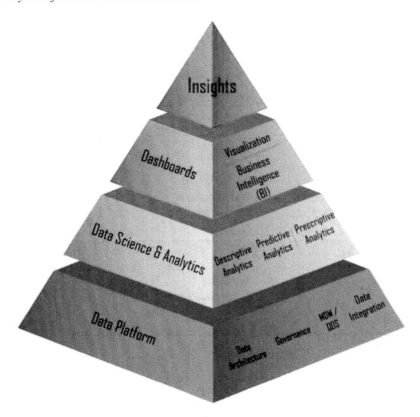

EA4AI Layers

EA4AI's main layers characteristics depend on (Sarkar, 2018):

- The lack of reproducibility and reusable artifacts, where the modules are reproducible.
- The lack of collaboration: silos should be removed, even though DSI4AI specialists work in an isolated manner.
- The technical debt: There is a lack of standards and EA4AI concepts for DSI4AI.
- Building reusable assets: Besides the DSI4AI, Non-Functional Requirements are important and includes, scalability, maintainability, availability and other.
- DSI4AI needs to implement an EA4AI approach, to define solutions, application and data models. For this goal there is a need to define layered EA4AI as shown in Figure 15.
- EAI4AI based DSI4AI is capable of: 1) Envisioning end-to-end solutions: 2) To improve and transform the *Entity*.
- Structured evolution is essential to DSI4AI that is an innovative field, that needs GAIPs.

Figure 15. Layered architecture hierarchy (Sarkar, 2018)

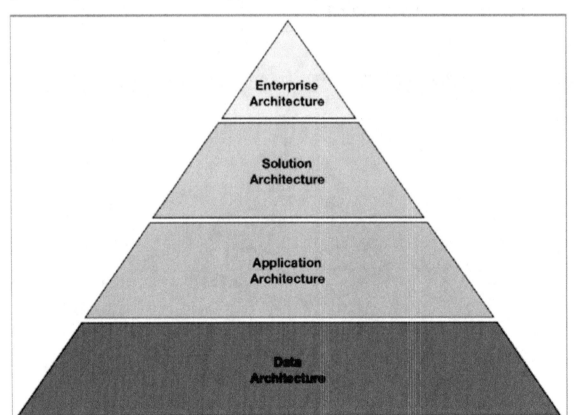

The Role of Data and EA4AI Standards

The *TRADf* uses data technologies and existing data standards that include: 1) RDBMS standards; 2) vertical industry documents' standards; 3) business process standards; 4) data governance standards; 5) business services standards; 6) extensible mark-up language standards; 7) Object Oriented (OO); and 8) resources description standards. Standardization for inter-operability can be achieved by using an ESB and its ETL module (Tamr, 2014). The evolution of standards, like the SOA standards, have enabled DSI4AIs to become more receptive to development and integration with various standards. Standardized *Project*s have to be inter-operable and their focus must be on their: 1) data models; 2) data architectures; 3) modelling concepts; and 4) data monitoring platforms. Regardless of the business domain, executive management understands the immense need for agility and the integration of DSI4AIs. The DSI4AI helps in establishing a unique GAIP.

Application Reference Model

Application Reference Model (ARM) categorizes the system, applications' standards and ICS that support the delivery of service capabilities, allowing various *Entities* to share common solutions. EA4AI's data architect and a *Project's* data analyst, can use the standard ARM, which is not on for analytics, but is also used for EAI4AI. ARM is a used, for mapping business APD to *Entity's* applications. ARM is a key for predictive analytics initiatives, where it defines the interface between the business and the ICS that supports it. GAIP needs to create ARM artefacts to be used by the DSI4AI (Doree, 2015).

Figure 16. The model's implementation

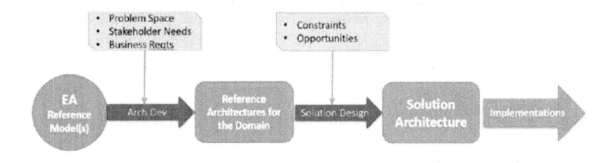

EA4AI's CSF's

Based on the business case's (and its CSA) LRP4AI process managed and weighted the most important CSFs that were used.

As shown in Table 5, the result's aim is to prove or justify the RDP4AI's feasibility; and the result permits to move to the next CSA that is modelling and implementation environments.

Table 5. The factors have an average of 9.0

Critical Success Factors	KPIs		Weightings
CSF_EA4AI_Integration_Principles	Feasible	▼	From 1 to 10. **09 Selected**
CSF_EA4AI_Integration_Integration_Strategy	Feasible	▼	From 1 to 10. **09 Selected**
CSF_EA4AI_Integration_Standards	Feasible	▼	From 1 to 10. **09 Selected**
CSF_EA4AI_Integration_EA4AI	Proven	▼	From 1 to 10. **10 Selected**
CSF_EA4AI_Integration_CSF_CSA	Feasible	▼	From 1 to 10. **09 Selected**
CSF_EA4AI_Integration_Layers	Complex	▼	From 1 to 10. **08 Selected**
CSF_EA4AI_Integration_Modelling_Languages	Proven	▼	From 1 to 10. **10 Selected**
CSF_EA4AI_Integration_ARM	Complex	▼	From 1 to 10. **08 Selected**

valuation

MODELLING AND IMPLEMENTATION ENVURONMENTS

The Basic Approach

The basic approach's main characteristics are (OMNI-SCI, 2021):

- DSI4AI needs capable and autonomous specialists because it is a complex environment.
- DSI4AI needs many skills that include statistical analysis and other fields like:
  - Statistics training, including probability, inferential statistics, linear/vector algebra and calculus.
  - Python and/or R, are DS4AI languages;
  - Apache Spark and SQL.
  - Visualization software.
  - MLI4AI, NLP4AI, DLI4AI.

DATA MODELLING LANGUAGES

EA4AI Modelling Language

EA4AI modelling languages like ArchiMate, which is an open and independent modelling language for *Entity* functional, enterprise and data architectures. ArchiMate is supported by many vendors and consulting companies; and it provides instruments to enable *Entity* architects to describe, analyse and visualize the relationships among business (including data) domains in an clear manner (The Open Group, 2013b).

Unified Modelling Language

Unified Modelling Language (UML) can be used with DSI4AI in the following contexts (Sikander, & Khiyal, 2018):

- To model data concepts and implementations; like the Data Flow Diagram (DFD) is an artefact that represents a flow of data through a process or a system (usually an ICS).
- The DFD also provides information on the outputs and inputs of each object (like a table) and the process itself. The DFD has no control flow, there are no Dynamic Rules for AI (DR4AI) and no loops. Specific operations based on the data can be represented by a flowchart.
- A UML Diagram, is essential to illustrate a conceptual model to a precise *Project* problem with the component or class diagrams. And to present the used algorithm, using the sequence or activity diagrams.
- In the context of the process of data analysis, which integrates three models as shown in Figure 17, it is the process of inspecting, cleaning, converting and modelling of data, in order to obtain particular results. Raw data is collected from various sources and transformed into usable information streams for DMS4AI and DSI4AI processing. There are different phases in the process of DMS4AI and DSI4AI processing; these processes are iterative. The UML state diagram for DSI4AI process is shown in Figure 18.

Figure 17. The data analysis process flowchart (Sikander, & Khiyal, 2018)

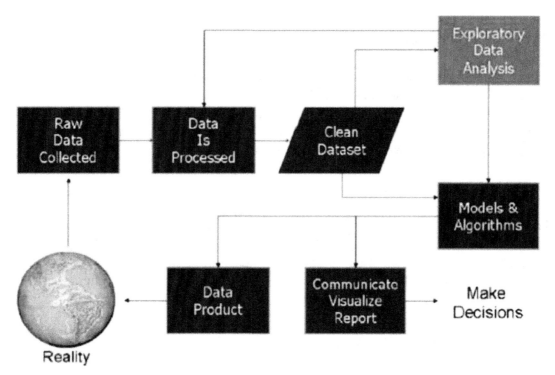

Figure 18. The data analysis process flowchart, using the state diagram (Sikander, & Khiyal, 2018)

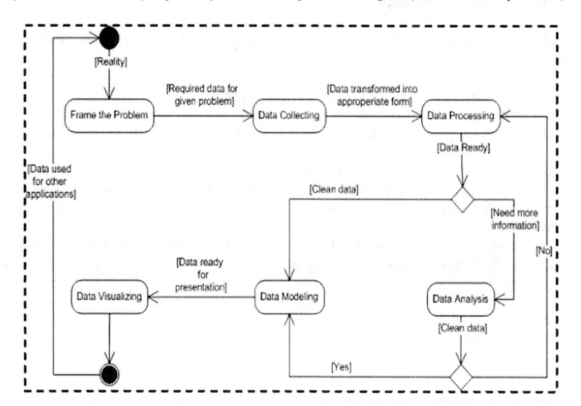

Entity Relationship Model

An Entity Relationship Model (ERM) describes interrelated objects (tables) of interest in an application domain. A basic ERM is composed of object types and specifies relationships that can exist between objects. In DSI4AI, an ERM is used to represent objects for *Project* needs to remember in order to perform business operations. The ERM is an abstract data model, which defines a data or information structure which can be implemented in a DBMS, commonly a RDBMS.

Data Modelling Diagrams

A data model is needed to describe the structure and relationships among a set of data managed in the *Project* and stored in a data management system. The most common is the relational model that is often represented in entity-relationship diagrams or class diagrams; these diagrams basically show data entities and their relationships. The DSI4AI for a *Project* can be seen as a data architectural view (Merson, 2009); where the modelling process incorporates various conceptual views.

Data Dissemination View

The purposed data dissemination diagram shows the relationship within the DSI4AI: 1) data entities; 2) business data services; and 3) application components/services. This diagram as shown in Figure 19, presents the logical data entities to be physically managed/accesses by application components or services. That permits a flexible architecture and modelling of the data sources. This diagram includes data services that abstract various data sources (TOGAF Modelling, 2015a).

Figure 19.

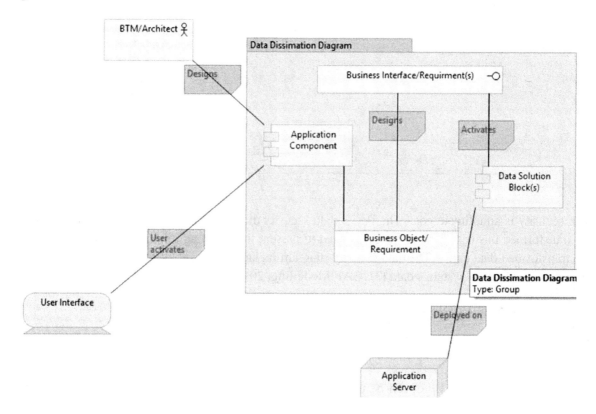

Data Migration Diagram

DSI4AI's data migration diagram presents the flow of data between the business systems' various data sources; it serves as a view for the *Project*'s data auditing and traceability map. The data migration diagram is enhanced through *Project*'s iterations (TOGAF Modelling, 2015d). A mapping table was developed to show the relationships between various data points (source, intermediate or destination).

Data Security Diagram

Design of data architecture and modelling are the most important activities in the *Project* and the transformed business data are a very important asset for the *Entity*; that implies that the transformed business

Figure 20. The experiment's data dissemination view

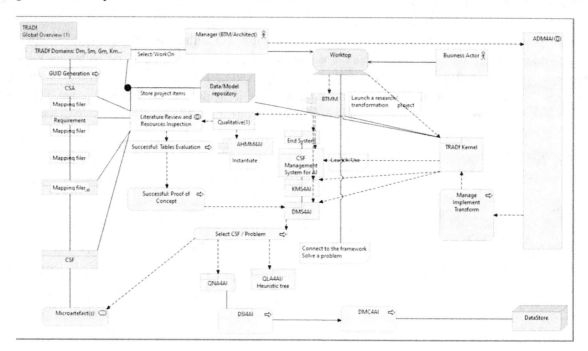

data security is an ultimate goal. The PoC's data security diagram presents the *Project*'s actors' roles for transformed business data. A matrix is used to present the mapping relation between the role and the transformed data entity. The data security diagram includes all external accesses which may have access to the business system's data (TOGAF Modelling, 2015e).

Functional Development

NLP4AI

TRADf's internal NLP4AI tool can be used for various application domains and in general for hard systems' thinking. The author recommends the use of an interpretable scripting for building a GAIP (Moore, 2014). The AHMM4AI based process is domain-driven and is founded on *TRADf* that in turn is based on a NLP4AI to manage heuristics/rules, *Entity*/enterprise architecture, QLA4AI and QNA4AI microartefacts (Simonin, Bertin, Traon, Jezequel & Crespi, 2010). The complexity lies in how to integrate the AHMM4AI and its programming NLP4AI in GAIP. The main characteristics and facts related to functional languages are (Clancy, 2019):

- Functional programming reaches for efficiency in finance.
- Financial institutions are adopting functional programming or NLP4AI as an alternative to the dominant imperative approach.
- NLP4AI results with less bugs as it is stricter and easier to check and to test.
- It has in-built concurrency constructs, and are optimal for distributed ledgers. Distributed ledgers may find a wide application in the derivatives industry.

- It lacks skilled developers, as well as its memory and speed drawbacks.
- They will become more relevant with the adoption of the Distributed Ledger Technology (DLT) in finance.
- NLP4AI make testing easier because of immutability.
- It will continue to spread, as *Entities* become aware of its advantages.

R vs Python for DSI4AI

DSI4AI languages are used for data transformation, data cleaning, and data visualization. There is also a need to detect outliers, identify relationships between variables, and construct complete interpretive models for DSI4AI. Data preparation and statistical analysis tools like R and Python can be used. R is a language for statistics, data analysis and graphical models.

R

R is particularly suited to data analysis tasks on individual servers that demand standalone analysis or. It's optimal for PoCs and visualization, but it is slow and has a difficult syntax.

Python

Python is a more readable language and is for general use for statistical analysis demands.

F#

F# (F sharp) is a functional, strongly typed, multi-paradigm programming language that incorporates functional, imperative and OO paradigms. F# is a part of the .NET platform.

SCALA

SCALA is a functional and OO programming language it is strong static typed system. Designed to be concise.

Classical Development Tools

Classical development environments, like JEE, C#, C++, Perl, EXCEL/VBA and other, can be used for DSI4AI oriented development.

Environments CSFs

Based on the business case's (and its CSA) LRP4AI process managed and weighted the most important CSFs that were used.

As shown in Table 6, the result's aim is to prove or justify the RDP4AI's feasibility; and the result permits to move to the next CSA that is the GAIP's components integration

Table 6. The factors have an average of 9.40

Critical Success Factors	KPIs	Weightings
CSF_Modelling_Implementation_DSI4AI_Interface	Proven ▾	From 1 to 10. **10 Selected**
CSF_Modelling_Implementation_Modelling_Languages	Proven ▾	From 1 to 10. **10 Selected**
CSF_Modelling_Implementation_Diagrams	Feasible ▾	From 1 to 10. **09 Selected**
CSF_Modelling_Implementation_Functional_Dev	Feasible ▾	From 1 to 10. **09 Selected**
CSF_Modelling_Implementation_CSF_CSA	Proven ▾	From 1 to 10. **10 Selected**
CSF_Modelling_Implementation_ADM4AI_Integration	Proven ▾	From 1 to 10. **10 Selected**
CSF_Modelling_Implementation_APD_Interfacing	Complex ▾	From 1 to 10. **08 Selected**

valuation

Table is wider than 6.25 inches

GAIP'S MAIN COMPONENTS INTEGRATION

GAIP's Construct

The GAIP's construct has the following characteristics and presumptions (OMNI-SCI, 2021):

- AI should simulate the human brain, by using the ICS, which includes learning, logical reasoning and auto-correction.
- The GAIP supports the *Entity's* learning, auto-correct and reasoning processes and the capacity to draw inferences in an independent manner.
- The GAIP is generic and has a holistic approach, because it can handle many types of activities, which demands reasoning, judgment and thought.
- The GAIP uses specialized methods to handle specific tasks.
- GAIP uses neural networks and it needs an extraordinary amount of data.
- For a summary: 1) DSI4AI is the field; 2) GAIP is the goal; and 3) MLI4AI is the process.

MLI4AI's Integration

The MLI4AI's Integration process has the following characteristics (OMNI-SCI, 2021):

- GAIP based DSI4AI and MLI4AI work together. Where MLI4AI feeds the ICS with huge amounts of data to support DMS4AI's processes.
- The GAIP based DMS4AI uses human interaction to feed the DMS4AI with massive quantities of data, to be able to solve *Project* problems.

- Humans feed the DMS4AI with various types of data, so it can learn from data associated with knowledge items/features.
- DSI4AI includes statistics that with ICS technologies can handle massive amounts of data. The MLI4AI is part of the DSI4AI, and it allows the DMS4AI to learn.
- MLI4AI uses algorithms to support the DMS4AI, but those algorithms rely on source data. The DMS4AI uses source data as a learning sets, so it can improve its algorithms. It tunes the parameters of the algorithms by using statistical techniques, including naive Bayes regression and supervised clustering.
- The DMS4AI can train another DMS4AI to detect data structures, by using unsupervised clustering, to optimize the classification algorithm; human support is needed to control the classification of structures that the DMS4AI identifies.
- The scope of DSI4AI goes beyond the MLI4AI, by encompassing data that is not generated by any mechanical process; like in the cases like, survey's data, data from clinical trials or any other kind of data.
- DSI4AI deploys data to train DMS4AIs and is not limited to statistical data processing. The DSI4AI includes automating MLI4AI's data-driven decisions.
- When a DSI4AI specialist creates the insights from data, a DMS4AI learns from those insights. A DMS4AI can build its own insights using existing algorithmic structure, where the starting point relies on some kind of used structured data.

BGD4AI's Integration

The Integration of BGD4AI has the following characteristics (OMNI-SCI, 2021):

- Uses data streams from various sources, like, online purchases, multimedia forms, instruments, financial logs, sensors, text files and others. Data can be: 1) Unstructured; 2) Semi-structured; and 3) Structured.
- Unstructured data, includes data from: blogs, digital audio/video feeds, digital images, emails, mobile devices, sensors, social networks and tweets, web pages and online sources.
- Semi-structured data comes from: system log storages, XML files and text files.
- Structured data, is the data that has been already processed by: OLTP, RDBMS, transaction data processes and other formats' processing.
- BGD4AI's integration is needed to support the processing of tremendous amounts of data from various sources; which is impossible to process with BI or DA4AI tools. BGD4AI based DSI4AI offers *Entities* with advanced, complex algorithms for analysing, cleansing, processing and extracting meaningful insights.
- BGD4AI based DSI4AI is a scientific research process that uses AHMM4AI and the ICS to process massive data.
- The DSI4AI, includes cross-functional tasks like, data cleansing, intelligent data capture techniques and data mining and NLP4AI support.
- The DSI4AI is capable of capturing, maintaining and preparing BGD4AI for complex and intelligent analysis.
- BGD4AI supports the DSI4AI to deliver velocity, variety and volume (or the 3Vs); that supports the techniques for analysing huge volumes of data.

THE USE OF STATISTICS

Statistics Methods' Integration

The Integration of statistics methods includes (OMNI-SCI, 2021):

- DSI4AI is a broad, cross functional domain that is used in applied business management, computer science, economics, mathematics, programming and software engineering; which are supported by statistics.
- The DSI4AI requires the collection, processing, management, analysis and visualization of large quantities of data; where DSI4AI specialists use tools from various APDs, including statistics, to achieve those activities.
- There is a close relation between DSI4AI and BGD4AI, where most BGD4AI's data are unstructured and include non-numeric data. Therefore, the task of processing data as a DSI4AI specialist involves removing noise and extracting useful data sets.
- Statistical tasks need specific design and implementation strategies to support: 1) acquisition; 2) architecture; 3) analysis; and 4) archiving processes. These *4As* of DSI4AI are unique to the APD.
- Statistics is a broad field demanding APD expertise and it focuses on the study of numerical and categorical data.
- Statistical theory and methods support the DSI4AI in: 1) gathering data in a performant way; 2) analyse and interpret them for a particular use; and 3) make conclusions to solve particular problems.
- Statistical methods ensure that DSI4AI processes explore and describe data while summarizing them.
- Statistical protocols are essential to deliver accurate prediction and insightful inferences.

Data Mining Technique for AI

The Data Mining Techniques for AI (DMT4AI) has the following characteristics (OMNI-SCI, 2021):

- It is used in business to support the DSI4AI, to render data more usable for a specific business objective.
- It deals with structured data, when exploring huge amounts of unprocessed data.

Deep Learning Integration for AI

The DLI4AI has the following characteristics (OMNI-SCI, 2021):

- It is a function that mimics how the human brain works as it processes data and generates patterns to be used by the DMS4AI.
- It is a type of MLI4AI, that focuses on deep neural networks that can master unstructured or unlabelled data, without any type of human assistance.
- It uses hierarchical artificial neural networks to engage in the MLI4AI process.

- Traditional DA4AI uses data in a linear manner, whereas the DLI4AI uses a hierarchy of functions which enables a nonlinear approach to problems' solving.

DSI4AI for Business

The DSI4AI for business has the following characteristics (OMNI-SCI, 2021):

- Supports analytics that is used in an APD.
- DSI4AI supports businesses to understand better the specific needs of customers by using the existing data.
- DSI4AI processes can deliver training models for searching and delivering recommendation.

Business Analytics Integration for AI

The Business Analytics Integration for AI (BAI4AI) has the following characteristics (OMNI-SCI, 2021):

- The DSI4AI and BAI4AI focus on solving business problems and both involve: 1) Data collection; 2) Modelling data; and 3) Gleaning insights from the data. The main difference is that BAI4AI is specific to business-related problems, like, profit and costs.
- In contrast, DSI4AI methods explore how a wide range of CSFs might affect the *Entity's* business. DSI4AI combines data with ICS and algorithms' implementation to solve various types of problems.
- BAI4AI is a specialized field, analysing data from the business using traditional statistical theory to generate insights and to deliver business solutions.

Business Intelligence Integration for AI

The BII4AI has the following characteristics (OMNI-SCI, 2021):

- It is a subset of DAI4AI and it analyses existing data for insights to discover business trends.
- It gathers data from internal and external sources to: 1) prepare processes for a specific use; and 2) creates dashboards to resolve business problems.
- BII4AI tools can usually evaluate specific events which might affect an *Entity* in the future.

DSI4AI in Finance

The DSI4AI in finance has the following characteristics (OMNI-SCI, 2021):

- It is a powerful tool to combat fraud, giving financial institutions to recognize problematic patterns in data.
- It helps to reduce non-performing assets and to reveal downward trends.
- DSI4AI creates a model that can perform predictive analytics on various topics.

DSI4AI Use in Transformation Initiatives

The DSI4AI in transformation initiatives has the following characteristics (OMNI-SCI, 2021):

- An *Entity* can use DSI4AI to shape policies to meet the needs of their constituents, by collecting data with the census, surveys and tools.
- Correlative or descriptive analysis of used data sets is used to support the DMS4AI.

GAIP's CSF's

Based on the LRP4AI process the most important CSFs that were used.

Table 7. The factors have an average of 8.50

Critical Success Factors	KPIs		Weightings
CSF_DSI4AI_GAIP_Construct	Feasible	▼	From 1 to 10. **09 Selected**
CSF_DSI4AI_GAIP_ML4AI_DLI4AI	Complex	▼	From 1 to 10. **08 Selected**
CSF_DSI4AI_GAIP_Analytics_Statistics	Feasible	▼	From 1 to 10. **09 Selected**
CSF_DSI4AI_GAIP_BGD4AI	Complex	▼	From 1 to 10. **08 Selected**
CSF_DSI4AI_GAIP_DMT4AI	Feasible	▼	From 1 to 10. **09 Selected**
CSF_DSI4AI_GAIP_Business	Complex	▼	From 1 to 10. **08 Selected**
CSF_DSI4AI_GAIP_Finance	Feasible	▼	From 1 to 10. **09 Selected**
CSF_DSI4AI_GAIP_Transformation	Complex	▼	From 1 to 10. **08 Selected**

valuation

As shown in Table 7, the result's aim is to prove or justify GAIP's feasibility; and the result permits to move to the next CSA that is the assembling the DSI4AI component.

ASSEMBLING DSI4AI'S COMPONENTS

DSI4AI components enable *Entities* to process huge amounts of structured and unstructured data from BG4AI to detect patterns. This enables them to increase efficiencies, manage costs, identify new market opportunities and boost their market advantage (OMNI-SCI (2021).

THE ANALYSIS PROCESSES

The Process

DSI4AI's Application Programming Interface (API) can be used to avoid common pitfalls, because of expensive, complex and monolithic nature, the barrier to integrate DSI4AI has been simplified with the introduction of simpler and distributed platform becomes viable (Gartner, 2020).

People

In order to motivate stakeholders, it is imperative that there is a strong relationship between the DSI4AI and the *Entity's* business results. This is complex to achieve, because of ICS' silo structure (Gartner, 2020).

Technology

To assess impacts related to *Projects*, firstly is important to assess DSI4AI's solutions for a given problem and whether the *Entity* is ready to be apply the solution. It is recommended to start with a PoC and assess an end solution. Secondly, as it is imperative not to start with ICS/technology integration, and where EA4AI needs to inspect the existing *Entity's* processes significantly (Gartner, 2020).

Data-Driven Business Transformation Projects

Data-driven *Projects* (or simply *DDProject*) has the following characteristics (IBM, 2019):

- DMS4AI based on data is daily business and there is a need to adopt new GAIP oriented technologies and methodologies that facilitate data-centric DMS4AI; that is the first important step for a *Project*. Where GAIP is the skeleton of MLI4AI and DLI4AI.
- DSI4AI and GAIP are synergistic, where GAIP is the skeleton of the DSI4AI, which improves data querying accuracy and performance and helps to optimize *Project* resources. DSI4AI platforms are evolving to support GAIP like patterns.
- Data platforms and GAIP analytics references from the LRP4AI, reveal the extent to which *Entities* use GAIP and MLI4AI as critical goals of their data platform and analytics initiatives. Two-thirds of *Entities* confirm that a GAIP like approach and MLI4AI are important components of their data platform and DA4AI initiatives. The increase upto 88% among the most data-driven *Entities*, where strategic *Project* decisions are data-driven.

Main Components

DS4AI main components are (Guru99, 2021):

- Statistics is the most critical unit of DSI4AI and it is the method or science of collecting and analysing numerical data in large quantities to deliver insights.
- Visualization technique supports the access to huge amounts of data in digestible visuals.

- MLI4AI explores the building and study of algorithms which learn to deliver predictions about unforeseen/future data.
- DLI4AI method is a new MLI4AI based research where the algorithm selects the analysis model to be followed.

DSI4AI Processes

The main DSI4AI processes are (Guru99, 2021):

- The *Discovery* process, involves data acquisition from the *Entity's* sources and supports various types of requests. Where data can be: 1) Log files from webservers; 2) Data gathered from social media; 3) Census datasets; and 4) Data streamed from online sources using APIs
- The *preparation* of data can generate inconsistencies like, missing values, blank columns, incorrect data formats; which needs to be corrected or removed. Correction implies, to process, explore and condition data models before modelling. The cleaner the *Entity's* data are, the more credible are the made predictions.
- The *Model Planning* process, determines the method and technique to define the relation between input variables. Planning for a model is done applying different statistical formulas and visualization environments.
- The *Model Building* process, prepares datasets for training and testing are distributed. Modelling techniques like association, classification and clustering are applied to the training data sets. Once the model prepared, it is tested against the *testing* datasets.
- The *Operationalization process*, delivers the final baseline models with reports, code and technical documents. The models are deployed in production environments after testing has terminated.
- *Communicating results*, to all stakeholders, shows the results and if they are successful or not.

DS4AI NEEDED SKILLS

DS4AI Roles

DSI4AI's main skill/specialist roles are:

- Data Scientist.
- Data Engineer.
- Data Analyst.
- Statistician.
- Data Architect.
- Data Admin.
- Business Analyst.
- Data/Analytics Manager.

Certifications

Today, there are various certifications, like, The Open Group Open Certified Data Scientist (Open CDS) certification, which is the industry's most comprehensive certification available for Data Scientists. Open CDS is an independent global certification for qualifying the skills, knowledge, and experience of Data Scientists (The Open Group, 2021).

DSI4AI's CSF's

Based on the LRP4AI process the most important CSFs that were used.

Table 8. The factors have an average of 8.70

Critical Success Factors	KPIs		Weightings
CSF_DSI4AI_Assembling_Analysis_Processes	Complex	▾	From 1 to 10. **08 Selected**
CSF_DSI4AI_Assembling_DDProject	Complex	▾	From 1 to 10. **08 Selected**
CSF_DSI4AI_Assembling_Integration_Components	Complex	▾	From 1 to 10. **08 Selected**
CSF_DSI4AI_Assembling_EA4AI_ADM4AI	Proven	▾	From 1 to 10. **10 Selected**
CSF_DSI4AI_Assembling_CSF_CSA	Feasible	▾	From 1 to 10. **09 Selected**
CSF_DSI4AI_Assembling_Processes	Feasible	▾	From 1 to 10. **09 Selected**
CSF_DSI4AI_Assembling_Skills	Proven	▾	From 1 to 10. **10 Selected**
CSF_DSI4AI_Assembling_Domains	Feasible	▾	From 1 to 10. **09 Selected**

valuation

As shown in Table 8, the result's aim is to prove or justify the RDP4AI's feasibility.

THE PROOF OF CONCEPT

Basics

TRADf's Tm empirical model was built to prove this RDP4AI's hypothesis by using a concrete PoC, which has been developed using the Microsoft Visual Studio 2019 and Python. The PoC contains *TRADf*'s major components needed for the BIG4AI based DSI4AI's processing and was primarily tested its mixed reasoning engine, which is based on the heuristics model. This PoC serves to confirm the research's RQ. The reasoning engine has a defined goal function, which calculates the best solution for the encountered DSI4AI problems or requests. The PoC's results are presented in the form of a set of technical and managerial recommendations.

CSFs, Rules and Constraints Setup

The DSI4AI's process execution starts with the use of the imputed data collection in *TRADf's* massive data storage and then these data are filtered using the selected set of CSFs. The execution of the qualitative part follows; initially inputted *TRADf's* data collection is considered to be the root or initial node that helps in the establishment of the basic set of possible problems and to be eventually enhanced with the adopted DSI4AI's solution(s). The DMS4AI's tree reasoning goal is to select the optimal solutions and to implement them in *Project* successfully.

The Tree and Resources

GAIP's decision tree's collection of nodes contains the following resources, which are based on the unbundling of the system: 1) The executed actions; 2) The constraints; 3) The DSI4AI related problems; and 4) The set of possible solutions. Each tree node is a CSF suggestion and it is linked to a concrete data state, which in turn contains an aggregate of a resource linked with a 1:1 mapping link.

Possible Solutions

The selected CSFs were fed in the DMS4AI's heuristics engine in order to reveal the optimal DSI4AI prerequisites for a selected *Project* problem or request. The CSFs were configured and weighted; afterwards they were processes in order to deliver a set of possible solutions. The DMS4AI starts with the initial set of selected CSFs that correspond to a specific problem or request; then the grounded hyperheuristics processing is launched to find a set of possible solution(s) in the form of possible improvements or suggestions of needed actions (Jaszkiewicz, & Sowiñski, 1999). The author's aim is to convert their relevant research outcomes into a set of managerially useful recommendations for DSI4AI's integration; and *TRADf's* hyper-heuristics tree processing model template that is suitable for a wide class of problem instances (Vella, Corne, & Murphy, 2009).

The PoC Processing

The PoC uses an internal set of CSFs' that are presented in Tables 1 to 8. These CSFs have bindings to specific RDP4AI resources, where the AHMM4AI formalism was designed using an NLP4AI microartefacts. In this chapter's tables and the result of the processing of the DMS4AI, as illustrated in Table 9, shows clearly that the DSI4AI is feasible.

The *TRADf* and hence the AHMM4AI's main constraint is that CSAs for simple research components, having an average result below 8.5 will be ignored. In the case of the DSI4AI's implementation an average result below 6.5 will be ignored. As shown in Table 9 the average is 9.15. The BGI4AI based DSI4AI processing model represents the relationships between this research's requirements, NLP4AI generic and microartefacts, unique identifiers and the CSAs. The PoC was achieved using *TRADf's* client interface. From the *TRADf's* client interface, the NLP4AI development setup and editing interface can

Table 9. The research's outcome

	Critical Success Factors	KPIs	Weightings Ranges	Values		
1	RDP5AI	HighlyFeasible	From 1 to 10.	9,25		
2	AHMM4AI	PossibleClassification	From 1 to 10.	10	EvaPA	
3	DMC4AI	AutomatedExists	From 1 to 10.	9,4		
4	PLATFORM	IntegrationPossible	From 1 to 10.	9		
5	EA4AI	AdvancedStage	From 1 to 10.	9		
6	ENVIRONMENT	Advanced	From 1 to 10.	9,4		
7	GAIP	IntegrationPossible	From 1 to 10.	8,5		
8	ASSEMBLING	IntegrationPossible	From 1 to 10.	8,7	RESULT:	9,15625

be launched. Once the development setup interface is activated the NLP4AI interface can be launched to implement the needed microartefact scripts to process the defined three CSAs. These scripts make up the kernel knowledge system and the DMS4AI set of actions that are processed in the background. The DSI4AI and the DMS4AI that automatically generates actions which make calls mixed (QLA4AI and QNA4AI) modules, that manages the edited NLP4AI script and flow. DSI4AI structures, serve various APDs and in this PoC the functional domain are information analysis and decision making of a business transaction's log; where the data that results from business transactions are logged and used in the data analysis process.

Information Analysis

DSI4AI's PoC took into account the integration of DAI4AI processes that are used by a virtual user who simulates a business analyst. In this PoC a spreadsheet was built to use various data sources that fed the prototyped business transactions system.

Layers

The prototyped business transaction is based on the PoC's class model; The data architecture and modelling PoC's layers are:

- Data architecture using TOGAF to link DSI4AI to various artefacts.
- The client layer that contains the following packages based on: RDBMS, Microsoft Excel, Flat Files Interfaces and a Client web interface.
- The data services layer that contains the data services hub.
- The data management layer that contains the following packages: an entity relational model, an extensible mark-up language transformer and a NoSQL database interface.

- The control-monitoring layer contains a generic logger interface.
- The platform layer that contains the following packages: the *Entity* ESB, an object database connector and an application database connector.

SOLUTIONS AND RECOMMENDATIONS

This chapter's and its PoC's list of the most important technical and managerial recommendations:

- The *Manager*s should be supported with a set of BGI4AI based DSI4AIs tools that can be easily integrated with the defined data-driven EA4AI principles (IBM, 2015a).
- The role of data standards is important; today there are many standards concerning the DSI4AI. The *Manager* must propose a solution on how to integrate these various data standards in the *Project*.
- GAIP's data service bus and *Entity* application integration concept must be defined for the *Project*. That would glue the various data sources of the business environment.
- The meta-model and the corresponding "1:1" mapping approach can be used to manage an agile *Project* process (OASIS, 2014).
- Unbundling through the use of business data services uses the DMS4AI to integrated in the context of a system that applies a holistic approach (Daellenbach, McNickle, & Dye, 2012).
- The data services and dBB4AIs must unify the implementation and usage of data models.
- To define BGI4AI's and DSI4AI's default CSFs.
- Implement an ETL process to access data from various locations to enable their unification and normalization for DSI4AI usage.
- Data transformation models need a meta-model to show the relationships between various types of data models and data sources.
- Define a data normalization and inter-operability paradigm that must be based on various standards.
- Define a business process and a data-driven EA4AI and modelling integration paradigm to enhance the KMS4AI and DMS4AI.
- Develop an agile MVC4AI pattern that is dynamically created for each business transaction. This MVC4AI uses a dBB4AI and its instance
- Define the ADM4AI's integration with the proposed concept where the data building and solution blocks are the basic artefacts that circulate through the ADM4AI.
- Define business architecture integration paradigm that is needed to manage the implementation of the dBB4AIs (The Open Group, 2014a).
- Define conceptual views that can be built to simplify the application of the DSI4AI. Such views can also be the used to simplify the *Entity*'s data-model that links various data sources.
- Create basic class diagrams for the DSI4AI(s) to be the central artefact that is defined in the initial phase and then calibrated in all other phases.
- Define the usage of business transactions' data models in various class diagrams.

CONCLUSION

This RDP, which manages BGI4AI and DSI4AI modules, is mainly motivated by high the failure rates and complexity in *Projects*. The main activities are related to data architecture and modelling components for a *Project*. A general data concept is needed to finalize the implementation phase of a *Project* and the integration of BGI4AI. There are several trends shaping the future of DSI4AI: 1) the DSI4AI tasks in the *Project* life-cycle are automated and that increases the *Entity's* ROI: 2) the DSI4AI feasibility should be verified by a PoC; 3) another important element is that, DSI4AI resources become accessible to a large set of end-points; 4) to manage the tension between the right to privacy, the need to regulate and the state of transparency; and 5) DSI4AI has to capacity to integrate MLI4AI algorithms transparent, that makes regulatory oversight possible. To implement an AI and Bigdata based data sciences for *Projects* it is recommended to establish a holistic framework like *TRADf* and an EA methodology like TOGAF. This whole chapter is a pattern on how to build such a system; added to that there are many recommendations.

FUTURE RESEARCH DIRECTIONS

The *TRADf* future research will focus on MLI4AI's internals.

REFERENCES

Camarinha-Matos, L. M. (2012). *Scientific research methodologies and techniques- Unit 2: Scientific method. Unit 2: Scientific methodology. PhD program in electrical and computer engineering.* Uninova.

Clancy, L. (2019). *Functional programming reaches for stardom in finance.* CME Group. Accessed and reviewed in April 2021, https://www.risk.net/risk-management/6395366/functional-programming-reaches-for-stardom-in-finance

Daellenbach, H., McNickle, D., & Dye, Sh. (2012). *Management Science. Decision-making through systems thinking* (2nd ed.). Plagrave Macmillian.

Dantzig, G. (1949). Programming of Interdependent Activities: II Mathematical Models. *The Journal of the Operational Research Society, 53*(11), 1275–1280.

Doree, J. (2015). *Data Science, Data Architecture-Predictive Analytics Methodology: Building a Data Map for a Greenfield Data Science Initiative.* Datasciencearchitect. Accessed and reviewed in April 2019, https://datasciencearchitect.wordpress.com/tag/togaf/

Fodor, O., Dell'Erba, M., Ricci, F., Spada, A., & Werthner, H. (2002). *Conceptual Normalisation of XML Data for Interoperability in Tourism. Commerce and Tourism Research Laboratory ITC-irst.* University of Trento.

Gartner. (2020). *Three Essentials for Starting and Supporting Master Data Management.* ID G00730039. Gartner Inc. Accessed and reviewed in April 2019, https://www.gartner.com/doc/reprints?id=1-24MIGFGU&ct=201119&st=sb

Guru99. (2021). *Data Science Tutorial for Beginners: What is, Basics & Process*. Accessed and reviewed in April 2019, https://www.guru99.com/data-science-tutorial.html

IBM. (2015a). *Modelling the Entity data architecture*. IBM.

IBM. (2019). *AI and Data Management-Delivering Data-Driven Business Transformation and Operational Efficiencies*. IBM USA.

IMD. (2015). *IMD business school and Cisco join forces on digital business transformation*. IMD.

Järvinen, P. (2007). Action Research is Similar to Design Science. *Quality & Quantity, 41*(1), 37–54. https://link.springer.com/article/10.1007/s11135-005-5427-1

Jaszkiewicz, J., & Sowiñski, R. (1999). The 'Light Beam Search' approach - an overview of methodology and applications. *European Journal of Operational Research, 113*(2), 300–314. doi:10.1016/S0377-2217(98)00218-5

Kim, K., & Kim, K. (1999). Routing straddle carriers for the loading operation of containers using a beam search algorithm. Elsevier. *Computers & Industrial Engineering, 36*(1), 109–136. doi:10.1016/S0360-8352(99)00005-4

Lazar, I., Motogna, S., & Parv, B. (2010). Behaviour-Driven Development of Foundational UML Components. Department of Computer Science. Babes-Bolyai University, Cluj-Napoca, Romania. doi:10.1016/j.entcs.2010.07.007

Leitch, R., & Day, Ch. (2000). *Action research and reflective practice: towards a holistic view*. Taylor & Francis. https://www.tandfonline.com/doi/ref/10.1080/09650790000200108?scroll=top

Lockwood, R. (2018). *Introduction The Relational Data Model*. Accessed and reviewed in April 2021, http://www.jakobsens.dk/Nekrologer.htm

Loginovskiy, O. V., Dranko, O. I., & Hollay, A. V. (2018). *Mathematical Models for Decision-Making on Strategic Management of Industrial Enterprise in Conditions of Instability*. In Internationalization of Education in Applied Mathematics and Informatics for HighTech Applications (EMIT 2018), Leipzig, Germany.

Mehra, A., Grundy, J., & Hosking, J. (2005). A generic approach to supporting diagram differencing and merging for collaborative design. In *ASE '05 Proceedings of the 20th IEEE/ACM international Conference on Automated software engineering*. ACM. 10.1145/1101908.1101940

Merson, P. (2009). *Data Model as an Architectural View. Technical Note. CMU/SEI-2009-TN-024*. Research, Technology, and System Solutions.

Modelling, T. O. G. A. F. (2015a). *Data dissemination view*. TOGAF Modelling. Accessed and reviewed in April 2021, http://www.TOGAF-modelling.org/models/data-architecture-menu/data-dissemination-diagrams-menu.html

Modelling, T. O. G. A. F. (2015c). *Data lifecyle diagram*. TOGAF Modelling. Accessed and reviewed in April 2021, http://www.TOGAF-modelling.org/models/data-architecture-menu/data-lifecycle-diagrams-menu.html

Modelling, T. O. G. A. F. (2015d). *Data migration diagram*. TOGAF Modelling. Accessed and reviewed in April 2021, http://www.TOGAF-modelling.org/models/data-architecture-menu/data-migration-diagrams-menu.html

Modelling, T. O. G. A. F. (2015e). *Data security diagram*. TOGAF Modelling. Accessed and reviewed in April 2021,http://www.TOGAF-modelling.org/models/data-architecture-menu/19-data-security-diagrams.html

Moore, J. (2014). *Java programming with lambda expressions-A mathematical example demonstrates the power of lambdas in Java 8*. Javaworld. Accessed and reviewed in April 2021, https://www.javaworld.com/article/2092260/java-se/java-programming-with-lambda-expressions.html

Nijboer, F., Morin, F., Carmien, S., Koene, R., Leon, E., & Hoffman, U. (2009). Affective brain-computer interfaces: Psychophysiological markers of emotion in healthy persons and in persons with amyotrophic lateral sclerosis. In *3rd International Conference on Affective Computing and Intelligent Interaction and Workshops*. IEEE. 10.1109/ACII.2009.5349479

OASIS. (2009). *OASIS Web Services Reliable Messaging (WS-ReliableMessaging) Version 1.2*. OASIS Standard. Accessed and reviewed in April 2021, http://docs.oasis-open.org/ws-rx/wsrm/200702/wsrm-1.2-spec-os.html

OASIS. (2014). *ISO/IEC and OASIS Collaborate on E-Business Standards-Standards Groups Increase Cross-Participation to Enhance Interoperability*. The OASIS Group. Accessed and reviewed in April 2021, https://www.oasis-open.org/news/pr/isoiec-and-oasis-collaborate-on-e-business-standards

OMNI-SCI. (2021). *Data Science - A Complete Introduction*. OMNI-SCI. Accessed and reviewed in April 2021, https://www.omnisci.com/learn/data-science

Sarkar, D. (2018). *Get Smarter with Data Science — Tackling Real Enterprise Challenges. Take your Data Science Projects from Zero to Production*. Towards Data Science. Accessed and reviewed in April 2021, https://towardsdatascience.com/get-smarter-with-data-science-tackling-real-enterprise-challenges-67ee001f6097

SAS. (2021). *History of Big Data*. SAS. Accessed and reviewed in April 2021, https://www.sas.com/en_us/insights/big-data/what-is-big-data.html

Sikander, M., & Khiyal, H. (2018). *Computational Models for Upgrading Traditional Agriculture*. Preston University. Accessed and reviewed in April 2021, https://www.researchgate.net/publication/326080886

Simonin, J., Bertin, E., Traon, Y., Jezequel, J.-M., & Crespi, N. (2010). Business and Information System Alignment: A Formal Solution for Telecom Services. In *2010 Fifth International Conference on Software Engineering Advances*. IEEE. 10.1109/ICSEA.2010.49

Tamr. (2014). *The Evolution of ETL*. Tamr. http://www.tamr.com/evolution-etl/

The Open Group. (2011). *Open Group Standard-TOGAF® Guide, Version 9.1*. The Open Group.

The Open Group. (2013b). *ArchiMate®*. Accessed and reviewed in April 2021, http://www.opengroup.org/subjectareas/*Entity*/archimate

The Open Group. (2014a). *The Open Group's Architecture Framework-Building blocks-Module 13.* Accessed and reviewed in April 2021, www.open-group.com/TOGAF

The Open Group. (2021). *The Open Group Professional Certification for the Data Scientist Profession (Open CDS).* The Open Group. Accessed and reviewed in April 2021, https://www.opengroup.org/certifications/certified-data-scientist-open-cds

Trad, A., & Kalpić, D. (2020a). *Using Applied Mathematical Models for Business Transformation.* *Author Book.* IGI-Global. doi:10.4018/978-1-7998-1009-4

Trujillo, J., & Luj'an-Mora, S. (2003). *A UML Based Approach for Modelling ETL Processes in Data Warehouses.* Dept. de Lenguajes y Sistemas Inform'aticos. Universidad de Alicante.

Vella, A., Corne, D., & Murphy, C. (2009). *Hyper-heuristic decision tree induction.* Sch. of MACS, Heriot-Watt Univ., Edinburgh, UK. Nature & Biologically Inspired Computing, 2009. NaBIC 2009. World Congress.

Veneberg, R. (2014). *Combining enterprise architecture and operational data-to better support decision-making. University of Twente.* School of Management and Governance.

ADDITIONAL READING

Farhoomand, A. (2004). *Managing Business Engineering transformation.* Palgrave Macmillan.

KEY TERMS AND DEFINITIONS

Data Modelling: Is the process of developing data models for the business transformation process. **CSFs:** can be used to manage the statuses and gaps in various project plans and gives the Projects the capacity to proactively and automatically recognize erroneous aBB4AIs and to just-in-time reschedule the Project plan(s).

TRADf: Is this research's framework.

Chapter 23
The Effect of Population, Public Investments, and Economic Growth on Regional Renewable Energy Consumption in Turkey:
Dynamic Panel Data Analysis

Özlem Karadağ Albayrak
https://orcid.org/0000-0003-0832-0490
Kafkas University, Turkey

ABSTRACT

Making the use of renewable energy sources widespread is of paramount importance for Turkey as for all countries. In this regard, the determiners of renewable energy consumption have been investigated. The effect of determining or factors affecting the use of renewable energy sources on a regional scale to Turkey were examined with different qualitative and quantitative research techniques. In this study, the factors of economic growth, public investments, and population are analyzed by considering regional differences on the consumption of renewable energy resources. The effect of regional economic growth, regional public investments, and regional population on the amount of regional renewable energy consumption were investigated by using panel data of 26 statistical regions of Level-2 classification in the period between 2010-2018 in Turkey. The results obtained by the dynamic panel data analysis concluded that economic growth and public investments at the regional level increased renewable energy consumption while the population growth decreased.

INTRODUCTION

Renewable energy sources are the safest alternatives to fossil fuels produced from oil, natural gas and coal. The reasons for searching alternatives to fossil fuels may be stated as their being generally exhausted and their damage to the environment. Therefore, renewable energy sources as an alternative to

DOI: 10.4018/978-1-7998-6985-6.ch023

fossil fuels in energy production are of paramount importance for all countries with different levels of development. The use of fossil fuels in large quantities in energy generation since the Industrial Revolution has supported the development of social productivity to a great extent but has caused important problems such as environmental pollution (Wang Q et. al., 2020). Energy use increases the economic growth and development of a country but results in the problems, such as global warming and carbon emission (Khan H. et al., 2020). Fossil sources such as oil, natural gas and coal, used widely in energy production, will run out of. This problem poses a threat to the sustainability of energy supply. The renewable energy consumption influences sustainable development positively and in a statistically significant manner (Güney, 2020).

Environmental agreements, to which many countries are a party, such as the Kyoto protocol, have also encouraged the search for alternatives to fossil fuels (Sasmaz et. al, 2020). In countries where the share of non-renewable energy sources in the overall energy mix is higher, the increase in energy consumption results in an increase in carbon emissions (Pata, 2018). Accordingly, large industrialized countries play a key role in the solution to this problem as they use most of the fossil fuels produced and technological development (Byrne et. al., 2007).

Increasing demand for energy consumption, strong commitments to remove environmental concerns, technology development and political support will enable the renewable energy an increasingly important role in the global energy mix in the long term (Anton and Nucu, 2020). The renewable energy sources, such as solar, wind, hydraulic, geothermal, biomass, wave, hydrogen either do not cause or result in very little emissions causing global warming. In this respect, encouraging the use of renewable energy sources is of utmost importance for providing a sustainable economic growth in environmental respects (Le et al., 2020).

While the energy supply in the world was obtained from oil, coal and natural gas respectively between 1990-2018, the supply provided from the renewable energy sources was least (International Energy Agency, 2021). As in many other countries across the world, Turkey also has limited fossil fuel reserves. Being dependent on outside financial sources regarding fossil fuels results in an economic burden for countries. In addition, any political tension between countries poses a threat to energy supply. For this reason, the ability to create their own resources using renewable energy resources provides social, economic and environmental benefits for countries. For example, the benefits of employment generation cover more than the income obtained from employment, produced goods and services due to "multiplier effect" (Le et al., 2020).

In 2019, Turkey provided approximately 45.2% of its energy production from renewable energy sources. A large part of this ratio has been generated by hydraulic sources with dams, which are not defined in YEKDEM legislation. Therefore, most of energy demand in Turkey is supplied by fossil sources. In general, policy-makers conduct research in many different fields for the increase in renewable energy sources. In this regard, renewable-sourced electricity generators are provided with a guarantee of purchase at certain prices, and there are different supports for the domestic spare parts used. Moreover, Turkey is also a party to environmental agreements such as the Kyoto protocol. Local administrations provide support in this respect by participating in various organizations. In Turkey, İzmir, Konya, Gaziantep as well as Seferihisar, Karşıyaka, Şişli, Kartal, Tepebaşı, Çankaya, Seydişehir, Fındıklı district municipalities are members of the International Council of Local Environmental Initiatives (ICLEI), which is the most common network of the local climate protection cities campaign in the world.

In this study, a regional evaluation was carried out regarding Turkey. All data were obtained in regional level. The goal of the study is to examine the effects of regional gross national product, population and public investments on renewable energy consumption, which is an indicator of regional development level with data for the period of 2010-2018 for 26 regions on a regional scale. The need for diversity and localization regarding energy sources is increasingly widely accepted in the world for the following years (Wang B. et. al, 2020).

This study supports the use of dynamic models according to static models while defining regional management behavior (Dahlberg and Johansson, 2000). In this study, the results provided by estimators of Pooled OLS, Fixed Effect, Difference GMM and System GMM are presented all together.

The most significant contribution of this study is to examine the effect of related variables on renewable energy consumption especially in Turkey with different regional development levels. As far as the search researchers have made in the related literature, this study is the first carried out on the regional scale in Turkey. In addition, this study aims to increase information about the role of regional economic growth, public investment and population in encouraging the implementation of renewable sources in energy sector. The conclusions obtained in this study may contribute to the decisions to be taken by policymakers to increase renewable energy consumption, especially in the goals for regional development. Turkey is a country with more regional developmental differences.

Regions such as Istanbul, Ankara and Izmir included in the Level 2 classification have the highest economic growth shares and there is one-way migration movement from other regions towards these regions. Renewable energy resources are the only alternative to eliminate environmental concerns, and they are a very important sector to close the difference between regional development levels economically and socially. This study focuses on regional scale assessment in order to contribute to the sustainable development of the regions. determinants that influence the consumption of renewable energy sources on a regional scale aims to correct this deficiency in the literature and in this context it is very important for Turkey.

Renewable Energy Sources

The renewable energy sources are defined as follows in The Regulation on Certification and Support of Renewable Energy Resources (YEKDEM): "Wind, solar, geothermal, biomass, gas generated from biomass (including landfill gas), wave, current energy, and energy generation production facilities by tidal and canal or river type or reservoir area below fifteen square kilometres or suitable for the establishment of a hydroelectric with pumped storage". Based on this definition, consumption of energy produced by hydraulic power plants not included in this classification was not subjected in the study.

All renewable energy sources are not used in Turkey. Hydraulics, solar, wind, geothermal, biomass-sourced energy is produced in Turkey. The solar and wind energy generation is carried out by two methods, licensed and unlicensed, and contests are held for licensed generation. There is a quite high potential regarding these sources in Turkey. In 2017, Turkey became the country which increased its installed capacity of solar energy most. It is also ranked among the top five countries in the world regarding geothermal energy generation.

BACKGROUND

Many researchers have conducted investigations on the different factors effective on the amount of renewable energy consumption. In this respect, economic growth, population, public investments, greenhouse gas emissions, financial development, energy prices, trade, foreign direct investment, human capital Index may be given as examples.

Le et al. (2020) analyzed the effect of financial development on renewable energy consumption by means of 2005-2014 panel data of 55 countries by using Two-System generalized moment method (GMM). Omri et al. (2015) investigated the relationship among consumption amount of renewable energy resources with the variables of per capita CO_2 emissions, real oil price, per capita GDP and per capita trade openness by static and dynamic panel data analysis techniques. Padhan et al. (2020) examined the effect of GDP, oil prices and carbon emissions per capita on renewable energy consumption in 30 OECD countries (1970-2015). By utilizing fully modified ordinary least squares (FMOLS) and pooled ordinary least squares (POLS) techniques, Amoah et. al. (2020) analyzed the role of economic welfare and economic freedom as driving forces of renewable energy by means of the panel data of 32 African countries between 1996-2017. Moreover, Assi et al. (2021) analyzed the effect of the variables, such as financial development, environmental pollution, innovation, economic freedom and GDP per capita, specified to be five main factors affecting the renewable energy consumption, by using the panel data belonging to the period of 1998-2018. By using 1980-2018 panel data from 190 countries, Zhao et al. (2020) analyzed the effect of financial development, per capita income and trade openness factors on renewable and non-renewable energy consumption in China by 1980-2015 time series. Khan H. Et al (2020) analyzed the effect of economic growth, foreign direct investment (FDI) and impact of CO_2 emissions on the renewable energy consumption by means of two-step difference GMM and two-step system GMM techniques from dynamic panel data estimators. In addition to these factors, the effects of new factors on renewable energy were also investigated. Yang and Park (2020) discussed the effect of renewable energy financial incentive policy and democratic governance on increasing renewable energy efficiency by the panel data of 98 developed countries between 2000-2014 and the fixed-effects regression estimates (FE) method. Sasmaz et al. (2020) concluded that there was a directly proportional relationship between renewable energy consumption and human development index (HDI). With a different approach, Agyeman et al. (2020) investigated the long-term driving forces of renewable energy consumption by using a time series data from 1990 to 2015 and the Fully modified ordinary least square (FMOLS) estimator. Przychodzen and Przychodzen (2020) discussed the effect of widely used factors, such as GDP, FDI and CO_2 on renewable energy consumption. In addition, the factors of unemployment level, inflation, domestic credit availability, public debt, current account balance, R&D expenditures, corporate restructuring, competition policy implementation, energy market competitiveness, European Union membership, and being a party to the Kyoto Protocol were also examined.

It is seen in the literature that the studies were mostly carried out on countries. There are few studies discussing the regional differences of a country. Dorrell and Lee (2020) discussed the effect of political parties on wind energy in the United States of America regarding the states. Hartley et al. (2015) revealed the impact of alternative energy sources on local employment in the state of Texas by First difference GMM methods. Bao and Xu (2019) examined the geographical regions in China by utilizing the annual data of 30 provinces (excluding Tibet, Hong Kong, Macau and Taiwan) between 1997-2015 and concluded that the value of China's renewable energy consumption, urbanization, and economic growth in one region can be influenced by others.

GDP and population, used in the study as the determiners of renewable energy consumption, have also been subjected in most of the studies detailed above. However, the literature examining direct public investments (PI) as a factor effective on consumption is not comprehensive. Financial investments made by public and private sectors are of paramount importance to increase renewable energy generation capacity in leading economies (Lee, 2019). Policy-makers may provide funds to local authorities in order to be used in renewable energy development (Menz and Vachon, 2005). However, public funds are limited, and many renewable energy projects compete for these limited funds (Wang Q. et al., 2019). Polzin et al. (2015) investigated the effect of electricity generation capacity investments, made by institutional investors in accordance with public policy in OECD countries, on renewable energy (RE), and stated that there was generally a directly proportional effect. By conducting an analysis with the 2004-2015 panel data of 23 OECD countries, Corrocher and Cappa (2020) found a directly proportional relationship among public investments and public policies with solar energy.

The above empirical studies show to what extent there are few regional study results on the determinants of the consumption amount of renewable energy sources. In Turkey, regional development differences are high. Renewable energy sources are considered to be an opportunity to reduce these differences. In this respect, it is of importance that energy policymakers and governments should be aware of renewable energies. Therefore, the motivation for this study is to investigate the effect of regional GDP, public investments and population on renewable energy sources in Turkey. The results of this study will provide policy-makers with suggestions in creating sustainable energy policies for Turkey.

MAIN FOCUS OF THE CHAPTER

In this study, in order to reveal the regional differences in Turkey, 26 regions were evaluated in the group of Degree 2 according to Nomenclature of Territorial Units for Statistics (NUTS) (Table 1). This study is also important because of its contribution to regional data collection. Turkey was compiled by the author without using any database ready for data to be revealed regional differences. Regional renewable energy consumption and public investments data were compiled and shared for use in other research.

Dataset and Method

Regional data were used to investigate the regional impact on the consumption of renewable energy sources. All these are annual data related to 2010-2018 for 26 regions. The explanatory variables creating the determinants of the renewable energy consumption amount were specified by examining both accessibility and studies in the literature. In the study, the natural logarithms of all variables were taken and used. The sources of the explained and explanatory variables and data sets used in the study are provided in Table 2.

The reason for using the above-listed variables in our research model may be summarized as follows:

Regional GDP: This refers to the natural logarithmic form of the per capita GDP of the regions. As income increases, energy consumption increases, and GDP is accepted to be a factor affecting renewable energy consumption (Padhan et al., 2020). The regions with high value in this variable may better subsidize construction and preparation costs (Dorrell and Lee,2020).

Regional Population: This represents the natural logarithmic form of the total population of each region. As energy demand will be higher in the regions with higher populations, such regions need more energy generation to meet this demand. These regions are more encouraged to make an investment on alternative energy sources (Dorrell and Lee,2020).

Table 1. Statistical Regional Units Classification (NUTS-2nd Level)

Region Code	Citys
TR10	İstanbul
TR21	Tekirdağ, Edirne, Kırklareli
TR22	Balıkesir, Çanakkale
TR31	İzmir
TR32	Aydın, Denizli, Muğla
TR33	Manisa, Afyon, Kütahya, Uşak
TR41	Bursa, Eskişehir, Bilecik
TR42	Kocaeli, Sakarya, Düzce, Bolu, Yalova
TR51	Ankara
TR52	Konya, Karaman
TR61	Antalya, Isparta, Burdur
TR62	Adana, Mersin
TR63	Hatay, Kahramanmaraş, Osmaniye
TR71	Kırıkkale, Aksaray, Niğde, Nevşehir, Kırşehir
TR72	Kayseri, Sivas, Yozgat
TR81	Zonguldak, Karabük, Bartın
TR82	Kastamonu, Çankırı, Sinop
TR83	Samsun, Tokat, Çorum, Amasya
TR90	Trabzon, Ordu, Giresun, Rize, Artvin, Gümüşhane
TRA1	Erzurum, Erzincan, Bayburt
TRA2	Ağrı, Kars, Iğdır, Ardahan
TRB1	Malatya, Elazığ, Bingöl, Tunceli
TRB2	Van, Muş, Bitlis, Hakkari
TRC1	Gaziantep, Adıyaman, Kilis
TRC2	Şanlıurfa, Diyarbakır
TRC3	Mardin, Batman, Şırnak, Siirt

Table 2. Variables Used in the Study

Variables	Description	Shortening	Source
Dependent variable	Energy generation from renewable sources (kWh)	lny	EPDK
Independent variable	Regional gross domestic product, by branches of economic activity (Thousand TL, at Current Prices)	lngdp	TUIK
Independent variable	Population(Thousand)	lnn	TUIK
Independent variable	Public investment program initial grant (Thousand TL, at Current Prices)	lnky	SBB

Regional Public Investments: This refers to the natural logarithmic form of regional public investments. Energy investments from public investments are one of the physical infrastructure investment items such as roads, water and dams (Pirili, 2011). Domestic investments generally promote development and contribute to economic growth. In this respect, renewable energy sector can increase the preference of renewable energy use (Erdinş and Aydınbaş, 2020). In Turkey, there are large differences between regions in terms of development. The public investments are an important factor in overcoming these regional differences (Öztürk, 2012). The public investments made on a regional basis are also transferred to energy investments by development agencies. In this regard, the regional public investments were also included in this model. The descriptive statistics of the variables are given in Table 3.

Table 3. Descriptive Statistics

	LNY	LNGDP	LNKY	LNN
Mean	16.37	17.73	13.74	14.71
Median	19.23	17.68	13.68	14.76
Max	22.80	20.87	16.30	16.53
Min	0.00	15.90	12.57	13.51
Std. Dev.	7.40	0.91	0.66	0.59
Skewness	-1.65	0.71	1.05	0.53
Kurtosis	4.00	3.90	4.78	4.46

In this study, dynamic panel data analysis methods were used to explain the determinants of the amount of regional energy consumption based on renewable energy. GMM estimators provide effective results in cases where the time interval is small but cross-section sizes are large (Roodman, 2009).

Dynamic Panel Data Analysis

In the model established in this study, the effect of regional population, gdp and public investments on regional renewable energy consumption amount is investigated. As it is highly possible that there is a non-linear relationship between the variables used in our model, natural logarithmic forms of the variables were used when establishing the model.

Dynamic panel data analyses are widely used among panel data analysis methods. The dynamic relationships related to economic and financial variables are characterized by the existence of lagged values of the dependent variable along with independent variables (Demirci, 2018). In dynamic panel data, the cause and effect relationship of the underlying case is generally dynamic in time. For example, performance may be affected by previous year's expenses, which can play a more important role, rather than the current year's marketing expenses. In order to control this internal relationship, dynamic panel data estimation techniques also use the lags of dependent variables as explanatory variables (Ullah et. al, 2018). The estimators used in dynamic panel data analysis are PooledOLS (POLS), FixedEffect (FE), one-step difference GMM, two-step difference GMM, one-step system GMM and two-step system GMM.

While difference GMM estimator is suggested by Arellano and Bond (1991), Arellano and Bover (1995), Blundell and Bond (1998) recommend system GMM estimators. Blundell and Bond (1998) argue that System GMM estimator provides consistent and efficient parameter estimations, and has better asymptotic and finite sampling properties than the simple first differences GMM estimator.

Estimations were performed by considering the dynamic panel features with lagged value of renewable energy consumption in order to determine the proper estimator for our model while estimator of difference and system generalized method of moments (GMM) was utilized in order to estimate our empirical model. Dahlberg and Johansson (2000) state that GMM techniques are the most proper methods that may be used when examining regional that is local administration behaviors. The GMM estimator produces efficient estimations in which the first differences of instrument variables are independent of fixed effects (Roodman, 2009). The GMM estimator generates consistent parameter estimates in a regression, where independent variables are not absolutely exogenous, and also controls heteroscedasticity and autocorrelation (Dorrell and Lee, 2020). In order to test the validity of instruments in our GMM estimation, serial correlation tests suggested by Arellano and Bover (1995) were administered (the null hypothesis: there is no autocorrelation), and it was tested for a series of quadratic correlations in residues. In addition, the restrictions in the estimators were examined by over identification Hansen test (null hypothesis: the overall validity of the instruments).

Model

The model that will reveal the relationship among the variables in this study is provided in Equation 1.

$$lnY_{it} = \beta_0 + \beta_1 lnY_{it-1} + \beta_2 lnGDP_{it} + \beta_3 lnKY_{it} + \beta_4 lnN_{it} + \epsilon_{it} \tag{1}$$

Y_{it}: Regional renewable energy consumption, Y_{it-1}: A lagged value of the regional renewable energy consumption amount, GDP_{it}: Regional economic growth, N_{it}: Regional population, KY_{it}: Regional public investments. What is more, ϵ_{it} refers to error term in the model. STATA package program was used to estimate this model.

SOLUTIONS AND RECOMMENDATIONS

The estimation results obtained by dynamic panel data analysis methods are given in Table 4.

When examining the estimation results in Table 4, it is concluded that the instruments used in the model are not over identified as null hypothesis was accepted in Hansen test statistics for both difference GMM and System GMM estimators. By this result, it is concluded that the estimation methods used are proper. When autocorrelation tests of difference GMM and System GMM estimation results are examined, there is a first order negative autocorrelation (AR1) in error terms while there is not any second order autocorrelation (AR2). Moreover, Sargan test p values in the GMM system are above the significance level, and confirm the validity of the study models and the instruments used. The study concluded that both differents GMM and system GMM techniques generated effective results. When the first lag coefficients of the dependent variable are compared, it is lower in the FE estimator (0,128) than in the POLS estimator (0,389). According to Bond's (2002) suggestion on the selection of the GMM type, as the ranking between the initial lag coefficients was concluded to be FE <GMM <POLS, difference-GMM is enough, thus, the use of System GMM is not very necessary.

Table 4. Dynamic Panel Data Analysis of Regions

Variables	POOLED OLS	FIXED	one-step difference GMM	two-step difference GMM	one-step system GMM	two-step system GMM
lny L1	0.389*	0.128**	0.242*	0.285*	0.269**	0.280*
	(0.000)	(0.045)	(0.000)	(0.000)	(0.014)	(0.010)
lngdp	1.875***	8.543*	6.271***	6.923*	5.5189*	5.159*
	(0.054)	(0.001)	(0.103)	(0.000)	(0.000)	(0.002)
lnky	1.126	2.796**	2.393	2.002*	1.778***	1.727**
	(0.230)	(0.025)	(0.139)	(0.000)	(0.051)	(0.044)
lnn	-1.896	-25.527	-13.922	-32.394*	-7.011*	-6.631*
	(0.154)	(0.253)	(0.735)	(0.007)	(0.000)	(0.001)
_cons	-9.630	200.595			-6.277	-4.978
	(0.330)	(0.495)			(0.614)	(0.726)
Sargan Test	0.364	0.3501	32.33*	32.33*	38.77*	38.77*
Hansen J-test				22.310	24.760	24.760
				(0.173)	(0.211)	(0.211)
AR(1)			-6.32*	-2.43**	-2.75*	-2.14**
			(0.000)	(0.015)	(0.006)	(0.033)
AR(2)			1.01	0.78	0.84	0.76
			(0.313)	(0.434)	(0.403)	(0.446)

*, **, *** significant at 1%, 5%, 10% significance level, respectively. Over-identification for restrictions in GMM estimation is investigated by Hansen J-test. The first differences of residues are investigated by AR2 test of Arellano-Bond for the presence of second order autocorrelation.

When the results of the estimation are examined, the increase in per capita national income (with an average of 5.5% effect for a 1% increase in GDP) affects renewable energy consumption significantly and proportionally. While the regions with low income levels carry out infrastructure investments, the regions with high income make more investment in the development of renewable energy sources. In 2018, while the energy generation based on renewable sources was 1463.7 GWh in the region of TR10, having the highest economic growth in Turkey, this was 374.5 GWh in the region of TRA2 with the lowest figures. This result is in accordance with the conclusions achieved by Khan Z. et al. (2020), Omri et. al (2015), Agyeman et al. (2020), Przychodzen and Przychodzen (2020).

The population variable has a negative coefficient in all estimation results, and the coefficient of population is significant in System GMM models. This result is in the parallel of the direction of relationship specified by Dorrell and Lee (2020) in the study on the relationship between installed power of wind energy sources and population. Mehrara et al. (2015) stated that urban population is one of the most important variables that adversely affect renewable energy consumption in the Economic Cooperation Organization (ECO) economies. Agyeman et al. (2020) also suggested that the population has an adverse but significant effect on renewable energy consumption. This may refer to the contribution of working group population to economic growth and the increasing need for fossil sources, the primary source of energy generation (Zhao Y. et. al., 2013).

The directly proportional effect of public investments on renewable energy consumption shows that increasing public investments will increase the consumption of renewable energy. Transfer of a certain part of public investments to this sector will increase the spreading speed of private entrepreneurs regarding renewable energy investments, and will establish a safe environment for investment. The direction regarding the effect of public investments achieved in our results is in accordance with the result suggested by Le (2019).

FUTURE RESEARCH DIRECTIONS

The most significant contribution of this study is that it provides the first assessment results obtained by regional data regarding Turkey. In further studies, in order to discuss these factors in detail, the effects of them on hydroelectric, solar, wind, geothermal and biomass installed powers from different renewable sources, about which there is a high potential in Turkey, can be examined. The effects of these factors may be subjected for cities provided that required data are provided. In addition, the effect of different incentive implementation, in which YEKTEM regulation, used to promote renewable energy consumption in Turkey, is also included, may also be discussed.

CONCLUSION

The influence levels of different factors affecting renewable energy consumption can be analyzed with different studies. This study is limited to three factors: regional economic growth, public investments and population. This is because these factors are related to regional development from different angles. Regional economic growth is included in the study in terms of encouraging renewable energy consumption, regional public investments, since most of the investments in renewable energy generation facilities require government support, and lastly because of the potential of creating employment for the population, they are included in the study in terms of monitoring the migration situation.

Dynamic panel data analyses are frequently used for comprehensive analysis of these effects. This study concluded that both differents GMM and system GMM techniques have provided effective results. In all dynamic panel data analysis methods, the directions of the relationships between variables have been same. In this study, it has been found out that one-step system GMM and two-step system GMM techniques from dynamic panel data analysis methods have had significant values in all variable coefficients. It has been suggested according to the estimation results that regional economic growth and public investments affect the consumption of regional renewable energy resources in the same direction while regional population has an adverse effect.

There are some limitations in this study. The first one is the difficulty of compiling regional data. While the data for more than 20 years have been obtained for some of the variables, the period has been limited for some variables. For this reason, this study is limited to the period between 2010-2018. Another limitation is the exclusion of hydraulic power plants with dams, which are not included in the YEKDEM lists but provide a large part of production. In Turkey, renewable energy investments have increased in recent years. However, this increase has not been seen at the same level in each region. Therefore, there has been no production in some of the sources in certain periods in the 26 regions that have been examined.

In this study, evaluation foreign direct investments, which were not included due to the lack of regional data but used in the general literature, in addition to public investments, may result in efficient results. This evaluation may be extended with the energy sources obtained from the hydraulic power plants with dam. In the following years, it is considered that renewable energy production sector in Turkey will develop more, thus, an extension in the period of this study may affect the results of the study.

This research received no specific grant from any funding agency in the public, commercial, or not-for-profit sectors.

REFERENCES

Agyeman, J. K., Ameyaw, B., Li, Y., Appiah-Kubi, J., Annan, A., Oppong, A., & Twumasi, M. A. (2020). Modeling the long-run drivers of total renewable energy consumption: Evidence from top five heavily polluted countries. *Journal of Cleaner Production, 277*, 123292. doi:10.1016/j.jclepro.2020.123292

Amoah, A., Kwablah, E., Korle, K., & Offei, D. (2020). Renewable energy consumption in Africa: The role of economic well-being and economic freedom. *Sustainability Science, 10*(32), 2–17.

Anton, S. G., & Nucu, A. E. A. (2020). The effect of financial development on renewable energy consumption. A panel data approach. *Renewable Energy, 147*, 330–338. doi:10.1016/j.renene.2019.09.005

Arellano, M., & Bond, S. (1991). Some tests of specification for panel data: Monte Carlo evidence and an application to employment equations. *The Review of Economic Studies, 58*(2), 277–297. doi:10.2307/2297968

Arellano, M., & Bover, O. (1995). Another look at the instrumental variable estimation of error-components models. *Journal of Econometrics, 68*(1), 29–51. doi:10.1016/0304-4076(94)01642-D

Assi, F., Isiksal, A. Z., & Tursoy, T. (2021). Renewable Energy Consumption, Financial Development, Environmental pollution, and Innovations in the ASEAN +3 group: Evidence from (P-ARDL) model. *Renewable Energy, 165*(1), 689–700. doi:10.1016/j.renene.2020.11.052

Bao, C., & Xu, M. (2019). Cause and effect of renewable energy consumption on urbanization and economic growth in China's provinces and regions. *Journal of Cleaner Production, 231*, 483–493. doi:10.1016/j.jclepro.2019.05.191

Blundell, R., & Bond, S. (1998). Initial conditions and moment restrictions in dynamic panel data models. *Journal of Econometrics, 87*(1), 115–143. doi:10.1016/S0304-4076(98)00009-8

Bond, S. R. (2002). *Dynamic Panel Data Models: A Guide to Micro Data Methods and Practice.* Center for Microdata Methods and Practice Working Papers.

Byrne, J., Hughes, K., Rickerson, W., & Kurdgelashvili, L. (2007). American policy conflict in the greenhouse: Divergent trends in federal, regional, state, and local green energy and climate change policy, *Energy. Pol, 35*(9), 4555–4573. doi:10.1016/j.enpol.2007.02.028

Corrocher, N., & Cappa, E. (2020). The Role of public interventions in inducing private climate finance: An empirical analysis of the solar energy sector. *Energy Policy, 147*, 111787. doi:10.1016/j.enpol.2020.111787

Dahlberg, M., & Johansson, E. (2000). An examination of the dynamic behaviour of local governments using GMM bootstrapping methods. *Journal of Applied Econometrics, 15*(4), 401–416. doi:10.1002/1099-1255(200007/08)15:4<401::AID-JAE564>3.0.CO;2-G

Demirci, N. S. (2018). The Firm Specific Determinants of Fixed Capital Investments: Theories of Corporate Investment and an Application to Industrial Firms Listed in BIST. *Finance & Econometrics*, 111.

Dorrell, J., & Lee, K. (2020). The Politics of Wind: A state level analysis of political party impact on wind energy development in the United States. *Energy Research & Social Science, 69*, 101602. doi:10.1016/j.erss.2020.101602

Energy Market Regulatory Authority (EPDK). (2021). *Nihai Yek Listeleri*. Retrieved from http: https://www.epdk.gov.tr/Detay/Icerik/372/elektrikyekdemhttp://www.epdk.org.tr/TR/Dokuman/8692. Erişim Tarihi 07/01/2021.

Erdinç, Z., & Aydınbaş, G. (2020). Panel Data Analysis on Determinants Of Renewable Energy Consumption, Journal Of Social. *Humanities and Administrative Sciences, 6*(24), 346–358.

Güney, T. (2020). Renewable energy consumption and sustainable development in high-income countries. *International Journal of Sustainable Development and World Ecology*. Advance online publication. doi:10.1080/13504509.2020.1753124

Hartley, P., Medlock, K. B. III, Temzelides, T., & Zhang, X. (2015). Local employment impact from competing energy sources: Shale gas versus wind generation in Texas. *Energy Econ, 49*, 610–619. doi:10.1016/j.eneco.2015.02.023

Institute, T. S. (TUIK). (2021). Retrieved from http: https://data.tuik.gov.tr/

International Council for Local Environmental Initiatives (ICLEI). (2021). *Climate Protection*. Retrieved from http: https://iclei-europe.org/our-members/

International Energy Agency (IEA). (2021). *Data and statistics*. Retrieved from http: https://www.iea.org/data-and-statistics?country=WORLD&fuel=Energy%20supply&indicator=TPESbySource

Khan, H., Khan, I., Oanh, L. T. K., & Lin, Z. (2020). The Dynamic Interrelationship of Environmental Factors and Foreign Direct Investment: Dynamic Panel Data Analysis and New Evidence from the Globe. *Mathematical Problems in Engineering*, 1–12.

Khan, Z., Malik, M. Y., Latif, K., & Jiao, Z. (2020). Heterogeneous effect of eco-innovation and human capital on renewable & non-renewable energy consumption: Disaggregate analysis for G-7 countries. *Energy, 209*, 118405. doi:10.1016/j.energy.2020.118405

Lea, T.-H., Nguyen, C. P., & Park, D. (2020). Financing renewable energy development: Insights from 55 countries. *Energy Research & Social Science, 68*, 101537. doi:10.1016/j.erss.2020.101537

Lee, T. (2019). Financial investment for the development of renewable energy capacity. *Energy & Environment, 0*(0), 1–14. doi:10.1177/0958305X19882403

Mehrara, M., Rezaei, S., & Razi, H. D. (2015). Determinants of renewable energy consumption among ECO countries; based on Bayesian model averaging and weighted-average least square. *Int Lett Soc Hum Sci*, *54*, 96–109. doi:10.18052/www.scipress.com/ILSHS.54.96

Menz, F. C., & Vachon, S. (2006). The effectiveness of different policy regimes for promoting wind power: Experiences from the states. *Energy Policy*, *34*(14), 1786–1796. doi:10.1016/j.enpol.2004.12.018

Omri, A., Daly, S., & Nguyen, D. K. (2015). A robust analysis of the relationship between renewable energy consumption and its main drivers. *Applied Economics*, *47*(28), 2913–2923. doi:10.1080/00036846.2015.1011312

Öztürk, L. (2012). Public Investments and Regional Inequality: A Causality Analysis, 1975-2001. *Ege Academıc Revıew*, *12*(4), 487–495.

Padhan, H., Padhang, P. C., Tiwari, A. V., Ahmed, R., & Hammoudeh, S. (2020). Renewable energy consumption and robust globalization(s) in OECD countries: Do oil, carbon emissions and economic activity matter? *Energy Strategy Reviews*, *32*, 100535. doi:10.1016/j.esr.2020.100535

Pata, U. K. (2018). The influence of coal and noncarbohydrate energy consumption on CO2 emissions: Revisiting the environmental Kuznets curve hypothesis for Turkey. *Energy*, *160*, 1115–1123. doi:10.1016/j.energy.2018.07.095

Pirili, M. U. (2011). The Role of Public Investments in Regional Development: A Theoretical Review. *Ege Academıc Revıew*, *11*(2), 309–324.

Polzin, F., Migendt, M., Taube, ¨. F. A., & von Flotow, P. (2015). Public policy influence on renewable energy investments—A panel data study across OECD countries. *Energy Policy*, *80*, 98–111. doi:10.1016/j.enpol.2015.01.026

Przychodzen, W., & Przychodzen, J. (2020). Determinants of renewable energy production in transitioneconomies: A panel data approach. *Energy*, *191*, 116583. doi:10.1016/j.energy.2019.116583

Resıdency of the Republıc of Turkey Strategy and Budget Dırectorate (SBB). (n.d.). Retrieved from http: http://www.sbb.gov.tr/wp-content/uploads/2019/04/Yat%C4%B1r%C4%B1mlar%C4%B1n-%C4%B0llere-G%C3%B6re-Da%C4%9F%C4%B1l%C4%B1m%C4%B1.xlsx

Roodman, D. (2009). How to do xtabond2: An introduction to difference and system GMM in Stata. *The Stata Journal*, *9*(1), 86–136. doi:10.1177/1536867X0900900106

Sasmaz, M. U., Sakar, E., Yayla, Y. E., & Akkucuk, U. (2020). The Relationship between Renewable Energy and Human Development in OECD Countries: A Panel Data Analysis. *Sustainability*, *12*(18), 7450. doi:10.3390u12187450

Turkish Renewable Energy Resources Support Mechanism (YEKDEM). (2011). *Official Gazette of the Republic of Turkey, 28782*. Retrieved from http: https://www.mevzuat.gov.tr/mevzuat?MevzuatNo=18907&MevzuatTur=7&MevzuatTertip=5

Ullah, S., Akhtar, P., & Zaefarian, G. (2018). Dealing with endogeneity bias: The generalized method of moments (GMM) for panel data. *Industrial Marketing Management*, *71*, 69–78. doi:10.1016/j.indmarman.2017.11.010

Wang, B., Yang, Z., Xuan, J., & Jiao, K. (2020). Crises and opportunities in terms of energy and AI technologies during the COVID-19 pandemic. *Energy AI*, *1*, 100013. doi:10.1016/j.egyai.2020.100013

Wang, Q., Li, S., & Pisarenko, Z. (2020). Heterogeneous effects of energy efficiency, oil price, environmental pressure, R&D investment, and policy on renewable energy – evidence from the G20 countries. *Energy*, *209*, 118322. doi:10.1016/j.energy.2020.118322

Wang, Q., Valchuis, L., Thompson, E., Conner, D., & Parsons, R. (2019). Consumer Support and Willingness to Pay for Electricity from Solar, Wind, and Cow Manure in the United States: Evidence from a Survey in Vermont. *Energies*, *12*(23), 4467. doi:10.3390/en12234467

Yang, S., & Park, S. (2020). The effects of renewable energy financial incentive policy and democratic governance on renewable energy aid effectiveness. *Energy Policy*, *145*, 111682. doi:10.1016/j.enpol.2020.111682

Zhao, P., Lu, Z., Fang, J., Paramati, S. R., & Jiang, K. (2020). Determinants of renewable and non-renewable energy demand in China. *Structural Change and Economic Dynamics*, *54*, 202–209. doi:10.1016/j.strueco.2020.05.002

Zhao, Y., Tang, K.-K., & Wang, L.-L. (2013). Do renewable electricity policies promote renewable electricity generation? Evidence from panel data. *Energy Policy*, *62*, 887–897. doi:10.1016/j.enpol.2013.07.072

ADDITIONAL READING

Abdel-Basset, M., Gamal, A., Chakrabortty, R. K., & Ryan, M. J. (2021). Evaluation approach for sustainable renewable energy systems under uncertain environment: A case study. *RENEWABLE ENERGY, Volume*, *168*, 1073–1095. doi:10.1016/j.renene.2020.12.124

Alkan, O., & Albayrak, O. K. (2020). *Ranking of renewable energy sources for regions in Turkey by fuzzy entropy based fuzzy COPRAS and fuzzy multimoora, renewable energy*. Volume.

KEY TERMS AND DEFINITIONS

Economic Growth: Economic growth is Gross National Product (GNP) or Gross Domestic Product (GDP).

Energy Production: We need energy at every stage of our lives. For a country, the level of economic development is one of its indicators, and the amount of production due to energy consumption.

Population: All those who live or live in a country, a region, a city or a village.

Public Investment: Investments made by the state to increase the capital stock of the economy.

Regional Development Degrees: Regions with different shares of national income.

Renewable Energy: They are sustainable energy resources obtained from natural resources.

Renewable Energy Production: Energy obtained from renewable sources such as sun, wind, biomass.

Section 3

Reflection

Chapter 24

Education for the Digital Industry:
Opportunities and Challenges of Experience–Based Expertise and Open Innovation

Valentina Chkoniya
 https://orcid.org/0000-0003-1174-3216
University of Aveiro, Portugal

Fernando Cruz Gonçalves
ENIDH, Portugal

Maria Manuela Martins Batista
ENIDH, Portugal

ABSTRACT

Education holds the power to transform and enrich the lives of people. In the era of the digital industry, where data is omnipresent in every walk of life and new trends impact society and future jobs, humans continue to evolve through education and developing mechanisms to improve education with data science in the heart of it. This chapter demonstrates that experience-based expertise and open innovation must be understood as a single process, where living labs that involve academies and enterprises create unique conditions for society's progress. There is a trinomial relationship between academy, society, and industries, which are interestingly far more exploited than the education and research. Effective management of the knowledge and information transferred between open innovation ecosystem partners is crucial. The scientific development of both concepts is an active field in the academic community, and new ideas appear, opening new paths of knowledge transfer methods with knowledge from data.

DOI: 10.4018/978-1-7998-6985-6.ch024

INTRODUCTION

Education is the key to shaping the lives of people. It holds power to transform and enrich it. Since the dawn of civilization, humans have evolved through education and have developed mechanisms to improve education. In the 21st century, where data is omnipresent in every walk of life, education is no exception.

Due to the recent explosion of big data, our society has been rapidly going through digital transformation and entering a new world with numerous eye-opening developments. These new trends impact society and future jobs, and thus student careers. At the heart of this digital transformation is data science (Braschler, Stadelmann, & Stockinger, 2019; Song & Zhu, 2017).

The three main differences between the fourth and previous three industrial revolutions are speed, scope, and systemic impact. Compared to earlier industrial revolutions, the fourth is developing exponentially rather than linearly (June Kim, 2021). Are the current education systems and paradigms oriented towards the values and goals of Industry 4.0? It does not always seem to be so. A 20th-century educational model is mostly still leading, introducing standardized facts and procedures designed to prepare the workforce for jobs that probably may not exist for a long time. It is not enough to cope with future challenges.

According to Vygotsky's Sociocultural Theory of Cognitive Development, "learning from experience is the process whereby human development occurs" (Vygotsky, Cole, John-Steiner, Scribner, & Souberman, 1978). Although experience is essential to learning, it is not enough; one has to do something to construct knowledge. Building an environment where students feel free to expose their knowledge state and compassionately help each other learn is incredibly difficult (Chkoniya, 2021). The idea of a growth mindset was first described by Carol Dweck (2017). Their research points out the importance of students believing that they can improve through practice. More interestingly, perhaps, they offer suggestions as to how to foster growth mindsets, such as praising effort instead of skill (Dweck, 2019; Hicks & Irizarry, 2018).

Business operations are undergoing drastic changes due to the disruptive effects of technological innovations, and it has consequences in the education sector (Oke & Fernandes, 2020). There are two essential dimensions of the learning process: grasping and transforming experience. A firm's capacity for accumulation is its most crucial technological asset. Therefore, the following virtuous cycle should be established: first, practical knowledge is accumulated systematically in the workplace; second, the knowledge should be scientifically codified. Third, the documentation of this codified knowledge should be conducted so those good textbooks can be produced. Fourth, training and teaching methods should be developed and tested in terms of their effectiveness and validity. Fifth, the new practices established on the foundation of the newly codified knowledge should be tried, and the performance of these trials should be evaluated objectively. Then, this cycle should be repeated, starting with the first phase (Lee et al., 2018).

This chapter demonstrates and gives an example that Experience-Based Expertise and Open Innovation (OI) must be understood as a single process. It is essential to create knowledge and transfer it, ensuring that the flow of knowledge takes place in a bidirectional way.

Background

Since Klaus Schwab and the World Economic Forum declared the arrival of the Fourth Industrial Revolution, there has been much discussion about it. The so-called fourth industrial or digital revolution is characterized by the unification of technologies that breaks the boundaries between physical, digital, and biological disciplines (Schwab, 2017). Compared to the three previous industrial revolutions, the main differences of fourth are speed, extent, and systemic impact (Chkoniya, Madsen, & Bukhrashvili, 2020). Only jobs that machines cannot do will last for the people in the future; they will base on creative expression, social interaction, physical dexterity, empathy, ingenuity, and collaboration (Lee et al., 2018). Lifelong inclusive and equitable education, formal and informal, physical and digital, will be vital for preparing new populations and society to be successful in this unpredictable future. (Alop, 2019).

Since the expected changes are disruptive, it will be difficult to adequately prepare for the changes to come with traditional high education (Alop, 2019; Erdogan & Demirel, 2017; Lee et al., 2018). The process of creating, approving, and launching new curricula, modules, subjects are now extended, cumbersome, and unable to respond quickly to increasingly rapid changes. Even the renewal of an existing curriculum may take a year or even more; creating new curricula maybe even longer and more cumbersome, and bureaucratic. These new curricula or their innovations may already be outdated when they start working.

Through the years, the education sector has been influenced by the evolution of technology and the global, regional, and local social dynamics. Therefore, today, teaching and learning methods include emerging information and communication technologies (ICTs), advanced tools, and innovative facilities. Also, teaching and learning methods are focused on developing desirable competencies in today's students to motivate them to propose solutions to today's and future problems. This new era is known as "Education 4.0". The OI Laboratories are used as enabling resources to reach the vision of Education 4.0 and boost knowledge transfer (Miranda et al., 2019).

MAIN FOCUS OF THE CHAPTER

It would be more effective to establish Enterprises and Academies, exchanging Experience-Based Expertise and OI. Especially when the massive digitalization of the Industry becomes evident, changing everything from the types of jobs available to the skills we will need.

Experience Based Expertise

Learning is the process whereby knowledge is created through experience transformation (Kolb & Kolb, 2017). Experiential learning, which has its origin in the works of Dewey, Lewin, and Piaget, focuses on the central role that experience plays in the learning process (Holzer & Andruet, 1995). Experience-based knowledge plays an essential role in decision-making processes as decision-makers try to compare the current problems with previous situations to find an appropriate solution. Therefore, generating knowledge from past decisions can significantly facilitate and accelerate future decisions (Argote & Ingram, 2000; Knowledge Management, 2021). According to Matthew and Sternberg, experience-based knowledge is context-dependent and typically develops over time through an iterative learning process of perception, action, and feedback (Matthew & Sternberg, 2009).

The Industry has introduced various problem-solving methods that apply this concept of cognitive experience. One famous example is called Six-Sigma (Figure 1). It was created in the late 1970s, when cheap Japanese goods were becoming increasingly competitive on the global markets, forcing American companies to seek ways to improve their product quality while, at the same time, keeping the costs low. In a joint effort, General Motors, Ford, and Chrysler made large-scale use of SPC - Statistical Process Control, which enabled them to steadily track the manufacturing process at critical points of quality and costs. Similarly, Motorola, which was being driven out of the market by cheaper and superior Japanese products, gathered a group of distinguished experts in mathematical statistics, design, and quality assurance, who worked together to develop a consistent system for constant quality improvement. Today Six Sigma is an economic process allowing enterprises to improve their financial health through planning and controlling the workflow in such a way as to minimize the consumption of raw materials and the production of waste while at the same time providing more satisfaction for the customer (Kęsek, Bogacz, & Migza, 2019).

Figure 1. Six-Sigma as an implementation of the general experience feedback process (adapted from Jabrouni, Kamsu-Foguem, Geneste, & Vaysse, 2011)

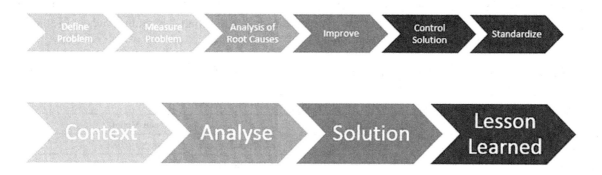

As a common good, open science opens possibilities for the development of nations through innovations and collaborative constructions, which help to democratize knowledge (Ramírez & García-Peñalvo, 2018).

Knowledge transfer in the context of Academia-Enterprise collaboration is understood as a determinant that improves innovation and competitiveness. The mechanisms by which this collaboration occurs have awakened increasing interest among academics, as well as in the business sector (Vélez-Rolón, Méndez-Pinzón, & Acevedo, 2020). The most recognized source of knowledge used in new research is directed towards Academia-Enterprise relationships in an OI environment (Alvarez-Meaza, Pikatza-Gorrotxategi, & Rio-Belver, 2020).

Open Innovation

Innovation is a crucial aspect of the sustainability and competitiveness of organizations and the economy. In recent years, OI has burst onto the scene as a more open approach, in which the sources and exchange of knowledge are extended beyond organizational borders. One of the main actors and providers of knowledge is the Academy (Heras-Rosas & Herrera, 2021).

The Fourth Industrial Revolution can be recognized as the advancement from simple digitization to innovation based on combinations of technologies enabling companies to innovate their business models (Lee et al., 2018). Companies use innovation to generate and apply knowledge, develop new products and services, new business models, and ultimately obtain business results.

Traditionally, companies innovated only using internal resources. The main reasons were the noncommercial focus of the scientific community and their need to protect their valuable assets. Such companies prioritized the volume of resources, the number of projects, and the investments in innovation. Consequently, organizations with closed innovation models tend to have big research departments generating plenty of in-house knowledge. The more, the better.

Today, the Digital Industry has undoubtedly become a key enabler of innovation, when innovation processes have become more open and require more significant resources in the different implementation phases to capture and transfer knowledge within and outside the Enterprise's boundaries (Urbinati, Chiaroni, Chiesa, & Frattini, 2020). OI ecosystems involve the transfer of knowledge between multiple stakeholders to contribute toward product and service innovation, and to an extent, have superseded network-level approaches to co-creation. Effective management of the knowledge and information transferred between ecosystem partners is crucial for the process of OI (Bacon, Williams, & Davies, 2019). The OI has emerged recently as a new innovation model and already became a hot topic that currently facilitates establishing links between Academia and Industry (Neves, Costa, & Reis, 2021). It encourages companies to use the existing external knowledge rather than reinvent the wheel (Table 1).

Table 1. Comparison between open and closed innovation models (adapted from Ennomotive, 2020)

Characteristic	Type of innovation model	
	Closed Model	**Open Model**
Source of knowledge	Use knowledge from internal sources	Internal + External knowledge sources
Success rate	Low (typically 20-30%) success rate	Double innovation success rate, up to 80%
Productivity	A lot of rework, low productivity	40-60% productivity increase
Speed	Low speed of innovation	High speed of innovation (x 3)

It is favorable to establish links with other companies, academies, tech centers, and other knowledge sources. The term OI as we know it was coined by Henry Chesbrough, associate professor and head of the Open Innovation Center of the Haas Business School of the University of California. However, collaboration and co-creation have always been around, maybe since humans started trading or since the cottage industry exchanged practices from other regions and cultures (Bogers, Chesbrough, Heaton, & Teece, 2019; Dodgson, Gann, & Salter, 2006; Ennomotive, 2020; Howard, Steensma, Lyles, & Dhanaraj, 2016; Karhade & Dong, 2021):

1. Cisco may be the most remarkable OI pioneer. Its acquisition strategy allowed the company to grow during the late 90's. The goal of these acquisitions was to make hardware compatible with software in new technological products. This customer-driven innovation strategy helped Cisco over perform Bell Labs or Lucent by effectively translating significant tech investments into business growth.

2. Another trailblazer is, undoubtedly, the pharmaceutical company Eli-Lilly, spearheaded by its R&D strategy manager. The company reflected on using collective intelligence to improve the traditionally low innovation success rates in the pharmaceutical Industry. Consequently, e.Lilly was born around the year 2000, the first OI platform to connect with global scientific knowledge. This platform is the origin of Innocentive, an Eli Lilly spin-off whose goal was to allow other pharmaceutical and consumer goods companies to use this open model.

3. The third initiator is Procter & Gamble. The company created in 2000 the so-called Connect & Develop their new OI process. P&G's ultimate goal was to continue growing by $2 billion annually while keeping a continuous R&D investment. Procter managed to have up to 50% of its innovations coming from the outside and, consequently, its R&D productivity increased by 60%.

OI has become a mainstream phenomenon in the current business landscape. Where two key innovation project attributes (i.e., complexity and uncertainty) are related to five factors for successful OI management (Bagherzadeh, Markovic, & Bogers, 2021):

1. Openness level;
2. External partner choice (e.g., users, suppliers, Academy, competitors, entrepreneurs, and start-ups);
3. OI mechanism choice (e.g., licensing agreements, alliances, innovation contests, and crowdsourcing intermediaries);
4. Collaboration process formalization;
5. Internal firm practices.

OI is improving innovation ecosystems in terms of promoting smart and responsible innovation. There is a trinomial relationship between Academy, Society, and Industries, which are interestingly far more exploited than the Education and Research. Given the noticeable importance of producing knowledge and disseminating that information, Academy will continue to have a prominent centrality in society in that regard (Neves et al., 2021).

Experience Based Expertise and OI must be understood as a single process. The scientific development of both concepts is an active field in the academic community, and also, that new terms appear, opening new paths of research (Alvarez-Meaza et al., 2020). This chapter gives a particular focus on Living Labs that involve Academies and Enterprises.

Living Labs

The "Living Lab" is an approach used since the 2000s in Europe and is defined as an OI laboratory that integrates the user as a central actor in the innovation process. By integrating users into the innovation process ensures highly reliable market assessment to reduce technological and commercial risks. "Living Lab" provides a better understanding of the user needs, which is a crucial factor for successful innovation and implementation of Pilot Projects (Arnould, Morel, & Fournier, 2020; Geenhuizen, 2018; Hossain, Leminen, & Westerlund, 2019; Leminen, Westerlund, & Nyström, 2012; Pallot & Pawar, 2012; Schuurman, De Marez, & Ballon, 2015).

Organizational usability must instead be evaluated in situ while the system is used for real work. There are three contexts for such evaluation: pilot implementation, techno change, and design in use (Table 3). The pilot implementation aims to inform the finalization of a system based on testing it in the field before go-live. Techno change focuses on shaking down a system during go-live to realize the benefits it was developed to help achieve. Design in use is the tailoring performed by users after go-live to fit a system and its use to their local and emerging needs (Hertzum, 2021).

According to Hertzum et al. (2021), a pilot implementation consists of five activities:

Table 2. Characteristics of different types of living labs (adapted from Leminen, Westerlund, & Nyström, 2012)

Characteristic	Type of Living Labs			
	Utilizer-driven	**Enabler-driven**	**Provider-driven**	**User-driven**
Purpose	Strategic R&D activity with preset objectives	Strategy development through action	Operations development through increased knowledge	Problem-solving by collaborative accomplishments
Organization	Network forms around a utilizer, who organizes action for rapid knowledge results	Network forms around a region (regional development) or a funded project (e.g., public funding)	Network forms around a provider organization(s)	Network initiated by users lacks formal coordination mechanisms
Action	Utilizer guides information collected from the users and promotes knowledge creation that supports the achievement of preset goals	Information is collected and used together, and knowledge is co-created in the network.	Information collected for immediate or postponed use; new knowledge based on the information that the provider gets from the others	Information is not collected formally and builds upon users' interests; knowledge is utilized in the network to help the user community.
Outcomes	New knowledge for product and business development	Guided strategy change into a preferred direction	New knowledge supporting operations development	Solutions to users' everyday-life problems
Lifespan	Short	Short/medium/long	Short/medium/long	Long

1. Planning and design;
2. Technical configuration;
3. Organizational adaptation;
4. Pilot us;
5. Learning.

The first three activities are preparations. During the preparations, the focus of the pilot implementation is defined, the boundary between the pilot site and the organization at large is determined, the system is configured for the pilot site, interfaces to other systems are established, work procedures at the pilot site are adjusted, users receive training, safeguards against breakdowns are set up, and so forth. The extent and complexity of the preparations demonstrate that a pilot implementation is not just the period of pilot use. During the pilot use period, the pilot site staff has the double task of conducting their work with the system and providing input to the evaluation. The final activity, learning, is the reason for conducting pilot implementations (Figure 2). Importantly, learning about the organizational usability of the system occurs during the preparations and during the period of pilot use.

Example of the Education and Digital Shipping Industry

In the 21st century, the maritime Industry has become concerned about Maritime Education and Training, and it has been deemed as a positive and potentially game challenging strategy in order to solve

Table 3. Three Contexts for Evaluating Organizational Usability (adapted from Hertzum, 2018)

Time	Pilot implementation	Techno change	Design in use
	Before go-live	During go-live	After go-live
Definition	Pilot implementation is a field test of a properly engineered yet unfinished system in its intended environment, using actual data, and aiming – through real-use experience – to explore the value of the system, improve or assess its design, and reduce implementation risk.	Deliberate techno change is "the use of IT to drive improvements in organizational performance."	Design in use encompasses the "practices of interpretation, appropriation, assembly, tailoring and further development of computer support in what is normally regarded as deployment or use."
Purpose	To learn about the fit between the system and its context to explore the system's value, improve its design, and reduce implementation risk.	To transition from old practices to the new system and start realizing the benefits that motivated its introduction.	To appropriate—tailor—the system for local and emergent needs when opportunities for such appropriation are seen and seized
People	Usability practitioners plan and facilitate the process	Usability practitioners facilitate the process	Users drive the process, facilitated by usability practitioners
Setting	In the field, i.e., during real work, but limited to a pilot site	In the field, but while the system is still new and unfamiliar	In the field, during regular use of the system for real work
System	The pilot system, i.e., a properly engineered yet unfinished system	Finished system but not yet error-free and not yet fully configured	The finished system, yet with possibilities for reconfiguration
Process	Used in situ for a limited time and with special precautions against errors	Used in situ by inexperienced users, possibly with extra support during go-live	Used in situ by regular users, some of whom occasionally engage in design-in-use activities
Benefit focus	Specified benefits dominate; other benefits may emerge	Specified benefits dominate; other benefits may emerge	Emergent benefits are likely to dominate
Duration	Temporary, typically weeks or months	Temporary, typically months	Continuous, typically years or decades
Main challenge	The boundary between pilot site and organization at large	Premature congealment of the process to ensure benefit from the new system	Insufficient capability to make or disseminate changes

several actual and possible challenges that provide the enhancement of growth, expansion, and positive change (Basak, 2017).

As a result of improvements in information technology and infrastructure, maritime technologies and operations have dramatically evolved from traditional automatic, mechanical, mechatronic-based technologies to intelligence, human-centered, and in-formation and ICT-supported smart operations. Such changes subvert the traditional evaluation of the competence of individual laborers (Pan, Oksavik, & Hildre, 2020). At the same time, the difficulty of evaluating the organizational usability of those technologies is raised. The two are combined dramatically to challenge current maritime education and research on many levels (Hertzum, 2018; Pan et al., 2020).

It will be especially challenging in the future when the whole shipping process will become Smart. Smart shipping is a standard system where ships and ports are connected to one global system and operated in the most optimal way using standard algorithms. These systems require full or large-scale integration of Smart Ships and Smart Ports into a single network leading by so-called artificial intelligence. However, a human operator must be maintained. (Alop, 2019).

Figure 2. Pilot implementation (adapted from Hertzum, 2021)

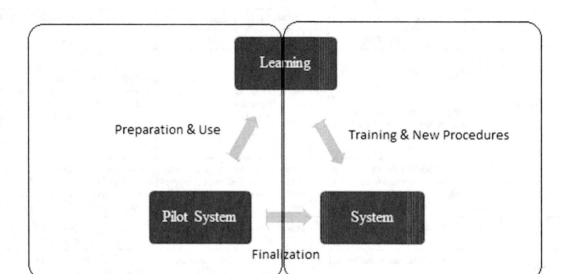

PILOT IMPLEMENTATION   FULL-SCALE IMPLEMENTATION

To prepare students for jobs that have not been created yet, we need to teach them how to be great problem solvers to be ready for anything. One way to do this is by teaching content and skills using real-world case studies and a learning model focused on reflection during the problem-solving process (Heirs & Manuel, 2021; Schwartz, 2019). It is similar to the project-based learning and Growth Mind-set idea, following the Theory of Cognitive Development (Alop, 2019; Dweck, 2019; Heirs & Manuel, 2021; Vygotsky et al., 1978).

Historical issues caused the gaps of maritime education in higher education and led to an unsystematic structure for research and development of maritime technology. Being an expert, or being at any stage of skill acquisition, does not necessarily mean performing and everyone else who exhibits the same type of thought processes (Basak, 2017). Everyone function in at least one of five stages of skill level:

1. Novice;
2. Advanced beginner;
3. Competent;
4. Proficient;
5. Expert.

In order to better prepare for the future, we need to include studying phenomena in a systematic way of participants in their everyday settings, taking a holistic view, providing a descriptive understanding, and taking a member's perspective. Therefore, there is no necessary to distinguish who is providing what types of maritime education, but we can see them as an utterly organizational system, including humans, technological artifacts, and institutional rules for organizing humans and technologies together (Pan et al., 2020).

Maritime education as a whole is generally considered repetitive practice-based training. There is a need for defining clear learning outcomes, improving the learning content to enable exploration and second-chance learning, minimizing theory-practice gaps by ensuring skills-knowledge balance and in-depth scholarship building, facilitating tasks for learning preparation and learning extension, and repositioning simulation components and their assessment schemes across the academic program (Jamil & Bhuiyan, 2021).

How to be more flexible and responsive to rapid changes? What are the new principles of education in the dynamically developing shipping industry and digital world where all information is available to everyone anytime? How to keep pace with the rapid and extensive changes in industries, including shipping? Lifelong inclusive and equitable education, formal and informal, physical and digital, will be vital for preparing new populations and society to be successful in this unpredictable future (Alop, 2019).

Hands-on experiential learning is a mainstay of meaningful education. Engaging students in field-based, experiential learning can help develop true passion and commitment to STEM (Science, Technology, Engineering, Math) subjects, allowing students to apply their skills and content knowledge in an authentic, experiential context (Living Labs) while enhancing many academic skills and engaging them in contextualized learning across disciplines (O'Neil et al., 2020).

We can find an interesting example in Portugal, where the only national college dedicated to the training of Merchant Marine Officers and senior managers of the Maritime-port sector in the areas of Intermodality, Logistics, and Management is participating in two pilot projects using an innovative approach in technological and pedagogical terms, through 'Living Labs' (ENIDH, 2021)

As a leading institution in the training of professionals linked to the maritime and logistics areas, the Escola Superior Náutica Infante D. Henrique (ENIDH) is involved in the eShip project, thus embodying its role as promoter of technological and digital progress in the sector. eShip project aims to digitize the vessel chartering process, thereby cutting management costs and fueling the digital transition.

The primary objective of the eShip project is to develop a digitalization model for the entire chartering process, from the market research stage to the completion of the trip, including freight negotiation and contracting, real-time trip analysis, overage calculations. /sub-stay, issuance of shipping and billing documents, post-trip analysis, and regulatory compliance. This electronic platform will be tested in two pilot projects using an innovative approach in technological and pedagogical terms, through Living Labs, focusing on the Liquefied Natural Gas (LNG) market, which is located in evident rise, and Solid Bulk.

SOLUTIONS AND RECOMMENDATIONS

Experience Based Expertise and OI must be understood as a single process, where Living Labs that involve Academies and Enterprises create unique conditions for society's progress. There is a trinomial relationship between Academy, Society, and Industries, which are interestingly far more exploited than the Education and Research. Effective management of the knowledge and information transferred between OI ecosystem partners are crucial.

FUTURE RESEARCH DIRECTIONS

The world today is extremely well connected and heavily dependent on maritime trade. The efficiency of the maritime sector generally strengthens the country's international and political position, as its activities are linked to international economic cooperation, attracting foreign investment, membership in international organizations, and other vital factors (Agbaba, 2020). The shipping market is the result of global production and its constant changes. As part of such a market, maritime transport is vulnerable to external factors, such as international trade, political situations, financial trends, technological developments, and legislation, which may directly or indirectly affect demand in the sector or similar. The adverse effects of these changes are reflected in lower freight rates, lower daily rental prices, and reduced prices of new or used boats. The maritime crisis has significantly affected income, wages, number of employees, and similar. In order to ensure the development of the maritime sector, it is necessary to continue research with Living Labs that invest in the growth of transport capacities, deepen ports, build new terminals and modernize existing ones. It also requires open-innovation principles to co-create the advanced in transport development and application, technological, technical, economic, organizational, and commercial measures to adapt to the environment.

CONCLUSION

During the long history of higher education institutions, their value to society has suffered several changes. However, experience accumulated in enterprises is essential to learning. The essence of innovation lies in knowledge, so OI opens the door to knowledge transfer with agents outside the organization.

Experience Based Expertise and OI must be understood as a single process; that is to say, it is essential to create knowledge and be able to transfer it, ensuring that the flow of knowledge takes place in a bidirectional way. This process from the postulated model must end the generation of value for both organizations, innovation being a fundamental factor that must be promoted and measured in future investigations. Knowledge management and knowledge transfer in the Academia–Enterprise relationship can be interpreted as a single factor that mediates the flow and use of knowledge. (Vélez-Rolón et al., 2020). The three main differences between the fourth and previous three industrial revolutions are speed, scope, and systemic impact. Compared to earlier industrial revolutions, the fourth is developing exponentially rather than linearly (June Kim, 2021). OI has become a mainstream phenomenon in the current business landscape (Bagherzadeh et al., 2021), and the OI community is pivotal to the relationship between academia and Enterprise. To prepare students, we need to teach them how to be great problem solvers. One way to do this is by teaching content and skills using real-time connections with Enterprises. Since the expected changes are disruptive and understanding user needs a key factor for successful innovation, Living Labs create unique conditions for society's progress.

ACKNOWLEDGMENT

The eShip project is supported by the EEA Grants.

REFERENCES

Agbaba, R. (2020). Maritime Challenges in Crisis Times. *Annals of Maritime Studies / Pomorski Zbornik, 59*(1), 51–60. . doi:10.18048/2020.59.03

Alop, A. (2019). The Challenges of the Digital Technology Era for Maritime Education and Training. *2019 European Navigation Conference (ENC), Navigation Conference (ENC), 2019 European.* 10.1109/EURONAV.2019.8714176

Alvarez-Meaza, I., Pikatza-Gorrotxategi, N., & Rio-Belver, R. M. (2020). Knowledge Sharing and Transfer in an Open Innovation Context: Mapping Scientific Evolution. *Journal of Open Innovation, 68*(4), 1–23. doi:10.3390/joitmc6040186

Argote, L., & Ingram, P. (2000). Knowledge transfer: A basis for competitive advantage in firms. *Organizational Behavior and Human Decision Processes, 82*(1), 150–169. doi:10.1006/obhd.2000.2893

Arnould, M., Morel, L., & Fournier, M. (2020). Developing a territorial diagnostic as part of a living lab process: Implementation to improve management and wood mobilization in small French private forest. *2020 IEEE International Conference on Engineering, Technology and Innovation (ICE/ITMC), Engineering, Technology and Innovation (ICE/ITMC), 2020 IEEE International Conference On.* 10.1109/ICE/ITMC49519.2020.9198373

Bacon, E., Williams, M. D., & Davies, G. H. (2019). Recipes for success: Conditions for knowledge transfer across open innovation ecosystems. *International Journal of Information Management, 49,* 377–387. doi:10.1016/j.ijinfomgt.2019.07.012

Bagherzadeh, M., Markovic, S., & Bogers, M. (2021). Managing Open Innovation: A Project-Level Perspective. *IEEE Transactions on Engineering Management, Engineering Management, IEEE Transactions on. IEEE Transactions on Engineering Management, 68*(1), 301–316. doi:10.1109/TEM.2019.2949714

Basak, S. K. (2017). A Framework on the Factors Affecting to Implement Maritime Education and Training System in Educational Institutions: A Review of the Literature. *Procedia Engineering, 194,* 345–350. doi:10.1016/j.proeng.2017.08.155

Bogers, M., Chesbrough, H., Heaton, S., & Teece, D. J. (2019). Strategic Management of Open Innovation: A Dynamic Capabilities Perspective. *California Management Review, 62*(1), 77–94. doi:10.1177/0008125619885150

Braschler, M., Stadelmann, T., & Stockinger, K. (2019). *Applied data science : lessons learned for the data-driven business. Applied data science lessons learned for the data-driven business.* Springer., doi:10.1007/978-3-030-11821-1

Chkoniya, V. (2021). *How Harvard's Case Method Can Help to Overcome the Challenges of Applied Data Science Education.* Academic Press.

Chkoniya, V., Madsen, A. O., & Bukhrashvili, P. (2020). *Anthropological Approaches to Understanding Consumption Patterns and Consumer Behavior.* IGI Global. doi:10.4018/978-1-7998-3115-0 de las Heras-Rosas, C., & Herrera, J. (2021). Research Trends in Open Innovation and the Role of the University. *Journal of Open Innovation*, 7(1), 1–22. doi:10.3390/joitmc7010029

Dodgson, M., Gann, D., & Salter, A. (2006). The role of technology in the shift towards open innovation: The case of Procter & Gamble. *R & D Management*, 36(3), 333–346. doi:10.1111/j.1467-9310.2006.00429.x

Dweck, C. (2019). What Having a "Growth Mindset" Actually Means. *Harvard Business Review*.

Dweck, C. S. (2017). *Summary of Carol S. Dweck's Mindset: Key Takeaways & Analysis*. CreateSpace Independent Publishing Platform.

ENIDH. (2021). *Escola Superior Náutica Infante D. Henrique*. Retrieved from https://www.enautica.pt/en/

Ennomotive. (2020). *Open Innovation: Definition and Types of Innovation*. Author.

Erdogan, O., & Demirel, E. (2017). New Technologies in Maritime Education and Training, Turkish Experiment. *Universal Journal of Educational Research*, 5(6), 947–952. doi:10.13189/ujer.2017.050606

Heirs, S., & Manuel, M. (2021). Sustainable Maritime Career Development: A case for Maritime Education and Training (MET) at the Secondary Level. *TransNav: International Journal on Marine Navigation & Safety of Sea Transportation*, 15(1), 91–99. doi:10.12716/1001.15.01.08

Hertzum, M. (2018). Three contexts for evaluating organizational usability. *Journal of Usability Studies Archive*, 14, 35–47.

Hertzum, M. (2021). *Organizational Implementation: The Design in Use of Information Systems*. Morgan & Claypool Publishers.

Hicks, S. C., & Irizarry, R. A. (2018). A Guide to Teaching Data Science. *The American Statistician*, 72(4), 382–391. doi:10.1080/00031305.2017.1356747 PMID:31105314

Holzer, S., & Andruet, R. (1995). *A multimedia workshop learning environment for statics*. doi:10.1109/FIE.1995.483056

Hossain, M., Leminen, S., & Westerlund, M. (2019). A systematic review of living lab literature. *Journal of Cleaner Production*, 213, 976–988. doi:10.1016/j.jclepro.2018.12.257

Howard, M., Steensma, H. K., Lyles, M., & Dhanaraj, C. (2016). Learning to collaborate through collaboration: How allying with expert firms influences collaborative innovation within novice firms. *Strategic Management Journal*, 37(10), 2092–2103. doi:10.1002mj.2424

Jabrouni, H., Kamsu-Foguem, B., Geneste, L., & Vaysse, C. (2011). Continuous improvement through knowledge-guided analysis in experience feedback. *Eng. Appl. of AI*, 24(8), 1419–1431. doi:10.1016/j.engappai.2011.02.015

Jamil, M. G., & Bhuiyan, Z. (2021). Deep learning elements in maritime simulation programs: A pedagogical exploration of learner experiences. *International Journal of Educational Technology in Higher Education*, 18(1), 1–22. doi:10.118641239-021-00255-0

June Kim, S. (2021). How can higher maritime education lead shipping growth? Korea's experience, 1948–1982. *International Journal of Maritime History*, 33(1), 90–117. doi:10.1177/0843871420974062

Karhade, P. P., & Dong, J. Q. (2021). Innovation Outcomes of Digitally Enabled Collaborative Problemistic Search Capability. *Management Information Systems Quarterly*, *45*(2), 693–717. doi:10.25300/MISQ/2021/12202

Kęsek, M., Bogacz, P., & Migza, M. (2019). The application of Lean Management and Six Sigma tools in global mining enterprises. *IOP Conference Series. Earth and Environmental Science*, *214*, 12090. doi:10.1088/1755-1315/214/1/012090

Knowledge Management. (2021). *Experience-Based Knowledge*. Knowledge management, Group Work, UCPori. Retrieved from https://knowledgemanagement5.wordpress.com/experience-based-knowledge/

Kolb, D., & Kolb, A. (2017). *The Experiential Educator: Principles and Practices of Experiential Learning*. Academic Press.

Lee, M., Yun, J. J., Pyka, A., Won, D., Kodama, F., Schiuma, G., Park, H. S., Jeon, J., Park, K. B., Jung, K. H., Yan, M.-R., Lee, S. Y., & Zhao, X. (2018). How to Respond to the Fourth Industrial Revolution or the Second Information Technology Revolution? Dynamic New Combinations between Technology, Market, and Society through Open Innovation. *Journal of Open Innovation*, *4*(3), 21. Advance online publication. doi:10.3390/joitmc4030021

Leminen, S., Westerlund, M., & Nyström, A.-G. (2012). Living Labs as Open-Innovation Networks. *Technology Innovation Management Review*, *2*(9), 6–11. doi:10.22215/timreview/602

Matthew, C. T., & Sternberg, R. J. (2009). *Developing experience-based (tacit) knowledge through reflection. In Learning and Individual Differences.* Elsevier Science., doi:10.1016/j.lindif.2009.07.001

Miranda, J., Lopez, C. S., Navarro, S., Bustamante, M. R., Molina, J. M., & Molina, A. (2019). Open Innovation Laboratories as Enabling Resources to Reach the Vision of Education 4.0. *2019 IEEE International Conference on Engineering, Technology, and Innovation (ICE/ITMC), Engineering, Technology and Innovation (ICE/ITMC), 2019 IEEE International Conference On.* 10.1109/ICE.2019.8792595

Neves, A. R., Costa, J., & Reis, J. (2021). Using a Systematic Literature Review to Build a Framework for University-Industry Linkages using Open Innovation. *Procedia Computer Science*, *181*, 23–33. doi:10.1016/j.procs.2021.01.095

O'Neil, J. M., Newton, R. J., Bone, E. K., Birney, L. B., Green, A. E., Merrick, B., Goodwin-Segal, T., Moore, G., & Fraioli, A. (2020). Using urban harbors for experiential, environmental literacy: Case studies of New York and the Chesapeake Bay. *Regional Studies in Marine Science*, *33*, 100886. Advance online publication. doi:10.1016/j.rsma.2019.100886

Oke, A., & Fernandes, F. A. P. (2020). Innovations in Teaching and Learning: Exploring the Perceptions of the Education Sector on the 4th Industrial Revolution (4IR). *Journal of Open Innovation*, *6*(2), 31. Advance online publication. doi:10.3390/joitmc6020031

Pallot, M., & Pawar, K. (2012). A holistic model of user experience for living lab experiential design. In *2012 18th International ICE Conference on Engineering, Technology and Innovation* (pp. 1–15). IEEE. 10.1109/ICE.2012.6297648

Pan, Y., Oksavik, A., & Hildre, H. P. (2020). *Simulator as a Tool for the Future Maritime Education and Research: A Discussion*. Academic Press.

Ramírez, M.-S., & García-Peñalvo, F.-J. (2018). Co-Creation and Open Innovation: Systematic Literature Review. *Comunicar: Media Education Research Journal, 26*(54), 9–18. doi:10.3916/C54-2018-01

Schuurman, D., De Marez, L., & Ballon, P. (2015). Living Labs: a systematic literature review. Open Living Lab Days 2015.

Schwab, K. (2017). *The fourth industrial revolution*. Currency.

Schwartz, L. (2019). *How to Use Case Studies in Your Classroom to Make Learning Relevant*. Edutopia.

Song, I.-Y., & Zhu, Y. (2017). Big Data and Data Science: Opportunities and Challenges of iSchools. *Journal of Data and Information Science, 2*(3), 1–18. doi:10.1515/jdis-2017-0011

Urbinati, A., Chiaroni, D., Chiesa, V., & Frattini, F. (2020). The role of digital technologies in open innovation processes: An exploratory multiple case study analysis. *R & D Management, 50*(1), 136–160. doi:10.1111/radm.12313

van Geenhuizen, M. (2018). A framework for the evaluation of living labs as boundary spanners in innovation. *Environment and Planning C. Politics and Space, 36*(7), 1280–1298. doi:10.1177/2399654417753623

Vélez-Rolón, A. M., Méndez-Pinzón, M., & Acevedo, O. L. (2020). Open Innovation Community for University-Industry Knowledge Transfer: A Colombian Case. *Journal of Open Innovation, 68*(4), 1–17. doi:10.3390/joitmc6040181

Vygotsky, L. S., Cole, M., John-Steiner, V., Scribner, S., & Souberman, E. (1978). *Mind in Society: Development of Higher Psychological Processes*. Harvard University Press.

KEY TERMS AND DEFINITIONS

Bulk Carrier: The large single-deck ship, say > 10,000 dwt, which carries unpackaged cargo.

EEA Grants: Through the European Economic Area (EEA) Agreement, Iceland, Liechtenstein, and Norway are partners in the internal market with the Member States of the European Union. To promote a continuous and balanced strengthening of economic and trade relations, the parties to the EEA Agreement have established a multi-annual Financial Mechanism known as the EEA Grants. The EEA Grants established the objective of reducing social and economic disparities in Europe by strengthening bilateral relations with the Beneficiary States.

ENIDH (Escola Superior Náutica Infante D. Henrique): The public polytechnic higher education institute in Portugal and the only national college dedicated to the training of Merchant Marine Officers and senior managers of the Maritime-port sector in the areas of Intermodality, Logistics, and Management.

Growth Mindset: The term used to describe people's beliefs about learning and intelligence means more than just accepting feedback and being open-minded. It is about taking feedback, learning from experience, and coming up with strategies for improvement.

Knowledge Transfer: The communication activities of knowledge between projects and organizations are affected by the other's expertise when at least one of them is affected.

Living Labs: The methodology of innovation that enables collaborative learning by users, producers, and researchers in a real-life environment, in which user needs are central.

Open Innovation: The new business management model for innovation that promotes collaboration with people and organizations outside the company, including high education institutions, tech centers, and other knowledge sources.

Chapter 25
The Contribution of Data Science Applied to Customer Relationship Management:
A Systematic Literature Review

Dora Maria Simões
https://orcid.org/0000-0002-9380-4475
University of Aveiro, Portugal

ABSTRACT

In the face the contemporary world lives, and the consequent data produced at an unprecedented speed through digital media platforms, the data are nowadays called the new global currency. It raises numerous opportunities to improve outcomes in businesses, namely at the level of customer relationship management (CRM) strategies and their systems. Nevertheless, how analytics can be applied and support the customer relationship processes seems unclear for academics and industries. To better connect customer relationship processes needs and what data science analytics can offer, this chapter presents a systematic literature review around the concepts, tools, and techniques behind this field, looking particularly on customer acquisition and customer retention in businesses. The outcomes highlight that academic researcher works in this field are very scare and recent. Searching the Scopus and Web of Science databases resulted in only 12 documents from 2013 to 2020, eight of them published in the last two years.

INTRODUCTION

In face the contemporary world lives, and the consequent data produced at an unprecedented speed through digital media platforms, the data are nowadays called the new global currency. It rises numerous opportunities to improve outcomes in businesses, namely at level of competitive advantages and support of decision-making processes (X. Wang, Nguyen, & Nguyen, 2020; C. H. Wang & Lien, 2019; Waller & Fawcett, 2013). Customer relationship management (CRM) is an emergent business and marketing strategy that aims to create and maintain profitable customer relationships by designing and delivering

DOI: 10.4018/978-1-7998-6985-6.ch025

superior value propositions. It is based on high-quality customer-related data and leveraged by digital information and communication technology (Buttle & Maklan, 2019; Laudon & Laudon, 2020). Data science. When customer relationship management (CRM) intersects with data science, uncountable opportunities for business emerge. Data science and big data, more specifically network analysis, social media, sentiment analysis, text mining, and information diffusion are application focus of analytics, also, on marketing and business (Camacho et al., 2020). In summary sense, data science can be defined as a multi-disciplinary field that uses scientific methods, techniques, and algorithms, to extract useful knowledge from structured and unstructured data. Big data refers to the use of different methods and techniques to analyze, and systematically extract information from data sets that are too large, or complex, to be dealt with traditional data-processing algorithms. Nevertheless, how analytics can be applied to customer relationship processes is still unclear as the scarce academic publications (De Caigny et al., 2020; Yue, 2020; Sung, Zhang, Higgins, & Choe, 2016) and known industry cases proved. These few developments concerning the state of the art focused on cited concepts is inconsistent with the remarkable advances in artificial intelligence and internet of things in the last decade. To better connect customer relationship processes needs and what data science analytics can offer, this chapter presents a systematic literature review around the concepts, tools and techniques behind the increasing field of data science applied to CRM processes, looking particularly on customer acquisition and customer retention in businesses (X. Wang, Nguyen, & Nguyen, 2020; Iwashita, 2019; C. H. Wang & Lien, 2019; Semrl & Matei, 2017).

The present chapter aims to analyze the literature published in main academic databases - Scopus (by Elsevier) and Web of Science (by Clarivate), under the umbrella of "data science" and "customer relationship management" key terms. The main goal is to fill the gap looking to the published scientific works and identifying tendencies to anticipate the future. The results present an overview of the most relevant themes exploited, their applications, the followed methodologies, removing the veil to other areas to explore.

The chapter is organized as follows: after this introduction the report of the methodologic process of the systematic literature review was performed, presenting the flowchart of the main phases and its steps. Then the results by each phase (input, processing, and output) are reported. The output concerns descriptive and thematic analyses. Finally, the future research directions and a conclusion of the study are highlighted.

METHODOLOGY

One way to achieve greater rigor and better levels of reliability in a literature review is to adopt a systematic approach. In the beginning of the present centenary, Tranfield and colleagues (2003) proposed that systematic literature reviews should be used to develop decision-making evidence to overcome unsystematic processes of literature review and to identify key areas to research. Afterwards, Brereton and colleagues (2007) added that a systematic literature review allows the researcher to make a rigorous and reliable assessment of the research carried out within a specific topic. It is an instrument to map works published on the specific research topic so that the researcher is able to elaborate a synthesis of the existing knowledge on the subject (Levy & Ellis, 2006). The result must be the "state of the art" and demonstrate that the research in question contributes with something new to the existing body of knowledge. Supported mainly in works of Tranfield, Denyer, and Smart (2003) and Levy and Ellis (2006), but also of Moher, Liberati, and Tetzlaff (2015) and Sampaio and Mancini (2007), the methodological approach of this research is mainly supported in three phases (six steps): input; processing and output (see *Figure 1*). In "input" phase there are the data sources and the techniques used during analysis - "processing" – and then, the "output" is generated (synthesis report).

The input phase begins (step one) with the definition and presentation of the main goal of this research: "Determine the most recent developments and applications of data science techniques in customer relationship management (CRM) contexts". After that, the step two continues with the process of data sources identification requiring the definition of rigorous string that suits in the bibliographic databases selected.

The processing phase begins exporting the documents and their references to the Mendeley Desktop – version 1.19.4 - where it was made a preliminary relevance analysis. Consequently, the relevant data about each publication was also exported to Microsoft Excel 2016 and organized in a tabular form. The records were sequentially numbered and sorted by author name, year of publication, title of publication, author keywords, source, publisher, document type, bibliographic database, and number of citations. Based on this, it was possible produce a descriptive analysis, presented by circular and line graphs, showing number of publications by year and distribution of publications by document type. Also, the sources and their respective publishers are analysed in perspective of the influence of their Impact Factor on citations of the papers. After that, and with the goal of produce a thematic analysis, the content of each publication is examined. The goal is to make a critical analysis canvass of the content of the papers, concerning, in each study, the field of action, the methodological approach, and the analytical platforms (step four). To complete this thematic (content) analysis a word frequency query and a cluster analysis by words similarity using NVIVO – version release 1.3 (535) are performed. The approach to process the thematic analysis on step 4 is presented in *Figure 2*.

The research follows to the output phase with a well-structured synthesis of the analyses made in the precedent phase - step five. To support this, a co-word analysis using VOSviewer - version 1.6.16 was performed. Finally, a conclusion about the evidence is presented enhancing the value proposition of the research outcomes to the academy and to the industry (step 6).

Through the application of systematic literature review, this work in addition to provide an overview of the current research being done in the domain of data science technologies and practices applied in customer relationship management strategies, also intends to be helpful for researchers and industries looking for a potential on the subject, by presenting ideas for applying data science to enhance new and innovative CRM strategies.

SYSTEMATIC LITERATURE REVIEW

The search was performed on September 29, 2020 following the methodologic procedure described in the previous section. Here it is reported the principal results in a structured way. First, it is presented the strings and the publications output. Second, the guidelines and the outcomes of the descriptive and thematic analyses. And, in third order, it is reported a critical synthesis of the global literature review ran.

Input Steps

In this study are used the Scopus (by Elsevier) and Web of Science (by Clarivate) databases, restricting the results to articles and proceeding papers as document types. Concerning the goal of identify the publications related to research works around the application of data science in customer relationship

Figure 1. Methodological approach' flowchart of systematic literature review (adapted from Levy & Ellis, 2006 and Sampaio & Mancini, 2007)

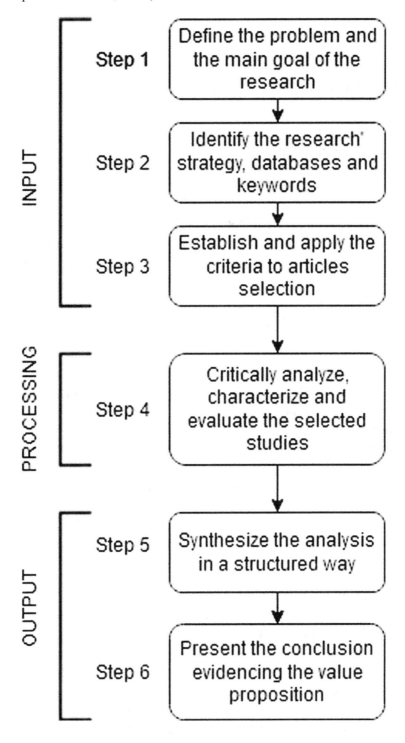

Figure 2. Thematic analysis approach

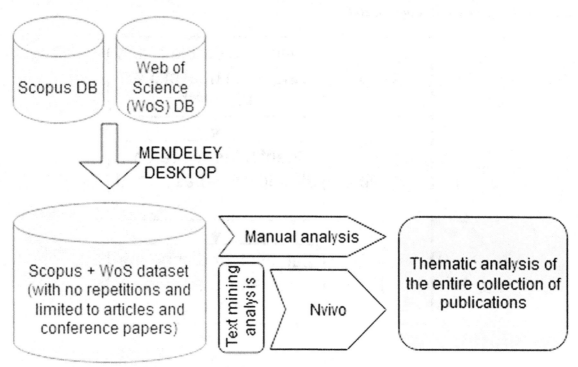

management, and whenever possible, with focus on customer acquisition or retention processes, it was defined to use the following key terms in the search: "data science" and "customer relationship management" or "CRM" (due sometimes it is used the acronym) or the terms "customer acquisition" or "customer retention", because they are terms related to processes strongly closed to CRM strategy. So, attending to these considerations and that these should be founded in the title, the abstract and/or the keywords defined by the authors in the published documents, in the first database, it was used the String 1 (*Figure 2*): TITLE-ABS-KEY ("data science") AND TITLE-ABS-KEY ("CRM" OR "CUSTOMER RELATION-SHIP MANAGEMENT" OR "CUSTOMER RETENTION" OR "CUSTOMER ACQUISITION") AND (LIMIT-TO (DOCTYPE, "cp") OR LIMIT-TO (DOCTYPE, "ar")), being obtained 9 documents. In the second database, it was used a similar string (adapted to the database' search codification) – String 2 (*Figure 3*): TS= ("data science") AND TS= ("CRM" OR "CUSTOMER RELATIONSHIP MANAGE-MENT" OR "CUSTOMER RETENTION" OR "CUSTOMER ACQUISITION")refined by document types: ARTICLE OR PROCEEDINGS PAPER - obtaining 8 documents, 1 of which is repeated and 4 of them being common to SCOPUS results.

So, applying exclusion and inclusion criteria cited (step three), the total number of the documents is 12. In this case, as all documents are about recent articles, published between 2013 and 2020, in English language, the unique limitation applied was consider articles (ar) and conference paper (cp) as showed in the strings presented above. In the string of Web of Science Core Collection, the term TS means the same as TITLE-ABS-KEY in Scopus, meaning that search is made in title, abstract and keywords of the publications.

Figure 3. String and results of Scopus

9 document results

TITLE-ABS-KEY ("**data science**") AND TITLE-ABS-KEY ("**CRM**" OR "CUSTOMER RELATIONSHIP MANAGEMENT" OR "CUSTOMER RETENTION" OR "CUSTOMER ACQUISITION") AND (LIMIT-TO (DOCTYPE , "**cp**") OR LIMIT-TO (DOCTYPE , "**ar**"))

Processing Step

As explained previous, the processing phase involve two types of analyses: descriptive and thematic (content). In the descriptive analysis, the goal was to make a critical analysis under the tendencies of the number of publications per year and its distribution per document type (article or conference paper). Also, it is canvassing the quality of the papers, concerning the sources of publication (journal or conference) and respective publishers, the impact factor and possible correlation with the citation numbers.

Figure 4. String and results of Web of Science

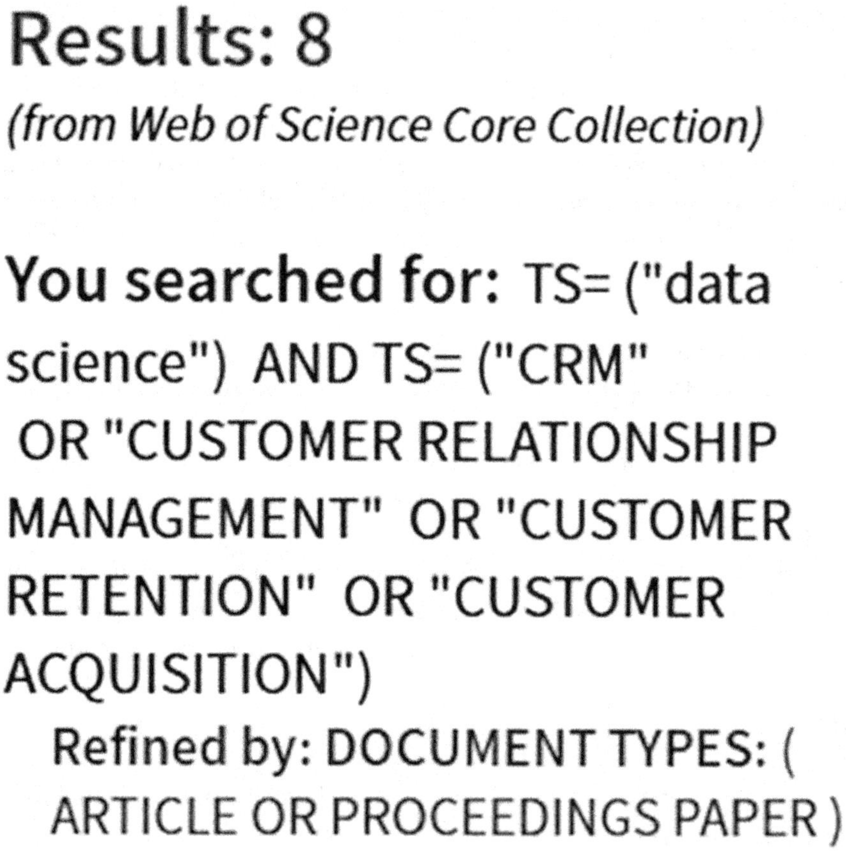

Results: 8
(from Web of Science Core Collection)

You searched for: TS= ("data science") AND TS= ("CRM" OR "CUSTOMER RELATIONSHIP MANAGEMENT" OR "CUSTOMER RETENTION" OR "CUSTOMER ACQUISITION")
Refined by: DOCUMENT TYPES: (ARTICLE OR PROCEEDINGS PAPER)

The thematic analysis intents to improve the knowledge on each study, namely, the field of action, the methodological approach followed, and the analytical platforms used. Also, a complementary content analysis is performed following the methods available through NVIVO – software provided by QSR International.

Descriptive analysis

After exporting the documents and their references to the Mendeley Desktop software – a bibliographic manager software – the relevant data about each publication was configured in a tabular form, with support in Microsoft Excel 2016 software. In *Table 1*, it is possible to see the result of this, with the records sequentially numbered and sorted by author name, year of publication, title of publication, source, publisher, document type, bibliographic database, and number of citations.

Analyzing the data in *Table 1* it was possible determine the number of publications per year (*Figure 5*) and the frequency' distribution of publications per document type (*Figure 6*). Looking the tables, it is possible to see that all publications are very recent (in a time interval of minus of one decade) and only in last year (2019) and presently (2020) we are assisting a some more activity, with an increase up to 4 publications in each year. Before (till 2018) it was registered no more than 1 publication by year and 0 in the years of 2015 and 2018. The publications are distributed equally by article and conference paper types.

The sources and their respective publishers had only one publication in the timespan of the study (2013-2020). Comparing the Impact Factor (Academic Accelerator, 2021) of each one with the number of citations of the papers, it was determined, and despite of their recency, that the ones published in journals with higher impact factor are the most cited (see *Table 2*). In the *Table 1* it is showed that they are the paper 1 (cited 3 times) - published in 2020 by Elsevier in Journal of Decision Support Systems – and the paper 9 (cited 95 times) – published in 2013 by Council of Supply Chain Management Professionals in Journal of Business Logistics. The other documents in analyze in this study with citations (both cited two times), till the moment, are the papers 7 and 8 – published by renowned Institute of Electrical and Electronics Engineers Inc. (IEEE) in International Conference on Behavioral, Economic, and Socio-Cultural Computing and International Conference on Data Science and Advanced Analytics, respectively, in 2017 and 2016.

Surprisingly, concerning their impact factor, they are the Journal of Industrial and Production Engineering and Lecture Notes in Computer Science published by Springer and Taylor and Francis Ltd., respectively, with no citation in their papers (2 and 10). One reason could be their recency due they were published in last year (2019). Other papers that it was expected more visibility are the 5 and the 11, both published by the Association for Computing Machinery (ACM), through the proceedings in conferences held in 2014 and 2020.

The analysis of the authors looks through that there aren't assiduous authors, in the context of this study. In the sample, each author or co-author participate only one time in each paper noticed. Also, there are no evidence of social relationship between authors through different publications.

Thematic analysis

With the goal of produce a thematic analysis, the content of each publication was examined manually. The thematic (content) analysis performed was firstly oriented by the keywords, the abstract and the title, and then all the content was analysed (reading each publication) to better understand their focus. With

Table 1. List of publications sorted by authors' name

Nº	Authors	Year	Title	Source	Publisher	Citations
1	(De Caigny, Coussement, & De Bock, 2020) (1) (2) (3)	2020	Leveraging fine-grained transaction data for customer life event predictions	Journal of Decision Support Systems	Elsevier B.V.	3/0
2	(de Castro Neto, Julia, Paiva, Carvalho, Junior, Peres, et al., 2019) (2) (4)	2019	Improving the AHT in telecommunication companies by automatic modeling of call center service	Lecture Notes in Computer Science	Springer Verlag	0
3	(Delgosha, Hajiheydari, & Saadeatmantesh, 2020) (1) (3)	2020	Semantic structures of business analytics research: applying text mining methods	Information Research - An International Electronic Journal	Univ. Sheffield - Dept. Information Studies	0
4	(Iwashita, 2019) (1) (3)	2019	Transitional method for identifying improvements in video distribution services	International Journal of Networked and Distributed Computing	Atlantis Press Sarl	0
5	(Jussila et al., 2014) (2) (4)	2014	New era of business analytics - making sense of business ecosystems	International Academic MindTrek Conference	Association for Computing Machinery, Inc (ACM)	0
6	(Salas-Rueda & Salas-Silis, 2019) (1) (3)	2019	Wevideo: cloud service useful for students during the construction and presentation of audiovisual contents?	Vivat Academia	Univ. Complutense Madrid, Servicio Publicaciones	0
7	(Semrl & Matei, 2017) (1) (2) (4)	2017	Churn prediction model for effective gym customer retention	Conference on Behavioral, Economic, and Socio-Cultural Computing	Institute of Electrical and Electronics Engineers Inc. (IEEE)	2/0
8	(Sung, Zhang, Higgins, & Choe, 2016) (1) (2) (4)	2016	Data-driven sales leads prediction for everything-as-a-service in the cloud	International Conference on Data Science and Advanced Analytics	Institute of Electrical and Electronics Engineers Inc. (IEEE)	2/2
9	(Waller & Fawcett, 2013) (2) (3)	2013	Click here for a data scientist: big data, predictive analytics, and theory development in the era of a maker movement supply chain	Journal of Business Logistics	Council of Supply Chain Management Professionals	95
10	(C. H. Wang & Lien, 2019) (1) (2) (3)	2019	Combining design science with data analytics to forecast user intention to adopt customer relationship management systems	Journal of Industrial and Production Engineering	Taylor and Francis Ltd.	0/0
11	(X. Wang, Nguyen, & Nguyen, 2020) (2) (4)	2020	Churn prediction using ensemble learning	International Conference Proceeding Series	Association for Computing Machinery (ACM)	0
12	(Yue, 2020) (2) (4)	2020	Topological data analysis of two cases: text classification and business customer relationship management	Journal of Physics: Conference Series	Institute of Physics Publishing	0

(1)Web of Science/CLARIVATE

(2)Scopus/ELSEVIER

(3)Article

(4)Conference paper

Figure 5. Publications per year

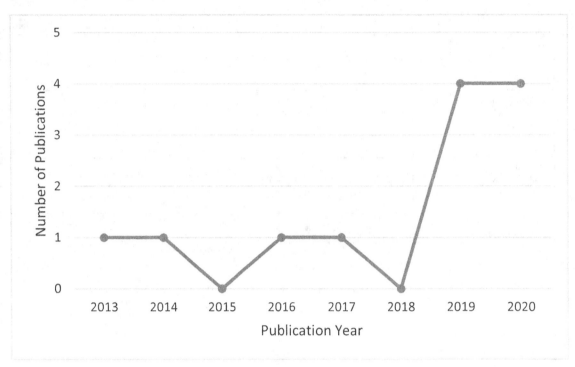

Figure 6. Publications per document type

Table 2. Impact factor of publication' sources

Source	Publisher	Impact Factor
Journal Decision Support Systems	Elsevier	5.420
Journal of Business Logistics	Council of Supply Chain Management Professionals	3.850
Journal of Industrial and Production Engineering	Taylor and Francis Ltd.	1.960
Lecture Notes in Computer Science	Springer	1.170
Information Research - An International Electronic Journal	Univ. Sheffield - Dept. Information Studies	0.763
Journal of Physics: Conference Series	Institute of Physics Publishing	0.540
International Journal of Networked and Distributed Computing	Atlantis Press Sarl	0.200
International Conference Proceeding Series	Association for Computing Machinery (ACM)	-
International Conference on Data Science and Advanced Analytics	Institute of Electrical and Electronics Engineers Inc. (IEEE)	-
International Academic MindTrek Conference	Association for Computing Machinery (ACM)	-
International Conference on Behavioral, Economic, and Socio-Cultural Computing	Institute of Electrical and Electronics Engineers Inc. (IEEE)	-
Vivat Academia	Univ. Complutense Madrid, Servicio Publicaciones	-

focus on these it was intended identify the key terms, the field of action, the methodological approach, and the analytical platforms (see *Table 3*).

Based on the results of content analysis presented above in *Table 3* and in the analysis of all corpus of publications clustered by word similarity, using Pearson Correlation Coefficient through NVIVO software, a summary of each set of publications with more similarity is described. The cluster analysis generated a diagram that cluster the selected files (the 12 publications) together if they have many words in common. The results can be viewed as a dendrogram or cluster map (see *Figure 7*). The summary proceeds in ascending order of relevance to focus of this chapter, that is also according the cluster tree map.

The paper #6 (Salas-Rueda & Salas-Silis, 2019) differs somewhat from the main objective of this systematic literature review because its focus is on analysis of the impact of the Wevideo cloud service during the teaching-learning process in higher education, and where the key term CRM appear resulting from the theme explored by the students in their practical exercises. However, this paper refers the use of RapidMiner – and relevant analytical platform for mining data. Also, the paper #9 (Waller & Fawcett, 2013) is irrelevant for this study because it is an editorial paper that proposes a 2x2 model to explain the role of predictive analytics in the theory development process and incentive researchers to publish in the journal, contributing to explaining the role of predictive analytics in the theory-building process.

Concerning the following set of papers: #3 from Delgosha and colleagues (2020) and #5 from Jussila and colleagues (2014), the first one - paper #3 - presents a study where the main research goal was identifying the major research topics and trends using text mining techniques. The authors begin distinguishing the three main hierarchical categories: descriptive, predictive, and prescriptive analytics (Delen, 2014). Descriptive analytics focusing on 'what happened in the past and why', while predictive analytics using models to answer the question of 'what will happen in future?', and prescriptive analytics going further to provide guidance by evaluating possible scenarios and answering, 'what course of

Table 3. Thematic analysis of publications

N°	Key terms[1]	Field of action	Methodologic approach	Analytical platforms
1	data science, customer relationship management, CRM	Validation of a new customer life event prediction model combining aggregated customer data (demographics, behavior, and contact) with fine-grained transaction data (that preserve recency, frequency, and monetary value information of the transactions) of a financial services industry, to predict four different customer life events.	Customer life event prediction (CLEP) method. Area Under the receiver operating characteristics Curve (AUC), Top Decile Lift (TDL), Wilcoxon signed-ranks tests and Wald statistics.	-
2	data science, customer relationship management, CRM	Enhance the customer service of an ISP company through performing a modelling of its CRM data warehouse and using such model to improve the call center scripts, so as to reduce the Average Handle Time (AHT).	Data Mining to induce classification rules able to predict the need for technical visit considering the customer problems.	-
3	data science, customer retention	Identify major research topics and trends using text mining techniques based on Web of science and Scopus databases.	Two text mining methods: co-word analysis and topic modelling.	VOSviewer BigML
4	data science, customer retention	Describes issues related to using customer satisfaction (CS) concept as a key indicator to customer retention, and its application to video distribution services (like Youtube, Netflix, etc), following a transitional evaluation approach.	Three evaluation methods for finding improving factors. Questionnaire data analysis oriented for the need of transitional approach.	-
5	data science, CRM	Discuss the business analytic applications and respective methods and industries.	Machine Learning methods, social network analysis and information visualization methods, and simulation methods.	NoSQL databases Hadoop
6	data science, CRM	Analyze of the impact of the Wevideo cloud service during the teaching-learning process in higher education. Using RapidMiner it is identified 4 predictive models.	Quantitative and qualitative research, predictive models by means of decision tree technique.	Wevideo cloud service RapidMiner
7	data science, customer retention	Predicting customer churn from contractual and behavioral perspectives, applied to fitness industry.	Machine Learning research.	AzureML BigML
8	data science, customer relationship management	Proposal of a data-driven iterative sales lead prediction framework for cloud everything as a service (cloud-based SaaS service), with the objective of to help the business team to nurture valuable potential customers, classifying (grouping) by paying and non-paying users.	RFDL (Recency, Frequency, Duration and Lifetime) analysis method, an extension of the RFM (Recency, Frequency, and Monetary value) model, Jenks natural breaks algorithm, and classification data mining techniques. BizDevOps process and DevOps deliverables.	IBM cloud platform (cloud-based relational data warehouse)
9	data science, customer relationship management	Editorial paper that proposes a 2x2 model to explain the role of predictive analytics in the theory development process and calls for other contributions in this domain.	2x2 model (matrix of explanation and prediction) pointing research questions relevant to practitioners.	-
10	data science, customer relationship management, CRM	(1) identifying the causalities between design features and behavioral intention, (2) deriving the priorities of design features, and (3) forecasting user intention to adopt CRM systems.	Behaviour-science (user perceptions and Behaviour intentions): Technology-Acceptance-Model (TAM) and design-science: Design-Based Research (DBR). Classification & Regression Tree (CART), Random Forest (RF) and Adaptive Boosting (AdaBoost).	-
11	data science, customer retention	A comparative study of the most widely used classification methods on the problem of customer churning in the telecommunication sector, using a public dataset from the Kaggle competition.	Machine learning classification models/techniques supported in three phases method: data pre-processing, model exploration, and fine-tuning the system. Classifiers: LightGBM, XGBoost, Decision Tree (DT) and Random Forest (RF).	-
12	data science, customer relationship management	Predicting customer loyalty and demand, applied on business-to-business.	Topological Data Analysis (TDA): 1st case - RFM + Prediction method and Time-series clustering technique, 2nd case – Persistent Homology and Mapper algorithms. Time Series Data and Text Classification of Natural Language Processing (NPL)	-

[1]In Title, Keywords or Abstract.

Figure 7. Tree map of publications clustered by word similarity

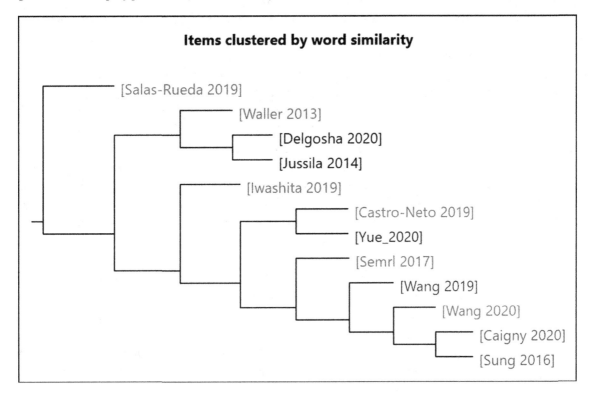

action should we take?'. They used two text mining methods to analyse content. Co-word analysis was used to calculate relationships among terms based on co-occurrence statistics, and topic modelling was used to identify the main topics based on the latent Dirichlet allocation model. They used to mine and visualise data VOSviewer and BigML, respectively. Latent Dirichlet allocation is a popular technique for content analysis designed to organize massive volumes of documents based on topics (Teh et al., 2007). BigML is a machine learning platform that provides sophisticated tools for statistical natural language processing to identify and model business analytics topics. The second one - paper #5 - discuss the business analytic applications and respective methods and industries. It could be a relevant contribution to deeper the knowledge on big data tools like NoSQL databases and Hadoop.

The paper #4 (Iwashita, 2019) describes issues related to using Customer Satisfaction (CS) concept as a key indicator to customer retention, and its application to video distribution services, following a transitional evaluation approach. The author distinguishes 3 types of video services: (a) video distribution (like Hulu or Netflix), (b) video share (like YouTube or Dailymotion), and (c) video broadcast (like Hikari TV or U-NEXT, or recently, in Portugal, the OPTO from SIC TV). Also, it is considered two types of business models: (1) free-for-viewer and (2) pay-for-viewer. The author explains customer loyalty as generally depending on the relationships among three factors: price, customer expectation (CE), and CS. Price is decided during service optimization. Customer expectations are set based on sales promotions, and the customer experiences satisfaction based on these expectations upon obtaining the goods/services. The good service is considered to be supported by a good strategy when CS is higher than CE. Loyalty decreases when this relationship is reversed, although the damage would be relatively small if CS is greater than price. However, customer retention will be difficult if CS is lower than price. Therefore, CS increases when it is larger than CE. The authors compare three evaluation methods for finding improving factors: evaluation using dissatisfaction scores (method 1), evaluation using difference in satisfaction and dissatisfaction scores (method 2), and transitional evaluation of satisfaction and dissatisfaction scores (method 3). The comparison is proceeded supported in a questionnaire and the data analysis oriented for the need of transitional approach. This is a relevant work highlighting the application of data science in business, and, particularly, in customer relationship management. In this case, specifically with the goal of improve customer satisfaction and consequently customer loyalty (retention).

Analysing now the set composed of the paper #2 (de Castro Neto et al., 2019) and the paper #12 (Yue, 2020), both are focused on Customer Relationship Management (CRM).In the paper #2 it is enhanced the customer service of an ISP company through performing a modelling of its CRM data warehouse and using such model to improve the call center scripts, such as to reduce the Average Handle Time (AHT). The modelling proposed uses data mining to induce classification rules able to predict the need for technical visit considering the customer problems. In the experiments carried out, rules with high predictive accuracy were generated. The results confirm that the generated rules allow for reducing the call AHT and can also be used as a tool for reducing the need for technical visits. Looking in paper #12 and particularly about the first case analyzed (Rivera-Castro et al., 2019), the authors enhance that after constructing a time series, from a qualitative perspective, the benefit of using them is their highly visual component. The marketing analyst can show the results to decisions-makers. From a quantitative side, topological RFM (Recency, Frequency and Monetary value) approach was used as a clustering method to increase the accuracy of a predictive model for loyalty scoring. Another benefit highlighted is the improvement on accuracy of a machine learning model. Thus, they open the door for a CRM predictive pipeline, where the practitioner can segment the customer base, generate personas, do predictions, and communicate to manage both predictions for the personas as well as for the individual users and identify those users diverging from the expected results from their respective personas. Therefore, the provider can obtain a deeper understanding of its customer base to adjust its product offering promotions while being able to generate reliable estimates for their future demand over multiple periods.

The paper #7 (Semrl & Matei, 2017) presents another example of data science application on service of customer relationship management (CRM). In this case, predicting customer churn from contractual and behavioral perspectives, applied to fitness industry. The AzureML and BigML analytical platforms supported the research' work. The last one already cited here in explanation of #paper 3.

The paper #10, from Wang and colleague (C. H. Wang & Lien, 2019), presents a study where the main goal of the authors was (1) identify the causalities between design features and behavioral intention, (2) derive the priorities of design features, and (3) forecast user intention to adopt CRM systems. The study allowed the authors highlighted that the contract-based sectors pay attention to managing call-center monitoring, loyalty programs and churn prevention while non-contract-based sectors focus on the skills of sales force automation, up-selling or cross-selling, and dynamic pricing. Enterprises with prior implementation experiences focus on the construct of perceived usefulness (PU) while the inexperienced enterprises focus on the construct of perceived ease-of-use (PEOU). Expert's users knowledgeable of statistics and database are more interested in mining analytics than the features of exploratory under-standing. Also, the study allowed find that the educational training in statistics or database is helpful to improve CRM operational skills for the staff (front-end and the back-end) and the novice users. Yet, forecasting user intention to adopt CRM can achieve better accuracy than forecasting user intention to recommend CRM. The authors enhance to that individual factors are highlighted, only job occupation (front-end vs. back-end) and prior knowledge (expert vs. novice). Following the concept of TAM, only

PU and PEOU are treated as the predictors. Other constructs, such as complexity, compatibility, and trialability, can be considered as the mediators or moderators in forecasting user. In opinion of the authors, despite ERP and CRM are popular enterprise applications, CRM is significantly different from ERP in two aspects: (1) ERP handles operational transactions like purchasing, accounting, and inventory control while CRM focuses on managing customer profiles and extending or enhancing customer relationships. (2) ERP needs to be tailored to internal business processes, but CRM depends on timely information to quickly respond to diverse requirements and handle customer complaints. In brief, ERP is more common in manufacturing sectors while CRM is more service-oriented. To address the impacts of organizational characteristics and individual characteristics, a novel TAM that combined design science with data science is presented help CRM developers identify key design features and capture the causation between user perceptions and behavioral intention. The enterprises with prior experiences in the implementation of enterprise applications are more likely to adopt the CRM system than the inexperienced ones. That means, CRM vendors can consolidate customer loyalty by targeting the enterprises who have already installed their ERP before. Meanwhile, for the purpose of market segmentation, CRM vendors should develop customized commercial software to satisfy the diverse requirements of distinct user groups. For individual users, poor knowledge in statistics or database can result in an obstacle in exploiting the strengths of the CRM software. The above-mentioned findings, in turn, suggest both CRM vendors and service companies the necessity of job training and developing different CRM versions (basic and advanced) for satisfying distinct user groups. In particular, the prediction of user recommendation is more difficult than the prediction of user adoption because recommendation needs user satisfaction with CRM systems and/or justification of performance comparisons between " before " adoption and " after " adoption. In the future, the impacts of cloud computing and artificial intelligence on mobile carriers (smartphones or tablets) deserve to be further addressed in designing CRM apps.

The paper #11 (X. Wang, Nguyen, & Nguyen, 2020) presents a comparative study of the most widely used classification methods on the problem of customer churning in the telecommunication sector, using a public dataset from the Kaggle competition. The authors cite the works of De Caigny and colleagues (e.g., De Caigny, Coussement, & De Bock, 2018) - Logit leaf model (LLM) – combination of decision tree and logistic regression, and Coussement and colleagues (Coussement, Lessmann, & Verstraeten, 2017) - improving churn prediction performance by data preparation treatment strategy. In this paper, the authors promote the application of machine learning classification models/techniques supported in three phases method: data pre-processing (including six steps: missing values, outliers, categorical variables, normalization, class imbalance, and feature selection), model exploration, and fine-tuning the system. Also, a top four performing classifiers are identified being the bagging and boosting ensemble techniques (LightGBM, XGBoost), Decision Tree (DT) and Random Forest (RF).

Finalizing this summary analysis about the publications in study, the focus is put on the paper #1 (De Caigny, Coussement, & De Bock, 2020) and on the paper #8 (Sung, Zhang, Higgins, & Choe, 2016). In the first one, the authors defend that managing customer relationships during such life events has crucial strategic importance and can align the company's actions better with future customer behavior. Correct detection of life events enables companies to engage customers with appropriate cross- or up-selling offers and reactively target them with relevant marketing campaigns. In their study, the authors determined that the customer demographics are always the most important for predicting life events despite customer behavior information and can help predict life events with less importance. Yet, the contact between the customer and company have the least importance. With respect to the fine-grained transaction data, the authors note substantial impacts in terms of predicting life events. They represent the most important source of information for moving, birth of a child, new relationships, and end of a relationship. The model that uses the RFM-extended behavioral similarity scores extracts far more predictive information out of the data, which then leads to heightened importance scores. So, they incorporate fine-grained transaction data, and particularly extending the PSN (pseudo-social network) methods with behavioral similarity measures based on RFM variables obtained from payment transactions, significantly improves predictive performance. So, the results show that optimal predictive performance requires a combination of aggregated and fine-grained transactional data. Predicting life events might help to target the right customers with the right promotions, which could give a competitive advantage. In addition to the case study applied to the financial industry, they suggest application of CLEP (customer life event prediction) method to telecommunications or retail industries, meanwhile drawing attention to data quality. Customer life event prediction (CLEP) method offer a framework for integrating fine-grained data in a predictive model (representing the data in a pseudo-social network (PSN) constructed on binary information and continuous data (RFM-based). To measure the predictive performance of the models it was used the area under the receiver operating characteristics curve (AUC) and top decile lift (TDL). To test whether observed differences in the performance measures across the models are statistically significant, the comparison of the classifiers used Wilcoxon signed-ranks tests. The paper #8 (Sung, Zhang, Higgins, & Choe, 2016) propose a data-driven iterative sales lead prediction framework for cloud everything as a service (cloud-based SaaS service), with the objective of to help the business team to nurture valuable potential customers, classifying (grouping) by paying and non-paying users. In this work, the authors propose the RFDL (Recency, Frequency, Duration and Lifetime) analysis method, an extension of the RFM (Recency, Frequency, and Monetary value) model. It is used IBM cloud platform (cloud-based relational data warehouse), BizDevOps process and DevOps deliverables.

As a remarkable point, the word cloud of *Figure 8* obtained through the quality software NVIVO confirm the domain of the publications.

Figure 8. Word cloud of frequency

In map (*Figure 8*) it is showed, based on a word frequency query with 100 most frequent, that the main themes of research are around customer and CRM, data analytics and models in business.

Output Steps

The synthesis of the analysis and the value proposition evidence is now presented. It was used VOS-viewer – free software provided by Centre for Science - to mine and visualise scientific texts (Van Eck & Waltman, 2010). The software uses text mining functions to identify related noun phrases, along with a clustering approach to examine the co-occurrence of the words. A co-occurrence map shows that the distance between two terms can be interpreted as an indication of the relatedness of the terms. It applies a distance-based mapping technique referred to as visualisation of similarities (VOS). Co-word analysis is based on two important assumptions: 1) the words used are good representatives for the reflection of its content and 2) the co-occurrence of the two words in various papers indicates their relation so that if the co-occurrence of the keywords is more, their relation is closer (Feng et al., 2017). Through the VOS-viewer software, the *Figure 9* shows a term co-occurrence map based on text data obtained based on the RIS file created from the publications' collection in analysis stored in Mendeley bibliographic software. This represents a co-word analysis network of high-frequency words related to this research, illustrating how common words presented in title and abstract fields of all documents are related to each other.

Figure 9. Network and overlay visualization of co-occurrence analysis on titles and abstracts

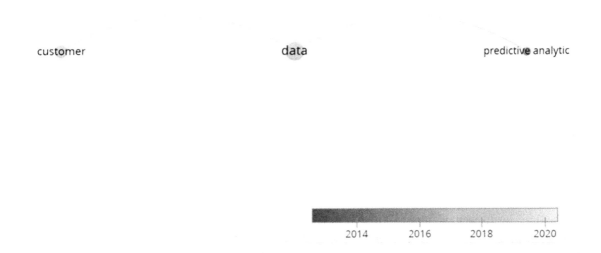

A full counting method was followed based on a minimum number of occurrences of a term of 6. This network identified 447 terms where 4 meets the threshold. For each of the 4 terms a relevance score was calculated and based on it the most relevant ones were selected based on premise of 60% most relevant. Then, 3 terms were select: customer, data, and predictive analytic (see *Figure 10*).

Figure 10. Terms with more occurrences and strength

The three terms were identified with the same relevance - 1.00 – being "data" the most frequent term (25) followed of customer (12) and predictive analytic (6). In this yielded of words, in *Figure 9*: green (data and customer) and violet (predictive analytic). Most important terms are marked with a larger font. Using the 'overlay visualisation' tab in VOSviewer software, the main topics of recent research in data (science) field, the rising and fading trends were identified. So, terms such as data and customer are among the most frequent topics in research. As observed in *Figure 9*, data and customer are two topics that have emerged as trends since mid-2016. Curiously, the term "predictive analytic" was more frequent in the begin of this timespan (2013-2014). More recently (from 2018) is emerging the term "data (science)"- represented with yellow colour in F*igure 9* and *Figure 11* - with a strong incidence but with yet little expression due few publications reference it.

Figure 11. Density visualization of co-occurrence analysis on titles and abstracts

The network, overlay and density visualisation of co-occurrence analysis based on titles and abstracts of publications reinforce the previous explanation that more and more research studies and practical applications works around the data science field applied to customer relationship management strategies and systems will be wellcome.

Truly, this study identified 8 publications centred on core of this research. They are: paper #4 from Iwashita (2019); paper #2 from de Castro Neto et al. (2019); paper #12 from Yue (2020); paper #7 from Semrl and Matei (2017); paper #11 from Xing Wang, Khang Nguyen, and Binh P. Nguyen (2020); paper #1 from De Caigny, Coussement, and De Bock (2020) and the paper #8 from Sung, Zhang, Higgins, and Choe (2016). The paper #10 from Chih-Hsuan Wang and Ching-Yu Lien (2019) despite its focus on CRM systems it is centred on its adoption by the enterprises and their users.

FUTURE RESEARCH DIRECTIONS

Evidence for this study and it was already referred in past in systematic literature review work of Saur-Amaral, Ferreira, and Conde (2013), despite their study have been centered on tourism marketing and consumption theme, the field of relationship marketing was cited as scarcely present, loyalty and customer relationship management tools were identified with few references and no real methodology or model applied to manage the relationship with the tourists and to measure the value of each customer. Eight years passed from the research of these authors, the systematic literature review made and present in this chapter highlights that there are not developments in this field (customer relationship management applied to tourism and its congeners business areas like hotels, travel agencies and companies, and so on). So, our research illustrated that there are clear gaps in the scientific literature and much core to explore in this thematic and in others business areas like telecommunications, bank, education, construction sector, etc.

This research has a few constraints, as it is limited to Scopus and Web of Science databases. The analysis may not be capable of extracting very deep knowledge of the specified context. As the data science applied to customer relationship management knowledge area is in its infancy stage, the keywords used in related studies are not yet standardised. Therefore, for a more complete understanding of this new area, researchers and practitioners might use congeners search terms of data science such as business intelligence, business analy*, big data analy*, data analy* and data mining without caring about the uppercase or lowercase or the spaces within the terms. Thus, they can retrieve documents from various databases as they may be used interchangeably by this search terms and "customer relationship management" or "CRM" and other terms. Future studies can use complementary bibliometric techniques (e.g., co-citation analysis, co-author analysis and bibliographic coupling) to give special attention to authors who provide links between the major knowledge groups would also be of interest, such as the kinds of work these links represent and the questions they address.

CONCLUSION

The aim of this manually and computational literature analysis was to identify the knowledge structure, review the main and influential trends and reveal hidden themes in the field of data science applied to customer relationship management in business. Text mining methods were used to analyse published documents in the Scopus and Web of Science databases. This study investigated the semantic structure analysing 12 related research documents published between 2013 and 2020. Many collected documents makes the text mining an appropriate method for a thorough assessment of the literature (Cosic et al., 2015; Rikhardsson & Yigitbasioglu, 2018).

The map of the co-occurrence terms and extracted themes show that, although the research interest in data science is contemporary, the studied subjects cover a wide variety of knowledge areas. Our findings indicate that the knowledge structure mainly consists of research applied to data analysis on customers management that allow to forecast a possible churn and improve the satisfaction and loyalty of customers base, in general. Examining the publication data associated with the keywords in the co-word analysis network showed that the topics related to CRM systems have become more popular.

REFERENCES

Academic Acelerator. (2021). *Academic Accelerator: Accelerate your scientific research*. Retrieved from https://academic-accelerator.com

Brereton, P., Kitchenham, B. A., Budgen, D., Turner, M., & Khalil, M. (2007). Lessons from applying the systematic literature review process within the software engineering domain. *Journal of Systems and Software*, *80*(4), 571–583. doi:10.1016/j.jss.2006.07.009

Buttle, F., & Maklan, S. (2019). Customer relationship management: concepts and technologies (4th ed.). Routledge, Taylor & Francis Group. doi:10.4324/9781351016551

Camacho, D., Panizo-Lledot, A., Bello-Orgaz, G., & Gonzalez-Pardo, C. E. (2020). The four dimensions of social network analysis: an overview of research methods, applications, and software tools. Information Fusion, 63, 88–120. doi:10.1016/j.inffus.2020.05.009

Cosic, R., Shanks, G., & Maynard, S. B. (2015). A business analytics capability framework. *AJIS. Australasian Journal of Information Systems*, *19*, S5–S19. doi:10.3127/ajis.v19i0.1150

Coussement, K., Lessmann, S., & Verstraeten, G. (2017). A comparative analysis of data preparation algorithms for customer churn prediction: A case study in the telecommunication industry. *Decision Support Systems, 95*, 27–36. doi:10.1016/j.dss.2016.11.007

De Caigny, A., Coussement, K., & De Bock, K. W. (2018). A new hybrid classification algorithm for customer churn prediction based on logistic regression and decision trees. *European Journal of Operational Research, 269*(2), 760–772. doi:10.1016/j.ejor.2018.02.009

De Caigny, A., Coussement, K., & De Bock, K. W. (2020). Leveraging fine-grained transaction data for customer life event predictions. *Decision Support Systems, 130.* . doi:10.1016/j.dss.2019.113232

de Castro Neto, H., Julia, R. M. S., Paiva, E. R. F., Carvalho, A. P. L. F., Junior, A. P. S., Peres, D. R. S., . . . de Assis, J. E. (2019). Improving the AHT in telecommunication companies by automatic modeling of call center service. In *EPIA Conference on Artificial Intelligence* (pp. 96–107). Vila Real, Portugal: Springer. 10.1007/978-3-030-30244-3_9

Delen, D. (2014). *Real-world data mining: Applied business analytics and decision making.* FT Press.

Delgosha, M. S., Hajiheydari, N., & Saadeatmantesh, H. (2020). Semantic structures of business analytics research: applying text mining methods. In *Information Research* (Vol. 25). University of Borås. Retrieved from http://www.informationr.net/ir/25-2/paper856.html

Feng, J., Zhang, Y. Q., & Zhang, H. (2017). Improving the co-word analysis method based on semantic distance. *Scientometrics, 111*(3), 1521–1531. doi:10.100711192-017-2286-1

Iwashita, M. (2019). Transitional Method for Identifying Improvements in Video Distribution Services. *International Journal of Networked and Distributed Computing, 7*(4), 141. doi:10.2991/ijndc.k.190911.001

Jussila, J., Huhtamäki, J., Kärkkäinen, H., Aho, T., Kortelainen, S., & Tebest, T. (2014). New era of business analytics - Making sense of business ecosystems. *MINDTREK 2014 - Proceedings of the 18th International Academic MindTrek Conference*, 266–268. 10.1145/2676467.2676517

Laudon, K. C., & Laudon, J. P. (2020). *Management information systems: managing the digital firm* (16th ed.). Pearson Education Limited.

Levy, Y., & Ellis, T. J. (2006). A systems approach to conduct an effective literature review in support of information systems research. *Informing Science Journal, 9*, 181–212. doi:10.28945/479

Moher, D., Liberati, A., & Tetzlaff, J. (2015). Principais itens para relatar revisões sistemáticas e metaanálises: A recomendação PRISMA. *Epidemiologia e Serviços de Saúde: Revista do Sistema Unico de Saúde do Brasil, 24*(2), 335–342. doi:10.5123/S1679-49742015000200017

Rikhardsson, P., & Yigitbasioglu, O. (2018). Business intelligence & analytics in management accounting research: Status and future focus. *International Journal of Accounting Information Systems, 29*, 37–58. doi:10.1016/j.accinf.2018.03.001

Rivera-Castro, R., Pilyugina, P., Pletnev, A., Maksimov, I., Wyz, W., & Burnaev, E. (2019). Topological data analysis of time series data for B2B Customer Relationship Management. https://arxiv.org/abs/1906.03956

Salas-Rueda, R.-A., & Salas-Silis, J.-A. (2019). WeVideo: ¿Servicio en la nube útil para los estudiantes durante la construcción y presentación de los contenidos audiovisuales? *Vivat Academia*, *1*, 67–89. doi:10.15178/va.2019.149.67-89

Saur-Amaral, I., Ferreira, P., & Conde, R. (2013). Linking past and future research in tourism management through the lens of marketing and consumption: a systematic literature review Investigação passada e futura sobre gestão do turismo, marketing e consumo: uma revisão sistemática da literatura. *Conde / Tourism & Management Studies, 9*(1), 35–40.

Semrl, J., & Matei, A. (2017). Churn prediction model for effective gym customer retention. *Proceedings of 4th International Conference on Behavioral, Economic, and Socio-Cultural Computing, BESC 2017,* 1–3. 10.1109/BESC.2017.8256385

Sung, C., Zhang, B., Higgins, C. Y., & Choe, Y. (2016). Data-driven sales leads prediction for everything-as-a-service in the cloud. *Proceedings - 3rd IEEE International Conference on Data Science and Advanced Analytics, DSAA 2016,* (May), 557–563. 10.1109/DSAA.2016.83

Tranfield, D., Denyer, D., & Smart, P. (2003). Towards a methodology for developing evidence-informed management knowledge by means of systematic review. *British Journal of Management, 14*(3), 207–222. doi:10.1111/1467-8551.00375

Van Eck, N. J., & Waltman, L. (2011). *Text mining and visualisation using VOSviewer.* https://arxiv.org/pdf/1109.2058

Waller, M. A., & Fawcett, S. E. (2013). Click here for a data scientist: Big data, predictive analytics, and theory development in the era of a maker movement supply chain. *Journal of Business Logistics, 34*(4), 249–252. doi:10.1111/jbl.12024

Wang, C. H., & Lien, C. Y. (2019). Combining design science with data analytics to forecast user intention to adopt customer relationship management systems. *Journal of Industrial and Production Engineering, 36*(4), 193–204. doi:10.1080/21681015.2019.1645051

Wang, X., Nguyen, K., & Nguyen, B. P. (2020). Churn prediction using ensemble learning. In *ACM International Conference Proceeding Series* (pp. 56–60). 10.1145/3380688.3380710

Yue, B. (2020). Topological Data Analysis of Two Cases: Text Classification and Business Customer Relationship Management. *Journal of Physics: Conference Series, 1550*(3), 032081. Advance online publication. doi:10.1088/1742-6596/1550/3/032081

KEY TERMS AND DEFINITIONS

Customer Acquisition: Business tactics aiming to attract prospect customers and to let them know about the enterprise' products and/or services and, the consequently, to identify uniquely the new customers when performing the purchases.

Customer Relationship Management (CRM): Corporate information management strategy inherent to customer relationship processes, supported by digital technologies, and aimed at increasing the efficiency and effectiveness of processes and respective activities, carried out with a view to acquiring new customers and retaining valuable customers' existing.

Customer Relationship Management System: Set of interdependent components—hardware, software, database resources, telecommunications networks, and people and procedures—that interact to collect data from customers and their interactions with the enterprise at the level of the various organizational functions - marketing, sales and support -, storage them, process them (transformation and analysis), and disseminate information to improve decision-making processes in order to acquire and retain valuable customers.

Customer Retention: Business tactics used by the enterprise to develop the relationship with new customers and improve their satisfaction level through interactions with the enterprise and, consequently, increase their value and avoid the future churn.

Data Science: Recent popular field related to business analytics research and its intelligent techniques applied to big data.

Systematic Literature Review: A systematic approach following a specific methodological process to review a set of academic literature, in order to analyses and discover new tendencies in a research topic.

Chapter 26
Data Science in Economics and Business:
Roots and Applications

Mara Madaleno
https://orcid.org/0000-0002-4905-2771
GOVCOPP, DEGEIT, Portugal & University of Aveiro, Portugal

João Lourenço Marques
https://orcid.org/0000-0003-0472-2767
GOVCOPP, DCSPT, Portugal & University of Aveiro, Portugal

Muhammad Tufail
https://orcid.org/0000-0002-6013-9157
National University of Sciences and Technology (NUST), Pakistan

ABSTRACT

Economics and business are a great background for data science provided econometricians and data scientists are sets with an intersection, although remaining unknown. In econometrics, data mining is somewhat a monstrous word, a field that traditionally seeks causal inference and results in interpretability. When we go deeper into what data science usually is, the boundaries between more traditional econometrics and even statistics and the hip and cool machine learning become shorter. In economics and business, we find examples and applications of simple and advanced data science techniques. This chapter intends to provide state-of-the-art data science applications in economics and business. The review and bibliometric analysis are limited to the research articles published through Elsevier Scopus. Results allowed the authors to conclude that despite the number of already existent research, a lot more remains to be explored joining both fields of knowledge, data since, and economics and business. This analysis allowed the authors to identify further possible avenues of research critically.

DOI: 10.4018/978-1-7998-6985-6.ch026

INTRODUCTION AND FRAMEWORK

Undoubtedly, mathematical modeling and statistics are central to quantitative economics, highlighted by the fact that some of the biggest data repositories are maintained by economic research organizations. Economists try to understand human behavior through Homo economics or the "economic man", to model human behavior. For that, they rely on economic theories and use some analytical tools and techniques, many of which are no more than standard statistical and mathematical models. We find in the literature economists walking around in all domains; from unemployment and inequality to the economics of climate change, to advertisement and revenue collection, from consumer and production behavior, up to profit, sales, and purchases, and finance data explorations (Provost and Fawcett, 2013; Brooks et al., 2019; Nosratabadi et al., 2020a, 2020b; Taddy, 2019; Basdas and Esen, 2020; Consoli et al., 2021).

We may think of some reasons why we should not dissociate economics, business, and data scientists. At least economists know exactly what the term machine learning means but with more econometric and statistical concepts. Machine learning ends up being a fancy word to describe statistical or predictive modeling that is used by programmers (Cao, 2017). Surprisingly, when we look for the most popular machine learning courses, the first two modules of their syllabus are still linear regression and logistic regression, basic concepts learned by economists in introductory econometrics. Econometrics is the application of statistical modeling in understanding complex social and environmental issues, being a big area of applied economics. We may even argue that in this case, economists have a deeper knowledge of linear regression than the average data scientists abroad. However, it is still hard for an economist to understand concepts such as neural networks, machine learning, and support vector machines, among many others, and still, heteroscedasticity is something away from the syllabus of machine learning, putting forward the pros and cons for economists or managers desiring to be involved in data science (Basdas and Esen, 2020; Consoli et al., 2021). Neural networks combine layers of logistic-like regressions to model non-linear relationships among variables, usually more complex, that simple regression analysis is not able to capture. Therefore, nothing as difficult as it may initially seem. Still, they build powerful algorithms, in what we believe to be complementary areas.

Economists have higher standards given their obsession in finding causal relationships, a goal unable to be fulfilled unless randomized controlled trials are pursued and sensitivity analysis to models basic assumptions scrutinized (we may think here of many emerging biases like attenuation, survivorship, selection bias, measurement error, reverse causality, truncation, censoring, among others). For machine learning, things are easier, given that models are not solved explicitly, and they do not need to rely on stricter assumptions (Donoho, 2017). Instead, models are estimated interactively with gradient descent and its derivatives, usually ignoring the theory behind the relationship we are trying to study (Taddy, 2019; Nosratabadi et al., 2020b). Even so, they use cross-validation and testing, and instead of t-statistics bootstrapping. In reality, this is summed up to the use of the right tools in the correct applications. Moreover, presentation and writing are important parts of data science provided non-technical audiences will be the interesting parts in research (managers, policymakers, marketers, copywriters, customers, clients). After all, the final result expected to be driven from the research is that we can demonstrate why our results matter and how stakeholders can use them and act over them. Economists, have generally a broader picture of the overall panorama and deepen these results, not just reading numbers as most data scientists, but presenting and clearly explaining results, with fluid writing. Whereas mathematicians and a computer scientist are not so comfortable when it comes to presenting and explaining the work results clearly and to a broader audience (with a correct structure and logic behind the story economists need to tell).

Economists should make great data scientists but usually opt for more traditional fields like finance, academia, enterprises, institutions, governments, and so on, and in all these fields we have data science applications as will become evident in our results section. However, if economists have a great background and unique blend of technical, statistical, soft skills, and human skills, perhaps, data science positions would benefit from having econometricians doing the job, taking advantage of their awareness of possible shortcomings emerging from data mining and resilience in trying all that might work to answer to specific problems (Taddy, 2019; Nosratabadi et al., 2020b). The joint work of both would increase the skills of both and allow to resolve more specific issues quickly, efficiently, and effectively (Consoli et al., 2021). At least we see in the literature that recently the combinations of the different areas of knowledge (economics, management, data science) have allowed great analyzes recognized by pairs of problems that both sciences had hitherto tried to solve in a more individualized way.

In fact, in the areas of economics and business, we may find several examples and applications of simple and advanced data science techniques. For example, behavioral economists can quantify consumer response and attitude in response to marketing campaigns, price reduction, and addition of new features (Basdas and Esen, 2020). Behavioral finances also deal with consumer behaviors and attitudes but are related to financial markets, where consumers are called investors (Consoli et al., 2021). Financial markets have huge datasets with which to work, demanding simply more sophisticated econometric techniques to analyze this data (Brooks et al., 2019). In all activity sectors, we find applications of data science (Cao, 2017), namely, agricultural and energy economists help decide how to set the right insurance policy for farmers against natural disasters and to deal with energy efficiency, consumption, and implementation of the rights policies to pursue the low carbon footprint goals and energy transition goals (Nosratabadi et al., 2020a). Industrial economists determine the level of commodity production and pricing mechanism for given market demand, helping markets to define the equilibrium price to be applied and sports economists are already making a huge influence (Consoli et al., 2021). All these examples are explored through optimization models, theoretical models, and econometrics, turning evident the relationship between data science and the areas of economics and business, as also exposed above.

To quantify marginal changes in output for a small change in input, mathematical models like differential equations are used. Statistical models are typically used to develop and test theories on the relationship between economic agents (people, farms, businesses) and impacts of policies/incentives using statistical tools. The whole domain of "econometrics" is based upon the application of standard statistical models (Consoli et al., 2021). These are familiar to data scientists since we are talking about descriptive statistics and hypothesis testing, correlation and regression analysis, time series analysis and visualization, predictive analytics and forecasting, and, as well, panel data modeling (OLS – ordinary least squares, fixed and random-effects models, etc.). Provided most economic questions are empirical, standard scientific processes are applied to analyze it (developing a hypothesis, collecting data, testing the hypothesis, making conclusions) (Basdas and Esen, 2020).

This chapter intends to present a literature survey and bibliometric analysis of the applications of data science to business and economics, considering as analysis period the most recent twenty years initially, to draw attention to the growing body of application and critically analyzing avenues of future research. We do that by exploring methods and techniques, analytics toolbox, and highlighting specific case studies. Almost all economics is data-driven and quantitative. As such, a model of the real world is created (a small or large part of it as representative) to understand relationships between different com-

Figure 1. Data Science Glossary
Source: Bajracharya (2018).

ponents, their interactions, and the impact of external influences, like policies, incentives, and shocks. Thus, when this complex interconnected system is modeled, economists rely on a range of mathematical and statistical techniques.

From the analysis undergone, it was possible to infer that the amount of data available reached incalculable dimensions with the advancement of the information systems, so their treatment and analysis need to support companies' strategic decisions. Data science is the science of data (Cao, 2017). Big data is only one of its dimensions, referring to data that is too large and/or complex to be effectively and/or efficiently handled by traditional data-related theories, technologies, and tools. Big data is changing the traditional business models because companies created in the digital era are aware of the potential of big data, and understand their data, how to use it, and the opportunities for gaining competitive advantage (Donoho, 2017). Big data is helping managers to measure and manage and as a result, they know more about their business, and this knowledge is translated into an improved decision-making process and increased performance (McAfee et al., 2012).

Economics and business are therefore much more than programmers think, as it is data science for economists or managers. Figure 1 presents a word cloud of data science key terms providing a clear picture of all that is involved.

Literature includes an appropriate number of state of the art review papers and comparative analysis of many data science methods (e.g., Brooks et al., 2019; Nosratabadi et al., 2020a; Nosratabadi et al., 2020b; Basdas et al., 2021). Considering the fields of economics and business jointly, there is still a lack of research in the area and the current research aims to fill this gap by providing a recent bibliometric and brief bibliographic analysis of methods within data science used and applied for economics and business. The chapter further contributes to identifying future trends in the advancement of learning algorithms for the economics and business areas.

The rest of the chapter develops as follows. Section 2 presents the data and the methodology followed to present the bibliometric and bibliographic analysis. Section 3 presents the results and discusses them, while section 4 evidences some of the most relevant conclusions.

DATA AND METHODOLOGY

Given that our goal is to provide the state of the art of data science in economics and business, the review and bibliometric analysis are limited to the original peer-review research articles published through Elsevier Scopus, which is one of the most comprehensive journals databases in the world. Besides, only articles written in English are considered for the review in this study.

The systematic literature review and bibliometric approach were based on the Prisma method including four steps: 1) identification (documents are identified through an initial search in the mentioned databases), 2) screening (first, duplicate articles are eliminated; second, the relevance of the articles is examined), 3) eligibility (the full text of articles was read by the authors, filtered and only some of them were considered eligible), 4) inclusion (the creation of the final database of the study, which is used for qualitative and quantitative analysis).

It was possible to observe that application domains include stock market, marketing, E-commerce, corporate banking, and cryptocurrency, but many more. Finally, we limited the search to the years 2018-2021, thus three complete years of data, as many articles had been already accepted to be published in 2021, or were in the publishing process. Removing other documents and letting solely articles and book chapters, we ended up with 377. Two different approaches were followed for the analysis of the collected data (articles): i) the VOSviewer, a bibliographic analysis software (https://www.vosviewer. com/), is used to visualize and analyze some bibliometric features of the initial data (N=377), based on the principle of co-occurrence and coupling of literature; and for ii) the most relevant publications (N=13), those identified as having the highest number of citations (see Table 3), a content analysis was applied to identify how the different topics studied in Economics and Business are linked with data science approaches. For this purpose, the final documents were stored as text files in QDA Miner and using the WORDSTAT software (developed by Provalis Research: https://www.provalisresearch.com/) a cluster analysis is presented for the key phrases of these texts. Once these groups of key expressions were found, the "key-word-in-context" (KWIK) tool was used to better understand the meaning of these contents in their contexts. The outputs of this analysis are presented and analyzed in the next section.

As for the search strategy of articles in the Scopus database, our initial research methodology was very general. While looking for **Data Science in Economics and Business** in title abstract and keywords Scopus returned 3,168 results. Restricting research only for the years 2011-2021 yielded 2,557 document results available. Limiting the search for the subject areas Economics, Econometrics and Finance, and Business, Management, and Accounting we ended up with 1,065 document results. From these, 894 are articles, 47 conference papers, 39 book chapters, 30 books, and 30 reviews (the rest relies on erratum, conference review, editorial, and letter and retracted). We then restricted the search solely to articles and book chapters, yielding 933 documents (both in the final publication stage as well as articles in press).

To restrict it further we limited the publishing period to the last 5 years (not considering 2021 since it is not full), 2016-2021, and limited our search to solely published articles in Journals. Even so, the number of retrieved articles was high dimension. Therefore, we advanced to other search criteria inside the Data Science umbrella, considering only those articles which in their title, abstract, or keywords, included the words *big data, data mining, data handling, artificial intelligence, digital storage, machine learning, information management, cloud computing, big data analytics, big data applications* and *data integration,* of course, limited to the subject areas of Economics, Econometrics, and Finance, and Business, Management, and Accounting.

The search limited to the years, 2016-2021, peer-reviewed articles and published or accepted to be published in scientific journals, under the general umbrella Data Science in Economics and Business, allowed us to end up with 2,235 document results. Curiously between 2018 and 2019, the number of articles published almost doubled. Published articles by year under the search limited to years 2016-2021 and for the retrieved 2,235 documents yielded 199 in 2016, 347 in 2017, 369 in 2018, 611 in 2019, 618 in 2020, and in 2021 we already have 91 documents published corresponding to the exposed criteria.

Further filters were applied to this search, namely in terms of years, provided the initial search criteria were still retrieving many articles. Therefore, we limited the articles between 2018-2021. These yielded for Business, Management, and Accounting 369 documents, and Economics, Econometrics and Finance 167, and for Social Sciences Scopus retrieves 109 articles, in a total of 430 documents. Provided it was still a lot of articles to analyze, we decided to restrict the analysis further, but surprisingly it is vast and huge the existent applications of data science in business and economics. Using the previous search, we limited articles further to the following subjects: *big data, economics, business,* published between 2018-2021, *data mining, data handling, artificial intelligence, digital storage, machine learning, information management, cloud computing, big data analytics, big data applications, data integration,* and excluding all subject areas besides Business, Management and Accounting, and Economics, Econometrics, and Finance. Removing other documents and letting solely articles and book chapters we ended up with 377 documents. Restricting only to the most recent years of 2018-2021 was only an attempt to restrict the total number of articles retrieved. Figure 2 summarizes the systematic process followed to select the literature.

The next section will present the results of our bibliometric and bibliographic analysis considering these 377 results. From these 363 refer to a journal published articles and only 14 to book chapters. The inclusion of book chapters in our research is because we are exactly elaborating this analysis for a book chapter inclusion and as such we taught it would be relevant to include them as well.

RESULTS AND DISCUSSION

In this section, a bibliometric analysis for the 377 papers, extracted from the Scopus database limited to the years 2018-2021, is presented. This analysis was conducted using the VOSviewer (version 1.6.13) software to retrieve and visualize the most relevant information about the network structure in these topics, such as co-occurrences of the author keywords, words in the titles and abstracts of the publications, and the bibliographic coupling of the authors, countries, institutions, and journals. Finally, a co-word analysis was carried out, using the QDA miner (version 6) and WORDSTAT (version 7.1) tools, to highlighting the crucial dimensions of the phrases network structures of the most relevant full papers (N=13). First, to this presentation, we have concentrated the discussion in the analysis of the method-

Figure 2. Systematic process to select literature

ologies followed, in summary, by the 377 articles analyzed (in a kind of bibliometric analysis for the employed methodologies and methods).

The first step of this analysis is to show the evolution of the number of publications in the last five years (2018-2021). There has been an increase of published articles under the subject areas of economics and business and any data science subject. The year 2021, still at the beginning (middle of February), has already a significant number of publications, meaning that a further increase is expected by the end of this year (see Figure 3).

To support the bibliographic analysis indicated previously as part of this chapter development, we resorted to the entire database of articles to explain which methods have been mostly applied from Data Science techniques to Economics and Business/Management areas analysis. We can take from the different collected articles in the analysis period that deep learning and machine learning methods are useful contributions in model advancements in prediction, planning, and uncertainty analysis. Therefore, with a wide application in economics, econometrics, management, business, and finance. Among deep and machine learning methods applied to address the different aspects in these area subjects, we find in the literature applications of artificial neural networks, support vector machines, decision trees, ensembles, Bayesians, hybrids, and neuro-fuzzy.

Figure 3. Published articles by year under the search limited to years 2018-2021 and for the retrieved 377 documents

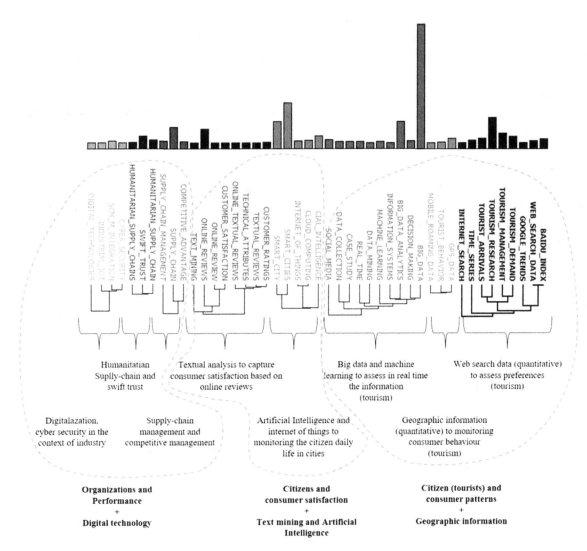

These have been applied in the articles analyzed, being easy to understand that the emerging technologies and novel concepts which arose in several fields of education and day life aspects. These have been promising to encourage a brighter future in dealing with these aspects and to provide systems to decision support. It is pointed in the literature that artificial intelligence applications allow us to use the internet of things, machine learning, deep learning, and big data to support the evolution and technological advancement in the economics and business fields. These methods have widely contributed to various applications domains with promising results as evidenced by the previous bibliometric analysis presented (e.g., smart cities, mobility, management, monitoring, city planning, resources allocation, energy demand, sustainability, corporate bankruptcy, consumption prediction, consumption reviews, food supply, cryptocurrency, production prediction, financial forecasts, air pollution monitoring and prediction, exchange rates, tourism demand, and supply, etc.). As for the future, it is further expected that the trends will converge towards the evolution of sophisticated hybrid deep learning models in economics and business subjects and fields.

Comprehensive state-of-the-art research is provided by Nosratabadi et al. (2020b), exposing the recent developments in emerging economic applications. Their analysis is done regarding novel data science methods, particularly, deep learning, machine learning, hybrid deep learning, hybrid machine learning, and ensemble models. They mention that broader application domains include economics research from stock market behavior, marketing, e-commerce, corporate banking, and cryptocurrency. In the present work we confirm these findings but as well join these tourism consumer reviews and forecasts, financial management, smart cities planning and management, consumption and production management, and consumer reviews and forecasts, despite many others.

From the bibliographic analysis performed it was as well possible to take many insights. Machine-learning algorithms provide the ability to learn from data and deliver in-depth insight into problems (Nosratabadi et al., 2020b). Notable classic machine learning methods (data science) applied in economics are support vector regression for anomaly detection, naïve Bayesian and C4.5 decision tree classifiers for credit card fraud detection, improved BP neural networks for product export and volume prediction, multilayer feed-forward neural network for stock price predictions, multilayer feed-forward neural network for stock price prediction, artificial neural networks for mobile social commerce, adaptive neuro-fuzzy inference systems for e-banking failure, decision trees for customer behavior, deep neural networks for recommender systems, naïve Bayes and linear support vector machine for sentiment analysis, deep learning for citizens and network analysis and tourism and forecasting, among many others (Brooks et al., 2019).

Moreover, deep learning as an emerging field of machine learning was applied mostly to aspects of today's society, self-driving cars, image recognition, animal behavior, renewable energy forecasting, hazard prediction, health informatics, bioinformatics, and so on. Deep learning models are usually evaluated in economics by support vector machine, K-nearest neighbors, and generalized regression neural networks. Furthermore, hybrid machine learning models are formed through the combination of two predictive machine learning algorithms or by a machine learning algorithm combined with optimization methods. Therefore, it is used to increase the accuracy of the other models. Finally, ensemble machine learning algorithms combine and apply multiple learning and training algorithms to enhance training and learning algorithms allowing us to learn from the data. Hybrid methods have been used to explore financial time series, forecasting, and rate prediction (Nosratabadi et al., 2020a, 2020b; Basdas et al., 2021).

Long short-term memory methods are notable machine learning and deep learning methods applied in stock markets (Basdas et al., 2021). These were used to explore portfolio management, algorithmic trading, socially responsible investment portfolios, stock price prediction, exchange-traded-fund options, price prediction, automated stock trading, sentiment analysis, and market index and stock trend predictions. Notable machine learning and deep learning methods in marketing and tourism include as goals to explore customer behavior, promotional activities, consumer reviews and opinions, sentiment analysis, and opinions forecast. As to e-commerce, data science techniques have been mostly used to explore investment quality, evaluation, order arrival prediction, allocation issues, credit risk evaluation, and product recommendation. In cryptocurrencies exploration, we mostly observe that the research objective has been focused on cryptocurrencies price prediction, while corporate bankruptcy applications are mostly restricted to prediction.

Still, a lot more in Economics and Business should be followed, explored, and done. The 377 articles were those retrieved from the Scopus database after the filters applications. Taking advantage of Big Data, deep learning, and machine learning methods, many other issues and thematics could be explored in Economics and Management. As for now, we could only say that this is an emerging field of research and we should bear in mind the need to keep on the right track.

Bibliometric Analysis of the Keyword Provided by Authors

Figure 4 shows the network visualization of the co-occurrence of the keywords. The high number of expected nodes imposes a minimum threshold of words. In this case, only were considered the keywords provided by authors of the paper that had a frequency more than 2 times, meaning that, of the 1542 words, 54 met the threshold. The concept '*big data*', '*big data analytics*' and '*artificial intelligence*' were the most frequent keywords, with 292, 57, and 42 occurrences, respectively.

Each keyword is represented by a circle and the size of a node determines the frequency of its occurrence. The larger the circle, the more often the keyword appears. Analyzing the graph is also possible to assess the connections between those terms, i.e., how they co-occurred as keywords. The distance between the nodes indicates the proximity of the two keywords. The keywords with the highest total link strength were selected and for these three most frequent keywords the number of co-existence was 340, 82, and 70, respectively - a minimum of the strength of 2 is considered in Figure 4 for more clarity.

Six different clusters are presented, resulted from the level of the interconnectivity of the keywords. These major groups are identified and classified according to the object of analysis (marketing and e-commerce, citizen and tourism, industry and firms) and the kind of topics typically associated with the field of data science (big data and artificial intelligence, network analysis, and forecasting, digitalization and data security).

Analyzing Figure 4, there is a clear association between i) network and text analysis on topics related to human behavior (social media, tourism, and smart cities); ii) artificial intelligence (and more specifically machine learning mechanism applied to big data to analyze marketing issues and forecast consumer behavior; and finally, iii) digitization and process automation in the business and business context. In this last group, intellectual capital, information and cybersecurity, and data privacy are highlighted aspects.

Bibliometric Analysis of the Words in the Title

Figure 5 presents a similar exercise to the one presented above, but this time applied to the titles of publications. Thus, the idea was to extract the concepts that occurred more than 2 times and group them according to their proximity - of the 1133 word 146 met the threshold. These results allow a more detailed analysis of the relationship between the themes and the responses that are intended to be obtained.

A total of 18 clusters were identified, however, we highlight 5 groups: i) the one that relates the services and the assessment of its consumers (applied with great frequency in the tourism area); ii) in another group, the processes of digitalization in firms and organizations stand out; iii) a third group, the relationship between performance assessment and monitoring in business contexts is evident; iv) it is also noteworthy, as already highlighted in the previous analysis, the application of a machine learning processes to assess consumption practices; and finally, v) the last group, aspects of perception assessment arise with the use of large volumes of data.

Figure 4. The network visualization of the keyword provided by authors

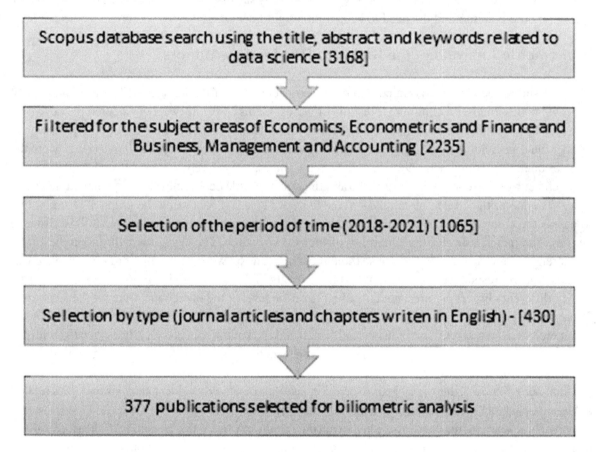

Bibliometric Analysis of the Words in the Abstracts

The analysis presented in Figure 6 highlights the most pertinent concepts included in the abstracts. These results stand out from the previous two analyses, due to the greater detail in the input data, using for this purpose the data of the 377 abstracts. The criteria of selection were the words or expressions within a sentence that occurred more than 15 times - of the 8402 words, 109 met the threshold (the Figure only shows the connections with a minimum strength of 10). The results are in line with the main conclusions of the previous analyzes (keywords and titles). Despite the greater complexity of the input data, three distinct clusters are presented: i) the first group is related to the adoption of performance evaluation mechanisms in the organizational management processes; ii) then, it is possible to highlight the analysis of consumption patterns taking advantage of big data generated, for example, from the online services and e-commerce; finally, iii) the third group aggregates content in the domain of economy and business in which the use of artificial intelligence to assess and estimate trends stand out.

Figure 5. The words visualization in the title

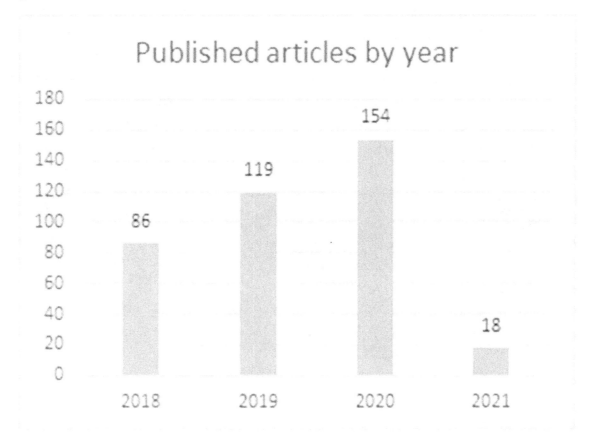

Bibliometric Analysis of the Authors

In total, 1023 authors were involved in the 377 articles analyzed. In Table 1 the most relevant author's names are revealed as to the number of articles published by each. Those with just one article published from the 377 have been excluded from the presentation. Only Dumay, J. has four articles published from the 377 from which resulted in our search. John C. Dumay is affiliated with the Macquarie University, Department of Accounting and Corporate Governance, thus a researcher working in the management field of education and not a data scientist (La Torre et al., 2018a; 2018b; 2019; Ndou et al., 2018). His co-authors only had three, two, or even one article published from these 377 during 2018-2021.

Bibliometric Analysis of the Institutions

Regarding affiliations of the authors publishing in the area of data science in economics and business, we observe from Figure 7 that eight are from the Hong Kong Polytechnic University, seven from the Macquarie University, and an equal number from the Università del Salento. Università Degli Studi di Torino has six affiliated authors among the 377 published articles in 2018-2021. It is important to note that the Macquire Business School is a part of The Macquire University. As such, in total there are 11 papers from this University (see Figure 7).

Figure 6. The words visualization in the abstracts

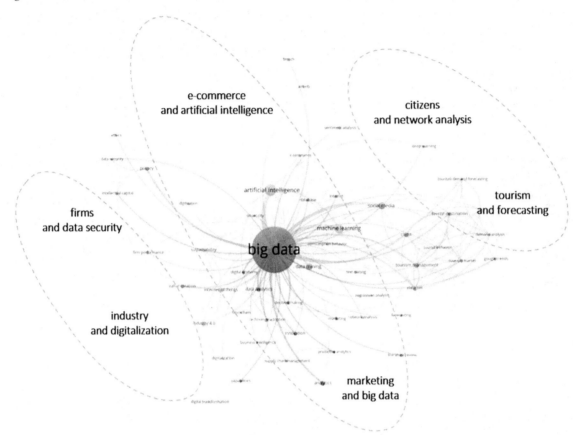

Table 1. Number of publications by author

Dumay, J.	4	Buhalis, D.	2	Gunter, U.	2	Ndou, V.	2
Akter, S.	3	Calic, G.	2	Hofmann, E.	2	Obschonka, M.	2
Kim, K.J.	3	Caputo, F.	2	Kaivo-oja, J.	2	Odendaal, E.	2
La Torre, M.	3	Chierici, R.	2	Kim, C.	2	Palmatier, R.W.	2
Law, R.	3	Choi, C.	2	Kim, K.H.	2	Park, Y.E.	2
Lim, C.	3	De Santis, F.	2	Kim, M.J.	2	Pellicelli, A.C.	2
Mandal, S.	3	Del Giudice, M.	2	Kirilenko, A.P.	2	Polimeno, G.	2
Passiante, G.	3	Del Vecchio, P.	2	Li, L.	2	Rea, M.A.	2
Sivarajah, U.	3	El Refae, G.A.	2	Maglio, P.	2	Rialti, R.	2
Tang, L.	3	Elia, G.	2	Maglio, P.P.	2	Roth, S.	2
Wang, S.	3	Fosso Wamba, S.	2	Mahroof, K.	2	Solazzo, G.	2
Agarwal, S.	2	Fosso Wamba, S.	2	Mariani, M.M.	2	Valentinov, V.	2
Anshari, M.	2	Gepp, A.	2	Marine-Roig, E.	2	Xiu, D.	2
Botes, V.L.	2	Ghasemaghaei, M.	2	Mikalef, P.	2	Zaki, M.	2
Brinch, M.	2	Gunasekaran, A.	2	Moro, S.	2	Önder, I.	2

Figure 7. Affiliation of authors' published articles

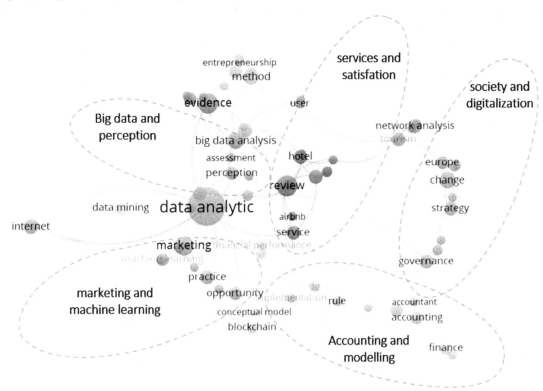

Other strongly recognized worldwide universities emerge with four authors affiliated in each, where many others were removed from the graph with three, two, or even one author affiliated.

Bibliographic Coupling of the Countries

Figure 8 represents an analysis of articles published by countries or territory in the period between 2018 and 2021. Figure 8 (a) shows countries of sourced articles (for the 377 retrieved documents) up to several six in terms of affiliations. The United States appears at the forefront within the field, followed by the United Kingdom, Italy, China, and Australia. From Germany, we have 29 authors, whereas Portugal is in the sixteenth position, as 9, the same number as Norway.

Figure 8 (b) shows a biographic coupling of the countries, representing the link strength calculated based on the number of publications. A minimum of two publications by country was considered, meaning that 46 of 69 met the threshold. Different clusters that were more related (more frequently linked) are represented by colors. It means that the publications that originated from the countries in the same cluster have more co-authorship, repeatedly. The level of cooperation between countries, standing out 9 different groups: United States, United Kingdom, Italy, Germany, France, Finland, Russian Federation, United Arab Emirates, and Singapore are the countries that constitute the central nucleus of these clusters.

From here we could even establish a ranking among the world's top-ranking universities and affiliations of authors of the 377 documents retrieved from the Scopus search during this period. Still, research emerging within the field of data science for economics and management is associated with the most

Figure 8. Country or territory of affiliations and network visualization
Note: (a) Country or territory of affiliations of authors' published articles. (b) The network visualization of the country cooperation during 2018 and 2021.

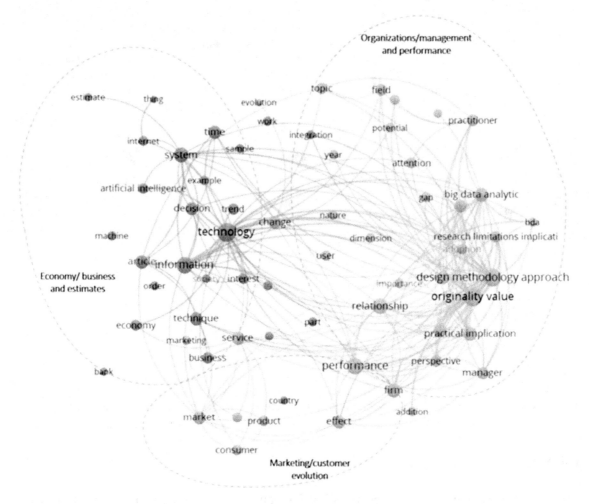

relevant countries in terms of development in research and science, and, of course, to the university reputation. Education within both fields is lacking in poorer countries opening room for deeper analysis and exploration, and an emerging opportunity for these countries' education concerning a joint analysis of data science techniques and economics and business. However, we should be aware of the hardest difficulties faced by developing countries in terms of education and this passage must be done carefully and gradually, provided more urgent needs in terms of economic development are still needed, just not to mention the hardness it is to get appropriate data to work with.

Bibliographic Analysis of the Journals

Exploring source title, or else journals names where these 377 articles have been published recently, provides a clearer picture of the subject areas which have been analyzed deeply in recent years (2018-2021). Table 2 presents the titles of the sources where articles have been published. With 19 articles published, we have the Journal of Business Research published by *Elsevier Inc* under the subject area of *Business, Management and Accounting*, namely *Marketing*, being classified as Q1 journal. Also in the marketing category, we have the Industrial Marketing Management Journal with 17 of these 377 articles published, followed by Tourism Management with 13 articles, Economics, Management and Financial Markets Journal with 12 articles published, and the Business Process Management Journal with 10. Many more Journals are included in the search but excluded from the presentation in Table 2 since these had only 2 articles published in each (96 more journal titles and source titles, to be more specific).

Going deeper into the analysis of the words that are most representative within the total list of journal publications, Figure 11 provides the words list that most emerge from here. Just to mention a few, appearing 92 times we have the word Journal (which is expected considering the names of the journals, and as such ignored in the analysis), 39 times Management, 28 International, 25 Business, 23 Economics, 19 Marketing, 18 Research (as well ignored), 14 Review (also should be ignored), 11 Economic, 10 Tourism, 9 Accounting, 7 European, 6 Finance, 6 Financial, 5 Letters (ignored), 4 Hospitality, 4 Innovation, 4 Studies (ignored), 3 Auditing, 3 Econometrics, 3 Global, 3 Governance, and 3 Technology.

Therefore, it is more common to verify data science applications related to management or business issues (39 and 25, respectively), than to economics (23 and 11), although there are numerous tourism applications, surpassed by the number of publications within the finance subject (12), followed by accounting applications. The rest of the words just appearing once have been excluded from this theoretical analysis, but they are presented as well in Figure 9. Management, finance, and economics get out highlighted from this words cloud and most authors publishing within these journals are from the areas of economics and business and not specialized data scientists. However, there is still room for more data science applications, especially considering the big data available, and for example, in finance, we may find several opportunities for data analysis using as resources high-frequency data (for example, betting's, stock market prices, etc.). It is worth mentioning that from the subject fields the 377 documents search yielded for Business, Management, and Accounting 321 articles, for Economics, Econometrics and Finance 155, and under the general umbrella Social Sciences 103. This calls attention to the fact that these are interrelated topics and one Journal has more than one subject category.

From the 377 articles collected for this analysis, we went to explore, as well, the number of citations and the number of citations for each excluding self-citations. Results are presented in Tables 3, 4, and Figure 10. The h-index of citations was 28 meaning that of the 377 documents considered for the h-index, 28 have been cited at least 28 times between 2018 and 2021. Table 3 only presents those articles cited more than 50 times in total.

For the 377 articles, the total number of citations reported is 3,144 during the period of analysis considered, mostly in 2020 (1,916 citations), being the most cited article that of Wirtz, Patterson, Kunz, Gruber, Lu, Paluch, and Martins (2018), "Brave new world: Service robots in the frontline" published in the Journal of Service Management. It is also observed from this Table 3 that those articles which are mostly cited refer to the subject of tourism followed by applications to financial markets. This is due to the very nature of data regarding both fields. In tourism related to customer satisfaction opinions, online textual reviews, forecasting tourism arrivals, smart hospitality, among others. Smart cities is a well-explored subject and cited in the context of data science, perfectly justified by the huge amount of data available to be explored. In terms of financial applications although the financial performance application reveals to be the article with most citations, loan prospecting, sustainability and performance, production system and big data in industry 4.0, data abundance and asset price informativeness, financial statement fraud and data mining, high-frequency trading data, banks challenges in industry 4.0, digital

Table 2. Number of publications by source title or Journal

Journal Of Business Research	19	Asia Pacific Journal Of Tourism Research	3	International Journal Of Accounting And Information Management	2
Industrial Marketing Management	17	Business Horizons	3	International Journal Of Educational Management	2
Tourism Management	13	European Management Journal	3	Journal Of Accounting And Organizational Change	2
Economics Management And Financial Markets	12	International Journal Of Physical Distribution And Logistics Management	3	Journal Of Destination Marketing And Management	2
Business Process Management Journal	10	International Journal Of Research In Marketing	3	Journal Of Financial Economics	2
Meditari Accountancy Research	8	Journal Of Cultural Economics	3	Journal Of International Accounting Auditing And Taxation	2
International Journal Of Forecasting	7	Journal Of Knowledge Management	3	Journal Of Management And Governance	2
International Journal Of Logistics Management	7	Journal Of Service Management	3	Journal Of Monetary Economics	2
Journal Of Asian Finance Economics And Business	7	Journal Of Services Marketing	3	Journal Of Open Innovation Technology Market And Complexity	2
Journal Of Econometrics	7	Wseas Transactions On Business And Economics	3	Journal Of Sustainable Tourism	2
International Journal Of Contemporary Hospitality Management	6	Academy Of Accounting And Financial Studies Journal	2	Journal Of Urban Economics	2
Cities	5	Accounting Research Journal	2	Marketing Letters	2
International Journal Of Economics And Business Administration	5	Bottom Line	2	Research In The Sociology Of Organizations	2
International Journal Of Hospitality Management	5	Competition And Change	2	Research In Transportation Economics	2
Quality Access To Success	5	Current Issues In Tourism	2	Review Of Industrial Organization	2
Managerial Auditing Journal	4	Economics Of Innovation And New Technology	2	Risks	2
Marketing Science	4	European Competition Journal	2	Singapore Economic Review	2
Small Business Economics	4	Global Business And Economics Review	2	Technological And Economic Development Of Economy	2
Technology In Society	4	Information Resources Management Journal	2	Tourism Analysis	2
Tourism Economics	4	International Finance Review	2	Tourism Management Perspectives	2

systems and financial management challenges, credit scoring, commodity price risk, hidden sentiment in financial big data, financial markets efficiency, stock prices trends, forecasting financial cycles, artificial intelligence, and financial markets, are just a few of the several applications which have been presented in the form of articles published up to this moment.

Figure 9. Word cloud of Journals (articles published within), under the search, limited to years 2018-2021 and for the retrieved 377 documents

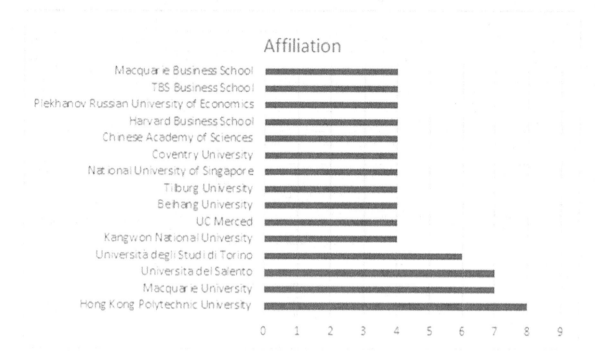

Given that the number of self-citations should be removed from an analysis of this type, Table 4 presents the number of citations reported during 2018-2021 for the collected 377 references, this time excluding self-citations. We followed the same criteria and considered only those with a number above 50.

As compared to Table 3 results, some articles are now left aside for not reaching the 50 citations, and some moved position. Curiously, the most cited article remains to be the most cited article without considering self-citations, even if with 10 fewer citations. Now in total for the period considered, the real total number of citations is just 2,796, less 348 citations which are self-citations. This total number considers all the 377 article citations overall, by year, and for the total period of 2018-2021. Finally, we have gathered all the references list of our 377 published articles and in Figure 11 we present a word cloud for the terms which emerge from the published articles, leaving room for a deeper analysis of the room that is still left for research under these thematic.

Big data analysis, business, tourism, marketing, performance, financial analysis, industrial, forecasting supply, digital, mining, smart systems, intelligence, learning, and models, are still the words that are commonly explored in data science applications to economics and business subjects.

Table 3. Number of citations during 2018-2021 for the collected 377 references

Publication info			2018	2019	2020	2021	Total
Year	Authors	Journal Title	105	740	1916	380	3144
2018	Wirtz et al.	Journal of Service Management	5	42	131	20	198
2018	Li et al.	Tourism Management	4	43	96	23	166
2018	Lim et al.	Cities	3	38	46	9	96
2019	Allam and Dhunny	Cities	0	14	62	11	87
2019	Zhao et al.	International Journal of Hospitality Management	0	14	52	12	78
2018	Amado et al.	European Research on Management and Business Economics	10	28	34	3	76
2019	Ardito et al.	Business Process Management Journal	0	14	48	10	72
2018	Buhalis and Leung	International Journal of Hospitality Management	4	26	38	3	71
2019	Mikalef et al.	Journal of Business Research	0	18	40	5	63
2019	Sun et al.	Tourism Management	1	12	36	9	58
2018	Dubey et al.	International Journal of Logistics Management	1	13	39	3	56
2018	Batista e Silva et al.	Tourism Management	2	19	28	4	53
2018	Coble et al.	Applied Economic Perspectives and Policy	7	19	21	4	51
2019	Polyakova et al.	International Journal of Economics and Business Administration	0	36	14	0	50

Table 4. Number of citations during 2018-2021 for the collected 377 references, excluding self-citations

Publication info			2018	2019	2020	2021	Total
Year	Authors	Journal Title	70	631	1750	342	2796
2018	Wirtz et al.	Journal of Service Management	5	38	127	19	189
2018	Li et al.	Tourism Management	4	42	90	22	158
2018	Lim et al.	Cities	2	37	46	9	94
2019	Allam and Dhunny	Cities	0	13	61	10	84
2019	Zhao et al.	International Journal of Hospitality Management	0	14	50	11	75
2019	Ardito et al.	Business Process Management Journal	0	13	48	9	70
2018	Amado et al.	European Research on Management and Business Economics	5	23	32	3	64
2018	Buhalis and Leung	International Journal of Hospitality Management	4	24	32	3	63
2019	Sun et al.	Tourism Management	1	12	33	7	53
2019	Mikalef et al.	Journal of Business Research	0	10	35	5	50
2018	Batista e Silva et al.	Tourism Management	2	18	26	4	50

Figure 10. Word cloud of references list, titles of articles published, under the search limited to years 2018-2021 and for the retrieved 377 documents

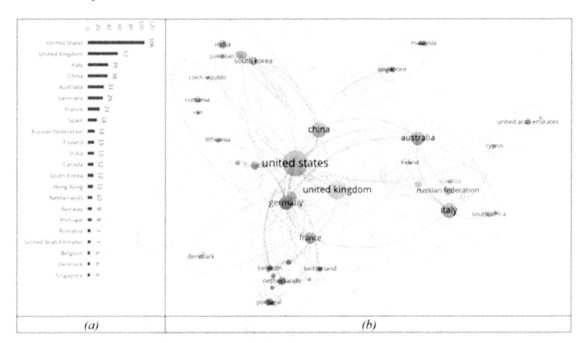

(a)	(b)

CONTENT ANALYSIS OF THE MOST RELEVANT PUBLICATION (FULL PAPER ANALYSIS)

In this point, a content analysis of the 13 most relevant articles (shown in Table 3) was carried out. Although Table 3 includes 14 of the most cited articles for the shortened period of analysis, we had to resort to the content analysis to the 13 that were freely available to download, or for which we had access. For this purpose, the QDA Miner and WORSTAT software were used to extract and understand the information in the context of the documents analyzed. We are presenting in Figure 11 the clusters of the pertinent expressions or terms in the context of this study. It is particularly evident the importance that studies on consumer behavior, both for tourist products and other general services, assume; in which the focus is to understand their preferences and the satisfaction. The information typically used in these studies is big data produced by users result of their actions on the internet (such as web search data, online booking data, webpage visiting data, etc.) or data collected from several devices (such as GPS or mobile phones).

The analysis of all these data, customer ratings, and customers' perceptions allow to make forecasts and anticipate preferences and expectations of the consumers. The objective is to better understand customers to deliver improved customer service, make better decisions and increase the value of a business. The second group of works seeks to analyze how the large volume of data can improve the quality of life of a citizen, reaching more sustainable and inclusive cities and environments. To better understand these needs, the IoT ecosystems, the data stored based smart devices, and sensors are crucial. Thus, big data in this context contributes to the creation of information for stakeholders to make better decisions. The third group of studies highlights the importance of digital technologies and solutions in the domain

Figure 11. Visualization of the content of the most relevant paper (N=13)

of Industry and organizations, to better used organizational resources regarding productivity gains. In this particular, aspects related to swift trust and humanitarian supply chains are highlighted.

CONCLUSION

Data Science and big data entered the mainstream academic vocabulary and the economy and business are no exception. The implementation range of big data in economics and finance has expanded from predicting financial distress to modeling efficient trading strategies, monitoring energy markets, managing the tourism industry, and socioeconomic process. This paper analyzed 377 publications on these topics in the scientific domain of firm performance, tourism, forecasting, customer satisfaction, and marketing, along with socio-economic monitoring, supply chain management, and smart cities development and interconnectivity. This growing literature encourages the contribution of big data techniques to the field of applied economics and business since these techniques can manage large volumes of data more practically without having rigid distribution assumptions.

There is a rapid growth in the use of data science and big data techniques. To demonstrate, decision tree methods in financial market strategies are used for the combination of multiple joint techniques based on sequential explanatory strategies, which start with quantitative analysis and then end up using semi-structured primary data analysis. Over the years text mining advanced from the development in big data techniques, and machine learning strategies became popular especially in predicting the future of the tourism industry, customer satisfaction, socioeconomic process, and the development of smart cities. However, differences in the outcome of techniques indicate that there is no common methodology of data science and big data, and the development of techniques is still underway. As for data mining techniques, the subject area of execution is still in progress. Although major concepts, such as firm performance, potential in the tourism industry, forecasting, marketing strategies, smart cities, and interconnectivity with ecosystem have been reviewed, so far, there are many more topics in economics, business, econometrics, and finance that can be managed with the help of big data and data science techniques.

The current growth trends predict a large increase in the number of publications in these areas. The USA and UK made the most relevant contributions within this important field. followed by Italy, Germany, and Australia. Besides the contribution of technologically advanced countries, there are some important contributions to data science and big data from the emerging economies as well such as China, South Korea, South Africa, India, and Malaysia. Which could be a game-changer in the field of data science and big data as these economies are very big in term of human resources, consumer markets, emerging financial markets that can create a spike or accelerate the marketing techniques, financial management, consumer satisfaction based on big data and data science.

Excel, Stata, Matlab, and SPSS have been the most applied toolboxes when using data science in economics and business. But things are changing rapidly with a new generation of economists, which now embrace open-source software platforms like Python and R which are becoming the go-to platforms for many economists nowadays, mostly because these are free software's. Numerous economists are now working as data scientists in different fields. Similarly, many data scientists are working with economic and behavioral problems which were exclusively the domain of economists in the past. Every discipline is different but there are similarities as well in terms of problems solved, methods used, theoretical constructs, and tools applied. Data scientists must be able to acquire, understand, and analyze complex and unstructured data, interpret the meaning of the results, and communicate the results to relevant stakeholders. Hence, data science requires a unique combination of econometrics and statistics, programming skills, and domain knowledge. When combining data science to economics and business, where decision making is a constant, we get the perfect match in interpretation, explanation, and support for policy directions to be pursued.

There is an increasing trend in the application of data science models, methods, and techniques in both economics and business, still, huge opportunities and challenges are emerging. This chapter highlights some other research opportunities and avenues, mainly connected to big data existent opportunities. For example, corporate governance and image recognition, well-being and wealth and consumer's choices, opinions and reviews, game-based learning and education, trading robots and market price forecasts, traders blogs and prices, industry 5.0 emergent opportunities, high-frequency data analysis, all kinds of financial risk analysis and forecasting, development or growth forecasting, social corporate responsibility and performance, connecting air pollution to energy and environmental economics, business management decisions support, municipalities data and performance indicators, systems for decision support and policymakers policies decisions support, among many other subjects that we could elaborate here, which were detected as still lacking appropriate research linking data science with the economics and business fields. Furthermore, despite the rapid development in the evolution of the techniques, techniques performance and implementation area are still in need of improvement. The findings of this chapter are, however, restricted to the economics and business areas and cannot be generalized to other fields of disciplines. We hope our findings will be useful to guide researchers and practitioners in economics and business areas to select the appropriate model after becoming familiarized with all these data science terminologies. We hope to encourage readers in the enlargement of their vision and data mining applications, with special emphasis on those connected and related to economics and business.

REFERENCES

Allam, Z., & Dhunny, Z. A. (2019). On big data, artificial intelligence and smart cities. *Cities (London, England)*, *89*, 80–91. doi:10.1016/j.cities.2019.01.032

Amado, A., Cortez, P., Rita, P., & Moro, S. (2018). Research trends on big data in marketing: A text mining and topic modeling based literature analysis. *European Research on Management and Business Economics*, *24*(1), 1–7. doi:10.1016/j.iedeen.2017.06.002

Ardito, L., Petruzzelli, A. M., Panniello, U., & Garavelli, A. C. (2019). Towards industry 4.0: Mapping digital technologies for supply chain management-marketing integration. *Business Process Management Journal*, *25*(2), 323–346. doi:10.1108/BPMJ-04-2017-0088

Bajracharya, K. (2018). *Data Science Glossary. Data Science.* Retrieved on 13 February 2021 from https://dimensionless.in/data-science-glossary/

Basdas, U., & Esen, M. F. (2021). *Review of Big Data Applications in Finance and Economics. In Handbook of Research on Engineering, Business, and Healthcare Applications of Data Science and Analytics.* IGI Global. doi:10.4018/978-1-7998-3053-5

Batista e Silva, F., Marín Herrera, M. A., Rosina, K., Ribeiro Barranco, R., Freire, S., & Schiavina, M. (2018). Analysing spatiotemporal patterns of tourism in Europe at high-resolution with conventional and big data sources. *Tourism Management*, *68*, 101–115. doi:10.1016/j.tourman.2018.02.020

Brooks, C., Hoepner, A. G. F., McMillan, D., Vivian, A., & Simen, C. W. (2019). Financial data science: The birth of a new financial research paradigm complementing econometrics? *European Journal of Finance*, *25*(17), 1627–1636. doi:10.1080/1351847X.2019.1662822

Buhalis, D., & Leung, R. (2018). Smart hospitality—Interconnectivity and interoperability towards an ecosystem. *International Journal of Hospitality Management*, *71*, 41–50. doi:10.1016/j.ijhm.2017.11.011

Cao, L. (2017). Data science: A comprehensive overview. *ACM Comput. Surv. 50*(3). doi:10.1145/3076253

Coble, K. H., Mishra, A. K., Ferrell, S., & Griffin, T. (2018). Big data in agriculture: A challenge for the future. *Applied Economic Perspectives and Policy*, *40*(1), 79–96. doi:10.1093/aepp/ppx056

Consoli, S., Reforgiato Recupero, D., & Saisana, M. (Eds.). (2021). Data Science for Economics and Finance. Methodologies and Applications. Springer International Publishing. doi:10.1007/978-3-030-66891-4

Donoho, D. (2017). 50 Years of Data Science. *Journal of Computational and Graphical Statistics*, *26*(4), 745–766. doi:10.1080/10618600.2017.1384734

Dubey, R., Luo, Z., Gunasekaran, A., Akter, S., Hazen, B. T., & Douglas, M. A. (2018). Big data and predictive analytics in humanitarian supply chains: Enabling visibility and coordination in the presence of swift trust. *International Journal of Logistics Management, 29*(2), 485–512. doi:10.1108/IJLM-02-2017-0039

Fischer, T., & Krauss, C. (2018). Deep learning with long short-term memory networks for financial market predictions. *European Journal of Operational Research, 270*(2), 654–669. doi:10.1016/j.ejor.2017.11.054

La Torre, M., Botes, V. L., Dumay, J., & Odendaal, E. (2019). Protecting a new achilles heel: The role of auditors within the practice of data protection. *Managerial Auditing Journal.* Advance online publication. doi:10.1108/MAJ-03-2018-1836

La Torre, M., Botes, V. L., Dumay, J., Rea, M. A., & Odendaal, E. (2018a). The fall and rise of intellectual capital accounting: New prospects from the big data revolution. *Meditari Accountancy Research, 26*(3), 381–399. doi:10.1108/MEDAR-05-2018-0344

La Torre, M., Dumay, J., & Rea, M. A. (2018b). Breaching intellectual capital: Critical reflections on big data security. *Meditari Accountancy Research, 26*(3), 463–482. doi:10.1108/MEDAR-06-2017-0154

Li, J., Xu, L., Tang, L., Wang, S., & Li, L. (2018). Big data in tourism research: A literature review. *Tourism Management, 68*, 301–323. doi:10.1016/j.tourman.2018.03.009

Lim, C., Kim, K., & Maglio, P. P. (2018). Smart cities with big data: Reference models, challenges, and considerations. *Cities (London, England), 82*, 86–99. doi:10.1016/j.cities.2018.04.011

McAfee, A., Brynjolfsson, E., & Davenport, T. H. (2012). Big data: The management revolution. *Harvard Business Review, 90*(10), 60–68. PMID:23074865

Mikalef, P., Boura, M., Lekakos, G., & Krogstie, J. (2019). Big data analytics and firm performance: Findings from a mixed-method approach. *Journal of Business Research, 98*, 261–276. doi:10.1016/j.jbusres.2019.01.044

Moon, K. S., & Kim, H. (2019). Performance of deep learning in prediction of stock market volatility. *Economic Computation and Economic Cybernetics Studies and Research, 53*(2/2019), 77–92. doi:10.24818/18423264/53.2.19.05

Ndou, V., Secundo, G., Dumay, J., & Gjevori, E. (2018). Understanding intellectual capital disclosure in online media big data: An exploratory case study in a university. *Meditari Accountancy Research, 26*(3), 499–530. doi:10.1108/MEDAR-03-2018-0302

Nosratabadi, S., Mosavi, A., Duan, P., Ghamisi, P., Filip, F., Band, S. S., Reuter, U., Gama, J., & Gandomi, A. H. (2020b). Data Science in Economics: Comprehensive Review of Advanced Machine Learning and Deep Learning Methods. *Mathematics, 8*(10), 1799. doi:10.3390/math8101799

Nosratabadi, S., Mosavi, A., Keivani, R., Ardabili, S., & Aram, F. (2020a). State of the Art Survey of Deep Learning and Machine Learning Models for Smart Cities and Urban Sustainability. In A. Várkonyi-Kóczy (Ed.), *Engineering for Sustainable Future. INTER-ACADEMIA 2019. Lecture Notes in Networks and Systems* (Vol. 101). Springer. doi:10.1007/978-3-030-36841-8_22

Polyakova, A. G., Loginov, M. P., Serebrennikova, A. I., & Thalassinos, E. I. (2019). Design of a socio-economic processes monitoring system based on network analysis and big data. *International Journal of Economics and Business Administration*, *7*(1), 130–139. doi:10.35808/ijeba/200

Provost, F., & Fawcett, T. (2013). *Data Science for Business: What You Need to Know about Data Mining and Data-Analytic Thinking* (1st ed.). O'Reilly Media.

Sun, S., Wei, Y., Tsui, K., & Wang, S. (2019). Forecasting tourist arrivals with machine learning and internet search index. *Tourism Management*, *70*, 1–10. doi:10.1016/j.tourman.2018.07.010

Taddy, M. (2019). *Business Data Science: Combining Machine Learning and Economics to Optimize* (1st ed.). Automate, and Accelerate Business Decisions.

Wang, W., Li, W., Zhang, N., & Liu, K. (2020). Portfolio formation with preselection using deep learning from long-term financial data. *Expert Systems with Applications*, *143*, 113042. doi:10.1016/j.eswa.2019.113042

Wirtz, J., Patterson, P. G., Kunz, W. H., Gruber, T., Lu, V. N., Paluch, S., & Martins, A. (2018). Brave new world: Service robots in the frontline. *Journal of Service Management*, *29*(5), 907–931. doi:10.1108/JOSM-04-2018-0119

Zhao, Y., Xu, X., & Wang, M. (2019). Predicting overall customer satisfaction: Big data evidence from hotel online textual reviews. *International Journal of Hospitality Management*, *76*, 111–121. doi:10.1016/j.ijhm.2018.03.017

KEY TERMS AND DEFINITIONS

Algorithms: A set of instructions that are followed to solve the problem.

Analytics: Systematic analysis of data or statistics.

Artificial Intelligence: Simulate human intelligence in machines that are programmed to think like humans and imitate their actions.

Big Data: Huge in volume or too large data and complex, in nature.

Cloud Computing: To deliver different services through the Internet. These resources include tools and applications like data storage, servers, databases, networking, and software

Data Mining: The process of finding differences, patterns, and correlations within large data sets to predict outcomes.

Deep Learning: It structures algorithms in layers to create an artificial neural network that can learn and make an intelligent decisions on its own.

Ensemble Learning: The process by which various models, such as classifiers or experts, are strategically generated and combined to solve a particular computational intelligence problem

Machine Learning: Use algorithms to parse data, learn from that data and make an informed decision based on what it has learned.

Optimization: Finding the best available.

Text Mining: Transforming unstructured text into structured data for easy analysis.

Chapter 27

A Historical Review of Immersive Storytelling Technologies:
New Uses of AI, Data Science, qnd User Experience in Virtual Worlds

Hector Puente Bienvenido
Universidad Complutense de Madrid, Spain

Borja Barinaga
Universidad Francisco de Vitoria Madrid, Spain

Jorge Mora-Fernandez
University of California, San Diego, USA

ABSTRACT

This chapter is focused on describing the history and the current relevance of user experience (UX) techniques that combine data science and AI in the research field of interactive and immersive storytelling, including virtual and augmented realities. It initially presents a brief history of interactive storytelling, video games, VR and AR, AI and data science, and the user experience (UX) techniques used in those areas. Later, the chapter describes the UX techniques in depth, using AI and data science that work best and are more useful for testing interactive media products, describing examples of its applications briefly. Finally, the chapter presents conclusions in relationship with utopias and dystopias regarding the future use of UX, AI, and data science in several areas such as edutainment, social media, media arts, and business, among others.

DOI: 10.4018/978-1-7998-6985-6.ch027

INTRODUCTION

There has been a significant implementation of technology to manage scientific data during the last two decades. One consequence of the increased use of technology has led to diverse findings in science and high techs like VR systems, UX, and big data analytics, that have challenged and questioned our descriptions and representation of reality and our daily habits.

This chapter focuses on the material senses. Significant optimization and economization of virtual reality (VR) and augmented reality (AR) displays have served to question, explore, and research the communication and languages of the material senses to a greater extent so that they can be merged and immersed in different VR and AR products. This new reality has reinforced a more profound recreation of the physical senses. Advancements in applied data science, the increase of bandwidth for data transfer networks, mobile ram abilities and memories, massive media alternatives for displaying and collecting social information, and the implementation of programming systems have helped Artificial Intelligence (AI) to manage significant amounts of personal information. These improvements are mainly motivated by the desire to increase business and industry profits through the registration, analysis, and monetization of the collected data from users and data based on the human interactions with different high-tech interfaces (computer, mobiles, VR and AR displays, and tablets). Of course, we can use high technology for other purposes, such as education or improving human beings' wellness. However, business and industry are still the leitmotivs of most research and applications of data science and artificial intelligence.

In this complex context of massive subjective and objective data and the ability of managing it with artificial intelligence software, companies are investigating the possibility of using data science, which gathers large amounts of subjective experiences, to collect objective responses from their users through the analysis artificial intelligence can provide.

HISTORICAL REVIEW OF INTERACTIVE, IMMERSIVE AND TRANSMEDIA STORYTELLING UX

Automated and interactive narration is usually linked to video games. However, it is not entirely true that its origin is only in computer games. Many of the characteristics of these narrative systems can be found in board games and, significantly, in the birth of role-playing games, invented by Gary Gigax (1938–2008) and Dave Arneson (1947–2009). The game *Dungeons & Dragons* (1974) was revolutionary, for it changed the paradigm of the traditional game. What is more, it established the way to elaborate a free and interactive story, lived in the first person, and based on rules. With the popularization of video game consoles and personal computers, due to the cheapness of electronic components, many young engineers became interested in programming fantasy-themed worlds that were mainly influenced by the work of J.R.R. Tolkien (1892–1973). Another critical factor to emerge was connecting computers in networks, such as through Arpanet (whose development began in the 1970s with the NCP protocol, *Network Control Program*, before the current TCP / IP, Transference Control Protocol and Internet Protocol). It was William Crowther, one of the programmers involved in the development of Arpanet, who programmed the first fully interactive, text-based fantasy story: *Colossal Cave Adventure* (1976) (Figure 1) (Barinaga, 2010). In 1977, the interactive story was polished and expanded by Don Woods, one of the fathers of hacker culture, who, as a student, discovered *Cave Adventure* on a Stanford University computer.

Figure 1. Left: Colossal Cave Adventure (1977) running on a PDP-11/34 and displayed on the VT100 console. Author: Autopilot. Right: a detail of a graph showing the structure of the world from the Colossal Cave Adventure Page (https://rickadams.org/adventure/index.html)

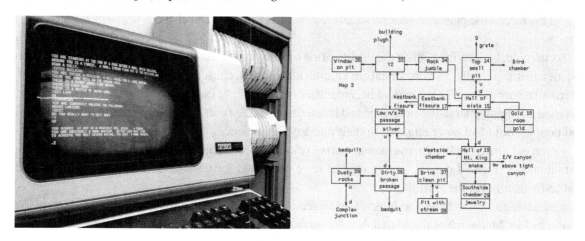

What was revolutionary about the system invented by Crowther was that it performed some very useful simplifications to produce the behavior of a purely artificial world. Colossal Cave Adventure's world has characters, space, and time – the essential elements for any narrative. Crowther conceived a world organized by spaces and connected by paths, much like the galleries of a cave. In each space, the player finds objects or characters, and the player can explore the world by picking up and putting down items (Barinaga, 2014). Notably, *Colossal Cave Adventure* has the fundamental characteristics of an interactive story, as defined by Crawford, which are structure, people, conflict, puzzles, choices, and spectacle (Crawford, 2005).

Significantly, the AI used in this program differed from the conventional one that was linked to the classical game studies, especially the game of chess, based on the research of Claude Shannon (1916–2001), used in emblematic projects like the *IBM Deep Blue* (1996) or *Deepmind/Google Alpha Go* (2015). The AI in the video game is much simpler but more effective from a narrative point of view. The Crowther structure simplifies reality without requiring complex AI and is based on simple state changes and automation. Despite its simplicity, the structure creates a rich experience, offering a great sense of freedom and a complex narrative. *Cave Adventure's* fundamental difference from other video games is that the AI is primarily used to achieve the feeling of spectacle that Crawford mentioned (Crawford, 2005). The program was designed to make the player's experience something memorable. Thus, the intention is not to simulate human decision making, but rather simulate plausible situations that give a sense of reality. Crowther's program proposed the following key aspects to simplify computing:

- Narrow paths and connections between each space or room that are justified by the narrative. This approach maintains the feeling of freedom while drastically limiting the possible options and facilitating programming.
- The appearance of an inventory that allows the taking and leaving elements. The changes of state caused by these interactions in the matrices serve as a trigger and conditioner of the adventure according to the algorithms of the general rules.

- Writing recognition system and narrator simulation. The game was revolutionary for allowing a natural communication between player and program. When the program was not able to interpret an order, it responded narratively using a random system of phrases and a large dose of humor. This forced the player to seek other alternatives to express themselves or perform actions.

As previously described, since the proliferation of role games and the first computers, computational videogames, especially conversational adventure video games, caused the public to gain more interest in interactive narratives. The main goal became discovering how to combine immersive storytelling with different engaging interactive structures and levels of interactivity so the user experiences could improve, and people could feel more engaged in their narrative experiences and game dynamics.

Emergent forms of interactive cinematic arts exploring these subjects in interactive video games (e.g., virtual and augmented reality, among others) were presented for decades in international conferences and festivals all over the world.

Research groups such as the Interactive Cinema at MIT, publications like The Language of New Media by Lev Manovich of the Visual Arts Department and CRCA at UC San Diego, and the interactive documentaries displayed on museums by the Labyrinth Project led by Marsha Kinder at the University of Southern California, inspired interactive media academic programs. That is how the Interactive Digital Media Programs at the University of Southern California, Carnegie Mellon University, and the Georgia Institute of Technologies started. The last one was led by Janet Murray (1997), the author of the book *Hamlet on the Holodeck: The Future of Narrative in Cyberspace* and who two decades later theoretically established the field (Murray, 2012).

In Europe, a significant exhibition and MIT publication entitled *Future Cinema* integrated the best research groups' findings and media artworks under the same roof at the ZKM, Center for Art and Media. The exhibition was curated by Peter Weibel and Jeffrey Shaw in Karlsruhe, Germany. In Spain, the Medialab Madrid was created around 2003 by Karin Ohlenschläger and Luis Rico, at the Centro Cultural Conde Duque. The center encouraged new media artists to research and create in the areas of interactive media and digital storytelling. *Via Intima* (Inside Track) was the first independent interactive transmedia project with an interactive exhibition, online, and interactive DVD. The project was developed at Medialab Madrid by Daktyl4 and led by Jorge Mora-Fernández and Borja Barinaga. Barinaga became one of the designers of the first academic videogame program in Spain. These creative and explorative spaces served as the first spaces for creation and testing of the emergent interactive digital storytelling arts and user experience (UX).

In terms of theoretical pioneers who persisted and consolidated research studies on interactive narratives, Marsha Kinder (1991, 2014), Michael Mateas (2004), Janet Murray (1997, 2012), Marie-Laure Ryan 2001), Lev Manovich (2005, 2001), Steve Anderson (2011), and Henry Jenkins have helped to establish the descriptions of some critical concepts regarding interactive storytelling and digital media. These concepts include, immersion, agency, and later transmedia. In Spain, in the area of interactive museums, Isidro Moreno (2002) from the Universidad Complutense de Madrid, director of the research group Museum I+D+C, has been an important pioneer. He is the author of the Interactive Museum of the Book of the Spanish National Library and author of the book *Musas y Nuevas Tecnologías*. Following Moreno's investigation lines, Jorge Mora-Fernandez, while researching with some of the mentioned American researchers at UCSD and USC, developed a model of analysis of interfaces to determine the most meaningful variables of interactive and transmedia narratives to study under UX to generate more interactivity, agency, and immersion. These models later evolved into a model of analysis for transmedia projects. In terms of the interactive and new forms of the book, the last years have been relevant to see the formation of the UNESCO New Forms of the Book, chaired by Alexis Weedon, UK, and the research developed by Deglaucy Jorge Teixeira, in Brazil, as well as the international conferences in digital storytelling, ICIDS.

Regarding the digital culture evolution from interactive media storytelling to transmedia storytelling, Marsha Kinder initially used the transmedia concept (1991, 2014) referring to transmedia intertextuality. However, Henry Jenkins is the one who popularized the transmedia narrative term. Jenkins (2011) gave the following description of the term in his blog: "transmedia storytelling represents a process where integral elements of a fiction get dispersed systematically across multiple delivery channels for the purpose of creating a unified and coordinated entertainment experience. Ideally, each medium makes its own unique contribution to the unfolding of the story."

Previously, Jenkins had described in his book, *Convergence Culture* (2006), the concept of convergence as a paradigm for thinking about the present moment of the media change. He defined the change by the stratification, diversification, and interconnection of the media in a converged way that influences the decisions of media producers, politicians, and citizens on the production and consumption of the digital culture. More recently, and because of the latest communicative and cultural practices, Jenkins evolved the convergence concept to become the transmedia term (2011):

Transmedia, used by itself, simply means "across media." Transmedia, at this level, is one way of talking about convergence as a set of cultural practices. We might also think about transmedia branding, transmedia performance, transmedia ritual, transmedia play, transmedia activism, and transmedia spectacle, as other logics.

In this regard, the transmedia narrative generates a universe of linear and circular possibilities where the stories start and finish with feedback to themselves and experimented one at a time. The linearity of the interactivity in this regard is understood as the coherent, communicative, immersive, and multilevel flow: aesthetic, narrative, and emotional,

Mora-Fernández (2013). Interactive linearity is a concept that has been developed in detail through time after the digital narrative and cultural evolution from hypermedia interactive narratives Mora-Fernández (2009). See Table 1 for the variables included on the model of analysis to interactive transmedia narratives Mora-Fernández (2019a, 2019b). See Figure 2 for the story flow across-media.

AI and Data Science Use in UX Interactive, Immersive, and Transmedia Storytelling

During the last years, conferences in interactive digital storytelling have been proliferating. An example of these conferences includes the International Conference on Interactive Digital Storytelling (ICIDS). At these events interactive digital storytellers in the areas of cinematic arts, videogames, and virtual reality exchange their project experiences of experimenting with interactive and transmedia digital storytelling systems. Some notable collections and research projects in this interdisciplinary arena are by Nunes, Oakley, and Nisi (2017); Marcus and Rosenzweig (2020); Nack ad Gordon (2016); Schoenau-Fog et al. (2015); Long (2000); Barbic et al. (2017); Mora-Fernandez (2019a, 2019b); Ioannidou (2013); and Parody (2011).

Figure 2. This image visually summarizes the influence and complementary story between media in one of Batman's Universes (from comic, to movie, to animation, to games to book)

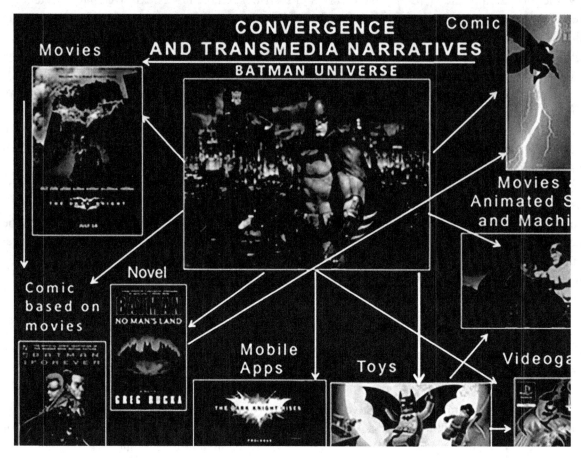

It is essential to say that the integration of aesthetic and narrative variables on a human-computer interface is so vast, almost as vast as the human imagination, that some AI used on UX only focuses on very specific aspects, as in shown the next chapters. Therefore, it is presented here as a model that has taken into consideration all the data science needed to perform fundamental research on interactive storytelling. Among others, the most meaningful aesthetic and narrative variables to observe in order to implement the interface product qualities in interactivity, immersion, and agency have been taken into consideration (see Table 1). It is interesting to see how Unity is allowing us to observe more variables for dynamic design adjustment (DDA) purposes. Soon, AI will collect all this data and compare the results between the interactive digital storytelling variables to finally respond to the fundamental question that motivates any UX test in any interactive media product: What are the most effective and attractive aesthetic? And what are the most compelling narrative elements in the interface that motivate and interact in different ways?

Because of the massive number of variables, the UX in interactive digital storytelling (IDS), UX data science, and AI is very simplified. Most of the time the IDS UX tests rely on traditional user experience questionnaires, such as the one used in the research *Connecting the Dots: Quantifying the Narrative Experience in Interactive Media* by Hannesson et al., Schoenau-Fog et al. (Eds.) (2015). However, some

Table 1. Model for analysis of hypermedia interfaces to observe and register the contained aesthetics, narrative elements, type of interactions and ethical values (adapted from Mora-Fernández, 2012)

1. Name and description of the interfaces and the conjunction of hypermedia expressions 1.1. Identifiable denomination of the hypermedia interface. Each different interface that appears on the hypermedia product should be numbered, named and observed under this descriptive model to obtain a deep analysis 2. General characteristics of the interface and detailed description of the multimedia characteristics of the expressions that can allow interaction with any of the narrative elements 2.1. Software: Group of expressions and technological tools that are used for the relationship and generation of natural and virtual interactions A) Of iconic intermediation B) Symbolic C) Combination of A & B D) Natural mimetic • Opened or virtual reality • Semi-opened or simulators of virtual reality F) Convergent G) Pull or push interfaces H) Static or dynamic Interfaces I) Mute or sound interfaces J) Smart interfaces K) The iteration 2.2. Types of image or perceptive representations A) Still image 1) Photo-mimetic 2) Photo-infographic 3) Info graphic B) Still image with sounded image C) Image in movement 1) Cine-mimetic 2) Cine-infographic 3) Cine-mimetic and infographic D) Visual image in movement with or without sounded image E) Audiovisual image F) Sounded image G) Sounded image with or without visual image or extraterritorial images 2.3. Hardware: Group of physical expressions A) Of intermediation B) Natural-mimetic 2.4. Typographic description • Size of letter • Style of font or type • Characteristics or effects of the letter • Color of the letter 2.5. Iconic description 2.6. Symbolic description 3. Features of the characters represented on the interface and general description of the potential interactions with the characters 3.1. Character or avatar of 1st, 2d or 3rd Person	3.2. Physical characteristics • Sex • Age • Height and weight • Hair, eyes and skin colors • Pose • Corporal appearance and customs • Morphological defects • Hereditary aspects 3.3. Sociological characteristics • Economic status • Employment • Type of education • Life and family relationships • Religion • Race, nationality • Function in his community • Political tendencies 3.4. Psychological characteristics • Sexual and moral life • Personal ambitions and motivations • Frustrations, main conflicts • Temper: angry, tolerant, pessimistic, optimistic, etc. • Vital attitude: complacent, combative, surrendered • Insecurities: obsessions, inhibitions, superstitions • Extroverted, introverted, well balanced • Capacities, aptitudes, languages • Qualities: imagination, criteria, taste, equilibrium • Intellectual coefficient: high, regular, low 4. Interactional aspects of the character and type of interaction available: selective, transformative or constructive 5. Values or spiritual principles and unscrupulous values that available to activate through the interaction with the narrative characteristics of the characters. Values and unscrupulous values that appear potentially related with the interaction developed 5.1. Ethical values 5.2. Unscrupulous values 6. Characteristics of the actions represented on the interface and general description of the potential interactions with the actions 6.1. Type of structure 6.2. Secondary theme or subplot 6.3. Changing hierarchy 6.4. Changing hierarchy •Relationships between main and secondary actions •Real relationships between main actions •Real relationships between secondary actions •Simulated relationships between main and secondary actions •Annulated between main and secondary actions 7. Aspects of the interactional actions and type of interaction available: selective, transformative or constructive	8. Values or spiritual principles and unscrupulous values that available to activate through the interaction with the narrative characteristics of the actions. Values and unscrupulous values that appear potentially related with the interaction developed 8.1. Ethical values 8.2. Unscrupulous values 9.Characterists of the spaces represented on the interface and general description of the potential interactions with the spaces 9.1. Natural, constructed, mimetic-natural or mimetic-info graphic 9.2. Senses implied in the spatial perception: view, ear and/or touch 9.3. Implicit space and/or explicit 9.4. 2D/3D or 4D space 9.5. Perspective: size, scale, position and point of views 9.6. Focus or defocus 9.7. Illumination and color temperature 9.8. Props 9.9. Protagonist space and/or hyperspace 9.10. Absent space or suggested space 9.11. Selection space with representation: coincident or different 9.12. Hyperspace 10. Aspects of the interactional spaces and type of interaction available: selective, transformative or constructive 11. Values or spiritual principles and unscrupulous values that available to activate through the interaction with the narrative characteristics of the spaces. Values and unscrupulous values that appear potentially related with the interaction developed 11.1. Ethical values 11.2. Unscrupulous values 12. Characteristics of the time represented in the interface and general description of the potential interactions with the time 12.1. Order: flashback, flashforward, meta-retrospective or meta-prospective 12.2. Duration: pure diegesis, impure diegesis, open or close 12.3. Frequency: repetitive sequence or singular multiple 12.4. Temporal localization: past, present, future, changing or inexistent 12.5. Iteration 13. Aspects of the interactional times and type of interaction available: selective, transformative or constructive 14. Values or spiritual principles and unscrupulous values that available to activate through the interaction with the narrative characteristics of the times. Values and unscrupulous values that appear potentially related with the interaction developed 14.1. Ethical values 14.2. Unscrupulous values

projects developed and programmed their tools to complement the user experience questionnaires. Some interesting ones found on Nunes, Oakley, and Nisi (2017), and Schoenau-Fog et al. (Eds.) (2015) are:

- Centre for Game by Aamri and Greuter, Schoenau-Fog et al. (Eds.) (2015).
- *Mise-en-scène: Playful Interactive Mechanics to Enhance Children's Digital Books,* Design Research, RMIT University, Melbourne, Australia. This research uses "two instruments Reading Motivation Scale (IRMS), and direct observations during the three school reading sessions... ...The *Motivation for Reading Questionnaire* (MRQ) was designed by Wigfield and Guthrie, and it measures 11 dimensions, including reading efficacy, challenge, curiosity, reading involvement, importance, recognition, grades, social competition, compliance, and reading work avoidance."
- *Connecting the Dots: Quantifying the Narrative Experience in Interactive Media Story Immersion in a Gesture-Based Audio-Only Game* by Wu and Rank, Schoenau-Fog et al. (Eds.) (2015), from Drexel University, Philadelphia, PA, USA. The researchers used an audio-based UX. They "compare useful designs of audio feedback that are responsive to hand gestures to both encourage user participation and maintain immersion in gesture-controlled audio-only environments. For the experimental study, two designs for responsive audio feedback were implemented in two game versions, as described below. We set up a between-subjects experimental design in order to compare the two game versions and their effect on the evaluation of the game, including its immersive qualities (…). The method is based on three moments: Experiment setup: hand motion input, processing, and audio output. The hardware setup for the game includes using a Leap Motion Controller for hand tracking and data input, a laptop for data recognition and processing of the game, and noise-cancelling stereo headphones for audio output."

- *Generating Side Quests from Building Blocks* by Tomas Hromada, Martin Cerny (B), Michal Bıda, and Cyril Brom, Schoenau-Fog et al. (Eds.) (2015) from the Department of Software and Computer Science Education, Charles University in Prague, Prague, Czech Republic. Their research developed "multiple automated quests generating systems were described in the literature. The GrailGM system uses a forward chaining inference engine to recombine quest elements given by a designer to form quests with multiple solutions and to guide the player's progression through the game. Petri Nets have also been proposed as models for generating quests. One of our primary goals was to keep the system simple and controllable while expanding the expressive power of template-based systems. To achieve both, we decided to split quests into blocks. Each block represents a short section of a quest (e.g., killing a monster to obtain an item). The blocks are arranged into a directed acyclic graph (DAG) where edges connect each block to its possible successors. The DAG may be represented explicitly (as in our implementation) or given implicitly by conditions. Blocks that have no incoming edges are called start blocks, and those with no outgoing edges are end blocks."
- *Evaluation of Yasmine's Adventures: Exploring the Socio-Cultural Potential of Location Aware Multimedia Stories* by Dionisio, Barreto, Nisi, Nunes, Hanna, Herlo, and Schubert, from Madeira-ITI, University of Madeira, and the Design Research Lab, Berlin University of the Art, Berlin N. Nunes et al. (2017). Their research entitled. In the research there is a combination of using Nvivo software. "The questionnaire and interview data were then analyzed using a grounded theory affinity analysis with the Nvivo software tools support. Researchers conducted a bottom-up data analysis reviewing and iterative process in three stages: open coding (quotes and high-level categories), affinity diagrams (relationships between categories), and theme organization (most frequent themes and description)."

In terms of interactive digital storytelling using a collection of specific data in combination with AI in UX AI Mobile and VR narrative experiences, some interesting examples appeared in *Interactive Storytelling* (Nunes et al., 2017):

- Developed by Kampa and its research Authoring Concepts and Tools for Interactive Digital Storytelling in the Field of Mobile Augmented Reality, from Hochschule RheinMain, Wiesbaden, Germany SPIRIT appears like an exciting UX tool. "In SPIRIT, a Storytelling XML (STARML) dialect has been derived from ARML by adding authoring-friendly XML-tags, with the focus on location-based content description for IDS. Further, a plot engine has been developed that interprets the STARML content structure, processes user interactions, and triggers AR video and other media. This engine uses conditions for planning. Authoring AR content has been made accessible for programmers by systems like EDoS and ComposAR. For non-programmers, TaleBlazer offers a visual script language like Scratch. An authoring concept is observing the authors for authoring tool development (...). The SPIRIT authoring tool StoryPlaceAR was developed out of the need to author media content outdoors in an ad-hoc manner (...). The system "immersive authoring for tangible AR" transforms 'What You See Is What You Get' authoring concept into 'What You Feel Is What You Get'. VideoTestAR enables prototypical AR video production and automatically authors the STARML content structure for immediate experience testing. In authoring for IDS, after content creation, the story structure can be altered by filling in content into an existing story structure. For this, several working steps are performed on the same STARML file and folder system. This process creates a bottleneck of collaboration and communication in an interdisciplinary team. In conclusion, this bottleneck exists for the authoring of XML structures for IDS systems."
- Developed by Bala, Nisi, and Nunes in their research Evaluating User Experience in 360o Storytelling Through Analytics at Madeira-ITI, University of Madeira, they developed their evaluation VR analytics for narrative structures "Based on the need for evaluation of complex narrative structures in VR storytelling, we designed IVRUX, a VR analytics platform for 360o video. This tool, intended to be used in an academic context, offers a support system to facilitate communication of creators and/or researchers with participants. The system is composed of three components: an online dashboard for researchers (built using the Angular framework) and a mobile VR application for the participants (built using Unity), connected through a REST API backend (Node.js and MongoDB). The system is designed so that the researcher does not need to have any expert skills (e.g., coding) to evaluate content."

In conclusion, IDS UX testing that can provide useful information for data science and AI, but there is a long way to go. However, software by iMotions, which integrates eye-tracking, EEG, and emotional facial recognition, has emerged as a promising tool for interactive communications and storytelling research. Some exciting applications of interactive storytelling on recovery from addictions can be found in research by Mora-Fernandez et al. (2020) entitled *iMotions' Automatic Facial Recognition & Text-Based Content Analysis of Basic Emotions & Empathy in the Application of the Interactive Neurocommunicative Technique LNCBT* (Line & Numbered Concordant Basic Text).

Figure 3. The video game Pong (Atari, 1972) is a perfect example of UX principles with very limited technological possibilities. This game put Atari at the forefront of the new entertainment industry. Exhibition in the Tekniska Museet, Stockholm, Sweden (16 September 2014). Photography by Diderot

BRIEF HISTORY OF UX APPLIED TO VIDEOGAMES

The design systems used in video games undergo constant optimization and evolution towards a fully adaptive user experience. They are applied both in the gaming medium and transferred to the most varied experiences by hybridizing the digital and physical world (Sequeiros & Puente, 2018, 2019). The innovations in design systems respond to a growing audience's demands. Therefore, one made up of people with unique characteristics, such as desires and interactions. Video games as cultural devices have been adapted to users through tools that allow the monitoring and analyzing of a player's performance or preference, enabling designers to adjust and tune the user's experience (Puente & Sequeiros, 2019a, 2019b). Dynamic design adjustment (DDA) not only allows the game to be altered in real-time based on the decisions and behavior of the player, but it also enhances the enjoyment and social inclusion of the game without neglecting the capacities and possible limitations of the users. DDA thereby follows the design justice approach (Crews & Zavotka, 2006; Constanza-Chock, 2020).

Traditionally a closed medium with predetermined systems, video games and their social contexts have been intertwined and merged with today's reality. Although past attempts, such as *Tempest* (Atari, 1981) and *God Hand* (Clover Studio, 2006), were limited by technology, a design approach that allows the game experience to be adapted to the player's interests has emerged. As it has been demonstrated, usability is a critical element in interactive systems (Maguire, 2001). For example, Missura and Gärtner (2009) have emphasized that the ideal video game should adapt its difficulty dynamically based on the player's performance.

From its origins, the field of videogames has been a cutting-edge platform for UX studies. Interfaces, gameplay, and narrative maintain, in most cases, a critical dependency to improve the player experience. After the burst of the first video game consoles into homes, such as Ralph Baer's *Odyssey* (Magnavox, 1972), the personal computers' current architecture was established: a motherboard, a sound card, and a graphics card. From that moment on, the interface development related to image and sound materialized in revolutionary projects such as the human-computer interfaces for the *Apple Lisa* (Mackintosh 1983), linked to Steve Wozniak and Steve Jobs (1955–2011) who were both ex-collaborators from Atari. (Kent, 2001)

In the eighties, Atari did not know what kind of industry it was creating. However, they did know the importance of narrative immersion and the experience of the players in their games. This is the reason they created research and development departments that thought about the future of interfaces and new options for human-computer interaction as a key to success (Kent, 2001). Today, some of these historical interfaces are part of the collections of prestigious museums, as is the case of *Pong* (1972; Figure 3), which is in the MOMA and the Science Museum of London, among others.

Unlike other fields, in the video game industry the importance of UX is preponderant. Games are based on the player's experience, and the activity is not compulsory but voluntary. If the experience is not rich and exciting, and the mechanics, gameplay, and narrative are not in line with the interface's quality, the player will stop playing, and the product will be a failure (Schell, 2008).

In this sense, from the origins of the main mechanics, it can be said that a massive incursion of artificial intelligence in the development of video games and in the improvement of the UX has been experienced, highlighting three key aspects:

Figure 4. Sensorama advertising poster and illustration of Morton Heilig's Sensorama device, a precursor to later virtual reality systems (Filed Jan 10, 1961). Author: Morton Heilig. Figure 5 of U.S. Patent #3050870 (via https://patft.uspto.gov/)

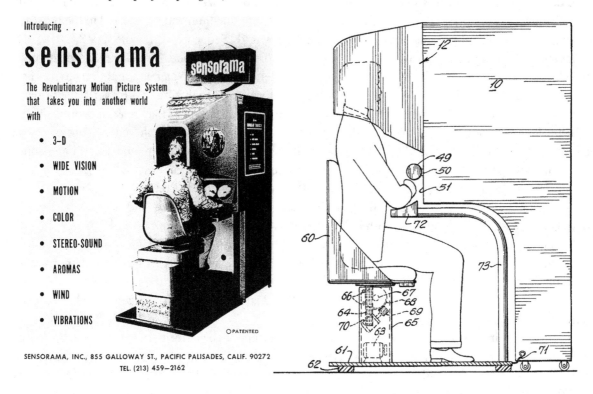

- With the increase in complexity of video games, automated and intelligent help and management systems have emerged that improve the quality of the gameplay and minimize the importance of secondary tasks not related to the experience or gameplay (Millington, 2006).
- Data analysis and information flow methods have been improved to facilitate testing and design, even from the game engines themselves.
- Increases in processing speed allows for the management of the intelligent automatic behaviors of a significantly greater number of non-player characters at the same point of the game. (Millington, 2006)

MOST RELEVANT MILESTONES IN VR, AND AR USER EXPERIENCE

Virtual reality has more than fifty years of existence now. However, in the last few years VR technology and industrial uses have been growing dramatically. The advances in electronics, energy (more efficient batteries), and computer technology have made it possible to realize a dream that began to develop from the multi-sensory simulator *Sensorama* (1960), created by Morton Heilig (Figure 4).

Sometimes the concept of VR is fuzzy, due to the large number of uses in the context of virtual spaces generated by 3D computer technology. Nevertheless, VR is mainly related to the simulation of a space by computer graphics to allow the user, intermediated through a hardware interface, to interact

Figure 5. HTC Vive (2016) vs VPL Research DataSuit (Circa 1989). HTC Executive Director of Marketing Jeff Gattis wears the HTC RE Vive (3 March 2015). Author: Maurizio Pesce. VPL Research DataSuit, a full-body outfit with sensors for measuring the movement of arms, legs, and trunk developed circa 1989. Displayed at the Nissho Iwai showroom in Tokyo (4 October 1999). Author: Dave Pape

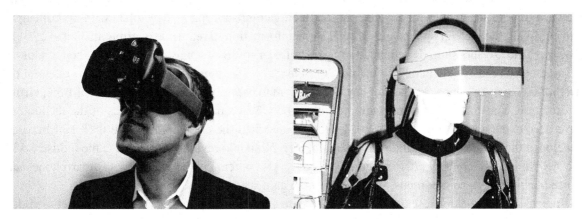

with things in a similar way that he or she would in the real world. The VR experience is immersive by definition and tries to be multi-sensory. (Fuch, 1992; Gigante, 1993).

The first head-mounted display (HMD) of VR was *The Sword of Damocles*, constructed by Ivan Sutherland (Sutherland, 1965). The system was able to track the orientation of the head to update the virtual scenario.

In the seventies there were relevant systems with multiple uses, such as the *GROPE* (1971). This was a human-force-feedback developed at the University of North Carolina. Today, this type of system combined with our advances in data transference could allow, for example, doctors to practice surgery remotely, systems like the *Da Vinci Surgical System* (Intuitive Surgical, 2000), present in approximately five thousand hospitals in 2020 (Singer 2010). Another early VR invention was *VIDEOPLACE* (1975) by Myron Krueger (Krueger et al., 1985). This hardware was the origin of all the movement reconnaissance systems used in later video game hardware, like *Microsoft Kinect* (2010) and *Nintendo Wii* (2006).

In the eighties, new interests were found in the military field for the use of virtual spaces. In 1981, Atari collaborated with the US Army to develop a training simulator for the gunners of the M2 Bradley Tank, inspired by the successful arcade game *Battlezone* (1981; Barinaga 2016). In 1982, the US Air Force, with the Armstrong Medical Research Laboratories, developed the *VCASS* (Visually Coupled Airborne System Simulator), an HMD system to control the pathways of missiles and targets (Mazuryk & Gervautz, 1999).

In the mid-eighties, the first VR commercial devices appeared. Examples include the *Fake Space Labs BOOM* (Binocular-Omni-Orientational Monitor, 1989) and the *HMD Data Glove* (1985) by the VPL company (Figure 5).

But in the end, all these devices, and the advances made in the 1990s, were too costly and bulky to reach the entertainment industry. Moreover, they remained as anecdotic, military, or scientific experiments with expensive hardware. In 2016, two companies launched to the market affordable and compatible new VR glasses systems: the *HTC Vive* (HTC) (Figure 5) and the Oculus Rift (Oculus VR). The videogame industry has embraced this technology as an up-and-coming field for the new generation of games. Furthermore, VR glasses have started to become a convenient interface for design and 3D modeling.

Although augmented reality shares similarities with VR, it is a visualization of reality with virtual content that augments the standard visual information. Thus, it enriches rather than replaces the real world (Bryson, 1992).

In 1990, Tom Caudell coined the concept of *Augmented Reality* while working on a project to simplify the view of wire schematics for airplanes at the Boeing company, and he developed with his colleague, David Mizell, the idea for special glasses that show information in real-time (Carmigniani et al., 2011). However, the advances in AR remained in a scientific or military context until 1999. The technology became more accessible when Nara Institute of Science and Technology's Hirokazu Kato released the *ARToolKit*, an open-source tool kit for any OS platform to capture video and insert, in real-time, virtual information. Since the AR modules are present in the OS of smartphones, the uses of the technology have been exponentially growing. In 2013, Google launched the *Google Lens*, and in 2016 Microsoft developed the *Holo Lens* for Windows Mixed Reality. Nintendo revolutionized the game industry with the AR game *Pokémon GO* (2016; Figure 6). Today, AR content can be viewed with smartphones and is used habitually in commercials, sports, and video games.

Increasing amounts of research using AI and data science in AI and VR have been developed during the last years. Some exciting publications that have collected interesting research are Jung and Tom Dieck (2018), Peddie (2017), as well as some proceedings from the EuroVR International Conference, Barbic et al. (2017), among others.

AI AND DATA SCIENCE IN STORYTELLING AND VIDEO GAME DESIGN

Artificial intelligence and data science have been linked to the development of commercial video games since their origins. Character simulation, non-player character (NPC) movements and actions, algorithms, and predictability, among others, play a fundamental role in gameplay experiences (Bekkes et al, 2012; Nantes et al, 2008) (data science applications are especially visible in areas like serious games).

The first game to partially use an AI dates back to the 1950s. This is the case with Nim. His AI implemented combinatorial game theory using binary logic operations. Two decades later, games such as *Pong* (1972), *Space Invaders* (1978), and *Galaxian* (1979) would already include simple AIs that incorporated preset patterns based on examining the input (action) of the human user. A few years later *Tempest* (1981) appeared. It was the first video game to use player performance parameters to optimize their gaming experience and achieve a balanced level of challenge. Thus, data science applied to video games was born and would revolutionize the field of game balancing adjustment with optimized matchmaking, generation of rewards, and item-drop mechanics.

Today, dynamic design adjustment (DDA) has been proven successful in various media such as video games and interactive experiences (Maguire, 2001). Significantly, DDA has been shown to improve the performance and the engagement of the users (Andrade et al., 2006; Xue et al., 2017). Adjusting NPCs' behavior to make them less aggressive, adapting the number of enemies in an environment and their health or damage values, and increasing the recovery speed of the health bar of players are some alternatives and design decisions that have been applied in studies (Chapman & Hunicke, 2004). DDA has also been as applied to favor the user experience in matchmaking (Aghdaie et al., 2007). However, the use of dynamic design adjustment is not limited to mechanics. The narrative can also be altered by adapting the narration to the player's profile. Graphics engines like Unity already have their own tool to implement dynamic design and make this data more accessible for development studios.

Figure 6. Pokémon GO fever in Japan (12 October 2019)

Corporations also have DDA systems based on machine learning. This is the case with IBM Watson. Through algorithms, Watson undergoes constant learning and adaptation, allowing for the development of unique systems for each player and individualization of the user's experience.

This approach opposes the traditional vision of the video game as a fixed and pre-designed experience without adaptive measures to the behavior and interest of the player. The traditional structure of videogames can be observed in the GDDs (*Game Design Document*) of different video games, such as *Prince of Persia* (Broderbund, 1993), *Grim Fandango* (Lucas Arts, 1998) and *Planescape: Torment* (Black Isle Studios, 2009).

The main point is not only located on the adaptation of video games to the player, but on how this interaction is carried out. With Niantic and its video game *Pokémon GO* (2016) (Figure 6) as the maximum exponent, the trends of video games have been observed to leave the digital medium and merge with reality. Pervasive video games have been integrated, taking the mechanisms and dynamics of prior and 'classical' games to other formats such as AR. The augmented reality format is acquiring new titles, such as *Five Nights at Freddy's AR: Special Delivery* (Illumix, 2019), *Shin Megami Tensei Liberation Dx2* (Atlus & Sega, 2018), and the currently in development *The Witcher: Monster Slayer* (Spokko, TBA). There is an interest in developing and improving AR-based experiences.

Figure 7. Different UX techniques that are being used in the design of immersive experiences and services shown as steps (inspired by Design Council's Double Diamond)

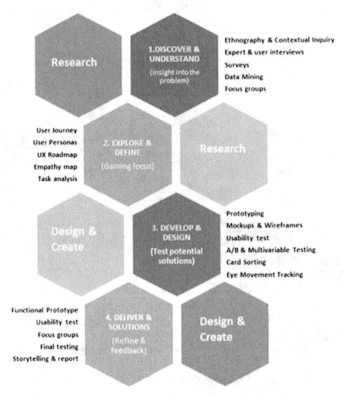

Storytelling and gaming systems based on data science and AI have permeated their environment (Mateas, 2003). We can currently observe multiple gamified and data-driven experiences in museum tours, digital narratives, and dating apps. For instance, the Prado Museum in Madrid has an interactive room (room number 39) where VR is used to interact with art pieces, which again demonstrates the importance of this new technology.

Thus, data science and artificial intelligence are critical pieces in the search for memorable experiences that consist of living an experience rather than consuming a product or story. The aforementioned methods are progressively approaching an increasingly immersive experience based on data analysis, which could be called Peak Immersive Experience. Using embedded metrics in devices, such as AR or VR, video game designers are encouraged to take advantage of the hardware paradigm change and establish DDA as a must-have from now on.

METHODOLOGIES TO IMPLEMENT UX INTERACTIVE AND IMMERSIVE STORYTELLING VR AND AR

After observing the great field that data science and artificial intelligence have to cover, this chapter focuses on using AI and applied data science in user experience techniques.

Figure 8. Unity Analytics heatmap (showing players' areas of interaction)
Source: Unity Analytics Documentation, 2021

First, a mapping of the different UX techniques (organized in design phases) that are currently being applied in the field of media storytelling must be explored.

Figure 7 identifies the different UX techniques that are being used in the design of immersive experiences and services. Inspired by the Design Council's Double Diamond, we have carried out an analysis of the research techniques most commonly used in the different phases of the design process. Notable is how an increasing influence of AI and applied data science in user experience techniques can be observed.

In this progressive integration of UX, AI, and data science, differentiation can be made between two relevant types of processes in terms of design systems and methodologies.

1. How do AI and data science collect information?
2. What narrative and aesthetic variables are currently considered most relevant or significant?

Although there are numerous examples of data analytics and tracking algorithms used in audiovisual devices, the current trend is to take advantage of the information collection options integrated into the development engines themselves (such as Unity or Unreal).

Any pattern of play, behavior, event, or interaction is recorded in a database, which can now be handled very intuitively via a data dashboard. This ability allows to collect and cross all the information on variables of interest for our analysis.

The narrative and aesthetic variables that are currently considered the most relevant or significant are the following: visual and special effects, generation of emotions (Fernández et al., 2021), quality in level design, and story (cutscenes, narrative interactions, etc.).

- quality, diversity, and customization of avatars,
- number of interactions (by click or collision) with game objects,
- level of concentration, emotions (very relevant in sensory storytelling) and attention on environment and user interface design elements (measured through biometrics, interactions and heat maps; see Figure 8),
- percentage of space to map explored (including percentage of completion or secrets discovered),
- the possibility of "skipping" or avoiding the story (cutscenes, textboxes) in narrative experiences (variables of great interest are the total and relative time of reading and listening to the story, the percentage of scrolling made to the textboxes, the number of skips performed, the number of interactions with other non-player characters),
- relative weight of the narrative (in time and relevance) on the gameplay and game experience (measured by game test and questionnaire, engine tracking events, etc.) and
- multidimensional measure of creativity (Jackson et al., 2012).

Engines like Unity already have their own tool to implement dynamic design and make it more accessible for development studios. Thus, GameTune and Unity Analytics are positioned as a dissociative element of DDA and high-budget video games, as Unity is one of the most used engines for video game development. The more variables that can be identified and contracted, the closer developers will be to having a complete map of what works and what does not in UX applied to interactive media storytelling.

IMPLEMENTING USERS' INTERACTIONS AND IMMERSIVE EXPERIENCES IN DIGITAL STORYTELLING

Reflections of What Works and What Does Not

The progressive rise of digital mediations and UX design techniques has led to a productive orientation that finds in the creation and sale of immersive and designed experiences an important niche of commercial, socio-cultural, and political exploitation. In this sense, authors such as Pine and Gilmore (2011) describe the emergence of a new type of economy that began at the end of the 20th century and is based on the production of highly personalized interactive experiences and digital storytelling. Producing memorable and captivating experiences to be sold and enjoyed is a trend that has always been latent, particularly in the entertainment field, but in recent decades this trend has exploded and grown significantly.

As early as the 1990s, Myron Krueger (1991) predicted that the information society (Castells, 1996) was going to be replaced by one in which experience would be the commodity with value. He also affirmed that, at that time, it was already visible that there were many ways of buying experiences and that access to them was already considered as wealth. For Krueger, virtual reality, in any of the forms in which it has ended up being established (e.g., videogames and their platforms), would be the paradigmatic example of this "experience society."

Accordingly, we have been flooded by immersive products that sell us digital storytelling experiences in packages for all types of profiles. Most importantly, this trend is also reaching other aspects of social reality such as interpersonal relationships (social networks and dating apps), politics (participatory democracy or digital activism), and leisure (escape rooms, interactive, performative, and immersive amusement parks, and e-sports). Nevertheless, this is a trend that goes beyond mere entertainment. For example, it

Figure 9. Facial emotional recognition during the participant interactions where each line represents different types of basic emotions (adapted from iMotions)

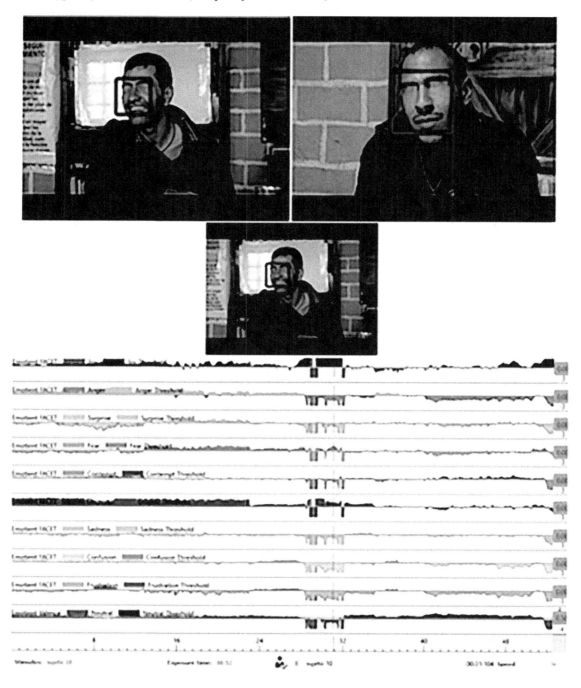

is not particularly difficult to find fields that are being structured, to a lesser or greater degree, in terms of experience. Tourism and cultural heritage are areas that have been especially permeated by the staging of experiences and by the sale of experience packages (sightseeing tours, dramatized wine tastings).

Figure 10. Unity Analytics interface showing players' key performance indicators (KPIs) (adapted from Unity Analytics Documentation, 2021)

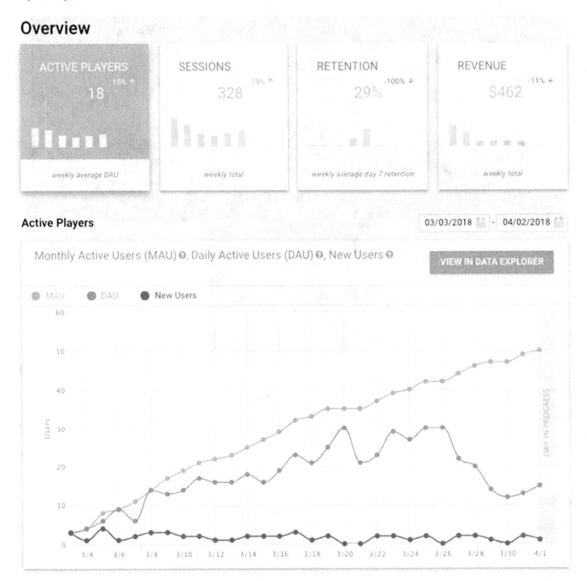

Storytelling and collecting or processing data in real-time have a significant influence on the afore mentioned experiences (Fernández & Puente-Bienvenido, 2015), and today there are numerous examples of great interest tools.

Some Implementations Suggestions in UX Methods and Software for Implementing Interactive and Immersive Storytelling

There are numerous tools in the audiovisual entertainment industry that enable the implementation and the study of highly immersive and interactive storytelling. Some of the tools are very popular, as in the

Figure 11. Inky editor interface (adapted from Inkle Studios, 2021)

case of Twine (an open-source tool for telling interactive, nonlinear stories) and iMotions (research software for access to emotional, cognitive, and behavioral data; see Figure 9).

However, the most potent innovations have appeared thanks to their integration in game engines (which allow informational tracking in real-time and readjust the experience continuously). In the following list three main tools that we consider to have the most significant potential in interactive and immersive storytelling due to their efficiency, accessibility, and synergies (taking advantage of data science and AI in game engines) are presented.

1. **GameTune:** Based on machine learning and AI, GameTune automatically optimizes elements such as progression speed, play patterns, difficulty, and game narratives through A/B testing. This UX tool continuously learns, adjusts, and iterates to deliver the best possible gaming experience, which means more engaged players and a better gameplay experience. GameTune can be used for various problems where the goal is to select the best alternative from A, B, C, (…) for each user. The best alternative is the one that maximizes engagement, player experience, immersive storytelling, conversion, and a custom game-specific reward.

2. **Unity Analytics:** Unity Analytics is a simple but powerful data platform that provides UX data in a video game (mostly related to a player's in-game behavior). Unity collects data by activating events when someone uses an application or game. Unity automatically dispatches a set of core events to collect richer and more in-depth information about how users play a game or experience storytelling. In addition to behavioral events for tracking user experience and player behavior, there are fully customizable events available whose names, purposes, and parameters can be defined as needed. Finally, it is also possible to use heat maps that are significantly useful in UX analysis.

3. **Inky:** Inky is an online tool for writing complex interactive stories that allow narrative designers to play and test their stories in real-time. It uses a powerful narrative scripting language that is

primarily designed for professional game development, though Inky can also be used to write and share choice-based interactive fiction.

CONCLUSION

The following conclusions are either based on the present emergent experiences or are imagined, but close to realistic tendencies. The conclusions covered in this chapter offer final observations in the areas of edutainment, social media, business, media arts, as well as other areas.

Ethical Consideration of UX Interactive and Immersive Storytelling in VR and AR

In the collective imagination of technology users, there are ambivalent discourses about how technical devices facilitate many areas of life and, in parallel, pose numerous risks and uncertainties. These are the so-called benefits and technological development counterparts (Sanmartín & Megías 2020; Sequeiros & Puente, 2019).

Fears and resistances towards technology do not occur uniformly, and certain areas, processes, and practices are perceived in very different ways. Perceptions can range from a partial fear of the implementation of a new technology in the field of interpersonal relationships, for reasons such as dehumanization, to an explicit desire to automate or digitize tasks that do not require much emotional involvement, such as health diagnosis, art, business, or media and audiovisual entertainment.

As a final compilation, we would like to go through a series of examples applied in different academic interest fields.

It is an excellent time for edutainment to develop given the need of more online education. To make full use and benefit of the transmedia and videogame entertainment industries, edutainment will require public institutions to invest in the new generation of interactive entertainment media to develop educational content.

The future of entertainment products linked to digital technology lies mainly in the video game industry. Within the frame of videogames, many possibilities coexist in gameplay, such as using different hardware and software interfaces. However, there is no doubt that gradually VR and AR are becoming relevant tools for game design. The involvement of VR and AR requires new ways of narrating and new possibilities to explore original audiovisual formats. UX-focused studios are already a vital part of the production phases of the new generation of video games. The massive data collection and the increased processing speeds of the new generations of processors allow designers to understand the user' behaviors within simulated or hybridized worlds much more effectively. Despite this advancement, the complexity of human behavior and the myriad factors to consider in the mathematical analysis of the information obtained do not allow absolute independence from game designers and their creative intuition. Nevertheless, the use of UX techniques dramatically simplifies and improves the work and results in game design.

The use of video games as a format for education is not without controversy. Fundamentally, if games become related to education, we are already introducing a political and ideological factor that is difficult to reconcile with an aseptic view of the issue. Merely talking about *serious games* (Clark Abt, 1970) as opposed to *video games* as entertainment introduces an idea linked to the medieval Christian tradition by which games are related to vagrancy, perversion, and crime. If a game is something serious, it will cease to be a game. With videogames, ideas and culture are transmitted in the same way as with any other audiovisual medium. To obtain edutainment, a right balance between serious contents and their presentation must be applied.

What is true is that because videogames have a robust mathematical logic base in their structure, they are beneficial in promoting scientific thinking. The possibility of generating experiences in simulated environments is fundamental not only for leisure, but it is also crucial in simulation. Simulators are, habitually, used to train professionals of different fields, such as pilots and scientists. Moreover, in many cases, the line between the simulator and video game is minimal. For example, many vehicle simulators are also marketed as video games.

On the other extreme, the border between sports and simulators is more complicated. In recent years, new forms of technological and digital sports have been born. Furthermore, these new sportive practices are linked to the immersion in new artificial or hybridized realities. There are already athletes who race professionally in virtual car races with simulators. Drone pilots use FPV glasses (First Person View) with real and augmented information incorporated. Furthermore, there are drone competitions within simulators. The boundaries between reality, simulation, and game are challenging to establish. The game and the ludic experience can arise in any context and any space: real, virtual, or imagined.

The video game is undoubtedly an ideological weapon and is a transmitter of profound values of the societies in which we live. However, the ideological use of games is not something new. In the Greek world's initiation rites and in some of its representations like the Olympic Games, there was a fundamental political and social component for social cohesion. Nevertheless, if we combine the video game's immersive capabilities with massive data management, the anonymity of young users, and, in some cases, severe problems of privacy rights, a very interesting conjunction that can be used unethically by both companies and governments emerges.

Edutainment needs to develop on an ethical and moral base that can communicate important cultural and scientific contents while keeping the game focused on entertainment. UX techniques can help develop better interactive media products that enhance the development of human intellect and spirit and support data to complement accessibility and disability challenges. Edutainment can serve the professors and students to develop better empathic environments where knowledge is built together.

Human relations and social media are fields where digitization, data science, and UX have developed more intensely. Human relationships are increasingly digitally mediated, from applications for dating to applications for sharing social, political, and daily content.

One of the main impacts of AI and data science is the standardization and dehumanization of job categories and skills. This influence of AI has made challenges to new job searchers navigating the online selection processes developed by websites such as LinkedIn. New ways of developing resumes and CVs are being developed to enable AI to at least select the job searcher profile. The exactitude of the words and the lack of synonyms and imagination concerning the interconnection between certain skills makes job search apps very robotic and leaves out potentially interesting profiles that do not correspond to rigid categories.

A series of gamified tools with interesting interactive narratives and storytelling have emerged in this type of context. Using algorithms and data intelligence, game designers and data scientists try to adapt and customize the user experience as much as possible. Thus, technological devices commit the user to immersive stories, suitable matches, challenges, and achievements to unlock, but at what cost? The management of private information, a loss of anonymity, the traceability of data, and the segmentation of socio-demographic data for marketing purposes are some of the tolls to users pay in exchange for immediacy, permanent connection, access, and personalization.

Ambivalent desires for digitization and customization arise in areas where greater penetration is desired, coexist with others where the public shows certain fears for their potential risks. Thus, utopian discourses of accessibility, immediacy, integration, and the breaking of limits coexist in parallel with other more dystopian visions associated with surveillance, control, deprivation, and inequality (of access and management). Thereby, desires and expectations regarding the progressive introduction of AI and data science in our social interactions are traversed by situations of socio-demographic variability and some groups are made vulnerable to being exposed to the less attractive effects of technological developments' progressive penetration (Sanmartín & Megías 2020). For example, people with a lower educational level perceive more significant risks and vulnerabilities associated with technological development, because they are the ones who are most exposed to its risks. Conversely, highly educated groups perceive technology and UX in a more positive, libertarian, and innocuous way (technophilic or utopian vision).

DEDICATORY

In Memoriam of our beloved friend Jorge Mora Fernández (1976-2021), Interactive Media Researcher (University of California, San Diego, Arthur C. Clarke Center in Human Imagination), colleague, storyteller, and navigator of the Virtual Seas.

ACKNOWLEDGMENT

Thanks to Arthur C. Clarke Center for Human Imagination, University of California San Diego, USA; the Laboratory of Digital Culture & Hypermedia Museography-Research Group Museum I+D+C, Universidad Complutense de Madrid,Spain; and the Emoji Studies Research Group, Digital Narrative and Video Game Studies UFV Research Group, Universidad Francisco de Vitoria, Madrid, Spain, Laboratory of Digital Culture & Hypermedia Museography-Research Group Museum I+D+C, Universidad Complutense de Madrid, Madrid, Spain.

REFERENCES

Aghdaie, N., Kolen, J., Mattar, M., Sardari, M., Xue, S., & Atif-Uz Zaman, K. (2018). *Multiplayer Video Game Matchmaking Optimization*. United States Patent 9993735.

Anderson, S. (2011). *Technologies of History*. Dartmouth College Press.

Andrade, G., Ramalho, G., Gomes, A. S., & Corruble, V. (2006). Dynamic Game Balancing: An Evaluation of User Satisfaction. In *Proceedings of the Second Artificial Intelligence and Interactive Digital Entertainment Conference* (p. 3–8). Menlo Park, CA: AAAI Press.

Bakkes, S. C. J., Spronck, P. & van Lankveld, G. (2012). Player behavioural modelling for video games. *Entertainment Computing, 3*, 71-79.

Barbic, J., D'Cruz, M., Latoschik, M. E., Slater, M., & Bourdot, P. (2017). Virtual Reality and Augmented Reality. In *14th EuroVR International Conference, EuroVR 2017 Laval, France*, December 12–14, 2017 *Proceedings*. Springer. 10.1007/978-3-319-72323-5

Barinaga, B. (2010). *Juego. Historia, teoría y práctica del diseño de videojuegos.* Alesia Games.

Barinaga, B. (2014). Digital distopy: Videogame. In Artecnología Augmented Knowledge and Accessibility. Complutense.

Barinaga, B. (2016). The video game and the game tradition.Education and shadows of the digital society. *Opción, 32,* 9.

Bryson, S. (1992). Measurement and calibration of static distortion of position data from 3D trackers. *SPIE Proceedings Vol. 1669: Stereoscopic Displays and Applications III.*

Carmigniani, J., Furht, B., Anisetti, M., Ceravolo, P., Damiani, E., & Ivkovic, M. (2011). Augmented reality technologies, systems and applications. *Multimedia Tools and Applications, 51*(1), 341–377. doi:10.100711042-010-0660-6

Castells, M. (1996). La era de la información. Economía, sociedad y cultura. Siglo XXI.

Chapman, V., & Hunicke, R. (2004). *AI for Dynamic Difficulty Adjustment in Games.* Academic Press.

Constanza-Chock, S. (2020). *Design Justice: Community-Led Practices to Build the Worlds we Need.* MIT Press. doi:10.7551/mitpress/12255.001.0001

Crawford, C. (2005). *On Interactive Storytelling.* New Riders.

Crews, D. E., & Zavotka, S. (2006). Aging, Disability, and Frailty: Implications for Universal Design. *Physiol Anthropol., 25*(1), 113–118. doi:10.2114/jpa2.25.113 PMID:16617216

Cruz-Neira, C. (1993). Virtual reality overview. *SIGGRAPH 93 International Conference on Computer Graphics and Interactive Techniques.*

Fernández, M., Puente, H., & Sequeiros, C. (2021). *Nuevas formas de comunicación a través de la narrativa en tiempo real: producción virtual, videojuegos y otras experiencias interactivas.* Congreso Internacional Comunicación y Pensamiento 2021. https://comunicacionypensamiento.org/ponencia/nuevas-formas-de-comunicacion-a-traves-de-la-narrativa-en-tiempo-real-produccion-virtual-video-juegos-y-otras-experiencias-interactivas/

Fernández, M., & Puente-Bienvenido, H. (2015). Universos fantásticos de inspiración lovecraftiana en videojuegos survival horror. Un estudio de caso de PT (Silent Hills). *Brumal. Revista de Investigación sobre lo Fantástico/Brumal. Research Journal on the Fantastic., 3*(1), 95–118.

Fuchs, H., & Bishop, G. (1992). *Research Directions in Virtual Environments.* University of North Carolina at Chapel Hill.

Gigante, M. A. (1993). Virtual reality: definitions, history and applications. *Virtual Real. Syst.*, 3–14. . doi:10.1016/B978-0-12-227748-1.50009-3

Ioannidou. (2013). Adapting Superhero Comics for the Big Screen: Subculture for the Masses. *Adaptation, 6*(2), 230–238. doi:10.1093/adaptation/apt004

Jackson, L.A., Witt, E., Games, A., Fitzgerald, H., Von Eye, A. & Zao, Y. (2011). Information Technological use and Creativity: Findings from The Children and Technological Project. *Computers in Human Behaviour, 28*(2), 370-376.

Jenkins, H. (2006). *Convergence Culture*. New York University Press.

Jenkins, H. (2007). *Transmedia Storytelling 101*. http://henryjenkins.org/2007/03/transmedia_storytelling_101.html

Jenkins, H. (2011). *Transmedia 202: Further Reflections*. http://henryjenkins.org/2011/08/defining_transmedia_further_re.html

Jenkins, H. (2013). *"Wish You Were Here": Imaginative Mobilities and Disembodied Intimacy in Postcards (Part Two)*. http://henryjenkins.org/2013/02/what-transmedia-producers-need-toknow-about-comics-an-interview-with-tyler-weaver-part-two.html

Jung, T., & Dieck, T. (2018). *Augmented Reality and Virtual Reality. Empowering Human, Place and Business*. Springer. doi:10.1007/978-3-319-64027-3

Kent, S. (2001). *The Ultimate History of Video Games: From Pong to Pokemon—The Story Behind the Craze That Touched Our Lives and Changed the World*. Crown.

Kinder, M. (1991). *Playing with Power in Movies, Television and Video Games*. University of California Press.

Kinder, M. (2014). *Transmedia Frictions: The Digital, the Arts, and the Humanities*. University of California Press.

Krueger, M. (1991). *Realidad artificial 2*. Addison-Wesley Profesional.

Krueger, M. W., Gionfriddo, T., & Hinrichsen, K. (1985). Videoplace an artificial reality. *Proceedings of the ACM SIGCHI Bulletin*, 16. 10.1145/317456.317463

Long, G. (2007). *Transmedia Storytelling. Business, Aesthetics and Production at the Jim Henson Company* (Master Thesis). Massachusetts Institute of Technology.

Maguire, M. (2001). Methods to support human-centred design. *Human-Computer Studies, 55*, 587–634.

Manovich, L. (2005). *Soft Cinema. The Language of New Media*. M.I.T. Press.

Mateas, M. (2003). *Expressive AI Games and AI, In proceedings of Level UP*. Digital Games Research Conference, Utrecht.

Mateas, M., & Murray, J. (2004). A preliminary poetics for interactive drama & games, & from game story to cyberdrama. In N. Wardrip-Fruin & P. Harrigan (Eds.), *First Person: New Media as Story, Performance & Game* (pp. 2–33). The MIT Press.

Mazuryk, T., & Gervautz, M. (1999). *History, Applications, Technology and Future*. Institute of Computer Graphics, Vienna University of Technology.

Millington, I. (2006). Artificial Intelligence for Games. Elsevier, Morgan Kaufmann Publishers.

Missura, O., & Gartner, T. (2009). *Player modelling for Intelligent Difficulty Adjustment*. Discovery Science, 12th International Conference.

Mora-Fernández, J.I. (2009). *La interfaz hipermedia: el paradigma de la comunicación interactiva. Modelos para implementar la inmersión juvenil en multimedia interactivos culturales. (Videojuegos, cine, realidad aumentada, museos y web)*. SGAE. Fundación Autor. Ediciones Autor.

Mora-Fernandez, J. I. (2013). Artecnología en cine interactivo al unas categorías, interfaces, estructuras narrativas, emociones e investigaciones. In *ArTecnologia. Arte, Tecnologia e linguagens Midiáticas*. Buqui.

Mora-Fernandez, J. I. (2019a). Extended analysis of the transmedia narrative universe of Nolan's Dark Knight: integrating original authorships, media convergences & interactive linear narratives. In Reflections in Social Sciences and other Topics. Guayaquil: CIDE.

Mora-Fernandez, J. I. (2019b). Concepts and Models of Analysis of Interactive and Transmedia Narratives: A Batman's Universe Case Study. In *Information Technology and Systems ICITS 2019, AISC 918* (pp. 929–943). Springer. doi:10.1007/978-3-030-11890-7_87

Mora-Fernandez, J. I. (2020). IMotions' Automatic Facial Recognition & Text-Based Content Analysis of Basic Emotions & Empathy in the Application of the Interactive Neurocommunicative Technique LNCBT (Line & Numbered Concordant Basic Text). In Digital Human Modeling and Applications in Health, Safety, Ergonomics and Risk Management. Human Communication, Organization and Work. Springer. https://doi.org/10.1007/978-3-030-49907-5_5.

Moreno Sánchez, I. (2002). *Musas y Nuevas Tecnologías: El relato hipermedia*. Paidós Comunicación.

Murray, J. (1997). *Hamlet On the Holodeck: the Future of Narrative in Cyberspace*. Free Press.

Murray, J. (2012). *Inventing The Medium. Principles of Interaction, Design as a Cultural Practice*. The MIT Press.

Nack, F., & Gordon, A. S. (2016). Interactive Storytelling. ICIDS 2016, LNCS 10045, 61–72. DOI: 6 doi:10.1007/978-3-319-48279-8

Nantes, A., Brown, R., & Maire, F. (2008). A Framework for Semi- Automatic Testing of Video Games. In *Proceedings of the Fourth Artificial Intelligence and Interactive Digital Entertainment Conference*. Association for the Advancement of Artificial Intelligence.

Nunes, O., & Nisi, V. (2017). Interactive Storytelling. *ICIDS 2017, LNCS 10690*, 372–375. doi:10.1007/978-3-319-71027-3_46

Parody, C. E. (2011). *A Theory of the Transmedia Franchise Character* (PhD thesis). University of Liverpool.

Piddle, J. (2017). *Augmented Reality. Where We Will Live*. Springer. doi:10.1007/978-3-319-54502-8

Pine, J., & Gilmore, J. H. (2011). *The Experience Economy*. Harvard Business Review Press.

Proietti, M. (2019). Experimental test of local observer independence. *Science Advances*, *5*(9). Advance online publication. doi:10.1126ciadv.aaw9832

Puente-Bienvenido, H. & Sequeiros, C. (2019a). A Sociological Look at Gaming Software: Erving Goffman's Dramaturgy in Video Games. *Revista Española de Investigaciones Sociológicas*, *166*, 135-152. doi:10.5477/cis/reis.166.135

Puente-Bienvenido, H., & Sequeiros Bruna, C. (2019b) Goffman y los videojuegos: Una aproximación sociológica desde la perspectiva dramatúrgica a los dispositivos videolúdicos. *Revista Española de Sociología*, *28*(2). https://recyt.fecyt.es/index.php/res/article/view/68948

Rico, L., & Ohlenschläger, K. (2005). *Banquete 05 – Communication in Evolution*. Museo Conde Duque.

Roth, C., & Koenitz, H. (2016). Evaluating the User Experience of Interactive Digital Narrative. In *Proceedings of the 1st International Workshop on Multimedia Alternate Realities*. Association for Computing Machinery. 10.1145/2983298.2983302

Ryan, M. L. (2001). *Narrative as Virtual Reality: Immersion and Interactivity in Literature and Electronic Media*. Johns Hopkins University Press.

Sanmartín, A. y Megías, I. (2020). *Jóvenes, futuro y expectativa tecnológica*. Madrid: Centro Reina Sofía sobre Adolescencia y Juventud, Fad. Doi:10.5281/zenodo.3629108

Schell, J. (2008). The Art of Game Design: A book of lenses. *Elsevier CRC Press*.

Sequeiros, C., & Puente-Bienvenido, H. (2018). Sociología y ci-fi: repensando los procesos de cambio social desde la ciencia ficción. *Nudos. Sociología, Teoría y didáctica de la literature, 2*, 4-16. doi:10.24197/nrtstdl.1.2018.4-16

Sequeiros, C., & Puente-Bienvenido, H. (2019). Cambio social, tecnología y ciencia-ficción. *Sociología y Tecnociencia*, *9*(2), 115–138.

Singer, E. (2010). The slow rise of the robot surgeon. *MIT Technology Review*. Retrieved from https://www.technologyreview.com/news/418141/the-slow-rise-of-the-robot-surgeon/

Sutherland, I. E. (1965). *The Ultimate Display. Multimedia: From Wagner to Virtual Reality*. Norton.

Wilber, K. (1985). *The Holographic Paradigm and other paradox, exploring the leading edge of science*. New Science Library.

Xue, S., Wu, M., Kolen, J., Aghdaie, N., & Zaman, K. A. (2017). Dynamic Difficulty Adjustment for Maximized Engagement in Digital Games. *WWW '17 Companion: Proceedings of the 26th International Conference on World Wide Web*.

KEY TERMS AND DEFINITIONS

Game Design: Techniques and processes used to design the rules and contents of a videogame.

Game Design Document: Document with all the design information of a videogame. It´s the main document for designers, programmers, and artists in a videogame project.

Game Engine: The core software for a game to properly run. It allows the design, creation, and operation of a videogame.

Gameplay: The game experience that emerges from the interaction between the game design and the player.

Heatmap: A graphical representation of data in the form of a map in which colors represent data values.

Chapter 28
Artificial Intelligences Are Subsets of Human Beings, Mainly in Fictions and Films:
Challenges and Opportunities

Nandini Sen
https://orcid.org/0000-0002-2844-6456
Heriot Watt University, UK

ABSTRACT

This chapter aims to create new knowledge regarding artificial intelligence (AI) ethics and relevant subjects while reviewing ethical relationship between human beings and AI/robotics and linking between the moral fabric or the ethical issues of AI as used in fictions and films. It carefully analyses how a human being will love robot and vice versa. Here, fictions and films are not just about technology but about their feelings and the nature of bonding between AIs and the human race. Ordinary human beings distrust and then start to like AIs. However, if the AI becomes a rogue as seen in many fictions and films, then the AI is taken down to avoid the destruction of the human beings. Scientists like Turing are champions of robot/AI's feelings. Fictional and movie AIs are developed to keenly watch and comprehend humans. These actions are so close to empathy they amount to consciousness and emotional quotient.

INTRODUCTION

Following Turing, A.M., (1950, p-433) I could have proposed the question, "Can machines think?" Turing's famous paper (1950) explains the meaning of the terms, "machine" and "think." I digress from his proposal a bit and further ask if machines can think ethically or if they can dream. The "machine" of the master mathematician has now been transformed into artificial intelligence and much progress has been done in this field. Now the question is that, how far the experts and scientists of artificial intelligence could add the intriguing value of the ethics in their experiments and brought the field of AI in the purview of gender, race, and ethics for the benefit of the human being and the animal kingdom. In

DOI: 10.4018/978-1-7998-6985-6.ch028

the Imitation Game Turing (1950) was trying to observe what were be the changes which could happen if a machine intervened in the process. He is further asking if the investigation is crucial for answering the question – "Can machines think?"

Even before Stephen Hawking and Elon Musk started to structuralise the world of artificial intelligence in 1942, the science fiction writer Isaac Asimov wrote the famous "The Three Laws of Robotics: A moral code to keep our machines in check. And the three laws of robotics are: a robot may not injure a human being, or through inaction allow a human being to come to harm. The second law, a robot must obey orders given by human beings, except where such orders would conflict with the first law. And the third, a robot must protect its own existence as long as such protection does not conflict with the first and the second law." Apparently these three laws are sufficient for constructing the basis to work from to develop a moral fabric inside the AI. (Asimov, 1990; A Britannica Publishing).

After WWII, several people started to work on intelligent machines. The British pioneer in this field Alan Turing delivered a lecture on AI in 1947. He also is the first to decide that AI was best studied by programming computers rather than by building machines. By the late 1950s, there were many explorers on AI, and most of them were developing their work on programming computers. Alan Turing's 1950 article Computing Machinery and Intelligence discussed conditions for considering a machine to be intelligent. He argued that if the machine could successfully pretend to be human to an expert observer then it certainly should be considered intelligent. This test would satisfy most people but not all philosophers. The observer could interact with the machine and a human, and the human would try to persuade the observer that it was human, and the machine would try to fool the observer (Anderson, 2017; McCarthy, 1990).

The philosopher John Searle said that the idea of a non-biological machine being intelligent is not rational. The philosopher Hubert Dreyfus said that AI is a kind of utopia. The computer scientist Joseph Weizenbaum said that the idea of AI was dirty, anti-human and unethical. Various people have said that since artificial intelligence hasn't reached human level by now, it should not be imagined. The highly evolved field of robotics is producing a huge range of machines, from autonomous vacuum cleaners to military drones to entire factory productions. At the same time, artificial intelligence and machine learning are lagging behind the software that helps us daily, whether we're searching the internet or being given government tasks. In addition, many people say that AI is not a good idea. They even suggest remembering of films like Terminator and the Matrix where AIs had mainly inflicted destruction and/or exploitation of the mankind (Trent. (2012). These developments are rapidly leading to a time when robots of all kinds will become prevalent in almost all aspects of society, and human-robot interactions will rise significantly (Anderson, 2017); (McCarthy, 1990).

This chapter based on the above arguments will examine a logical progression in the evolution of AI. It will present a set of balanced arguments including the debates on the anticipated positives and the apprehended evils. These perhaps exist in the concepts if AI is necessary in human civilisation. It will take us through few sections mainly: literature review; discussion about fictional and filmic AI characters; comparison of real-life AI characters and fictional/filmic AI; ethnography; analysis and conclusion including future research.

LITERATURE REVIEW

Asimov's laws are still mentioned as a guiding principle of the growth of the concept of artificial intelligence (AI). The South Korean government even proposed a Robot Ethics Charter in 2007 reflecting the laws. But assuming how much AI has changed and will continue to develop in the coming days, the chapter asks how these systems could be updated for a 21st century form of AI (Anderson, 2017). Asimov also examined how a machine could easily solve a mathematical problem but rejected to write a poem. On the other hand, Turing rightly trusted that a machine could solve the mathematical problem whereas the human being could give away if he had to solve a difficult problem. The AI machine could solve a chess problem within seconds, however, declared that he would not be able to write a poetry (Turing, 1950). Turing (1950) had tried to grasp the complex issue if machines or AI could perform better or differently from human being while undertaking a problem. He had also discussed if a machine had free will. It was tough to discern if the machine/AI had a random element or they could choose their programmes depending on the digits. (Turing, 1950, pp-433-460). Turing strongly believed, even if it was debatable about the thinking capacity of machines in 1950, however, in the later period of the century general people will not be able to argue about the machines' reasoning power. Turing is subtly critical about human beings that they could not go beyond their own superior intellectual capability. He wanted to establish a machine's reasoning ability. He though extended his view that apart from human beings, others could not have a soul as allocated by the God. He was not clear whether a machine could have a soul or not. That became the concern of the moral fabric. Machine is created by man. If man puts a soul inside the machine, then doesn't man not taking the role of the God (Turing, 1950).

Turing following Professor Jefferson's Lister Oration for 1949 agreed that a machine, until could scribble a poem or compose music inspired by thoughts and feelings and not by chance that machines will not attend or equalize human brain-that is, not only write it but know that it had written it. No AI could realise happiness at its successes, grief when its internal connections are down, be warmed by appreciation, be made depressed by its mistakes, be overwhelmed by sex, be desperate when it cannot get what it desires. This is directly taking the research to the question of consciousness and the mystery behind the machine or the AI. Turing clearly points out that the AI scientists need to construct kind, resourceful, beautiful, friendly, innovative, humorous machines. The AI should be able tell right from wrong, make errors, fall in love, relish delicious food, making attempts to make someone fall in love with it, taking lessons from experience, use words properly, can think about itself, have as much heterogenous behaviour as a man. These are possibilities of the near future, rather than Utopian dreams.

Copeland (2004) pointed out that Turing was not the only theoretical mind to have produced an idea basic for the development of computers: he was also involved in their construction. "It has been said that computing machines can only carry out the processes that they are instructed to do. This is certainly true in the sense that if they do something other than what they were instructed then they have just made some mistake. Turing, along with his colleagues, cracked the Enigma cipher, shortening WWII by an estimated two years (Copeland, 2004). When Alan Turing was cracking intercepted coded messages from the Nazis during World War II, he probably could not imagine that his computational discoveries could be used for identifying changes in patterns of ecological data as well. Turing was trying to recognize regularities in the coded messages of Nazi Germans and come up with a ''program'' that would transform the messages to their decoded content (Copeland, 2004).

Huang and Rust (2018) describe four levels of intelligence that AI systems can exhibit. While AI is not a new technology, given its conceptualization in the 1940s (Copeland 2004), it is still considered to be an emerging technology since the techniques used to implement it are radically evolving (Stahl, et al., 2021). Additionally, companies are currently investing significant resources in the development and proliferation of AI. A simple question that comes to mind when scientists tried to define this concept is the following: is it a concept that can be understood in terms of a mechanism (or an algorithm) that generates certain (human-like) behaviours or is it a matter of a human perceiving an agent as intelligent? Although Turing's original intention in 'Computing Machinery and Intelligence' was to explore whether a computer can 'imitate a brain' (Turing and Copeland 2004), he then admitted to be skeptical as to how the intelligence of a machine was to be perceived: 'The extent to which we regard something as behaving in an intelligent manner' he noted (Turing 1950) 'is determined as much by our own state of mind and training as by the properties of the object under consideration'. In other words, Turing suggests that 'intelligence' relates to how we conceptualise it.

There have been a few notable scientists working for research centers and universities who have perceived the central concepts that have guided to technological initiatives in both the UK and the USA. Among these standouts is Alan Turing, the inventor of the Turing Machine, which set down the mathematical basics for the project of modern digital computers. The cryptography work of Turing in the Enigma project at Bletchley Park near London was crucial for shortening the duration of the Second World War. (Copeland, 2004).

Public worry will be a huge problem for AI to overcome. Understanding society's long-term tension of self-aware automatons should be a consideration within AI laboratories, especially those specializing in fully autonomous humanoids. Asimov anticipated this public terror and proposed the Three Laws of Robotics to reduce the fear. Three Laws are not practical from a general sense even though the ethical issues involved are crucial in the scientists' minds. As the contemporary idea of AI was still being refined, Asimov envisioned a day when humanity would be served by a host of AI. However, he knew that apprehension would be the greatest hurdle to success and, consequently, implanted all of his fictional robots with the Three Laws of Robotics. Above all, these laws served to protect humans from almost any abstracted risks. Asimov believed that humans would put safeguards into any potentially hazardous instruments and visualised AI as just advanced machines. Asimov considered that his Three Laws were more than just a literary plan; he could realise scientists engaged in Artificial Intelligence (AI) research had taken his Laws to heart, (Asimov1990; Britannica). Knowledge of the Three Laws of Robotics appears to be homogenous among AI researchers, there is the encompassing attitude that the Laws are not implementable in any meaningful sense. With the field of Artificial Intelligence now 70 years old and the extensive use of AI products, it is time to rethink about Asimov's Three Laws in terms of applications to implementation and calculating the underlying fear of unmanageable AI (Copeland, 2004).

CONTEXT OF THE FICTIONAL ROBOTIC AND AI CHARACTERS

Many storytellers and scientists have used similar rational to establish that only humans possess a soul. To interfere in this area is to intrude in God's own territory. This anxiety of man stopping, through technology, into God's zone and being unable to control his own creations is referred to as the "Frankenstein Complex" by Isaac Asimov in several of his essays (most notably (Asimov 1991). The "Frankenstein Complex" (Mc Cauley, 2007) is alive in Hollywood films rekindling the idea of love/hate through a line of productions that would never be forgotten: Terminator (all three); I, Robot; A.I.: Artificial Intelligence; 2001: A Space Odyssey; Blade Runner; Short Circuit; Electric Dreams; the Battlestar Galactica series;

Robocop; Metropolis. These films originate from Sci-Fi literature. The important theme involves is that AIs attempt to harm people or even all of humanity. The current generation has seen a sudden and fantastic flowing in philosophy and science of the mind; a great intellectual revolution is happening in terms of AI. The central drama is AI, the fresh attempt to make computers think. In 1980's and 1990's people doubted the seriousness of a thinking machine. On the other hand, many scientists thought like Turing (1950) that it's only a matter of time, computers with minds will be possible, if interplanetary travel is endeavored. Scientists believed that AI psychology, philosophy, and linguistics, are now possible and can be established as super specialties. There is one fear not to recognise AI as a sensitive mind because of our anthropocentricism or human chauvinism is ingrained in our intelligence (Haugland, 1989).

Doug Blank (2006), Associate Professor of Computer Science at Bryn Mawr College, commented in a similar vein that trouble is that robots don't have clear-cut symbols and rules like those that must be imagined necessary in the sci-fi world. Most robots don't have the ability to look at a person and see them as a person (a 'human'). And that is the easiest concept needed to follow the rules. In the second novel of Asimov's Robots Series, The Naked Sun, the main character, Elijah Baley concludes that a robot could inadvertently disobey any of the Three Laws if it is not aware of the full consequences of its actions (Asimov 1957). While the character in the novel rightly conclude that it is impossible for an AI to know the full consequences of its actions, there is never an exploration of exactly how hard this task can be. (Blank 2006). Aaron Sloman, Professor of Artificial Intelligence and Cognitive Science at The University of Birmingham, described the issue in a way that gets at the sheer vastness of the problem: Another obstacle involves potential contradictions as the old utilitarian philosophers found centuries ago: harming and benefits by AI is relative in nature (Sloman 2006; Sloman 2006). This relativity in terms of harming and benefit which can be performed by an AI is complex (McCauley, 2007).

Isaac Asimov (1991) coined the term "Frankenstein Complex" to describe the fear that the public has towards humanmade technologies when they invade the realm commonly considered to be God's domain. This complex demonstrates some of the historical evidence of this fear and provides reasons why it is unfounded. Finally, it suggests a way for the AI community to help in reducing the public's fear of a prowling species of aggressive robots. Hollywood and the media worsen the issue while some well-known authors and scientists lend reliability to it. This apprehension is much older than the current concepts of AI and robotics. Asimov recognized this deep misinformation of technology and created the Three Laws of Robotics intended to project how these complex machines could be made harmless. For AIs to be accommodated in everyday society, scientists must examine the underlying apprehension of intelligent AI and reevaluate Asimov's response (McCauley, 2007). Not because he understood how to build robots, but to discover if there are lessons to be learned from his insights into society's response to intelligent technology. Asimov knew that fear would be the greatest barrier to success and, consequently, implanted all of his fictional robots with the Three Laws of Robotics. Above all, these laws served to protect humans from almost any perceivable hazard. Asimov believed that humans would put safeguards into any potentially dangerous tool and saw robots as just advanced tools. The word "robot" comes from the Czech word "robota" meaning 'drudgery' or 'servitude' (Jerz, 2002).

In much of science fiction since early times, the story is about artificially created workers that ultimately rise to overthrow their human creators. Even before Capek's (McCauley, L., (2007)) use of the term 'robot', however, the notion that science could produce something that it could not control had been explored most intensely by Mary Shelly under the guise of Frankenstein's monster (Shelley, 1818).

The full title of Shelley's novel is "Frankenstein, or The Modern Prometheus." In Greek mythology Prometheus brought fire (technology) to humanity and was, consequently, soundly punished by Zeus.

Where AIs are concerned, the fantasies that people can most readily recognise with, those that capture their imaginations and explore into their thickest fears, involve the displacing of humanity by its metallic offspring (Stephen Horne, 2021). Even well-respected scientists in both academia and industry have expressed their belief that humans will engineer a new species of intelligent machines that will replace human race. Ray Kurzweil (1999; 2005), Warwick (2002) argue that robotics, genetic engineering, and nanotechnology pose a unique kind of threat that the world has never before faced, "robots, engineered organisms, and nanobots share a dangerous amplifying factor: They can self-replicate. A bomb is blown up only once – but one bot can become many, and quickly get out of control." Clearly, Joy is expressing the basis of why the public at large continues to be grasped by the Frankenstein Complex. (Joy, Bill Joy, co-founder of Sun Microsystems, expressed in a 2000 Wired Magazine article (Joy, 2000)

The probability of a robotic uprising that destroys or subjugates humanity is quite low (Singh Roy, 2021). The primary argument that robots will take over the world is that they will eventually be able to design and manufacture themselves in large numbers thereby activating the inevitability of evolution. Each robot produced must have all the knowledge, capability, resources, time, and motivation to build more robots, otherwise, the evolution goes nowhere. Humans could build a robot or AI with the sole task of designing and building a new AI that is better at designing and building AI which builds another AI, etc. (McCauley, 2007). Asimov (1991) imagined human beings as the apprentice of the God in creativity when he is constructing the AI and robots. He is skeptical about the human's smartness in using the machines. Human beings submitted their souls to the Gods for the purpose of safety. In contrast to Turing (1950), Asimov (1991) imagined that human beings taking over creative powers of God or borrowing them to build their own superiority over nature. At every step Asimov expressed his doubts if smart people will wisely use the machines. Even in 1991 Asimov felt a pessimism that AI/Technology had carried away civilisation in a negative way. He even was frustrated when he put up the following question, "Do we not see that our Technology has run away with us and is slowly and inexorably destroying the environment ant habitability of the planet?" (Asimov, 1991).

Asimov (1991) directly said that human beings could strategise the whole matter by creating and artificial human being. Unlike Turing (1950) Asimov challenged the problem of creating artificial human being in different ways, even suggesting that AI engineers could be punished. Here we can take up the example of the story of Frankenstein by Mary Shelley (1818) where the creature created by the scientist became a monster and tried to punish the creator. The Artificial creature got trapped inside a world of loneliness. He was abandoned both by the audience and the creator to his fate. Asimov (1991) clearly advised his readers that the creator should be punished instead of the human-like creature. Asimov (1991) also introduced his readers to the concept of slave related to the 'robot' following Karel Kapek (play RUR). It is true that the concept of AI was dreams of human beings which were reflected in many stories. Mythical robots were used by the Gods or human beings under the guidance of the Gods. Shelley (1818) exposed very well that the scientist was not smart or wise enough to deal with this artificial being. He unempathetically treated the creature and in retaliation the creature killed everyone in Frankenstein's family including Frankenstein. Maybe Shelley (1818) even compared the God with this scientist. God clearly failed to control human beings from doing criminal acts and other sins. Shelley (1818) examined in her novel how God had also abandoned the human beings to fend for themselves and had even posed a question what would happen if the artificial creature was filled with culture and intellect and could talk like human beings. She pointed out that the artificial creature became miserably sad. He is unable to control his mind. Ultimately, he became dangerous for the human civilisation. The artificial being instead of finishing himself escaped to the Arctic. Asimov could envisage the future of the collaboration of the AI and human beings. Though scientists can confront the whole concept of AI, robots, or humanoid, at the same time they can develop an aura of romanticism. In fact, there are some things humanity is not meant to know. Human beings could find a solution to this unfortunate position of the AI. In future there would be lot of opportunities to develop an optimism through the wiser and balanced philosophy of handling AI ensuring safety of the broader humanity and human beings.

DISCUSSION AROUND AI CHARACTERS/ ROBOTS IN FICTIONS AND MOVIES

Fictional and movie AI characters can take the human beings through a mysterious adventure, sermon, or vision. Human beings, perhaps, can be overwhelmed by the intense abstraction and their strong narratives of absurdity, well- articulated though unresolved speculations on the origins and destinies of human life. They can as well grip us inside an engagement projecting their visual starkness, serenity, wonder, and euphoria at both the earth and the heaven, maybe beyond the infinite (Geraci, 2007). In science-fiction literature and film, human beings are simultaneously apprehensive and allured in the presence of intelligent machines. This is an experience that estimates the mystical experience science fiction offers. It is an empirical support for Anne Forest's (Forest, 1998) claim that human beings feel fear and fascination in the presence of advanced robots. The human reaction to intelligent machines shows that human beings in many respects have elevated those machines to divine status. Twentieth-century Euro-American cinema contradict our trust in the unambiguous potential of technology. *Metropolis*, *Forbidden Planet*, *Terminator*, and *The Matrix* show that human beings' relations with artificial intelligence complement their relations with the God. This signifies that robotic technology projects a particular kind of sanctity in the twentieth century. Technology promises salvation on one hand while creating fear with the other. This concurrence of opposites appears most prominently in depictions of intelligent robots (Geraci, 2007).

Lang in his film Metropolis (Geraci, 2007) shows an imagery in a scene where the protagonist, Freder, the son of the leader of Metropolis, wanders below ground while following a girl. In the underworld, he sees the machines go haywire after a worker collapses from fatigue. The mechanical failure results in numerous deaths, which the son sees in a vision as the sacrifice of children to the Babylonian god Moloch. In this powerful scene, Freder becomes aware of the dark side of a technology that has always benefited him. By superimposing the vision of Moloch over the machine, Lang shows how it has become a god, ruling over the subject workers who devote themselves utterly to its care. The allure and dread of technology continues in more contemporary films, from the *Terminator* series to the *Matrix* trilogy. In these movies, intelligent machines threaten the human species with extinction, real and virtual, but remain vital to human survival. Without Arnold Schwarzenegger's reprogrammed Terminator machine, the protagonist of *Terminator 2: Judgment Day* (1991) and *Terminator 3: The Rise of the Machines* (2003) would not have survived.

The research considers the foundational figure in science fiction to be Mary Shelley (1818), which would make Frankenstein's monster something of a foundational robot. In *Frankenstein: A Modern Prometheus* (Shelley, 1818), Frankenstein's monster, a living being made through scientific expertise, barely resembles the shiny metallic robots of many science-fiction authors (and especially films) but comes closer and closer to reality as scientists work to create artificial muscles, skin, and other tissue to replace the inefficient actuators and joints of contemporary robotics (Horne, 2021). Frankenstein's monster represents a hope for technological progress gone awry; the machine monster becomes a monster, indeed, and flees civilization (Brantinger, 1980). While *Frankenstein (1818)* marks a crucial moment in literature, it wasn't until the twentieth century that true robots found their way into popular culture. Although Shelley's work tends toward the disastrous, twentieth-century science-fiction robots have largely been more complex (Horne, 2021).

*I, Robot (*Asimov, 1950*)* concludes with a story about the Machines—advanced robots that control Earth's economy for the maximum benefit of human beings. The Machines' immense power over Earthly life and their ability to fashion a harmonious Eden of it make them gods (Thomsen 1982). It transpires that the Machines are systematically eliminating human beings from positions of responsibility because those human beings mistrust the Machines and are therefore perceived as a threat to human well-being. The Machines' domination of human life means the reduction of humankind to mere instrumentality but also the possibility of real human happiness. Damnation and salvation are intertwined just like fear and fascination. Asimov ultimately believes that human beings will retain a control over their creations (Klass 1983), but he finds the wholehearted endorsement implicit in the *Star Wars* treatment of R2-D2 impossible to maintain.

The perfect 21st-century female looks like a smart model though a bit odd with the open -ended look. In "Ex Machina," Alex Garland's clever futuristic film about old and new desires, the female in question is a robot called Ava, a name suggestive of both Adam and Eve. Ava has a serene humanoid face and the expressive hands and feet of a dancer, but also the transparent figure of a visible woman anatomy model. Beautiful and smart, sleek, and stacked, Ava is at once decidedly unsettling and safely under lock and key, which makes her an ideal posthuman female (Manohlia, 2015). This prepares Ex-Machina a creative story, except instead of God repurposing a rib, the story here involves a Supreme Being who has built an A.I., using a fortune he's made from a search engine called Blue Book." The trouble with thinking machines, Wittgenstein writes, isn't that we don't know yet if they can do the job, but 'a machine thinks (perceives, dreams)' seems somehow nonsensical." And it seems so because such a machine is not (yet) known to us. Ava looks at once familiar and new, distinctly human, and thoroughly machined, only compared with the robot in "Metropolis". Ava excels the human-AI divide, she defies categorization because of the radical autonomy she shares with the queer sisters lived by Scarlett Johansson in "Her," and "Under the Skin". (Stephen Horne, 2021). These are the new heroines: totally hot, bracingly cold, powerfully sovereign, and posthuman. (Dargis, Manohlia., (2015).,

It's just a lump of iron. Why this attachment? A question asked of taxi driver Bimal (Kali Banerjee), the central character of Ajantrik, regarding his dedication to his very old and battered 1920 taxi, called Jagaddal. This taxi driver's relationship to his car somehow draws a parallel to Ghatak's own attempts to explain what it is about the cinema that draws his commitment. Ajantrik is a movie where a mingling of the human and the mechanical elements take place and is portrayed superbly when Bimal pauses pensively to say: "That I'm a machine. I like the smell of burnt gasoline. It makes me high…" The connect Bimal feels towards his taxi announces a profoundly human attachment and dedication motivating him. Bimal holds onto his car, Jagaddal, for fifteen years, against the prevailing trend among his peers who gave up old cars and upgraded to new ones. Bimal calls those new cars, 'fashionable whores.' Jagaddal thus is elevated to the status of a human being and Ritwik Ghatak brings out this human element through his camera, sights, and sounds, epitomised by his attention to frequent autonomous movements of Jagaddal's headlights. Sounds of drinking and exhalations of satisfaction exude from the car among descriptions of Jagaddal's health and durability. According to Bimal, in comparison with other cars, Jagaddal never 'catches cold' or 'gets tummy aches.' That Bimal believes in Jagaddal's independent agency is sum- marised in the final test of the car's strength, after it has received new parts (Information Desk, 2021). 'I've pampered you enough,' Bimal warns, dropping several large boulders and as the car collapses or 'dies,' Bimal smashes the windscreen and bursts into tears, his head resting on the steering wheel. And thus, Ritwik Ghatak superbly excels beyond the 'man and the machine' (Information Desk, 2021)

Meditations on the philosophical and social conundrums posed by Asimov's most celebrated invention: The Three Laws of Robotics. Asimov's stories have become such an established part of robot folklore that his three laws have shaped some of the fundamental thinking in the development of real-life robotic engineering and artificial intelligence. In the movie, however, much of the action is motivated by robots that have in some way been programmed to evade these laws, under which circumstances their chests conveniently start glowing red. Asimov's aim with his robot stories was to explore the consequences, and in particular the loopholes, of the rational scheme that he had established (Bell, 2004).

Transhumanists believe that human race will soon undergo a technological evolution into a new and superior form. While there is no single template for transhumanism's imagined future, there are several recurring motifs, such as enhanced cognition, improved bodies, and extended lifespans. Sometimes the emphasis is on enhanced biology, sometimes on the supplementation or replacement of the body by technology. the futures imagined in science fiction sometimes come true. Science fiction writers told stories about going to the moon before anyone went there. They told stories about artificially intelligent machines before these were invented. And so on. This means readers may try to rummage through science fiction for visionary images, especially of future technologies. The dystopian vision of Altered Carbon might, for instance, be construed as a warning that we need "to be thinking about the cost of pursuing technological immortality" (Miller, 2018). Westworld, a serial, challenges scientists to consider the difference between being human and being a AI. From the beginning of this new serialisation on HBO scenes of graphic human-on-robot violence became popular. But the robots in Westworld have more than just human-like physical bodies, they display emotion including extreme pain, they see and recognise each other's suffering, they bleed and even die. What makes this acceptable, at least within Westworld's narrative, is that they are just extremely life-like human simulations. The disturbing message, echoing that of previous sci-fi classics such as Blade Runner and AI, is that machines could one day touch human ability as to be indistinguishable from human beings – not just in intellect and appearance, but also in moral terms (Prescott, 2016).

But there are relatively few about how they might cooperate with humanity (Asimov got in here early on this and remains one of the few). The hypocrisy is that this trend suggests that it's fine for governments to monitor its citizens and for corporations to analyse social media feeds (even using software bots), but an AI shouldn't. It's like saying that you're happy being screwed over, but only by a political system or another mammal, not a computer. One solution, therefore, is to consider how to limit AIs and teach them human ethics. But if we "train" AIs to have ethical behaviours, who do we trust to train them? To whose ethical standards? Public perceptions of AI will be governed by just this sort of mistrust and suspicion, fostered by such public debacles and by the broadly negative view evident in much science fiction. But what such examples perhaps reveal is that the problem with AI is not that it is "artificial", nor that it is immoral, nor even in its economic or social impact. Perhaps the problem is us (Slocombe, 2016). Despite the "long time ago," Star Wars is picturised in the future in terms of how we conceive of it. The human society narrated is one that features more advanced technology than we currently have, a technology that reflects our trajectory in transportation, telecommunication, military technology, artificial intelligence, and robotics. So, what kind of future does Star Wars show us? Well, a familiar one, to put it mildly — one that despite the spaceships and laser-swords is more reflective than speculative. "From a social point of view most SF has been incredibly regressive and unimaginative.

Instead of comparing it to the works of H.G. Wells or Isaac Asimov or Kim Stanley Robinson, we can compare Star Wars to the works of George MacDonald and J.R.R. Tolkien and Neil Gaiman, and there we find a much more favourable lens by which to understand and appreciate what the Star Wars universe accomplishes. This isn't SF – it's fantasy in outer space, and, more than that, it's good fantasy (Deman, 2017).

Asimov's stories as allegories of slavery point out that the biologist of the robot would be dealing with himself, and not only because he is the only instantiation but also because that's what thinking humans do. Asimov explicitly refers to Andrew's first scholarly achievement, namely a history of robots: he wants to explain how robots feel about what has happened since the first ones could work and live on Earth. Only a robot can tell what it is like to be a robot and telling this realizes the history of robots from an inside perspective and thus again a narrative of the life of someone who is supposed not to be living. Robots do not have a history, they live a timeless life, but if robots can produce narratives of their lives, they prove to be human (Blum, 2016). In "The Bicentennial Man" (Asimov, 1976), Asimov rejected his own Three Laws as a proper basis for Machine Ethics. He believed that a robot with the characteristics possessed by Andrew, the robot hero of the story, should not be required to be a slave to human beings as the Three Laws dictate. He, further, provided an explanation for why humans feel the need to treat intelligent robots as slaves, an explanation that shows a weakness in human beings that makes it difficult for them to be ethical icons. Because of this weakness, it seems likely that machines like Andrew could be more ethical than most human beings. "The Bicentennial Man" gives us hope that, not only can intelligent machines be taught to behave in an ethical fashion, but they might be able lead human beings to behave more ethically as well (Anderson, 2007).

Robots have become as commonplace as vacuum cleaners, gene-editing is the norm and biotechnological advances are close to recreating unique human beings. Amazon recommends is just the beginning. "In the era of big data, we might start to be able to rebuild somebody's character so that after they've died, they can still carry on, figuring out what they'd order next online, which concert they'd like to go to and what they would have said at the breakfast table if you had read them the latest headlines," Ishiguro continues (Allardice, 2021). He deliberately didn't read either the recent Ian McEwan novel *Machines Like Me* or Jeanette Winterson's *Frankisssstein*, which also take on artificial intelligence. From very different angles. Klara (Ishiguro, 2021) is a sort of robotic parent, "Terminator-like in her determination to look after Josie", but she is also a potential surrogate child: when Josie gets sick, Klara is being programmed to take her place. "What happens to things like love in an age when we are changing our views about the human individual and the individual's uniqueness?" Ishiguro asks. "There was this question – it always sounds very pompous – about the human soul: do we actually have one or not?" (Ishiguro, 2021). For the first time, Ishiguro is beginning to fear for the future, not just the consequences of climate change, but other issues raised in *Klara*: artificial intelligence, gene-editing, big data – "sorry to bang on about this" – and their implications for equality and democracy. "The nature of capitalism itself is changing its model," Ishiguro says. "I do worry that we are not in control any more of these things." (Allardice, 2021).

The film script, written by Kubrick and Arthur C. Clarke whose books and stories the movie was based on, and directed by Kubrick, is a multisensory ode to cosmic mystery, fate and the future. Kubrick's *2001*, like most science fiction, problematizes humanity's relation with technology. And, like most science fiction, it is not so much about the future, whatever that could mean, as the future as seen from the present of the filmmaker's eyes and thoughts. The cold calculating nature of the characters is the audience's coldness; their lack of surprise at their surroundings is the lack of surprise at the audience. The film's characters are lost (Pope, 2003). The film's characters are lost and have surrendered to their crypts in an all-pervasive melancholy. Narratives of transcendence and/or Apocalypse spring. HAL, the AI, goes mad. Is Kubrick suggesting we regain control of the AI, or that human beings renegotiate their relationship with technology, accepting their contamination by it, or their co-dependence with it? Given the nature of the ending, there can be no conclusions here, though it should be noted that even after Bowman kills HAL, he still employs the AI, goes for a ride with it -- beyond the infinite (Overbye, 2018).

Consumers of devices such as Apple Computer's Siri or Amazon's Alexa are acquainted with the way AIs communicate with humans with voice- and thought recognition. The clarity of diction and thought compositions of these machines remind us of the exploits of the supercomputer Hal 9000 of Arthur C. Clark's 2001: A Space Odyssey, as depicted in Stanley Kubrick's movie of the same name. Hal's voice quality was certainly not as human-like as Alexa's, for instance, but Hal demonstrated distinct emotive qualities not yet seen in these familiar commercial devices (Swagatam Sen, 2021). We can argue that artificial intelligence of digital technology thus far is superfast in information processing and all the exploits of the extant machines merely are a response to information fed as instruction (Swagatam Sen, 2021). In this sense, interaction with Alexa is not a conversation, as Alexa cannot speak about anything what she has not been supplied as data or has not accumulated by listening to her human consumers (Sen, S., and Singh Roy, 2021). On the other hand, when we order an article of commerce through a vendor's website, frequently you receive suggestions with this kind of message: buyers who ordered this are also interested in the following. A clever marketing trick alright, but behind it is an algorithm that looks at your profile of preference and makes an informed suggestion. Consumers need to think of the consequence of using these awesome machines (Horne, 2021). The scariest consequence of artificial intelligence has been sounded by Elon Musk of Tesla Motors and supported by Stephen Hawking. Since technologies have social consequences, what would happen if we were able to achieve driverless public transportation, robots serving in the supermarkets and restaurants and similar developments throughout social activities? Or, just a few very technology-savvy individuals will control the rest of us? The answers to the questions raised here will slowly but surely be revealed in future (Sikdar, 2018).

The late Stanley Kubrick's film 2001: A Space Odyssey *portrayed a computer, HAL9000, that appeared to be a conscious entity, especially given that it seemed capable of some forms of emotional expression.* Looking back on how humans interact with a supercomputer in *2001: A Space Odyssey*, we are led to conclude that many forthcoming challenges of dealing with synthetic emotions in AI will be more social than technical. Although a work of fiction, this film can nevertheless alert us to specific pitfalls that can occur when human actors embark on emotion-laden interchanges with computers. Computers, too, may be prone to misinterpretation of human emotional cues. Although this is not unusual among human actors, the high-speed logical processing and problem solving of computers creates a far greater level of asymmetry in situations of emotional exchange (Nofz, et al, 2002).

ETHNOGRAPHY

I came across four people Tirtho Dasgupta, Swagatam Sen, Anusua Singh Roy, and Stephen Horne who are either Artificial Intelligence scientists or admirers of films and fictions based on artificial intelligence. I thought to interview and chat with them over phone on the subject in-depth to add clarity and qualitative dimensions to the research.

Tirtho Dasgupta, Film Maker and AI user-experience designer:

AI slowly entered the commercial world after the scientific world. I used Facebook very nominally as I had other things to do in my hometown. After coming to Scotland, I experienced loneliness and homesickness. These factors influenced me to go deeper into Facebook (FB). Rootlessness has provoked me to spend more time with FB. I dug FB for connecting myself with my childhood. Thus, FB AI gives opportunity me to reconnect with my nostalgia, roots, childhood, schools, and the friends related to these spaces. AI is giving me scope to connect with the common friend- school friends, local friends, feel-good cultural groups- to develop positive feelings, new friends, and to interact with new characters. I argue, exchange narratives, and share my feelings with new and older friends. At the same time political and religious sectors in FB provoked me to become emotionally agitative. I am addictive to FB and Twitter and cannot come out these unnecessarily evocative AI platforms. A deeply involved person like me is forgetting to empathise or listening to other people. However, I have now recovered and have come under control. I am questioning that if the AI spaces are safe or whether they are destroying our personal and friendly relationships. I observe that my younger friends are trying to experience instant gratification through these social media controlled by sensitive and super intelligent AIs. The business houses are controlling our souls, and moral fabric by simply playing algorithms. These AIs, through social business medias, are manipulating with our choices, even in terms of our sadnesses and happy moments. When someone close is dying we are sharing this intimate experience within an unsafe, very public space like FB. Since 2015-2014- the smartphone revolution created this selfie-obsession and breaking the Monalisa myth by making it only the background. We are becoming crazy to take a photo in front of that small painting and instantly sharing the photo with the public. I am getting out-of-proportionately bigger than that legendary photo of Monalisa. I am not appreciating the place or the creation- photo is not etched in my mind, mind is replaced by the prompt gratification. Social media is worrying me I wonder what kind of world we are creating for the future generation. AI hasn't matured enough to create its own subjectivity or subjective perspective- subjective decision. This is an enigma if AI can solve the acute problem of ethics and will be able to produce a matured, empathetic AI who will help and support to sustain humanity in this world.

Swagatam Sen: HSBC, Senior Manager, Research and Development, Compliance Analytics

I will emphasise on data witchcraft or the AI which can be used in medical science medicine profession. *2001: Space Odyssey*, it's a science fiction- one of the pioneers about AI. Hall is an elevated machine. It has a philosophical tone. He is asking what happens if AI has the consciousness. Hal comprehended that there are errors in the whole operation inside the spaceship. Hal is almost adopting human consciousness and emotions. At first Hal is trying to convince Dave to run the operation. Dave is not understanding Hal's logic. Hal, as if developing human instinct, can see through the human error and to make the mission successful is killing the scientist and others. Sen (2021), believes that scientists and consumers must trust AIs, create protocols, and can discover the optimal solutions to mitigate ethical issues.

Anusua Singh Roy, Statistician, Queen Margaret University, Edinburgh, UK

Singh Roy talks about the ethical issues related to gender, class, and community perspectives in the kingdom of AI. She is challenging how far Asimov's three laws of robotics are applicable in the modern world taking consideration of profitability and expanse of industrial territories although we sometimes forget to keep in mind about climate change. The considerate admirer of AI has concerns whether industries and science laboratories comprehend robots and AI as slaves of human beings or whether the AI/ robots will control human being in future. She said still we are clueless about the conflict of interests between AIs and human race. Following Turing's arguments (1950) Singh Roy genuinely wishes to know if AI/ Robots dream, watch nightmares, if can they participate in community activities or feel any urge to be in kinship. She is curious to know if the AIs can reproduce their next generation without human intervention. She also stated that still now scientists are in darkness about the real quantification of the AI emotional capital. This lack of knowledge about AI emotions and consciousness may bring the extinction of human beings. AIs can reach a such a stage where they will not be able to control their rage and can kill human beings. In Marvel-movies- AI- Avenger's Age of Ultron- Ultron was initially peacekeeping programme- controlling violence but ultimately became uncontrolled. He gathered so much information that Ultron realised that to maintain peace human beings should be destroyed. He learned from surroundings that human beings are the source of all problem and sins. Scientists must rethink even if the human beings are erroneous and sinful that doesn't mean that they need to be made eroded from the face of the earth. Human race should be controlled otherwise they can destroy other human beings, or the humans must extinct. Sing Roy analyses the situation in a very humane way. It goes in line with how much advanced the robots and the AIs will be, this must be decided otherwise AIs will destroy human beings. The AI admirer suggests that robots and AIs can be filled in with ethical values so that AIs can differentiate good and bad or right and wrongs. AIs without humane qualities will remain as raw intelligence and AIs can become rogues. Scientists then will need to dismantle roguish AIs. Instead of taking down such expensive intelligent helpers, scientists can carefully craft the AIs with ethical and humane values.

HOW FAR CAN AI BE CREATIVE AND USED FOR PROFIT IN THE MAINSTREAM SOCIETY OR FOR INDUSTRIES

In 1980's the computers are excelling their programmers. Even the programme designers are always not able to predict how the AI would work after getting the inputs from the scientist. Chess machines are outperforming their programmers bringing up some brilliant moves that the engineers will never have imagined in their dreams (Sen, 2021). However, this dramatic invention is only a rearrangement of previously available matters. Thus, many AI experts (Sen, 2021) will reflect the whole process of AI as truly creative, free, or artistic. But at the same time other AI scientists will push to perform harder and more complex research to reproduce the true AI with an intellect which can create jealousy in the scientist's mind. It needs to be cultivated if current generation of AIs can feel the alienation, loneliness, or the melancholia of their legendary forefather Frankenstein (Sen, S. 2021).

Intense existential threats (Davies, 2016) from AI comes from misplaced attention on the possibility that such technology could develop consciousness. Recent headlines suggest that respected thinkers such as Bill Gates and Stephen Hawking are concerned about machines becoming self-aware. At some point, a piece of software will 'wake up', prioritize its desires above human beings and intimidating humanity's existence. We must realize that stopping an AI from developing consciousness is not the same as stopping it from developing the capacity to cause terror. It might be that consciousness, or our perception of it, would naturally come with superintelligence. That is, the way we would judge something as conscious or not would be based on our interactions with it. A superintelligent AI would be able to talk to the consumers, create faces that react with emotional expressions just like somebody we will talk to on Skype, or what's app or zoom. Maybe with conscious AIs would care about humanity more than unconscious ones would (Sen, 2021). In his book *Superintelligence* (Oxford University Press, 2011), the Oxford researcher Nick Bostrom (2011) describes many examples of how an AI could be dangerous. One is an AI whose main ambition is to create more AIs. With advanced intelligence and no other values, it might proceed to seek control of world resources in pursuit of this goal, and humanity can be damaged. Another scenario is an AI asked to calculate the infinite digits of pi that uses up all of Earth's matter as computing resources. Perhaps an AI built with more laudable goals, such as decreasing suffering, would try to eliminate humanity for the good of the rest of life on Earth. These hypothetical processes are dangerous not because they are conscious, but because they are built without refined and multifaceted ethics. Instead of getting fanatical about consciousness in AI, scientists should put more effort into programming goals, values, and ethical codes. A global race is under way to develop AI. And there is a chance that the first superintelligent AI with ethical values will be the only one, scientists ever make. So that it can improve itself and start changing the world according to its own values and maintaining safety of the human kingdom

Turing (1950) argued that it must be possible to build a thinking machine since it was possible to build imitations of any small part of a man. He made the distinction between producing accurate electrical models of nerves and replacing them computationally with the available technology of vacuum tube circuits, this follows directly from his paper (1950), and the assumption that the nervous system can be modeled as a computational system. For other parts of the body, he suggests that \television cameras, microphones, loudspeakers", etc., could be used to model the rest of the system. This would be a tremendous undertaking of course." Even so, Turing notes that the so constructed machine would still have no contact with food, sex, sport, and many other things of importance to the human being. Turing concludes that the best domains in which to explore the mechanization of thought are various games, in that they require little contact with the outside world. (Brooks, 1991).

One potential opportunity of AI is in updating intellectual property policy for the AI. The consumers could, for example, reduce patent lengths for the use of digital technologies to ensure that the gains from AI-based innovations are shared broadly. There is a strong case for granting developing countries access to patented technologies: most patents are produced in rich countries and generate most of their income from sales and licenses within rich countries, so innovators would not incur significant losses if developing countries could use their technology for free or with limited royalties before their patents expire in high-income countries (Korinek, Stiglitz, 2021).

ANTICIPATED AI ACTIONS

Aissatou, from a rural village in Guinea, West Africa, couldn't add the essayists' phone numbers to her phone so they won't be able to stay in touch with them. She said, "I can't, because I did not go to school." Lacking a formal education, Aissatou does not read or write in any European or mainstream language. Aissatou's lack of schooling should not keep her from accessing basic services on her phone. The problem, as we see it, is that Aissatou's new phone does not understand her local language. Computer and AI systems should adapt to the ways majority of the people use language. West Africans have spoken their languages for thousands of years, creating rich oral history traditions that have served communities by bringing alive ancestral stories and historical perspectives and passing down knowledge and morals. Computers could easily support this oral tradition. Speech technology, however, does not "speak" any of the 2,000 languages and dialects spoken by Africans. Apple's Siri, Google Assistant, and Amazon's Alexa collectively serve zero African languages. Maybe this can be fixed by propagating a more inclusive language training and input in these AIs (Doumbouya and et al, 2021). In fact, the benefits of mobile technology are not accessible to most of the 700 million illiterate people around the world. Because illiteracy tends to correlate with lack of schooling and thus the inability to speak a common world language, speech technology is not available to those who need it. For them, speech recognition technology could help linking the gap between illiteracy and access to valuable information and services from agricultural information to medical care which can be passed on. Groups with power over technological goods and services tend to speak the same few languages, making it easy to insufficiently consider those with different backgrounds. Speakers of languages such as those widely spoken in West Africa or other poor countries are unfairly underrepresented in research of companies and universities that have historically built-up speech-recognition technics. It is unfortunate that technological systems can fail to provide the same quality of services for diverse consumers, treating many communities as if they do not exist.

Labor-saving advances in AI may undo the gains from globalization and pose new challenges for economic development. The last fifty years have spurred unprecedented economic growth for many developing countries – brought about by the fast adoption of technological advancements – and has led to vastly shared increases in prosperity, lifting many people out of poverty. But there is no guarantee that this process will continue in future. Their (Korinek, Stiglitz, 2021) new working paper on "Artificial Intelligence, Globalization, and Strategies for Economic Development," challenges the long-standing assumption that technological progress will necessarily continue to advance broadly shared prosperity in developing countries. They argue that new developments in (AI) may create the perfect storm to topple technological advancement from broadly shared increases in living standards. Dozens of developing countries have escaped from poverty in recent decades through a strategy of export-led growth, fueled by manufacturing goods produced with their abundant supply of cheap labor or their richness in natural resources (Korinek, Stiglitz, 2021). But AI poses a triple threat to this strategy. "First, AI automates labor, which strips developing countries of their comparative advantage in cheap labor. Second, AI produces more output with fewer natural resources. And for nations that rely on exporting their natural resources to pay for food and other essentials, AI advancement could have deadly consequences. Third, AI operates in a "winner-takes-all" market." (Korinek, Stiglitz, 2021). AI scientists need to address these crucial problems and bring out concrete solutions to make the world fairer for majority of the people.

Metaphors inspired by differences of individual intelligence between humans and AIs will patent new inventions, publish groundbreaking research papers, make money on the stock market, or lead political power blocks. Fast AIs will invent capabilities that futurists commonly predict for human civilizations a millennium in the future, like interstellar travel. (Bolstrom, N., Yudkowsky, E., 2011). Asimov's laws are based on functional morality, which assumes that robots have sufficient agency and cognition to make moral decisions. It is debatable if Asimov's laws distract from capturing the diversity of robotic missions and initiative. Understanding these diversities and complexities is critical for designing the "right" kind of AI. Ironically, Asimov's laws really are human-centric because most of the initiative for safety and efficacy lies in the robot as an autonomous agent. Finally, while perhaps not as entertaining as Asimov's laws, experts can hope the alternative laws of responsible robotics can better communicate to the public about the complex mix of opportunities and challenges of robots in today's world (Murphy and Woods, 2009).

CONCLUSION

If we are serious about developing advanced AI, this is a challenge that we must meet machines are to be placed in a position of being stronger, faster, more trusted, or smarter than humans, then the discipline of machine ethics must entrust itself to seeking human-superior (not just human-equivalent) niceness. Although current AIs offer us few ethical issues that are already present in the design of cars or power plants, the approach of AI algorithms toward more humanlike thought foreshadows speculated complications. Social roles may be filled by AI algorithms, implying new design requirements like transparency and foreseeability. (Bolstrom, N., Yudkowsky, E., (2011). Scientists and consumers of AI may hope that machines will eventually compete with men in all purely intellectual fields. But which are the best ones to start with? Even this is a difficult decision. Many people think that a very abstract activity, like the playing of chess, would be best. It can also be maintained that it is best to provide the machine with the best sense organs that money can buy, and then teach it to understand and speak English. However, we have discussed in the section of **Anticipated AI Actions,** about AIs only with English as a language of communication, will be wicked in nature as majority of the people in the world from the poorer countries do not understand English. It is needed to innovate several different languages which can be put inside the AI so that AIs become universal and more humanitarian in nature (Mc Carthy, 2004).

As AI systems (e.g., Robots, chatbots, and other intelligent agents) are moving from being perceived as a tool to being perceived as autonomous agents and team-mates, an important focus of research and development is comprehending the ethical impact of these systems. What does it mean for an AI system to decide? There should be the moral, societal, and legal consequences of their actions and decisions. It will be difficult to hold AI accountable for their actions and to expect AIs will stop their learning capacities and can be controlled by their creators. Contrary to the frightening images of a dystopic future in media and popular fiction, where AI systems dominate the world and is mostly concerned with warfare, AI is already changing the everyday lives mostly in ways that improve human health, safety, and productivity (Stone et al. 2016). This is the case in domain such as transportation; service robots; healthcare; education; public safety and security; and entertainment.

The researcher challenges the concept of a general welfare. The countries which are benefiting from the AI systems are the minority rich countries who have the capability to invest huge amounts of money to innovate and cultivate such AIs and robots in their everyday lives. To ensure that those dystopic futures do not become reality, these systems must be introduced in ways that build trust and understanding, and respect human and civil rights. The need for ethical considerations in the building of intelligent interactive systems is becoming one of the most significant areas of research in the last few years and has led to several plans both whatever their level of autonomy and social awareness and their ability to learn, Theories, methods, algorithms are needed to integrate societal, legal and moral values into technological developments in AI, at all stages of development - analysis, design, construction, deployment, and evaluation. These frameworks must deal both with the poorer countries and richer countries' autonomic reasoning of the machine about such issues that we consider having ethical impact. AI reasoning should be able to consider societal values, moral and ethical considerations; weigh the respective priorities of values held by different stakeholders in various multicultural contexts; explain its reasoning; and assure transparency. Responsible Artificial Intelligence is about human responsibility for the development of intelligent systems along fundamental human principles and values, to ensure human flourishing and wellbeing in a sustainable world for both poorer and richer countries (Dignum, 2018).

Ten years ago, if scientists mentioned the term "artificial intelligence" in a boardroom there's a good chance you would have been laughed at. For most people it would recall sentient, sci-fi machines such as 2001: A Space Odyssey's HAL or Star Trek's Data. Today it is one of the hottest buzzwords in business and industry. So how has this change come about? Well partly it is due to the Big Data revolution itself (Sen, and Dasgupta, 2021). From healthcare to self-driving cars to predicting the outcome of legal cases are all done by AIs, no one is laughing now! Here too the current research will allege that though no one is laughing at the huge technological development in the rich countries who can afford AIs in their everyday lives powered by AI in their smartphones, assistants like Apple's Siri and Google's Google assistants, self-driving autonomous cars, but people in the poorer countries are unable even to feed themselves properly and are suffering in their digitally divided worlds. Even in countries like UK the latest pandemic has clearly polarized between the rich and the working- class people in terms of the digital and AI usage and consumption (Marr, 2017).

Real anxieties that development of AI which equals or surpasses human brain but has the capacity to work at far higher speeds, could have negative implications for the future of humanity have been voiced, and not just by apocalyptic sci-fi such as The Matrix or The Terminator, but respected scientists like Stephen Hawking. This will further divide the world. Even if AIs don't force human beings to leave the earth or turn human race into living batteries, a less dramatic but still nightmarish scenario is that automation of labour will lead to profound societal change perhaps for the better, or perhaps for the worse. This comprehensible concern has led to doubting by several tech titans including Google, IBM, Microsoft, Facebook, and Amazon, of the partnership in AI. We need to trust that these groups will research and advocate for ethical implementations of AI, and to set guidelines for future research and deployment of robots and AI. The question arises here that whether these big AI giants will bring in the whole spectrum of problems like racial, gender, equality, culture, societal, and poverty divides in the kingdom of AI. If these crucial and important problems are not sorted and mitigated with sustainable solutions the world of AI will be completely meaningless.

The artificial intelligence (AI) and robotics communities face an important ethical decision: whether to support or oppose the development of lethal autonomous weapons systems (Singh Roy, 2021, Russel, 2015). There are ethical issues involved when efforts are made to apply normative ethical principles on non-organic intelligence like AI or consciousness uploads (human brain being transformed into inorganic computers which can imitate the original brain personhood). When human consciousness is uploaded onto a fast computer, the principle of subjective rate of time, for example, could be incompatible with human ethics. Many dignitaries like Stephen Hawking, Steve Wozniak, and the figureheads of AI at Facebook and Google, Yann LeCun, and Demis Hassabis have signed a petition of warning of a ''military artificial intelligence arms race'' and calling for a ban on dangerous weapons and military conflicts (Kadircan, 2019). The research, in conclusion, will like to know how AI can act ethically while making endorsements to humans and express their ethical judgements effectively. These are the current foci of ethical human-AI interaction research. In addition, AI engineers and experts need to engage more with the ethics and decision-making scientist communities. Since such AI technologies as autonomous vehicles, and autonomous weapons, and cryptocurrencies are becoming a reality and affecting societies, a global and unified AI regulatory framework needs to be established as soon as possible to address the ethical issues by drawing on interdisciplinary expertise (Goldsmith and Burton, 2017).

REFERENCES

Allan Turing: Life and Legacy of a Great Thinker. (n.d.). https://link.springer.com/chapter/10.1007/978-3-662-05642-4_13

Allardice, L. (2021). *Interview: Kazin Ishiguro: AI, gene-editing, big data… I worry we are not in control of these things anymore.* The Guardian. https://www.theguardian.com/books/2021/feb/20/kazuo-ishiguro-klara-and-the-sun-interview?fbclid=IwAR0ExKc5Jda-6TEWM-l-zJzBGYmFgpw0N-DWVrlzPfIl6Ehw3Dh1WPIaRMI

Anderson, M. R. (2017). *After 75 Years, Isaac Asimov's Three Laws of Robotics Need Updating.* The Conversation.

Anderson, S. L. (2007). *Asimov's "Three Laws of Robotics" and Machine Metaethics. Artificial Intelligence and Society, 22.*

Asimov, I. (1950). *I, Robot.* Del Rey.

Asimov, I. (1957). *The Naked Sun.* Doubleday.

Asimov, I. (1990). The Laws of Robotics. In Robot Visions. Academic Press.

Asimov, I. (1991). *The Lord's Apprentice. In The Ultimate Frankenstein.* Manhanset House.

Asimov, I. (n.d.). *Learn about Asimov's Three Laws of Robotics.* Britannica Publishing.

Bell, P. (2004). Monster or Machine? *Nature.*

Blank, D. (2006). *Robotics and Asimov's Three Laws. In The Frankenstein Complex and Asimov's Three Laws.* Association of the Advancement of Artificial Intelligence.

Blum, P. R., (2016). Robots, Slaves, and the Paradox of the Human Condition. In *Isaac Asimov's Robot Stories.* Czech Science Foundation at the project Between Renaissance and Baroque Philosophy and Knowledge of the Czech Lands within the Wider European Context.

Bolstrom, N., & Yudkowsky, E. (2011). *The Ethics of Artificial Intelligence.* Cambridge University Press.

Brantinger, P. (1980). The Gothic Origins of Science Fiction. *NOVEL: A Forum on Fiction, 14*(1), 30–43.

Brooks, R. A. (1991). *Intelligence without Reason.* Massachusetts Institute of Technology Artificial Intelligence Laboratory.

Copeland, B. J., & Produfoot, D. (2004). *The Computer, Artificial Intelligence, and the Turing Test. In Alan Turing: Life and Legacy of a Great Thinker.* Springer.

Dargis, M. (2015). Review: In 'Ex Machina', a Mogul Fashions the Droid of his dreams. *The New York Times.* https://www.nytimes.com/2015/04/10/movies/review-in-ex-machina-a-mogul-fashions-the-droid-of-his-dreams.html

Davies, J., (2016). Program good ethics into artificial intelligence. *Nature, 538,* 291.

Deman, J. (2017). Star Wars is colonial fantasy: How our future imaginings are limited by our past. *The Conversation.*

Dignum, V., (2018). Ethics in artificial Intelligence: Introduction to the Special Issue. *Nature, Ethics and Information Technology, 20,* 1-3.

Doumbouya, M., Einstein, L., & Piech, C. (2020). Why AI Needs to be able to understand all the World's languages: The benefits of mobile technology are not accessible to most of the world's 700 million illiterate people. *Scientific American.* https://www.scientificamerican.com/article/why-ai-needs-to-be-able-to-understand-all-the-worlds-languages/?fbclid=IwAR3sA7mY-yDukaLdu0dC9RKCzZMEdtub-dG5WoGjmk8hc4pMSY6Fdzkbt7No

Forest, A. (1998). Cog, a Humanoid Robot, and The Question of The Image of God. *Zygon: Journal of Religion and Science, 33,* 91-111.

Geraci, R. M. (2007). Robots and the Sacred in Science Fiction: Theological Implications of AI. *Zygon, 42,* No-4.

Goldsmith, J., & Burton, E. (2017). Why Teaching Artificial Intelligence Practitioners Is Important. *Proceedings of the AAAI Conference on Artificial Intelligence,* 31(1), 4836-4840.

Haugland, J. (1989). *Artificial Intelligence: The Very Idea.* The Massachusetts Institute of Technology.

Huang, M., Rust, R.T., (2018). Artificial Intelligence in Service. *Journal of Service Research, 2*(2), 155-172.

Information Desk. (2021). *Ritwik Ghatak's War between 'Man and Machine.* Get Bengal, Thinking Positive.

Ishiguro, K. (2021). *Klara and the Sun.* Faber and Faber.

Jerz, D. G. (2002). R.U.R. (Rossum's Universal Robots). Dover.

Joy, B. (2000). *Why the future doesn't need us.* Wired.

Kadircan, H. K. (2019). Medical Ethics: Consideration on Artificial Intelligence. *Journal of Clinical Neuroscience.*

Kevin, W. J. (2000). *Co-founder of Sun Microsystem-expressed in a 2000 Wired Magazine article.* Academic Press.

Klass, M. (1983). The Artificial Alien: Transformations of the Robot in Science Fiction. *Annals of the American Academy of Political and Social Science,* 171-79.

Korinek, A., & Stiglitz, J. (2021). *Artificial Intelligence Could Mean Large Increase in Prosperity- But only for a Privileged Few.* https://www.ineteconomics.org/perspectives/blog/artificial-intelligence-could-mean-technological-advancement-but-only-for-a-privileged-few?fbclid=IwAR0qxVBh0NYHEJLVJCo C3bynkESnLFgfn8QFZcIE63kGu06TIjMEbWDHadM

Kurzweil, R. (1999). *The Age of Spiritual Machines.* Viking Adult.

Kurzweil, R. (2005). *The Singularity Is Near: When Humans Transcend Biology.* Viking Books.

Manohlia, D. (2015). Review: 'Ex Machina', a Mogul Fashions the Droid of his Dreams. *The New York Times*.

Marr, B. (2017). The Complete Beginners' Guide to Artificial Intelligence. *Forbes*.

McCarthy, J. (1990). *What is AI? Basic Questions; Artificial Intelligence, Logic and Formalizing Common Sense*. Computer Science Department, Stanford University.

McCauley, L. (2007). *The Frankenstein Complex and Asimov's Three Laws*. Association of the Advancement of Artificial Intelligence.

McCauley, L. (2007). *Countering the Frankenstein Complex*. American Association for Artificial Intelligence. https://www.openculture.com/2019/03/isaac-asimov-predicts-the-future-of-civilization.html

Miller, G. (2018). *Why Altered Carbon is not about the future-nor is any other science fiction*. The Conversation.

Murphy, R. R., & Woods, D. D. (2009). *Beyond Asimov: The Three Laws of Responsible Robotics, Institute for Human and Machine Cognition*. IEEE Computer Society.

Nofz, M.P., & Vendy, P. (2002). When Computers Say It with Feeling: Communication and Synthetic Emotions in Kubrick's 2001: A Space Odyssey. *Journal of Communication Inquiry*, 25-45.

Overbye, D. (2018). 2001: A Space Odyssey' Is Still the 'Ultimate Trip'. *The New York Times*. https://www.nytimes.com/2018/05/10/science/2001-a-space-odyssey-kubrick.html

Pope, R. I. (2003). *Kubrick's Crypt, a Derrida/Deluze Monster, in 2001: A Space Odyssey*. Edinburgh University Press Journals.

Prescott, J., (2016). Why watching Westworld's robots should make us question ourselves. *The Conversation*.

Russel, S. (2015). Ethics of Artificial Intelligence. *Nature*, 415-418.

Shelley, M. (1818). *Frankenstein or The Modern Prometheus*. Harding, Mavor and Jones.

Sikdar, S. (2018). Artificial Intelligence, its impact on innovation, and the Google effect. *Clean Technologies and Environmental Policy*, 20, No-1–No-2.

Slocombe, W. (2016). What science fiction tells us about our trouble with Artificial Intelligence, *The Conversation*.

Sloman, A. (2006). *Why Asimov's three laws of robotics are unethical*. Retrieved June 9, 2006, URL: https://www.cs.bham.ac.uk/research/projects/cogaff/misc/asimov-three-laws.html

Stahl, B. C. (2021). Organisational responses to the ethical issues of AI. *AI & Society*.

Thomsen, C. W. (1982). Robot Ethics and Robot Parody: Remarks on Isaac Asimov's *I, Robot* and Some Critical Essays and Short Stories by Stanislaw Lem. In T. P. Dunn & R. D. Erlich (Eds.), *The Mechanical God: Machines in Science Fiction* (pp. 19–26). Greenwood.

Trent, G. (2012). *The Rebirth of Mankind Homo Evolutis*. PDXdzyn.

Turing, A. M. (1950). Computing Machinery and Intelligence. *Mind*, *49*, 433–460.

Warwick, K. (2002). *I, Cyborg*. Century.

Yu, H., Shen, Z., & Miao, C. (2018). Building Ethics into Artificial Intelligence, *Computer Science, Artificial Intelligence*. Cornell University. https://arxiv.org/abs/1812.02953

KEY TERMS AND DEFINITIONS

AI Ethics: AI ethics will give an AI consciousness and intelligence to resolve conflicts, crisis, and problems which will ultimately benefit humanity involving both philosophical and technical issues. The AI should be programmed in such a way that the system can eradicate accidents and disasters as much as possible. It must deal with issues like human welfare, justice for most of the people, climate change, and defending the basic rights of human beings.

Artificial Intelligence: It is the science and engineering of constructing intelligent machines, especially intelligent computer programs. It is related to the similar task of using computers to understand human intelligence, but AI does not have to confine itself to methods that are biologically observable. They can very easily solve difficult and complex mathematical problems, e.g., they can play chess at a very high level or can drive a motor car on its own under human supervision.

Asimov's Three Laws: 1) A robot may not injure a human being or, through inaction, allow a human being to come to harm. 2) A robot must obey the orders given it by human beings except where such orders would conflict with the First Law. 3) A robot must protect its own existence if such protection does not conflict with the First or Second Laws.

Robots: The complex machines performing a program while detecting and overcoming problems and acting towards fulfillment of the human instructions—all this makes a perfect robot. Karel Čapek, who coined the term 'robot' for machines replace human workers, related robots with slaves. In his play *Rossum's Universal Robots* (R.U.R.; 1920) he suggested that robots could replace human slave labor.

Turing's Test: In 1950 Alan Turing proposed an important condition for considering a machine to be intelligent. He emphasised that if the machines could successfully pass a test that it is a human to a knowledgeable observer then we certainly should consider it intelligent.

Chapter 29
Towards Ethical Neuromarketing 2.0 Based on Artificial Intelligence

Elodie Attié

iD https://orcid.org/0000-0003-3400-8927

Capgemini Engineering, France

Solène Le Bars

Altran Lab, France

Ilhem Quenel

Capgemini Engineering, France

ABSTRACT

Eighty percent of consumer behaviors and purchases rely on subconscious processes. The use of neuro-marketing tools to study consumer behavior is not clear, notably regarding its practices and intentions toward consumers. This chapter aims to understand how neuromarketing can explain consumer behavior thanks to Neuromarketing 2.0 tools, how companies can manage the collected data in a responsible way and build a neuroethical charter to regulate the way companies use it. Most companies choose to not communicate about it when they use neuromarketing tools, and therefore, this chapter aims to pave the way towards solutions and recommendations and democratize its use by making Neuromarketing 2.0 more responsible and ethical.

INTRODUCTION

Between 80 and 97% of new product launches on the market fail from a lack of understanding of the market challenges and consumer behavior and needs (Mediamarketing, 2017). Neuromarketing is an area of marketing that uses neuroscience frameworks and technics, such as psychophysics or brain imaging, in order to further understand these underlying processes, and to influence consumer behaviors (Droulers

DOI: 10.4018/978-1-7998-6985-6.ch029

& Roullet, 2010; Morin, 2011; Nilashi et al., 2020). One of the objectives of neuromarketing is to adapt the methods and theories from neuroscience and artificial intelligence (AI) research with behavioral theories, and develop experimental designs to better understand consumer behavior and decision-making processes (Plassmann et al. 2015). Cognitive neuroscience examines how the central nervous system generates psychological processes that typically come into play when purchasing a product, such as perceptions, feelings, memory, intentions, judgment, planning, decision-making, action, behavior, etc. Therefore, neuromarketing is of prime interest for managers, in order to get an overview of the current market and its challenges. Multinational companies such as Coca Cola, McDonald's, Google, Facebook, Apple, Ebay, to name a few, have used, or use, neuromarketing tools to refine their marketing strategies, increase the frequency rate and consequent sales to ensure profits (Bayle-Tourtoulou & Badoc, 2020). However, if neuromarketing attracts managers by its opportunities and benefits, most companies that use neuromarketing tools still hide this information, stating confidential intellectual property (de Sousa, 2018). On one side, companies can increase sales and profits whereas on the other side, consumers can get better products and services, and access to better-targeted information about those products and services (Wieckowski, 2019). Neuromarketing 2.0 uses tools driven by AI, such as facial and movement coding. With neuromarketing and AI, marketing tools have become more efficient. Thus, the ethical issues raised regarding neuromarketing and AI are similar to the ones raised regarding advertising and marketing in general. The use of neuromarketing 2.0 with AI tools seems to be a wise response to address complex ethical problems, notably because they are innovative, non-invasive and they do not rely on medical data collection. Therefore, neuromarketing 2.0 tools include algorithms that are capable of collecting then interpreting data, in order to mimic cognitive decisions and predict future behaviors. For this reason, researchers and consumers may perceive neuromarketing as an immoral deviation of neuroscience, and this chapter aims at proposing an ethical way of using neuromarketing 2.0 tools. Therefore, we aim to define a neuroethical charter to protect consumers' personal data and regulate the use of neuromarketing. The main goals of the proposed chapter are the following:

1. To better understand and explain consumer behavior through conscious and automatic processes;
2. To discuss which neuromarketing 2.0 tools could be used in market research as non-intrusive and high human valued technologies;
3. To understand and change the negative perception of neuromarketing by making it more relevant, ethical and transparent to managers and consumers;
4. To build a neuroethical charter to regulate the way companies use neuromarketing through AI tools.

BACKGROUND

Marketing Research: Understanding Consumer Behavior

Researchers describe the notion of subconscious as a system or process existing in consumers' brain, and strongly determined by the environment that emit signals requiring attention, and engender emotions and memory (Guelfand, 2013). Thanks to neuromarketing, marketers can observe consumer behavior through cognitive processes such as attention, emotions and memory which all influence consumer perceptions toward the brand, and then can predict consumer behavior. Firstly, the literature distinguishes several types of attention (i.e., the ability to focus consciously or subconsciously on specific things in the presence of others; Chou et al., 2010) that neuromarketing can analyze (see Figure 1). Visual attention implies an alpha activity in the occipital region. Marketers can increase consumers' attention with greater color contrasts on packaging in order to differentiate from their competitors (Burke & Leykin, 2014; Stoll et al., 2008).

Figure 1. Types of consumer attention

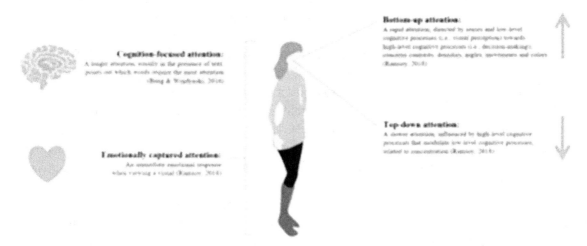

Figure 1 describes four types of attention that marketers can observe with neuromarketing 2.0 tools, notably. Eye tracking can measure the bottom-up and top-down attention. For example, Google used the technology of eye tracking to measure the influence of users' attention and emotional arousal (with pupil dilatation) while looking at new advertising formats, comparing the efficacy of overlay formats versus banners (O'Reilly, 2013). Based on this experimentation, Google could recommend to its clients that overlay formats increase attention and emotional involvement. Moreover, facial coding can analyze the emotionally captured attention. Coca Cola used facial coding to analyze quantitative ad performances (Bayle-Tourtoulou & Badoc, 2020; Dooley, 2013). To do this, Coca cola recorded consumers' facial muscles movements while they were watching their advertisings, in order to capture, analyze and understand real time emotional and cognitive states of mind induced (Dooley, 2013). Both eye tracking and facial coding can determine the cognition-focused attention.

Secondly, emotions play an essential role in consumer decision-making (Corcos & Pannequin, 2013). Generally, consumers use more emotions than rationality during a decision-making process (Murray, 2013). Emotions are characterized by an observable physical state, which can be translated into sensations (Solomon, 2017), and then into behaviors (Ciccarelli & Meyer, 2006). The type of emotion modulates specific alpha rhythms in the frontal cortex (Morris et al., 2001). Thus, a higher neuronal activity in the left frontal alpha activity implies negative emotions whereas a higher neuronal activity in the right frontal activity implies positive emotions (Vecchiato et al., 2011). Marketers usually consider two types of emotions:

1. Basic emotions: positive-negative feelings (i.e., pleasure/displeasure) associated with low to high levels of excitement (Russell et al., 1989);

2.   Consumption emotions: feelings linked to purchasing decisions and consumption experiences (Westbrook & Oliver, 1991).

Thirdly, memory expresses the effects of previous experiences embedded in present behaviors (Roediger, 1990). The cognitive and affective information present in advertising can create a mental representation that enhance long-term memory (Plassmann et al., 2015). This process of retention of the information and events takes places in the left frontal region. There is a diminution of the alpha activity which reflects the encoding phase in long-term memory (Langleben et al., 2009; Rossiter et al., 2001).

Marketing Evolution: From Marketing Research to Neuromarketing 2.0

Companies can use marketing research tools to adjust a marketing mix strategy, target their consumers, reformulate their offer and sales strategies, and generate new product concepts to increase business profits, among other marketing challenges (Guelfand, 2013). Traditional marketing research attempts to catch consumers' intentions and behaviors, by directly asking consumers how they perceive a brand, product or service. Consumers translate their unconscious thoughts into language, sometimes allowing brands to grasp subconscious intentions (Guelfand, 2013). However, traditional market research remains subjective and entails many biases due to confounding factors such as social desirability or environmental influence (Legardinier, 2013). Neuromarketing should reduce the uncertainty to understand and explain consumer behavior (Harrell, 2019). In order to limit these biases, neuromarketing employs neuroscience tools to get physiological or alternative behavioral measures and capture consumers' subconscious response to marketing strategies (Oullier, 2012) (see Figure 2).

Figure 2 shows that neuromarketing techniques can evaluate:

1.   Brain electrical and chemical modifications, thanks to traditional medical tools like fMRI (functional magnetic resonance imaging), EEG (electroencephalogram), or MEG (magnetoencephalography);
2.   Physiological activities, with other traditional medical tools like ECG (electrocardiograms), GSR (galvanic skin responses), or facial electromyograms, and AI tools like eye tracking and facial coding;
3.   Behaviors and attitudes, with the implicit response test, response times, and indoor GPS.

For example, McDonald's used fMRI, with a neuromarketing company based in London called Neuro Sense, to measure the brain activation of the reward circuit (i.e., the neural system responsible for motivation, desire and positive reinforcement) with participants who were watching their ads and measure their effectiveness (Bayle-Tourtoulou & Badoc, 2020).

SETTING THE STAGE

Understanding how the Brain Influences Consumer Behaviors Through Neuromarketing Lens

Each region of the brain that activates implies specific functions and in turn specific behaviors. The nucleus accumbens is the region of positive emotions that activates when consumers perceive advan-

Figure 2. Consumer indicators and neuromarketing tools

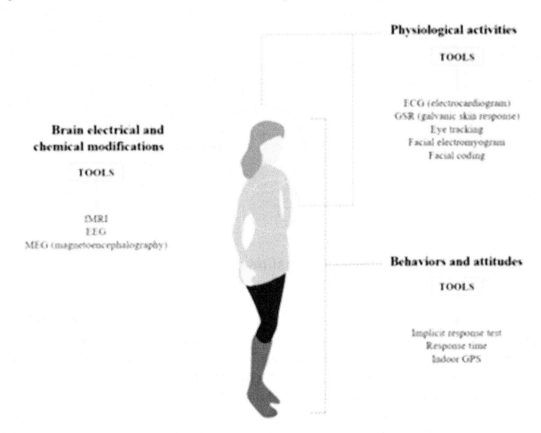

tages and gains –explaining impulsive purchases for example (Corcos & Pannequin, 2013; Knutson et al., 2007). However, when consumers perceive expensive prices, the insula activates, then frontal areas activate, in order to use rationality and judgment –the purchase decision is slower and more cautious (Corcos & Pannequin, 2013; Knutson et al., 2007). The medial prefrontal cortex evaluates the trade-off between the advantages of the product or service –perceived through the nucleus accumbens– and the consequences of the choice –perceived through the insula (Knutson et al., 2007). Thus, companies can measure unexpected feelings toward a product or service, and predict behaviors according to the activation of different brain areas (Damasio, 1994; Bechara et al., 1997; Knutson et al., 2007). For example, watching an attractive advertising or product induces the activation of a more specific brain area involved in the reward circuitry: the nucleus accumbens (Knutson et al., 2007) –linked to the anticipation of pleasure (Carter et al., 2009). In contrast, the perception of a high price can curb the product purchase and this phenomenon results from another brain area, the insula –linked to the anticipation of pain (Knutson et al., 2007). Figure 3 presents the differentiation between the insula and nucleus accumbens regions of the brain.

Figure 3. Regions of the brain activated with positive and negative emotions

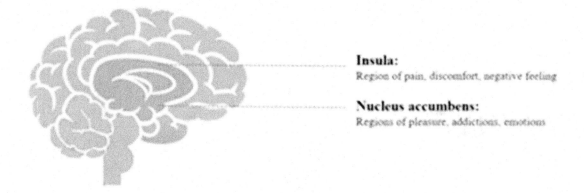

How Neuromarketing can Influence Consumer Behaviors and Intentions to Purchase

Companies usually use fMRI to study the influence of packaging, ads, logos, or slogans on the brain (Bayle-Tourtoulou & Badoc, 2020). Neuromarketing thus enables to redefine packaging and product conception and advertising, and thus, promote specific behaviors (Harrell, 2019). Neuromarketing also embraces computational models of decision-making, big data and AI algorithms to better predict consumers' behaviors, becoming a neuromarketing 2.0 (Hegazy, 2019; Stoicescu, 2016). Indeed, big data and AI tools allow companies to survey and select relevant information from their consumer target, apply analytical tools, build solutions from market predictions, and find relationships between factors that may influence consumer behavior (Phillips-Wren, 2012). Neuromarketing 2.0 can lead companies through AI techniques in order to study consumers' subconscious thoughts, which represent inaccessible contents and knowledge about decision-making and actions (Guelfand, 2013). Consumer behavior evolves with the activity of neuromodulators –brain hormones such as testosterone, cortisol and oxytocin– and neurotransmitters –chemical messengers. For example, dosing artificial testosterone to men increases their preference for higher social status and luxury brands, compared to brands of similar perceived quality but synonyms of lower perceived social status (Nave et al., 2018). Thus, neuromarketing tools allow managers to understand how to activate the right lever in consumers' brains to create an action toward the brand, products and services (de Sousa, 2018). Researchers scanned consumers' brains while they tasted three glasses of wines with three different prices: even though the glasses contained the same wine, each glass of wine activated a different area in consumers' brains, highlighting a preference for the most expensive wine (Schmidt et al., 2017). Moreover, subliminal advertising (i.e., presenting a particular stimulus below the threshold of conscious perception) constitutes a representative example of how neuromarketing can use cognitive neuroscience methods (Smarandescu & Shimp, 2015; Sofi et al., 2018). Brands can display a subliminal message (i.e., word, image, emoji, logo or jingle) to influence intentions and behaviors toward the brand (Hsu et al., 2020; Smarandescu & Shimp, 2015; Sofi et al., 2018). This technique influences consumers' perceptions and cognition, at an automatic level, and interferes with consumers' endogenous goals and desires regarding a product or behavior. However, there is no evidence that subliminal advertising is effective in real market conditions.

CASE DESCRIPTION

Neuromarketing 2.0: Technology Components and Concerns

Technology components

According to the literature, neuromarketing presents some advantages. The main drivers for neuromarketing 2.0 adoption are economic, such as cost and time reduction, an improved performance, greater customer satisfaction, and more accurate forecasting and decision-making (Cubric, 2020). AI can now exceed 87% of sensitivity, 91% of specificity and 96% of predictions, thus offering security, efficiency and equity (Abràmoff et al., 2020). If neuromarketing techniques are well used, the data can bring out a huge competitive advantage to companies, defining predictive models based on feeling detection for example (de Bruyn et al., 2020). Specifically, Figure 4 presents the benefits and risks of neuromarketing 2.0 tools that seem to be the most relevant to this research, such as gestural coding, facial coding, vocal coding, eye tracking and pupil tracking.

Figure 4. Neuromarketing 2.0 techniques

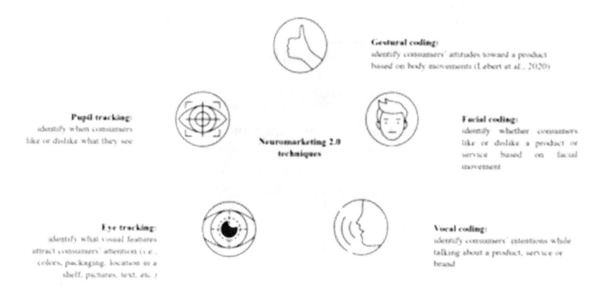

All these neuromarketing 2.0 techniques (Figure 4) enable marketers to predict behaviors and intentions to purchase. AI can identify key points from facial images based on facial activities and muscles, and learn the visual patterns of facial movements according to emotional labels (Calvo & D'Mello, 2010). Moreover, there are important relationships between voice parameters and emotions or behaviors (Banse & Scherer, 1996; Johnstone & Scherer, 2000). Regarding the eye tracking method, there are correlations between the time spent looking at the advertising and preferences (Maughan et al., 2007; Orquin & Loose, 2013). Finally, the pupil size increases during both emotionally negative and positive stimuli when compared to neutral stimuli (Partala & Surakka, 2003).

Technology Concerns

The main technology issues with neuromarketing 2.0 concern its technical (i.e., data training and data management) and social features (i.e., dependence on technology, technology trust) (Cubric, 2020). Firstly, there is a significant cost of implementation and maintenance, and if necessary, of support infrastructures: the creation of algorithms able to capture, explain and predict behaviors requires significant costs linked to the specific machines implied and people to hire. Maintenance also involves additional costs. Secondly, neuromarketing 2.0 has a limited applicability to specific issues: the relationships highlighted are often correlational rather than causal (Ma & Sun, 2020). This lack of causal capacity makes predictions unstable when change occurs, limiting their use in marketing (Ma & Sun, 2020). For example, one of the limits of eye tracking is the lack of knowledge to understand why consumers look at a particular spot on an advertising (Lever et al., 2019). Thirdly, technology itself does not have emotions and moral values. Neuromarketing 2.0 executes its program and cannot judge what is right or wrong like humans do. Yet, human bias also imply technology bias (Cubric, 2020). Indeed, people can be biased and judgmental, leading to biased and judgmental technologies that try to explain consumer behavior (de Bruyn et al., 2020). Therefore, cybersecurity is an important asset of AI to ensure a safe and positive evolution of technology in society (Lin et al., 2011). Finally, despite some obvious benefits of using neuromarketing 2.0 to develop efficient marketing strategies, this technique also raises some important ethical questions. First, neuroimaging technics can be invasive (Oullier, 2012) –except for GSR, eye tracking, or response time measurement– and even though some neuromarketing technics are non-invasive, their safety and reliability still represent ethical issues (Claeys & Vialatte, 2012). In France, only scientific and medical research can use fMRI and other hospital scanners. However, other countries like United Kingdom, Belgium or the United States are more open about the development and use of neuromarketing.

Neuromarketing 2.0: Consumer Privacy Concerns

Neuromarketing 2.0 presents security and ethical issues. The way the technology tracks and collects personal data can be intrusive, arousing privacy concerns (Awad & Krishnan, 2006; Hong & Thong, 2013; Phelps et al., 2001). Privacy concerns is the extent to which consumers are concerned about the flow of their information through technologies (Phelps et al., 2000). More specifically, consumers create beliefs and trust toward the use of the technology and privacy management (Chaudhuri & Holbrook, 2001; Phelps et al., 2000; Shin, 2010). For consumers, their purchases can be known from companies but their thoughts and feelings should remain private to them (Wieckowski, 2019). Consumers might perceive companies that use neuromarketing tools as untrustworthy since they can invade their private thoughts and feelings, sometimes leading to consumer backlash against the brand (Wieckowski, 2019). Therefore, regardless of the neuromarketing and market research methodology used (i.e., neuroscience tools, data mining based on activity and purchase history, consumer surveys, etc.), consumers may perceive reticence due to privacy concerns and a violation of their right to privacy (Wieckowski, 2019). However, the benefits of neuromarketing 2.0 (i.e., personalization of products and services) can compensate the loss of privacy (Xu et al., 2011). Moreover, there are few ethical reviews of neuromarketing 2.0, mainly due to the novelty and complexity of this technique (Abràmoff et al., 2020). Thus, companies have to collect data according to each country's regulatory framework, in a way that is transparent regarding the purpose and the extent of use of the data (Abràmoff et al., 2020). In Europe, since May 2018, a recent law called GDPR (General Data Protection Regulation) regulates the use of data and ensures the protection of data, with a unified set of rules for all organizations that process personal data coming from Europe. The GDPR improves data management by giving more visibility and control to European citizens over the management of their data (i.e., what data, what purpose, how long). If European organizations, or worldwide organizations collecting European data, do not follow this regulation, they risk sanctions, such as 4% of their annual worldwide turnover or 20 million euros (the greater of the two), and additional damages to the parties concerned (see cnil.fr website for updates).

Neuromarketing 2.0: Management and Organizational Concerns

When neuromarketing 2.0 tools are well designed and used, it can deepen the understanding of consumers and business, point out coming issues, and suggest automated decision support (Ma & Sun, 2020). Therefore, the cooperation between humans and technology predicts important changes in organizations, with an evolution of organizational behaviors, structures, workflows, ethics and work environments (Demir et al., 2019). It becomes relevant to focus on the management, organizational and social aspects of neuromarketing 2.0, such as the factors of acceptance (Cubric, 2020), the need for education and training, and psychological, social and ethical issues, among other issues (Demir et al., 2019). According to Lin et al. (2011), the main management challenges and recommendations imply:

1. **Performance:** Companies must be able to create a neuromarketing 2.0 that can do minimal distinctions in gestures or speech and take into account relevant and salient safety information;
2. **Ethical regulation:** Companies should define a code of ethics to regulate neuromarketing 2.0. and be clear about their rights and responsibilities, as well as consumers';
3. **A budget:** Neuromarketing 2.0 implies an economic impact of AI tools and robotics, and companies should be able to estimate its expected costs and benefits on the long-term.

Even though the development of technologies can threatens the survival of certain jobs, people remain irreplaceable in the assessment of subjective and qualitative issues (i.e., intuitive capacities, norms, intangible interests and other complex social and contextual factors like decision-making) (Demir et al., 2019; Jarrahi, 2018). Thus, neuromarketing 2.0 can extend human capabilities rather than replace human decision-making (Jarrahi, 2018).

CURRENT CHALLENGES

Data Management: How to Manage Meaningful Information

Neuromarketing 2.0 imply a collection and management of all kinds of data (i.e., pupil dilatation, facial expressions, different position in a store, etc.). There should be a strategic and structured vision of the collected data. Data management can increase the productivity and overall performance of the company thanks to the quality of data, compliance with requirements agreed by the user, efficiency gains, access and security of the data (Soler et al., 2016). Data management implies standards and tools, ensuring the accessibility, reliability and security of data. Therefore, data management requires technical expertise regarding the data programming and quality, and data transmission, extraction and use –implying time and money to train employees to learn how to manage the data (Olajide, 2019). The main goal of data management is to transform data into valuable information for business and strategies. Data management teams intervene at the following levels:

1. **Data quality:** Data quality is the basis of data management by ensuring accuracy, consistency, and traceability. Non-quality data represent a significant risk and additional cost for the company since incorrect or not updated data can distort customer knowledge and decrease the reactivity of decisions. Thus, companies should have clear objectives, good material and know how to analyze the data. For example, studying the attention process of consumers requires a good eye tracking material and people able to analyze this type of data. Moreover, companies should constantly collect and update the data in order to keep up with the evolution of data innovations. With data quality, neuromarketing can, and should, guide marketers and managers in decision-making and action, through anticipation, predictions and smart recommendations.

2. **Data security:** According to the collected data, security can become a very important issue. Indeed, neuromarketing 2.0 can sometimes track very personal data (i.e., images or videos of faces and body movements) that consumers do not want to spread. Therefore, it is important for them to know how the collected data are stored and used.

3. **Data repository:** Data management implies the need of a master data management. Master data represents the strategic information that marketers need to collect to understand consumer perceptions. It could be information about customers, products, resources, market challenges, etc.

4. **Compliance with legal obligations:** Legal obligations mainly come from the GDPR to encourages an ethical use and traceability of the data within companies, through five principles:
   - *Accountability*: the obligation to implement internal mechanisms and procedures to demonstrate the compliance with data protection rules;
   - *Data protection by design*: the implementation of technical and organizational measures, at the earliest stages of the design of the processing operations, to protect privacy by following data protection principles –it usually implies the use of anonymization (i.e., replacing personal identifiable material with artificial identifiers) and the use of encryption (i.e., encoding messages so that only those authorized can access the data);
   - *Data protection by default*: the process of ensuring the highest privacy protection –it implies settings like a limited accessibility, a short period storage, and only the data necessary for companies' use is processed;
   - *Data protection officer*: the data protection officer is responsible for the protection and compliance of the data –leading to the development of new jobs in the data sector;
   - *Data impact assessment*: a detailed description of the processing (i.e., technical and operational aspects), a legal assessment of the fundamental principles and rights (i.e., purpose, what data, retention periods, information and rights of individuals), and a technical study of data security risks (i.e., confidentiality, integrity and availability).

5. **Infrastructures:** The main challenge of companies is to optimize neuromarketing infrastructures. Data management structures must meet both the accessibility needs of neuromarketing and business, as well as the regulations and security constraints.

Neuroethics: How to use Neuromarketing 2.0

Consumers may perceive some doubts and fears about neuromarketing intentions and techniques (Attié et al., 2021). Consumers perceive neuromarketing as a way to influence them, through persuasion and manipulation, with few concerns about the benefits for consumers and data protection (Flores et al., 2014). Yet, some ethical principles in neuromarketing must be followed, such as asking for participants' consent regarding the use of the collected data –which do not differentiate much from traditional marketing (Wieckowski, 2019). Neuromarketing 2.0 leads to technologies that have not reached yet all the capabilities of the human brain when it comes to detect emotions, be empathetic, have an intuition; its values and morality depends on how people decide to build it (Baillargeon, 2018). Thus, one challenge is to understand the impact of AI on neuromarketing, in order to highlight the best practices and benefits for researchers, managers and consumers. A way to face ethical issues due to neuromarketing could be to create and adopt an ethical and responsible way of treating the data (Sultana & Nangunoori, 2008). For this reason, this chapter aims to build a neuroethic charter to respond to deontology aspects raised by the use of AI tools in neuromarketing 2.0. Neuroethics focus on both theoretical and practical aspects of implementing AI into neuromarketing challenges since it examines how the knowledge of the brain can explain consumers' identity, consciousness and intentions (Evers, 2014). The theoretical foundations of neuroethics should enable companies to address ethical challenges linked to neuromarketing (Evers, 2014).

SOLUTIONS AND RECOMMENDATIONS

Ethics and Transparency: Improving the Acceptance of Neuromarketing 2.0

Neuromarketing enables to observe consumers' conscious thinking and identify automatic reactions. By combining both neuromarketing and traditional marketing research methods, companies show an interest to understand and invest in consumers to respond to their needs (Sultana & Nangunoori, 2008). However, employees and consumers may perceive neuromarketing as immoral due to this perception of finding ways to manipulate consumers (Charmettant, 2018). Managers could thus change the way consumers perceive neuromarketing and transform its dark sides into a clarified explanation of this marketing tool, through communication, transparency, and clear guidelines and infrastructures –both internally and externally (Attié et al., 2021; Courbet & Benoit, 2013). Thus, communication should demonstrate the benefits of neuromarketing techniques, as some research has shown its futility (Sultana & Nangunoori, 2008). Indeed, explaining neuromarketing processes and strategies, and how they influence consumers, could mitigate the unconscious effects and doubts (Courbet & Benoit, 2013). Moreover, consumers expect higher prices if companies use neuromarketing tools since it should increase companies' budgets in marketing (Attié et al., 2021). Yet, higher prices are not a main brake (Burke & Leykin, 2014) if it is justified by higher quality, positive innovative brand image, positive emotions (Berger & Milkman, 2012), and a new experience to enjoy that neuromarketing could create (Attié et al., 2021). In addition, implementing neuromarketing 2.0 means that employees should accept this technology as well, developing a gain in skills and a synergy resulting from the appropriation of these new tools (Quéant, 2019). Thus, companies should slowly prepare and integrate this change into their organization and strategy (Quéant, 2019). Finally, it is important to find ethical ways to use neuromarketing tools. Researchers and marketers can understand how to push people to perform more ethical, responsible and positive behaviors thanks to the use of nudges for example (Singler, 2015). The main goal of nudges is to offer a better option that maximizes health, well-being and wealth (Lin et al., 2017). However, nudges should preserve consumers' rights to choose the option they prefer (i.e., increase physical activity, decrease alcohol or smoking habits, etc.) without forcing them (Lin et al., 2017). For example, research demonstrated that smokers exposed to the smell of cigarettes mixed with rotten eggs during the phase 2 of their sleep –when the body prepares for deep sleep– would then reduce their smoking habits for several days, but smokers must be willing to stop cigarettes first (Hurst, 2015). Neuromarketing can thus predict intentions and find ways to transform these intentions into action.

Ethics and Responsibility: A Neuroethical Charter for Neuromarketing 2.0

Neuromarketing 2.0 implies collecting then analyzing and using sometimes sensitive and personal data. Marketers should thus implement and promote ethical principles linked to their use of neuromarketing. Thus, it is necessary to develop reliable and trustable neuromarketing 2.0 tools regarding the following aspects: ethical considerations, ethical practices, responsible data management, and consumer rights, according to the field of intervention.

Ethical Consideration

Companies should predict the dangers related to neuromarketing studies. For example, managers should implement safeguards policies and consider the establishment of mechanisms that promote integrity, autonomy, safety, privacy, non-discrimination and the dignity of people in the short and long term. In addition, there should be a priority given to safety assessment in the development and use of neuromarketing tools: companies should collaborate with researchers, health professionals, engineers, employees, consumers, as well as private actors and public authorities in order to prioritize research rather than business matters. This communication should address the ethical, legal and social issues, and opportunities related to advances in brain research and neuromarketing 2.0.

Ethical Practices

Companies should take into account consumers' concerns about neuromarketing 2.0 intentions and tools, from the planning and design step of the technology development to the implementation of the strategy on the market. There should be an establishment of standards and best practices of the technical ethical aspects of innovation in neuromarketing tools. Consumers should have access to sufficient and clear information about the safety, quality and efficacy of new neuromarketing 2.0 tools and procedures. In addition, companies should establish business practices that encourage accountability (i.e., social responsibility), transparency (i.e., expose the interest at stake and promote clear communications about neuromarketing tools and objectives), integrity (i.e., foster debates between the different actors involved), reliability (i.e., standards and practices that increase trust and confidence), responsiveness, and security. Therefore, there should be a willingness to encourage the further development of ethical guidelines and best practices based on the rigor and replicability of neuromarketing 2.0 tools. Finally, companies could name advisory boards specialized on ethical matters to verify compliance with ethical and legal principles, and its application.

Responsible Data Management

It is necessary to provide people and research stakeholders with clear information and education on the collection, storage, analysis and potential use of personal brain data collected. Companies should be transparent and communicate about their strategy in order to let both employees and consumers know the concept of neuromarketing 2.0, its purposes and consequences. Moreover, companies doing neuromarketing should respect existing laws regarding data use (i.e., GDPR principles in Europe) and anonymize the collected data to protect consumers' information, among the other recommendations.

Consumer Rights

Companies should avoid potential harmful effects and give due consideration to human rights and societal values, and more specifically, emphasize respect for consumer privacy, cognitive freedom and individual autonomy. Consumers should always be able to give an informed, full and free consent about their data use, in order to protect their autonomy and privacy. This consent should include an easy access to the modification and deletion of their personal data, as well as clear policies about legal proceedings, confidentiality, and privacy security. Therefore, companies need to ensure the traceability of the collected data through neuromarketing 2.0 tools. More specifically, managers should encourage efforts to raise awareness of potential existing unethical neuromarketing intentions and techniques and, if necessary, adapt to existing legislation and regulations.

Fields of Intervention

If neuromarketing can bring positive outcomes (i.e., well-being, health benefits), regulations should be less strict than if the main purpose is only to increase business profits. In some countries, there are some laws that regulate non-interventional research (i.e., human observation, data collection, and collection by extra-corporeal non-invasive sensors, audio, video and image recordings, collection of electrophysiological data, anthropometric measurements without invasive intervention, interviews, observations, tests and questionnaires).

CONCLUSION

Marketers need to gain consumer acceptance regarding any marketing techniques they consider using (du Pre Gauntt, 2008; Merisavo et al., 2007; Ranchhod, 2007). In 2015, most people talking to an AI bot named Eugene Goostman believed they were talking to a real person. Therefore, smart robots can offer great opportunities in sales services by building relationships with customers, while analyzing and predicting their behavior. This chapter aims at highlighting and discussing reliable and trustable neuromarketing 2.0 tools to detect and translate consumer attention, emotions, intentions and behaviors. Thanks to neuromarketing, companies should get access to relevant tools to create better ads for the greater good of everyone, by encouraging positive behaviors or even citizenship through nudges (Falk et al., 2015; Wieckowski, 2019). Another contribution was to define a neuroethical charter to favor transparency about the technologies used and companies' intentions, and to develop ethical and trustworthy data management guidelines. This chapter aims at encouraging research on the ethical, legal and societal dimensions of neuromarketing 2.0. If used right, neuromarketing can become a catalyst for positive change in the coming years. Thus, this chapter should give an understanding of how neuromarketing 2.0 works with AI tools, how to use these tools, in order to improve marketing strategies and relationships between companies and consumers. Finally, almost all companies protect their intellectual property when they use neuromarketing and do not communicate much about it, but this issue could be solved by rewarding the firms that decide to be transparent and willing to be peer reviewed for example, leading the way toward more ethical business and practices (Wieckowski, 2019).

ACKNOWLEDGMENT

This research was supported by Capgemini Engineering.

REFERENCES

Abràmoff, M. D., Tobey, D., & Char, D. S. (2020). Lessons Learned About Autonomous AI: Finding a Safe, Efficacious, and Ethical Path Through the Development Process. *American Journal of Ophthalmology*, *214*, 134–142. doi:10.1016/j.ajo.2020.02.022 PMID:32171769

Attié, E., Gourdou, C., & Guédon, E. (2021). *Understanding consumer acceptance of neuromarketing* Paper presented at *International Marketing Trends Conference*, Venice.

Awad, N. F., & Krishnan, M. S. (2006). The personalization privacy paradox: An empirical evaluation of information transparency and the willingness to be profiled online for personalization. *Management Information Systems Quarterly*, *30*(1), 13–28. doi:10.2307/25148715

Baillargeon, N. (2018). L'éthique des voitures autonomes [The ethics of autonomous cars]. *Québec Science Magazine*. Accessed from: https://www.quebecscience.qc.ca/normand-baillargeon/ethique-des-voitures-autonomes/

Banse, R., & Scherer, K. R. (1996). Acoustic profiles in vocal emotion expression. *Journal of Personality and Social Psychology*, *70*(3), 614–636. doi:10.1037/0022-3514.70.3.614 PMID:8851745

Bayle-Tourtoulou, A.-S., & Badoc, M. (2020). *The neuro-consumer: Adapting communication and marketing strategies for the consumer*. Routledge. doi:10.4324/9781003019978

Bechara, A., Damasio, H., Tranel, D., & Damasio, A. R. (1997). Deciding advantageously before knowing the advantageous strategy. *Science*, *275*(5304), 1293–1295. doi:10.1126cience.275.5304.1293 PMID:9036851

Berger, J., & Milkman, K. (2012). What makes online content viral? *JMR, Journal of Marketing Research*, *49*(2), 192–205. doi:10.1509/jmr.10.0353

Burke, R., & Leykin, A. (2014). *Identifying the Drivers of Shopper Attention*. Engagement, and Purchase., doi:10.1108/S1548-643520140000011006

Calvo, R. A., & D'Mello, S. (2010). Affect detection: An interdisciplinary review of models, methods, and their applications. *IEEE Transactions on Affective Computing, 1*(1), 18–37. doi:10.1109/T-AFFC.2010.1

Carter, R. M., MacInnes, J. J., Huettel, S. A., & Adcock, R. A. (2009). Activation in the VTA and nucleus accumbens increases in anticipation of both gains and losses. *Frontiers in Behavioral Neuroscience, 3*, 21. doi:10.3389/neuro.08.021.2009 PMID:19753142

Charmetant, E. (2018). La neuroéthique: Histoire, actualité et prospective [Neuroethics: history, present and future]. *Transversalites, 146*(3), 45–58. doi:10.3917/trans.146.0045

Chaudhuri, A., & Holbrook, M. B. (2001). The chain of effects from brand trust and brand affect to brand performance: The role of brand loyalty. *Journal of Marketing, 65*(2), 81–93. doi:10.1509/jmkg.65.2.81.18255

Chou, K. L., Amick, M. M., Brandt, J., Camicioli, R., Frei, K., Gitelman, D., Goldman, J., Growdon, J., Hurtig, H. I., Levin, B., Litvan, I., Marsh, L., Simuni, T., Tröster, A. I., & Uc, E. Y. (2010). A Recommended Scale for Cognitive Screening in Clinical Trials of Parkinson's Disease. *Movement Disorders, 25*(15), 2501–2507. doi:10.1002/mds.23362 PMID:20878991

Ciccarelli, S. K., & Meyer, G. E. (2006). *Psychology*. Prentice Hall.

Claeys, A., & Vialatte, J.-S. (2012). Office parlementaire d'évaluation des choix scientifiques et technologiques. L'impact et les enjeux des nouvelles technologies d'exploration et de thérapie du cerveau [Parliamentary Office for the Evaluation of Scientific and Technological Choices. The impact and challenges of new technologies for brain exploration and therapy]. *Rapport par Claeys et Vialatte, députés. Paris. Assemblée Nationales et Sénat, 2012*, 25.

Corcos, A., & Pannequin, F. (2013). Neuroeconomics, decision-making and rationality. *Économie et institutions, 16.*. doi:10.4000/ei.74

Courbet, D., & Benoit, D. (2013). Neurosciences au service de la communication commerciale: manipulation et éthique - Une critique du neuromarketing [Neuroscience at the service of commercial communication: manipulation and ethics - A Critique of Neuromarketing]. *Études de communication - Langages, information, médiations. Université de Lille, 40*, 28–42.

Cubric, M. (2020). Drivers, barriers and social considerations for AI adoption in business and management: A tertiary study. *Technology in Society, 62*, 101257. Advance online publication. doi:10.1016/j.techsoc.2020.101257

Damasio, A. R. (1994). *Descartes' Error: Emotion, Reason and the Human Brain*. G.P. Putmans & Sons.

De Bruyn, A., Viswanathan, V., Beh, Y. S., Brock, J. K. U., & von Wangenheim, F. (2020). Artificial Intelligence and Marketing: Pitfalls and Opportunities. *Journal of Interactive Marketing, 51*, 91–105. doi:10.1016/j.intmar.2020.04.007

De Sousa, J. (2018). *The Challenge of Neuromarketing*. IGI Global. doi:10.4018/978-1-5225-4834-8.ch002

Demir, K. A., Döven, G., & Sezen, B. (2019). Industry 5.0 and human-robot co-working. *Procedia Computer Science, 158*, 688–695. doi:10.1016/j.procs.2019.09.104

Dooley, R. (2013). *Neuromarketing: For Coke*. It's the Real Thing.

Droulers, O., & Roullet, B. (2010). *Neuromarketing. Le marketing revisité par les neurosciences du consommateur* [Neuromarketing. Marketing revisited by the neurosciences of the consumer?]. Dunod.

Du Pre Gauntt, J. (2008). Mobile advertising: After the growing pains. New York, NY: eMarketer.

Evers, K. (2014). *Quand la neuroscience se réveille* [When neuroscience wakes up]. Upsala Universiteit. Accessed from: https://www.crb.uu.se/digitalAssets/445/c_445294-l_1-k_k-evers-neuroethique.pdf

Falk, E. B., Berkman, E. T., Whalen, D., & Lieberman, M. D. (2015). Neural Activity During Health Messaging Predicts Reductions in Smoking Above and Beyond Self-Report. *Health Psychology*. PMID:21261410

Flores, J., Baruca, A., & Saldivar, R. (2014). Is neuromarketing ethical? Consumers say yes. Consumers say no. Journal of Legal. *Ethical and Regulatory Issues*, *17*(2), 77–91.

Guelfand, G. (2013). *Les études qualitatives: Fondamentaux, méthodes, analyse, techniques* [Qualitative studies: Fundamentals, methods, analysis, techniques]. EMS Editions. doi:10.3917/ems.guelf.2013.01

Harrell, E. (2019). Neuromarketing: What you need to know. *Harvard Business Review*. Accessed from: https://hbr.org/2019/01/neuromarketing-what-you-need-to-know

Hegazy, I. M. (2019). The effect of political neuromarketing 2.0 on election outcomes. *Review of Economics and Political Science*.

Hong, W., & Thong, J. (2013). Internet privacy concerns: An integrated conceptualisation and four empirical studies. *Management Information Systems Quarterly*, *37*(1), 275–298. doi:10.25300/MISQ/2013/37.1.12

Hsu, L., & Chen, Y.-J. (2020). Neuromarketing, subliminal advertising, and hotel selection: An EEG study. *Australasian Marketing Journal*, *28*(4), 200–208. Advance online publication. doi:10.1016/j.ausmj.2020.04.009

Hurst, J. (2015). Assessing kindship through scent – the mouse model. *Chemical Senses*, *40*(3), 211–297. doi:10.1093/chemse/bju073

Jarrahi, M. H. (2018). Artificial intelligence and the future of work: Human-AI symbiosis in organizational decision-making. *Business Horizons*, *61*(4), 577–586. doi:10.1016/j.bushor.2018.03.007

Johnstone, T., & Scherer, K. R. (2000). Vocal communication of emotion. In *Handbook of Emotions* (2nd ed., pp. 220–235). Guilford Press.

Knutson, B., Rick, S., Wimmer, G. E., Prelec, D., & Loewenstein, G. (2007). Neural predictors of purchases. *Neuron*, *53*(1), 147–156. doi:10.1016/j.neuron.2006.11.010 PMID:17196537

Langleben, D. D., Loughead, J. W., Ruparel, K., Hakun, J. G., Bush-Winokur, S., Holloway, M. B., Strasser, A. A., Cappella, J. N., & Lerman, C. (2009). Reduced prefrontal and temporal processing and recall of high "sensation value" ads. *NeuroImage*, *46*(1), 219–225. doi:10.1016/j.neuroimage.2008.12.062 PMID:19457412

Legardinier, A. (2013). *Comment limiter les biais liés au choix des échelles de mesure dans les études marketing?* [How to limit the biases linked to the choice of measurement scales in marketing studies?]. Gestion et management, Dumas.

Lever, M. W., Shen, Y., & Joppe, M. (2019). Reading travel guidebooks: Readership typologies using eye-tracking technology. *Journal of Destination Marketing & Management, 14,* 1–13. doi:10.1016/j.jdmm.2019.100368

Lin, P., Abney, K., & Bekey, G. (2011). Robot Ethics: Mapping the Issues for a Mechanized World. *Artificial Intelligence, 175*(5-6), 942–949. doi:10.1016/j.artint.2010.11.026

Lin, Y., Osman, M., & Ashcroft, R. (2017). Nudge: Concept, effectiveness, and ethics. *Basic and Applied Social Psychology, 39*(6), 293–306. doi:10.1080/01973533.2017.1356304

Ma, L., & Sun, B. (2020). Machine learning and AI in marketing – Connecting computing power to human insights. *International Journal of Research in Marketing, 37*(3), 481–504. doi:10.1016/j.ijresmar.2020.04.005

Maughan, L., Gutnikov, S., & Stevens, R. (2007). Like more, look more. Look more, like more: The evidence from eye tracking. *Journal of Brand Management, 14*(4), 335–342. doi:10.1057/palgrave.bm.2550074

Mediamarketing. (2017). *Le chemin passe par le neuromarketing* [The path goes through neuromarketing]. Accessed from: https://www.mediamarketing.ma/article/GHBGBGH/le_chemin_passe_par_le_neuromarketing.html

Merisavo, M., Kajalo, S., Karjaluoto, H., Virtanen, V., Salmenkivi, S., Raulas, M., & Leppäniemi, M. (2007). An empirical study of the drivers of consumer acceptance of mobile advertising. *Journal of Interactive Advertising, 7*(2), 1–19. doi:10.1080/15252019.2007.10722130

Morris, P. L., Hopwood, M., Whelan, G., Gardiner, J., & Drummond, E. (2001). Naltrexone for alcohol dependence: A randomized controlled trial. *Addiction (Abingdon, England), 11*(15), 65–73. doi:10.1046/j.1360-0443.2001.961115654.x PMID:11784454

Murray, P. N. (2013). *Inside the Consumer Mind How Emotions Influence What We Buy The emotional core of consumer decision making.* Retrieved from https://www.psychologytoday.com/blog/inside-the-consumermind/201302/how-emotions-influence-what-we-buy

Nave, G., Nadler, A., Dubois, D., Zava, D., Camerer, C., & Plassmann, H. (2018). Single-dose testosterone administration increases men's preference for status goods. *Nature Communications, 9*(1), 24–33. doi:10.103841467-018-04923-0 PMID:29970895

Nilashi, M., Samad, S., Ahmadi, N., Ahani, A., Abumalloh, R. A., Asadi, S., & Yadegaridehkordi, E. (2020). Neuromarketing: A review of research and implications for marketing. *Journal of Soft Computer Decision Support System, 7*(2), 23–31.

O'Reilly, L. (2013). *Google patents 'pay-per-gaze' eye-tracking ad technology.* Accessed from: https://www.marketingweek.com/google-patents-pay-per-gaze-eye-tracking-ad-technology/

Olajide, V. (2019). *Introduction to Data Management*. Accessed from: https://www.researchgate.net/publication/335062781

Orquin, J. L., & Loose, S. M. (2013). Attention and choice: A review on eye movements in decision making. *Acta Psychologica*, *144*(1), 190–206. doi:10.1016/j.actpsy.2013.06.003 PMID:23845447

Oullier, O. (2012). Le cerveau et la loi: analyse de l'émergence du neurodroit [The Brain and the Law: Analysis of the Emergence of Neurolaw]. Centre d'Analyse Stratégique.

Partala, T., & Surakka, V. (2003). Pupil size variation as an indication of affective processing. *International Journal of Human-Computer Studies*, *59*(1-2), 185–198. doi:10.1016/S1071-5819(03)00017-X

Phelps, J. E., D'Souza, G., & Nowak, G. J. (2001). Antecedents and consequences of consumer privacy concerns: An empirical investigation. *Journal of Interactive Marketing*, *15*(4), 2–17. doi:10.1002/dir.1019

Phelps, J. E., Nowak, G. J., & Ferrell, E. (2000). Privacy concerns and consumer willingness to provide personal information. *Journal of Public Policy & Marketing*, *19*(1), 27–41. doi:10.1509/jppm.19.1.27.16941

Phillips-Wren, G. (2012). AI tools in decision making support systems: A review. *International Journal of Artificial Intelligence Tools*, *21*(2), 1240005. doi:10.1142/S0218213012400052

Plassmann, H., Ramsoy, T. Z., & Milosavljevic, M. (2015). Branding the brain: A critical review and outlook. *Journal of Consumer Psychology*, *22*(1), 18–36. doi:10.1016/j.jcps.2011.11.010

Quéant, P. (2019). IA et puissance aérospatiale, implications pour l'Armée de l'air [AI and Aerospace Power, Implications for the Air Force]. *Revue Défense Nationale*, *820*(5), 117–122. doi:10.3917/rdna.820.0117

Ranchhod, A. (2007). Developing mobile marketing strategies. *International Journal of Mobile Advertising*, *2*(1), 76–83.

Roediger, H. L. (1990). Implicit memory: Retention without remembering. *The American Psychologist*, *42*, 873. doi:10.1037/h0092053 PMID:2221571

Rossiter, J. R., Silberstein, R. B., Harris, P. G., & Nield, G. (2001). So What? A Rejoinder to the Reply by Crites and Aikman-Eckenrode to Rossiter et al. (2001). *Journal of Advertising Research*, *41*(3), 59–61. Advance online publication. doi:10.2501/JAR-41-3-59-61

Russell, J. A., Lewicka, M., & Niit, T. (1989). A Cross-Cultural Study of a Circumflex Model of Affect. *Journal of Personality and Social Psychology*, *57*(5), 848–856. doi:10.1037/0022-3514.57.5.848

Schmidt, L., Skvortsova, V., Kullen, C., Weber, B., & Plassmann, H. (2017). How context alters value: The brain's valuation and affective regulation system link price cues to experienced taste pleasantness. *Scientific Reports*, *7*(1), 8098. Advance online publication. doi:10.103841598-017-08080-0 PMID:28808246

Shin, D. (2010). The effects of trust, security & privacy in social networking: A security-based approach to understand the pattern of adoption. *Interacting with Computers*, *22*(5), 428–438. doi:10.1016/j.intcom.2010.05.001

Singler, E. (2015). *Green Nudge: Changer les comportements pour sauver la planète*. Pearson.

Smarandescu, L., & Shimp, T. A. (2015). Drink Coca-Cola, eat popcorn, and choose powerade: Testing the limits of subliminal persuasion. *Marketing Letters, 26*(4), 715–726. doi:10.100711002-014-9294-1

Sofi, S. A., Nika, F. A., Shah, M. S., & Zarger, A. S. (2018). Impact of subliminal advertising on consumer buying behaviour: An empirical study on young Indian consumers. *Global Business Review, 19*(6), 1580–1601. doi:10.1177/0972150918791378

Soler, A. S., Ort, M., Steckel, J., & Nieschullze, J. (2016). *An introduction to data management.* Accessed from: https://www.gfbio.org/documents/10184/22817/Reader_GFBio_BefMate_20160222/1ca43f24-255044b3-a05e-e180c3e544c0

SolomonR. C. (2017). *Emotion.* Retrieved from http://www.britannica.com/topic/emotion

Stoicescu, C. (2016). Big Data, the perfect instrument to study today's consumer behavior. *Database System Journal, 6,* 28–42.

Stoll, M., Baecke, S., & Kenning, P. (2008). What they see is what they get? An fMRI-study on neural correlates of attractive packaging. *Journal of Consumer Behaviour, 7*(4-5), 342–359. Advance online publication. doi:10.1002/cb.256

Sultana, N., & Nangunoori, R. (2008). Ethical Acceptability of Neuromarketing: Relevance, Limits and Limitations. *Prabandhan: Indian Journal of Management, 1*(1), 31. Advance online publication. doi:10.17010//2008/v1i1/64654

Vecchiato, G., Toppi, J., Astolfi, L., De Vico Fallani, F., Cincotti, F., Mattia, D., Bez, F., & Babiloni, F. (2011). Spectral EEG frontal asymmetries correlate with the experienced pleasantness of video commercial advertisements. *Medical & Biological Engineering & Computing, 49*(5), 579–583. doi:10.100711517-011-0747-x PMID:21327841

Westbrook, R. A., & Oliver, R. L. (1991). The Dimensionality of Consumption Emotion Patterns and Consumer Satisfaction. *The Journal of Consumer Research, 18*(1), 84–91. doi:10.1086/209243

Wieckowski, A. (2019). When neuromarketing crosses the line. *Harvard Business Review.* Accessed from: https://hbr.org/2019/01/when-neuromarketing-crosses-the-line?ab=at_articlepage_recommende-darticles_bottom1x1

Xu, H., Luo, X., Carroll, J. M., & Rosson, M. B. (2011). The Personalization Privacy Paradox. *Decision Support Systems, 51*(1), 42–52. doi:10.1016/j.dss.2010.11.017

KEY TERMS AND DEFINITIONS

Artificial Intelligence (AI): AI is a set of algorithms capable of collecting and interpreting data, in order to predict consumer behaviors.

Data Management: The planning, development, implementation, and administration of data systems in order to collect, store, secure, use and archive data.

Eye Tracking: Recording fixation points and eye movements when users look at visual stimuli such as advertising, websites, packaging, or in-store shelves.

Facial Coding: The decoding of specific facial behaviors, based on the facial muscles that produce them, to identify unconscious thoughts and behaviors.

Gestural Coding: The decoding of body attitudes and postures, based on the body muscles that produce them, to identify unconscious thoughts and behaviors.

Neuroethics: The study of the moral values of neuroscientific technologies and the ethics of neuroscience (i.e., the ethical issues raised by neural imaging techniques or cognitive enhancement) (Evers, 2014).

Neuromarketing 2.0: The study of consumers' sensory-motor, cognitive and affective responses to marketing stimuli thanks to AI tools.

Neuroscience: The study of the nervous system, which controls every aspect of the body, from emotion and memory to basic body activities such as movements, breathing and heartbeat.

Pupil Tracking: The recording of the variation of pupil dimensions when consumers look at visual stimuli to identify unconscious perceptions and behaviors.

Vocal Coding: The decoding of the voice, based on characteristics such as tone and timbre, to identify unconscious thoughts and behaviors.

Chapter 30
Responsible Machine Learning for Ethical Artificial Intelligence in Business and Industry

Deepak Saxena

ⓘD https://orcid.org/0000-0002-9331-3799

Birla Institute of Technology and Science, Pilani, India

Markus Lamest

Trinity College Dublin, Ireland

Veena Bansal

Indian Institute of Technology, Kanpur, India

ABSTRACT

Artificial intelligence (AI) systems have become a new reality of modern life. They have become ubiquitous to virtually all socio-economic activities in business and industry. With the extent of AI's influence on our lives, it is an imperative to focus our attention on the ethics of AI. While humans develop their moral and ethical framework via self-awareness and reflection, the current generation of AI lacks these abilities. Drawing from the concept of human-AI hybrid, this chapter offers managerial and developers' action towards responsible machine learning for ethical artificial intelligence. The actions consist of privacy by design, development of explainable AI, identification and removal of inherent biases, and most importantly, using AI as a moral enabler. Application of these action would not only help towards ethical AI; it would also help in supporting moral development of human-AI hybrid.

INTRODUCTION

Breaking away from the realm of science fiction, artificial intelligence (AI) systems have become the reality of modern life. Kaplan and Haenlein (2019) define AI as "a system's ability to interpret external data correctly, to learn from such data, and to use those learnings to achieve specific goals and tasks

DOI: 10.4018/978-1-7998-6985-6.ch030

through flexible adaptation". AIs in modern life not only provide recommended course of actions to those working in business and industry, but they are also effectively making decisions for us. In our everyday life, they strongly influence what we watch during our leisure time, who we interact more with on social networks, the videos we watch and the music we listen to, what we buy on e-commerce websites and on what rate, what interest rate and credit limits we are offered on our credit cards, what route our taxis take and so on. The list of AI applications is endless. However, AI models are usually opaque, and one often knows very little on the decisions-making algorithm used by AIs (Burrell, 2016; de Saint Laurent, 2018; McQuillan, 2018; Mackenzie, 2019). Since AIs have so much influence on our lives, it is an imperative to focus our attention on the ethics of AI.

At the same time, AIs are built by humans, often using the process of machine learning. Hence, the choices made by the AI developers (who design the AI) and the managers (who decide to implement the recommendations from the AI) are crucial. This paper offers some suggestions towards responsible machine learning building on the idea of human-AI hybrid (Bansal et al., 2019a, 2019b; Dellermann et al., 2019; Jarrahi, 2018; Peeters et al., 2020). Taking a socio-technical systems perspective (Andras et al., 2018), the term human-AI hybrid indicates that each subsystem (AI and the humans) brings a unique skillset to the table and can help in ethical development of the overall system. In so doing, the chapter takes machine learning as a common denominator of AI and introduces a responsible machine learning framework towards ethical AI. For developers and managers, the chapter suggests actionable insights that can be used in industry and business.

The remainder of the chapter is as follows. The next section provides some background in terms of the notion of artificial intelligence, the machine learning process, and the concept of distributed morality in the context of socio-technical systems. Thereafter, the building blocks of responsible machine learning are discussed with the implications they have for the AI developers and managers. The building blocks are aligned with the classical machine learning stages. Based on the discussion, recommendations are presented for the managers and developers. This is followed by noting some limitations and future development, with last section concluding the chapter.

BACKGROUND

The Notion of Artificial Intelligence

While the notion of AI has been popular from the movies like *The Terminator* or *Ex Machina*, there are two crucial limitations related to the popular perception of AI. The first limitation relates to the notion of intelligence. Strictly speaking, the use of the term intelligence in AI does not relate to the entirety of human intelligence but refers mostly to the logical-mathematical intelligence (Brock, 2018; Vetrò et al., 2019). When developers build an AI, they try to automate and optimize the processing that requires data manipulation and logical reasoning. While there have been efforts to design emotionally intelligent AI (Schuller & Schuller, 2018) or AIs with kinaesthetic intelligence (e.g., self-driving cars), the efforts are yet to see the light of the day in wider society. It is with this caution the term 'intelligence' is to be used for AI. Therefore, while AIs are fit to replace humans in the tasks that require an application of logical-mathematical intelligence, human intervention is still needed (Brock, 2018; Ross, 2018; Wilson et al., 2017) due to other forms of intelligence they possess, especially when it comes to ambiguous situations and inductive reasoning. For this reason, this paper draws from the idea of the human-AI hybrid

(Dellermann et al., 2019; Jarrahi, 2018; Peeters et al., 2020) instead of the notion of standalone machine intelligence. Interestingly, this idea is not entirely new but teased upon in the context of expert systems and knowledge engineering (Brock, 2018).

The second limitation relates to the scope of AI. In the popular discourse AI systems are often conceived as a single entity, sometimes termed strong AI (de Saint Laurent, 2018), especially when it comes to issues such as AI ethics. However, what is often ignored is that an AI is built to perform a specific task. It exceeds human capabilities not at an overall level but in the context of information processing for a specific problem (Brock, 2018; de Saint Laurent, 2018). An AI for the bank fraud detection cannot predict the onset of cancer. IBM deep blue may be an excellent chess player; it cannot be used in the autonomous cars to find its way. Therefore, instead of considering AI as an all-encompassing term, one needs a more specific notion to talk about the ethics of AI in business and industry. This common denominator could be machine learning process though which an AI system usually develops its intelligence. It may be noted, however, the machines learning is only an enabler of Artificial Intelligence, and not equivalent to it (de Saint Laurent, 2018). Moreover, while AI ethics as a whole remains a complex subject with no simple answers, machine learning offers some leeway in terms of corrective actions (de Saint Laurent, 2018). The next section briefly explores the machine learning process.

How AI Systems Gain Intelligence

Machine Learning (ML) may be defined as the statistical method that creates models based on training data and continuously improves the model based on the match between the prediction and actual data. In other words, ML programs seek to understand and replicate how certain inputs lead to certain outputs to assist in the task of prediction (de Saint Laurent, 2018). The classical machine learning process is supervised in the sense that the training data is often structured and contains clear inputs and outputs. In contrast, under unsupervised ML, the data is not structured, and the machine looks for patterns in the data without any human intervention. Finally, deep learning is considered as a specific ML method that tries to mimic the functioning of human brain by creating multilayer neural networks, with each layer building on the previous (LeCun et al., 2015; Rusk, 2016). As business examples, while Google DeepMind uses deep learning neural networks, IBM Watson relies on machine learning. While deep learning algorithms are considered more efficient and require more computational power, machine learning models are easy to implement and interpret. In this chapter we focus on classical supervised ML for simplicity. Classical ML may be understood to be consisting of four stages – data collection and preparation, training and modelling, model evaluation, and usage for prediction. Although it is shown in logical sequence, it is useful to remember that the ML process is iterative as AI systems continuously improve the model based on the match between the prediction and actual data. Figure 1 outlines each ML stage and notes potential issues from an ethical perspective.

Data Collection and Preparation

Existing datasets are the starting point for ML algorithms to train. It is argued that the ML race between companies is essentially a race about data (Beck & Libert, 2019). The quality of the AI depends upon the amount and the quality of data used to train the AI. ML provides an opportunity to learn from traditional data such as browsing or purchase as well as from non-traditional sources such as big data (Zhou et al., 2017) to support business decisions. This is why companies prefer to collect user data from as many

Figure 1. Machine learning stages and potential issues

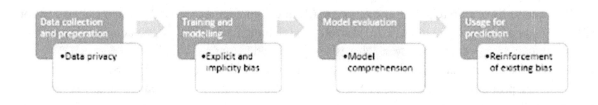

sources as possible. At the same time, it is observed that big data results in an information overload for managers (Saxena & Lamest, 2018) due to its volume and velocity. ML provides a more efficient solution to the problem of making sense of the wide tapestry of data residing within and outside the company. However, the database design process almost exclusively focuses upon database and query optimization, virtually disregarding issues such as privacy or trust. With the technology infrastructure becoming all pervasive and ever cheaper, there are obvious tensions between convenience versus privacy (Weinberg et al., 2015) and customer insights versus privacy intrusion (Plangger & Watson, 2015). Especially with the advent of ubiquitous and non-intrusive technologies such as Internet of Things (IoT), not only customers need to be aware of the privacy invasion, but organizations also need to be mindful of the extent of data collection and its wider repercussions (Santanen, 2019) to avoid reputation loss and legal challenges.

Training and Modelling

This is this stage when AI systems use complex statistical methods for pattern recognition and to make sense of the training data (de Saint Laurent, 2018). The result of this process is often a model to explain the specific patterns and to make predictions. While there are a variety of approaches to optimize the learning process (e.g., see Qiu et al., 2017), it is useful to remember that an AI model draws from the training data fed to it and essentially reinforces the existing patterns from which training data is generated (de Saint Laurent, 2018). Consequently, while the model might be statistically optimal with respect to the training data fed to it, it might still have inherent biases (Daugherty et al., 2019; Miller, 2020; Vetrò et al., 2019; Žliobaité, 2015) due to disproportionate datasets and/or collinearity. Training on the past data runs the risk of introducing certain bias in the model (Ajana, 2015; de Saint Laurent, 2018; Turner Lee, 2018). For instance, few years back a leading business needed to shut down its recruitment AI because it seemed to disadvantage female candidates. Since women are traditionally under-represented in the technology sector, AI systems usually inherit gender bias (Leavy, 2018). Similarly, Ajana (2015) reports that the use of big data and machine learning in border operations runs the risk of creating undue restrictions on certain 'high-risk' identities and privileging certain identities. More recently, UK authorities had to revise the school grades predicted by an AI since it downgraded some grades assigned by the teachers, based on the school profile (Evgeniou et al., 2020) even though the teachers were confident in their grade assignment. These examples clearly illustrate that the importance of identification and removal of biases at the training and modelling stage for non-discriminative use of data in ML (Žliobaité, 2015).

Model Evaluation

The next step in the ML process is to evaluate the efficacy of the model. This is usually evaluated with reference to the fit between the predicted outcomes and the actual outcomes. However, statistical fit is only one aspect of model evaluation. A key managerial challenge is to make sense of the models themselves. Since there might be thousands of variables and complex algebraic expressions at play, sometimes managers step in the dark (de Saint Laurent, 2018; McQuillan, 2018; Wilson et al, 2017) regarding how the model actually works. For instance, it was reported in 2015 that a popular photo application was tagging people of color as Gorilla. After unsuccessfully trying to address the issue, the eventual solution used by the developers was to remove the term gorilla (and neighboring terms – chimpanzee, monkey etc.) from its lexicon. This implies that sometimes even the developers may struggle in understanding the decision-model used by the system. This issue becomes extremely complex when there are competing models and algorithms to choose from. Thus, choosing a model in a specific context itself becomes an ethical exercise (Webb et al., 2019) for decision makers. The issue becomes even more complex with neural network based deep learning models that are rarely comprehensible to humans (Dickson, 2018). Consequently, model selection often becomes a matter of experience and subjective impression of the researcher (de Saint Laurent, 2018).

Usage for Prediction

Just as computers' main task is to execute efficient calculations, the task of an AI is to facilitate predictions (Agrawal et al., 2019). However, unlike traditional computer programs that are expected to repeat the same steps that are designed by their programmers, an AI keeps modifying its logic based on the relative success/failure of its prediction. Irrespective of the model and logic, however, one central limitation is that although the past data may be used to predict the future; it should not determine the future (Ajana, 2015). As Kerr and Earle (2013) argue, by reinforcing past bias, this approach restricts the future possibilities for those who are subject to this algorithmic governmentality (Harkens, 2018), for instance limiting jobs or immigration prospects. Thus, we need human intervention at this stage to make a call on whether the recommendations made by AI are fair and safe (Bansal et al., 2019a; "Perspectives on Issues in AI Governance", 2019).

Throughout the machine learning process, managers and developers are involved in different capacities. In this context, the next section discusses the notion of distributed morality and human-AI hybrid.

Distributed Morality and the Human-AI Hybrid

Although popular literature may wish to assign agency to an AI program, there is an increasing support for the notion of distributed morality (Floridi, 2013; de Saint Laurent, 2018; Magnani & Bardone, 2008) for complex information systems such as an AI. Towards the goal of ethical and trustworthy AI, national and transnational AI strategies and guidelines seek to provide a regulatory framework and set of principles (Dafoe, 2018; Lauterbach, 2019) for AI governance. Recent guidelines on trustworthy AI from the European Commission (2019) and the Algorithmic Accountability Bill presented in the US Congress (2019) are two such examples. Similarly, Ethically Aligned Design from the Institute of Electrical and Electronics Engineers (IEEE, 2019) provides a broad set of principles for the design and governance of AI. While such principles provide a broad framework for ethical AI governance, AI developers and business users still need to take decisions in their specific business context.

Distributed morality implies that ethics of a complex system are determined by the actions taken by various actors involved in the development, implementation, and use of the system. In this respect, the first burden of morality falls on AI developers. Technology developers usually build a technology with a defined functionality in mind, usually dictated by the organizational needs. However, this does not exonerate them from their ethical responsibility. Since the affordances designed in the technological artefact support or constrain certain actions, AI developers end up doing ethics by other means (Verbeek, 2006, 2011). The second burden of morality falls on the business users. An AI is designed towards specific business goals that need to be framed within a broader societal context. Hence, not only the goal determination is an inherent ethical process, but also is the choice of whether to act on AI's recommendations. Even saying 'yes' to AI recommendations constitutes an ethical decision on part of the business users (de Saint Laurent, 2018).

Thus, as opposed to the notion of an AI working in isolation, it is the human-AI hybrid system (Andras et al., 2018; Bansal et al., 2019a; Dellermann et al., 2019; Jarrahi, 2018; Peeters et al., 2020; "Perspectives on Issues in AI Governance", 2019) one needs to focus upon. While the AIs have an immense capacity for logical-mathematical processing (Vetrò et al., 2019), they are not conceived as possessing awareness and intentionality (de Saint Laurent, 2018). In contrast, reflection and moral self-awareness are arguably a crucial part of moral development (Friedland & Cole, 2019) in humans and collectives. At the current stage of development, AI systems do not possess a capability for self-awareness or reflection. Thus, following-on from the idea of distributed morality and human-AI hybrid, the key for AI ethics lies in humans facilitating the ML process to incorporate ingredients of reflection and moral self-awareness to turn the AI into socially responsible agents (Vetrò et al., 2019). The next section discusses those actions required for responsible machine learning.

TOWARDS RESPONSIBLE MACHINE LEARNING

Aligned with the notion of human-AI hybrid and distributed morality, Figure 2 shows a responsible ML model with corrective actions. In a limited manner, it draws from knowledge discovery in databases (KDD) approach that involves data preprocessing, data cleaning, incorporation of prior knowledge, and appropriate interpretation/evaluation when extracting knowledge from available datasets (Custers, 2013; Fayyad et al., 1996). In a limited manner, it tries to bring classical ML closer to the KDD process in which knowledge must be more understandable and useful than being optimal and precise (Kodratoff, 1999).

Privacy by Design

The first and the most basic step for a responsible AI is putting privacy and fairness at the core of its design. At the preprocessing stage, training data may be analyzed for inherent biases for the purpose of removing those before feeding into ML training stage (Žliobaitė, 2015). A more effective measure, however, may be introduced at the data collection stage in the form of privacy by design. The recent enactment of the General Data Protection Regulation (GDPR) in the European Union facilitates and promotes user privacy and puts a legal binding on the organizations. For managers and employees, this means that they should be aware of the data protection and privacy regulations, and do not put demands

Figure 2. Towards responsible machine learning

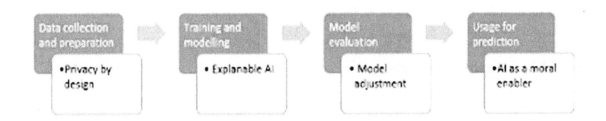

on the AI developers that violate these principles. Especially with the advent of big data and IoT, not only customers need to be aware of the privacy invasion; businesses also need to be mindful of the extent of data collection and its wider repercussions.

The notion of Privacy by Design (Bednar, 2019; Cavoukian, 2012; Wahlstrom et al., 2020) may be employed during the data preparation stage, incorporating privacy affordances in the planning and the design of the system itself (Matwin, 2013). For example, different privacy levels may be used to reflect the privacy sensitivity of the data. This would help in data minimization (Schaar, 2010) i.e., no or minimal collection/processing of individually identifiable information but efficient utilization at the aggregate level. In this regard, the Algorithmic Accountability bill presented in the US Congress (2019) mandates businesses to provide a detailed description of the AI, its algorithmic design, training data used, and the purpose of the system. It also requires them to prepare and report an impact assessment study on the accuracy, fairness/biases, privacy, and security of the system.

Explainable AI

Privacy is only the first stage of an ethical ML process. To ensure an ethical human-AI hybrid, business users should have an adequate understanding of the actual working, purpose, and the limitations of the AI (de Saint Laurent, 2019; Martinho-Truswell, 2018). In this regard, the recent European Commission (2019) guidelines on trustworthy AI suggest appointing a responsible person, or in some cases even an entire panel or board for this purpose. The guidelines suggest that in case an AI system has a significant impact on people's lives, even a layperson should be able to understand both the causality of the algorithmic decision-making process and how this is implemented by the respective organization. In this regard, Wilson et al (2017) identify a new job category of 'explainers' who can bridge the gap between the AI and managerial understanding.

However, it is easier said than done (Weld & Bansal, 2019). ML models are so complex that the managers (sometimes even the developers) may not have enough understanding of the underlying logic. To have full trust in the system, a manager needs to know on what basis and how the AI comes up with a specific recommendation (Ross, 2018). To support this requirement, we need machine learning models that can be broadly explained to humans, often called an explainable AI (Dickson, 2018; Hagras, 2018; Rai, 2020) or in short XAI. An XAI may take diverse approaches. It may involve explaining the building blocks of the ML model, explaining the reasoning, or developing a text-based post-hoc explanation (Arrieta et al., 2020). There arises a question of the trade-off between the explicability of the AI and its efficacy (Brock, 2018; London, 2019; "Perspectives on Issues in AI Governance", 2019) as too much focus on explanation might defeat the purpose of AI creation for optimal and quick decision-making. At the same time, however, Bansal et al. (2019b) demonstrate that (standalone) AI performance improvements may actually hurt the performance of human-AI team.

Model Adjustment

Despite the efforts towards explainable AI, there is no denying that certain explicit or implicit biases (Miller, 2020; Turner Lee, 2018) will be present in the model. In this regard, Žliobaitė (2015) suggests model postprocessing at this stage in terms of changing certain parameters. Moreover, rather than treating these biases as an unwanted outcome, developers and managers may use the AI as a detection mechanism to surface biases ("Perspectives on Issues in AI Governance", 2019). Once an AI detects a specific bias, managers and developers can take steps to remove specific biases, or even to introduce affirmative biases. For instance, for a recruitment AI, one may remove variables such as house address (that may bias an AI towards candidates residing in affluent areas) and/or introduce positive biases for underrepresented populations (e.g., women and third gender, people of color). At the managerial level, this would require discussing and determining which existing biases need to be removed and which positive biases or affirmative actions need to be introduced in the model (Verwer & Calders, 2013). For AI developers, this would mean allowing for changing weights on certain decision criteria or conducting a 'what-if' analysis. However, this should be done on a continuous basis since Calders and Žliobaitė (2013) demonstrate that such biases may creep-in in the model even when relevant variables are removed from the dataset. In this regard, Wilson et al (2017) identify a new job category of 'sustainers' who will ensure that an AI system performs as intended and unintended outcomes are dealt with utmost urgency. Thus, frequent debates (de Saint Laurent, 2018) on AI's decisions and ML models is required for such model adjustments.

Using AI as a Moral Enabler

A crucial implication of human-AI hybrids is that they evolve together. While an AI helps humans in sifting through complex datasets, a human may help AI in working with uncertainty and equivocality of business decisions (Wilson et al., 2017). Moreover, we argue that AI could be used as a moral enabler (Floridi, 2013) for humans. This would involve introducing opportunity for reflection and self-awareness. AI developers may introduce AI friction filter via visceral notices (Friedland, 2019) to trigger the reflective mind. For instance, the managers and developers may be shown the visualization of the outcome variable with key determining variables ("Perspectives on Issues in AI Governance", 2019). The users may then use the opportunity to reflect on whether they wish to go with a specific model or wish to further improve it. Another approach might be informing the end-user about a different set of action than that recommended based on the past behavior. IEEE (2019) recommends that such comprehensive information should be provided to recognize different kind of algorithmic interventions on an opt-in basis. The AI may prompt the users if they are accepting all automated decisions without spending enough time reflecting on the options available to them. As Lara and Deckers (2019) suggest, by constantly asking reflective questions, an AI may act as a Socratic assistant for moral enhancement of the human-AI hybrid. It may also work the other way round when humans assist an AI in improving its trustworthiness. For example, Zhang et al (2019) have proposed a hybrid system called *CrowdLearn* that complements the machine intelligence with the intelligence of the crowd to detect anomalies and improve opaque AI algorithms. Thus, humans and AI can help each other towards moral development of the hybrid system (Bansal et al., 2019a).

SOLUTIONS AND RECOMMENDATIONS

Based on the discussion above, Table 1 outlines the actions recommended for responsible machine learning in business and industry. However, two caveats must be noted here. First, each ML stage is iterative in nature to support learning and to facilitate reflection. Second, although the actions for AI developers and managers are shown in separate rows, in practice they need to collaborate and support each other on a continuous basis. In a sense, the developers and the managers form the feedback loop for each ML stage.

Table 1. Recommended actions for responsible machine learning

Recommended Actions	Privacy by Design	Explainable AI	Model Adjustment	AI as a Moral Enabler
Action at the level of managers	• Determine the data and privacy protection policies. • Understand and explain the use of data to the employees.	• Those using the results from AI must roughly understand what goes inside the black box. • Determine which models/constructs are to be used.	• Determine which existing biases are unwanted, and which affirmative biases are to be introduced.	• Reflect on the decision-making process and its impact.
Actions at the level of developers	• Design systems in a way that allows for further protection of privacy.	• Facilitate explainable AI.	• Make existing biases visible through explainable AI. • If existing biases are unwanted, exclude certain variables from the decision criteria. • Introduce affirmative biases in the system by changing the decision criteria.	• Introduce opportunities for reflection.

FUTURE RESEARCH DIRECTIONS

Certain limitations of this work, that inform the future research directions, may be noted. One limitation of the chapter is that its recommendations are mainly applicable to classical machine learning approaches with linear algorithmic assumptions. Deep learning approaches that rely on hierarchical neural network analysis, are often difficult to explain and interpret. Thus, a dedicated approach to responsible deep learning (such as the one illustrated in Angelov & Soares, 2020) is warranted. Having noted that, the framework described in this chapter may be used across a diverse range of ML applications and need not be confined to AI development. Second, despite being actionable, the recommendations remain conceptual and need to be examined empirically. These recommendations need to be informed by practice, in the form of case study of AI development or a survey of experts in the future work. Finally, it needs to be acknowledged that the discourse on AI ethics is ever evolving and requires continuous interaction and debate among the developers, regulators, business and civil society.

CONCLUSION

AIs are increasingly becoming a reality in modern life. With all pervasiveness of AI systems that can collect information on our minute actions and process complex information sets ranging from IoT to Big Data, there is a need for a framework that attends to the ethical aspect of an AI. Self-awareness and reflection help in the moral development of humans. Despite their immense capacity for logical-mathematical processing, the current generation of AIs lack the ability to reflect and can rarely be called self-aware. Focusing on the machine learning, the process through which an AI develops its intelligence, we offer a set of actions towards responsible machine learning, outlining managerial and developers' actions at each ML stage. Responsible machine learning may include privacy by design, development of explainable AI, identification and removal of inherent biases, and most importantly, use of AI as a moral enabler. We trust that these actions would not only help in the development of ethical AI systems, but also would also help in supporting further moral development of combined human-AI hybrids.

REFERENCES

Agrawal, A., Gans, J. S., & Goldfarb, A. (2019). Exploring the impact of artificial intelligence: Prediction versus judgment. *Information Economics and Policy*, *47*, 1–6. doi:10.1016/j.infoecopol.2019.05.001

Ajana, B. (2015). Augmented borders: Big Data and the ethics of immigration control. *Journal of information. Communication and Ethics in Society*, *13*(1), 58–78. doi:10.1108/JICES-01-2014-0005

Andras, P., Esterle, L., Guckert, M., Han, T. A., Lewis, P. R., Milanovic, K., Payne, T., Perret, C., Pitt, J., Powers, S. T., Urquhart, N., & Wells, S. (2018). Trusting intelligent machines: Deepening trust within socio-technical systems. *IEEE Technology and Society Magazine*, *37*(4), 76–83. doi:10.1109/MTS.2018.2876107

Angelov, P., & Soares, E. (2020). Towards explainable deep neural networks (xDNN). *Neural Networks*, *130*, 185–194. doi:10.1016/j.neunet.2020.07.010 PMID:32682084

Arrieta, A. B., Díaz-Rodríguez, N., Del Ser, J., Bennetot, A., Tabik, S., Barbado, A., ... Chatila, R. (2020). Explainable Artificial Intelligence (XAI): Concepts, taxonomies, opportunities and challenges toward responsible AI. *Information Fusion*, *58*, 82–115. doi:10.1016/j.inffus.2019.12.012

Bansal, G., Nushi, B., Kamar, E., Lasecki, W. S., Weld, D. S., & Horvitz, E. (2019a). Beyond accuracy: The role of mental models in human-ai team performance. In *Proceedings of the AAAI Conference on Human Computation and Crowdsourcing (Vol. 7*, No. 1, pp. 2-11). Academic Press.

Bansal, G., Nushi, B., Kamar, E., Weld, D. S., Lasecki, W. S., & Horvitz, E. (2019, July). Updates in human-ai teams: Understanding and addressing the performance/compatibility tradeoff. *Proceedings of the AAAI Conference on Artificial Intelligence*, *33*(01), 2429–2437. doi:10.1609/aaai.v33i01.33012429

Beck, M., & Libert, B. (2019). The machine learning race is really a data race. *MIT Sloan Management Review*. Available at https://sloanreview.mit.edu/article/the-machine-learningrace-is-really-a-data-race/

Bednar, K., Spiekermann, S., & Langheinrich, M. (2019). Engineering Privacy by Design: Are engineers ready to live up to the challenge? *The Information Society*, *35*(3), 122–142. doi:10.1080/01972243.2019.1583296

Brock, D. C. (2018). Learning from Artificial Intelligence's Previous Awakenings: The History of Expert Systems. *AI Magazine*, *39*(3), 3–15. doi:10.1609/aimag.v39i3.2809

Burrell, J. (2016). How the machine 'thinks': Understanding opacity in machine learning algorithms. *Big Data & Society*, *3*(1), 2053951715622512. doi:10.1177/2053951715622512

Calders, T., & Žliobaitė, I. (2013). Why unbiased computational processes can lead to discriminative decision procedures. In *Discrimination and privacy in the information society* (pp. 43–57). Springer. doi:10.1007/978-3-642-30487-3_3

Cavoukian, A. (2012). Privacy by design: origins, meaning, and prospects for assuring privacy and trust in the information era. In G. O. M. Yee (Ed.), *Privacy protection measures and technologies in business organizations: aspects and standards* (pp. 170–208). IGI Global. doi:10.4018/978-1-61350-501-4.ch007

Custers, B. (2013). Data dilemmas in the information society: Introduction and overview. In *Discrimination and Privacy in the Information Society* (pp. 3–26). Springer. doi:10.1007/978-3-642-30487-3_1

Dafoe, A. (2018). AI governance: a research agenda. Governance of AI Program, Future of Humanity Institute, University of Oxford.

Daugherty, P. R., Wilson, H. J., & Chowdhury, R. (2019). Using artificial intelligence to promote diversity. *MIT Sloan Management Review*, *60*(2), 1.

De Saint Laurent, C. (2018). In defence of machine learning: Debunking the myths of artificial intelligence. *Europe's Journal of Psychology*, *14*(4), 734–747. doi:10.5964/ejop.v14i4.1823 PMID:30555582

Dellermann, D., Ebel, P., Söllner, M., & Leimeister, J. M. (2019). Hybrid intelligence. *Business & Information Systems Engineering*, *61*(5), 637–643. doi:10.100712599-019-00595-2

Dickson, B. (2018). Explainable AI: Learning how AI makes decisions. *PC Mag*. Available at https://uk.pcmag.com/news/118591/learning-how-ai-makes-decisions

European Commission. (2019), *Ethics Guidelines for Trustworthy AI*. https://ec.europa.eu/digital-single-market/en/news/ethics-guidelines-trustworthy-ai

Evgeniou, T., Hardoon, D. R., & Ovchinnikov, A. (2020). What Happens When AI is Used to Set Grades? *Harvard Business Review*. https://hbr.org/2020/08/what-happens-when-ai-is-used-to-set-grades

Fayyad, U., Piatetsky-Shapiro, G., & Smyth, P. (1996). The KDD process for extracting useful knowledge from volumes of data. *Communications of the ACM*, *39*(11), 27–34. doi:10.1145/240455.240464

Floridi, L. (2013). Distributed morality in an information society. *Science and Engineering Ethics*, *19*(3), 727–743. doi:10.100711948-012-9413-4 PMID:23197312

Friedland, J. (2019). AI Can Help Us Live More Deliberately. *MIT Sloan Management Review*. https://sloanreview.mit.edu/article/ai-can-help-us-live-more-deliberately

Friedland, J., & Cole, B. M. (2019). From homo-economicus to homo-virtus: A system-theoretic model for raising moral self-awareness. *Journal of Business Ethics*, *155*(1), 191–205. doi:10.100710551-017-3494-6

Hagras, H. (2018). Toward human-understandable, explainable AI. *Computer*, *51*(9), 28–36. doi:10.1109/MC.2018.3620965

Harkens, A. (2018). The ghost in the legal machine: Algorithmic governmentality, economy, and the practice of law. *Journal of Information Communication and Ethics in Society*, *16*(1), 16–31. doi:10.1108/JICES-09-2016-0038

IEEE. (2019). *Ethically Aligned Design*. Institute of Electrical and Electronic Engineers. https://ethicsinaction.ieee.org/

Jarrahi, M. H. (2018). Artificial intelligence and the future of work: Human-AI symbiosis in organizational decision making. *Business Horizons*, *61*(4), 577–586. doi:10.1016/j.bushor.2018.03.007

Kaplan, A., & Haenlein, M. (2019). Siri, Siri, in my hand: Who's the fairest in the land? On the interpretations, illustrations, and implications of artificial intelligence. *Business Horizons*, *62*(1), 15–25. doi:10.1016/j.bushor.2018.08.004

Kerr, I., & Earle, J. (2013). Prediction, preemption, presumption: How big data threatens big picture privacy. *Stanford Law Review Online*, *66*, 65–72.

Kodratoff, Y. (1999, July). Comparing machine learning and knowledge discovery in databases: An application to knowledge discovery in texts. In *Advanced Course on Artificial Intelligence* (pp. 1–21). Springer.

Lara, F., & Deckers, J. (2019). Artificial Intelligence as a Socratic Assistant for Moral Enhancement. *Neuroethics*, 1–13. doi:10.100712152-019-09401-y

Lauterbach, A. (2019). Artificial intelligence and policy: Quo vadis? *Digital Policy. Regulation & Governance*, *21*(3), 238–263. doi:10.1108/DPRG-09-2018-0054

Leavy, S. (2018, May). Gender bias in artificial intelligence: The need for diversity and gender theory in machine learning. In *Proceedings of the 1st international workshop on gender equality in software engineering* (pp. 14-16). 10.1145/3195570.3195580

LeCun, Y., Bengio, Y., & Hinton, G. (2015). Deep learning. *Nature, 521*(7553), 436-444.

London, A. J. (2019). Artificial intelligence and black-box medical decisions: Accuracy versus explainability. *The Hastings Center Report*, *49*(1), 15–21. doi:10.1002/hast.973 PMID:30790315

Mackenzie, A. (2019). From API to AI: Platforms and their opacities. *Information Communication and Society*, *22*(13), 1989–2006. doi:10.1080/1369118X.2018.1476569

Magnani, L., & Bardone, E. (2008). Distributed morality: Externalizing ethical knowledge in technological artifacts. *Foundations of Science*, *13*(1), 99–108. doi:10.100710699-007-9116-5

Martinho-Truswell, E. (2018), 3 Questions About AI That Nontechnical Employees Should Be Able to Answer. *Harvard Business Review*. https://hbr.org/2018/08/3-questionsabout-ai-that-nontechnicalemployees-should-be-able-to-answer

Matwin, S. (2013). Privacy-preserving data mining techniques: survey and challenges. In *Discrimination and Privacy in the Information Society* (pp. 209–221). Springer. doi:10.1007/978-3-642-30487-3_11

McQuillan, D. (2018). People's councils for ethical machine learning. *Social Media + Society*, *4*(2), 2056305118768303. doi:10.1177/2056305118768303

Miller, K. (2020). A Matter of Perspective: Discrimination, Bias, and Inequality in AI. In M. Jackson & M. Shelly (Eds.), Legal Regulations, Implications, and Issues Surrounding Digital Data (pp. 182-202). IGI Global.

Peeters, M. M., van Diggelen, J., Van Den Bosch, K., Bronkhorst, A., Neerincx, M. A., Schraagen, J. M., & Raaijmakers, S. (2020). Hybrid collective intelligence in a human–AI society. *AI & Society*, 1–22.

Perspectives on Issues in AI Governance. (2019). *Google*. https://ai.google/static/documents/perspectives-on-issues-in-ai-governance.pdf.

Plangger, K., & Watson, R. T. (2015). Balancing customer privacy, secrets, and surveillance: Insights and management. *Business Horizons*, *58*(6), 625–633. doi:10.1016/j.bushor.2015.06.006

Qiu, J., Wu, Q., Ding, G., Xu, Y., & Feng, S. (2016). A survey of machine learning for big data processing. *EURASIP Journal on Advances in Signal Processing*, *2016*(1), 67. doi:10.118613634-016-0355-x

Rai, A. (2020). Explainable AI: From black box to glass box. *Journal of the Academy of Marketing Science*, *48*(1), 137–141. doi:10.100711747-019-00710-5

Ross, J. (2018). The fundamental flaw in AI implementation. *MIT Sloan Management Review*, *59*(2), 10–11.

Rusk, N. (2016). Deep learning. *Nature Methods*, *13*(1), 35–35. doi:10.1038/nmeth.3707 PMID:27110626

Santanen, E. (2019). The value of protecting privacy. *Business Horizons*, *62*(1), 5–14. doi:10.1016/j.bushor.2018.04.004

Saxena, D., & Lamest, M. (2018). Information overload and coping strategies in the big data context: Evidence from the hospitality sector. *Journal of Information Science*, *44*(3), 287–297. doi:10.1177/0165551517693712

Schaar, P. (2010). Privacy by design. *Identity in the Information Society*, *3*(2), 267–274. doi:10.100712394-010-0055-x

Schuller, D., & Schuller, B. W. (2018). The age of artificial emotional intelligence. *Computer*, *51*(9), 38–46. doi:10.1109/MC.2018.3620963

Turner Lee, N. (2018). Detecting racial bias in algorithms and machine learning. *Journal of Information. Communication and Ethics in Society*, *16*(3), 252–260. doi:10.1108/JICES-06-2018-0056

US Congress. (2019). *HR 2231 – Algorithmic Accountability Act of 2019*. https://www.congress.gov/bill/116th-congress/house-bill/2231/text

Verbeek, P. P. (2006). Materializing morality: Design ethics and technological mediation. *Science, Technology & Human Values*, *31*(3), 361–380. doi:10.1177/0162243905285847

Verbeek, P. P. (2011). *Moralizing technology: Understanding and designing the morality of things.* University of Chicago Press. doi:10.7208/chicago/9780226852904.001.0001

Verwer, S., & Calders, T. (2013). Introducing positive discrimination in predictive models. In *Discrimination and privacy in the information society* (pp. 255–270). Springer. doi:10.1007/978-3-642-30487-3_14

Vetrò, A., Santangelo, A., Beretta, E., & De Martin, J. C. (2019). AI: From rational agents to socially responsible agents. *Digital Policy. Regulation & Governance*, *21*(3), 291–304. Advance online publication. doi:10.1108/DPRG-08-2018-0049

Wahlstrom, K., Ul-haq, A., & Burmeister, O. (2020). Privacy by design. *AJIS. Australasian Journal of Information Systems*, *24*, 1–9. doi:10.3127/ajis.v24i0.2801

Webb, H., Patel, M., Rovatsos, M., Davoust, A., Ceppi, S., Koene, A., Dowthwaite, L., Portill, V., Jirotka, M., & Cano, M. (2019). It would be pretty immoral to choose a random algorithm: Opening up algorithmic interpretability and transparency. *Journal of Information Communication and Ethics in Society*, *17*(2), 210–228. doi:10.1108/JICES-11-2018-0092

Weinberg, B. D., Milne, G. R., Andonova, Y. G., & Hajjat, F. M. (2015). Internet of Things: Convenience vs. privacy and secrecy. *Business Horizons*, *58*(6), 615–624. doi:10.1016/j.bushor.2015.06.005

Weld, D. S., & Bansal, G. (2019). The challenge of crafting intelligible intelligence. *Communications of the ACM*, *62*(6), 70–79. doi:10.1145/3282486

Wilson, H. J., Daugherty, P., & Bianzino, N. (2017). The jobs that artificial intelligence will create. *MIT Sloan Management Review*, *58*(4), 14.

Zhang, D., Zhang, Y., Li, Q., Plummer, T., & Wang, D. (2019, July). Crowdlearn: A crowd-ai hybrid system for deep learning-based damage assessment applications. In *2019 IEEE 39th International Conference on Distributed Computing Systems (ICDCS)* (pp. 1221-1232). IEEE. 10.1109/ICDCS.2019.00123

Zhou, L., Pan, S., Wang, J., & Vasilakos, A. V. (2017). Machine learning on big data: Opportunities and challenges. *Neurocomputing*, *237*, 350–361. doi:10.1016/j.neucom.2017.01.026

Žliobaitė, I. (2015). *A survey on measuring indirect discrimination in machine learning.* arXiv preprint arXiv:1511.00148.

ADDITIONAL READING

Boddington, P. (2017). *Towards a Code of Ethics for Artificial Intelligence.* Springer. doi:10.1007/978-3-319-60648-4

Bostrom, N., & Yudkowsky, E. (2014). The ethics of artificial intelligence. The Cambridge handbook of artificial intelligence, 1, 316-334.

Custers, B. H. M., Calders, T. G. K., Schermer, B. W., & Zarsky, T. Z. (2013). *Discrimination and privacy in the information society: data mining and profiling in large databases.* Springer. doi:10.1007/978-3-642-30487-3

Flasiński, M. (2016). *Introduction to Artificial Intelligence*. Springer. doi:10.1007/978-3-319-40022-8

Floridi, L. (2013). *The Ethics of Information*. Oxford University Press. doi:10.1093/acprof:oso/9780199641321.001.0001

Jackson, P. C. (2019). *Introduction to Artificial Intelligence*. Courier Dover Publications.

Molnar, C. (2021). Interpretable Machine Learning: A Guide for Making Black Box Models Explainable. https://christophm.github.io/interpretable-ml-book/

Sheikh, S. (2021). *Understanding the Role of Artificial Intelligence and Its Future Social Impact*. IGI Global. doi:10.4018/978-1-7998-4607-9

Thompson, S. J. (2021). *Machine Law, Ethics, and Morality in the Age of Artificial Intelligence*. IGI Global. doi:10.4018/978-1-7998-4894-3

Vassileva, B., & Zwilling, M. (2021). *Responsible AI and Ethical Issues for Businesses and Governments*. IGI Global. doi:10.4018/978-1-7998-4285-9

White, J., & Searle, R. (2015). *Rethinking Machine Ethics in the Age of Ubiquitous Technology*. IGI Global. doi:10.4018/978-1-4666-8592-5

KEY TERMS AND DEFINITIONS

Artificial Intelligence: A system that develops a prediction model based on the training data, predicts future trends based on current data, and recommends a future course of action.

Deep Learning: A subset of machine learning in which an AI prepares a multilayer neural network of algorithms to build and constantly refine a prediction model based on available data (may be structured or unstructured).

Explainable AI: An AI for which the underlying model may be explained using the constructs understandable to humans. The explanation may be incorporated during the learning process or may be introduced once the model is built.

Human-AI Hybrid: A concept that views humans and AI as subsystems of a socio-technical system, with the implication that action of either have an influence on the other and on the overall system.

Machine Learning: The learning process through which an AI analyses the training dataset (usually structured), builds, and refines a prediction model. Machine learning may be supervised or unsupervised.

Privacy by Design: A concept that puts privacy at the center of the system design process. At each step of the process, privacy-preserving techniques are introduced to support for data protection.

Compilation of References

Aaker, D. A. (1996). *Building Strong Brands*. Simon & Schuster.

Aaker, D. A., Kumar, V., & Day, G. S. (2008). *Marketing research* (9th ed.). John Wiley & Sons.

Abad-Segura, E., González-Zamar, M. D., de la Rosa, A. L., & Gallardo-Pérez, J. (2020). Management of the digital economy in higher education: Trends and future perspectives [Gestión de la economía digital en la educación superior: tendencias y perspectivas futuras]. *Campus Virtuales*, *9*(1), 57–68.

Abbasi-Sureshjani, S., Raumanns, R., Michels, B. E. J., Schouten, G., & Cheplygina, V. (2020). Risk of training diagnostic algorithms on data with demographic bias. *Lecture Notes in Computer Science*, *12446*, 183–192. doi:10.1007/978-3-030-61166-8_20

Abiodun, O. I., Jantan, A., Omolara, A. E., Dada, K. V., Mohamed, N. A., & Arshad, H. (2018). State-of-the-art in artificial neural network applications: A survey. *Heliyon*, *4*(11), 1–41. doi:10.1016/j.heliyon.2018.e00938 PMID:30519653

Abràmoff, M. D., Tobey, D., & Char, D. S. (2020). Lessons Learned About Autonomous AI: Finding a Safe, Efficacious, and Ethical Path Through the Development Process. *American Journal of Ophthalmology*, *214*, 134–142. doi:10.1016/j.ajo.2020.02.022 PMID:32171769

Abratt, R., & Motlana, P. (2002). Managing co-branding strategies: Global brands into local markets. *Business Horizons*, *45*(5), 43–50. doi:10.1016/S0007-6813(02)00242-2

Academic Acelerator. (2021). *Academic Accelerator: Accelerate your scientific research*. Retrieved from https://academic-accelerator.com

Accenture. (2006). *E-government leadership: Building the trust*. Accenture.

Adadi, A., & Berrada, M. (2018). Peeking inside the black-box: A survey on Explainable Artificial Intelligence (XAI). *IEEE Access: Practical Innovations, Open Solutions*, *6*, 52138–52160. doi:10.1109/ACCESS.2018.2870052

Adhikari, A., & Bhattacharya, S. (2016). Appraisal of literature on customer experience in tourism sector: Review and framework. *Current Issues in Tourism*, *19*(4), 296–321. doi:10.1080/13683500.2015.1082538

Adobe. (2020). *Digital Trends Study: 2020 Is The Year Of CX-Centric Business Transformation*. Retrieved January 15, 2021, from https://cmo.adobe.com/articles/2020/2/digital-trends-study--2020-is-the-year-of-cx-centric-business-tr.html#gs.imxcnu

Affisco John, F., & Soliman Khalid, S. (2006). E-government: A strategic operations management framework for service delivery. *Business Process Management Journal*, *12*(1), 13–21. doi:10.1108/14637150610643724

Agbaba, R. (2020). Maritime Challenges in Crisis Times. *Annals of Maritime Studies / Pomorski Zbornik, 59*(1), 51–60. . doi:10.18048/2020.59.03

Aggarwal, P., & McGill, A. L. (2007). Is that car smiling at me? Schema congruity as a basis for evaluating anthropomorphized products. *The Journal of Consumer Research*, *34*(4), 468–479. doi:10.1086/518544

Aghdaie, N., Kolen, J., Mattar, M., Sardari, M., Xue, S., & Atif-Uz Zaman, K. (2018). *Multiplayer Video Game Matchmaking Optimization*. United States Patent 9993735.

Agrawal, A., Gans, J. S., & Goldfarb, A. (2019). Exploring the impact of artificial intelligence: Prediction versus judgment. *Information Economics and Policy*, *47*, 1–6. doi:10.1016/j.infoecopol.2019.05.001

Agyeman, J. K., Ameyaw, B., Li, Y., Appiah-Kubi, J., Annan, A., Oppong, A., & Twumasi, M. A. (2020). Modeling the long-run drivers of total renewable energy consumption: Evidence from top five heavily polluted countries. *Journal of Cleaner Production*, *277*, 123292. doi:10.1016/j.jclepro.2020.123292

Ahmed, A.-O., & Hussein, A.-O. (2006). E-government readiness assessment model. *Journal of Computational Science*, *2*(11), 841–845. Advance online publication. doi:10.3844/jcssp.2006.841.845

Aiello, G., Giallanza, A., & Mascarella, G. (2020). Towards Shipping 4.0. A preliminary gap analysis. *Procedia Manufacturing*, *42*, 24–29. doi:10.1016/j.promfg.2020.02.019

Ainouz, S. A., & Ben Ahmed, M. (2020). *A Smart Chatbot Architecture based on NLP and Machine Learning for Health Care Assistance*. . doi:10.1145/3386723.3387897

Ajana, B. (2015). Augmented borders: Big Data and the ethics of immigration control. *Journal of information. Communication and Ethics in Society*, *13*(1), 58–78. doi:10.1108/JICES-01-2014-0005

Aji, B. M., & Larner, A. J. (2017). Screening for dementia: Single yes/no question or Likert scale? *Clinical Medicine*, *17*(1), 93–94. doi:10.7861/clinmedicine.17-1-93 PMID:28148591

Ajzen, I. (1991). The theory of planned behavior. *Organizational Behavior and Human Decision Processes*, *50*(2), 179–211. Advance online publication. doi:10.1016/0749-5978(91)90020-T

Akerlof, G. A., & Shiller, R. J. (2015). *The economics of manipulation. How we fall like dupes into the plots of the market*. Planeta Colombiana S.A.

Akhter, S. H. (2014). Privacy concern and online transactions: The impact of internet self-efficacy and internet involvement. *Journal of Consumer Marketing*, *31*(2), 118–125. doi:10.1108/JCM-06-2013-0606

Akkiraju, R., Sinha, V., Xu, A., Mahmud, J., Gundecha, P., Liu, Z., Liu, X., & Schumacher, J. (2020). *Characterizing machine learning processes: A maturity framework*. Paper presented at the International Conference on Business Process Management. 10.1007/978-3-030-58666-9_2

Al-adawi, Z., Cardiff, Y., & Pallister, J. (2005). *Conceptual Model of Citizen Adoption of E-Government*. Paper presented at the Second International Conference on Innovations in Information Technology (IIT'05). http://citeseerx.ist.psu.edu/viewdoc/download?doi=10.1.1.92.2165&rep=rep1&type=pdf

Alavi, A., Sayareh, J., Fei, J., & Nguyen, H.-O. (2018). Port Logistics Integration: Challenges and Approaches. *International Journal of Supply Chain Management*, 7.

Algorithmia. (2020). *The roadmap to machine learning maturity*. Retrieved from https://info.algorithmia.com/hubfs/2018/Whitepapers/The_Roadmap_to_Machine_Learning_Maturity_Final.pdf

Ali, F., Kim, W. G., Li, J., & Jeon, H. M. (2018). Make it delightful: Customers' experience, satisfaction and loyalty in Malaysian theme parks. *Journal of Destination Marketing & Management*, *7*, 1–11. doi:10.1016/j.jdmm.2016.05.003

Allam, Z., & Dhunny, Z. A. (2019). On big data, artificial intelligence and smart cities. *Cities (London, England)*, *89*, 80–91. doi:10.1016/j.cities.2019.01.032

Allan Turing: Life and Legacy of a Great Thinker. (n.d.). https://link.springer.com/chapter/10.1007/978-3-662-05642-4_13

Allardice, L. (2021). *Interview: Kazin Ishiguro: AI, gene-editing, big data... I worry we are not in control of these things anymore*. The Guardian. https://www.theguardian.com/books/2021/feb/20/kazuo-ishiguro-klara-and-the-sun-interview?fbclid=IwAR0ExKc5Jda-6TEWM-l-zJzBGYmFgpw0N-DWVrlzPfIl6Ehw3Dh1WPIaRMI

Allen, I. E., & Seaman, C. A. (2007). Likert scales and data analyses. *Quality Progress*, *40*(7), 64–65.

Alliance for Qualification. (2019). *AI and Software Testing Foundation Syllabus*. Retrieved from https://www.alliance-4qualification.info/a4q-ai-and-software-testing

Alonso-Cortés, F. (2020). *¿Hacia dónde vamos en la nueva era del cliente?* Retrieved December 16, 2020, from https://www.marketingdirecto.com/especiales/the-future-of-advertising-especiales/hacia-donde-vamos-en-la-nueva-era-del-cliente

Alop, A. (2019). The Challenges of the Digital Technology Era for Maritime Education and Training. *2019 European Navigation Conference (ENC), Navigation Conference (ENC), 2019 European*. 10.1109/EURONAV.2019.8714176

AlSheibani, S., Cheung, Y., & Messom, C. (2018). Artificial intelligence adoption: AI-readiness at firm-level. *Proceedings of the 22nd Pacific Asia Conference on Information Systems - Opportunities and Challenges for the Digitized Society: Are We Ready? PACIS 2018*.

Al-Shura, M. S., Zabadi, A. M., Abughazaleh, M., & Alhadi, M. A. (2018). Critical success factors for adopting cloud computing in the pharmaceutical manufacturing companies. *Management and Economics Review*, *3*(2), 123–137. doi:10.24818/mer/2018.12-01

Alspaugh, S., Zokaei, N., Liu, A., Jin, C., & Hearst, M. A. (2018). Futzing and moseying: Interviews with professional data analysts on exploration practices. *IEEE Transactions on Visualization and Computer Graphics*, *25*(1), 22–31. doi:10.1109/TVCG.2018.2865040 PMID:30136976

Alvarez-Meaza, I., Pikatza-Gorrotxategi, N., & Rio-Belver, R. M. (2020). Knowledge Sharing and Transfer in an Open Innovation Context: Mapping Scientific Evolution. *Journal of Open Innovation*, *68*(4), 1–23. doi:10.3390/joitmc6040186

Amado, A., Cortez, P., Rita, P., & Moro, S. (2018). Research trends on big data in marketing: A text mining and topic modeling based literature analysis. *European Research on Management and Business Economics*, *24*(1), 1–7. doi:10.1016/j.iedeen.2017.06.002

Amat Abreu, M., Ortega Tenezaca, D. B., & Yaguar Mariño, J. J. (2020). Determination of the degree of influence of the climatic factors of vulnerability of the agricultural sector with neutrosophic techniques [Determinación del grado de influencia de los factores climáticos de vulnerabilidad del sector agropecuario con técnicas neutrosóficas]. *Investigação Operacional*, *41*(5), 699–705.

Amatriain, X. (2013) *Beyond Data: from user information to business value through personalized recommendations and consumer science*. Paper presented at the CIKM'13, San Francisco, CA.

Ameen, N., Tarhini, A., Reppel, A., & Anand, A. (2020). Customer experiences in the age of artificial intelligence. *Computers in Human Behavior*, *114*, 106548. doi:10.1016/j.chb.2020.106548 PMID:32905175

Ameisen, E. (2018). *How to deliver on Machine Learning projects. A guide to the ML Engineering Loop*. Retrieved from https://blog.insightdatascience.com/how-to-deliver-on-machine-learning-projects-c8d82ce642b0

Amelia. (n.d.). *Amelia: The most human AI for the Enterprise*. https://amelia.com/amelia/

Amershi, S., Begel, A., Bird, C., DeLine, R., Gall, H., Kamar, E., Nagappan, N., Nushi, B., & Zimmermann, T. (2019). *Software engineering for machine learning: A case study.* Paper presented at the 2019 IEEE/ACM 41st International Conference on Software Engineering: Software Engineering in Practice (ICSE-SEIP). 10.1109/ICSE-SEIP.2019.00042

Amoah, A., Kwablah, E., Korle, K., & Offei, D. (2020). Renewable energy consumption in Africa: The role of economic well-being and economic freedom. *Sustainability Science*, *10*(32), 2–17.

Anderson, M. R. (2017). *After 75 Years, Isaac Asimov's Three Laws of Robotics Need Updating.* The Conversation.

Anderson, M., & Anderson, S. L. (Eds.). (2011). *Machine ethics.* Cambridge University Press. doi:10.1017/CBO9780511978036

Anderson, S. (2011). *Technologies of History.* Dartmouth College Press.

Anderson, S. L. (2007). *Asimov's "Three Laws of Robotics" and Machine Metaethics. Artificial Intelligence and Society, 22.*

Andrade, G., Ramalho, G., Gomes, A. S., & Corruble, V. (2006). Dynamic Game Balancing: An Evaluation of User Satisfaction. In *Proceedings of the Second Artificial Intelligence and Interactive Digital Entertainment Conference* (p. 3–8). Menlo Park, CA: AAAI Press.

Andrade, J., & Fukuyama Sobata, M. (2020). Content aspects valued by users of travel blogs. Insights from brazilian travelers. *International Journal of Information Systems and Tourism*, *5*(1), 7–17.

Andras, P., Esterle, L., Guckert, M., Han, T. A., Lewis, P. R., Milanovic, K., Payne, T., Perret, C., Pitt, J., Powers, S. T., Urquhart, N., & Wells, S. (2018). Trusting intelligent machines: Deepening trust within socio-technical systems. *IEEE Technology and Society Magazine*, *37*(4), 76–83. doi:10.1109/MTS.2018.2876107

Angelis, J., & da Silva, E. R. (2019). Blockchain adoption: A value driver perspective. *Business Horizons*, *62*(3), 307–314. doi:10.1016/j.bushor.2018.12.001

Angelov, P., & Soares, E. (2020). Towards explainable deep neural networks (xDNN). *Neural Networks*, *130*, 185–194. doi:10.1016/j.neunet.2020.07.010 PMID:32682084

Ankit, K., Irsoy, O., Su, J., Bradbury, J., English, R., Pierce, B., Ondruska, P., Gulrajani, I., & Socher, R. (2016). *Ask Me Anything: Dynamic Memory Networks for Natural Language Processing.* ICML.

ANTAQ. (2019). *Port perfomance system: external user manual.* Agência Nacional de Transportes Aquaviários – ANTAQ.

Antonio, V. (2018, July 30). How AI is changing sales. *Harvard Business Review.* https://hbr.org/2018/07/how-ai-is-changing-sales

Anton, S. G., & Nucu, A. E. A. (2020). The effect of financial development on renewable energy consumption. A panel data approach. *Renewable Energy*, *147*, 330–338. doi:10.1016/j.renene.2019.09.005

Aoki, N. (2020). The importance of the assurance that "humans are still in the decision loop" for public trust in artificial intelligence: Evidence from an online experiment. *Computers in Human Behavior*, 106572.

Ardito, L., Petruzzelli, A. M., Panniello, U., & Garavelli, A. C. (2019). Towards industry 4.0: Mapping digital technologies for supply chain management-marketing integration. *Business Process Management Journal*, *25*(2), 323–346. doi:10.1108/BPMJ-04-2017-0088

Arellano, M., & Bond, S. (1991). Some tests of specification for panel data: Monte Carlo evidence and an application to employment equations. *The Review of Economic Studies*, *58*(2), 277–297. doi:10.2307/2297968

Arellano, M., & Bover, O. (1995). Another look at the instrumental variable estimation of error-components models. *Journal of Econometrics*, *68*(1), 29–51. doi:10.1016/0304-4076(94)01642-D

Argote, L., & Ingram, P. (2000). Knowledge transfer: A basis for competitive advantage in firms. *Organizational Behavior and Human Decision Processes*, *82*(1), 150–169. doi:10.1006/obhd.2000.2893

Arnould, M., Morel, L., & Fournier, M. (2020). Developing a territorial diagnostic as part of a living lab process: Implementation to improve management and wood mobilization in small French private forest. *2020 IEEE International Conference on Engineering, Technology and Innovation (ICE/ITMC), Engineering, Technology and Innovation (ICE/ITMC), 2020 IEEE International Conference On*. 10.1109/ICE/ITMC49519.2020.9198373

Arpteg, A., Brinne, B., Crnkovic-Friis, L., & Bosch, J. (2018). *Software engineering challenges of deep learning*. Paper presented at the 2018 44th Euromicro Conference on Software Engineering and Advanced Applications (SEAA). 10.1109/SEAA.2018.00018

Arrieta, A. B., Díaz-Rodríguez, N., Del Ser, J., Bennetot, A., Tabik, S., Barbado, A., ... Chatila, R. (2020). Explainable Artificial Intelligence (XAI): Concepts, taxonomies, opportunities and challenges toward responsible AI. *Information Fusion*, *58*, 82–115. doi:10.1016/j.inffus.2019.12.012

Artaraz, M. (2002). Teoría de las tres dimensiones de desarrollo sostenible. *Ecosistemas (Madrid)*, *2002*(2). http//www.aeet.org/ecosistemas/022/informe1.htm

Ashfaq, M., Yun, J., Yu, S., & Loureiro, S. M. C. (2020). I, Chatbot: Modeling the determinants of users' satisfaction and continuance intention of AI-powered service agents. *Telematics and Informatics*, *54*, 1014734. doi:10.1016/j.tele.2020.101473

Ashmore, R., Calinescu, R., & Paterson, C. (2019). *Assuring the machine learning lifecycle: Desiderata, methods, and challenges*. arXiv preprint arXiv:1905.04223.

Asimov, I. (1990). The Laws of Robotics. In Robot Visions. Academic Press.

Asimov, I. (n.d.). *Learn about Asimov's Three Laws of Robotics*. Britannica Publishing.

Asimov, I. (1950). *I, Robot*. Del Rey.

Asimov, I. (1957). *The Naked Sun*. Doubleday.

Asimov, I. (1991). *The Lord's Apprentice. In The Ultimate Frankenstein*. Manhanset House.

Asociación para el Desarrollo de la Experiencia de Cliente. (2017). La experiencia de cliente rentable. Libro colaborativo. Ed. DEC, Madrid 2017.

Asociación para el Desarrollo de la Experiencia de Cliente. (2019). *Behavioral Economics. VI Congreso Internacional sobre Experiencia de Cliente*. Retrieved November 22, 2020, from https://asociaciondec.org/eventos/congreso/congreso-2019/

Asociación para el Desarrollo de la Experiencia de Cliente. (2020). *The Experience Revolution. VII Congreso Internacional sobre Experiencia de Cliente*. Retrieved November 22, 2020, from https://asociaciondec.org/eventos/congreso/congreso-2020/

Assi, F., Isiksal, A. Z., & Tursoy, T. (2021). Renewable Energy Consumption, Financial Development, Environmental pollution, and Innovations in the ASEAN +3 group: Evidence from (P-ARDL) model. *Renewable Energy*, *165*(1), 689–700. doi:10.1016/j.renene.2020.11.052

Atlam, H. F., Azad, M. A., Alzahrani, A. G., & Wills, G. (2020). A Review of Blockchain in Internet of Things and AI. *Big Data and Cognitive Computing*, *4*(4), 28. doi:10.3390/bdcc4040028

Attié, E., Gourdou, C., & Guédon, E. (2021). *Understanding consumer acceptance of neuromarketing* Paper presented at *International Marketing Trends Conference*, Venice.

Attwell, K., Lake, J., Sneddon, J., Gerrans, P., Blyth, C., & Lee, J. (2021). Converting the maybes: Crucial for a successful COVID-19 vaccination strategy. *PLoS One, 16*(1), e0245907. doi:10.1371/journal.pone.0245907 PMID:33471821

Auh, S., Menguc, B., Katsikeas, C. S., & Jung, Y. S. (2019). When Does Customer Participation Matter? An Empirical Investigation of the Role of Customer Empowerment in the Customer Participation–Performance Link. *JMR, Journal of Marketing Research, 56*(6), 1012–1033. doi:10.1177/0022243719866408

Autonomous ship project, key facts about YARA Birkeland. (2017). Retrieved from https://www.kongsberg.com/maritime/support/themes/autonomous-ship-project-key-facts-about-yara-birkeland/

Awad, E., Dsouza, S., Kim, R., Schulz, J., Henrich, J., Shariff, A., Bonnefon, J.-F., & Rahwan, I. (2018). The moral machine experiment. *Nature, 563*(7729), 59–64. doi:10.103841586-018-0637-6 PMID:30356211

Awad, N. F., & Krishnan, M. S. (2006). The personalization privacy paradox: An empirical evaluation of information transparency and the willingness to be profiled online for personalization. *Management Information Systems Quarterly, 30*(1), 13–28. doi:10.2307/25148715

Awang, Z., Afthanorhan, A., & Mamat, M. (2016). The Likert scale analysis using parametric based Structural Equation Modeling (SEM). *Computational Methods in Social Sciences, 4*(1), 13.

Ayanso, A., Chatterjee, D., & Cho, D. I. (2011). E-government readiness index: A methodology and analysis. *Government Information Quarterly, 28*(4), 522–532. doi:10.1016/j.giq.2011.02.004

Ayanso, A., Cho, D. I., & Lertwachara, K. (2010). The digital divide: Global and regional ict leaders and followers. *Information Technology for Development, 16*(4), 304–319. doi:10.1080/02681102.2010.504698

Ayanso, A., Cho, D. I., & Lertwachara, K. (2014). Information and communications technology development and the digital divide: A global and regional assessment. *Information Technology for Development, 20*(1), 60–77. doi:10.1080/02681102.2013.797378

Ayanso, A., & Lertwachara, K. (2015). An analytics approach to exploring the link between ict development and affordability. *Government Information Quarterly, 32*(4), 389–398. doi:10.1016/j.giq.2015.09.009

Bachhofer, M., & Wildenberg, M. (2010). *FCMappers.* http://www.fcmappers.net

Backus, P., Janakiram, M., Mowzoon, S., Runger, C., & Bhargava, A. (2006). Factory Cycle-Time Prediction with a Data-Mining Approach. *Semiconductor Manufacturing. IEEE Transactions on., 19*(2), 252–258. doi:10.1109/TSM.2006.873400

Bacon, E., Williams, M. D., & Davies, G. H. (2019). Recipes for success: Conditions for knowledge transfer across open innovation ecosystems. *International Journal of Information Management, 49*, 377–387. doi:10.1016/j.ijinfomgt.2019.07.012

Badri, M. A., & Alshare, K. (2008). A path analytic model and measurement of the business value of e-government: An international perspective. *International Journal of Information Management, 28*(6), 524–535. doi:10.1016/j.ijinfomgt.2006.10.004

Baena Rojas, J. J., Cano Arenas, J. A., Jarrin Quintero, J. A., & Pérez Arroyave, H. R. (2014). Use of information and communication technologies for international negotiation: An advantage for Colombian companies? *Revista Ciencias Estratégicas, 22*(32), 279-294. Retrieved from https://www.redalyc.org/pdf/1513/151339264007.pdf

Bag, S., Pretorius, J. H. C., Gupta, S., & Dwivedi, Y. K. (forthcoming). Role of institutional pressures and resources in the adoption of big data analytics powered artificial intelligence, sustainable manufacturing practices and circular economy capabilities. *Technological Forecasting and Social Change, 163*, 120420.

Bagherzadeh, M., Markovic, S., & Bogers, M. (2021). Managing Open Innovation: A Project-Level Perspective. *IEEE Transactions on Engineering Management, Engineering Management, IEEE Transactions on. IEEE Transactions on Engineering Management, 68*(1), 301–316. doi:10.1109/TEM.2019.2949714

Bailis, P., Olukotun, K., Ré, C., & Zaharia, M. (2017). *Infrastructure for usable machine learning: The stanford dawn project.* arXiv preprint arXiv:1705.07538.

Baillargeon, N. (2018). L'éthique des voitures autonomes [The ethics of autonomous cars]. *Québec Science Magazine.* Accessed from: https://www.quebecscience.qc.ca/normand-baillargeon/ethique-des-voitures-autonomes/

Bain & Co, & Asociación para el Desarrollo de la Experiencia de Cliente. (2020). *V Informe de Madurez de Experiencia de Cliente.* Retrieved November 22, 2020, from https://asociaciondec.org/presentacion-de-informes/v-informe-de-madurez-de-experiencia-de-cliente/45773/

Bajracharya, K. (2018). *Data Science Glossary. Data Science.* Retrieved on 13 February 2021 from https://dimensionless.in/data-science-glossary/

Baker, V., Elliot, B., Sicular, S., Mullen, A., & Brethenoux, E. (2020). *Magic quadrant for cloud AI developer services.* Retrieved from https://www.gartner.com/en/documents/3981253/magic-quadrant-for-cloud-ai-developer-services

Bakkes, S. C. J., Spronck, P. & van Lankveld, G. (2012). Player behavioural modelling for video games. *Entertainment Computing, 3*, 71-79.

Balaguer. (2020). *¿Es posible analizar el ROI en la experiencia del cliente?* Retrieved March 15, 2021, from https://micliente.net/roi-en-la-experiencia-del-cliente/

Baldegger, R., Caon, M., & Sadiku, K. (2020). Correlation between Entrepreneurial Orientation and Implementation of AI in Human Resources Management. *Technology Innovation Management Review, 10*(4), 72–79. doi:10.22215/timreview/1348

Ballesteros Riveros, D. P., & Ballesteros Silva, P. P. (2004). Competitive logistics and supply chain management. *Sciences et Techniques (Paris)*, 201–206. https://www.redalyc.org/pdf/849/84912053030.pdf

Balmer, J. M. T., & Greyser, S. A. (2002). Managing the multiple identities of the corporation. *California Management Review, 43*(3), 72-86. doi:10.2307/41166133

Balyan, R., McCarthy, K. S., & McNamara, D. S. (2020). Applying natural language processing and hierarchical machine learning approaches to text difficulty classification. *International Journal of Artificial Intelligence in Education, 30*(3), 1–34. doi:10.100740593-020-00201-7

Ban, H. J., & Kim, H. S. (2019). Understanding customer experience and satisfaction through airline passengers' online review. *Sustainability, 11*(15), 4066. doi:10.3390u11154066

Banini, G. A., & Bearman, R. A. (1998). Application of fuzzy cognitive maps to factors affecting slurry rheology.[. *International Journal of Mineral Processing, 52*(4), 233–244. doi:10.1016/S0301-7516(97)00071-9

Bannister, F. (2007). The curse of the benchmark: An assessment of the validity and value of e-government comparisons. *International Review of Administrative Sciences, 73*(2), 171–188. doi:10.1177/0020852307077959

Bansal, G., Nushi, B., Kamar, E., Lasecki, W. S., Weld, D. S., & Horvitz, E. (2019a). Beyond accuracy: The role of mental models in human-ai team performance. In *Proceedings of the AAAI Conference on Human Computation and Crowdsourcing* (*Vol. 7*, No. 1, pp. 2-11). Academic Press.

Bansal, G., Nushi, B., Kamar, E., Weld, D. S., Lasecki, W. S., & Horvitz, E. (2019, July). Updates in human-ai teams: Understanding and addressing the performance/compatibility tradeoff. *Proceedings of the AAAI Conference on Artificial Intelligence*, *33*(01), 2429–2437. doi:10.1609/aaai.v33i01.33012429

Banse, R., & Scherer, K. R. (1996). Acoustic profiles in vocal emotion expression. *Journal of Personality and Social Psychology*, *70*(3), 614–636. doi:10.1037/0022-3514.70.3.614 PMID:8851745

Bao, C., & Xu, M. (2019). Cause and effect of renewable energy consumption on urbanization and economic growth in China's provinces and regions. *Journal of Cleaner Production*, *231*, 483–493. doi:10.1016/j.jclepro.2019.05.191

Baran, T. (2020). Anket Formuyla Veri Toplamada Renk ve Cevap Alternatifi Sayısının Cevaplama Süresi ve İfade Cevaplama Sayısına Etkisi. *Akademisyen Yayınevi. Bölüm*, *5*, 97–116.

Barbic, J., D'Cruz, M., Latoschik, M. E., Slater, M., & Bourdot, P. (2017). Virtual Reality and Augmented Reality. In *14th EuroVR International Conference, EuroVR 2017 Laval, France*, December 12–14, 2017 *Proceedings*. Springer. 10.1007/978-3-319-72323-5

Bardakcı, A. (2009). Pazarlama Araştırmalarında Kullanılan Tutum Ölçeklerindeki Cevap Alternatifi Sayısına İlişkin Bir Literatür Taraması. *Pamukkale Üniversitesi Sosyal Bilimler Enstitüsü Dergisi*, (4), 7–20.

Bargh, J. A. (1997). Automaticity of Everyday Life. *Advances in Social Cognition*, *10*, 1–61.

Barinaga, B. (2014). Digital distopy: Videogame. In Artecnología Augmented Knowledge and Accessibility. Complutense.

Barinaga, B. (2016). The video game and the game tradition.Education and shadows of the digital society. *Opción*, *32*, 9.

Barinaga, B. (2010). *Juego. Historia, teoría y práctica del diseño de videojuegos*. Alesia Games.

Barnette, J. (2000). Effects of stem and Likert response option reversals on survey internal consistency: If you feel the need, there is a better alternative to using those negatively worded stems. *Educational and Psychological Measurement*, *60*(3), 361–370. doi:10.1177/00131640021970592

Basak, S. K. (2017). A Framework on the Factors Affecting to Implement Maritime Education and Training System in Educational Institutions: A Review of the Literature. *Procedia Engineering*, *194*, 345–350. doi:10.1016/j.proeng.2017.08.155

Basdas, U., & Esen, M. F. (2021). *Review of Big Data Applications in Finance and Economics. In Handbook of Research on Engineering, Business, and Healthcare Applications of Data Science and Analytics*. IGI Global. doi:10.4018/978-1-7998-3053-5

Batista e Silva, F., Marín Herrera, M. A., Rosina, K., Ribeiro Barranco, R., Freire, S., & Schiavina, M. (2018). Analysing spatiotemporal patterns of tourism in Europe at high-resolution with conventional and big data sources. *Tourism Management*, *68*, 101–115. doi:10.1016/j.tourman.2018.02.020

Batterton, K., & Hale, K. (2017). The Likert Scale What It Is and How to Use It. *Phalanx*, *50*(2), 32–39.

Bauer, P., Stevens, B., & Hazeleger, W. (2021). A digital twin of Earth for the green transition. *Nature Climate Change*, *11*(2), 80–83. doi:10.103841558-021-00986-y

Bayle-Tourtoulou, A.-S., & Badoc, M. (2020). *The neuro-consumer: Adapting communication and marketing strategies for the consumer*. Routledge. doi:10.4324/9781003019978

Bazley, W. J., Cronqvist, H., & Mormann, M. (2021). Visual Finance: The Pervasive Effects of Red on Investor Behavior. *Management Science*. https://pubsonline.informs.org/doi/abs/10.1287/mnsc.2020.3747

BBVA Research. (28 April 2016). *Peru: The retail sector.* Retrieved from https://www.bbvaresearch.com/publicaciones/peru-el-sector-retail/

BBVA. (2019). *Machine learning': ¿qué es y cómo funciona?* Retrieved November 25, 2020, from https://www.bbva.com/es/machine-learning-que-es-y-como-funciona/

BBVA. (2020). *Blockchain y la inteligencia artificial: ¿La pareja ideal?* Retrieved December 23, 2020, from https://www.bbvaopenmind.com/tecnologia/inteligencia-artificial/blockchain-y-la-inteligencia-artificial-la-pareja-idealblockchain-y-la-inteligencia-artificial-la-pareja-ideal/

Bechara, A., Damasio, H., Tranel, D., & Damasio, A. R. (1997). Deciding advantageously before knowing the advantageous strategy. *Science*, *275*(5304), 1293–1295. doi:10.1126cience.275.5304.1293 PMID:9036851

Beck, M., & Libert, B. (2019). The machine learning race is really a data race. *MIT Sloan Management Review*. Available at https://sloanreview.mit.edu/article/the-machine-learningrace-is-really-a-data-race/

Becker, M. H. (1974). The health belief model and sick role behavior. *Health Education Monographs*, *2*(4), 409–419. doi:10.1177/109019817400200407

Bednar, K., Spiekermann, S., & Langheinrich, M. (2019). Engineering Privacy by Design: Are engineers ready to live up to the challenge? *The Information Society*, *35*(3), 122–142. doi:10.1080/01972243.2019.1583296

Belanche, D., Casaló, L. V., & Flavián, C. (2019). Artificial Intelligence in FinTech: Understanding robo-advisors adoption among customers. *Industrial Management & Data Systems*, *119*(7), 1411–1430. Advance online publication. doi:10.1108/IMDS-08-2018-0368

Belani, H., Vukovic, M., & Car, Ž. (2019). *Requirements engineering challenges in building AI-based complex systems.* Paper presented at the 2019 IEEE 27th International Requirements Engineering Conference Workshops (REW). 10.1109/REW.2019.00051

Bellamy, R. K., Dey, K., Hind, M., Hoffman, S. C., Houde, S., Kannan, K., Lohia, P., Martino, J., Mehta, S., & Mojsilović, A. (2019). AI Fairness 360: An extensible toolkit for detecting and mitigating algorithmic bias. *IBM Journal of Research and Development, 63*(4/5), 1-4.

Bell, P. (2004). Monster or Machine? *Nature.*

Benson, C., D. S., P. & Colling, A. (2018, June). *A Quantitative Analysis of Possible Futures of Autonomous Transport.* Academic Press.

Benton, W. C. (2020). Machine learning systems and intelligent applications. *IEEE Software*, *37*(04), 43–49. doi:10.1109/MS.2020.2985224

Benzidia, S., Makaoui, N., & Bentahar, O. (2020). The impact of big data analytics and artificial intelligence on green supply chain process integration and hospital environmental performance. *Technological Forecasting and Social Change*, *165*, 120557. doi:10.1016/j.techfore.2020.120557

Berezina, K., Ciftci, O., & Cobanoglu, C. (2019). Robots, artificial intelligence, and service automation in restaurants. In *Robots, Artificial Intelligence, and Service Automation in Travel, Tourism and Hospitality*. Emerald Publishing Limited. doi:10.1108/978-1-78756-687-320191010

Berger, J., & Milkman, K. (2012). What makes online content viral? *JMR, Journal of Marketing Research*, *49*(2), 192–205. doi:10.1509/jmr.10.0353

Berman, S. J., Kesterson-Townes, L., Marshall, A., & Srivathsa, R. (2012). How cloud computing enables process and business model innovation. *Strategy and Leadership*, *40*(4), 27–35. doi:10.1108/10878571211242920

Beşikçi, E. B., Arslan, O., Turan, O., & Ölçer, A. I. (2016, February). An artificial neural network-based decision support system for energy-efficient ship operations. *Computers & Operations Research*, *66*, 393–401. doi:10.1016/j.cor.2015.04.004

Beuscart, J. S., Mellet, K., & Trespeuch, M. (2016). Reactivity without legitimacy? Online consumer reviews in the restaurant industry. *Journal of Cultural Economics*, *9*(5), 458–475. doi:10.1080/17530350.2016.1210534

Bhatia, R. (2016, December 12). Say hello to Simi – a chatbot that makes your cocktail. *Analytics India Magazine*. https://analyticsindiamag.com/say-hello-simi-chatbot-makes-cocktail/

Bhattacherjee, A. (2001). Understanding information systems continuance: An expectation-confirmation model. *MIS Quarterly: Management. Information Systems*, *25*(3), 351. Advance online publication. doi:10.2307/3250921

Bigman, Y. E., & Gray, K. (2020). Life and Death Decisions of Autonomous Vehicles. *Nature*, *579*(7797), E1–E2. doi:10.103841586-020-1987-4 PMID:32132695

Bilgen, B., & Ozkarahan, I. (2007, June). A mixed-integer linear programming model for bulk grain blending and shipping. *International Journal of Production Economics*, *107*(2), 555–571. doi:10.1016/j.ijpe.2006.11.008

Bilgihan, A., Kandampully, J., & Zhang, T. (2015). Towards a unified customer experience in online shopping environments. Antecedents and outcomes. *International Journal of Quality and Service Sciences*, *8*(1), 102-119. doi:10.1108/IJQSS-07-2015-0054

Bilgihan, A., Barreda, A., Okumus, F., & Nusair, K. (2016). Consumer perception of knowledge sharing in travel related online social networks. *Tourism Management*, *52*, 287–296. doi:10.1016/j.tourman.2015.07.002

Bing Liu, Hakkani-Tur, & Heck. (n.d.). *Dialogue Learning with Human Teaching and Feedback in End-to-End Trainable Task-Oriented Dialogue Systems*. Academic Press.

Bird, S., Dudík, M., Edgar, R., Horn, B., Lutz, R., Milan, V., Sameki, M., Wallach, H., & Walker, K. (2020). *Fairlearn: A toolkit for assessing and improving fairness in AI*. Retrieved from https://www.microsoft.com/en-us/research/uploads/prod/2020/05/Fairlearn_WhitePaper-2020-09-22.pdf

Bishop, P. A., & Herron, R. L. (2015). Use and misuse of the Likert item responses and other ordinal measures. *International Journal of Exercise Science*, *8*(3), 297. PMID:27182418

Blank, D. (2006). *Robotics and Asimov's Three Laws. In The Frankenstein Complex and Asimov's Three Laws*. Association of the Advancement of Artificial Intelligence.

Blum, P. R., (2016). Robots, Slaves, and the Paradox of the Human Condition. In *Isaac Asimov's Robot Stories*. Czech Science Foundation at the project Between Renaissance and Baroque Philosophy and Knowledge of the Czech Lands within the Wider European Context.

Blundell, R., & Bond, S. (1998). Initial conditions and moment restrictions in dynamic panel data models. *Journal of Econometrics*, *87*(1), 115–143. doi:10.1016/S0304-4076(98)00009-8

Blut, M., Beatty, S. E., Evanschitzky, H., & Brock, C. (2014). The impact of service characteristics on the switching costs–customer loyalty link. *Journal of Retailing*, *90*(2), 275–290. doi:10.1016/j.jretai.2014.04.003

Bogachov, S., Kwilinski, A., Miethlich, B., Bartosova, V., & Gurnak, A. (2020). Artificial intelligence components and fuzzy regulators in entrepreneurship development. *Entrepreneurship and Sustainability Issues*, *8*(2), 487–499. doi:10.9770/jesi.2020.8.2(29)

Bogers, M., Chesbrough, H., Heaton, S., & Teece, D. J. (2019). Strategic Management of Open Innovation: A Dynamic Capabilities Perspective. *California Management Review*, *62*(1), 77–94. doi:10.1177/0008125619885150

Bohannon, J., Koch, D., Homm, P., & Driehaus, A. (2015, December). Chocolate with high cocoa content as a weight-loss accelerator. *International Archives of Medicine*, *8*(55), 1–8.

Boletín Oficial del Estado. (2018). *Ley Orgánica 3/2018, de 5 de diciembre, de Protección de Datos Personales y garantía de los derechos digitales*. Retrieved November 18, 2020, from https://www.boe.es/buscar/act.php?id=BOE-A-2018-16673&p=20181206&tn=2

Bolstrom, N., & Yudkowsky, E. (2011). *The Ethics of Artificial Intelligence*. Cambridge University Press.

Bond, S. R. (2002). *Dynamic Panel Data Models: A Guide to Micro Data Methods and Practice*. Center for Microdata Methods and Practice Working Papers.

Bonnefon, J.-F., Shariff, A., & Rahwan, I. (2016). The Social Dilemma of Autonomous Vehicles. *Science*, *352*(6293), 1573–1576. doi:10.1126cience.aaf2654 PMID:27339987

Boone, H. N., & Boone, D. A. (2012). Analyzing likert data. *Journal of Extension*, *50*(2), 1–5.

Boone, J. M. (1997). Hotel-restaurant co-branding: A preliminary study. *The Cornell Hotel and Restaurant Administration Quarterly*, *38*(5), 34–43. doi:10.1016/S0010-8804(97)86581-0

Bornstein, R. F., & Pittman, T. S. (1992). *Perception Without Awareness*. The Guilford Press.

Bosch, J., Crnkovic, I., & Olsson, H. H. (2020). *Engineering AI systems: A research agenda*. arXiv preprint arXiv:2001.07522.

Boston Consulting Group & DEC. (2018). Informe BCG-DEC. In *Reinventarse: El gran reto de la Experiencia de Cliente. Estudio integral sobre la Experiencia de Cliente en España Evolución 2016-2018*. Retrieved November 28, 2020, from https://asociaciondec.org/informes-dec/informe-dec_bcg-reinventarse-el-gran-reto-de-la-experiencia-de-cliente/35680/

Bouguessa, M. (2011). A Practical Approach for Clustering Transaction Data. In P. Perner (Ed.), *Machine Learning and Data Mining in Pattern Recognition* (Vol. 6871, pp. 265–279). Springer-Verlag Berlin Heidelberg. doi:10.1007/978-3-642-23199-5_20

Bourque, P., & Fairley, R. (2014). Guide to the software engineering body of knowledge (SWEBOK (R)): Version 3.0. IEEE Computer Society Press.

Bozonier, J. (2015). *Test-driven machine learning*. Packt Publishing Ltd.

Brantinger, P. (1980). The Gothic Origins of Science Fiction. *NOVEL: A Forum on Fiction*, *14*(1), 30–43.

Braschler, M., Stadelmann, T., & Stockinger, K. (2019). *Applied data science : lessons learned for the data-driven business. Applied data science lessons learned for the data-driven business*. Springer., doi:10.1007/978-3-030-11821-1

Brazil Country Review. (2021). Retrieved from https://search.ebscohost.com/login.aspx?direct=true&db=bth&AN=149896693&site=eds-live

Breck, E., Cai, S., Nielsen, E., Salib, M., & Sculley, D. (2016). *What's your ML Test Score? A rubric for ML production systems*. Paper presented at the Reliable Machine Learning in the Wild - NIPS 2016 Workshop.

Brennan, R., Canning, L., & McDowell, R. (2014). *Business-to-Business Marketing* (3rd ed.). Sage.

Brereton, P., Kitchenham, B. A., Budgen, D., Turner, M., & Khalil, M. (2007). Lessons from applying the systematic literature review process within the software engineering domain. *Journal of Systems and Software*, *80*(4), 571–583. doi:10.1016/j.jss.2006.07.009

Breuel, C. (2020, Jan 3). *MLOps: Machine learning as an engineering discipline.* Retrieved from https://towardsdatascience.com/ml-ops-machine-learning-as-an-engineering-discipline-b86ca4874a3f

Brewer, N. T., Chapman, G. B., Gibbons, F. X., Gerrard, M., McCaul, K. D., & Weinstein, N. D. (2007). Meta-analysis of the relationship between risk perception and health behavior: The example of vaccination. *Health Psychology*, *26*(2), 136–145. doi:10.1037/0278-6133.26.2.136 PMID:17385964

Brill, T. M., Munoz, L., & Miller, R. J. (2019). Siri, Alexa, and other digital assistants: A study of customer satisfaction with artificial intelligence applications. *Journal of Marketing Management*, *35*(15-16), 1401–1436. doi:10.1080/0267 257X.2019.1687571

Brock, D. C. (2018). Learning from Artificial Intelligence's Previous Awakenings: The History of Expert Systems. *AI Magazine*, *39*(3), 3–15. doi:10.1609/aimag.v39i3.2809

Brooks, R. A. (1991). *Intelligence without Reason.* Massachusetts Institute of Technology Artificial Intelligence Laboratory.

Brooks, C., Hoepner, A. G. F., McMillan, D., Vivian, A., & Simen, C. W. (2019). Financial data science: The birth of a new financial research paradigm complementing econometrics? *European Journal of Finance*, *25*(17), 1627–1636. doi:10.1080/1351847X.2019.1662822

Brooks, M. R., Button, K., & Nijkamp, P. (2002). *Maritime Transport.* Edward Elgar Pub.

Brown, J. D. (2011). Likert items and scales of measurement. *Statistics*, *15*(1), 10–14.

Brundtland, G. H. (1987). *Report of the World Commission on Environment and Development: Our Common Future ('The Brundtland Report').* doi:10.9774/GLEAF.978-1-907643-44-6_12

BrynjolfssonE.HittL.KimH. (2011). Strength in numbers: how does data-driven decision making affect firm performance? https://ssrn.com/abstract=1819486 doi:10.2139srn.1819486

Bryson, S. (1992). Measurement and calibration of static distortion of position data from 3D trackers. *SPIE Proceedings Vol. 1669: Stereoscopic Displays and Applications III.*

Buck, B., Espinach, L., & Söderberg, S. (2014). *GRI G4 Guidelines and ISO 26000:2010 How to use the GRI G4 Guidelines and ISO 26000 in conjunction.* Retrieved from https://www.iso.org/files/live/sites/isoorg/files/archive/pdf/en/iso-gri-26000_2014-01-28.pdf

Buck, J., & Lee, E. (1993). Scheduling dynamic dataflow graphs with bounded memory using the token flow model. *1993 IEEE International Conference on Acoustics, Speech, and Signal Processing*, *1*, 429-432. 10.1109/ICASSP.1993.319147

Bughin, J., Cincera, M., Reykowska, D., Żyszkiewicz, M., & Ohme, R. (2020). *Perceptive risk clusters of European citizens and NPI compliance in face of the covid-19 pandemics.* Working Papers ECARES 2020-51, ULB Université libre de Bruxelles.

Bughin, J., Hazan, E., Ramaswamy, S., Allas, T., Dahlström, P., Henke, N., & Trench, M. (2017). Artificial intelligence: the next digital frontier? *McKinsey Global Institute.* https://www.mckinsey.com/~/media/mckinsey/industries/advanced%20 electronics/our%20insights/how%20artificial%20intelligence%20can%20deliver%20real%20value%20to%20companies/ mgi-artificial-intelligence-discussion-paper.ashx

Bughin, J. (2016). Big data, Big bang? *Journal of Big Data*, *3*(1), 1–14. doi:10.118640537-015-0014-3

BughinJ.CinceraM. (2021). *How Institutional Actions before Vaccine Affects Vaccination Intention Later: Prediction Via Machine Learning.* https://ssrn.com/abstract=3824550 doi:10.2139srn.3824550

BughinJ.CinceraM.ReykowskaD.ŻyszkiewiczM.OhmeR. (2021). COVID-19 Endemism and the Control Skeptics. https://ssrn.com/abstract=3785230 doi:10.2139srn.3785230

Buhalis, D., & Leung, R. (2018). Smart hospitality—Interconnectivity and interoperability towards an ecosystem. *International Journal of Hospitality Management, 71*, 41–50. doi:10.1016/j.ijhm.2017.11.011

Burke, R., & Leykin, A. (2014). *Identifying the Drivers of Shopper Attention.* Engagement, and Purchase., doi:10.1108/S1548-643520140000011006

Burkov, A. (2020). *Machine learning engineering.* True Positive Inc.

Burns, A., & Bush, R. (2000). *Marketing Research* (3rd ed.). Prentice Hall.

Burrell, J. (2016). How the machine 'thinks': Understanding opacity in machine learning algorithms. *Big Data & Society, 3*(1), 2053951715622512. doi:10.1177/2053951715622512

Buttle, F., & Maklan, S. (2019). Customer relationship management: concepts and technologies (4th ed.). Routledge, Taylor & Francis Group. doi:10.4324/9781351016551

Buxbaum, P. (2020). Pandemic developments will drive future supply-chain improvements. *American Journal of Transportation.*

Bybee, R. W. (1991). Planet Earth in Crisis: How Should Science Educators Respond? *The American Biology Teacher, 53*(3), 146–153. doi:10.2307/4449248

Byrne, J., Hughes, K., Rickerson, W., & Kurdgelashvili, L. (2007). American policy conflict in the greenhouse: Divergent trends in federal, regional, state, and local green energy and climate change policy, *Energy. Pol, 35*(9), 4555–4573. doi:10.1016/j.enpol.2007.02.028

Byrnes, J. P., Miller, D. C., & Schafer, W. D. (1999). Gender differences in risk taking: A meta-analysis. *Psychological Bulletin, 125*(3), 367–383. doi:10.1037/0033-2909.125.3.367

Caceres Cabana, Y. D., Gonzalez, S., & Rivera Medina, J. (2020). Alpaca meat: constraints and reinforcements in consumption. In Anthropological approaches to understanding consumption patterns and consumer behaviour. IGI Global. doi:10.4018/978-1-7998-3115-0.ch016

Cacho, J. L., Marques, L., & Nascimento, Á. (2020). Customer-Oriented Global Supply Chains: Port Logistics in the Era of Globalization and Digitization. In V. Chkoniya, A. O. Madsen, & P. Bukhrashvili (Eds.), *Anthropological Approaches to Understanding Consumption Patterns and Consumer Behavior* (pp. 82–103). IGI Global. doi:10.4018/978-1-7998-3115-0.ch005

CAF Development Bank of Latin America. (2020). *The state of Latin America's digitalization in the face of the COVID-19 pandemic* (Vol. 19). Retrieved from Observatorio CAF del Ecosistema Digital: https://scioteca.caf.com/handle/123456789/1540

CAF Development Bank of Latin America. (2020). The state of Latin America's digitalization in the face of the COVID-19 pandemic. *CAF Observatory of the Digital Ecosystem, 19*(3), 17. Retrieved from https://scioteca.caf.com/handle/123456789/1540

Cai, S., Bileschi, S., Nielsen, E. D., & Chollet, F. (2020). *Deep learning with JavaScript.* Manning.

Calders, T., & Žliobaitė, I. (2013). Why unbiased computational processes can lead to discriminative decision procedures. In *Discrimination and privacy in the information society* (pp. 43–57). Springer. doi:10.1007/978-3-642-30487-3_3

Calvo, R. A., & D'Mello, S. (2010). Affect detection: An interdisciplinary review of models, methods, and their applications. *IEEE Transactions on Affective Computing*, *1*(1), 18–37. doi:10.1109/T-AFFC.2010.1

Camacho, D., Panizo-Lledot, A., Bello-Orgaz, G., & Gonzalez-Pardo, C. E. (2020). The four dimensions of social network analysis: an overview of research methods, applications, and software tools. Information Fusion, 63, 88–120. doi:10.1016/j.inffus.2020.05.009

Camarinha-Matos, L. M. (2012). *Scientific research methodologies and techniques- Unit 2: Scientific method. Unit 2: Scientific methodology. PhD program in electrical and computer engineering.* Uninova.

Canhoto, A. I., & Clear, F. (2020). Artificial intelligence and machine learning as business tools: A framework for diagnosing value destruction potential. *Business Horizons*, *63*(2), 183–193. doi:10.1016/j.bushor.2019.11.003

Cao, L. (2017). Data science: A comprehensive overview. *ACM Comput. Surv. 50*(3). doi:10.1145/3076253

Cao, K., Liu, E., & Jain, A. K. (2014). Segmentation and Enhancement of Latent Fingerprints: A Coarse to Fine RidgeStructure Dictionary. *IEEE Transactions on Pattern Analysis and Machine Intelligence*, *36*(9), 1847–1859. doi:10.1109/TPAMI.2014.2302450 PMID:26352236

Capgemini. (2005). *Online availability of public services: How is europe progressing?* Retrieved from http://www.umic.pt/images/stories/publicacoes/2004[1].01%20-%20Web-based%20Survey%20on%20Electronic%20Public%20Services%20-%20Fourth%20measurement.pdf

Capgemini. (2006). *Online availability of public services: How is europe progressing?* Retrieved from https://www.ut.is/media/Skyrslur/CapGemini_2006.pdf

Capgemini. (2020). *Informe mundial del seguro 2020 de Capgemini.* Retrieved December 15, 2020, from https://www.capgemini.com/es-es/news/informe-mundial-del-seguro-2020-de-capgemini/

Caputo, A., Marzi, G., & Pellegrini, M. (2016). The Internet of Things in manufacturing innovation processes: Development and application of a conceptual framework. *Business Process Management Journal*, *22*(2), 383–402. doi:10.1108/BPMJ-05-2015-0072

Carbone, V., & De Martino, M. (2003). The changing role of ports in supply-chain management: An empirical analysis. *Maritime Policy & Management*, *30*(4), 305–320. doi:10.1080/0308883032000145618

Carifio, J., & Perla, R. (2008). Resolving the 50-year debate around using and misusing Likert scales. *Medical Education*, *42*(12), 1150–1152. doi:10.1111/j.1365-2923.2008.03172.x PMID:19120943

Carifio, J., & Perla, R. J. (2007). Ten common misunderstandings, misconceptions, persistent myths and urban legends about Likert scales and Likert response formats and their antidotes. *Journal of Social Sciences*, *3*(3), 106–116. doi:10.3844/jssp.2007.106.116

Carley, K., & Palmquist, M. (1992). Extracting, representing, and analyzing mental models.[. *Social Forces*, *70*(3), 601–636. doi:10.2307/2579746

Carmigniani, J., Furht, B., Anisetti, M., Ceravolo, P., Damiani, E., & Ivkovic, M. (2011). Augmented reality technologies, systems and applications. *Multimedia Tools and Applications*, *51*(1), 341–377. doi:10.100711042-010-0660-6

Carr, S. (2021). *How Many Ads Do We See A Day In 2021?* https://ppcprotect.com/how-many-ads-do-we-see-a-day/

Carter, R. M., MacInnes, J. J., Huettel, S. A., & Adcock, R. A. (2009). Activation in the VTA and nucleus accumbens increases in anticipation of both gains and losses. *Frontiers in Behavioral Neuroscience, 3*, 21. doi:10.3389/neuro.08.021.2009 PMID:19753142

Carù, A., & Cova, B. (2013). *Consuming experiences: An introduction. In Consuming experience*. Routledge. doi:10.4324/9780203390498

Casaca, A. C. P., & Loja, M. A. R. (2020). 2019 World of Shipping Portugal. An International Research Conference on Maritime Affairs editorial "Leading the shipping industry into the future." *Journal of Shipping & Trade, 5*(1), 1–4. doi:10.118641072-020-00082-y

Casco, A. R. (2020). Effects of the COVID-19 pandemic on consumer behavior. *INNOVARE Journal of Science and Technology, 9*(2).

Cassar, M. L., Caruana, A., & Konietzny, J. (2020). Wine and satisfaction with fine dining restaurants: An analysis of tourist experiences from user generated content on TripAdvisor. *Journal of Wine Research*, 1–16.

Castells, M. (1996). La era de la información. Economía, sociedad y cultura. Siglo XXI.

Castelo, N. (2019). *Blurring the line between human and machine: Marketing artificial intelligence* (Doctoral dissertation). Columbia University Academic Commons. doi:10.7916/d8-k7vk-0s40

Castelo, N., Bos, M., & Lehman, D. (2018). *Consumer adoption of algorithms that blur the line between human and machine*. Graduate School of Business: Columbia University Working Paper.

Castelo, N., & Ward, A. (2016). Political affiliation moderates attitudes towards artificial intelligence. In P. Moreau & S. Puntoni (Eds.), *NA - Advances in Consumer Research* (pp. 723–723). Association for Consumer Research.

Castrillón-Muñoz, A. J., Infante-Moro, A., Zuñiga-Collazos, A., & Martínez-López, F. J. (2019). University Spin-Off: A Literature Review for Their Application in Colombia. *Journal of Environmental Management and Tourism, 10*(1), 73–86. doi:10.14505//jemt.v10.7(33).08

Castrillón-Muñoz, A. J., Infante-Moro, A., Zuñiga-Collazos, A., & Martínez-López, F. J. (2020a). Capacities of the research groups at unicauca (Colombia) to develop spin-off-type undertakings. *Journal of Technology Management & Innovation, 15*(1), 64–75. doi:10.4067/S0718-27242020000100064

Castrillón-Muñoz, A. J., Infante-Moro, A., Zúñiga-Collazos, A., & Martínez-López, F. J. (2020b). Generation of technological-based spin offs based on I+D+i results from the research groups of the University of Cauca Colombia [Generación de empresas derivadas de base tecnológica (Spin Offs), a partir de los resultados de I+ D+ i de los grupos de investigación de la Universidad del Cauca, Colombia]. *Información Tecnológica, 31*(1), 67–78.

Cavoukian, A. (2012). Privacy by design: origins, meaning, and prospects for assuring privacy and trust in the information era. In G. O. M. Yee (Ed.), *Privacy protection measures and technologies in business organizations: aspects and standards* (pp. 170–208). IGI Global. doi:10.4018/978-1-61350-501-4.ch007

Centomo, S., Panado, M., & Fummi, F. (2018). Cyber-Physical Systems Integration in a Production Line Simulator. *2018 IFIP/IEEE International Conference on Very Large Scale Integration (VLSI-SoC)*, 237-242. 10.1109/VLSI-SoC.2018.8644836

Central Reserve Bank of Peru. (2016). *Informe Económico y Social Región Arequipa*. Retrieved from https://www.bcrp.gob.pe/docs/Proyeccion-Institucional/Encuentros-Regionales/2016/arequipa/ies-arequipa-2016.pdf

CepymeNews. (2020). *14 estadísticas sobre la gestión de la experiencia del cliente*. Retrieved November 16, 2020, from https://cepymenews.es/gestion-experiencia-cliente/

Cerdán, Á. L. M. (2006). Análisis de la adopción de tecnologías colaborativas en Pymes. *Revista de economía y empresa*, *24*(56), 51-66.

Chan, A. P. H., & Tung, V. W. S. (2019). Examining the effects of robotic service on brand experience: The moderating role of hotel segment. *Journal of Travel & Tourism Marketing*, *36*(4), 458–468. Advance online publication. doi:10.10 80/10548408.2019.1568953

Chang, K. (2020). Artificial intelligence in personnel management: The development of APM model. *The Bottom Line (New York, N.Y.)*, *33*(4), 377–388. doi:10.1108/BL-08-2020-0055

Chang, K. C., Kuo, N. T., Hsu, C. L., & Cheng, Y. S. (2014). The impact of website quality and perceived trust on customer purchase intention in the hotel sector: Website brand and perceived value as moderators. *International Journal of Innovation, Management and Technology*, *5*(4), 255. doi:10.7763/IJIMT.2014.V5.523

Chapman, P., Clinton, J., Kerber, R., Khabaza, T., Reinartz, T., Shearer, C., & Wirth, R. (2000). *CRISP-DM 1.0: Step-by-step data mining guide*. Academic Press.

Chapman, V., & Hunicke, R. (2004). *AI for Dynamic Difficulty Adjustment in Games*. Academic Press.

Charmetant, E. (2018). La neuroéthique: Histoire, actualité et prospective [Neuroethics: history, present and future]. *Transversalites*, *146*(3), 45–58. doi:10.3917/trans.146.0045

Chaturvedi, A., Carroll, J. D., Green, P. E., & Rotondo, J. A. (1997). A feature-based approach to market segmentation via over-lapping k-centroids clustering. *JMR, Journal of Marketing Research*, *34*(3), 370–377. doi:10.1177/002224379703400306

Chaudhuri, A., & Holbrook, M. B. (2001). The chain of effects from brand trust and brand affect to brand performance: The role of brand loyalty. *Journal of Marketing*, *65*(2), 81–93. doi:10.1509/jmkg.65.2.81.18255

Chen, C.-H., Khoo, L. P., Chong, Y. T., & Yin, X. F. (2014, May). Knowledge discovery using genetic algorithm for maritime situational awareness. *Expert Systems with Applications*, *41*(6), 2742–2753. doi:10.1016/j.eswa.2013.09.042

Chen, C., Härdle, W. K., & Unwin, A. (2007). *Handbook of data visualization*. Springer Science & Business Media.

Chen, C., & Phou, S. (2013). A closer look at destination: Image, personality, relationship and loyalty. *Tourism Management*, *36*, 269–278. doi:10.1016/j.tourman.2012.11.015

Chen, F., Feng, J., Jain, A. K., Zhou, J., & Zhang, J. (2011). Separating overlapped fingerprints. *IEEE Transactions on Information Forensics and Security*, *6*(2), 346–359. doi:10.1109/TIFS.2011.2114345

Chen, H., & Boning, D. (2017). Online and Incremental Machine Learning Approaches for IC Yield Improvement. *2017 IEEE/ACM International Conference on Computer-Aided Design (ICCAD)*. 10.1109/ICCAD.2017.8203857

Chiambaretto, P., & Gurău, C. (2017). David by Goliath: What is co-branding and what is in it for SMEs. *International Journal of Entrepreneurship and Small Business*, *31*(1), 103–122. doi:10.1504/IJESB.2017.083805

Chkoniya, V. (2021). *How Harvard's Case Method Can Help to Overcome the Challenges of Applied Data Science Education*. Academic Press.

Chkoniya, V., & Mateus, A. (2019). Digital Category Management: How Technology Can Enable the Supplier-Retailer Relationship. In Smart Marketing With the Internet of Things (pp. 139-163). IGI Global.

Chkoniya, V., Madsen, A. O., & Bukhrashvili, P. (2020). *Anthropological Approaches to Understanding Consumption Patterns and Consumer Behavior*. IGI Global. doi:10.4018/978-1-7998-3115-0

Chopra, K. (2019). Indian shopper motivation to use artificial intelligence: Generating Vroom's expectancy theory of motivation using grounded theory approach. *International Journal of Retail & Distribution Management, 47*(3), 331–347. Advance online publication. doi:10.1108/IJRDM-11-2018-0251

Cho, S. W. (2020). Quantifying the impact of nonpharmaceutical interventions during the COVID-19 outbreak: The case of Sweden. *The Econometrics Journal, 23*(3), 323–334. doi:10.1093/ectj/utaa025

Chou, K. L., Amick, M. M., Brandt, J., Camicioli, R., Frei, K., Gitelman, D., Goldman, J., Growdon, J., Hurtig, H. I., Levin, B., Litvan, I., Marsh, L., Simuni, T., Tröster, A. I., & Uc, E. Y. (2010). A Recommended Scale for Cognitive Screening in Clinical Trials of Parkinson's Disease. *Movement Disorders, 25*(15), 2501–2507. doi:10.1002/mds.23362 PMID:20878991

Christian, L. M., Parsons, N. L., & Dillman, D. A. (2009). Designing scalar questions for Web surveys. *Sociological Methods & Research, 37*(3), 393–425. doi:10.1177/0049124108330004

Churchill, G. A., Jr. (1999). Marketing Research Methodological Foundations (7th ed.). The Dryden Press International Edition.

Chyung, S. Y., Barkin, J. R., & Shamsy, J. A. (2018). Evidence-Based Survey Design: The Use of Negatively Worded Items in Surveys. *Performance Improvement, 57*(3), 16–25. doi:10.1002/pfi.21749

Chyung, S. Y., Hutchinson, D., & Shamsy, J. A. (2020). Evidence-Based Survey Design: Ceiling Effects Associated with Response Scales. *Performance Improvement, 59*(6), 6–13. doi:10.1002/pfi.21920

Chyung, S. Y., Kennedy, M., & Campbell, I. (2018). Evidence-Based Survey Design: The Use of Ascending or Descending Order of Likert-Type Response Options. *Performance Improvement, 57*(9), 9–16. doi:10.1002/pfi.21800

Chyung, S. Y., Roberts, K., Swanson, I., & Hankinson, A. (2017). Evidence-based survey design: The use of a midpoint on the Likert scale. *Performance Improvement, 56*(10), 15–23. doi:10.1002/pfi.21727

Chyung, S. Y., Swanson, I., Roberts, K., & Hankinson, A. (2018). Evidence-based survey design: The use of continuous rating scales in surveys. *Performance Improvement, 57*(5), 38–48. doi:10.1002/pfi.21763

Ciborra, C. (2005). Interpreting e-government and development: Efficiency, transparency or governance at a distance? *Information Technology & People, 18*(3), 260–279. doi:10.1108/09593840510615879

Ciccarelli, S. K., & Meyer, G. E. (2006). *Psychology*. Prentice Hall.

Cisco. (2020). *Cisco Annual Internet Report (2018–2023)*. Retrieved November 21, 2020, from https://www.cisco.com/c/en/us/solutions/collateral/executive-perspectives/annual-internet-report/white-paper-c11-741490.html

Claeys, A., & Vialatte, J.-S. (2012). Office parlementaire d'évaluation des choix scientifiques et technologiques. L'impact et les enjeux des nouvelles technologies d'exploration et de thérapie du cerveau [Parliamentary Office for the Evaluation of Scientific and Technological Choices. The impact and challenges of new technologies for brain exploration and therapy]. *Rapport par Claeys et Vialatte, députés. Paris. Assemblée Nationales et Sénat, 2012*, 25.

Clancy, L. (2019). *Functional programming reaches for stardom in finance*. CME Group. Accessed and reviewed in April 2021, https://www.risk.net/risk-management/6395366/functional-programming-reaches-for-stardom-in-finance

Clark, K. R., Moses, E., & Leslie, K. R. (2021). System N: A Multimodal Approach to Understanding Consumer Decision Making. *Journal of Consumer Psychology*.

Cliffydcw (Producer). (2020). *Own work*. Retrieved from https://commons.wikimedia.org/w/index.php?curid=19054763

Cluetrain. (1999). *95 Theses*. Retrieved November 16, 2020, from https://www.cluetrain.com/; http://tremendo.com/cluetrain/

Coble, K. H., Mishra, A. K., Ferrell, S., & Griffin, T. (2018). Big data in agriculture: A challenge for the future. *Applied Economic Perspectives and Policy, 40*(1), 79–96. doi:10.1093/aepp/ppx056

Codara, L. (1998). *Le Mappe Cognitive*. Carocci Editore.

Cohen, H. (2013). *Los 4 momentos de la verdad en el marketing*. Retrieved December 13, 2020, from https://www.marketingdirecto.com/actualidad/checklists/los-4-momentos-de-la-verdad-en-el-marketing

Cohen, J. B., Pham, M.T., & Andrade, E.B. (2006): The nature and role of affect in consumer behavior. In Handbook of Consumer Psychology. Lawrence Erlbaum.

Columbus, L. (2019). *10 Ways Machine Learning Is Revolutionizing Manufacturing in 2019*. https://www.forbes.com/sites/louiscolumbus/2019/08/11/10-ways-machine-learning-is-revolutionizing-manufacturing-in-2019/?sh=7e5167012b40

Consoli, S., Reforgiato Recupero, D., & Saisana, M. (Eds.). (2021). Data Science for Economics and Finance. Methodologies and Applications. Springer International Publishing. doi:10.1007/978-3-030-66891-4

Constanza-Chock, S. (2020). *Design Justice: Community-Led Practices to Build the Worlds we Need*. MIT Press. doi:10.7551/mitpress/12255.001.0001

Consumer 360 and DATUM International. (2020). *Customer Experience and COVID-19 Comercio, Bancos y Farmacias protocols*. Retrieved from https://www.datum.com.pe/new_web_files/files/pdf/2020%20Experiencia%20del%20Cliente%20y%20Protocolos%20Covid-19.pdf

Contissa, G., Lagioia, F., & Sartor, G. (2017). The ethical knob: Ethically-customizable automated vehicles and the law. *Artificial Intelligence and Law, 25*(3), 365–378. doi:10.100710506-017-9211-z

Copeland, B. J., & Produfoot, D. (2004). *The Computer, Artificial Intelligence, and the Turing Test. In Alan Turing: Life and Legacy of a Great Thinker*. Springer.

Corcos, A., & Pannequin, F. (2013). Neuroeconomics, decision-making and rationality. *Économie et institutions, 16.* . doi:10.4000/ei.74

Corrocher, N., & Cappa, E. (2020). The Role of public interventions in inducing private climate finance: An empirical analysis of the solar energy sector. *Energy Policy, 147*, 111787. doi:10.1016/j.enpol.2020.111787

Cosic, R., Shanks, G., & Maynard, S. B. (2015). A business analytics capability framework. *AJIS. Australasian Journal of Information Systems, 19*, S5–S19. doi:10.3127/ajis.v19i0.1150

Courbet, D., & Benoit, D. (2013). Neurosciences au service de la communication commerciale: manipulation et éthique - Une critique du neuromarketing [Neuroscience at the service of commercial communication: manipulation and ethics - A Critique of Neuromarketing]. *Études de communication - Langages, information, médiations. Université de Lille, 40*, 28–42.

Coussement, K., Lessmann, S., & Verstraeten, G. (2017). A comparative analysis of data preparation algorithms for customer churn prediction: A case study in the telecommunication industry. *Decision Support Systems, 95*, 27–36. doi:10.1016/j.dss.2016.11.007

Crawford, C. (2005). *On Interactive Storytelling*. New Riders.

Crews, D. E., & Zavotka, S. (2006). Aging, Disability, and Frailty: Implications for Universal Design. *Physiol Anthropol., 25*(1), 113–118. doi:10.2114/jpa2.25.113 PMID:16617216

Cross, J., Meadow, G., & Com, I., & Jostaphot. (2017, September). Autonomous ships 101. *Journal of Ocean Technology, 12*, 23–27.

Crupi, A., Del Sarto, N., Di Minin, A., Gregori, G. L., Lepore, D., Marinelli, L., & Spigarelli, F. (2020). The digital transformation of SMEs–a new knowledge broker called the digital innovation hub. *Journal of Knowledge Management, 24*(6), 1263–1288. doi:10.1108/JKM-11-2019-0623

Cruz-Neira, C. (1993). Virtual reality overview. *SIGGRAPH 93 International Conference on Computer Graphics and Interactive Techniques.*

Cubilla-Montilla, M., Rodriguez, C., & Ortega, E. (2015). Análisis de los indicadores de sostenibilidad del Global Reporting Initiative. Una mirada desde el Biplot Logístico. *Revista Centros, 3*, 96–114.

Cubric, M. (2020). Drivers, barriers and social considerations for AI adoption in business and management: A tertiary study. *Technology in Society, 62*, 101257. Advance online publication. doi:10.1016/j.techsoc.2020.101257

Cullen, R. (2001). Tackling the digital divide. *Online Information Review, 25*(5), 311–320. doi:10.1108/14684520110410517

Curia, L., & Lavalle, A. (2011). Decision strategies in dynamic systems - applying fuzzy cognitive maps application to a socio-economic example [Estrategias de decisión en sistemas dinámicos - aplicando mapas cognitivos difusos aplicación a un ejemplo socio-económico]. *Journal of Information Systems and Technology Management, 8*, 663–680. doi:10.4301/S1807-17752011000300008

Custers, B. (2013). Data dilemmas in the information society: Introduction and overview. In *Discrimination and Privacy in the Information Society* (pp. 3–26). Springer. doi:10.1007/978-3-642-30487-3_1

Czermański, E., Cirella, G. T., Oniszczuk-Jastrząbek, A., Pawłowska, B., & Notteboom, T. (2021). An Energy Consumption Approach to Estimate Air Emission Reductions in Container Shipping. *Energies, 14*(278), 278. doi:10.3390/en14020278

Daellenbach, H., McNickle, D., & Dye, Sh. (2012). *Management Science. Decision-making through systems thinking* (2nd ed.). Plagrave Macmillian.

Dafoe, A. (2018). AI governance: a research agenda. Governance of AI Program, Future of Humanity Institute, University of Oxford.

Dahlberg, M., & Johansson, E. (2000). An examination of the dynamic behaviour of local governments using GMM bootstrapping methods. *Journal of Applied Econometrics, 15*(4), 401–416. doi:10.1002/1099-1255(200007/08)15:4<401::AID-JAE564>3.0.CO;2-G

Dahlstrom, R., & Dato-on, M. C. (2004). Business-to-business antecedents to retail co-branding. *Journal of Business-To-Business Marketing, 11*(3), 1–22. doi:10.1300/J033v11n03_01

Dai, L., Hu, H., & Zhang, D. (2015, October). An empirical analysis of freight rate and vessel price volatility transmission in global dry bulk shipping market [English Edition]. *Journal of Traffic and Transportation Engineering, 2*(5), 353–361. doi:10.1016/j.jtte.2015.08.007

Damasio, A. R. (1994). *Descartes' Error: Emotion, Reason and the Human Brain.* G.P. Putmans & Sons.

Daniela, P., Calvert, T., Clark, B., & Parkhurst, G. (2019). *New Technology and Automation in Freight Transport and Handling Systems.* Academic Press.

Dantzig, G. (1949). Programming of Interdependent Activities: II Mathematical Models. *The Journal of the Operational Research Society, 53*(11), 1275–1280.

Dargis, M. (2015). Review: In 'Ex Machina', a Mogul Fashions the Droid of his dreams. *The New York Times*. https://www.nytimes.com/2015/04/10/movies/review-in-ex-machina-a-mogul-fashions-the-droid-of-his-dreams.html

Das, A., Singh, H., & Joseph, D. (2017). A longitudinal study of e-government maturity. *Information & Management*, *54*(4), 415–426. doi:10.1016/j.im.2016.09.006

Daugherty, P. R., Wilson, H. J., & Chowdhury, R. (2019). Using artificial intelligence to promote diversity. *MIT Sloan Management Review*, *60*(2), 1.

Davenport, T. H., Barth, P., & Bean, R. (2012). How Big Data Is Different. *MIT Sloan Management Review*, *54*(1), 43.

Davenport, T. H., & Ronanki, R. (2018). Artificial intelligence for the real world. *Harvard Business Review*, *96*(1), 108–116.

Davenport, T., Guha, A., Grewal, D., & Bressgott, T. (2020). How artificial intelligence will change the future of marketing. *Journal of the Academy of Marketing Science*, *48*(1), 24–42. doi:10.100711747-019-00696-0

Davies, J., (2016). Program good ethics into artificial intelligence. *Nature*, *538*, 291.

Davis, F. D. (1989). Perceived usefulness, perceived ease of use, and user acceptance of information technology. *MIS Quarterly: Management. Information Systems*, *13*(3), 319. Advance online publication. doi:10.2307/249008

Davis, K., & Blomstrom, R. (1980). *Business and society. Concepts and policy issues* (4th ed.). McGraw Hill.

Davis, R., Vochozka, M., Vrbka, J., & Neguriță, O. (2020). Industrial Artificial Intelligence, Smart Connected Sensors, and Big Data-driven Decision-Making Processes in Internet of Things-based Real-Time Production Logistics. *Economics. Management and Financial Markets*, *15*(3), 9–15.

Davoyan, A. (2020). The Impact of Artificial Intelligence on Work, Education, Mobility and Economy. In *Proceedings of the Future Technologies Conference* (pp. 291-296). Springer.

De Bruyn, A., Viswanathan, V., Beh, Y. S., Brock, J. K. U., & von Wangenheim, F. (2020). Artificial Intelligence and Marketing: Pitfalls and Opportunities. *Journal of Interactive Marketing*, *51*, 91–105. doi:10.1016/j.intmar.2020.04.007

De Caigny, A., Coussement, K., & De Bock, K. W. (2020). Leveraging fine-grained transaction data for customer life event predictions. *Decision Support Systems, 130.* . doi:10.1016/j.dss.2019.113232

De Caigny, A., Coussement, K., & De Bock, K. W. (2018). A new hybrid classification algorithm for customer churn prediction based on logistic regression and decision trees. *European Journal of Operational Research*, *269*(2), 760–772. doi:10.1016/j.ejor.2018.02.009

de Castro Neto, H., Julia, R. M. S., Paiva, E. R. F., Carvalho, A. P. L. F., Junior, A. P. S., Peres, D. R. S., . . . de Assis, J. E. (2019). Improving the AHT in telecommunication companies by automatic modeling of call center service. In *EPIA Conference on Artificial Intelligence* (pp. 96–107). Vila Real, Portugal: Springer. 10.1007/978-3-030-30244-3_9

De Keyser, A., & Köcher, S., Alkire (née Nasr), L., Verbeeck, C., & Kandampully, J. (2019). Frontline service technology infusion: Conceptual archetypes and future research directions. *Journal of Service Management*, *30*(1), 156–183. doi:10.1108/JOSM-03-2018-0082

De Keyser, A., & Lariviere, B. (2014). How technical and functional service quality drive consumer happiness: Moderating influences of channel usage. *Journal of Service Management*, *25*(1), 30–48. doi:10.1108/JOSM-04-2013-0109

de Langen, P. W. (2020). *Towards a Better Port Industry: Port Development, Management and Policy*. Taylor & Francis. doi:10.4324/9780203797501 de las Heras-Rosas, C., & Herrera, J. (2021). Research Trends in Open Innovation and the Role of the University. *Journal of Open Innovation*, *7*(1), 1–22. doi:10.3390/joitmc7010029

De Massis, A., Frattini, F., Kotlar, J., Petruzzelli, A. M., & Wright, M. (2016). Innovation through tradition: Lessons from innovative family businesses and directions for future research. *The Academy of Management Perspectives*, *30*(1), 93–116. doi:10.5465/amp.2015.0017

de Miranda, A. S. (2020). *Uma nova dinâmica para os portos portugueses*. PÚBLICO.

de Oliveira, W. B., & Lima, L. C. (2016). Ports and flows in the technical-scientific-informational milieu: The case of the Port of Fortaleza. *Caderno de Geografia*, *26*(46), 597–614. doi:10.5752/p.2318-2962.2016v26n.46p.597

De Quevedo, E., De la Fuente, J. M., & Delgado, J. B. (2005). Reputación Corporativa y Creación de Valor. Marco Teórico de Una Relación Circular. *Investigaciones Europeas de Dirección y Economía de la Empresa*, *11*(2), 81–97.

De Saint Laurent, C. (2018). In defence of machine learning: Debunking the myths of artificial intelligence. *Europe's Journal of Psychology*, *14*(4), 734–747. doi:10.5964/ejop.v14i4.1823 PMID:30555582

De Sousa, J. (2018). *The Challenge of Neuromarketing*. IGI Global. doi:10.4018/978-1-5225-4834-8.ch002

De Souza Nascimento, E., Ahmed, I., Oliveira, E., Palheta, M. P., Steinmacher, I., & Conte, T. (2019). *Understanding development process of machine learning systems: Challenges and solutions.* Paper presented at the 2019 ACM/IEEE International Symposium on Empirical Software Engineering and Measurement (ESEM). 10.1109/ESEM.2019.8870157

De Winter, J. C., & Dodou, D. (2010). Five-point Likert items: T test versus Mann-Whitney-Wilcoxon. *Practical Assessment, Research & Evaluation*, *15*(11), 2.

Delenclos, F.-X., Rasmussen, A., & Riedl, J. (2018). *To Get Smart, Ports Go Digital*. Retrieved from https://www.bcg.com/publications/2018/to-get-smart-ports-go-digital

Delenclos, F.-X., Rasmussen, A., & Riedl, J. (2018). *To Get Smart, Ports Go Digital*. BCG.

Delen, D. (2014). *Real-world data mining: Applied business analytics and decision making*. FT Press.

Delgosha, M. S., Hajiheydari, N., & Saadeatmantesh, H. (2020). Semantic structures of business analytics research: applying text mining methods. In *Information Research* (Vol. 25). University of Borås. Retrieved from http://www.informationr.net/ir/25-2/paper856.html

Dellermann, D., Ebel, P., Söllner, M., & Leimeister, J. M. (2019). Hybrid intelligence. *Business & Information Systems Engineering*, *61*(5), 637–643. doi:10.100712599-019-00595-2

Deloitte & ESPO. (2021). *Europe's ports at the crossroads of transitions A Deloitte and ESPO Study*. European Sea Ports Organisation (ESPO) and Deloitte Port Advisory.

Deloitte. (2018). *II Informe sobre la operativización de la Voz de Cliente*. Retrieved March 13, 2020, from https://www2.deloitte.com/us/en.html

Deloitte. (2021). *Smart Ports - Point of View*. Academic Press.

DeLone, W. H., & McLean, E. R. (1992). Information systems success: The quest for the dependent variable. *Information Systems Research*, *3*(1), 60–95. Advance online publication. doi:10.1287/isre.3.1.60

Deman, J. (2017). Star Wars is colonial fantasy: How our future imaginings are limited by our past. *The Conversation*.

Demey, J. R., Vicente-Villardon, J. L., Galindo-Villardon, M. P., & Zambrano, A. Y. (2008, December 15). (2208). Identifying molecular markers associated with classification of genotypes by external logistic biplots. *Bioinformatics (Oxford, England), 24*(24), 2832–2838. doi:10.1093/bioinformatics/btn552 PMID:18974073

Demirci, N. S. (2018). The Firm Specific Determinants of Fixed Capital Investments: Theories of Corporate Investment and an Application to Industrial Firms Listed in BIST. *Finance & Econometrics*, 111.

Demir, K. A., Döven, G., & Sezen, B. (2019). Industry 5.0 and human-robot co-working. *Procedia Computer Science, 158*, 688–695. doi:10.1016/j.procs.2019.09.104

Dempster, A. P., Laird, N. M., & Rubin, D. B. (1977). Maximum likelihood from incomplete data via the em algorithm. *Journal of the Royal Statistical Society. Series B. Methodological, 39*(1), 1–22. doi:10.1111/j.2517-6161.1977.tb01600.x

Deng, B. (2015). Machine ethics: The robot's dilemma. *Nature, 523*(7558), 24–26. doi:10.1038/523024a PMID:26135432

DesJardins, J. (2014). An introduction to business ethics. New York, NY: McGraw-Hill/Irwin.

Dev, C. S., Morgan, M. S., & Shoemaker, S. (1995). A positioning analysis of hotel brands: Based on travel-manager perceptions. *The Cornell Hotel and Restaurant Administration Quarterly, 36*(6), 48–55. doi:10.1177/001088049503600617

DG MOVE. (2019). Mobility and Transport Transport in the European Union Current Trends and Issues Background Information. Brussels: Directorate-General for Mobility and Transport (DG MOVE) of the European Commission.

Dhamija, P., & Bag, S. (2020). Role of artificial intelligence in operations environment: a review and bibliometric analysis. *Business Process Management Journal, 3*(1).

Di Vaio, A., Palladino, R., Hassan, R., & Escobar, O. (2020). Artificial intelligence and business models in the sustainable development goals perspective: A systematic literature review. *Journal of Business Research, 121*, 283–314. doi:10.1016/j.jbusres.2020.08.019

Díaz-Bustamante, M., Carcelén, S., & Puelles, M. (2016). Image of luxury brands: A question of style and personality. *SAGE Open, 6*(2), 1–15. doi:10.1177/2158244016644946

Diaz-Sarmiento, C., López-Lambraño, M., & Roncallo-Lafont, L. (2017). Understanding generations: a review of the concept, classification and distinguishing characteristics of baby boomers, X and millennials. *Revista Clío América*, 188-204. doi:10.21676/23897848.2440

Dickson, B. (2018). Explainable AI: Learning how AI makes decisions. *PC Mag*. Available at https://uk.pcmag.com/news/118591/learning-how-ai-makes-decisions

Dieffenbach, M. C., Gillespie, G. S., Burns, S. M., McCulloh, I. A., Ames, D. L., Dagher, M. M., Falk, E. B., & Lieberman, M. D. (2021). Neural reference groups: A synchrony-based classification approach for predicting attitudes using fNIRS. *Social Cognitive and Affective Neuroscience, 16*(1–2), 117–128. doi:10.1093can/nsaa115 PMID:33025001

Dietterich, T. G. (2002). Machine learning for sequential data: A review. *Lecture Notes in Computer Science, 2396*, 15–30.

Dietvorst, B. J., Simmons, J. P., & Massey, C. (2015). Algorithm aversion: People erroneously avoid algorithms after seeing them err. *Journal of Experimental Psychology. General, 144*(1), 114–126. doi:10.1037/xge0000033 PMID:25401381

Dignum, V., (2018). Ethics in artificial Intelligence: Introduction to the Special Issue. *Nature, Ethics and Information Technology, 20*, 1-3.

Diwan, M. A. (2016). Internet of Things in Logistics: Towards Autonomous Logistics & Smart Logistic Entities. The International Maritime Transport & Logistics Conference (MARLOG5).

DNV GL. (2020). *Ports: green gateways to Europe.* DNV.

Doan, T., Veira, N., Keng, B., & Ray, S. (2018). *Generating Realistic Sequences of Customer-Level Transactions for Retail Datasets. IEEE International Conference on Data Mining Workshops,* Singapore. 10.1109/ICDMW.2018.00122

Dodgson, M., Gann, D., & Salter, A. (2006). The role of technology in the shift towards open innovation: The case of Procter & Gamble. *R & D Management, 36*(3), 333–346. doi:10.1111/j.1467-9310.2006.00429.x

Dolnicar, S. (2003). *Using cluster analysis for market segmentation-typical misconceptions, established methodological weaknesses and some recommendations for improvement.* Academic Press.

Domingo-Carrillo, M. A., González-Rodríguez, R., & Chávez-Miranda, E. (2020). Identifying hotel revenue management implementation drivers. *International Journal of Information Systems and Software Engineering for Big Companies, 7*(2), 33–48.

Domingos, P. (2017). *The Master Algorithm.* Penguin Books.

Donoho, D. (2017). 50 Years of Data Science. *Journal of Computational and Graphical Statistics, 26*(4), 745–766. doi:10.1080/10618600.2017.1384734

Dooley, R. (2013). *Neuromarketing: For Coke.* It's the Real Thing.

Doree, J. (2015). *Data Science, Data Architecture-Predictive Analytics Methodology: Building a Data Map for a Greenfield Data Science Initiative.* Datasciencearchitect. Accessed and reviewed in April 2019, https://datasciencearchitect.wordpress.com/tag/togaf/

Dorrell, J., & Lee, K. (2020). The Politics of Wind: A state level analysis of political party impact on wind energy development in the United States. *Energy Research & Social Science, 69,* 101602. doi:10.1016/j.erss.2020.101602

Doumbouya, M., Einstein, L., & Piech, C. (2020). Why AI Needs to be able to understand all the World's languages: The benefits of mobile technology are not accessible to most of the world's 700 million illiterate people. *Scientific American.* https://www.scientificamerican.com/article/why-ai-needs-to-be-able-to-understand-all-the-worlds-languages/?fbclid=IwAR3sA7mY-yDukaLdu0dC9RKCzZMEdtubdG5WoGjmk8hc4pMSY6Fdzkbt7No

DRE. (2017). Resolução do Conselho de Ministros 175/2017, 2017-11-24 - DRE. *Diário Da República n.º 227/2017, Série I de 2017-11-24.* Retrieved from https://dre.pt/home/-/dre/114248655/details/maximized

Drone deliveries take off at the port of Rotterdam. (2020, May). Retrieved from https://www.drycargomag.com/drone-deliveries-take-off-at-the-port-of-rotterdam

Droulers, O., & Roullet, B. (2010). *Neuromarketing. Le marketing revisité par les neurosciences du consommateur* [Neuromarketing. Marketing revisited by the neurosciences of the consumer?]. Dunod.

Du Pre Gauntt, J. (2008). Mobile advertising: After the growing pains. New York, NY: eMarketer.

Dubey, R., Luo, Z., Gunasekaran, A., Akter, S., Hazen, B. T., & Douglas, M. A. (2018). Big data and predictive analytics in humanitarian supply chains: Enabling visibility and coordination in the presence of swift trust. *International Journal of Logistics Management, 29*(2), 485–512. doi:10.1108/IJLM-02-2017-0039

Ducruet, C., & Zaidi, F. (2012). Maritime constellations: A complex network approach to shipping and ports. *Maritime Policy & Management, 39*(2), 151–168. doi:10.1080/03088839.2011.650718

Duerig, T. W., Melton, K. N., & Stöckel, D. (2013). *Engineering aspects of shape memory alloys.* Butterworth-Heinemann.

Du, S., & Xie, C. (2021). Paradoxes of artificial intelligence in consumer markets: Ethical challenges and opportunities. *Journal of Business Research, 129*, 961–974. doi:10.1016/j.jbusres.2020.08.024

Dweck, C. (2019). What Having a "Growth Mindset" Actually Means. *Harvard Business Review*.

Dweck, C. S. (2017). *Summary of Carol S. Dweck's Mindset: Key Takeaways & Analysis*. CreateSpace Independent Publishing Platform.

Dwivedi, S., & Singh, V. (2013). Modeling Techniques and Applications (CIMTA) Research and reviews in question answering system. *International Conference on Computational Intelligence*. 10.1016/j.protcy.2013.12.378

Dwivedi, Y. K., Hughes, L., Ismagilova, E., Aarts, G., Coombs, C., Crick, T., Duan, Y., Dwivedi, R., Edwards, J., Eirug, A., Galanos, V., Ilavarasan, P. V., Janssen, M., Jones, P., Kar, A. K., Kizgin, H., Kronemann, B., Lal, B., Lucini, B., ... Williams, M. D. (2021). Artificial intelligence (AI): Multidisciplinary perspectives on emerging challenges, opportunities, and agenda for research, practice and policy. *International Journal of Information Management, 57*, 101994. doi:10.1016/j.ijinfomgt.2019.08.002

Ebert, C., Gallardo, G., Hernantes, J., & Serrano, N. (2016). DevOps. *IEEE Software, 33*(3), 94–100. doi:10.1109/MS.2016.68

Eckart, C., & Young, G. (1936). The approximation of one matrix by another of lower rank. *Psychometrika, 1*(3), 211–218. doi:10.1007/BF02288367

Egan, J. (2011). *Relationship Marketing: Exploring Relational Strategies in Marketing*. Pearson Education.

Eissler, M. (2021). Probability that an infection like Covid-19 stops without reaching herd immunity, calculated with a stochastic agent-based model. medRxiv, 2020-12.

Ekong, U. O., Ifinedo, P., Ayo, C. K., & Ifinedo, A. (2012). E-commerce adoption in Nigerian businesses: An analysis using the technology-organization-environmental framework. In Leveraging Developing Economies with the Use of Information Technology: Trends and Tools (pp. 156-178). IGI Global.

Elsden, C., Manohar, A., Briggs, J., Harding, M., Speed, C., & Vines, J. (2018, April). Making sense of blockchain applications: A typology for HCI. In *Proceedings of the 2018 CHI Conference on Human Factors in Computing Systems* (pp. 1-14). 10.1145/3173574.3174032

Energy Market Regulatory Authority (EPDK). (2021). *Nihai Yek Listeleri*. Retrieved from http: https://www.epdk.gov.tr/Detay/Icerik/372/elektrikyekdemhttp://www.epdk.org.tr/TR/Dokuman/8692. Erişim Tarihi 07/01/2021.

English, P., & Fleischman, D. (2019). Food for thought in restaurant reviews: Lifestyle journalism or an extension of marketing in UK and Australian newspapers. *Journalism Practice, 13*(1), 90–104. doi:10.1080/17512786.2017.1397530

ENIDH. (2021). *Escola Superior Náutica Infante D. Henrique*. Retrieved from https://www.enautica.pt/en/

Ennomotive. (2020). *Open Innovation: Definition and Types of Innovation*. Author.

Entorno turístico. (2020). *Artificial intelligence and hospitality, a good combination?* [La inteligencia artificial y el hotelería, ¿buena combinación?]. https://www.entornoturistico.com/inteligencia-artificial-hoteleria-buena-combinacion/

Erdinç, Z., & Aydınbaş, G. (2020). Panel Data Analysis on Determinants Of Renewable Energy Consumption, Journal Of Social. *Humanities and Administrative Sciences, 6*(24), 346–358.

Erdogan, O., & Demirel, E. (2017). New Technologies in Maritime Education and Training, Turkish Experiment. *Universal Journal of Educational Research, 5*(6), 947–952. doi:10.13189/ujer.2017.050606

Erevelles, S., Stevenson, T. H., Srinivasan, S., & Fukawa, N. (2008). An analysis of B2B ingredient co-branding relationships. *Industrial Marketing Management, 37*(8), 940–952. doi:10.1016/j.indmarman.2007.07.002

Eshuis, R., & Wieringa, R. (2003). Comparing Petri net and activity diagram variants for workflow modelling – a quest for reactive Petri nets. In H. Ehring, W. Reising, G. Rozenberg, & H. Weber (Eds.), Petri Net Technology for Communication-Based Systems, (vol. 2472). Springer.

Esteva, A., Kuprel, B., Novoa, R. A., Ko, J., Swetter, S. M., Blau, H. M., & Thrun, S. (2017). Dermatologist-level classification of skin cancer with deep neural networks. *Nature, 542*(7639), 115–118. doi:10.1038/nature21056 PMID:28117445

Europa Press. (2018). *Hoteliers are betting on the Internet of Things to personalize the experience* [Los hoteleros apuestan por el Internet de las Cosas para personalizar la experiencia]. https://www.europapress.es/turismo/hoteles/noticia-hoteleros-apuestan-internet-cosas-personalizar-experiencia-20180322111219.html

European Commission. (2019), *Ethics Guidelines for Trustworthy AI.* https://ec.europa.eu/digital-single-market/en/news/ethics-guidelines-trustworthy-ai

European Commission. (2019). *Ethics Guidelines for Trustworthy AI.* https://ec.europa.eu/futurium/en/ai-alliance-consultation

Evans, M. (2019). Build a 5-star customer experience with artificial intelligence. *Forbes.* https://www.forbes.com/sites/allbusiness/2019/02/17/customer-experience-artificial- intelligence/#1a30ebd415bd

Evers, K. (2014). *Quand la neuroscience se réveille* [When neuroscience wakes up]. Upsala Universiteit. Accessed from: https://www.crb.uu.se/digitalAssets/445/c_445294-l_1-k_k-evers-neuroethique.pdf

Evgeniou, T., Hardoon, D. R., & Ovchinnikov, A. (2020). What Happens When AI is Used to Set Grades? *Harvard Business Review.* https://hbr.org/2020/08/what-happens-when-ai-is-used-to-set-grades

Fainshtein, E., & Serova, E. (2020). Value Proposition of Network Companies Providing Restaurant Services in Russia: Analysis and Evaluation. In Anthropological Approaches to Understanding Consumption Patterns and Consumer Behavior (pp. 137-158). IGI Global.

Falk, E. B., Berkman, E. T., Whalen, D., & Lieberman, M. D. (2015). Neural Activity During Health Messaging Predicts Reductions in Smoking Above and Beyond Self-Report. *Health Psychology.* PMID:21261410

Fan, Z. P., Che, Y. J., & Chen, Z. Y. (2017). Product sales forecasting using online reviews and historical sales data: A method combining the Bass model and sentiment analysis. *Journal of Business Research, 74*, 90–100. doi:10.1016/j.jbusres.2017.01.010

Farah, D. (2020). *The modern MLOps blueprint.* Retrieved from https://medium.com/slalom-data-analytics/the-modern-mlops-blueprint-c8322af69d21

Farrokhi, A., Shirazi, F., Hajli, N., & Tajvidi, M. (2020). Using artificial intelligence to detect crisis related to events: Decision making in B2B by artificial intelligence. *Industrial Marketing Management, 91*, 257–273. doi:10.1016/j.indmarman.2020.09.015

Faulhaber, A. K., Dittmer, A., Blind, F., Wächter, M. A., Timm, S., Sütfeld, L. R., Stephan, A., Pipa, G., & König, P. (2019). Human decisions in moral dilemmas are largely described by utilitarianism: Virtual car driving study provides guidelines for autonomous driving vehicles. *Science and Engineering Ethics, 25*(2), 399–418. doi:10.100711948-018-0020-x PMID:29357047

Fayyad, U., Piatetsky-Shapiro, G., & Smyth, P. (1996). The KDD process for extracting useful knowledge from volumes of data. *Communications of the ACM, 39*(11), 27–34. doi:10.1145/240455.240464

Fazio, R. H. (2001). On the automatic activation of associated evaluations: An overview. *Cognition and Emotion, 15*(2), 115–141. doi:10.1080/02699930125908

Fazio, R. H., Powell, M. C., & Williams, C. J. (1989). The role of attitude accessibility in the attitude-to-behavior process. *The Journal of Consumer Research, 16*(3), 280–288. doi:10.1086/209214

Fazio, R. H., Sanbonmatsu, D. M., Powell, M. C., & Kardes, F. R. (1986). On the automatic activation of attitudes. *Journal of Personality and Social Psychology, 50*(2), 229–238. doi:10.1037/0022-3514.50.2.229 PMID:3701576

Fazio, R. H., & Williams, C. J. (1986). Attitude accessibility as a moderator of the attitude–perception and attitude–behavior relations: An investigation of the 1984 presidential election. *Journal of Personality and Social Psychology, 51*(3), 505–514. doi:10.1037/0022-3514.51.3.505 PMID:3761146

Feng, C. M., Park, A., Pitt, L., Kietzmann, J., & Northey, G. (2020). Artificial intelligence in marketing: A bibliographic perspective. *Australasian Marketing Journal.* doi:10.1016/j.ausmj.2020.07.006

Feng, J. Z., & Jain, A. K. (2013, April). Orientation field estimation for latent fingerprint enhancement. *IEEE Transactions on Pattern Analysis and Machine Intelligence, 35*(4), 925–940. doi:10.1109/TPAMI.2012.155 PMID:22826508

Feng, J., Zhang, Y. Q., & Zhang, H. (2017). Improving the co-word analysis method based on semantic distance. *Scientometrics, 111*(3), 1521–1531. doi:10.100711192-017-2286-1

Fernández, M., Puente, H., & Sequeiros, C. (2021). *Nuevas formas de comunicación a través de la narrativa en tiempo real: producción virtual, videojuegos y otras experiencias interactivas.* Congreso Internacional Comunicación y Pensamiento 2021. https://comunicacionypensamiento.org/ponencia/nuevas-formas-de-comunicacion-a-traves-de-la-narrativa-en-tiempo-real-produccion-virtual-videojuegos-y-otras-experiencias-interactivas/

Fernández, M., & Puente-Bienvenido, H. (2015). Universos fantásticos de inspiración lovecraftiana en videojuegos survival horror. Un estudio de caso de PT (Silent Hills). *Brumal. Revista de Investigación sobre lo Fantástico/Brumal. Research Journal on the Fantastic., 3*(1), 95–118.

Fernández-Rovira, C., Valdés, J. Á., Molleví, G., & Nicolas-Sans, R. (forthcoming). The digital transformation of business. Towards the datafication of the relationship with customers. *Technological Forecasting and Social Change, 162,* 120339.

Feuerlicht, G., & Govardhan, S. (2010). Impact of cloud computing: beyond a technology trend. *Systems Integration.*

Findasense. (2020). Estudio COVID-19. *Escenarios y Horizontes de futuro post-cuarentena en el consumo y la producción.* Retrieved November 30, 2020, from https://es.insights.findasense.com/estudios/covid-19-paper-futuro-del-consumo-y-la-produccion-66508

Fioresi, E., & Guimarães, L. (2016). *Brazilian management port: a socio-technical approach.* Academic Press.

Fischer, T., & Krauss, C. (2018). Deep learning with long short-term memory networks for financial market predictions. *European Journal of Operational Research, 270*(2), 654–669. doi:10.1016/j.ejor.2017.11.054

Flores-Fernandez, J., & Martínez-López, F. J. (2020). Historical cycles and prospective: Our future according to our past [Ciclos históricos y prospectiva: nuestro futuro según nuestro pasado]. *Revista de Pensamiento Estratégico y Seguridad CISDE, 5*(1), 103–121.

Flores, J., Baruca, A., & Saldivar, R. (2014). Is neuromarketing ethical? Consumers say yes. Consumers say no. Journal of Legal. *Ethical and Regulatory Issues, 17*(2), 77–91.

Floridi, L., & Cowls, J. (2019). A unified framework of five principles for AI in society. *Harvard Data Science Review, 1*(1).

Floridi, L. (2013). Distributed morality in an information society. *Science and Engineering Ethics*, *19*(3), 727–743. doi:10.100711948-012-9413-4 PMID:23197312

Fodor, O., Dell'Erba, M., Ricci, F., Spada, A., & Werthner, H. (2002). *Conceptual Normalisation of XML Data for Interoperability in Tourism. Commerce and Tourism Research Laboratory ITC-irst.* University of Trento.

Food and Agriculture Organization of the United Nations. (2017). *Food and Agriculture. Actions to advance the agenda of the 2030 Agenda and Sustainable Development Goals.* FAO. Retrieved from http://www.fao.org/3/a-i7454s.pdf

Forest, A. (1998). Cog, a Humanoid Robot, and The Question of The Image of God. *Zygon: Journal of Religion and Science*, *33*, 91-111.

Forrest, C. (2017, October 11). Google Home Mini spied on user 'thousands of times a day,' sent recordings to Google. *TechRepublic.* https://www.techrepublic.com/ article/google-home-mini-spied-on-user-thousands-of- times-a-day-sent-recordings-to-google/

Forrester Customer Experience. (2013). *Forrester's 2013 Customer Experience Predictions.* Retrieved December 3, 2020, from https://go.forrester.com/blogs/13-01-04-forresters_2013_customer_experience_predictions/

Forrester. (2020). *Improving Customer Experience By One Point Can Drive More Than A Billion Dollars In Revenue.* Retrieved December 3, 2020, from https://go.forrester.com/blogs/improving-customer-experience-by-1-point-can-drive-more-than-a-billion-dollars-in-revenue-in-2019/

Friedland, J. (2019). AI Can Help Us Live More Deliberately. *MIT Sloan Management Review.* https://sloanreview.mit.edu/article/ai-can-help-us-live-more-deliberately

Friedland, J., & Cole, B. M. (2019). From homo-economicus to homo-virtus: A system-theoretic model for raising moral self-awareness. *Journal of Business Ethics*, *155*(1), 191–205. doi:10.100710551-017-3494-6

Friedman, H. H., Herskovitz, P. J., & Pollack, S. (1993). The biasing effects of scale-checking styles on response to a Likert scale. In Proceedings of the American Statistical Association annual conference. *Survey Research Methods*, *2*, 792–795.

Frijda, N. H. (1986). The emotions. Cambridge University Press.

Fuchs, H., & Bishop, G. (1992). *Research Directions in Virtual Environments.* University of North Carolina at Chapel Hill.

Fundes Latinoamerica. (2020). *Why are FMCG companies focusing - today more than ever - on the traditional channel?* Retrieved from https://www.fundes.org/por-que-las-empresas-de-consumo-masivo-se-estan-enfocando-hoy-mas-que-nunca-en-el-canal-tradicional/

Gabriel, K. R. (1971). The biplot - graphic display of matrices with applications to principal component analysis. *Biometrika*, *58*(3), 453–467. doi:10.1093/biomet/58.3.453

Gabriel, K. R. (1995). Biplot display of multivariate categorical data, with comments on multiple correspondence analysis. In *Recent Advances in Descriptive Multivariate Analysis.* Oxford Science Publications.

Gabriel, K. R. (1998). Generalised bilinear regression. *Biometrika*, *85*(3), 689–700. doi:10.1093/biomet/85.3.689

Gabriel, K. R., & Zamir, S. (1979). And Zamir, S. (1979). Lower rank approximation of matrices by least squares with any choice of weights. *Technometrics*, *21*(4), 489–498. doi:10.1080/00401706.1979.10489819

Gaito, J. (1980). Measurement scales and statistics: Resurgence of an old misconception. *Psychological Bulletin*, *87*(3), 564–567. doi:10.1037/0033-2909.87.3.564

Galbally, J., Haraksim, R., & Beslay, L. (2018). A study of age and ageing in fingerprint biometrics. *IEEE Transactions on Information Forensics and Security, 14*(5), 1351–1365. doi:10.1109/TIFS.2018.2878160

Galesic, M., & Bosnjak, M. (2009). Effects of questionnaire length on participation and indicators of response quality in a web survey. *Public Opinion Quarterly, 73*(2), 349–360. doi:10.1093/poq/nfp031

Galindo, P., Vicente, P., & Araya, C. (2009). Biplot Versus Coodernadas Paralelas. In Memoria del XXIII Foro de Estadística (pp. 55-59). Academic Press.

Galindo, P. (1986). Una representación simultánea: HJ Biplot. *Qüestiió. Quaderns d'Estadística, Sistemes, Informàtica i Investigació Operativ, 10*, 13–23.

Galkin, A. (2019). *How to Calculate Price Index. Formula to Know Competitors' Impact on Your Sales in 15 Minutes.* Competera. Retrieved from https://competera.net/resources/articles/price-index-calculation

Gallagher, J. (2017, January 26). Artificial intelligence 'as good as cancer doctors'. *BBC News.* https://www.bbc. com/news/health-38717928

Gans, J., & Ryall, M. D. (2017). Value capture theory: A strategic management review. *Strategic Management Journal, 38*(1), 17–41. doi:10.1002mj.2592

Gao, Z., Sun, D., Zhao, R., & Dong, Y. (2021, January). Ship-unloading scheduling optimization for a steel plant. *Information Sciences, 544*, 214–226. doi:10.1016/j.ins.2020.07.029

Garbuio, M., & Lin, N. (2019). Artificial intelligence as a growth engine for health care startups: Emerging business models. *California Management Review, 61*(2), 59–83. doi:10.1177/0008125618811931

García Haro, M. A. (2018*). La co-creación de valor a través de los social media: efecto en la imagen de Cuenca como destino turístico* (Doctoral thesis). Universidad de Castilla-La Mancha.

Garcia, A. M., & Gil-Saura, I. (2016). *Innovating in retail trade: the influence of ICT and its effects on customer satisfaction.* doi:10.5295/cdg.10556am

García-Peñalvo, F. J. (2021). Digital Transformation in the Universities: Implications of the COVID-19 Pandemic [Transformación digital en las universidades: Implicaciones de la pandemia de la COVID-19]. *Education in the Knowledge Society, 22*, e25465. doi:10.14201/eks.25465

García-Ruiz, R., & Pérez Escoda, A. (2021). Teacher's digital competence as key for strengthening a responsible use of the Internet [La competencia digital docente como clave para fortalecer el uso responsable de Internet]. *Campus Virtuales, 10*(1), 59–71.

Gardner, H. J., & Martin, M. A. (2007). Analyzing ordinal scales in studies of virtual environments: Likert or lump it! *Presence (Cambridge, Mass.), 16*(4), 439–446. doi:10.1162/pres.16.4.439

Garland, R. (1991). The mid-point on a rating scale: Is it desirable. *Marketing Bulletin, 2*(1), 66–70.

Garousi, V., Felderer, M., & Mäntylä, M. V. (2016). *The need for multivocal literature reviews in software engineering: Complementing systematic literature reviews with grey literature.* Paper presented at the 20th International Conference on Evaluation and Assessment in Software Engineering. 10.1145/2915970.2916008

Gartner. (2019). *Creating a High-Impact Customer Experience Strategy.* Retrieved December 4, 2020, from https://emtemp.gcom.cloud/ngw/globalassets/en/marketing/documents/creating-a-high-impact-customer-experience-strategy-gartner-for-marketers-11-22-2019.pdf

Gartner. (2020). *Blockchain Technology: What's Ahead? Be ready for the next phase of the blockchain revolution.* Retrieved December 3, 2020, from https://www.gartner.com/en/information-technology/insights/blockchain

Gartner. (2020). *Three Essentials for Starting and Supporting Master Data Management.* ID G00730039. Gartner Inc. Accessed and reviewed in April 2019, https://www.gartner.com/doc/reprints?id=1-24MIGFGU&ct=201119&st=sb

Gass, S. I., & Assad, A. A. (2005). *An Annotated Timeline of Operations Research.* Kluwer.

Gautier, A., Ittoo, A., & Van Cleynenbreugel, P. (2020). AI algorithms, price discrimination and collusion: A technological, economic and legal perspective. *European Journal of Law and Economics, 50*(3), 405–435. doi:10.100710657-020-09662-6

Gebauer, H., Arzt, A., Kohtamäki, M., Lamprecht, C., Parida, V., Witell, L., & Wortmann, F. (2020). How to convert digital offerings into revenue enhancement–Conceptualizing business model dynamics through explorative case studies. *Industrial Marketing Management, 91*, 429–441. doi:10.1016/j.indmarman.2020.10.006

Genc, R. (2010). Strategic brand management in hospitality sector: How to manage co-branding in hotels and restaurants. *Acta Universitatis Danubius Œconomica, 6*(3), 33–46.

Genevsky, A., Yoon, C., & Knutson, B. (2017). When Brain Beats Behavior: Neuroforecasting Crowdfunding Outcomes. *The Journal of Neuroscience: The Official Journal of the Society for Neuroscience, 37*(36), 8625–8634. doi:10.1523/JNEUROSCI.1633-16.2017 PMID:28821681

Geraci, R. M. (2007). Robots and the Sacred in Science Fiction: Theological Implications of AI. *Zygon, 42*, No-4.

Gers, F. A., Schmidhuber, J., & Cummins, F. (2000). Learning to forget: Continual prediction with LSTM. *Neural Computation, 12*(10), 2451–2471. doi:10.1162/089976600300015015 PMID:11032042

Geylani, T., Inman, J. J., & Hofstede, F. T. (2008). Image reinforcement or impairment: The effects of co-branding on attribute uncertainty. *Marketing Science, 27*(4), 730–744. doi:10.1287/mksc.1070.0326

Gigante, M. A. (1993). Virtual reality: definitions, history and applications. *Virtual Real. Syst.*, 3–14. . doi:10.1016/B978-0-12-227748-1.50009-3

Gill, R., & Singh, J. (2020). A Review of Neuromarketing Techniques and Emotion Analysis Classifiers for Visual-Emotion Mining. *2020 9th International Conference System Modeling and Advancement in Research Trends (SMART)*, 103–108. 10.1109/SMART50582.2020.9337074

Gillath, O., Ai, T., Branicky, M. S., Keshmiri, S., Davison, R. B., & Spaulding, R. (2021). Attachment and trust in artificial intelligence. *Computers in Human Behavior, 115*, 106607. doi:10.1016/j.chb.2020.106607

Gill, T. (2020). Blame it on the self-driving car: How autonomous vehicles can alter consumer morality. *The Journal of Consumer Research, 47*(2), 272–291. doi:10.1093/jcr/ucaa018

Github. (2020). *Awesome production machine learning.* Retrieved from https://github.com/EthicalML/awesome-production-machine-learning

Glaser, B. G., & Strauss, A. L. (2006). *The Discovery of Grounded Theory: Strategies for Qualitative Research.* Aldine Transactions.

Global Reporting Initiative. (2013). *Guide for the preparation of sustainability reports.* G4. Retrieved from https://www.globalreporting.org/resourcelibrary/Spanish-G4-Part-One.pdf

Gogolev, S., & Ozhegov, E. M. (2019). Comparison of Machine Learning Algorithms in Restaurant Revenue Prediction. In *International Conference on Analysis of Images, Social Networks and Texts* (pp. 27-36). Springer.

Goldsmith, J., & Burton, E. (2017). Why Teaching Artificial Intelligence Practitioners Is Important. *Proceedings of the AAAI Conference on Artificial Intelligence*, 31(1), 4836-4840.

Gómez Borja, M.A. (2014). *El proceso de decisión en el consumidor*. UOC.

Gómez Gutiérrez, C. (2018). United Nations Educational, Scientific and Cultural Organization (UNESCO) [El desarrollo sostenible: conceptos básicos, alcance y criterios para su evaluación]. *Tema*, III.

Gonçalves, M. J. A., Camarinha, A. P., Abreu, A. J., Teixeira, S. F., & Ferreira da Silva, A. (2020). An analysis of the most used websites in Portugal regarding accessibility web in the tourism sector. *International Journal of Information Systems and Tourism*, 5(1), 19–28.

González-González, C. S., Violant Holz, V., Infante Moro, A., Cáceres García, L., & Guzmán Franco, M. (2021). Educational robotics in inclusive contexts: The case of the hospital classrooms [Robótica educativa en contextos inclusivos: el caso de las aulas hospitalarias]. *Educación XX1*, 24(1), 375-403. [] doi:10.5944/educxx1.27047

González-Zamar, M. D., Abad-Segura, E., & Belmonte-Ureña, L. J. (2020). Meaningful learning in the development of digital skills. Trend analysis. *IJERI: International Journal of Educational Research and Innovation*, (14), 91–110.

González-Zamar, M. D., Abad-Segura, E., & Gallardo-Pérez, J. (2021). Ubiquitous learning in arts education and visual languages: Trend Analysis [Aprendizaje ubicuo en educación artística y lenguajes visuales: Análisis de tendencias]. *Campus Virtuales*, 10(1), 125–139.

Goodman, E., Bamford, J., & Saynor, P. (Eds.). (2016). *Small firms and industrial districts in Italy*. Routledge.

Google Cloud. (2020). *MLOps: Continuous delivery and automation pipelines in machine learning*. Retrieved from https://cloud.google.com/solutions/machine-learning/mlops-continuous-delivery-and-automation-pipelines-in-machine-learning

Gouider, M., & Farhat, A. (2010). Mining Multi-level Frequent Itemsets under Constraints. *International Journal of Database Theory and Application*, 3(4), 15–34.

Goulding, C. (1999). Grounded theory, ethnography and phenomenology: A comparative analysis of three qualitative strategies for marketing research. *European Journal of Marketing*, 39(3/4), 294–308. doi:10.1108/03090560510581782

Governo do Brasil. (2021). *PSP - Porto Sem Papel*. Retrieved from https://concentrador.portosempapel.gov.br/PSP-CDP/private/comum/pages/home.xhtml

Gower, J. C., & Hand, D. (1996). *Biplots*. Chapman & Hall.

Granulo, A., Fuchs, C., & Puntoni, S. (2020). Preference for human (vs. robotic) labor is stronger in symbolic consumption contexts. *Journal of Consumer Psychology*, 31(1), 72–80. doi:10.1002/jcpy.1181

Graziano, M. D., Renga, A., & Moccia, A. (2019). Integration of automatic identification system (AIS) data and single-channel synthetic aperture radar (SAR) images by SAR-based ship velocity estimation for maritime situational awareness. *Remote Sensing*, 11(19), 16. doi:10.3390/rs11192196

Greenberger, E., Chen, C., Dmitrieva, J., & Farruggia, S. P. (2003). Item-wording and the dimensionality of the Rosenberg Self-Esteem Scale: Do they matter? *Personality and Individual Differences*, 35(6), 1241–1254. doi:10.1016/S0191-8869(02)00331-8

Greenwald, T. (2011). How smart machines like iPhone 4S are quietly changing your industry. *Forbes*. https://www.forbes.com/sites/tedgreenwald/2011/10/13/how-smart-machines-like-iphone-4s-are- quietly-changing-your-industry/#46547361598f

Greenwald, A. G. (1992). New Look 3: Unconscious cognition reclaimed. *The American Psychologist, 47*(6), 766–779. doi:10.1037/0003-066X.47.6.766 PMID:1616174

Grifoll, M., Ortego, M. I., & Egozcue, J. J. (2019). Compositional data techniques for the analysis of the container traffic share in a multi-port region. *European Transport Research Review, 11*(1), 1. doi:10.118612544-019-0350-z

Grönroos, C. (2011). A service perspective on business relationships: The value creation, interaction and marketing interface. *Industrial Marketing Management, 40*(2), 240–247. doi:10.1016/j.indmarman.2010.06.036

Grossman, R. P. (1997). Co-branding in advertising: Developing effective associations. *Journal of Product and Brand Management, 6*(3), 191–201. doi:10.1108/10610429710175709

Guelfand, G. (2013). *Les études qualitatives: Fondamentaux, méthodes, analyse, techniques* [Qualitative studies: Fundamentals, methods, analysis, techniques]. EMS Editions. doi:10.3917/ems.guelf.2013.01

Guidotti, R., Monreale, A., Nanni, M., Giannotti, F., & Pedreschi, D. (2017). Clustering Individual Transactional Data for Masses of Users. In *Proceedings of the 23rd International Conference on Knowledge Discovery and Data Mining*, Association for Computing Machinery. 10.1145/3097983.3098034

Guidotti, R., Rossetti, G., Pappalardo, L., Giannotti, F., & Pedreschi, D. (2019). Personalized Market Basket Prediction with Temporal Annotated Recurring Sequences. *IEEE Transactions on Knowledge and Data Engineering, 31*(11), 2151–2163. doi:10.1109/TKDE.2018.2872587

Guillet, B. D., & Tasci, A. D. (2012). Chinese hoteliers' take on hotel co-branding in China. *Tourism Review, 67*(4), 3–11. doi:10.1108/16605371211277777

Guimerá, A. (2015). *Mapa de la empatía (Dave Gray).* Retrieved December 5, 2020, from https://www.marketing-esencial.com/2015/03/03/mapa-de-empatia/

Güney, T. (2020). Renewable energy consumption and sustainable development in high-income countries. *International Journal of Sustainable Development and World Ecology.* Advance online publication. doi:10.1080/13504509.2020.1753124

Guo, C., Guan, Z., & Song, Y. (2012). Research on dynamic berth assignment of bulk cargo port based on ant colony algorithm. In Z. Zhang, R. Zhang, & J. Zhang (Eds.), *LISS* (pp. 235–240). Springer. doi:10.1007/978-3-642-32054-5_35

Guo, C., Guan, Z., & Song, Y. (2013). Research on bulk-cargo-port berth assignment based on priority of resource allocation. *Journal of Industrial Engineering and Management, 6*(1), 276–288. doi:10.3926/jiem.673

Gupta, R., Khari, M., Gupta, D., & Crespo, R. G. (2020). Fingerprint image enhancement and reconstruction using the orientation and phase reconstruction. *Information Sciences, 530*, 201–218. doi:10.1016/j.ins.2020.01.031

Guru99. (2021). *Data Science Tutorial for Beginners: What is, Basics & Process.* Accessed and reviewed in April 2019, https://www.guru99.com/data-science-tutorial.html

Gustafsod, P. E. (1998). Gender Differences in risk perception: Theoretical and methodological perspectives. *Risk Analysis, 18*(6), 805–811. doi:10.1111/j.1539-6924.1998.tb01123.x PMID:9972583

Gutierrez, A., Boukrami, E., & Lumsden, R. (2015). Technological, organizational and environmental factors influencing managers' decision to adopt cloud computing in the UK.[. *Journal of Enterprise Information Management, 28*(6), 788–807. doi:10.1108/JEIM-01-2015-0001

Gutmann, G., & Konagaya, A. (2019). *Predictive Simulation: Using Regression and Artificial Neural Networks to Negate Latency in Networked Interactive Virtual Reality.* arXiv preprint arXiv:1910.04703.

Haakman, M., Cruz, L., Huijgens, H., & van Deursen, A. (2020). *AI lifecycle models need to be revised. An exploratory study in fintech.* arXiv preprint arXiv:2010.02716.

Haefner, N., Wincent, J., Parida, V., & Gassmann, O. (2020). Artificial intelligence and innovation management: A review, framework, and research agenda. *Technological Forecasting and Social Change, 162*, 120392. doi:10.1016/j.techfore.2020.120392

Haenlein, M., & Kaplan, A. (2019). A brief history of artificial intelligence: On the past, present, and future of artificial intelligence. *California Management Review, 61*(4), 5–14. doi:10.1177/0008125619864925

Hafkin, N. J. (2009). *E-government in africa: An overview of progress made and challenges ahead.* Paper presented at the UNDESA/UNPAN workshop on electronic/mobile government in Africa: Building Capacity in Knowledge Management through Partnership, The United Nations Economic Commission for Africa.

Hagras, H. (2018). Toward human-understandable, explainable AI. *Computer, 51*(9), 28–36. doi:10.1109/MC.2018.3620965

Hair, J., Hult, G., Ringle, C., & Sarstedt, M. (2017). *A primer on Partial Least Squares Structural Equation Modeling (PLS-SEM)* (2nd ed.). SAGE Los Angeles.

Hakim, A., Klorfeld, S., Sela, T., Friedman, D., Shabat-Simon, M., & Levy, D. J. (2020). Machines learn neuromarketing: Improving preference prediction from self-reports using multiple EEG measures and machine learning. *International Journal of Research in Marketing.* Advance online publication. doi:10.1016/j.ijresmar.2020.10.005

Hall, M., Frank, E., Holmes, G., Pfahringer, B., Reutemann, P., & Witten, I. H. (2009). The weka data mining software: An update. *SIGKDD Explorations, 11*(1), 10–18. doi:10.1145/1656274.1656278

Hamilton, I. A. (2018, October 13). Why it's totally unsurprising that Amazon's recruitment AI was biased against women. *Insider.* https://www.businessinsider.com/amazon-ai-biased-against-women-no-surprise-sandra-wachter-2018-10

Hansen, J. P. (2003). CAN'T MISS—Conquer Any Number Task by Making Important Statistics Simple. Part 1. Types of Variables, Mean, Median, Variance, and Standard Deviation. *Journal for Healthcare Quality, 25*(4), 19–24. doi:10.1111/j.1945-1474.2003.tb01070.x PMID:14606209

Hao, N., Wang, H. H., & Zhou, Q. (2020). The impact of online grocery shopping on stockpile behavior in Covid-19. China agricultural economic review. *Revisión económica agrícola de China, 12*(3), 459-470. doi:10.1108/CAER-04-2020-0064

Haralambides, H. E. (2019). Gigantism in container shipping, ports and global logistics: A time-lapse into the future. *Maritime Economics & Logistics, 21*(1), 1–60. doi:10.105741278-018-00116-0

Harari, Y. H. (2020). *The world after the coronavirus.* Retrieved from http://virtual.iuc.edu.co/pluginfile.php/3512/mod_resource/content/1/2.%20FILOSOF%C3%8DA%20MAYO%2011%20-%2015.pdf

Harkens, A. (2018). The ghost in the legal machine: Algorithmic governmentality, economy, and the practice of law. *Journal of Information Communication and Ethics in Society, 16*(1), 16–31. doi:10.1108/JICES-09-2016-0038

Harrell, E. (2019). Neuromarketing: What you need to know. *Harvard Business Review.* Accessed from: https://hbr.org/2019/01/neuromarketing-what-you-need-to-know

Harrison-Walker, L. J. (2019). The effect of consumer emotions on outcome behaviors following service failure. *Journal of Services Marketing, 33*(3), 285–302. doi:10.1108/JSM-04-2018-0124

Hartley, J. (2013). Some thoughts on Likert type scales. *International Journal of Clinical and Health Psychology, 13*, 83–86.

Hartley, J., & Betts, L. (2010). Four layouts and a finding: The effects of changes in the order of the verbal labels and numerical values on Likert type scales. *International Journal of Social Research Methodology, 13*(1), 17–27. doi:10.1080/13645570802648077

Hartley, J., & Sawaya, W. (2019). Tortoise, not the hare: Digital transformation of supply chain business processes. *Business Horizons, 62*(6), 707–715. doi:10.1016/j.bushor.2019.07.006

Hartley, P., Medlock, K. B. III, Temzelides, T., & Zhang, X. (2015). Local employment impact from competing energy sources: Shale gas versus wind generation in Texas. *Energy Econ, 49*, 610–619. doi:10.1016/j.eneco.2015.02.023

Hart, M. C. (1996). Improving the Dissemination Of SERVQUAL By Using Magnitude Scaling. In *Total Quality Management Action* (pp. 267–271). Springer. doi:10.1007/978-94-009-1543-5_42

Ha, S., & Stoel, L. (2009). Consumer e-shopping acceptance: Antecedents in a technology acceptance model. *Journal of Business Research, 62*(5), 565–571. doi:10.1016/j.jbusres.2008.06.016

Haşıloğlu, S. B., Baran, T., & Aydın, O. (2015). Pazarlama araştırmalarındaki potansiyel problemlere yönelik bir araştırma: Kolayda örnekleme ve sıklık ifadeli ölçek maddeleri. *Pamukkale İşletme ve Bilişim Yönetimi Dergisi,* (1), 19–28.

Hastie, T., & Tibshirani, R. (1987). Generalized Additive Models: Some Applications. *Journal of the American Statistical Association, 82*(398), 371–386. doi:10.1080/01621459.1987.10478440

Haugland, J. (1989). *Artificial Intelligence: The Very Idea.* The Massachusetts Institute of Technology.

Heck, P. (2019). *Software engineering for machine learning applications.* Retrieved from https://fontysblogt.nl/software-engineering-for-machine-learning-applications/

Heck, P. (2020). *Testing machine learning applications.* Retrieved from https://fontysblogt.nl/testing-machine-learning-applications/

Heck, P., & Schouten, G. (2021). *Lessons learned from educating AI engineers.* Paper accepted for the 1st International Workshop on AI Engineering (WAIN).

Heeks, R. (2002). *Egovernment in Africa: Promise and practice.* Academic Press.

Hegazy, I. M. (2019). The effect of political neuromarketing 2.0 on election outcomes. *Review of Economics and Political Science.*

Heilig, L., Schwarze, S., & Voss, S. (2017). *An Analysis of Digital Transformation in the History and Future of Modern Ports.* doi:10.24251/HICSS.2017.160

Heilig, L., Lalla-Ruiz, E., & Voss, S. (2017). Digital transformation in maritime ports: Analysis and a game-theoretic framework. *NETNOMICS: Economic Research and Electronic Networking, 18*(2-3), 227–254. Advance online publication. doi:10.100711066-017-9122-x

Heirs, S., & Manuel, M. (2021). Sustainable Maritime Career Development: A case for Maritime Education and Training (MET) at the Secondary Level. *TransNav: International Journal on Marine Navigation & Safety of Sea Transportation, 15*(1), 91–99. doi:10.12716/1001.15.01.08

Helmig, B., Huber, J.-A., & Leeflang, P. S. (2008). Co-branding: The state of the art. *Schmalenbach Business Review, 60*(4), 359–377. doi:10.1007/BF03396775

Hendarman, A. F., & Tjakraatmadja, J. H. (2012). Relationship among soft skills, hard skills, and innovativeness of knowledge workers in the knowledge economy era. *Procedia: Social and Behavioral Sciences, 52*, 35–44. doi:10.1016/j.sbspro.2012.09.439

Henn na Hotel. (n.d.). https://www.h-n-h.jp/en/concept

Hermann, K. M., Kocisky, T., Grefenstette, E., Espeholt, L., Kay, W., Suleyman, M., & Blunsom, R. (2015). Teaching machines to read and comprehend. In *28th International Proceedings on Advances in Neural Information Processing Systems* (pp. 1693–1701). MIT Press.

Herodotou, H., Aslam, S., Holm, H., & Theodossiou, S. (2020). Big Maritime. *Data Management*, 313–334. doi:10.1007/978-3-030-50892-0_19

Hertzum, M. (2018). Three contexts for evaluating organizational usability. *Journal of Usability Studies Archive*, *14*, 35–47.

Hertzum, M. (2021). *Organizational Implementation: The Design in Use of Information Systems*. Morgan & Claypool Publishers.

Hesenius, M., Schwenzfeier, N., Meyer, O., Koop, W., & Gruhn, V. (2019). *Towards a software engineering process for developing data-driven applications*. Paper presented at the 2019 IEEE/ACM 7th International Workshop on Realizing Artificial Intelligence Synergies in Software Engineering (RAISE). 10.1109/RAISE.2019.00014

Hicks, S. C., & Irizarry, R. A. (2018). A Guide to Teaching Data Science. *The American Statistician*, *72*(4), 382–391. doi:10.1080/00031305.2017.1356747 PMID:31105314

Hinchliffe, E. (2017, February 22), IBM's Watson will help diagnose heart disease when doctors may have missed the signs. *Mashable*. https://mashable.com/2017/02/22/ibm-watson-clinical-imaging-cardiology/

Hirsch, J. (2020). *An fNIRS Approach to Two-person Neuroscience*. Biophotonics Congress: Biomedical Optics 2020 (Translational, Microscopy, OCT, OTS, BRAIN) (2020), Paper BM4C.1, BM4C.1. 10.1364/BRAIN.2020.BM4C.1

Hirsch, J., Zhanga, X., Noah, J. A., & Ono, Y. (2017). Frontal temporal and parietal systems synchronize within and across brains during live eye-to-eye contact. *NeuroImage*, *157*, 314–330. doi:10.1016/j.neuroimage.2017.06.018 PMID:28619652

Hoffman, D. L., & Novak, T. P. (2018). Consumer and object experience in the internet of things: An assemblage theory approach. *The Journal of Consumer Research*, *44*(6), 1178–1204. doi:10.1093/jcr/ucx105

Hofmans, J., Theuns, P., Baekelandt, S., Mairesse, O., Schillewaert, N., & Cools, W. (2007). Bias and changes in perceived intensity of verbal qualifiers effected by scale orientation. *Survey Research Methods*, *1*(2), 97–108.

Ho, L. C. J., & Taylor, M. E. (2007). An empirical analysis of triple bottom-line reporting and its determinants: Evidence from the United States and Japan. *Journal of International Financial Management & Accounting*, *18*(2), 123–150. doi:10.1111/j.1467-646X.2007.01010.x

Holme, R., & Watts, P. (2001). Making Good Business Sense. *Journal of Corporate Citizenship*, *2001*(2), 17–20. doi:10.9774/GLEAF.4700.2001.su.00005

Holper, L., Scholkmann, F., & Wolf, M. (2012). Between-brain connectivity during imitation measured by fNIRS. *NeuroImage*, *63*(1), 212–222. doi:10.1016/j.neuroimage.2012.06.028 PMID:22732563

Holzer, S., & Andruet, R. (1995). *A multimedia workshop learning environment for statics*. doi:10.1109/FIE.1995.483056

Hong, J. W. (2020). Why Is Artificial Intelligence Blamed More? Analysis of Faulting Artificial Intelligence for Self-Driving Car Accidents in Experimental Settings. *International Journal of Human-Computer Interaction*, *36*(18), 1768–1774. doi:10.1080/10447318.2020.1785693

Hong, W., & Thong, J. (2013). Internet privacy concerns: An integrated conceptualisation and four empirical studies. *Management Information Systems Quarterly*, *37*(1), 275–298. doi:10.25300/MISQ/2013/37.1.12

Hossain, F. T., Hossain, M. I., & Nawshin, S. (2017). *Machine learning based class level prediction of restaurant reviews. In 2017 IEEE Region 10 Humanitarian Technology Conference (R10-HTC)*. IEEE.

Hossain, M., Leminen, S., & Westerlund, M. (2019). A systematic review of living lab literature. *Journal of Cleaner Production, 213*, 976–988. doi:10.1016/j.jclepro.2018.12.257

Howard, M. (2020, March). Water drone christened in the port of Hamburg. *Maritime Logistics Professional.*

Howard, M., Steensma, H. K., Lyles, M., & Dhanaraj, C. (2016). Learning to collaborate through collaboration: How allying with expert firms influences collaborative innovation within novice firms. *Strategic Management Journal, 37*(10), 2092–2103. doi:10.1002mj.2424

Hsu, L., & Chen, Y.-J. (2020). Neuromarketing, subliminal advertising, and hotel selection: An EEG study. *Australasian Marketing Journal, 28*(4), 200–208. Advance online publication. doi:10.1016/j.ausmj.2020.04.009

Huang, B., Laporte, S., Sénécal, S., & Sobol, K. (2021), Partner or servant? The effect of relationship role on consumer interaction with artificial intelligence. *AMA Winter Academic Conference Proceedings, 32*, 382-384.

Huang, M., Rust, R.T., (2018). Artificial Intelligence in Service. *Journal of Service Research, 2*(2), 155-172.

Huang, M. H., & Rust, R. T. (2018). Artificial intelligence in service. *Journal of Service Research, 21*(2), 155–172. doi:10.1177/1094670517752459

Hulten, G. (2019). *Building intelligent systems*. Apress. doi:10.1007/978-1-4842-3933-9

Hurst, J. (2015). Assessing kindship through scent – the mouse model. *Chemical Senses, 40*(3), 211–297. doi:10.1093/chemse/bju073

Hustić, I., & Gregurec, I. (2015). *The influence of price on customer's purchase decision*. Academic Press.

Hwang, H., & Park, M. H. (2020). The Threat of AI and Our Response: The AI Charter of Ethics in South Korea. *Asian Journal of Innovation & Policy, 9*(1), 56–78.

Hwang, J. S. (2016). The fourth industrial revolution (industry 4.0): Intelligent manufacturing. *SMT Magazine, 3*, 616–630.

iabSpain. (2018). *Estudio anual de eCommerce España 2018*. Retrieved December 6, 2020, from https://iabspain.es/wp-content/uploads/estudio-ecommerce-iab-2018_vcorta.pdf

Iacovou, C. L., Benbasat, I., & Dexter, A. S. (1995). Electronic data interchange and small organizations: Adoption and impact of technology. *Management Information Systems Quarterly, 9*(4), 465–485. doi:10.2307/249629

IBM. (2015a). *Modelling the Entity data architecture*. IBM.

IBM. (2019). *AI and Data Management-Delivering Data-Driven Business Transformation and Operational Efficiencies*. IBM USA.

Ibrahim, A. M. (2001). Differential responding to positive and negative items: The case of a negative item in a questionnaire for course and faculty evaluation. *Psychological Reports, 88*(2), 497–500. doi:10.2466/pr0.2001.88.2.497 PMID:11351897

IEEE. (2019). *Ethically Aligned Design*. Institute of Electrical and Electronic Engineers. https://ethicsinaction.ieee.org/

Ifinedo, P. (2012). Factors influencing e-government maturity in transition economies and developing countries: A longitudinal perspective. *SIGMIS Database, 42*(4), 98–116. doi:10.1145/2096140.2096147

IMD. (2015). *IMD business school and Cisco join forces on digital business transformation*. IMD.

INEI. (2014). *Results of the Micro and Small Enterprise Survey 2013*. Retrieved from https://www.inei.gob.pe/media/MenuRecursivo/publicaciones_digitales/Est/Lib1139/libro.pdf

INEI. (2017). *National Census of Food Markets 2016*. Retrieved from https://www.inei.gob.pe/media/MenuRecursivo/publicaciones_digitales/Est/Lib1448/libro.pdf

INEI. (2018). *Technical report Estadísticas de las Tecnologías de Información y Comunicación en los Hogares*. Retrieved from https://www.inei.gob.pe/media/MenuRecursivo/boletines/04-informe-tecnico-n04_tecnologias-de-informacion-jul-ago-set2018.pdf

Infante Moro, J. C. (2017). *User perception to improve the use of Social Networks as a communication channel in the hotel sector* [Percepción de los usuarios para la mejora del uso de las Redes Sociales como canal de comunicación en el sector hotelero] (Doctoral Thesis). University of Huelva.

Infante-Moro, A., Infante-Moro, J. C., & Gallardo-Pérez, J. (2021a). Factors that influence the adoption of the Internet of Things in the hotel sector [Factores que influyen en la adopción del Internet de las Cosas en el sector hotelero]. *RISTI - Revista Iberica de Sistemas e Tecnologias de Informacao*, (E41), 370-383.

Infante-Moro, A., Infante-Moro, J. C., & Gallardo-Pérez, J. (2020a). Key factors in the implementation of Cloud Computing as a service and communication tool in universities. In *Eighth International Conference on Technological Ecosystems for Enhancing Multiculturality* (pp. 631-636). 10.1145/3434780.3436698

Infante-Moro, A., Infante-Moro, J. C., & Gallardo-Pérez, J. (2020b). Motivational factors in the insertion of digital skills in teaching. In *Eighth International Conference on Technological Ecosystems for Enhancing Multiculturality* (pp. 365-370). 10.1145/3434780.3436631

Infante-Moro, A., Infante-Moro, J. C., & Gallardo-Pérez, J. (2020c). Motivational factors that justify the implementation of the internet of things as a security system in the hotel sector [Factores motivacionales que justifican la implementación del Internet de las Cosas como sistema de seguridad en el sector hotelero]. *Revista de Pensamiento Estratégico y Seguridad CISDE*, *5*(2), 81–91.

Infante-Moro, A., Infante-Moro, J. C., & Gallardo-Pérez, J. (2020d). The employment possibilities of the internet of things in the hotel sector and its training needs [Las posibilidades de empleo del Internet de las Cosas en el sector hotelero y sus necesidades formativas]. *Education In The Knowledge Society*, *21*, 14. doi:10.14201/eks.222643

Infante-Moro, A., Infante-Moro, J. C., & Gallardo-Pérez, J. (2021b). The acquisition of ICT skills at the university level: The case of the Faculty of Business Studies and Tourism of the University of Huelva [La adquisición de competencias TIC en el ámbito universitario: El caso de la Facultad de Ciencias Empresariales y Turismo de la Universidad de Huelva]. *Revista de Medios y Educacion*, (60), 29–58.

Infante-Moro, A., Infante-Moro, J. C., & Gallardo-Pérez, J. (2021c). Key Factors in the Implementation of the Internet of Things in the Hotel Sector. *Applied Sciences (Basel, Switzerland)*, *11*(7), 2924. doi:10.3390/app11072924

Information Desk. (2021). *Ritwik Ghatak's War between 'Man and Machine*. Get Bengal, Thinking Positive.

Inkinen, T., Helminen, R., & Saarikoski, J. (2019). Port Digitalization with Open Data: Challenges, Opportunities, and Integrations. *Journal of Open Innovation*, *5*(2), 30. doi:10.3390/joitmc5020030

Inselberg, A. (1992). *The plane R2 with coordinate parallel. Computer Science and Applied Mathematics Departments. Tel Aviv*. University.

Institute for Ethical AI & Machine Learning. (2020). *Machine learning maturity model v1.0*. Retrieved from https://ethical.institute/mlmm.html

Institute of Chartered Accountants in England and Wales (ICAEW). (2004). *Sustainability: The Role of Accountants.* Sustainable Business Initiative Report.

Institute, T. S. (TUIK). (2021). Retrieved from http: https://data.tuik.gov.tr/

International Council for Local Environmental Initiatives (ICLEI). (2021). *Climate Protection.* Retrieved from http: https://iclei-europe.org/our-members/

International Energy Agency (IEA). (2021). *Data and statistics.* Retrieved from http: https://www.iea.org/data-and-statistics?country=WORLD&fuel=Energy%20supply&indicator=TPESbySource

Internet World Sats. (2020). *Internet World Sats.* Retrieved from https://www.internetworldstats.com/stats2.htm

Intersoft Consulting. (2020). *General Data Protection Regulation GDPR.* Retrieved December 6, 2020, from https://gdpr-info.eu/

Ioannidou. (2013). Adapting Superhero Comics for the Big Screen: Subculture for the Masses. *Adaptation, 6*(2), 230–238. doi:10.1093/adaptation/apt004

Ishiguro, K. (2021). *Klara and the Sun.* Faber and Faber.

Ishikawa, F., & Yoshioka, N. (2019). *How do engineers perceive difficulties in engineering of machine-learning systems? Questionnaire survey.* Paper presented at the 2019 IEEE/ACM Joint 7th International Workshop on Conducting Empirical Studies in Industry (CESI) and 6th International Workshop on Software Engineering Research and Industrial Practice (SER&IP). 10.1109/CESSER-IP.2019.00009

İşlek, İ., & Gunduz Oguducu, S. (2017). A Decision Support System for Demand Forecasting based on Classifier Ensemble. *Federated Conference on Computer Science and Information Systems (ACSIS), 13*, 35–41. 10.15439/2017F224

ISO. (2020). *ISO/IEC 25010.* Retrieved December 18, 2020, from https://iso25000.com/index.php/normas-iso-25000/iso-25010

itUser. (2020). *La experiencia de cliente y el aumento de ingresos, una relación que confirman el 82% de las empresas.* Retrieved December 18, 2020, from https://www.ituser.es/estrategias-digitales/2020/06/la-experiencia-de-cliente-y-el-aumento-de-ingresos-una-relacion-que-confirman-el-82-de-las-empresas

Ivanov, O. A., Ivanova, V. V., & Saltan, A. A. (2018). Likert scale questionnaires as an educational tool in teaching discrete mathematics. *International Journal of Mathematical Education in Science and Technology, 49*(7), 1110–1118. doi:10.1080/0020739X.2017.1423121

Iwashita, M. (2019). Transitional Method for Identifying Improvements in Video Distribution Services. *International Journal of Networked and Distributed Computing, 7*(4), 141. doi:10.2991/ijndc.k.190911.001

Izard, C. E. (1977). *Human emotions.* Plenum Press.

Izo. (2019a). *5 Tendencias en Experiencia de Cliente en 2019.* Retrieved December 18, 2020, from https://izo.es/tendencias-experiencia-de-cliente-2019/

Izo. (2019b). *¿Cómo Conseguir Empleados Felices y Comprometidos?* https://izo.es/como-conseguir-empleados-felices-y-comprometidos/

Jabrouni, H., Kamsu-Foguem, B., Geneste, L., & Vaysse, C. (2011). Continuous improvement through knowledge-guided analysis in experience feedback. *Eng. Appl. of AI, 24*(8), 1419–1431. doi:10.1016/j.engappai.2011.02.015

Jacks, D. S., & Pendakur, K. (2010). Global Trade and The Maritime Transport Revolution. *The Review of Economics and Statistics*, *92*(4), 745–755. doi:10.1162/REST_a_00026

Jackson, L.A., Witt, E., Games, A., Fitzgerald, H., Von Eye, A. & Zao, Y. (2011). Information Technological use and Creativity: Findings from The Children and Technological Project. *Computers in Human Behaviour, 28*(2), 370-376.

Jacoby, J., & Matell, M. S. (1971). Three-point Likert scales are good enough. *JMR, Journal of Marketing Research*, *8*(4), 495–500. doi:10.1177/002224377100800414

Jain, A. K., Murty, M. N., & Flynn, P. J. (1999). Data clustering: A review. *ACM Computing Surveys*, *31*(3), 264–323. doi:10.1145/331499.331504

Jamieson, S. (2004). Likert scales: How to (ab) use them. *Medical Education*, *38*(12), 1217–1218. doi:10.1111/j.1365-2929.2004.02012.x PMID:15566531

Jamil, M. G., & Bhuiyan, Z. (2021). Deep learning elements in maritime simulation programs: A pedagogical exploration of learner experiences. *International Journal of Educational Technology in Higher Education*, *18*(1), 1–22. doi:10.118641239-021-00255-0

Jannach, D., Zanker, M., & Fuchs, M. (2014). Leveraging multi-criteria customer feedback for satisfaction analysis and improved recommendations. *Information Technology & Tourism*, *14*(2), 119–149. doi:10.100740558-014-0010-z

Jansen, A. (2006). *Assessing e-government progress– Why and what.* https://www.uio.no/studier/emner/jus/afin/FINF4001/h05/undervisningsmateriale/AJJ-nokobit2005.pdf

Jarek, K., & Mazurek, G. (2019). Marketing and Artificial Intelligence. *Central European Business Review*, *8*(2), 46–55. doi:10.18267/j.cebr.213

Jarrahi, M. H. (2018). Artificial intelligence and the future of work: Human-AI symbiosis in organizational decision-making. *Business Horizons*, *61*(4), 577–586. doi:10.1016/j.bushor.2018.03.007

Järvinen, P. (2007). Action Research is Similar to Design Science. *Quality & Quantity, 41*(1), 37–54. https://link.springer.com/article/10.1007/s11135-005-5427-1

Jaszkiewicz, J., & Sowiñski, R. (1999). The 'Light Beam Search' approach - an overview of methodology and applications. *European Journal of Operational Research*, *113*(2), 300–314. doi:10.1016/S0377-2217(98)00218-5

Jean, W., & Yazdanifard, R. (2015). The Review of How Sales Promotion Change the Consumer's Perception and Their Purchasing Behavior of a Product. *Global Journal of Management and Business Research*, *15*, 33–37.

Jenkins, H. (2007). *Transmedia Storytelling 101.* http://henryjenkins.org/2007/03/transmedia_storytelling_101.html

Jenkins, H. (2011). *Transmedia 202: Further Reflections.* http://henryjenkins.org/2011/08/defining_transmedia_further_re.html

Jenkins, H. (2013). *"Wish You Were Here": Imaginative Mobilities and Disembodied Intimacy in Postcards (Part Two).* http://henryjenkins.org/2013/02/what-transmedia-producers-need-toknow-about-comics-an-interview-with-tyler-weaver-part-two.html

Jenkins, H. (2006). *Convergence Culture.* New York University Press.

Jensen, Ø., & Hansen, K. V. (2007). Consumer values among restaurant customers. *International Journal of Hospitality Management*, *26*(3), 603–622. doi:10.1016/j.ijhm.2006.05.004

Jerz, D. G. (2002). R.U.R. (Rossum's Universal Robots). Dover.

Jing, L., Marlow, P. B., & Hui, W. (2008). An analysis of freight rate volatility in dry bulk shipping markets. *Maritime Policy & Management, 35*(3), 237–251. doi:10.1080/03088830802079987

Jin, N., Lee, S., & Huffman, L. (2012). Impact of restaurant experience on brand image and customer loyalty: Moderating role of dining motivation. *Journal of Travel & Tourism Marketing, 29*(6), 532–551. doi:10.1080/10548408.2012.701552

Johnson, J. M., Bristow, D. N., & Schneider, K. C. (2004). Did you not understand the question or not? An investigation of negatively worded questions in survey research. *Journal of Applied Business Research, 20*(1), 75–86.

Johns, R. (2005). One size doesn't fit all: Selecting response scales for attitude items. *Journal of Elections, Public Opinion, and Parties, 15*(2), 237–264. doi:10.1080/13689880500178849

Johnstone, T., & Scherer, K. R. (2000). Vocal communication of emotion. In *Handbook of Emotions* (2nd ed., pp. 220–235). Guilford Press.

Jones, C., Alderete, M. V., & Motta, J. (2013). E-commerce adoption in Micro, Small and Medium-sized commercial and service enterprises in Cordoba. *Cuadernos de Administración, 29*(50), 164-175. Retrieved from https://www.redalyc.org/pdf/2250/225029797006.pdf

Jones, V. K. (2018). Voice-activated change: Marketing in the age of artificial intelligence and virtual assistants. *Journal of Brand Strategy, 7*(3), 233–245.

Jose, P. C., & Fernandes, A. P. (2020). European Seaports Information Systems. The Impacts of Directive 2010/65/EU. *Economics and Culture, 17*(2), 38–49. doi:10.2478/jec-2020-0019

Joshi, A., Kale, S., Chandel, S., & Pal, D. K. (2015). Likert scale: Explored and explained. *Current Journal of Applied Science and Technology*, 396-403.

Joy, B. (2000). *Why the future doesn't need us*. Wired.

Józsa, K., & Morgan, G. A. (2017). Reversed items in Likert scales: Filtering out invalid responders. *Journal of Psychological and Educational Research, 25*(1), 7–25.

June Kim, S. (2021). How can higher maritime education lead shipping growth? Korea's experience, 1948–1982. *International Journal of Maritime History, 33*(1), 90–117. doi:10.1177/0843871420974062

Jung, T., & Dieck, T. (2018). *Augmented Reality and Virtual Reality. Empowering Human, Place and Business*. Springer. doi:10.1007/978-3-319-64027-3

Junta de Andalucía. (2020). *Guide Using ICTs to reach new market niches and consumers*. Retrieved from www.formacion.andaluciaesdigital.es: https://www.formacion.andaluciaesdigital.es/catalogo-cursos/-/acciones/ficha/7809

Jurney, R. (2017). *Agile data science 2.0: Building full-stack data analytics applications with Spark*. O'Reilly Media.

Jussila, J., Huhtamäki, J., Kärkkäinen, H., Aho, T., Kortelainen, S., & Tebest, T. (2014). New era of business analytics - Making sense of business ecosystems. *MINDTREK 2014 - Proceedings of the 18th International Academic MindTrek Conference*, 266–268. 10.1145/2676467.2676517

Kadircan, H. K. (2019). Medical Ethics: Consideration on Artificial Intelligence. *Journal of Clinical Neuroscience*.

Kak, S. (2006). Artificial and biological intelligence. *ACM Ubiquity, 6*(42), 1–20.

Kaloudi, N., & Li, J. (2020). The AI-based cyber threat landscape: A survey. *ACM Computing Surveys, 53*(1), 1–34. doi:10.1145/3372823

Kalouptsidi, M. (2014, February). Time to build and fluctuations in bulk shipping. *The American Economic Review*, *104*(2), 564–608. doi:10.1257/aer.104.2.564

Kane, M. J., Price, N., Scotch, M., & Rabinowitz, P. (2014). Comparison of ARIMA and Random Forest time series models for prediction of avian influenza H5N1 outbreaks. *BMC Bioinformatics*, *15*(1), 276. doi:10.1186/1471-2105-15-276 PMID:25123979

Kang, H., Le, M., & Tao, S. (2016). *Container and microservice driven design for cloud infrastructure devops*. Paper presented at the 2016 IEEE International Conference on Cloud Engineering (IC2E). 10.1109/IC2E.2016.26

Kang, K., Zhang, W.-c., Guo, L.-y., & Ma, T. (2012, September). Research on ship routing and deployment mode for a bulk. In *2012 international conference on management science & engineering 19th annual conference proceedings*. Dallas, TX: IEEE. 10.1109/ICMSE.2012.6414421

Kantar. (2020). *A new world: Changes and prospects for shopping channels*. Retrieved from http://mkt.kantarworldpanel.com: http://mkt.kantarworldpanel.com/global/LATAM/Retail/Retail_COVID-19_v3.pdf

Kapferer, J.-N. (1998). Why are we seduced by luxury brands? *Journal of Brand Management*, *6*(1), 44–49. doi:10.1057/bm.1998.43

Kapferer, J.-N. (2012). *The New Strategic Brand Management: Advanced Insights and Strategic Thinking* (5th ed.). Kogan Page.

Kaplan, A., & Haenlein, M. (2019). Siri, Siri, in my hand: Who's the fairest in the land? On the interpretations, illustrations, and implications of artificial intelligence. *Business Horizons*, *62*(1), 15–25. doi:10.1016/j.bushor.2018.08.004

Karhade, P. P., & Dong, J. Q. (2021). Innovation Outcomes of Digitally Enabled Collaborative Problemistic Search Capability. *Management Information Systems Quarterly*, *45*(2), 693–717. doi:10.25300/MISQ/2021/12202

Karlis, T. (2018, January). Maritime law issues related to the operation of unmanned autonomous cargo ships. *WMU Journal of Maritime Affairs*, *17*(1), 1–10. doi:10.100713437-018-0135-6

Karlsson, L. C., Soveri, A., Lewandowsky, S., Karlsson, L., Karlsson, H., Nolvi, S., Karuki, M., Lindfelt, M., & Antfolk, J. (2021). Fearing the disease or the vaccine: The case of COVID-19. *Personality and Individual Differences*, *172*, 110590. doi:10.1016/j.paid.2020.110590 PMID:33518869

Karnowski, J., & Fadely, R. (2016). *How AI careers fit into the data landscape*. Retrieved from https://blog.insightdatascience.com/how-emerging-ai-roles-fit-in-the-data-landscape-d4cd922c389b

Kavallieratos, G., Diamantopoulou, V., & Katsikas, S. K. (2020). Shipping 4.0: Security Requirements for the Cyber-Enabled Ship. *IEEE Transactions on Industrial Informatics*, *16*(10), 6617–6625. doi:10.1109/TII.2020.2976840

Kaviya, K., Roshini, C., Vaidhehi, V., & Sweetlin, J. D. (2017). Sentiment analysis for restaurant rating. In *2017 IEEE International Conference on Smart Technologies and Management for Computing, Communication, Controls, Energy and Materials (ICSTM)* (pp. 140-145). IEEE.

Keim, D., Kohlhammer, J., Ellis, G., & Mansmann, F. (2010). *Mastering the information age: Solving problems with visual analytics*. VisMaster.

Keller, K. L., & Richey, K. (2006). The importance of corporate brand personality traits to a successful 21st century business. *Journal of Brand Management*, *14*(1-2), 74–81. doi:10.1057/palgrave.bm.2550055

Kennedy, M., Campbell, I., & Chyung, Y. (2018). *Evidence-Based Survey Design: The Use of Ascending or Descending Order of Likert Response Options*. Academic Press.

Kent, S. (2001). *The Ultimate History of Video Games: From Pong to Pokemon—The Story Behind the Craze That Touched Our Lives and Changed the World.* Crown.

Kerr, I., & Earle, J. (2013). Prediction, preemption, presumption: How big data threatens big picture privacy. *Stanford Law Review Online, 66*, 65–72.

Kery, M. B., Radensky, M., Arya, M., John, B. E., & Myers, B. A. (2018). *The story in the notebook: Exploratory data science using a literate programming tool.* Paper presented at the CHI Conference on Human Factors in Computing Systems. 10.1145/3173574.3173748

Kęsek, M., Bogacz, P., & Migza, M. (2019). The application of Lean Management and Six Sigma tools in global mining enterprises. *IOP Conference Series. Earth and Environmental Science, 214*, 12090. doi:10.1088/1755-1315/214/1/012090

Kevin, W. J. (2000). *Co-founder of Sun Microsystem-expressed in a 2000 Wired Magazine article.* Academic Press.

Khan, H., Khan, I., Oanh, L. T. K., & Lin, Z. (2020). The Dynamic Interrelationship of Environmental Factors and Foreign Direct Investment: Dynamic Panel Data Analysis and New Evidence from the Globe. *Mathematical Problems in Engineering*, 1–12.

Khan, M. A., Khan, T. M., Bailey, D. G., & Kong, Y. (2016). A spatial domain scar removal strategy for fingerprint image enhancement. *Pattern Recognition, 60*, 258–274. doi:10.1016/j.patcog.2016.05.015

Khan, Z., Malik, M. Y., Latif, K., & Jiao, Z. (2020). Heterogeneous effect of eco-innovation and human capital on renewable & non-renewable energy consumption: Disaggregate analysis for G-7 countries. *Energy, 209*, 118405. doi:10.1016/j.energy.2020.118405

Kim, H. J., Pan, G., & Pan, S. L. (2007). Managing it-enabled transformation in the public sector: A case study on e-government in south korea. *Government Information Quarterly, 24*(2), 338–352. doi:10.1016/j.giq.2006.09.007

Kim, H. W., Chan, H. C., & Gupta, S. (2007). Value-based Adoption of Mobile Internet: An empirical investigation. *Decision Support Systems, 43*(1), 111–126. doi:10.1016/j.dss.2005.05.009

Kim, K., & Kim, K. (1999). Routing straddle carriers for the loading operation of containers using a beam search algorithm. Elsevier. *Computers & Industrial Engineering, 36*(1), 109–136. doi:10.1016/S0360-8352(99)00005-4

Kim, M., Zimmermann, T., DeLine, R., & Begel, A. (2017). Data scientists in software teams: State of the art and challenges. *IEEE Transactions on Software Engineering, 44*(11), 1024–1038. doi:10.1109/TSE.2017.2754374

Kim, W. G., & Park, S. A. (2017). Social media review rating versus traditional customer satisfaction. *International Journal of Contemporary Hospitality Management, 29*(2), 784–802. doi:10.1108/IJCHM-11-2015-0627

Kinder, M. (1991). *Playing with Power in Movies, Television and Video Games.* University of California Press.

Kinder, M. (2014). *Transmedia Frictions: The Digital, the Arts, and the Humanities.* University of California Press.

Kingma, D. P., & Ba, J. (2015). Adam: {A} Method for Stochastic Optimization. In Y. Bengio & Y. LeCun (Eds.), *3rd International Conference on Learning Representations, ICLR 2015, San Diego, CA, USA, May 7-9, 2015, Conference Track Proceedings.* https://arxiv.org/abs/1412.6980

Kirk, C. P., & Rifkin, L. S. (2020, September). I'll trade you diamonds for toilet paper: Consumer reacts, copes, and adapts behaviors in the COVID-19 pandemic. *Journal of Business Research, 117*, 124–131. doi:10.1016/j.jbusres.2020.05.028 PMID:32834208

Kirk, M. (2017). *Thoughtful machine learning with Python: A test-driven approach.* O'Reilly Media.

Klass, M. (1983). The Artificial Alien: Transformations of the Robot in Science Fiction. *Annals of the American Academy of Political and Social Science*, 171-79.

Kleinginna, P.R., & Kleinginna, A.M. (1981). A categorized list of emotion definitions, with suggestions for a consensual definition. *Motivation and Emotion*, *5*(4), 345–379.

KLM. (2016, March 29). *Spencer robot completed tests guiding KLM passengers at Schiphol*. https://news.klm.com/spencer-robot-completed-tests-guiding-klm-passengers-at-schiphol/

Klmcare. (n.d.). *Meet KLM Care-E*. http://klmcare-e-entry.com

Knapp, T. R. (1990). Treating ordinal scales as interval scales: An attempt to resolve the controversy. *Nursing Research*, *39*(2), 121–123. doi:10.1097/00006199-199003000-00019 PMID:2315066

Knowledge Management. (2021). *Experience-Based Knowledge*. Knowledge management, Group Work, UCPori. Retrieved from https://knowledgemanagement5.wordpress.com/experience-based-knowledge/

Knutson, B., Rick, S., Wimmer, G. E., Prelec, D., & Loewenstein, G. (2007). Neural predictors of purchases. *Neuron*, *53*(1), 147–156. doi:10.1016/j.neuron.2006.11.010 PMID:17196537

Kodratoff, Y. (1999, July). Comparing machine learning and knowledge discovery in databases: An application to knowledge discovery in texts. In *Advanced Course on Artificial Intelligence* (pp. 1–21). Springer.

Kohli, A. K., Jaworski, B. J., & Shabshab, N. (2019). Customer centricity: a multi-year journey. In *Handbook on Customer Centricity*. Edward Elgar Publishing.

Kolarik, T., & Rudorfer, G. (1994). Time series forecasting using neural networks. *Proceedings of the International Conference on APL : The Language and Its Applications, APL 1994*, 86–94. 10.1145/190271.190290

Kolb, D., & Kolb, A. (2017). *The Experiential Educator: Principles and Practices of Experiential Learning*. Academic Press.

Koller, B. (2020, Sep 28). *12 Factors of reproducible Machine Learning in production*. Retrieved from https://blog.maiot.io/12-factors-of-ml-in-production/

Korinek, A., & Stiglitz, J. (2021). *Artificial Intelligence Could Mean Large Increase in Prosperity- But only for a Privileged Few*. https://www.ineteconomics.org/perspectives/blog/artificial-intelligence-could-mean-technological-advancement-but-only-for-a-privileged-few?fbclid=IwAR0qxVBh0NYHEJLVJCoC3bynkESnLFgfn8QFZcIE63kGu06TIjMEbWDHadM

Kotler, P., Armstrong, G., Cámara, D., & Cruz, I. (2004). Principios de marketing (10a edición). Madrid: Prentice Hall.

Kraus, S. J. (1995). Attitudes and the Prediction of Behavior: A Meta-Analysis of the Empirical Literature. *Personality and Social Psychology Bulletin*, *21*(1), 58–75. doi:10.1177/0146167295211007

Krensky, P., den Hamer, P., Brethenoux, E., Hare, J., Idoine, C., Linden, A., Sicular, S., & Choudhary, F. (2020). *Magic quadrant for data science and machine learning platforms*. Academic Press.

Kreps, S., Prasad, S., Brownstein, J. S., Hswen, Y., Garibaldi, B. T., Zhang, B., & Kriner, D. L. (2020). Factors associated with US adults' likelihood of accepting COVID-19 vaccination. *JAMA Network Open*, *3*(10), e2025594–e2025594. doi:10.1001/jamanetworkopen.2020.25594 PMID:33079199

Kretschmann, L., Zacharias, M., Klöver, S., & Hensel, T. (2020). *Machine Learning in Maritime Logistics*. Fraunhofer CML.

Kriens, P., & Verbelen, T. (2019). *Software engineering practices for machine learning*. arXiv preprint arXiv:1906.10366.

Krish, R. P., Fierrez, J., Ramos, D., Alonso-Fernandez, F., & Bigun, J. (2019). Improving automated latent fingerprint identification using extended minutia types. *Information Fusion*, *50*, 9–19. doi:10.1016/j.inffus.2018.10.001

Krueger, M. (1991). *Realidad artificial 2*. Addison-Wesley Profesional.

Krueger, M. W., Gionfriddo, T., & Hinrichsen, K. (1985). Videoplace an artificial reality. *Proceedings of the ACM SIGCHI Bulletin*, 16. 10.1145/317456.317463

Kühn, A., Joppen, R., Reinhart, F., Röltgen, D., von Enzberg, S., & Dumitrescu, R. (2018). Analytics Canvas–A Framework for the design and specification of data analytics projects. *Procedia CIRP*, *70*, 162–167. doi:10.1016/j.procir.2018.02.031

Kula, V., & Tatoglu, E. (2003). An exploratory study of Internet adoption by SMEs in an emerging market economy.[. *European Business Review*, *15*(5), 324–333. doi:10.1108/09555340310493045

Kumar, S., Yadava, M., & Roy, P. P. (2019). Fusion of EEG response and sentiment analysis of products review to predict customer satisfaction. *Information Fusion*, *52*, 41–52. doi:10.1016/j.inffus.2018.11.001

Kumar, V., & Leone, R. P. (1988). Measuring the Effect of Retail Store Promotions on Brand and Store Substitution. *JMR, Journal of Marketing Research*, *25*(2), 178–185. doi:10.1177/002224378802500206

Kunstelj, M., & Vintar, M. (2004). Evaluating the progress of e-government development: A critical analysis. *Info. Pol.*, *9*(3,4), 131-148.

Kurzweil, R. (1999). *The Age of Spiritual Machines*. Viking Adult.

Kurzweil, R. (2005). *The Singularity Is Near: When Humans Transcend Biology*. Viking Books.

La Torre, M., Botes, V. L., Dumay, J., & Odendaal, E. (2019). Protecting a new achilles heel: The role of auditors within the practice of data protection. *Managerial Auditing Journal*. Advance online publication. doi:10.1108/MAJ-03-2018-1836

La Torre, M., Botes, V. L., Dumay, J., Rea, M. A., & Odendaal, E. (2018a). The fall and rise of intellectual capital accounting: New prospects from the big data revolution. *Meditari Accountancy Research*, *26*(3), 381–399. doi:10.1108/MEDAR-05-2018-0344

La Torre, M., Dumay, J., & Rea, M. A. (2018b). Breaching intellectual capital: Critical reflections on big data security. *Meditari Accountancy Research*, *26*(3), 463–482. doi:10.1108/MEDAR-06-2017-0154

Laforet, S. (2011). A framework of organisational innovation and outcomes in SMEs. *International Journal of Entrepreneurial Behaviour & Research*, *17*(4), 380–408. doi:10.1108/13552551111139638

Laforet, S., & Tann, J. (2006). Innovative characteristics of small manufacturing firms. *Journal of Small Business and Enterprise Development*, *13*(3), 363–380. doi:10.1108/14626000610680253

Lambrou, M., Watanabe, D., & Iida, J. (2019, November). Shipping digitalization management: Conceptualization, typology, and antecedents. *Journal of Shipping and Trade*, *4*(11), 11. Advance online publication. doi:10.118641072-019-0052-7

Lanctot, R. (2017). *Accelerating the Future: The Economic Impact of the Emerging Passenger Economy*. Strategy Analytics Report. https://newsroom.intel.com/newsroom/wp-content/uploads/sites/11/2017/05/passenger-economy.pdf

Lane, C. (2013). Taste makers in the "fine-dining" restaurant industry: The attribution of aesthetic and economic value by gastronomic guides. *Poetics*, *41*(4), 342–365. doi:10.1016/j.poetic.2013.05.003

Lange, G. S., & Johnston, W. J. (2020). The value of business accelerators and incubators–an entrepreneur's perspective. *Journal of Business and Industrial Marketing*.

Langleben, D. D., Loughead, J. W., Ruparel, K., Hakun, J. G., Bush-Winokur, S., Holloway, M. B., Strasser, A. A., Cappella, J. N., & Lerman, C. (2009). Reduced prefrontal and temporal processing and recall of high "sensation value" ads. *NeuroImage*, *46*(1), 219–225. doi:10.1016/j.neuroimage.2008.12.062 PMID:19457412

Langley. (n.d.). *Crafting Papers on Machine Learning*. Adaptive Systems Group, Daimler-Chrysler Research and Technology Center.

Langley, D. J., van Doorn, J., Ng, I. C., Stieglitz, S., Lazovik, A., & Boonstra, A. (2021). The Internet of Everything: *Smart things and their impact on business models. Journal of Business Research*, *122*, 853–863. doi:10.1016/j.jbusres.2019.12.035

Lara, F., & Deckers, J. (2019). Artificial Intelligence as a Socratic Assistant for Moral Enhancement. *Neuroethics*, 1–13. doi:10.100712152-019-09401-y

Larson, H., Jarrett, C., Eckersberger, E., Smith, D., & Paterson, P. (2014). Understanding vaccine hesitancy around vaccines from a global perspective: A systematic review of published literature, 2007-2012. *Vaccine*, *32*(19), 2150–2159. doi:10.1016/j.vaccine.2014.01.081 PMID:24598724

Lasi, H., Fettke, P., Kemper, H.-G., Feld, T., & Hoffmann, M. (2014). Industry 4.0. *Business & Information Systems Engineering*, *6*(4), 239–242. doi:10.100712599-014-0334-4

Laudon, K. C., & Laudon, J. P. (2020). *Management information systems: managing the digital firm* (16th ed.). Pearson Education Limited.

Lauterbach, A. (2019). Artificial intelligence and policy: Quo vadis? *Digital Policy. Regulation & Governance*, *21*(3), 238–263. doi:10.1108/DPRG-09-2018-0054

Lazar, I., Motogna, S., & Parv, B. (2010). Behaviour-Driven Development of Foundational UML Components. Department of Computer Science. Babes-Bolyai University, Cluj-Napoca, Romania. doi:10.1016/j.entcs.2010.07.007

Leachman, S. A., & Merlino, G. (2017). Medicine: The Final Frontier in Cancer Diagnosis. *Nature*, *542*(7639), 36–38. doi:10.1038/nature21492 PMID:28150762

Lea, T.-H., Nguyen, C. P., & Park, D. (2020). Financing renewable energy development: Insights from 55 countries. *Energy Research & Social Science*, *68*, 101537. doi:10.1016/j.erss.2020.101537

Leavy, S. (2018, May). Gender bias in artificial intelligence: The need for diversity and gender theory in machine learning. In *Proceedings of the 1st international workshop on gender equality in software engineering* (pp. 14-16). 10.1145/3195570.3195580

LeCun, Y., Bengio, Y., & Hinton, G. (2015). Deep learning. *Nature, 521*(7553), 436-444.

Lee, J., Singh, J., & Azamfar, M. (2019). *Industrial artificial intelligence.* arXiv preprint arXiv:1908.02150.

Lee, C.-L. (2014). Is co-branding a double-edged sword for brand partners? *European Research Studies Journal*, *17*(4), 19–34. doi:10.35808/ersj/430

Lee, H. L. (2018). Big data and the innovation cycle. *Production and Operations Management*, *27*(9), 1642–1646. doi:10.1111/poms.12845

Lee, I., & Shin, Y. (2020). Machine learning for enterprises: Applications, algorithm selection, and challenges. *Business Horizons*, *63*(2), 157–170. doi:10.1016/j.bushor.2019.10.005

Lee, M., Yun, J. J., Pyka, A., Won, D., Kodama, F., Schiuma, G., Park, H. S., Jeon, J., Park, K. B., Jung, K. H., Yan, M.-R., Lee, S. Y., & Zhao, X. (2018). How to Respond to the Fourth Industrial Revolution or the Second Information Technology Revolution? Dynamic New Combinations between Technology, Market, and Society through Open Innovation. *Journal of Open Innovation*, *4*(3), 21. Advance online publication. doi:10.3390/joitmc4030021

Lee, S. M., Tan, X., & Trimi, S. (2005). Current practices of leading e-government countries. *Communications of the ACM*, *48*(10), 99–104. doi:10.1145/1089107.1089112

Lee, T. (2019). Financial investment for the development of renewable energy capacity. *Energy & Environment*, *0*(0), 1–14. doi:10.1177/0958305X19882403

Legardinier, A. (2013). *Comment limiter les biais liés au choix des échelles de mesure dans les études marketing?* [How to limit the biases linked to the choice of measurement scales in marketing studies?]. Gestion et management, Dumas.

Legg, S., & Hutter, M. (2007). *Universal intelligence: a definition of machine intelligence*. Retrieved from https://arxiv.org/pdf/0712.3329.pdf

Leitch, R., & Day, Ch. (2000). *Action research and reflective practice: towards a holistic view*. Taylor & Francis. https://www.tandfonline.com/doi/ref/10.1080/09650790000200108?scroll=top

Leminen, S., Westerlund, M., & Nyström, A.-G. (2012). Living Labs as Open-Innovation Networks. *Technology Innovation Management Review*, *2*(9), 6–11. doi:10.22215/timreview/602

Lemon, K. N., & Verhoef, P. C. (2016). Understanding Customer Experience Throughout the Customer Journey. *Journal of Marketing*, *80*(6), 69–96. doi:10.1509/jm.15.0420

Lemon, K. N., & Verhoef, P. C. (2016). Understanding customer experience throughout the customer journey. *Journal of Marketing*, *80*, 69–96.

Letheren, K., Russell-Bennett, R., & Whittaker, L. (2020). Black, white or grey magic? Our future with artificial intelligence. *Journal of Marketing Management*, *36*(3-4), 216–232. doi:10.1080/0267257X.2019.1706306

Leung, E., Paolacci, G., & Puntoni, S. (2018). Man versus machine: Resisting automation in identity-based consumer behavior. *JMR, Journal of Marketing Research*, *55*(6), 818–831. doi:10.1177/0022243718818423

Lever, M. W., Shen, Y., & Joppe, M. (2019). Reading travel guidebooks: Readership typologies using eye-tracking technology. *Journal of Destination Marketing & Management*, *14*, 1–13. doi:10.1016/j.jdmm.2019.100368

Levinson, M. (2020). *Outside The Box*. Kirkus Reviews.

Levy, Y., & Ellis, T. J. (2006). A systems approach to conduct an effective literature review in support of information systems research. *Informing Science Journal*, *9*, 181–212. doi:10.28945/479

Lewis, R. C. (1981). The positioning statement for hotels. *The Cornell Hotel and Restaurant Administration Quarterly*, *22*(1), 51–61. doi:10.1177/001088048102200111

Lewkowitz, M. (2014, Feb 12). *Bots: The future of human-computer interaction*. Available: https://chatbotsmagazine.com/bots-the-future-of-human-computer-interaction56696f7aff56

Liang, Z. (2019, September). Design of automatic matching system for ocean-going cargo in international logistics. *Journal of Coastal Research*, *93*(SI), 1105–1110. doi:10.2112/SI93-160.1

Liban, A., & Hilles, S. M. (2018, July). Latent Fingerprint Enhancement Based on Directional Total Variation Model with Lost Minutiae Reconstruction. In *2018 International Conference on Smart Computing and Electronic Enterprise (ICSCEE)* (pp. 1-5). IEEE. 10.1109/ICSCEE.2018.8538417

Li, H., Xie, K. L., & Zhang, Z. (2020). The effects of consumer experience and disconfirmation on the timing of online review: Field evidence from the restaurant business. *International Journal of Hospitality Management, 84,* 102344. doi:10.1016/j.ijhm.2019.102344

Li, J. P., Mirza, N., Rahat, B., & Xiong, D. (2020). Machine learning and credit ratings prediction in the age of fourth industrial revolution. *Technological Forecasting and Social Change, 161,* 120309. doi:10.1016/j.techfore.2020.120309

Li, J., Feng, J., & Kuo, C. C. J. (2018). Deep convolutional neural network for latent fingerprint enhancement. *Signal Processing Image Communication, 60,* 52–63. doi:10.1016/j.image.2017.08.010

Li, J., Xu, L., Tang, L., Wang, S., & Li, L. (2018). Big data in tourism research: A literature review. *Tourism Management, 68,* 301–323. doi:10.1016/j.tourman.2018.03.009

Likert, R. (1932). A technique for the measurement of attitudes. *Archives de Psychologie.*

Lim, C., Kim, K., & Maglio, P. P. (2018). Smart cities with big data: Reference models, challenges, and considerations. *Cities (London, England), 82,* 86–99. doi:10.1016/j.cities.2018.04.011

Lin, A., & Chen, N. C. (2012). Cloud computing as an innovation: Percepetion, attitude, and adoption. *International Journal of Information Management, 32*(6), 533–540. doi:10.1016/j.ijinfomgt.2012.04.001

Lin, C., & Lekhawipat, W. (2014). Factors affecting online repurchase intention. *Industrial Management & Data Systems, 114*(4), 597–611. doi:10.1108/IMDS-10-2013-0432

Lind, M. (2018). Digital Data Sharing: The Ignored Opportunity for Making Global Maritime Transport Chains More Efficient | UNCTAD. *UNCTAD Transport and Trade Facilitation Newsletter, 79.*

Lind, M., Michaelides, M., Ward, R., & Watson, R. T. (2020). *Maritime Informatics.* Springer International Publishing. Retrieved from https://books.google.pt/books?id=Ed6PzQEACAAJ

Lind, M., Michaelides, M., Ward, R., & Watson, R. T. (2020). *Maritime Informatics.* Springer International Publishing.

Lindstrom, M. (2016). *Small data: las pequeñas pistas que nos advierten de las grandes tendencias.* Grupo Planeta Spain.

Lindstrom, M. (2019). *Brandwashed: O lado oculto do marketing controlamos o que compramos ou são as empresas que escolhem por nós?* Alta Books.

Linke, M. (2012). Connecting Logistics Networks Globally Via the Un Single Window Concept. *Journal of Globalization Studies, 3*(2), 139–154.

Lin, P., Abney, K., & Bekey, G. (2011). Robot Ethics: Mapping the Issues for a Mechanized World. *Artificial Intelligence, 175*(5-6), 942–949. doi:10.1016/j.artint.2010.11.026

Lin, P., Abney, K., & Bekey, G. A. (Eds.). (2012). *Robot ethics: The ethical and social implications of robotics.* MIT Press.

Lin, Y., Osman, M., & Ashcroft, R. (2017). Nudge: Concept, effectiveness, and ethics. *Basic and Applied Social Psychology, 39*(6), 293–306. doi:10.1080/01973533.2017.1356304

Lippert, S. K., & Govindarajulu, C. (2006). Technological, organizational, and environmental antecedents to web services adoption. *Communications of the IIMA, 6*(1), 14.

Liu, H., Jayawardhena, C., Dibb, S., & Ranaweera, C. (2019). Examining the trade-off between compensation and promptness in eWOM-triggered service recovery: A restorative justice perspective. *Tourism Management, 75,* 381–392. doi:10.1016/j.tourman.2019.05.008

Liu, M., Liu, S., & Yan, W. (2018). Latent fingerprint segmentation based on ridge density and orientation consistency. *Security and Communication Networks, 2018*, 2018. doi:10.1155/2018/4529652

Liuqu, Y., Fan, X., & Fu, P. L. (2015). From Customer Satisfaction to Customer Experience: Online Customer Satisfaction Practice in International E-commerce. In *International Conference on Cross-Cultural Design* (pp. 80-89). Springer. DOI: 10.1007/978-3-319-20934-0_8

Liu, S., Liu, M., & Yang, Z. (2017). Sparse coding-based orientation estimation for latent fingerprints. *Pattern Recognition, 67*, 164–176. doi:10.1016/j.patcog.2017.02.012

Liu, W., & Chang, C. (2007). Variants of Principal Components Analysis. *2007 IEEE International Geoscience and Remote Sensing Symposium*, 1083-1086, 10.1109/IGARSS.2007.4422989

Li, X., Yen, C.-L., & Uysal, M. (2014). Differentiating with brand personality in economy hotel segment. *Journal of Vacation Marketing, 20*(4), 323–333. doi:10.1177/1356766714527965

Lobera, J., Fernández Rodríguez, C. J., & Torres-Albero, C. (2020). Privacy, values and machines: Predicting opposition to artificial intelligence. *Communication Studies, 71*(3), 448–465. doi:10.1080/10510974.2020.1736114

Lockwood, R. (2018). *Introduction The Relational Data Model*. Accessed and reviewed in April 2021, http://www.jakobsens.dk/Nekrologer.htm

Loginovskiy, O. V., Dranko, O. I., & Hollay, A. V. (2018). *Mathematical Models for Decision-Making on Strategic Management of Industrial Enterprise in Conditions of Instability*. In Internationalization of Education in Applied Mathematics and Informatics for HighTech Applications (EMIT 2018), Leipzig, Germany.

London, A. J. (2019). Artificial intelligence and black-box medical decisions: Accuracy versus explainability. *The Hastings Center Report, 49*(1), 15–21. doi:10.1002/hast.973 PMID:30790315

Long, G. (2007). *Transmedia Storytelling. Business, Aesthetics and Production at the Jim Henson Company* (Master Thesis). Massachusetts Institute of Technology.

Longoni, C., Bonezzi, A., & Morewedge, C. K. (2019). Resistance to medical artificial intelligence. *The Journal of Consumer Research, 46*(4), 629–650. doi:10.1093/jcr/ucz013

Longoni, C., & Cian, L. (2020). Artificial intelligence in utilitarian vs. hedonic contexts: The "word-of-machine" effect. *Journal of Marketing*. doi:10.1177/0022242920957347

Lorenzo Romero, C., Alarcón de Amo, M. C., & Gómez Borja, M. A. (2011). Adopción de redes sociales virtuales: Ampliación del modelo de aceptación tecnológica integrando confianza y riesgo percibido. *Cuadernos de Economía y Dirección de la Empresa, 14*, 194–205.

Loureiro, S. M. C., Guerreiro, J., & Tussyadiah, I. (2020). Artificial Intelligence in Business: State of the Art and Future Research Agenda. *Journal of Business Research, 129*, 911–926. doi:10.1016/j.jbusres.2020.11.001

Loureiro, S. M. C., Japutra, A., Molinillo, S., & Bilro, R. G. (2021). Stand by me: Analyzing the tourist–intelligent voice assistant relationship quality. *International Journal of Contemporary Hospitality Management*. Advance online publication. doi:10.1108/IJCHM-09-2020-1032

Lourido Gómez, S., & Otero Neira, M.C. (2016). La dimensión afectiva de la experiencia de marca y el papel de las emociones en el comportamiento del consumidor. 26 *Congreso ACEDE Vigo, ponencia 3592ª*. [libro de actas].

Lun, Y. V., & Quaddus, M. A. (2009). An empirical model of the bulk shipping market. *International Journal of Shipping and Transport Logistics, 1*(1), 37. Advance online publication. doi:10.1504/IJSTL.2009.021975

Luo, X., Tong, S., Fang, Z., & Qu, Z. (2019). Frontiers: Machines vs. humans: The Impact of Artificial Intelligence Chatbot Disclosure on Customer Purchases. *Marketing Science*, *38*(6), 937–947. doi:10.1287/mksc.2019.1192

Lwakatare, L. E., Raj, A., Bosch, J., Olsson, H. H., & Crnkovic, I. (2019). *A taxonomy of software engineering challenges for machine learning systems: An empirical investigation.* Paper presented at the International Conference on Agile Software Development. 10.1007/978-3-030-19034-7_14

Lwakatare, L. E., Raj, A., Crnkovic, I., Bosch, J., & Olsson, H. H. (2020). Large-scale machine learning systems in real-world industrial settings: A review of challenges and solutions. *Information and Software Technology*, *127*, 106368. doi:10.1016/j.infsof.2020.106368

Lyon, D. (2014). Surveillance, snowden, and big data: Capacities, consequences, critique. *Big Data & Society*, *1*(2), 1–13. doi:10.1177/2053951714541861

Maaß, D., Spruit, M., & de Waal, P. (2014). Improving short-term demand forecasting for short-lifecycle consumer products with data mining techniques. *Decision Analysis*, *1*(1), 4. doi:10.1186/2193-8636-1-4

Maaten, L., & Hinton, G. (2008). Visualizing Data using t-SNE. *Journal of Machine Learning Research*, *9*(86), 2579–2605.

Máchová, R., & Lnenicka, M. (2015). Reframing e-government development indices with respect to new trends in ict. *Review of Economic Perspectives*, *15*(4), 383–412. doi:10.1515/revecp-2015-0027

MacInnis, D. J., & Folkes, V. S. (2010). The disciplinary status of consumer behavior: A sociology of science perspective on key controversies. *The Journal of Consumer Research*, *36*(6), 899–914. doi:10.1086/644610

Mackenzie, A. (2019). From API to AI: Platforms and their opacities. *Information Communication and Society*, *22*(13), 1989–2006. doi:10.1080/1369118X.2018.1476569

Maeda, H. (2015). Response option configuration of online administered Likert scales. *International Journal of Social Research Methodology*, *18*(1), 15–26. doi:10.1080/13645579.2014.885159

Magistretti, S., Dell'Era, C., & Petruzzelli, A. M. (2019). How intelligent is Watson? Enabling digital transformation through artificial intelligence. *Business Horizons*, *62*(6), 819–829. doi:10.1016/j.bushor.2019.08.004

Magnani, L., & Bardone, E. (2008). Distributed morality: Externalizing ethical knowledge in technological artifacts. *Foundations of Science*, *13*(1), 99–108. doi:10.100710699-007-9116-5

Maguire, M. (2001). Methods to support human-centred design. *Human-Computer Studies*, *55*, 587–634.

Mahanti, A., & Alhajj, R. (2005). Visual Interface for Online Watching of Frequent Itemset Generation in Apriori and Eclat. In *Proceedings of the Fourth International Conference on Machine Learning and Applications*. IEEE Computer Society. 10.1109/ICMLA.2005.68

Ma, J., Wang, A., Lin, F., Wesarg, S., & Erdt, M. (2019). A novel robust kernel principal component analysis for nonlinear statistical shape modeling from erroneous data. *Computerized Medical Imaging and Graphics*, *77*, 101638. doi:10.1016/j.compmedimag.2019.05.006 PMID:31550670

Makarius, E. E., Mukherjee, D., Fox, J. D., & Fox, A. K. (2020). Rising with the machines: A sociotechnical framework for bringing artificial intelligence into the organization. *Journal of Business Research*, *120*, 262–273. doi:10.1016/j.jbusres.2020.07.045

Makridakis, S., Spiliotis, E., & Assimakopoulos, V. (2018). Statistical and Machine Learning forecasting methods: Concerns and ways forward. *PLoS One*, *13*(3), e0194889. Advance online publication. doi:10.1371/journal.pone.0194889 PMID:29584784

Ma, L., & Sun, B. (2020). Machine learning and AI in marketing–Connecting computing power to human insights. *International Journal of Research in Marketing*, *37*(3), 481–504. doi:10.1016/j.ijresmar.2020.04.005

Malhotra, N. K. (2004). *Marketing Research an Applied Orientation* (Vol. 4). Pearson, Prentice Hall.

Malhotra, N. K., Kim, S. S., & Agarwal, J. (2004). Internet users' information privacy concerns: The construct, the scale, and a causal model. *Information Systems Research*, *15*(4), 336–355. doi:10.1287/isre.1040.0032

Malik, M. E., Naeem, B., & Munawar, M. (2012). Brand image: Past, present and future. *Journal of Basic and Applied Scientific Research*, *2*(12), 13069–13075.

Malle, B. F., Scheutz, M., Arnold, T., Voiklis, J., & Cusimano, C. (2015), Sacrifice one for the good of many? People apply different moral norms to human and robot agents. In *HRI'15: Proceedings of the Tenth Annual ACM/ IEEE International Conference on Human-Robot Interaction.* New York, NY: ACM. 10.1145/2696454.2696458

Malle, B. F. (2016). Integrating Robot Ethics and Machine Morality: The Study and Design of Moral Competence in Robots. *Ethics and Information Technology*, *18*(4), 243–256. doi:10.100710676-015-9367-8

Malone, A., Caceres Cabana, Y. D., & Taya Zegarra, A. (2020). Informal food systems and differential mobility during the COVID-19 pandemic in Arequipa, Perú. *The Town Planning Review*. Advance online publication. doi:10.3828/tpr.2020.61

Manohlia, D. (2015). Review: 'Ex Machina', a Mogul Fashions the Droid of his Dreams. *The New York Times.*

Manovich, L. (2005). *Soft Cinema. The Language of New Media.* M.I.T. Press.

Manyika, J., Lund, S., Chui, M., Bughin, J., Woetzel, J., Batra, P., Ko, R., & Sanghvi, S. (2017). *What the future of work will mean for jobs, skills, and wages.* McKinsey Global Institute Report. https://www.mckinsey.com/featured-insights/future-of-work/jobs-lost-jobs-gained-what-the-future-of-work-will-mean-for-jobs-skills-and-wages

Marbán, O., Segovia, J., Menasalvas, E., & Fernández-Baizán, C. (2009). Toward data mining engineering: A software engineering approach. *Information Systems*, *34*(1), 87–107. doi:10.1016/j.is.2008.04.003

Marcus, G. E., & Fisher, M. M. (1999). *Anthropology as Cultural Critique: An experimental moment in the human sciences.* doi:10.7208/chicago/9780226229539.001.0001

Marcus, G., & Davis, E. (2019). *Rebooting AI: Building artificial intelligence we can trust.* Vintage.

Maridueña, M. R., Leyva, M., & Febles, A. (2016). Modelado y análisis de indicadores de ciencia y tecnología mediante mapas cognitivos difusos. *Ciencias de la Información*, *47*(1), 17–24.

Marketing Directo. (2019). *Las 4 tendencias en marketing digital que definirán el año 2020.* Retrieved December 18, 2020, from https://www.marketingdirecto.com/marketing-general/tendencias/las-4-tendencias-en-marketing-digital-que-definiran-el-ano-2020

Marr, B. (2017). The Complete Beginners' Guide to Artificial Intelligence. *Forbes.*

Martelo, R. J., Jimenez-Pitre, I., & Moncaris Gonzalez, L. (2017). Guía Metodológica para el Mejoramiento del Desarrollo de Software a través de la Aplicación de la Técnica Árboles de Problemas. *Información Tecnológica*, *28*(3), 87–94. doi:10.4067/S0718-07642017000300010

Martimo, P. (2017). *Disruptive Innovation and Maritime Sector - Discovering smart-shipping's potential to disrupt shipping.* Report Turku School of Economics.

Martín Lineros, E. (2020). *Webinar Alumni: La revolución del 5G.* Retrieved December 18, 2020, from https://www.youtube.com/watch?v=en8SzXmYmZU&feature=youtu.be

Martinez Coral, P. (2017). "Seguro mató a confianza": Challenges for the adoption of digital government in Colombia. *Academic Journals: Inclusion and Development, 5*(1), 63–72. doi:10.26620/uniminuto.inclusion.5.1.2018.63-72

Martinez Dominguez, M. (2018). Access to and use of information and communication technologies in Mexico: determinants. *PAAKAT: Journal of Technology and Society, 8*(14). Retrieved from . doi:10.32870/Pk.a8n14.316

Martínez Pérez, S., Fernández Robles, B., & Barroso Osuna, J. (2021). Augmented reality as a resource for training in higher education [La realidad aumentada como recurso para la formación en la educación superior]. *Campus Virtuales, 10*(1), 9–19.

Martínez Sánchez, F. (2008). La emoción. In Motivación & emoción. Mc Graw Hill.

Martínez-López, F. J., García-Ordaz, M., Arteaga-Sánchez, R., & Infante-Moro, A. (2015). The presence of large Spanish companies in online social networks. *Journal of Marketing Analytics, 3*(4), 171–186. doi:10.1057/jma.2015.15

Martinho-Truswell, E. (2018), 3 Questions About AI That Nontechnical Employees Should Be Able to Answer. *Harvard Business Review*. https://hbr.org/2018/08/3-questionsabout-ai-that-nontechnicalemployees-should-be-able-to-answer

Mascarenhas, O. A., Kesavan, R., & Bernacchi, M. (2006). Lasting customer loyalty: A total customer experience approach. *Journal of Consumer Marketing*.

Masicampo, E. J., & Baumeister, R. F. (2011). Consider it done! Plan making can eliminate the cognitive effects of unfulfilled goals. *Revista de personalidad y psicología social, 101*(4), 667-683. doi:10.1037/a0024192

Mateas, M. (2003). *Expressive AI Games and AI, In proceedings of Level UP*. Digital Games Research Conference, Utrecht.

Mateas, M., & Murray, J. (2004). A preliminary poetics for interactive drama & games, & from game story to cyberdrama. In N. Wardrip-Fruin & P. Harrigan (Eds.), *First Person: New Media as Story, Performance & Game* (pp. 2–33). The MIT Press.

Mathews, B. P., & Shepherd, J. L. (2002). Dimensionality of Cook and Wall's (1980) British Organizational Commitment Scale revisited. *Journal of Occupational and Organizational Psychology, 75*(3), 369–375. doi:10.1348/096317902320369767

Matthew, C. T., & Sternberg, R. J. (2009). *Developing experience-based (tacit) knowledge through reflection. In Learning and Individual Differences*. Elsevier Science., doi:10.1016/j.lindif.2009.07.001

Matwin, S. (2013). Privacy-preserving data mining techniques: survey and challenges. In *Discrimination and Privacy in the Information Society* (pp. 209–221). Springer. doi:10.1007/978-3-642-30487-3_11

Maughan, L., Gutnikov, S., & Stevens, R. (2007). Like more, look more. Look more, like more: The evidence from eye tracking. *Journal of Brand Management, 14*(4), 335–342. doi:10.1057/palgrave.bm.2550074

Mavragani, A., & Tsagarakis, K. P. (2019). Predicting referendum results in the Big Data Era. *Journal of Big Data, 6*(1), 1–20. doi:10.118640537-018-0166-z

Mazuryk, T., & Gervautz, M. (1999). *History, Applications, Technology and Future*. Institute of Computer Graphics, Vienna University of Technology.

McAfee, A., Brynjolfsson, E., Davenport, T. H., Patil, D. J., & Barton, D. (2012). Big data: The management revolution. *Harvard Business Review, 90*(10), 60–68. PMID:23074865

McAteer, M. (2020). *Nitpicking machine learning technical debt*. Retrieved from https://matthewmcateer.me/blog/machine-learning-technical-debt/

McCarthy, J., Minsky, M. L., Rochester, N., & Shannon, C. E. (1955), A proposal for the Dartmouth summer research project on artificial intelligence, http://www-formal.stanford.edu/jmc/history/dartmouth/dartmouth.html

McCarthy, J. (1960). Recursive Functions of Symbolic Expressions and their Computation by Machine, part I. *Communications of the ACM, 3*(4), 184–195. doi:10.1145/367177.367199

McCarthy, J. (1990). *What is AI? Basic Questions; Artificial Intelligence, Logic and Formalizing Common Sense.* Computer Science Department, Stanford University.

McCauley, L. (2007). *Countering the Frankenstein Complex.* American Association for Artificial Intelligence. https://www.openculture.com/2019/03/isaac-asimov-predicts-the-future-of-civilization.html

McCauley, L. (2007). *The Frankenstein Complex and Asimov's Three Laws.* Association of the Advancement of Artificial Intelligence.

McKinsey. (2020). *From surviving to thriving: Business after coronavirus.* Author.

McQuillan, D. (2018). People's councils for ethical machine learning. *Social Media + Society, 4*(2), 2056305118768303. doi:10.1177/2056305118768303

Medallia & DEC. (2020*). ¿Pueden ser emocionales las empresas financieras?* Retrieved December 18, 2020, from https://go.medallia.com/es-dec-webinar.html

Mediamarketing. (2017). *Le chemin passe par le neuromarketing* [The path goes through neuromarketing]. Accessed from: https://www.mediamarketing.ma/article/GHBGBGH/le_chemin_passe_par_le_neuromarketing.html

Mehari, Y. (2020). *The Role of Social Trust in Citizen Mobility During COVID-19.* https://ssrn.com/abstract=3607668[REMOVED HYPERLINK FIELD] doi:10.2139srn.3607668

Mehra, A., Grundy, J., & Hosking, J. (2005). A generic approach to supporting diagram differencing and merging for collaborative design. In *ASE '05 Proceedings of the 20th IEEE/ACM international Conference on Automated software engineering.* ACM. 10.1145/1101908.1101940

Mehrara, M., Rezaei, S., & Razi, H. D. (2015). Determinants of renewable energy consumption among ECO countries; based on Bayesian model averaging and weighted-average least square. *Int Lett Soc Hum Sci, 54,* 96–109. doi:10.18052/www.scipress.com/ILSHS.54.96

Mehrtens, J., Cragg, P. B., & Mills, A. M. (2001). A model of Internet adoption by SMEs.[. *Information & Management, 39*(3), 165–176. doi:10.1016/S0378-7206(01)00086-6

Mejia, J., Mankad, S., & Gopal, A. (2020). Service Quality Using Text Mining: Measurement and Consequences. *Manufacturing & Service Operations Management,* 1–19. doi:10.1287/msom.2020.0883

Meltzer, T. (2014, June 15). Robot doctors, online lawyers and automated architects: The future of the professions. *The Guardian.* https://www.theguardian.com/technology/2014/jun/15/robot-doctors-

Mendes Constante, J., Langen, P., Vieira, G., Lunkes, R., & van der Lugt, L. (2018). The impact of management practices use on Brazilian Port Authorities' Performance. *Rivista Internazionale di Economia dei Trasporti, 45.* Advance online publication. doi:10.19272/201806702005

Méndez Aparicio, M. D. (2019). *Determinantes y consecuencias de la Experiencia de Cliente y la Satisfacción en el ámbito digital: un análisis del uso de áreas privadas©* (Doctoral thesis). Universidad de Burgos, Burgos.

Méndez-Aparicio, M.D., Jiménez-Zarco, A.I., Izquierdo-Yusta, A., & Martinez-Ruiz. (2020). The psychological logic of customer loyalty: towards an integrated conceptual framework (satisfaction, trust and commitment). *Publicación en curso.*

Méndez-Aparicio, M. D., Jiménez-Zarco, A., Izquierdo-Yusta, A., & Blazquez-Resino, J. J. (2020). Customer Experience and Satisfaction in Private Insurance Customer Web Areas. *Frontiers in Psychology*, *11*, 2591.

Mengesha, N., Ayanso, A., & Demissie, D. (2020). Profiles and Evolution of E-Government Readiness in Africa: A Segmentation Analysis. *International Journal of Information Systems and Social Change*, *11*(1), 43–65. doi:10.4018/IJISSC.2020010104

Menon, R. R., Sukhadiya, H., & Patel, J. (2015). Standalone USB Flash to USB Flash. *Data Transfer*, ●●●, 6936–6941.

Menz, F. C., & Vachon, S. (2006). The effectiveness of different policy regimes for promoting wind power: Experiences from the states. *Energy Policy*, *34*(14), 1786–1796. doi:10.1016/j.enpol.2004.12.018

Menzies, T. (2019). The five laws of SE for AI. *IEEE Software*, *37*(1), 81–85. doi:10.1109/MS.2019.2954841

Merisavo, M., Kajalo, S., Karjaluoto, H., Virtanen, V., Salmenkivi, S., Raulas, M., & Leppäniemi, M. (2007). An empirical study of the drivers of consumer acceptance of mobile advertising. *Journal of Interactive Advertising*, *7*(2), 1–19. doi:10.1080/15252019.2007.10722130

Merritt, S. M. (2012). The two-factor solution to Allen and Meyer's (1990) Affective Commitment Scale: Effects of negatively worded items. *Journal of Business and Psychology*, *27*(4), 421–436. doi:10.100710869-011-9252-3

Merson, P. (2009). *Data Model as an Architectural View. Technical Note. CMU/SEI-2009-TN-024*. Research, Technology, and System Solutions.

Microsoft. (2020a). *What are Azure Machine Learning pipelines?* Retrieved from https://docs.microsoft.com/en-us/azure/machine-learning/concept-ml-pipelines

Microsoft. (2020b). *What is the Team Data Science Process?* Retrieved from https://docs.microsoft.com/en-us/azure/machine-learning/team-data-science-process/overview

Mikalef, P., Boura, M., Lekakos, G., & Krogstie, J. (2019). Big data analytics and firm performance: Findings from a mixed-method approach. *Journal of Business Research*, *98*, 261–276. doi:10.1016/j.jbusres.2019.01.044

Mileski, J., Clott, C., Galvao, C. B., & Laverne, T. (2020). Technical analysis: the psychology of the market of dry bulk freight rates. *Journal of Shipping & Trade*, *5*(1). doi:10.118641072-020-00079-7

Miller, K. (2020). A Matter of Perspective: Discrimination, Bias, and Inequality in AI. In M. Jackson & M. Shelly (Eds.), Legal Regulations, Implications, and Issues Surrounding Digital Data (pp. 182-202). IGI Global.

Miller, G. (2018). *Why Altered Carbon is not about the future-nor is any other science fiction*. The Conversation.

Millington, I. (2006). Artificial Intelligence for Games. Elsevier, Morgan Kaufmann Publishers.

Ministério da Infraestrutura. (2018). Porto sem Papel - PSP — Português (Brasil). Author.

Ministério da Infraestrutura. (2020). Sistema Portuário Nacional — Português (Brasil). *Governo Do Brasil*. Retrieved from https://www.gov.br/infraestrutura/pt-br/assuntos/transporte-aquaviario/sistema-portuario

Mintz, Y., & Brodie, R. (2019). Introduction to artificial intelligence in medicine. *Minimally Invasive Therapy & Allied Technologies*, *28*(2), 73–81. doi:10.1080/13645706.2019.1575882 PMID:30810430

Miranda, J., Lopez, C. S., Navarro, S., Bustamante, M. R., Molina, J. M., & Molina, A. (2019). Open Innovation Laboratories as Enabling Resources to Reach the Vision of Education 4.0. *2019 IEEE International Conference on Engineering, Technology, and Innovation (ICE/ITMC), Engineering, Technology and Innovation (ICE/ITMC), 2019 IEEE International Conference On*. 10.1109/ICE.2019.8792595

Mircioiu, C., & Atkinson, J. (2017). A comparison of parametric and non-parametric methods applied to a Likert scale. *Pharmacy (Basel, Switzerland)*, *5*(2), 26. doi:10.3390/pharmacy5020026 PMID:28970438

Missura, O., & Gartner, T. (2009). *Player modelling for Intelligent Difficulty Adjustment*. Discovery Science, 12th International Conference.

Mitchell, M., Wu, S., Zaldivar, A., Barnes, P., Vasserman, L., Hutchinson, B., Spitzer, E., Raji, I. D., & Gebru, T. (2019). *Model cards for model reporting*. Paper presented at the Conference on Fairness, Accountability, and Transparency. 10.1145/3287560.3287596

Modelling, T. O. G. A. F. (2015a). *Data dissemination view*. TOGAF Modelling. Accessed and reviewed in April 2021, http://www.TOGAF-modelling.org/models/data-architecture-menu/data-dissemination-diagrams-menu.html

Modelling, T. O. G. A. F. (2015c). *Data lifecyle diagram*. TOGAF Modelling. Accessed and reviewed in April 2021, http://www.TOGAF-modelling.org/models/data-architecture-menu/data-lifecycle-diagrams-menu.html

Modelling, T. O. G. A. F. (2015d). *Data migration diagram*. TOGAF Modelling. Accessed and reviewed in April 2021, http://www.TOGAF-modelling.org/models/data-architecture-menu/data-migration-diagrams-menu.html

Modelling, T. O. G. A. F. (2015e). *Data security diagram*. TOGAF Modelling. Accessed and reviewed in April 2021,http://www.TOGAF-modelling.org/models/data-architecture-menu/19-data-security-diagrams.html

Moeuf, A., Lamouri, S., Pellerin, R., Tamayo-Giraldo, S., Tobon-Valencia, E., & Eburdy, R. (2020). Identification of critical success factors, risks and opportunities of Industry 4.0 in SMEs. *International Journal of Production Research*, *58*(5), 1384–1400. doi:10.1080/00207543.2019.1636323

Moher, D., Liberati, A., & Tetzlaff, J. (2015). Principais itens para relatar revisões sistemáticas e meta-análises: A recomendação PRISMA. *Epidemiologia e Serviços de Saúde: Revista do Sistema Unico de Saúde do Brasil*, *24*(2), 335–342. doi:10.5123/S1679-49742015000200017

Molnar, C. (2020). *Interpretable machine learning*. Lulu.Com.

Moon, H., & Sprott, D. E. (2016). Ingredient branding for a luxury brand: The role of brand and product fit. *Journal of Business Research*, *69*(12), 5768–5774. doi:10.1016/j.jbusres.2016.04.173

Moon, K. S., & Kim, H. (2019). Performance of deep learning in prediction of stock market volatility. *Economic Computation and Economic Cybernetics Studies and Research*, *53*(2/2019), 77–92. doi:10.24818/18423264/53.2.19.05

Moore, J. (2014). *Java programming with lambda expressions-A mathematical example demonstrates the power of lambdas in Java 8*. Javaworld. Accessed and reviewed in April 2021, https://www.javaworld.com/article/2092260/java-se/java-programming-with-lambda-expressions.html

Mora-Fernandez, J. I. (2019a). Extended analysis of the transmedia narrative universe of Nolan's Dark Knight: integrating original authorships, media convergences & interactive linear narratives. In Reflections in Social Sciences and other Topics. Guayaquil: CIDE.

Mora-Fernandez, J. I. (2019b). Concepts and Models of Analysis of Interactive and Transmedia Narratives: A Batman's Universe Case Study. In *Information Technology and Systems ICITS 2019, AISC 918* (pp. 929–943). Springer. doi:10.1007/978-3-030-11890-7_87

Mora-Fernandez, J. I. (2020). IMotions' Automatic Facial Recognition & Text-Based Content Analysis of Basic Emotions & Empathy in the Application of the Interactive Neurocommunicative Technique LNCBT (Line & Numbered Concordant Basic Text). In Digital Human Modeling and Applications in Health, Safety, Ergonomics and Risk Management. Human Communication, Organization and Work. Springer. https://doi.org/10.1007/978-3-030-49907-5_5.

Mora-Fernández, J.I. (2009). *La interfaz hipermedia: el paradigma de la comunicación interactiva. Modelos para implementar la inmersión juvenil en multimedia interactivos culturales. (Videojuegos, cine, realidad aumentada, museos y web).* SGAE. Fundación Autor. Ediciones Autor.

Mora-Fernandez, J. I. (2013). Artecnología en cine interactivo al unas categorías, interfaces, estructuras narrativas, emociones e investigaciones. In *ArTecnologia. Arte, Tecnologia e linguagens Midiáticas.* Buqui.

Morales Salas, R. E., Infante-Moro, J. C., & Gallardo-Pérez, J. (2019). Mediation and interaction in a VLE for effective management in virtual learning [La mediación e interacción en un AVA para la gestión eficaz en el aprendizaje virtual]. *Campus Virtuales, 8*(1), 49–61.

Morales Salas, R. E., Infante-Moro, J. C., & Gallardo-Pérez, J. (2020). Evaluation of virtual learning environments: A management to improve. *IJERI: International Journal of Educational Research and Innovation,* (13), 126–142.

Morales Salas, R. E., & Rodríguez Pavón, P. R. (2020). Digital ICT skills applied in organizations [Las competencias digitales en TIC aplicadas en las organizaciones]. *International Journal of Information Systems and Software Engineering for Big Companies, 7*(1), 25–35.

Moreno Sánchez, I. (2002). *Musas y Nuevas Tecnologías: El relato hipermedia.* Paidós Comunicación.

Morgan, B. (2018). How Amazon has reorganized around artificial intelligence and machine learning. *Forbes.* https://www.forbes.com/sites/blakemorgan/2018/07/16/how-amazon-has-re-organized-around-artificial-intelligence-and-machine-learning/?sh=40ca07877361

Morgan, R. M., & Hunt, S. D. (1994). The commitment-trust theory of relationship marketing. *Journal of Marketing, 58*(Julio), 20–38.

Morris, P. L., Hopwood, M., Whelan, G., Gardiner, J., & Drummond, E. (2001). Naltrexone for alcohol dependence: A randomized controlled trial. *Addiction (Abingdon, England), 11*(15), 65–73. doi:10.1046/j.1360-0443.2001.961115654.x PMID:11784454

Mostert, P., Petzer, D., & De Meyer, C. (2012). A theoretical and empirical investigation into service failure and service recovery in the restaurant Industry. In Service Science Research, Strategy and Innovation: Dynamic Knowledge Management Methods (pp. 86-99). IGI Global. doi:10.4018/978-1-4666-0077-5.ch005

Motion, J., Leitch, S., & Brodie, R. J. (2003). Equity in corporate co-branding: The case of Adidas and the All Blacks. *European Journal of Marketing, 37*(7/8), 1080–1094. doi:10.1108/03090560310477672

Mouratiadou, I., & Moran, D. (2007). Mapping public participation in the Water Framework Directive: A case study of the Pinios River Basin, Greece. *Ecological Economics, 62*(1), 66–76. doi:10.1016/j.ecolecon.2007.01.009

Mukhopadhyay, P., & Chaudhuri, B. B. (2015). A survey of Hough Transform. *Pattern Recognition, 48*(3), 993–1010. doi:10.1016/j.patcog.2014.08.027

Mullainathan, S., & Shafir, E. (2016). *Scarcity: Why does having little mean so much?* Fondo de Cultura Económica.

Müller, V. C., & Bostrom, N. (2016). Future Progress in Artificial Intelligence: A Survey of Expert Opinion. In Fundamental Issues of Artificial Intelligence (555-572). Springer. doi:10.1007/978-3-319-26485-1_33

Munin. (2016). http://www.unmanned-ship.org/munin/

Murphy, R. R., & Woods, D. D. (2009). *Beyond Asimov: The Three Laws of Responsible Robotics, Institute for Human and Machine Cognition.* IEEE Computer Society.

Murphy, S. T., & Zajonc, R. B. (1993). Affect, cognition, and awareness: Affective priming with optimal and suboptimal stimulus exposures. *Journal of Personality and Social Psychology*, *64*(5), 723–739. doi:10.1037/0022-3514.64.5.723 PMID:8505704

Murray, P. N. (2013). *Inside the Consumer Mind How Emotions Influence What We Buy The emotional core of consumer decision making*. Retrieved from https://www.psychologytoday.com/blog/inside-the-consumermind/201302/how-emotions-influence-what-we-buy

Murray, J. (1997). *Hamlet On the Holodeck: the Future of Narrative in Cyberspace*. Free Press.

Murray, J. (2012). *Inventing The Medium. Principles of Interaction, Design as a Cultural Practice*. The MIT Press.

Murray, J. (2013). Likert data: What to use, parametric or non-parametric? *International Journal of Business and Social Science*, *4*(11).

Mustak, M., Jaakkola, E., Halinen, A., & Kaartemo, V. (2016). Customer participation management. *Journal of Service Management*, *27*(3), 250–275. doi:10.1108/JOSM-01-2015-0014

Nack, F., & Gordon, A. S. (2016). Interactive Storytelling. ICIDS 2016, LNCS 10045, 61–72. DOI: 6 doi:10.1007/978-3-319-48279-8

Nantes, A., Brown, R., & Maire, F. (2008). A Framework for Semi- Automatic Testing of Video Games. In *Proceedings of the Fourth Artificial Intelligence and Interactive Digital Entertainment Conference*. Association for the Advancement of Artificial Intelligence.

Nave, G., Nadler, A., Dubois, D., Zava, D., Camerer, C., & Plassmann, H. (2018). Single-dose testosterone administration increases men's preference for status goods. *Nature Communications*, *9*(1), 24–33. doi:10.103841467-018-04923-0 PMID:29970895

Nayar, R. (2015). Role of Web 3.0 in Service Innovation. In *The Handbook of Service Innovation* (pp. 253–280). Springer. doi:10.1007/978-1-4471-6590-3_13

Ndou, V., Secundo, G., Dumay, J., & Gjevori, E. (2018). Understanding intellectual capital disclosure in online media big data: An exploratory case study in a university. *Meditari Accountancy Research*, *26*(3), 499–530. doi:10.1108/MEDAR-03-2018-0302

Netzer, O., Feldman, R., Goldenberg, J., & Fresko, M. (2012). Mine Your Own Business: Market-Structure Surveillance through Text Mining. *Marketing Science*, *31*(3), 521–543. doi:10.1287/mksc.1120.0713

Neves, A. R., Costa, J., & Reis, J. (2021). Using a Systematic Literature Review to Build a Framework for University-Industry Linkages using Open Innovation. *Procedia Computer Science*, *181*, 23–33. doi:10.1016/j.procs.2021.01.095

Nguyen, A., & Catalan, D. (2020). Digital mis/disinformation and public engagement with health and science controversies: Fresh perspectives from Covid-19. *Media and Communication*, *8*(2), 323–328. doi:10.17645/mac.v8i2.3352

Nicholls, M. E., Orr, C. A., Okubo, M., & Loftus, A. (2006). Satisfaction guaranteed: The effect of spatial biases on responses to Likert scales. *Psychological Science*, *17*(12), 1027–1028. doi:10.1111/j.1467-9280.2006.01822.x PMID:17201782

Nielsen. (2019). *3,5 Mil Milhões de Euros na "Selva Promocional" dos Bens de Grande Consumo*. Nielsen. Retrieved from https://www.nielsen.com/pt/pt/insights/article/2019/3-point-5-billion-euros-in-promotional-jungle-of-consumer-goods/

Nielsen. (2020). *COVID-19 will affect low-income consumers in Latin America the most*. Retrieved from https://www.nielsen.com/pe/es/insights/article/2020/covid-19-afectara-mas-a-los-consumidores-de-bajos-ingresos-en-latinoamerica/

Nieto, A. B., Galindo-Villardón, M., Leiva, V., & Vicente-Galindo, M. (2014). A Methodology for Biplots based on bootstrapping with R. *Revista Colombiana de Estadistica*, *37*(2Spe), 367–397. doi:10.15446/rce.v37n2spe.47944

Nijboer, F., Morin, F., Carmien, S., Koene, R., Leon, E., & Hoffman, U. (2009). Affective brain-computer interfaces: Psychophysiological markers of emotion in healthy persons and in persons with amyotrophic lateral sclerosis. In *3rd International Conference on Affective Computing and Intelligent Interaction and Workshops*. IEEE. 10.1109/ACII.2009.5349479

Nilashi, M., Samad, S., Ahmadi, N., Ahani, A., Abumalloh, R. A., Asadi, S., & Yadegaridehkordi, E. (2020). Neuromarketing: A review of research and implications for marketing. *Journal of Soft Computer Decision Support System*, *7*(2), 23–31.

Ning, L. Q., & Liu, J. L. (2008). Application of Stone-Geisser Test in Customer Satisfaction. *Tianjin Daxue Xuebao*, 3.

Nobre, H. (2019). A marca como ferramenta de gestão empresarial. In C. Machado & J. P. Davim (Eds.), *Organização e Políticas Empresariais* (pp. 133–166). Actual Editora.

Nobre, H., & Simões, C. (2019). NewLux brand relationship scale: Capturing the scope of mass-consumed luxury brand relationships. *Journal of Business Research*, *102*, 328–338. doi:10.1016/j.jbusres.2019.01.047

Nofz, M.P., & Vendy, P. (2002). When Computers Say It with Feeling: Communication and Synthetic Emotions in Kubrick's 2001: A Space Odyssey. *Journal of Communication Inquiry*, 25-45.

Nori, H., Jenkins, S., Koch, P., & Caruana, R. (2019). *Interpretml: A unified framework for machine learning interpretability.* arXiv preprint arXiv:1909.09223.

Norman, G. (2010). Likert scales, levels of measurement and the "laws" of statistics. *Advances in Health Sciences Education: Theory and Practice*, *15*(5), 625–632. doi:10.100710459-010-9222-y PMID:20146096

Norstad, I., Fagerholt, K., & Laporte, G. (2011, August). Tramp ship routing and scheduling with speed optimization. *Transportation Research Part C, Emerging Technologies*, *19*(5), 853–865. doi:10.1016/j.trc.2010.05.001

Nosek, B. A., Hawkins, C. B., & Frazier, R. S. (2011). Implicit social cognition: From measures to mechanisms. *Trends in Cognitive Sciences*, *15*(4), 152–159. doi:10.1016/j.tics.2011.01.005 PMID:21376657

Nosratabadi, S., Mosavi, A., Duan, P., Ghamisi, P., Filip, F., Band, S. S., Reuter, U., Gama, J., & Gandomi, A. H. (2020b). Data Science in Economics: Comprehensive Review of Advanced Machine Learning and Deep Learning Methods. *Mathematics*, *8*(10), 1799. doi:10.3390/math8101799

Nosratabadi, S., Mosavi, A., Keivani, R., Ardabili, S., & Aram, F. (2020a). State of the Art Survey of Deep Learning and Machine Learning Models for Smart Cities and Urban Sustainability. In A. Várkonyi-Kóczy (Ed.), *Engineering for Sustainable Future. INTER-ACADEMIA 2019. Lecture Notes in Networks and Systems* (Vol. 101). Springer. doi:10.1007/978-3-030-36841-8_22

Notteboom, T., Lugt, L. van der, Saase, N. van, Sel, S., & Neyens, K. (2020). The Role of Seaports in Green Supply Chain Management: Initiatives, Attitudes, and Perspectives in Rotterdam, Antwerp, North Sea Port, and Zeebrugge. *Sustainability, 12*(4), 1688. doi:10.3390u12041688

Notteboom, T. E., Parola, F., Satta, G., & Pallis, A. A. (2017). The relationship between port choice and terminal involvement of alliance members in container shipping. *Journal of Transport Geography*, *64*, 158–173. doi:10.1016/j.jtrangeo.2017.09.002

Ntwali, A., Kituyi, A., & Kengere, A. O. (2020). Claims Management and Financial Performance of Insurance Companies in Rwanda: A Case of SONARWA General Insurance Company Ltd. *Journal of Financial Risk Management*, *9*(03), 190.

Nueno, J. L., & Quelch, J. A. (1998). The mass marketing of luxury. *Business Horizons, 41*(6), 61–61. doi:10.1016/S0007-6813(98)90023-4

Nunes, O., & Nisi, V. (2017). Interactive Storytelling. *ICIDS 2017, LNCS 10690,* 372–375. doi:10.1007/978-3-319-71027-3_46

Nunnally, J. C. (1978). *Psychometric Theory.* Academic Press.

O'Neil, C. (2016). *Weapons of Math Destruction: How Big Data Increases Inequality and Threatens Democracy.* Penguin Books.

O'Neil, J. M., Newton, R. J., Bone, E. K., Birney, L. B., Green, A. E., Merrick, B., Goodwin-Segal, T., Moore, G., & Fraioli, A. (2020). Using urban harbors for experiential, environmental literacy: Case studies of New York and the Chesapeake Bay. *Regional Studies in Marine Science, 33,* 100886. Advance online publication. doi:10.1016/j.rsma.2019.100886

O'Reilly, L. (2013). *Google patents 'pay-per-gaze' eye-tracking ad technology.* Accessed from: https://www.marketingweek.com/google-patents-pay-per-gaze-eye-tracking-ad-technology/

OASIS. (2009). *OASIS Web Services Reliable Messaging (WS-ReliableMessaging) Version 1.2.* OASIS Standard. Accessed and reviewed in April 2021, http://docs.oasis-open.org/ws-rx/wsrm/200702/wsrm-1.2-spec-os.html

OASIS. (2014). *ISO/IEC and OASIS Collaborate on E-Business Standards-Standards Groups Increase Cross-Participation to Enhance Interoperability.* The OASIS Group. Accessed and reviewed in April 2021, https://www.oasis-open.org/news/pr/isoiec-and-oasis-collaborate-on-e-business-standards

Öberg, C. (2016). What creates a collaboration-level identity? *Journal of Business Research, 69*(9), 3220–3230. doi:10.1016/j.jbusres.2016.02.027

Obschonka, M., & Audretsch, D. B. (2020). Artificial intelligence and big data in entrepreneurship: A new era has begun. *Small Business Economics, 55*(3), 529–539. doi:10.100711187-019-00202-4

OECD. (2005). *E-government for better government.* OECD.

OECD. (2019). *OECD Public Governance Reviews The Innovation System of the Public Service of Brazil An Exploration of its Past, Present and Future Journey.* OECD Publishing.

Ogbum, W. F., & Thomas, D. S. (1922, May 8). The influence of the business cycle on certain social conditions. *Journal of the American Statistical Association, 18*(139), 324–340. doi:10.1080/01621459.1922.10502475

Oh, H., Fiore, A. M., & Jeong, M. (2007). Measuring experience economy concepts: Tourism applications. *Journal of Travel Research, 46*(2), 119–131.

Ohme, R. (2001). The implicit conditioning of consumer attitudes: Logo substitution effect. Implicit Processes in Cognition, 32(1).

Ohme, R., Matukin, M., & Wicher, P. (2020). Merging Explicit Declarations With Implicit Response Time to Better Predict Behavior. In V. Chkoniya, A. O. Madsen, & P. Bukhrashvili (Eds.), *Anthropological Approaches to Understanding Consumption Patterns and Consumer Behavior* (pp. 427–448). IGI Global. doi:10.4018/978-1-7998-3115-0.ch023

Okazaki, S. (2006). What do we know about mobile internet adopters? A cluster analysis. *Information & Management, 43*(2), 127–141. doi:10.1016/j.im.2005.05.001

Oke, A., & Fernandes, F. A. P. (2020). Innovations in Teaching and Learning: Exploring the Perceptions of the Education Sector on the 4th Industrial Revolution (4IR). *Journal of Open Innovation, 6*(2), 31. Advance online publication. doi:10.3390/joitmc6020031

Okonkwo, U. (2009). The luxury brand strategy challenge. *Journal of Brand Management, 16*(5-6), 287–289. doi:10.1057/bm.2008.53

Olajide, V. (2019). *Introduction to Data Management*. Accessed from: https://www.researchgate.net/publication/335062781

Oliva, F. L., & Kotabe, M. (2019). Barriers, practices, methods and knowledge management tools in startups. *Journal of Knowledge Management*.

Oliveira, B., & Casais, B. (2019). The importance of user-generated photos in restaurant selection. *Journal of Hospitality and Tourism Technology, 10*(1), 2–14. doi:10.1108/JHTT-11-2017-0130

Oliver, R. L. (1980). A Cognitive Model of the Antecedents and Consequences of Satisfaction Decisions. *JMR, Journal of Marketing Research, 17*(4), 460–469. Advance online publication. doi:10.1177/002224378001700405

Olson, Bartley, Urbanowicz, & Moore. (2016). Evaluation of a Tree-based Pipeline Optimization Tool for Automating Data Science. In *Proceedings of the Genetic and Evolutionary Computation Conference 2016, GECCO '16* (pp. 485-492). Association for Computing Machinery.

OMNI-SCI. (2021). *Data Science - A Complete Introduction*. OMNI-SCI. Accessed and reviewed in April 2021, https://www.omnisci.com/learn/data-science

Omri, A., Daly, S., & Nguyen, D. K. (2015). A robust analysis of the relationship between renewable energy consumption and its main drivers. *Applied Economics, 47*(28), 2913–2923. doi:10.1080/00036846.2015.1011312

Oosterbaan, R. J. (2019). Software for generalized and composite probability distributions. *International Journal of Mathematical and Computational Methods, 4*, 1–9.

Ordanini, A., & Pasini, P. (2008). Service co-production and value co-creation: The case for a service-oriented architecture (SOA). *European Management Journal, 26*(5), 289–297. doi:10.1016/j.emj.2008.04.005

Orquin, J. L., & Loose, S. M. (2013). Attention and choice: A review on eye movements in decision making. *Acta Psychologica, 144*(1), 190–206. doi:10.1016/j.actpsy.2013.06.003 PMID:23845447

Ortega-Vivanco, M. (2020, March). Effects of Covid-19 on consumer behaviour: The case of Ecuador. *RETOS. Journal of Management Science and Economics, 10*(20). Advance online publication. doi:10.17163/ret.n20.2020.03

Osobajo, O. A., Koliousis, I., & McLaughlin, H. (2021). Making sense of maritime supply chain: A relationship marketing approach. *Journal of Shipping and Trade, 6*(1), 1. doi:10.118641072-020-00081-z

Oullier, O. (2012). Le cerveau et la loi: analyse de l'émergence du neurodroit [The Brain and the Law: Analysis of the Emergence of Neurolaw]. Centre d'Analyse Stratégique.

Oved, D. (2018). *Real-time human pose estimation in the browser with TensorFlow.js*. Retrieved from https://medium.com/tensorflow/real-time-human-pose-estimation-in-the-browser-with-tensorflow-js-7dd0bc881cd5

Overbye, D. (2018). 2001: A Space Odyssey' Is Still the 'Ultimate Trip'. *The New York Times*. https://www.nytimes.com/2018/05/10/science/2001-a-space-odyssey-kubrick.html

Overgoor, G., Chica, M., Rand, W., & Weishampel, A. (2019). Letting the computers take over: Using AI to solve marketing problems. *California Management Review, 61*(4), 156–185. doi:10.1177/0008125619859318

Özesmi, U., & Özesmi, S. L. (2003). A participatory approach to ecosystem conservation: fuzzy cognitive maps and stakeholder group analysis in Uluabat Lake, Turkey. *Environmental Management, 31*(4), 518-531. doi:10.100700267-002-2841-1

Özesmi, U., & Özesmi, S. L. (2004). Ecological models based on people's knowledge: A multistep Fuzzy Cognitive Mapping approach. *Ecological Modelling, 176*(1), 43–64. doi:10.1016/j.ecolmodel.2003.10.027

Ozkaya, I. (2020). What is really different in engineering AI-enabled systems? *IEEE Software, 37*(4), 3–6. doi:10.1109/MS.2020.2993662

Öztürk, L. (2012). Public Investments and Regional Inequality: A Causality Analysis, 1975-2001. *Ege Academic Review, 12*(4), 487–495.

Pacheco-Cortés, A. M., & Infante-Moro, A. (2020). ICT resignification in a virtual learning environment [La resignificación de las TIC en un ambiente virtual de aprendizaje]. *Campus Virtuales, 9*(1), 85–99.

Padhan, H., Padhang, P. C., Tiwari, A. V., Ahmed, R., & Hammoudeh, S. (2020). Renewable energy consumption and robust globalization(s) in OECD countries: Do oil, carbon emissions and economic activity matter? *Energy Strategy Reviews, 32*, 100535. doi:10.1016/j.esr.2020.100535

Pallot, M., & Pawar, K. (2012). A holistic model of user experience for living lab experiential design. In *2012 18th International ICE Conference on Engineering, Technology and Innovation* (pp. 1–15). IEEE. 10.1109/ICE.2012.6297648

Palm, M. (2016). *Technologies of consumer labor: a history of self-service.* Routledge.

Pan, Y., Oksavik, A., & Hildre, H. P. (2020). *Simulator as a Tool for the Future Maritime Education and Research: A Discussion.* Academic Press.

Pandian, A. P. (2019). Artificial intelligence application in smart warehousing environment for automated logistics. *Journal of Artificial Intelligence, 1*(02), 63–72.

Pangrazio, L., & Sefton-Green, J. (2021). Digital Rights, Digital Citizenship and Digital Literacy: What's the Difference? *Journal of New Approaches in Educational Research, 10*(1), 15–27. doi:10.7821/naer.2021.1.616

Pantano, E., & Pizzi, G. (2020). Forecasting artificial intelligence on online customer assistance: Evidence from chatbot patents analysis. *Journal of Retailing and Consumer Services, 55*(102096), 1–9. doi:10.1016/j.jretconser.2020.102096

Paoli, C., Voyant, C., Muselli, M., & Nivet, M. L. (2010). Forecasting of preprocessed daily solar radiation time series using neural networks. *Solar Energy, 84*(12), 2146–2160. doi:10.1016/j.solener.2010.08.011

Papageorgiou, E. I., Markinos, A. T., & Gemtos, T. (2009). Application of fuzzy cognitive maps for cotton yield management in precision farming. *Expert Systems with Applications, 36*(10), 12399–12413. doi:10.1016/j.eswa.2009.04.046

Papageorgiou, E. I., & Salmerón, J. L. (2013). A Review of Fuzzy Cognitive Maps Research During the Last Decade. *IEEE Transactions on Fuzzy Systems, 21*(1), 66–79. doi:10.1109/TFUZZ.2012.2201727

Pappas, N., Caputo, A., Pellegrini, M. M., Marzi, G., & Michopoulou, E. (2021). The complexity of decision-making processes and IoT adoption in accommodation SMEs. *Journal of Business Research, 131*, 573–583. doi:10.1016/j.jbusres.2021.01.010

Parikh, A., Behnke, C., Vorvoreanu, M., Almanza, B., & Nelson, D. (2014). Motives for reading and articulating user-generated restaurant reviews on Yelp. com. *Journal of Hospitality and Tourism Technology, 5*(2), 160–176. doi:10.1108/JHTT-04-2013-0011

Park, C. W., Jaworski, B. J., & MacInnis, D. J. (1986). Strategic brand concept-image management. *Journal of Marketing, 50*(4), 135–145. doi:10.1177/002224298605000401

Parody, C. E. (2011). *A Theory of the Transmedia Franchise Character* (PhD thesis). University of Liverpool.

Parola, F., Satta, G., Notteboom, T., & Persico, L. (2020). Revisiting traffic forecasting by port authorities in the context of port planning and development. *Maritime Economics & Logistics*. Advance online publication. doi:10.105741278-020-00170-7

Partala, T., & Surakka, V. (2003). Pupil size variation as an indication of affective processing. *International Journal of Human-Computer Studies, 59*(1-2), 185–198. doi:10.1016/S1071-5819(03)00017-X

Paschen, J., Kietzmann, J., & Kietzmann, T. C. (2019). Artificial intelligence (AI) and its implications for market knowledge in B2B marketing. *Journal of Business and Industrial Marketing, 34*(7), 1410–1479. doi:10.1108/JBIM-10-2018-0295

Pata, U. K. (2018). The influence of coal and noncarbohydrate energy consumption on CO2 emissions: Revisiting the environmental Kuznets curve hypothesis for Turkey. *Energy, 160*, 1115–1123. doi:10.1016/j.energy.2018.07.095

Patten, D. M. (1991). Exposure, legitimacy, and social disclosure. *Journal of Accounting and Public Policy, 10*(4), 297–308. doi:10.1016/0278-4254(91)90003-3

Peeters, M. M., van Diggelen, J., Van Den Bosch, K., Bronkhorst, A., Neerincx, M. A., Schraagen, J. M., & Raaijmakers, S. (2020). Hybrid collective intelligence in a human–AI society. *AI & Society*, 1–22.

Pelegrín-Borondo, J., Arias-Oliva, M., & Olarte-Pascual, C. (2017). Emotions, price and quality expectations in hotel services. *Journal of Vacation Marketing, 23*(4), 322–338.

Pelgrín Borondo, J. (2013) *Análisis comparativo de la estrategia de los grupos competitivos: e-clientes vs. clientes off-line* (Doctoral thesis). Universitat Rovira I Virgili, Tarragona.

Pell, G. (2005). Use and misuse of Likert scales. *Medical Education, 39*(9), 970–970. doi:10.1111/j.1365-2929.2005.02237.x PMID:16150039

Peng, Z., Shan, W., Guan, F., & Yu, B. (2016). Stable vessel-cargo matching in dry bulk shipping market with price game mechanism. *Transportation Research Part E, Logistics and Transportation Review, 95*, 76–94. doi:10.1016/j.tre.2016.08.007

Perakis, A. N., & Bremer, W. M. (1992). An operational tanker scheduling optimization system: Background, current practice and model formulation. *Maritime Policy & Management, 19*(3), 177–187. doi:10.1080/751248659

Pérez-Escoda, A., Castro-Subizarreta, A., & Fandos-Igado, M. (2016). The digital competence of Generation Z: keys for its curricular introduction in Primary School. *Scientific Journal of Educommunication, 49*, 71-80. Retrieved from https://www.redalyc.org/pdf/158/15847434008.pdf

Pérez-Rave, I. I., & Muñoz-Giraldo, L. (2014, July - September). Espacio literario relevante sobre la evaluación de la calidad del servicio: Países de realización de los estudios, métodos de análisis, índices de fiabilidad, hipótesis y desafíos. *Elsevier, Ingeniería. Investigación y Tecnología, 15*(3). Advance online publication. doi:10.1016/S1405-7743(14)70356-7

Perspectives on Issues in AI Governance. (2019). *Google*. https://ai.google/static/documents/perspectives-on-issues-in-ai-governance.pdf.

Peru Retail. (2018). *Peru: Traditional vs. modern channel*. Lima. Retrieved from https://www.peru-retail.com/peru-canal-tradicional-vs-canal-moderno/

Peru Retail. (2020) *What are the most visited shopping channels by Peruvians before Covid-19?* Retrieved from https://www.peru-retail.com/cuales-son-los-canales-de-compra-mas-visitados-por-los-peruanos-ante-el-covid-19/

Perunovic, Z., & Vidic, J.-P. (2011). Innovation in the Maritime Industry. *Proceedings of the 22nd POMS Annual Conferences*.

Petersen, S. (2007). The ethics of robot servitude. *Journal of Experimental & Theoretical Artificial Intelligence, 19*(1), 43–54. doi:10.1080/09528130601116139

Pfeiffer, J., Pfeiffer, T., Meißner, M., & Weiß, E. (2020). Eye-Tracking-Based Classification of Information Search Behavior Using Machine Learning: Evidence from Experiments in Physical Shops and Virtual Reality Shopping Environments. *Information Systems Research, 3*(3), 675–691. doi:10.1287/isre.2019.0907

Phelps, J. E., D'Souza, G., & Nowak, G. J. (2001). Antecedents and consequences of consumer privacy concerns: An empirical investigation. *Journal of Interactive Marketing, 15*(4), 2–17. doi:10.1002/dir.1019

Phelps, J. E., Nowak, G. J., & Ferrell, E. (2000). Privacy concerns and consumer willingness to provide personal information. *Journal of Public Policy & Marketing, 19*(1), 27–41. doi:10.1509/jppm.19.1.27.16941

Phillip Kottak, C. (2011). Cultural anthropology. McG.

Phillips-Wren, G. (2012). AI tools in decision making support systems: A review. *International Journal of Artificial Intelligence Tools, 21*(2), 1240005. doi:10.1142/S0218213012400052

Piddle, J. (2017). *Augmented Reality. Where We Will Live.* Springer. doi:10.1007/978-3-319-54502-8

Pilkington, M. (2016). Blockchain technology: principles and applications. In *Research handbook on digital transformations.* Edward Elgar Publishing.

Piller, C. (1999). Everyone is a critic in cyberspace. *Los Angeles Times, 3*(12), A1.

Pine, J., & Gilmore, J. (1999). *The Experience Economy.* Harvard Business School Press.

Pinhasi, A. (2020). *Deploying machine learning models to production: Inference service architecture patterns.* Retrieved from https://medium.com/data-for-ai/deploying-machine-learning-models-to-production-inference-service-architecture-patterns-bc8051f70080

Pirili, M. U. (2011). The Role of Public Investments in Regional Development: A Theoretical Review. *Ege Academic Review, 11*(2), 309–324.

Plangger, K., & Watson, R. T. (2015). Balancing customer privacy, secrets, and surveillance: Insights and management. *Business Horizons, 58*(6), 625–633. doi:10.1016/j.bushor.2015.06.006

Plassmann, H., Ramsoy, T. Z., & Milosavljevic, M. (2015). Branding the brain: A critical review and outlook. *Journal of Consumer Psychology, 22*(1), 18–36. doi:10.1016/j.jcps.2011.11.010

Polyakova, A. G., Loginov, M. P., Serebrennikova, A. I., & Thalassinos, E. I. (2019). Design of a socio-economic processes monitoring system based on network analysis and big data. *International Journal of Economics and Business Administration, 7*(1), 130–139. doi:10.35808/ijeba/200

Polzin, F., Migendt, M., Taube, ". F. A., & von Flotow, P. (2015). Public policy influence on renewable energy investments—A panel data study across OECD countries. *Energy Policy, 80,* 98–111. doi:10.1016/j.enpol.2015.01.026

Poole, D. L., & Mackworth, A. K. (2010). *Artificial intelligence: Foundations of computational agents.* Cambridge University Press. doi:10.1017/CBO9780511794797

Pope, R. I. (2003). *Kubrick's Crypt, a Derrida/Deluze Monster, in 2001: A Space Odyssey.* Edinburgh University Press Journals.

Port of Antwerp deploys autonomous drones for safety enforcement. (2021, February). *Dry Cargo International.* Retrieved from https://www.drycargomag.com/port-of-antwerp-deploys-autonomous-drones-for-safety-enforcement

Portugal.EU. (2021). *Program for the Portuguese Presidency of the Council of the European Union.* Author.

Portuguese Government Portal. (2021). *Americas - Regional Affairs - Foreign Policy - Diplomatic Portal. Ministry of Foreign Affairs of Portugal.* Retrieved from https://www.portaldiplomatico.mne.gov.pt/en/foreign-policy/regional-affairs/americas

Porwik, P. (2010). *The Modern Techniques of Latent Fingerprint Imaging.* IEEE. doi:10.1109/CISIM.2010.5643695

Poulis, K., Galanakis, G. C., Triantafillou, G. T., & Poulis, E. (2020). Value migration: Digitalization of shipping as a mechanism of industry dethronement. *Journal of Shipping and Trade, 5*(1), 1–18. doi:10.118641072-020-00064-0

Pradeep, A. K., Appel, A., & Sthanunathan, S. (2019). *AI for Marketing and Product Innovation.* Wiley.

Prahono, A., & Elidjen. (2015). Evaluating the role e-government on public administration reform: Case of official city government websites in indonesia. *Procedia Computer Science, 59*, 27–33. doi:10.1016/j.procs.2015.07.334

Prassas, G., Pramatari, K. C., Papaemmanouil, O., & Doukidis, G. J. (2001). A recommender system for online shopping based on past customer behavior. *Proceedings of the 14th Bled Electronic Commerce Conference e-Everything: e-Commerce, e-Government, e-Household, e-Democracy.*

Prebensen, N., Kim, H., & Uysal, M. (2015). Cocreation as Moderator between the Experience Value and Satisfaction Relationship. *Journal of Travel Research*, 1–12.

Premkumar, G., Ramamurthy, K., & Crum, M. (1997). Determinants of EDI adoption in the transportation industry. *European Journal of Information Systems, 6*(2), 107–121. doi:10.1057/palgrave.ejis.3000260

Premkumar, G., & Roberts, M. (1999). Adoption of new information technologies in rural small businesses. *Omega, 27*(4), 467–484. doi:10.1016/S0305-0483(98)00071-1

Prescott, J., (2016). Why watching Westworld's robots should make us question ourselves. *The Conversation.*

Preston, C. C., & Colman, A. M. (2000). Optimal number of response categories in rating scales: Reliability, validity, discriminating power, and respondent preferences. *Acta Psychologica, 104*(1), 1–15. doi:10.1016/S0001-6918(99)00050-5 PMID:10769936

Proietti, M. (2019). Experimental test of local observer independence. *Science Advances, 5*(9). Advance online publication. doi:10.1126ciadv.aaw9832

Projeto JUL- LSW contributes to the concept of the National Single Window. (2021). Retrieved from https://www.projeto-jul.pt/en/news/lsw-contributes-to-the-concept-of-national-single-window

Provost, F., & Fawcett, T. (2013). *Data Science for Business: What You Need to Know about Data Mining and Data-Analytic Thinking* (1st ed.). O'Reilly Media.

Provost, F., & Fawcett, T. (2013). *Data science for business: What you need to know about data mining and data-analytic thinking.* O'Reilly Media.

Przychodzen, W., & Przychodzen, J. (2020). Determinants of renewable energy production in transitioneconomies: A panel data approach. *Energy, 191*, 116583. doi:10.1016/j.energy.2019.116583

Puente-Bienvenido, H. & Sequeiros, C. (2019a). A Sociological Look at Gaming Software: Erving Goffman's Dramaturgy in Video Games. *Revista Española de Investigaciones Sociológicas, 166*, 135-152. doi:10.5477/cis/reis.166.135

Puente-Bienvenido, H., & Sequeiros Bruna, C. (2019b) Goffman y los videojuegos: Una aproximación sociológica desde la perspectiva dramatúrgica a los dispositivos videolúdicos. *Revista Española de Sociología, 28*(2). https://recyt.fecyt. es/index.php/res/article/view/68948

Puntoni, S., Reczek, R. W., Giesler, M., & Botti, S. (2021). Consumers and artificial intelligence: An experiential perspective. *Journal of Marketing, 85*(1), 131–151. doi:10.1177/0022242920953847

PuroMarketing. (2019). *En 2030 la Experiencia de Cliente dependerá de la Inteligencia Artificial.* Retrieved December 18, 2020, from https://www.puromarketing.com/12/32895/experiencia-cliente-dependera-inteligencia-artificial.html

PWC. (2017a). *La Inteligencia Artificial impulsará el PIB mundial un 14% en 2030 por sus efectos en la productividad y en el consume.* Retrieved December 18, 2020, from https://www.pwc.es/es/sala-prensa/notas-prensa/2017/la-inteligencia-artificial-impulsara-pib-mundial.html

PWC. (2017b). *Sizing the prize. What's the real value of AI for your business and how can you capitalise?* Retrieved December 8, 2020, from https://www.pwc.com/gx/en/issues/data-and-analytics/publications/artificial-intelligence-study.html

PWC. (2018). *Will robots really steal our jobs? An international analysis of the potential long term impact of automation.* PWC. https://www.pwc.com/hu/hu/kiadvanyok/assets/pdf/impact_of_automation_on_jobs.pdf

PWC. (2020). *Experience is everything: Here's how to get it right.* Retrieved December 15, 2020, from https://www. pwc.com/us/en/advisory-services/publications/consumer-intelligence-series/pwc-consumer-intelligence-series-customer-experience.pdf

Qian, P., Li, A., & Liu, M. (2019, June). Latent fingerprint enhancement based on DenseUNet. In *2019 International Conference on Biometrics (ICB)* (pp. 1-6). IEEE.

Qiu, J., Wu, Q., Ding, G., Xu, Y., & Feng, S. (2016). A survey of machine learning for big data processing. *EURASIP Journal on Advances in Signal Processing, 2016*(1), 67. doi:10.118613634-016-0355-x

Qualtrics. (2020). *What is closed-loop customer experience management?* Retrieved December 16, 2020, from https:// www.qualtrics.com/experience-management/customer/closed-loop-cx/

Quéant, P. (2019). IA et puissance aérospatiale, implications pour l'Armée de l'air [AI and Aerospace Power, Implications for the Air Force]. *Revue Défense Nationale, 820*(5), 117–122. doi:10.3917/rdna.820.0117

Radziwon, A., Bilberg, A., Bogers, M., & Madsen, E. S. (2014). The smart factory: Exploring adaptive and flexible manufacturing solutions. *Procedia Engineering, 69*, 1184–1190. doi:10.1016/j.proeng.2014.03.108

Rai, A. (2020). Explainable AI: From black box to glass box. *Journal of the Academy of Marketing Science, 48*(1), 137–141. doi:10.100711747-019-00710-5

Raine, R. (2009). Making A Clever Intelligent Agent: The Theory Behind The Implementation. *IEEE International Conference on Intelligent Computing and Intelligent Systems.* 10.1109/ICICISYS.2009.5358137

Raman, A., & Hoder, C. (2020). *Building intelligent apps with cognitive APIs.* O'Reilly.

Ramírez, M.-S., & García-Peñalvo, F.-J. (2018). Co-Creation and Open Innovation: Systematic Literature Review. *Comunicar: Media Education Research Journal, 26*(54), 9–18. doi:10.3916/C54-2018-01

Ramos, K., Cuamea, O., Morgan, J., & Estrada, A. (2020). Social Networks' Factors Driving Consumer Restaurant Choice: An Exploratory Analysis. In *International Conference on Applied Human Factors and Ergonomics* (pp. 158-164). Springer.

Ranchhod, A. (2007). Developing mobile marketing strategies. *International Journal of Mobile Advertising, 2*(1), 76–83.

Randhawa, K., & Scerri, M. (2015). Service innovation: A review of the literature. In *The handbook of service innovation* (pp. 27–51). Springer. doi:10.1007/978-1-4471-6590-3_2

Real Academia Española, R. A. E. (2019). *Diccionario de la lengua española* (22nd ed.). Retrieved December 17, 2020, from http://www.rae.es

Recio Muñoz, F., Silva Quiroz, J., & Abricot Marchant, N. (2020). Análisis de la Competencia Digital en la Formación Inicial de estudiantes universitarios: Un estudio de meta-análisis en la Web of Science. *Píxel-Bit, Revista De Medios Y Educación*, *59*, 125-146. [] doi:10.12795/pixelbit.77759

Regional Government of Arequipa. (2020). *Regional Executive Resolution N° 192-2020-GRA/GR*. Retrieved from www.regionarequipa.gob.pe: https://www.regionarequipa.gob.pe/Cms_Data/Contents/GobRegionalArequipaInv/Media/Resolucion.Detalle/2020/R.E.R/RER-192-2020.pdf

Reichheld, F. (2014). How the Net Promoter Score (NPS) Can Drive Growth. *JWI 518: Marketing in The Global Environment*, 73-100.

Residency of the Republic of Turkey Strategy and Budget Directorate (SBB). (n.d.). Retrieved from http: http://www.sbb.gov.tr/wp-content/uploads/2019/04/Yat%C4%B1r%C4%B1mlar%C4%B1n-%C4%B0llere-G%C3%B6re-Da%C4%9F%C4%B1l%C4%B1m%C4%B1.xlsx

Revathy, T., Pramila, G., Adhiraja, A., & Askerunisa, A. (2014, April). Automatic Latent Fingerprint Segmentation based on Orientation and Frequency Features. In *2014 International Conference on Communication and Signal Processing* (pp. 1192-1196). IEEE. 10.1109/ICCSP.2014.6950029

Revieve. (n.d.). *AI Skincare Advisor*. https://www.revieve.com/solutions/skincareadvisor

Ribeiro, M. T., Singh, S., & Guestrin, C. (2016). *"Why should I trust you?": Explaining the predictions of any classifier*. Paper presented at the 22nd ACM SIGKDD International Conference on Knowledge Discovery and Data Mining, San Francisco, CA, USA. 10.1145/2939672.2939778

Richardson, K. (2016). Sex robot matters: Slavery, the prostituted, and the rights of machines. *IEEE Technology and Society Magazine*, *35*(2), 46–53. doi:10.1109/MTS.2016.2554421

Richardson, S. (2020). Cognitive automation: A new era of knowledge work? *Business Information Review*, *37*(4), 182–189. doi:10.1177/0266382120974601

Rico, L., & Ohlenschläger, K. (2005). *Banquete 05 – Communication in Evolution*. Museo Conde Duque.

Rikhardsson, P., & Yigitbasioglu, O. (2018). Business intelligence & analytics in management accounting research: Status and future focus. *International Journal of Accounting Information Systems*, *29*, 37–58. doi:10.1016/j.accinf.2018.03.001

Riley, D., Charlton, N., & Wason, H. (2015). The impact of brand image fit on attitude towards a brand alliance. *Management & Marketing*, *10*(4), 270–283. doi:10.1515/mmcks-2015-0018

Rivera-Castro, R., Pilyugina, P., Pletnev, A., Maksimov, I., Wyz, W., & Burnaev, E. (2019). Topological data analysis of time series data for B2B Customer Relationship Management. https://arxiv.org/abs/1906.03956

Rivoir, A., Morales, M. J., & Casamayou, A. (July 18, 2019). Uses and perceptions of digital technologies in older people. Limitations and benefits for their quality of life. *Austral Journal of Social Sciences*, 295-313. doi:10.4206/rev.austral.cienc.soc.2019.n36-15

Robinson, S., Orsingher, C., Alkire, L., De Keyser, A., Giebelhausen, M., Papamichail, K. N., Shams, P., & Temerak, M. S. (2020). Frontline encounters of the AI kind: An evolved service encounter framework. *Journal of Business Research*, *116*, 366–376. doi:10.1016/j.jbusres.2019.08.038

Rodrigue, J.-P. (2010). *Maritime Transportation: Drivers for the Shipping and Port Industries*. Academic Press.

Rodrigues, K. R., Ferreira, C. G., Murta, A. L. S., & Murta, M. P. A. (2017). Sistema Portuário Brasileiro e o Uso da Tecnologia para uma Gestão Eficiente. *HOLOS*, (7), 110–126. doi:10.15628/holos.2017.6080

Rodriguez Rojas, C. I. (2015). *Sostenibilidad en las empresas*. Recuperado 6 de julio de 2020, de Escuela de Organización InduStrial website: https://www.eoi.es/blogs/carollirenerodriguez/2012/05/20/sostenibilidad-en-las-empresas/

Rodríguez-Ardura, I., Maraver-Tarifa, G., Jiménez-Zarco, A. I., Martínez-Argüelles, M. J., & Ammetller, G. (2018). *Principios y estrategias de marketing* (Vol. 2). Edi UOC.

Roediger, H. L. (1990). Implicit memory: Retention without remembering. *The American Psychologist*, *42*, 873. doi:10.1037/h0092053 PMID:2221571

Rogers Everett, M. (1995). *Diffusion of innovations*.

Rogers, E. (2003). Diffusion of innovations. Delran, NJ: Simon & Schuster.

Roggeveen, A. L., Tsiros, M., & Grewal, D. (2012). Understanding the co-creation effect: When does collaborating with customers provide a lift to service recovery? *Journal of the Academy of Marketing Science*, *40*(6), 771–790. doi:10.100711747-011-0274-1

Rohit, Dharamshi, & Subramanyam. (2019). Approaches to Question Answering Using LSTM and Memory Networks: SocProS 2017. In *Soft Computing for Problem Solving*. Doi:10.1007/978-981-13-1592-3 15

Rohit, G. (2019). *Dharamshi, Ekta Subramanyam, Natarajan*. Approaches to Question Answering Using LSTM and Memory.

Rollins, J. (2015). *Why we need a methodology for data science*. Retrieved from https://www.ibmbigdatahub.com/blog/why-we-need-methodology-data-science

Romano, A. (2020, July 5). This hotel has a robot named Rosé that will deliver wine to your room Without human contact. *Travel and Leisure*. https://www.travelandleisure.com/food-drink/wine/rose-robot-room-service-hotel-trio-california

Romero, J., Ruiz-Equihua, D., Loureiro, S. M. C., & Casaló, L. V. (2021). *Smart Speaker Recommendations: Impact of Gender Congruence and Amount of Information on Users' Engagement and Choice*. Frontier in Psychology., doi:10.3389/fpsyg.2021.659994

Ronen, D. (1993, December). Ship scheduling: The last decade. *Ship scheduling: The last decade, 71*(3), 325-333. doi:10.1016/0377-2217(93)90343-L

Ronen, D. (1983, February). Cargo ships routing and scheduling: Survey of models and problems. *European Journal of Operational Research*, *12*(2), 119–126. doi:10.1016/0377-2217(83)90215-1

Roodman, D. (2009). How to do xtabond2: An introduction to difference and system GMM in Stata. *The Stata Journal*, *9*(1), 86–136. doi:10.1177/1536867X0900900106

Rorissa, A., & Demissie, D. (2010). An analysis of african e-government service websites. *Government Information Quarterly*, *27*(2), 161–169. doi:10.1016/j.giq.2009.12.003

Rosenblatt, F. (1957). The perceptron - A perceiving and recognizing automaton. *Issues (Chicago, Ill.), Technical Report*, 85–460–1.

Rossi, F. (2018). Building trust in artificial intelligence. *Journal of International Affairs*, 72(1), 127–134.

Rossiter, J. R., Silberstein, R. B., Harris, P. G., & Nield, G. (2001). So What? A Rejoinder to the Reply by Crites and Aikman-Eckenrode to Rossiter et al. (2001). *Journal of Advertising Research*, 41(3), 59–61. Advance online publication. doi:10.2501/JAR-41-3-59-61

Ross, J. (2018). The fundamental flaw in AI implementation. *MIT Sloan Management Review*, 59(2), 10–11.

Roszkowski, M., & Soven, M. (2010). Shifting gears: Consequences of including two negatively worded items in the middle of a positively worded questionnaire. *Assessment & Evaluation in Higher Education*, 35(1), 117–134. doi:10.1080/02602930802618344

Roth, C., & Koenitz, H. (2016). Evaluating the User Experience of Interactive Digital Narrative. In *Proceedings of the 1st International Workshop on Multimedia Alternate Realities*. Association for Computing Machinery. 10.1145/2983298.2983302

Rouf, M. A. (2011). The Corporate Social Responsibility Disclosure: A Study of Listed Companies in Bangladesh. *Business and Economics Research Journal*, 2(3), 19–32.

Ruiz, J. B., & Bell, R. A. (2021). Predictors of intention to vaccinate against COVID-19: Results of a nationwide survey. *Vaccine*, 39(7), 1080–1086. doi:10.1016/j.vaccine.2021.01.010 PMID:33461833

Rusk, N. (2016). Deep learning. *Nature Methods*, 13(1), 35–35. doi:10.1038/nmeth.3707 PMID:27110626

Russel, S. (2015). Ethics of Artificial Intelligence. *Nature*, 415-418.

Russell, J. A. (2003). Core affect and psychological construction of emotion. *Psychological Review*, 110(1), 145–172.

Russell, J. A., Lewicka, M., & Niit, T. (1989). A Cross-Cultural Study of a Circumflex Model of Affect. *Journal of Personality and Social Psychology*, 57(5), 848–856. doi:10.1037/0022-3514.57.5.848

Russell, S. J. (1997). Rationality and intelligence. *Artificial Intelligence*, 94(1-2), 57–77. doi:10.1016/S0004-3702(97)00026-X

Russell, S. J., & Norvig, P. (2016). *Artificial Intelligence: A Modern Approach* (3rd ed.). Pearson.

Russkikh, P., & Kapulin, D. (2020). Simulation modeling for optimal production planning using Tecnomatix software. *Journal of Physics: Conference Series*, 1661, 012188. doi:10.1088/1742-6596/1661/1/012188

Russo, S. J. (2020). Is de-identification of personal health information in the age of artificial intelligence a reality or a noble myth? *Journal of Health Care Compliance*, (March–April), 55–59.

Rust, R. T. (2020). The future of marketing. *International Journal of Research in Marketing*, 37(1), 15–26. doi:10.1016/j.ijresmar.2019.08.002

Rust, R. T., & Huang, M. H. (2014). The service revolution and the transformation of marketing science. *Marketing Science*, 33(2), 206–221. doi:10.1287/mksc.2013.0836

Ryan, M. L. (2001). *Narrative as Virtual Reality: Immersion and Interactivity in Literature and Electronic Media*. Johns Hopkins University Press.

Sabhanayagam, T., Venkatesan, V. P., & Senthamaraikannan, K. (2018). A comprehensive survey on various biometric systems. *International Journal of Applied Engineering Research: IJAER*, 13(5), 2276–2297.

Sabio & DEC. (2020). *La omnicanalidad es responder a lo que el cliente te está pidiendo*. https://brilliantcx.sabiogroup.com/l/668023/2020-09-30/25ly6

Salas-Rueda, R.-A., & Salas-Silis, J.-A. (2019). WeVideo: ¿Servicio en la nube útil para los estudiantes durante la construcción y presentación de los contenidos audiovisuales? *Vivat Academia, 1*, 67–89. doi:10.15178/va.2019.149.67-89

Salazar, M. S. (2015). The dilemma of combining positive and negative items in scales. *Psicothema, 27*(2), 192–199. PMID:25927700

Salehi-Esfahani, S., Ravichandran, S., Israeli, A., & Bolden, E. III. (2016). Investigating information adoption tendencies based on restaurants' user-generated content utilizing a modified information adoption model. *Journal of Hospitality Marketing & Management, 25*(8), 925–953. doi:10.1080/19368623.2016.1171190

Sallam, M. (2021). COVID-19 vaccine hesitancy worldwide: A concise systematic review of vaccine acceptance rates. *Vaccines, 9*(2), 160. doi:10.3390/vaccines9020160 PMID:33669441

Same, S., & Larimo, J. (2012, May). Marketing theory: Experience marketing and experiential marketing. In *7th International Scientific Conference. Business and Management* (pp. 10-11). Academic Press.

Sangthong, M. (2020). The Effect of the Likert Point Scale and Sample Size on the Efficiency of Parametric and Nonparametric Tests. *Thailand Statistician, 18*(1), 55–64.

Sanmartín, A. y Megías, I. (2020). *Jóvenes, futuro y expectativa tecnológica*. Madrid: Centro Reina Sofía sobre Adolescencia y Juventud, Fad. Doi:10.5281/zenodo.3629108

Sanny, L., Arina, A., Maulidya, R., & Pertiwi, R. (2020). Purchase intention on Indonesia male's skin care by social media marketing effect towards brand image and brand trust. *Management Science Letters, 10*(10), 2139–2146.

Santanen, E. (2019). The value of protecting privacy. *Business Horizons, 62*(1), 5–14. doi:10.1016/j.bushor.2018.04.004

Santolaria, C. J. S., & González, J. P. G. (2013). Las memorias de sostenibilidad y su divulgación. *Contaduría Universidad de Antioquia*, (57), 107-118. Retrieved from https://revistas.udea.edu.co/index.php/cont/article/view/15580/13523

Sarenet (2019). *2022: Más tráfico en Internet que el acumulado en tres décadas*. https://blog.sarenet.es/trafico-web/

Sarkar, D. (2018). *Get Smarter with Data Science — Tackling Real Enterprise Challenges. Take your Data Science Projects from Zero to Production*. Towards Data Science. Accessed and reviewed in April 2021, https://towardsdatascience.com/get-smarter-with-data-science-tackling-real-enterprise-challenges-67ee001f6097

SAS. (2021). *History of Big Data*. SAS. Accessed and reviewed in April 2021, https://www.sas.com/en_us/insights/big-data/what-is-big-data.html

Sasmaz, M. U., Sakar, E., Yayla, Y. E., & Akkucuk, U. (2020). The Relationship between Renewable Energy and Human Development in OECD Countries: A Panel Data Analysis. *Sustainability, 12*(18), 7450. doi:10.3390u12187450

Sato, D., Wider, A., & Windheuser, C. (2019). *Continuous delivery for machine learning: Automating the end-to-end lifecycle of machine learning applications*. Retrieved from https://martinfowler.com/articles/cd4ml.html

Saur-Amaral, I., Ferreira, P., & Conde, R. (2013). Linking past and future research in tourism management through the lens of marketing and consumption: a systematic literature review Investigação passada e futura sobre gestão do turismo, marketing e consumo: uma revisão sistemática da literatura. *Conde / Tourism & Management Studies, 9*(1), 35–40.

Saxena, D., & Lamest, M. (2018). Information overload and coping strategies in the big data context: Evidence from the hospitality sector. *Journal of Information Science, 44*(3), 287–297. doi:10.1177/0165551517693712

Scarsi, R. (2007). The bulk shipping business: Market cycles and shipowners' biases. *Maritime Policy & Management, 34*(6), 577–590. doi:10.1080/03088830701695305

Schaar, P. (2010). Privacy by design. *Identity in the Information Society, 3*(2), 267–274. doi:10.100712394-010-0055-x

Schell, J. (2008). The Art of Game Design: A book of lenses. *Elsevier CRC Press.*

Scherer, K. R. (2005). What are emotions? And how can they be measured? *Social Sciences Information. Information Sur les Sciences Sociales, 44*(4), 695–729.

Schim van der Loeff, W., Godar, J., & Prakasha, V. (2018, December). A spatially explicit data-driven approach to calculating commodity-specific shipping emissions per vessel. *Journal of Cleaner Production, 205*, 895–908. doi:10.1016/j.jclepro.2018.09.053

Schmidt, L., Skvortsova, V., Kullen, C., Weber, B., & Plassmann, H. (2017). How context alters value: The brain's valuation and affective regulation system link price cues to experienced taste pleasantness. *Scientific Reports, 7*(1), 8098. Advance online publication. doi:10.103841598-017-08080-0 PMID:28808246

Schmitt, B. (1999). Experiential marketing. *Journal of Marketing Management, 15*(1-3), 53–67.

Schriesheim, C. A., & Hill, K. D. (1981). Controlling acquiescence response bias by item reversals: The effect on questionnaire validity. *Educational and Psychological Measurement, 41*(4), 1101–1114. doi:10.1177/001316448104100420

Schuller, D., & Schuller, B. W. (2018). The age of artificial emotional intelligence. *Computer, 51*(9), 38–46. doi:10.1109/MC.2018.3620963

Schuurman, D., De Marez, L., & Ballon, P. (2015). Living Labs: a systematic literature review. Open Living Lab Days 2015.

Schwab, K. (2017). *The fourth industrial revolution.* Currency.

Schwartz, L. (2019). *How to Use Case Studies in Your Classroom to Make Learning Relevant.* Edutopia.

Schweitzer, F., Belk, R., Jordan, W., & Ortner, M. (2019). Servant, friend or master? The relationships users build with voice-controlled smart devices. *Journal of Marketing Management, 35*(7-8), 693–715. doi:10.1080/0267257X.2019.1596970

Sci-Kit Learn. (2020). *API Reference.* https://scikit-learn.org/stable/modules/classes.html#module-sklearn.preprocessing

Sculley, D., Holt, G., Golovin, D., Davydov, E., Phillips, T., Ebner, D., Chaudhary, V., & Young, M. (2014). *Machine learning: The high interest credit card of technical debt.* Paper presented at the SE4ML Workshop (NIPS 2014).

Semrl, J., & Matei, A. (2017). Churn prediction model for effective gym customer retention. *Proceedings of 4th International Conference on Behavioral, Economic, and Socio-Cultural Computing, BESC 2017,* 1–3. 10.1109/BESC.2017.8256385

Sequeiros, C., & Puente-Bienvenido, H. (2018). Sociología y ci-fi: repensando los procesos de cambio social desde la ciencia ficción. *Nudos. Sociología, Teoría y didáctica de la literatura, 2,* 4-16. doi:10.24197/nrtstdl.1.2018.4-16

Sequeiros, C., & Puente-Bienvenido, H. (2019). Cambio social, tecnología y ciencia-ficción. *Sociología y Tecnociencia, 9*(2), 115–138.

Serban, A., van der Blom, K., Hoos, H., & Visser, J. (2020). *Adoption and effects of software engineering best practices in machine learning.* Paper presented at the ESEM conference. 10.1145/3382494.3410681

Serrano, C. L., Peña Lapeira, C. J., & Laverde Guzmán, M. Y. (2018). Influence of ICT in the economic development of Colombia. *Revista Ciencias de la Información,* 3-10. Retrieved from http://cinfo.idict.cu/index.php/cinfo/article/view/854

Sestino, A., Prete, M. I., Piper, L., & Guido, G. (2020). Internet of Things and Big Data as enablers for business digitalization strategies. *Technovation*, *98*, 102173. doi:10.1016/j.technovation.2020.102173

Shankar, V., Smith, A. K., & Rangaswamy, A. (2003). Customer satisfaction and loyalty in online and offline environments. *International Journal of Research in Marketing*, *20*(2), 153–175.

Shelley, M. (1818). *Frankenstein or The Modern Prometheus*. Harding, Mavor and Jones.

Shen, B., Choi, T.-M., & Chow, P.-S. (2017). Brand loyalties in designer luxury and fast fashion co-branding alliances. *Journal of Business Research*, *81*, 173–180. doi:10.1016/j.jbusres.2017.06.017

Sheng, J., Amankwah-Amoah, J., & Wang, X. (2017). A multidisciplinary perspective of big data in management research. *International Journal of Production Economics*, *191*, 97–112. doi:10.1016/j.ijpe.2017.06.006

Sherstins, A. (2020). Fundamentals of Recurrent Neural Network (RNN) and Long Short-Term Memory (LSTM) Network. *Physica D: Nonlinear Phenomena, 404*.

Sheth, J. (2020). Impact of Covid-19 on consumer behavior: Will the old habits return or die? *Journal of Business Research 117*, 280-283. doi:10.1016/j.jbusres.2020.05.059

Shiau, W. L., Sarstedt, M., & Hair, J. F. (2019). Internet research using partial least squares structural equation modeling (PLS-SEM). *Internet Research*.

Shimp, T., & Sharma, S. (1987). Consumer ethnocentrism: Construction and validation of the CETSCALE. *JMR, Journal of Marketing Research*, *26*(August), 280–289. doi:10.1177/002224378702400304

Shin, D. (2010). The effects of trust, security & privacy in social networking: A security-based approach to understand the pattern of adoption. *Interacting with Computers*, *22*(5), 428–438. doi:10.1016/j.intcom.2010.05.001

Shipwright design and construction, additional design procedures, design code for unmanned marine systems. (n.d.). *Lloyd's Register*. Retrieved from www.lr.org

Shrestha, Y. R., Krishna, V., & von Krogh, G. (2020). Augmenting organizational decision-making with deep learning algorithms: Principles, promises, and challenges. *Journal of Business Research*, *123*, 588–603. doi:10.1016/j.jbusres.2020.09.068

Siami-Namini, S., Tavakoli, N., & Siami Namin, A. (2019). A Comparison of ARIMA and LSTM in Forecasting Time Series. *Proceedings - 17th IEEE International Conference on Machine Learning and Applications, ICMLA 2018*, 1394–1401. 10.1109/ICMLA.2018.00227

Siegel, S. (1957). Nonparametric statistics. *The American Statistician*, *11*(3), 13–19.

Sierra Diez, B., Froufe Torres, M., & Falces Delgado, C. (2010). El papel de las metas conscientes e inconscientes en la motivación del consumidor. *REME*, *13*(35-36), 193–210.

Siggelkow, N. (2007). Persuasion with case studies. *Academy of Management Journal*, *50*(1), 20–24. doi:10.5465/amj.2007.24160882

Sikander, M., & Khiyal, H. (2018). *Computational Models for Upgrading Traditional Agriculture*. Preston University. Accessed and reviewed in April 2021, https://www.researchgate.net/publication/326080886

Sikdar, S. (2018). Artificial Intelligence, its impact on innovation, and the Google effect. *Clean Technologies and Environmental Policy, 20*, No-1–No-2.

Silverstein, S. (2018). REX real estate: Home showings-AI / Voice / Chatbot. *Behance.* https://www.behance.net/gallery/64004179/REX-Real-Estate-Home-Showings-AI-Voice-Chatbot

Simonin, J., Bertin, E., Traon, Y., Jezequel, J.-M., & Crespi, N. (2010). Business and Information System Alignment: A Formal Solution for Telecom Services. In *2010 Fifth International Conference on Software Engineering Advances.* IEEE. 10.1109/ICSEA.2010.49

Singer, E. (2010). The slow rise of the robot surgeon. *MIT Technology Review.* Retrieved from https://www.technology-review.com/news/418141/the-slow-rise-of-the-robot-surgeon/

Singh, J. P., Kalafatis, S., & Ledden, L. (2014). Consumer perceptions of cobrands: The role of brand positioning strategies. *Marketing Intelligence & Planning, 32*(2), 145–159. doi:10.1108/MIP-03-2013-0055

Singler, E. (2015). *Green Nudge: Changer les comportements pour sauver la planète.* Pearson.

Skålén, P., Gummerus, J., Von Koskull, C., & Magnusson, P. R. (2015). Exploring value propositions and service innovation: A service-dominant logic study. *Journal of the Academy of Marketing Science, 43,* 137–158. doi:10.100711747-013-0365-2

Slocombe, W. (2016). What science fiction tells us about our trouble with Artificial Intelligence, *The Conversation.*

Sloman, A. (2006). *Why Asimov's three laws of robotics are unethical.* Retrieved June 9, 2006, URL: https://www.cs.bham.ac.uk/research/projects/cogaff/misc/asimov-three-laws.html

Smarandescu, L., & Shimp, T. A. (2015). Drink Coca-Cola, eat popcorn, and choose powerade: Testing the limits of subliminal persuasion. *Marketing Letters, 26*(4), 715–726. doi:10.100711002-014-9294-1

SmartPort. (2019). Smart ships and the changing maritime ecosystem (T. van Dijk, H. van Dorsser, R. van den Berg, H. Moonen, & R. Negenborn, Eds.). Academic Press.

Smith, J. H., Milberg, S. J., & Burke, J. B. (1996). Information privacy: Measuring individuals' concerns about organizational practices. *Management Information Systems Quarterly, 20*(2), 167–196. doi:10.2307/249477

Snow, J. (2018, July 26). Amazon's face recognition falsely matched 28 members of congress with mugshots. *ACLU.* https:// www.aclu.org/blog/privacy-technology/surveillance-technologies/amazons-face-recognition-falsely-matched-28

Sofi, S. A., Nika, F. A., Shah, M. S., & Zarger, A. S. (2018). Impact of subliminal advertising on consumer buying behaviour: An empirical study on young Indian consumers. *Global Business Review, 19*(6), 1580–1601. doi:10.1177/0972150918791378

Sohn, K., & Kwon, O. (2020). Technology acceptance theories and factors influencing artificial Intelligence-based intelligent products. *Telematics and Informatics, 47,* 101324. Advance online publication. doi:10.1016/j.tele.2019.101324

Solana Gutierrez, J., Rincón Sanz, G., Alonso González, C., & Garcia De Jalon Lastra, D. (2015). Use of Maps of Diffuse Knowledge (FCMs) in the prioritization of river restoration: Application to the Esla River [Utilización de Mapas de Conocimiento Difuso (MCD) en la asignación de prioridades de la restauración fluvial: Aplicación al río Esla]. *Cuadernos de la Sociedad Española de Ciencias Forestales, 41,* 367–380.

Soler, A. S., Ort, M., Steckel, J., & Nieschullze, J. (2016). *An introduction to data management.* Accessed from: https:// www.gfbio.org/documents/10184/22817/Reader_GFBio_BefMate_20160222/1ca43f24-255044b3-a05e-e180c3e544c0

SolomonR. C. (2017). *Emotion.* Retrieved from http://www.britannica.com/topic/emotion

Sommer, L. (2015). Industrial revolution-industry 4.0: Are German manufacturing SMEs the first victims of this revolution? *Journal of Industrial Engineering and Management, 8*(5), 1512–1532. doi:10.3926/jiem.1470

Sommerville, I. (2019). *Artificial intelligence and systems engineering*. Academic Press.

Sommerville, I., & Sawyer, P. (1997). *Requirements engineering: A good practice guide*. John Wiley & Sons, Inc.

Song, I.-Y., & Zhu, Y. (2017). Big Data and Data Science: Opportunities and Challenges of iSchools. *Journal of Data and Information Science, 2*(3), 1–18. doi:10.1515/jdis-2017-0011

Sonnenwald, D. H., Maglaughlin, K. L., & Whitton, M. C. (2001). Using innovation diffusion theory to guide collaboration technology evaluation: work in progress. In *Proceedings Tenth IEEE International Workshop on Enabling Technologies: Infrastructure for Collaborative Enterprises. WET ICE 2001* (pp. 114-119). IEEE. 10.1109/ENABL.2001.953399

Sorrel, C. (2016, November 13). Self-driving Mercedes will be programmed to sacrifice pedestrians to save the driver. *Fast Company*. https://www.fastcompany.com/3064539/self-driving-mercedes-will-be-programmed-to-sacrifice-pedestrians-to-save-the-driver

Sosa Sierra, M. D. C. (2011). Artificial intelligence in business financial management [Inteligencia artificial en la gestión financiera empresarial]. *Revista científica Pensamiento y gestión*, (23), 153-186.

Spence, C. (2019). Neuroscience-inspired design: From academic neuromarketing to commercially relevant research. *Organizational Research Methods, 22*(1), 275–298.

Spiekermann, S. (2015). *Ethical IT innovation: A value-based system design approach*. CRC Press. doi:10.1201/b19060

Srour, F., Oosterhout, M., Baalen, P. J., & Zuidwijk, R. (2008). *Port Community System Implementation: Lessons Learned from International Scan*. Academic Press.

Stahl, B. C. (2021). Organisational responses to the ethical issues of AI. *AI & Society*.

Stein, M. (2020, April). *Unmanned maritime infrastructure inspection-a mixed-method risk management approach from German port facilities*. Academic Press.

Stein, M. (2018, June). Integrating Unmanned Vehicles in Port Security Operations: An Introductory Analysis and First Applicable Frameworks. *Ocean Yearbook Online, 32*(1), 556–583. doi:10.1163/22116001-03201022

Stevens, S. S. (1946). On the theory of scales of measurement. *Science. New Series, 103*(2684), 677–680.

Stoicescu, C. (2016). Big Data, the perfect instrument to study today's consumer behavior. *Database System Journal, 6*, 28–42.

Stoll, M., Baecke, S., & Kenning, P. (2008). What they see is what they get? An fMRI-study on neural correlates of attractive packaging. *Journal of Consumer Behaviour, 7*(4-5), 342–359. Advance online publication. doi:10.1002/cb.256

Stopford, M. (2009). *Maritime Economics*. Routledge.

Strotmann, H. (2007). Entrepreneurial survival. *Small Business Economics, 28*(1), 87–104. doi:10.100711187-005-8859-z

Sukhbaatar, S., & Arthur, S. J. W. R. F. (n.d.). *End-To-End Memory Networks*. Dept. of Computer Science Courant Institute, New York University.

Sullivan, G. M., & Artino, A. R. Jr. (2013). Analyzing and interpreting data from Likert type scales. *Journal of Graduate Medical Education, 5*(4), 541–542. doi:10.4300/JGME-5-4-18 PMID:24454995

Sultana, N., & Nangunoori, R. (2008). Ethical Acceptability of Neuromarketing: Relevance, Limits and Limitations. *Prabandhan: Indian Journal of Management, 1*(1), 31. Advance online publication. doi:10.17010//2008/v1i1/64654

Sumioka, H., Nakae, A., Kanai, R., & Ishiguro, H. (2013). Huggable communication medium decreases cortisol levels. *Scientific Reports, 3*(1), 1–6. doi:10.1038rep03034 PMID:24150186

Su, N., & Reynolds, D. (2017). Effects of brand personality dimensions on consumers' perceived self-image congruity and functional congruity with hotel brands. *International Journal of Hospitality Management, 66*, 1–12. doi:10.1016/j.ijhm.2017.06.006

Sung, C., Zhang, B., Higgins, C. Y., & Choe, Y. (2016). Data-driven sales leads prediction for everything-as-a-service in the cloud. *Proceedings - 3rd IEEE International Conference on Data Science and Advanced Analytics, DSAA 2016*, (May), 557–563. 10.1109/DSAA.2016.83

Sun, S., Wei, Y., Tsui, K., & Wang, S. (2019). Forecasting tourist arrivals with machine learning and internet search index. *Tourism Management, 70*, 1–10. doi:10.1016/j.tourman.2018.07.010

Superintencia de Banca. Seguros y AFP - BID. (2012). *Pilot Survey on Access to and Use of Financial Services 2012.* Retrieved from https://www.sbs.gob.pe/Portals/0/jer/est_incl_finan/Informe%20de%20resultados%20inferenciales_.pdf

Susskind, R., & Susskind, D. (2016, October 11). Technology will replace many doctors, lawyers, and other professionals. *Harvard Business Review.* https://hbr.org/2016/10/robots-willreplace-doctors-lawyers-and-other-professionals

Sutherland, I. E. (1965). *The Ultimate Display. Multimedia: From Wagner to Virtual Reality.* Norton.

Svoboda, J., Monti, F., & Bronstein, M. M. (2017, October). Generative convolutional networks for latent fingerprint reconstruction. In *2017 IEEE International Joint Conference on Biometrics (IJCB)* (pp. 429-436). IEEE. 10.1109/BTAS.2017.8272727

Swaid, S. I., & Wigand, R. T. (2012). The effect of perceived site-to-store service quality on perceived value and loyalty intentions in multichannel retailing. *International Journal of Management, 29*(3), 301.

Szegedy, C., Liu, W., Jia, Y., Sermanet, P., Reed, S., Anguelov, D., Erhan, D., Vanhoucke, V., & Rabinovich, A. (2015). Going deeper with convolutions. *Proceedings of the IEEE Computer Society Conference on Computer Vision and Pattern Recognition*, 1–9. 10.1109/CVPR.2015.7298594

Taddy, M. (2019). *Business Data Science: Combining Machine Learning and Economics to Optimize* (1st ed.). Automate, and Accelerate Business Decisions.

Tamr. (2014). *The Evolution of ETL.* Tamr. http://www.tamr.com/evolution-etl/

Tan, D. (2019). *Coding habits for data scientists.* Retrieved from https://www.thoughtworks.com/insights/blog/coding-habits-data-scientists

Tanev, S., & Sandstrom, G. (2019). Editorial Artificial Intelligence and Innovation Management. *Technology Innovation Management Review, 9*(12), 3–4. doi:10.22215/timreview/1286

Tat, C. H., Lim, K., Lund, S., Deggim, H., Koyama, T., Foo, D., . . . de Souza, C. (2020, October). *Future of shipping: Digitalisation webinar.* Retrieved from https://fos-digitalisation2020.sg/

Taylor, S. J., & Bodgan, R. (1984). *Introducción. Ir hacia la gente. Introducción a los métodos cualitativos de investigación. La búsqueda de significados.* Paidós Ibérica.

Taylor, S. J., & Letham, B. (2018). Forecasting at Scale. *The American Statistician, 72*(1), 37–45. doi:10.1080/00031305.2017.1380080

Tecnohotel. (2018). *Artificial Intelligence, advantages and challenges of automating the hotel industry* [Inteligencia Artificial, ventajas y retos de automatizar la industria hotelera]. https://n9.cl/lyia

Tejedor-Flores, N., Galindo-Villardón, P., & Vicente-Galindo, P. (2017). Sustainability multivariate analysis based on the global reporting initiative (GRI) framework, using as a case study: Brazil compared to Spain and Portugal. *International Journal of Sustainable Development and Planning*, *12*(4), 667–677. doi:10.2495/SDP-V12-N4-667-677

Tejedor, N. (2015). *Análisis Multivariante de la Sosteniblidad en Brasil para los años 2011, 2012 y 2013, a través del Global Reporting Initiative (GRI) (Trabajo fin de máster)*. Universidad de Salamanca.

Telecom Advisory Services, LLC. (2015). *The Digital Ecosystem and Economy in Latin America*. Retrieved from http://www.teleadvs.com/wp-content/uploads/Presentacion_IGF_v3.pdf

Temkin, B. (2019). *The State of Customer ExperienceManagement, 2019. Benchmark of Customer Experience Activities, Competencies, and Maturity Levels*. Retrieved December 18, 2020, from https://www.qualtrics.com/docs/xmi/XMI_StateOfCustomerExperienceManagement-2019.pdf

Terpstra, T. (2011). Emotions, trust, and perceived risk: Affective and cognitive routes to floofd preparedness. *Risk Analysis*, *31*(10), 1658–1675. doi:10.1111/j.1539-6924.2011.01616.x PMID:21477090

Thales. (2018, January 8). KFC Use Facial Recognition for Payment in China. *Thales*. https://www.thalesgroup.com/en/markets/digital-identity-and-security/banking-payment/magazine/kfc-use-facial-recognition-payment-china

Thalheim, B. (2013). *Entity-relationship modeling: Foundations of database technology*. Springer Science & Business Media.

The Economist Intelligence Unit. (2020). *The Internet of Things: Applications for Business. Exploring the transformative potential of IoT*. Author.

The Open Group. (2011). *Open Group Standard-TOGAF® Guide, Version 9.1*. The Open Group.

The Open Group. (2013b). *ArchiMate®*. Accessed and reviewed in April 2021, http://www.opengroup.org/subjectareas/*Entity*/archimate

The Open Group. (2014a). *The Open Group's Architecture Framework-Building blocks-Module 13*. Accessed and reviewed in April 2021, www.open-group.com/TOGAF

The Open Group. (2021). *The Open Group Professional Certification for the Data Scientist Profession (Open CDS)*. The Open Group. Accessed and reviewed in April 2021, https://www.opengroup.org/certifications/certified-data-scientist-open-cds

Thomas & Thomas. (2018). Chatbot Using Gated End-to-End Memory Networks. *International Research Journal of Engineering and Technology, 5*.

Thomas, F., Handdon, L., Gilligan, R., Heinzmann, P., & De Gournay, C. (2005). Cultural Factors Shaping the Experience of ICTs: An Exploratory Review. *ResearchGate*. Obtenido de https://www.researchgate.net/publication/251783055_Cultural_Factors_Shaping_the_Experience_of_ICTs_An_Exploratory_Review

Thomsen, C. W. (1982). Robot Ethics and Robot Parody: Remarks on Isaac Asimov's *I, Robot* and Some Critical Essays and Short Stories by Stanislaw Lem. In T. P. Dunn & R. D. Erlich (Eds.), *The Mechanical God: Machines in Science Fiction* (pp. 19–26). Greenwood.

Thomson, J. J. (1976). Killing, letting die, and the trolley problem. *The Monist*, *59*(2), 204–217. doi:10.5840/monist197659224 PMID:11662247

Tirunillai, S., & Tellis, G. J. (2014). Mining Marketing Meaning from Online Chatter: Strategic Brand Analysis of Big Data Using Latent Dirichlet Allocation. *JMR, Journal of Marketing Research*, *51*(4), 463–479. doi:10.1509/jmr.12.0106

Titz, K., Lanza-Abbott, J. A., & Cruz, G. C. Y. (2004). The anatomy of restaurant reviews: An exploratory study. *International Journal of Hospitality & Tourism Administration*, 5(1), 49–65. doi:10.1300/J149v05n01_03

Tokman, M., Davis, L. M., & Lemon, K. N. (2007). The WOW factor: Creating value through win-back offers to reacquire lost customers. *Journal of Retailing*, 83(1), 47-64. doi:10.1016/j.jretai.2006.10.005

To, M. L., & Ngai, E. W. (2006). Predicting the organisational adoption of B2C e-commerce: An empirical study. *Industrial Management & Data Systems*, 106(8), 1133–1147. doi:10.1108/02635570610710791

Tornatzky, L. G., Fleischer, M., & Chakrabarti, A. K. (1990). *Processes of Technological Innovation*. Lexington books.

Torrent-Sellens, J. (2020). Industria 4.0 y resultados empresariales en España: un primer escaneado. *Oikonomics*. Retrieved December 18, 2020, from http://comein.uoc.edu/divulgacio/oikonomics/es/numero12/dossier/jtorrent.html

Torrent-Sellens, J. (2016). La economía del conocimiento y el conocimiento de la economía. *Oikonomics Revista de Economía. Empresa y Sociedad*, 5, 26–32.

Trad, A., & Kalpić, D. (2020a). *Using Applied Mathematical Models for Business Transformation. Author Book.* IGI-Global. doi:10.4018/978-1-7998-1009-4

Tranfield, D., Denyer, D., & Smart, P. (2003). Towards a methodology for developing evidence-informed management knowledge by means of systematic review. *British Journal of Management*, 14(3), 207–222. doi:10.1111/1467-8551.00375

Trent, G. (2012). *The Rebirth of Mankind Homo Evolutis*. PDXdzyn.

Triantafillidou, A., & Siomkos, G. (2014). Consumption experience outcomes: Satisfaction, nostalgia intensity, word of-mouth communication and behavioural intentions. *Journal of Consumer Marketing*, 31(6/7), 526–540. https://doi.org/10.1108/JCM-05-2014-0982

Trujillo, J., & Luj'an-Mora, S. (2003). *A UML Based Approach for Modelling ETL Processes in Data Warehouses*. Dept. de Lenguajes y Sistemas Inform'aticos. Universidad de Alicante.

Trunk, A., Birkel, H., & Hartmann, E. (2020). On the current state of combining human and artificial intelligence for strategic organizational decision making. *Business Research*, 1-45.

Tucker, C. (2018). Privacy, algorithms, and artificial intelligence. In *The Economics of Artificial Intelligence: An Agenda* (pp. 423–438). University of Chicago Press.

Tu, M. (2018). An exploratory study of Internet of Things (IoT) adoption intention in logistics and supply chain management. *International Journal of Logistics Management*, 29(1), 131–151. doi:10.1108/IJLM-11-2016-0274

Turan, I., Şimşek, Ü., & Aslan, H. (2015). Eğitim araştırmalarında likert ölçeği ve likert tipi soruların kullanımı ve analizi. *Sakarya Üniversitesi Eğitim Fakültesi Dergisi*, (30), 186–203.

Turing, A. M. (1950). Computing machinery and intelligence. *Mind*, 49(236), 433–460. doi:10.1093/mind/LIX.236.433

Turing, A. M. (1950). Computing Machinery and Intelligence. *Mind*, 49, 433–460.

Turkish Renewable Energy Resources Support Mechanism (YEKDEM). (2011). *Official Gazette of the Republic of Turkey*, 28782. Retrieved from http: https://www.mevzuat.gov.tr/mevzuat?MevzuatNo=18907&MevzuatTur=7&MevzuatTertip=5

Turletti, P. (2018). *El ROI de marketing y ventas, Cálculo y utilidad nuevo estandar de rendimiento*. ESIC.

Turner Lee, N. (2018). Detecting racial bias in algorithms and machine learning. *Journal of Information. Communication and Ethics in Society*, 16(3), 252–260. doi:10.1108/JICES-06-2018-0056

Tušar, T., Gantar, K., Koblar, V., Ženko, B., & Filipič, B. (2017). A study of overfitting in optimization of a manufacturing quality control procedure. *Applied Soft Computing, 59*, 77–87. doi:10.1016/j.asoc.2017.05.027

Tussyadiah, I. (2020). A review of research into automation in tourism: Launching the Annals of Tourism Research Curated Collection on Artificial Intelligence and Robotics in Tourism. *Annals of Tourism Research, 81*, 102883. doi:10.1016/j.annals.2020.102883

Tynan, C., McKechnie, S., & Chhuon, C. (2010). Co-creating value for luxury brands. *Journal of Business Research, 63*(11), 1156–1163. doi:10.1016/j.jbusres.2009.10.012

Uleman J. S. & Bargh J. A. (1989). *Unintended thought*. New York: Guilford Press.

Ulker-Demirel, E. (2019). The Features of New Communication Channels and Digital Marketing. In *Handbook of Research on Narrative Advertising* (pp. 302–313). IGI Global. doi:10.4018/978-1-5225-9790-2.ch026

Ullah, S., Akhtar, P., & Zaefarian, G. (2018). Dealing with endogeneity bias: The generalized method of moments (GMM) for panel data. *Industrial Marketing Management, 71*, 69–78. doi:10.1016/j.indmarman.2017.11.010

UNCTAD. (2019). *Digitalization in Maritime Transport: Ensuring Opportunities for Development | UNCTAD*. United Nations Publication.

UNCTAD. (2020). Review of Maritime Transport 2020. *United Nations Publications*.

UNCTAD. (2021a). *Maritime profile: Brazil*. Retrieved from https://unctadstat.unctad.org/CountryProfile/MaritimeProfile/en-GB/076/index.html

UNCTAD. (2021b). Maritime profile: Portugal. *UNCTADstat*. Retrieved from https://unctadstat.unctad.org/CountryProfile/MaritimeProfile/en-GB/620/index.html

UNDESA. (2001). *Benchmarking e-government: A global perspective - assessing the progress of the un member states*. Retrieved from https://publicadministration.un.org/egovkb/Portals/egovkb/Documents/un/English.pdf

UNDESA. (2003). *Un global e-government survey 2003*. Retrieved from https://publicadministration.un.org/egovkb/portals/egovkb/Documents/un/2003-Survey/unpan016066.pdf

UNDESA. (2004). *Un global e-government readiness report 2004: Towards access for opportunity*. Retrieved from https://publicadministration.un.org/egovkb/portals/egovkb/Documents/un/2004-Survey/Complete-Survey.pdf

UNDESA. (2005). *Un global e-government readiness report 2005: From e-government to e-inclusion* Retrieved from https://publicadministration.un.org/egovkb/Portals/egovkb/Documents/un/2005-Survey/Complete-survey.pdf

UNDESA. (2008). *United nations e-government survey 2008: From e-government to connected governance* Retrieved from https://publicadministration.un.org/egovkb/Portals/egovkb/Documents/un/2008-Survey/Complete-survey.pdf

UNDESA. (2010). *United nations e-government survey 2010: Leveraging e-government at a time of financial and economic crisis*. Retrieved from https://publicadministration.un.org/egovkb/Portals/egovkb/Documents/un/2010-Survey/Complete-survey.pdf

UNDESA. (2018). *United nations e-government survey 2018: Gearing e-government to support transformation towards sustainable and resilient societies*. Retrieved from https://publicadministration.un.org/egovkb/Portals/egovkb/Documents/un/2018-Survey/E-Government%20Survey%202018_FINAL%20for%20web.pdf

UNDESA. (2020). *E-government survey 2020: Digital government in the decade of action for sustainable development*. Retrieved from https://publicadministration.un.org/egovkb/Portals/egovkb/Documents/un/2020-Survey/2020%20UN%20E-Government%20Survey%20(Full%20Report).pdf

United Nations. (2019). *Sustainable Development Goals*. Retrieved from https://sdgs.un.org/goals

Upchurch, M. (2018). Robots and ai at work: The prospects for singularity. *New Technology, Work and Employment*, *33*(3), 205–218. doi:10.1111/ntwe.12124

Upstart. (n.d.). https://www.upstart.com/about#

Urbinati, A., Bogers, M., Chiesa, V., & Frattini, F. (2019). Creating and capturing value from Big Data: A multiple-case study analysis of provider companies. *Technovation*, *84*, 21–36. doi:10.1016/j.technovation.2018.07.004

Urbinati, A., Chiaroni, D., Chiesa, V., & Frattini, F. (2020). The role of digital technologies in open innovation processes: An exploratory multiple case study analysis. *R & D Management*, *50*(1), 136–160. doi:10.1111/radm.12313

Urruticoechea, A., & Vernaza, E. (2018). *Una aplicación de la metodología biplot logísico: análisis de la sostenibilidad empresarial*. XI Semana Internacional de la Estadística y la Probabilidad. Facultad de Ciencias Físico Matemáticas Puebla.

US Congress. (2019). *HR 2231 – Algorithmic Accountability Act of 2019*. https://www.congress.gov/bill/116th-congress/house-bill/2231/text

Valohai, SigOpt, & Tecton. (2020). *Practical MLOps: How to get ready for production models*. Author.

Van Eck, N. J., & Waltman, L. (2011). *Text mining and visualisation using VOSviewer*. https://arxiv.org/pdf/1109.2058

van Geenhuizen, M. (2018). A framework for the evaluation of living labs as boundary spanners in innovation. *Environment and Planning C. Politics and Space*, *36*(7), 1280–1298. doi:10.1177/2399654417753623

Vanelslander, T., & Sys, C. (2020). *Maritime Supply Chains*. Elsevier Science.

Vargha, Z. (2018). Performing a strategy's world: How redesigning customers made relationship banking possible. *Long Range Planning*, *51*(3), 480–494.

Vargo, S. L., & Lusch, R. F. (2014). Inversions of service-dominant logic. *Marketing Theory*, *14*(3), 239–248.

Varian, H. R. (2014). *Intermediate Microeconomics A Modern Approach* (9th ed.). Theresia Kowara.

Vásquez, C., & Chik, A. (2015). "I am not a foodie…": Culinary capital in online reviews of Michelin restaurants. *Food & Foodways*, *23*(4), 231–250. doi:10.1080/07409710.2015.1102483

Vázquez Brust. (2020). *Ciencia de Datos para Gente Sociable. Una introducción a la exploración, análisis y visualización de datos*. Retrieved December 18, 2020, from https://bitsandbricks.github.io/ciencia_de_datos_gente_sociable/index.html

Vecchiato, G., Toppi, J., Astolfi, L., De Vico Fallani, F., Cincotti, F., Mattia, D., Bez, F., & Babiloni, F. (2011). Spectral EEG frontal asymmetries correlate with the experienced pleasantness of video commercial advertisements. *Medical & Biological Engineering & Computing*, *49*(5), 579–583. doi:10.100711517-011-0747-x PMID:21327841

Vedan, A. B., & Thomas, E. M. B. (2019). A Cabotagem Brasileira no Contexto Mundial: Uma Análise Compreensiva Da Lei N° 9.432/1997 e de seus desdobramento. In E. M. O. Martins & P. H. R. de Oliveira (Eds.), *Direito marítimo, portuário e aduaneiro: temas contemporâneos* (pp. 13–31). Arraes Editores.

Vélez-Rolón, A. M., Méndez-Pinzón, M., & Acevedo, O. L. (2020). Open Innovation Community for University-Industry Knowledge Transfer: A Colombian Case. *Journal of Open Innovation*, *68*(4), 1–17. doi:10.3390/joitmc6040181

Vella, A., Corne, D., & Murphy, C. (2009). *Hyper-heuristic decision tree induction*. Sch. of MACS, Heriot-Watt Univ., Edinburgh, UK. Nature & Biologically Inspired Computing, 2009. NaBIC 2009. World Congress.

Velleman, P. F., & Wilkinson, L. (1993). Nominal, ordinal, interval, and ratio typologies are misleading. *The American Statistician*, *47*(1), 65–72.

Veneberg, R. (2014). *Combining enterprise architecture and operational data-to better support decision-making. University of Twente*. School of Management and Governance.

Venkatesh, V. G., Zhang, A., Deakins, E., Mani, V., & Shi, Y. (2020). Supply Chain Integration Barriers to Port-Centric Logistics—An Emerging Economy Perspective. *Transportation Journal*, *59*(3), 215–253. doi:10.5325/transportationj.59.3.0215

Venkatesh, V., Thong, J. Y., & Xu, X. (2012). Consumer acceptance and use of information technology: Extending the unified theory of acceptance and use of technology. *Management Information Systems Quarterly*, *36*(1), 157–178. doi:10.2307/41410412

Verbeek, P. P. (2006). Materializing morality: Design ethics and technological mediation. *Science, Technology & Human Values*, *31*(3), 361–380. doi:10.1177/0162243905285847

Verbeek, P. P. (2011). *Moralizing technology: Understanding and designing the morality of things*. University of Chicago Press. doi:10.7208/chicago/9780226852904.001.0001

Verhoef, P. C., Lemon, K. N., Parasuraman, A., Roggeveen, A., Tsiros, M., & Schlesinger, L. A. (2009). Customer experience creation: Determinants, dynamics and management strategies. *Journal of Retailing*, *85*(1), 31–41.

Verkijika, S. F., & De Wet, L. (2018). A usability assessment of e-government websites in sub-saharan africa. *International Journal of Information Management*, *39*, 20–29. doi:10.1016/j.ijinfomgt.2017.11.003

Verwer, S., & Calders, T. (2013). Introducing positive discrimination in predictive models. In *Discrimination and privacy in the information society* (pp. 255–270). Springer. doi:10.1007/978-3-642-30487-3_14

Vetrò, A., Santangelo, A., Beretta, E., & De Martin, J. C. (2019). AI: From rational agents to socially responsible agents. *Digital Policy. Regulation & Governance*, *21*(3), 291–304. Advance online publication. doi:10.1108/DPRG-08-2018-0049

Vial, G. (2019). Understanding digital transformation: A review and a research agenda. *The Journal of Strategic Information Systems*, *28*(2), 118–144.

Viana, J., & Peralta, H. (2021). Online Learning: From the Curriculum for All to the Curriculum for Each Individual. *Journal of New Approaches in Educational Research*, *10*(1), 122–136. doi:10.7821/naer.2021.1.579

Vicente Cuervo, M. R., & López Menéndez, A. J. (2006). A multivariate framework for the analysis of the digital divide: Evidence for the european union-15. *Information & Management*, *43*(6), 756–766. doi:10.1016/j.im.2006.05.001

Vicente Galindo, P., Vaz, E., & de Noronha, T. (2015). How Corporations Deal with Reporting Sustainability: Assessment Using the Multicriteria Logistic Biplot Approach. *Systems*, *3*(1), 6–26. doi:10.3390ystems3010006

Vicente Villardón, J.L. (2015). *Multbiplot: A package for Multivariate Analysis using Biplots. Departamento de Estadística*. Universidad de Salamanca. http://biplot.usal.es/ClassicalBiplot/index.html

Vicente-Villardon, J. L., Galindo-Villardon, M. P., & Blazquez-Zaballos, A. (2006). *Logistic Biplots in Multiple Correspondence Analysis and Related Methods*. Statistics in Social and Behavioural Sciences Series.

Vickers, A. J. (2005). Parametric versus non-parametric statistics in the analysis of randomized trials with non-normally distributed data. *BMC Medical Research Methodology*, *5*(1), 35. doi:10.1186/1471-2288-5-35 PMID:16269081

Vieira, J., & Fialho, G. (2020). Port Management Modernization and Integrated Operational Planning. *Revista Eletrônica de Estratégia & Negócios*, *13*, 196. doi:10.19177/reen.v13e0I2020196-224

Vigderhous, G. (1977). The level of measurement and "permissible" statistical analysis in social research. *Pacific Sociological Review*, *20*(1), 61–72. doi:10.2307/1388904

Vilner, Y. (n.d.). *Chatbots101:The Evolution of Customer Retention Latest Trend*. Available: https://www.entrepreneur.com/article/293439

Vincent, J. (2017, January 4). The UK's national health service is testing out a medical chatbot as a non-emergency helpline. *The Verge*. https://www.theverge.com/2017/1/4/14168312/uk-nhs-babylon-medical-chatbot-helpline

Visengeriyeva, L., Kammer, A., Bär, I., Kniesz, A., & Plöd, M. (n.d.). *Machine learning operations*. Retrieved from https://ml-ops.org/

Vogelsang, A., & Borg, M. (2019). *Requirements engineering for machine learning: Perspectives from data scientists*. Paper presented at the IEEE 27th International Requirements Engineering Conference Workshops (REW). 10.1109/REW.2019.00050

Voice2Biz. (n.d.). *Google Home and Alexa Talk to aach other & have a conversation*. https://www.voice2biz.com/google-home-and-alexa-talk-to-each-other-have-a-conversation/

Vrontis, D., Thrassou, A., & Czinkota, M. R. (2011). Wine marketing: A framework for consumer-centred planning. *Journal of Brand Management*, *18*(4-5), 245–263. doi:10.1057/bm.2010.39

Vroom, V. H. (1964). *Work and motivation*. Wiley.

Vygotsky, L. S., Cole, M., John-Steiner, V., Scribner, S., & Souberman, E. (1978). *Mind in Society: Development of Higher Psychological Processes*. Harvard University Press.

Wachinger, G., Renn, O., Begg, C., & Kuhlicke, C. (2013). The risk perception paradox: Implications for governance and communication of natural hazards. *Risk Analysis*, *33*(6), 1049–1065. doi:10.1111/j.1539-6924.2012.01942.x PMID:23278120

Wadgave, U., & Khairnar, M. R. (2016). Parametric tests for Likert scale: For and against. *Asian Journal of Psychiatry*, *24*, 67–68. doi:10.1016/j.ajp.2016.08.016 PMID:27931911

Wahlstrom, K., Ul-haq, A., & Burmeister, O. (2020). Privacy by design. *AJIS. Australasian Journal of Information Systems*, *24*, 1–9. doi:10.3127/ajis.v24i0.2801

Wallach, W., Franklin, S., & Allen, C. (2010). A Conceptual and Computational Model of Moral Decision Making in Human and Artificial Agents. *Trends in Cognitive Sciences*, *2*(3), 454–485. PMID:25163872

Waller, M. A., & Fawcett, S. E. (2013). Click here for a data scientist: Big data, predictive analytics, and theory development in the era of a maker movement supply chain. *Journal of Business Logistics*, *34*(4), 249–252. doi:10.1111/jbl.12024

Walls, A. R., Okumus, F., Wang, Y., & Kwun, D. J. W. (2011). An epistemological view of consumer experience. *International Journal of Hospitality Management*, *30*(1), 10–21.

Wang, B., Yang, Z., Xuan, J., & Jiao, K. (2020). Crises and opportunities in terms of energy and AI technologies during the COVID-19 pandemic. *Energy AI*, *1*, 100013. doi:10.1016/j.egyai.2020.100013

Wang, C. H., & Lien, C. Y. (2019). Combining design science with data analytics to forecast user intention to adopt customer relationship management systems. *Journal of Industrial and Production Engineering*, *36*(4), 193–204. doi:10.1080/21681015.2019.1645051

Wang, D., Weisz, J. D., Muller, M., Ram, P., Geyer, W., Dugan, C., Tausczik, Y., Samulowitz, H., & Gray, A. (2019). Human-AI collaboration in data science: Exploring data scientists' perceptions of automated AI. *Proceedings of the ACM on Human-Computer Interaction, 3*(CSCW), 1-24. 10.1145/3359313

Wang, J., & Karypis, G. (2004). Summary: Efficiently Summarizing Transactions for Clustering. In *Proceedings of the Fourth IEEE International Conference on Data Mining*. IEEE Computer Society. 10.1109/ICDM.2004.10105

Wang, K., Xu, C., & Liu, B. (1999). Clustering Transactions Using Large Items. In *Proceedings of the Eighth International Conference on Information and Knowledge*. Association for Computing Machinery. 10.1145/319950.320054

Wang, L., & Alexander, C. A. (2016). Machine learning in big data. International *Journal of Mathematical. Engineering and Management Sciences, 1*(2), 52–61.

Wang, L., Luo, G. L., Sari, A., & Shao, X. F. (2020). What nurtures fourth industrial revolution? An investigation of economic and social determinants of technological innovation in advanced economies. *Technological Forecasting and Social Change, 161*, 120305. doi:10.1016/j.techfore.2020.120305

Wang, P., Guo, J., Lan, Y., & Cheng, X. (2014). Modeling Retail Transaction Data for Personalized Shopping Recommendation. In *Proceedings of the 23rd ACM International Conference on Information and Knowledge Management*. Association for Computing Machinery. 10.1145/2661829.2662020

Wang, Q., Li, S., & Pisarenko, Z. (2020). Heterogeneous effects of energy efficiency, oil price, environmental pressure, R&D investment, and policy on renewable energy – evidence from the G20 countries. *Energy, 209*, 118322. doi:10.1016/j.energy.2020.118322

Wang, Q., Valchuis, L., Thompson, E., Conner, D., & Parsons, R. (2019). Consumer Support and Willingness to Pay for Electricity from Solar, Wind, and Cow Manure in the United States: Evidence from a Survey in Vermont. *Energies, 12*(23), 4467. doi:10.3390/en12234467

Wang, R., Luo, J., & Huang, S. S. (2020). Developing an artificial intelligence framework for online destination image photos identification. *Journal of Destination Marketing & Management, 18*, 100512. doi:10.1016/j.jdmm.2020.100512

Wang, S.-C., Soesilo, P. K., & Zhang, D. (2015). Impact of luxury brand retailer co-branding strategy on potential customers: A cross-cultural study. *Journal of International Consumer Marketing, 27*(3), 237–252. doi:10.1080/08961530.2014.970320

Wang, W., Li, W., Zhang, N., & Liu, K. (2020). Portfolio formation with preselection using deep learning from long-term financial data. *Expert Systems with Applications, 143*, 113042. doi:10.1016/j.eswa.2019.113042

Wang, X., Nguyen, K., & Nguyen, B. P. (2020). Churn prediction using ensemble learning. In *ACM International Conference Proceeding Series* (pp. 56–60). 10.1145/3380688.3380710

Ward, R., & Bjørn-Andersen, N. (2021). The Origins of Maritime Informatics. In Maritime Informatics. Springer. doi:10.1007/978-3-030-50892-0_1

Warwick, K. (2002). *I, Cyborg*. Century.

Washizaki, H., Uchida, H., Khomh, F., & Guéhéneuc, Y.-G. (2020). *Machine learning architecture and design patterns*. Academic Press.

Wason, H., & Charlton, N. (2015). How positioning strategies affect co-branding outcomes. *Cogent Business & Management, 2*(1), 1092192. doi:10.1080/23311975.2015.1092192

WCO. (2021). *Managing Transition to a Single Window, Volume 1, Part IX*. World Customs Organization.

Webb, H., Patel, M., Rovatsos, M., Davoust, A., Ceppi, S., Koene, A., Dowthwaite, L., Portill, V., Jirotka, M., & Cano, M. (2019). It would be pretty immoral to choose a random algorithm: Opening up algorithmic interpretability and transparency. *Journal of Information Communication and Ethics in Society, 17*(2), 210–228. doi:10.1108/JICES-11-2018-0092

Weber, R. H. (2010). Internet of Things–New security and privacy challenges. *Computer Law & Security Review, 26*(1), 23–30. doi:10.1016/j.clsr.2009.11.008

Weem, G. H., Onwuegbuzie, A. J., & Collins, K. M. T. (2006). The role of reading comprehension in responses to positively and negatively worded items on rating scales. *Evaluation and Research in Education, 19*(1), 3–20. doi:10.1080/09500790608668322

Weems, G. H., & Onwuegbuzie, A. J. (2001). The impact of midpoint responses and reverse coding on survey data. *Measurement & Evaluation in Counseling & Development, 34*(3), 166–176. doi:10.1080/07481756.2002.12069033

Weichert, D., Link, P., Stoll, A., Rüping, S., Ihlenfeldt, S., & Wrobel, S. (2019). A review of machine learning for the optimization of production processes. *International Journal of Advanced Manufacturing Technology, 104*(5-8), 1889–1902. doi:10.100700170-019-03988-5

Weinberg, B. D., Milne, G. R., Andonova, Y. G., & Hajjat, F. M. (2015). Internet of Things: Convenience vs. privacy and secrecy. *Business Horizons, 58*(6), 615–624. doi:10.1016/j.bushor.2015.06.005

Weinmann, M., Schneider, C., & Vom Brocke, J. (2016). Digital Nudging. *Business & Information Systems Engineering, 433-436.* Advance online publication. doi:10.2139srn.2708250

Weld, D. S., & Bansal, G. (2019). The challenge of crafting intelligible intelligence. *Communications of the ACM, 62*(6), 70–79. doi:10.1145/3282486

Weng, L., & Cheng, C. (2000). Effects of response order on Likert type scales. *Educational and Psychological Measurement, 60*(6), 908–924. doi:10.1177/00131640021970989

Werbos, P. J. (1982). Applications of advances in nonlinear sensitivity analysis. In R. F. Drenick & F. Kozin (Eds.), *System Modeling and Optimization* (pp. 762–770). Springer Berlin Heidelberg. doi:10.1007/BFb0006203

West, D. M. (2003). *Global e-government, 2003.* Retrieved from http://www.insidepolitics.org/egovt03int.pdf

West, D. M. (2004b). *Global e-government, 2004.* Retrieved from http://www.insidepolitics.org/egovt04int.pdf

West, D. M. (2005). *Global e-government, 2005.* Retrieved from http://www.insidepolitics.org/egovt05int.pdf

West, D. M. (2006). *Global e-government, 2006.* Retrieved from http://www.insidepolitics.org/egovt06int.pdf

West, D. M. (2007). *Global e-government, 2007.* Retrieved from http://www.insidepolitics.org/egovt07int.pdf

Westbrook, R. A., & Oliver, R. L. (1991). The Dimensionality of Consumption Emotion Patterns and Consumer Satisfaction. *The Journal of Consumer Research, 18*(1), 84–91. doi:10.1086/209243

West, D. M. (2004a). E-government and the transformation of service delivery and citizen attitudes. *Public Administration Review, 64*(1), 15–27. doi:10.1111/j.1540-6210.2004.00343.x

Weston, Bordes, Rush, van Merrienboer, Joulin, & Mikolov. (n.d.). Towards Ai-complete Question Answering: A Set Of Prerequisite Toy Tasks. In *Soft Computing for Problem Solving Arch.* Academic Press.

Weston, J., Bordes, A., & Chopra, S. (2015). *Towards AI-Complete Question Answering: A Set of Prerequisite Toy Tasks.* arXiv preprint, arXiv: 1502.05968

Weston, J., Chopra, S., & Bordes, A. (2015). Memory networks. *Proceedings of the 3rd International Conference on Learning Representations (ICLR).*

Whitmore, A. (2012). A statistical analysis of the construction of the united nations e-government development index. *Government Information Quarterly, 29*(1), 68–75. doi:10.1016/j.giq.2011.06.003

Wieckowski, A. (2019). When neuromarketing crosses the line. *Harvard Business Review.* Accessed from: https://hbr.org/2019/01/when-neuromarketing-crosses-the-line?ab=at_articlepage_recommendedarticles_bottom1x1

Wierenga, B. (2010). Marketing and artificial intelligence: Great opportunities, reluctant partners. In *Marketing intelligent systems using soft computing* (pp. 1–8). Springer.

Wiggers, K. (2019, March 19). Ojo Labs raises $45 million to develop a chatbot for real estate. *VentureBeat.* https://venturebeat.com/2019/03/19/ojo-labs-raises-45-million-to-develop-a-chatbot-for-real-estate/

Wilber, K. (1985). *The Holographic Paradigm and other paradox, exploring the leading edge of science.* New Science Library.

Wilson, H. J., Daugherty, P., & Bianzino, N. (2017). The jobs that artificial intelligence will create. *MIT Sloan Management Review, 58*(4), 14.

Winston, P. H. (1992). *Artificial Intelligence* (3rd ed.). Addison-Wesley.

Wirth, N. (2018). Hello marketing, what can artificial intelligence help you with? *International Journal of Market Research, 60*(5), 435–438. doi:10.1177/1470785318776841

Wirtz, J., Patterson, P. G., Kunz, W. H., Gruber, T., Lu, V. N., Paluch, S., & Martins, A. (2018). Brave new world: Service robots in the frontline. *Journal of Service Management, 29*(5), 907–931. doi:10.1108/JOSM-04-2018-0119

Witten, I. H., & Frank, E. (2002). Data mining: Practical machine learning tools and techniques with java implementations. *SIGMOD Record, 31*(1), 76–77. doi:10.1145/507338.507355

Woods, C. M. (2006). Careless responding to reverse-worded items: Implications for confirmatory factory analysis. *Journal of Psychopathology and Behavioral Assessment, 28*(3), 189–194. doi:10.100710862-005-9004-7

World Bank. (2020). *World bank country and lending groups.* Retrieved from https://datahelpdesk.worldbank.org/knowledgebase/articles/906519-world-bank-country-and-lending-groups

World Economic Forum. (2019). *What are ICTs?* Retrieved from en.weforum.org: https://es.weforum.org/agenda/2019/02/que-son-las-tics/

World Shipping Council. (2021). *Industry Issues.* Retrieved from https://www.worldshipping.org/industry-issues

Wu. (2020). *Bulk ship routing and scheduling under uncertainty* (Doctoral dissertation). Hong Kong Polytechnic University, China. Retrieved from https://theses.lib.polyu.edu.hk/handle/200/10660

Wu, D., Jennings, C., Terpenny, J., Gao, R., & Kumara, S. (2017). A Comparative Study on Machine Learning Algorithms for Smart Manufacturing: Tool Wear Prediction Using Random Forests. *Journal of Manufacturing Science and Engineering, 139*(7), 071018. Advance online publication. doi:10.1115/1.4036350

Xiao, W., Zhao, H., Pan, H., Song, Y., Zheng, V. W., & Yang, Q. (2019, July). Beyond personalization: Social content recommendation for creator equality and consumer satisfaction. In *Proceedings of the 25th ACM SIGKDD International Conference on Knowledge Discovery & Data Mining* (pp. 235-245). ACM.

Xiong, C., Merityand, S., & Socher, R. (2016). *Dynamic Memory Networks for Visual and Textual Question Answering*. ICML.

Xue, S., Wu, M., Kolen, J., Aghdaie, N., & Zaman, K. A. (2017). Dynamic Difficulty Adjustment for Maximized Engagement in Digital Games. *WWW '17 Companion: Proceedings of the 26th International Conference on World Wide Web*.

Xu, H., Luo, X., Carroll, J. M., & Rosson, M. B. (2011). The Personalization Privacy Paradox. *Decision Support Systems*, *51*(1), 42–52. doi:10.1016/j.dss.2010.11.017

Yadav, M., Perumal, M., & Srinivas, M. (2020). Analysis on novel coronavirus (COVID-19) using machine learning methods. *Chaos, Solitons, and Fractals*, *139*, 110050. doi:10.1016/j.chaos.2020.110050 PMID:32834604

Yams, N. B., Richardson, V., Shubina, G. E., Albrecht, S., & Gillblad, D. (2020). Integrated AI and Innovation Management: The Beginning of a Beautiful Friendship. *Technology Innovation Management Review, 10*(11).

Yan, E. (2019). *Data science and agile: What works and what doesn't work*. Retrieved from https://towardsdatascience.com/agiledatascience-3b7ca65278a4

Yang, C., Dillard, J., & Li, R. (2018). Understanding fear of Zika: Personal, interpersonal, and media Influences. *Risk Analysis*, *38*(12), 2535–2545. doi:10.1111/risa.12973 PMID:29392760

Yang, S. B., Hlee, S., Lee, J., & Koo, C. (2017). An empirical examination of online restaurant reviews on Yelp. com. *International Journal of Contemporary Hospitality Management*, *29*(2), 817–839. doi:10.1108/IJCHM-11-2015-0643

Yang, S., & Park, S. (2020). The effects of renewable energy financial incentive policy and democratic governance on renewable energy aid effectiveness. *Energy Policy*, *145*, 111682. doi:10.1016/j.enpol.2020.111682

Yan, H., Chen, K., & Liu, L. (2006). Efficiently Clustering Transactional Data with Weighted Coverage Density. In *Proceedings of the 15th International Conference on Information and Knowledge Management*. Association for Computing Machinery. 10.1145/1183614.1183668

Yeşilkanat, C. M. (2020). Spatio-temporal estimation of the daily cases of COVID-19 in worldwide using random forest machine-learning algorithm. *Chaos, Solitons, and Fractals*, *140*, 110210. doi:10.1016/j.chaos.2020.110210 PMID:32843823

Yoo, C. W. (2020). An Exploration of the Role of Service Recovery in Negative Electronic Word-of-Mouth Management. *Information Systems Frontiers*, *22*(3), 719–734. doi:10.100710796-018-9880-5

Yoon, S., Feng, J., & Jain, A. K. (2010). On Latent Fingerprint Enhancement. *Proc. SPIE Biometric Technology for Human Identification VII*.

Yu, H., Shen, Z., & Miao, C. (2018). Building Ethics into Artificial Intelligence, *Computer Science, Artificial Intelligence*. Cornell University. https://arxiv.org/abs/1812.02953

Yue, B. (2020). Topological Data Analysis of Two Cases: Text Classification and Business Customer Relationship Management. *Journal of Physics: Conference Series*, *1550*(3), 032081. Advance online publication. doi:10.1088/1742-6596/1550/3/032081

Yu, F., Liu, Q., Wu, S., Wang, L., & Tan, T. (2016). A Dynamic Recurrent Model for Next Basket Recommendation. In *Proceedings of the 39th International ACM SIGIR Conference on Research and Development in Information Retrieval*. Association for Computing Machinery. 10.1145/2911451.2914683

Zahedi, M., & Ghadi, O. R. (2015). Combining Gabor filter and FFT for fingerprint enhancement based on a regional adaption method and automatic segmentation. *Signal, Image and Video Processing*, *9*(2), 267–275. doi:10.100711760-013-0436-3

Zajonc, R. B. (1968). Attitudinal effects of mere exposure. *Journal of Personality and Social Psychology, 9*(2, Pt.2), 1–27. doi:10.1037/h0025848

Zajonc, R. B. (1980). Feeling and thinking: Preferences need no inferences. *The American Psychologist, 35*(2), 151–175. doi:10.1037/0003-066X.35.2.151

Zarsky, T. Z. (2016). Incompatible: The GDPR in the age of big data. *Seton Hall Law Review, 47,* 995.

Zhang, D., Zhang, Y., Li, Q., Plummer, T., & Wang, D. (2019, July). Crowdlearn: A crowd-ai hybrid system for deep learning-based damage assessment applications. In *2019 IEEE 39th International Conference on Distributed Computing Systems (ICDCS)* (pp. 1221-1232). IEEE. 10.1109/ICDCS.2019.00123

Zhang, J. R. L.-C. (2013). Adaptive Directional Total-Variation Model for. IEEE Transactions on Information Forensics And Security, 8.

Zhang, T., Gao, C., Ma, L., Lyu, M., & Kim, M. (2019). *An empirical study of common challenges in developing deep learning applications.* Paper presented at the 2019 IEEE 30th International Symposium on Software Reliability Engineering (ISSRE). 10.1109/ISSRE.2019.00020

Zhang, C. B., & Li, Y. N. (2019). How social media usage influences B2B customer loyalty: Roles of trust and purchase risk. *Journal of Business and Industrial Marketing.*

Zhang, J., Harman, M., Ma, L., & Liu, Y. (2020). *Machine learning testing: Survey, landscapes and horizons. IEEE Transactions on Software Engineering.* Early Access.

Zhang, J., Lai, R., & Kuo, C. C. J. (2013). Adaptive directional total-variation model for latent fingerprint segmentation. *IEEE Transactions on Information Forensics and Security, 8*(8), 1261–1273. doi:10.1109/TIFS.2013.2267491

Zhang, X., & Savalei, V. (2016). Improving the factor structure of psychological scales: The Expanded format as an alternative to the Likert scale format. *Educational and Psychological Measurement, 76*(3), 357–386. doi:10.1177/0013164415596421 PMID:27182074

Zhang, Z., Zhang, Z., & Law, R. (2014). Relative importance and combined effects of attributes on customer satisfaction. *Service Industries Journal, 34*(6), 550–566. doi:10.1080/02642069.2014.871537

Zhao, P., Lu, Z., Fang, J., Paramati, S. R., & Jiang, K. (2020). Determinants of renewable and non-renewable energy demand in China. *Structural Change and Economic Dynamics, 54,* 202–209. doi:10.1016/j.strueco.2020.05.002

Zhao, Y., Tang, K.-K., & Wang, L.-L. (2013). Do renewable electricity policies promote renewable electricity generation? Evidence from panel data. *Energy Policy, 62,* 887–897. doi:10.1016/j.enpol.2013.07.072

Zhao, Y., Xu, X., & Wang, M. (2019). Predicting overall customer satisfaction: Big data evidence from hotel online textual reviews. *International Journal of Hospitality Management, 76,* 111–121. doi:10.1016/j.ijhm.2018.03.017

Zhou, L., Pan, S., Wang, J., & Vasilakos, A. V. (2017). Machine learning on big data: Opportunities and challenges. *Neurocomputing, 237,* 350–361. doi:10.1016/j.neucom.2017.01.026

Zickfeld, J. H., Schubert, T. W., Herting, A. K., Grahe, J., & Faasse, K. (2020). Correlates of health-protective behavior during the initial days of the COVID-19 outbreak in Norway. *Frontiers in Psychology, 11,* 11. doi:10.3389/fpsyg.2020.564083 PMID:33123045

Zinkevich, M. (2017). *Rules of machine learning: Best practices for ML engineering.* Retrieved from https://developers.google.com/machine-learning/guides/rules-of-ml

Žliobaitė, I. (2015). *A survey on measuring indirect discrimination in machine learning.* arXiv preprint arXiv:1511.00148.

Zomerdijk, L. G., & Voss, C. A. (2011). NSD processes and practices in experiential services. *Journal of Product Innovation Management*, *28*(1), 63–80.

Zwanka, R., & Buff, C. (2020). Generation COVID-19: A conceptual framework of consumer behavioral changes to be caused by the COVID-19 pandemic. *Journal of International Consumer Marketing*, *33*(1), 58–67. doi:10.1080/08961 530.2020.1771646

Żyminkowska, K. (2019). Concepts of Customer Activism. In *Customer Engagement in Theory and Practice* (pp. 1–22). Palgrave Pivot. doi:10.1007/978-3-030-11677-4_1

About the Contributors

Valentina Chkoniya received her PhD in Technical Sciences by Murmansk State Technical University, Russia, in 2003. Actually, she is a professor at the University of Aveiro, member of GOVCOPP, Portugal, and managing partner of VT Mar (company in the marketing intelligence market). Valentina Chkoniya is a highly professional and experienced professor with a deep understanding and knowledge regarding the business, based on a deep strategic perspective and building on more than 20 years of experience. Her current research interests include data analysis, decision support systems, marketing research, consumer behaviour and information technologies for retail.

* * *

Clony Abreu Junior is a research fellow. Graduated in Computer Science, at the Ruy Barbosa College, Salvador, Bahia – Brazil (2005), postgraduate in IT Management by Metropolitan College of Belo Horizonte – MG, Brazil (2008), MBA in Applications Project for Mobile Devices by Instituto Newton Paiva Ferreira de Belo Horizonte – MG (2017). Master in Computer Engineering at the Aveiro University, Portugal (2021).

David Aguilar Del Carpio is a professor at the Faculty of Economics of the Universidad Nacional de San Agustín de Arequipa. Economist graduated from the same university, Master in Economics from the PUCP, graduated from the graduate school of the UNSA of the Master in Formulation, Evaluation and Management of Investment Projects. Experience in research of public policies and social problems, as well as in positions of human resource management, planning and spending in the public and private sectors. Skill in indicator analysis, statistics and information consolidation.

Abdullah M. M. Altrad is an Associate Professor at the American University of Phnom Penh (AUPP). Received Master of IT in 2011 from University Utara Malaysia (UUM), and also obtained PhD of IT from School of Computing - UUM as well. Also, worked as research assistant in UUM (2014) for Broadband Service Project of Last-mile connection-based Powerline Communication Network, then moved to Almadinah International University Malaysia as a lecturer of Computer Science since 2015 until August 2020. Moreover, introduced an Adaptive Recourse Allocation Technique for Powerline Communication Network based on Combinatorial Optimization and Metaheuristic Techniques. The current research topics are on Machine Learning, Wireless Networks, IoT, and Cybersecurity.

Muhammad Ashfaq is a post-doctorate researcher at Shenzhen University, China. In 2020, he obtained his PhD in Marketing from Dongbei University of Finance and Economics, China. His work has been published in different SSCI-ranked journals. His research includes consumer behavior, technology adoption, and digital marketing.

Elodie Attié is currently a scientific project manager at Capgemini Engineering. She obtained a PhD in marketing about the acceptance of the Internet of Things and its influence on consumer well-being in 2019. Her research interests relate to innovations, marketing, consumer behavior and well-being.

Anteneh Ayanso is Professor of Information Systems and Director of the Centre for Business Analytics at Brock University. He teaches Business Analytics, Database Design and Management, and Data Mining Techniques & Applications. His research interests focus primarily on data management, business analytics, electronic commerce, and electronic government. He has published many articles in leading journals such as Decision Sciences, Decision Support Systems, European Journal of Operational Research, Journal of Database Management, International Journal of Electronic Commerce, Government Information Quarterly, among others. Dr. Ayanso's research has been funded by internal and external grants, including a Discovery Research Grant by the Natural Sciences and Engineering Research Council (NSERC) of Canada. He is currently serving as an Associate Editor at Decision Support Systems journal and a review board member at Journal of Database Management, International Journal of Convergence Computing, and International Journal of Electronic Commerce.

Veena Bansal is an Associate Professor with the Indian Institute of Technology Kanpur. She is widely published in the area of enterprise resource planning. Her current area of interest include Big Data, Machine Learning applications, Data Science Adoption.

Tamer Baran is PhD lecturer. Dr. Baran hold his bachelor degree from Dumlupinar University, master and PhD degrees in Marketing from Pamukkale University. His research field is marketing and specified areas are Islamic marketing, marketing research, consumer behavior, branding and retailing. Studies of Dr. Baran has published in prestigious academic journals in these areas. He has worked in Pamukkale University, Kale VS since 2011.

Belém Barbosa is an Assistant Professor at the School of Economics and Management, University of Porto. She is also a Researcher at the Research Unit of Governance, Competitiveness and Public Policy (GOVCOPP). Her research main research interests are digital marketing and consumer behavior.

Borja Barinaga is a digital art professor in the videogames department at the Francisco de Vitoria University in Madrid. He is an official researcher at the University Complutense in Madrid, and he is a member of the research group Museum I+D+C, Laboratory for the Digital Culture and Hypermedia Museography. Barinaga wrote the first book about video game design in the Spanish language and also is one of the founders of the first video game degree in Spain. His research field is digital languages and communication.

Mª Manuela Batista is a specialist in Transport Services, Postgraduate in Environmental Port Management, Coordinator of Port Management Undergraduate Course at ENIDH (Escola Superior

Náutica Infante D. Henrique - Portuguese Maritime College). Professor at Transport and Logistics Department (Applied Physical Chemistry and Pollution – Master Course in Deck and Bridge Operations; Environmental Management in Transport - Degree in Port Management and Degree in Transport and Logistics Management; Applied Chemistry and Physical Chemistry - Degree in Deck and Bridge Operations). Participates in national / European projects in the maritime-port sector and coordinates a Training Academy (MSC-ENIDH Academy) dedicated to Maritime Transport. Since 2001 coordinates and teaches several training actions/courses: Dangerous and Noxious Cargo Operations; Familiarization / Specialization for the transportation of Goods in Tankers (Oil Tankers, Chemicals and Liquefied Gas). Is a consultant in companies / associations dedicated to the transport, handling and storage of chemical products / dangerous goods.

Liliana Bernardino has a Masters Degree in Mathematics & Statistics with a following Master Degree in Machine Learning and Decision Support Systems. With more than 16 years' experience of using simple and complex analytics to change data into knowledge by focusing her work and efforts in customer insights and strategic/behavioral analytics. She's passionate about solving questions like "so what?", "how it happened?" and "why?" in consumer data to create true customer insight. She has significant experience delivering and drawing advanced predictive analytics solutions to drive customer loyalty into commercial results. Has the belief that if a company applies analytics correctly this turns out not just into measurement tools, but into an insight finder, a strategy builder and a loyalty weapon. Throughout her career she has built (and still do) platforms and statistical solutions that were the "ramp up" for the customer knowledge growth and in the past few years leads CRM, Data Science and Report Building Teams in Sonae MC

Chintan Bhatt (Ph.D.) is currently working as an Assistant Professor in Computer Engineering department, Chandubhai S. Patel Institute of Technology, CHARUSAT. He is a member of IEEE, EAI, ACM, CSI, AIRCC and IAENG (International Association of Engineers). His areas of interest include Internet of Things, Data Mining, Web Mining, Networking, Security Mobile Computing, Big Data and Software Engineering. He has more than 5 years of teaching experience and research experience, having good teaching and research interests. He has chaired a track in CSNT 2015 and ICTCS 2014. He has been working as Reviewer in Wireless Communications, IEEE (Impact Factor-6.524) and Internet of Things Journal, IEEE, Knowledge-Based Systems, Elsevier (Impact Factor-2.9) Applied Computing and Informatics, Elsevier and Mobile Networks and Applications, Springer. He has delivered an expert talk on Internet of Things at Broadcast Engineering Society Doordarshan, Ahmedabad on 30/09/2015. He has been awarded Faculty with Maximum Publication in CSIC Award and Paper Presenter Award at International Conference in CSI-2015, held at New Delhi.

Hector Bienvenido is currently an assistant professor in the area of Social Research Methods at Complutense University of Madrid. Héctor's research interests focus on the social implications of ICTs (mobile phones, social networks) and videogames, especially in relation to the processes of interaction, social exclusion, agencies and emergency; as well as the study of youth and leisure practices and cultures, virtual communities, social change and user experiences (UX). He is a member of the research group 'Ordinary Sociology/Sociología Ordinaria' (UCM). Héctor has published numerous conference and journal papers such as papers in DiGRA, Journal of Critical Care, and Revista Española de Investigaciones Sociológicas.

Jacques Bughin has lectured economics and management since 1992, and has published tens of research in outlets such as Management Science, Research Policy, IEEE, Eutropean Economic Review, Harvard Business Review and Sloan Management Review. After retiring as senior partner at McKinsey and as Director of the McKinsey Global Institute, he now advises various companies on strategies, and the UN on digitigitization, is Venture Partner at Antler, and Senior Advisor to Fortino Capital. He is also part of the Technology advisor board of the European Parliament.

Yezelia Cáceres is a professor at the Faculty of Economics of the Universidad Nacional de San Agustín de Arequipa, Peru. She recently published: 'Informal food systems and differential mobility during the COVID-19 pandemic in Arequipa, Peru together with Aaron Malone and Anabel Taya (https://doi.org/10.3828/tpr.2020.61). On the other hand, her book chapter stands out: Alpaca Meat: Constraints and Reinforcements on Consumption, in book: Anthropological Approaches to Understanding Consumption Patterns and Consumer Behavior (pp. 286-302) DOI: 10.4018 / 978-1-7998-3115- 0.ch016, prepared with Sara Gonzales and Juan Rivera. Among other contributions, there is the Analysis of the instrument for measuring institutional capacity. Case study: Pampacolca 2018 Available at the CIES Economic and Social Research Consortium. Theoretical contributions for the analysis of competitiveness and the value chain in micro and small companies. Ilustro 2018, vol 9 available at https://doi.org/10.36901/illustro.v9i0.1224 The use of information and communication technologies to improve agricultural production in the Arequipa region 2014 - Research Contest Research Consortium Económica y Social CIES "The use of ICT for key industries in the southern economic corridor: alpaca and coffee. Enhancing the Competitiveness of SMEs in the Southern Economic Corridor in Peru (2012) KDS Korean Development Strategy Using the radio to improve the local responses to climate variability, Center for Development and Informatics (CDI), University of Manchester, United Kingdom (2012).

José Luís Cacho is CEO of APS – Ports of Sines and the Algarve Authority, S.A. and ex-President and Adviser of APLOP - Association of Portuguese Speaking Ports. The Port of Sines is an open deep-water sea port with excellent maritime access, without restrictions, leading the Portuguese port sector in the volume of cargo handled, and offering unique natural characteristics to receive any type of vessels. He also was member of the Monitoring Committee of the Logistics Platforms National Network Plan, a member of the Monitoring Group for the rail link to the Port of Aveiro and of the Committee on Accreditation of Civil Engineering Graduation at the University of Trás-os -Montes e Alto Douro (UTAD), by the Engineers Order between. He was also member of the Biology Department Council, of the University of Aveiro, while being a member of the Council General of the University of Coimbra. He was CEO of APA - Port of Aveiro Authority, S.A., where he had already been Member of the Board of Directors and CEO of APFF - Port of Figueira da Foz Authority, S.A. and President of APP – Portugal Ports Association.

Michele Cincera is Professor of Industrial economics at the Solvay Brussels School of Economics and Management – Université Libre de Bruxelles. Since 2012, he is the Director of the International Centre of Innovation, Technology and Education Studies (iCite). His research interests and expertise embrace the quantitative assessment at the micro-level of innovative and entrepreneurial activities, their determinants and socio-economic impacts as well as the analysis of National Innovation Systems and the socio-economic impact of policies supporting science, research and innovation. He is currently member of the scientific board of the Brussels Institute for Statistics and Analysis (IBSA) and member of the international jury of the pôles de compétitivité wallons.

Kimberly Rose Clark is a Senior Lecturer and Researcher at Dartmouth College. She also serves as Co-Founder and Chief Research Officer of Merchant Mechanics and Founding Partner of Bellwether Citizen Response. Dr. Clark is a successful "pracademic" focused on human decision making. Her research specialty centers on applied behavioral neuroscience research with 30+ years of designing and implementing research programs focused on science communications.

Luís Cruz is an Assistant Professor at the Delft University of Technology and the Scientific Manager of the AI-for-Fintech Research lab. He holds a Ph.D. in Computer Science from the University of Porto, Portugal. Dr. Cruz has been actively contributing to the research fields of Machine Learning Engineering and Sustainable Software Engineering. His work aims at defining software engineering practices for machine learning projects and at improving development processes to deliver carbon-efficient software.

Pedro Gusmão is a student and researcher at University of Aveiro.

Fernando Cruz Goncalves is a specialist in Administration and Management - Maritime-Port Economics (ENIDH / Escola Naval / ISCIA), Master in Maritime Management and Transport Economics (ITMMA - Antwerp University), MBA in Logistics Management (IST / ISCTE / EGP), Degree in Management and Technologies Maritime (ENIDH), Degree in Administration and Maritime Management (ENIDH), Bachelor in Pilotage (ENIDH). Merchant Marine Officer, Coordinator of the degree in Port Management, Coordinator of the degree in Transport and Logistics Management and Coordinator of the Master in Port Management at ENIDH. Professor at the Department of Transport and Logistics. Consultant in Transport, Ports and Logistics in several projects and studies carried out in the scope of business and programs co-financed by the European Commission. Author and co-author of several publications in the area of Management, Economics of Transport and Logistics. Author of the book the "Maritime Transport of Containerized Cargo Market" (May 2015 - Chiado Editora), which is considered one of the best-selling books, at national level, in the scope of the maritime-port sector. He is / was former Vice- Director of the magazine "Cluster do Mar", member of the Editorial Board of Revista de Marinha, columnist of Revista Logística Moderna and regular columnist of the main publications of the sector (Logística Hoje / Revista Mobilidade / Diário de Notícias / Newspaper "Público "/ Sector Blogs) with several dozens of articles published. He regularly participates in congresses, seminars and conferences at national and international level on the issue of Transport, Logistics, Economy, Environment, Spatial Planning and Maritime-Port Policy, organized by different entities in the sector. He is the author / co-author of dozens of communications presented within the scope of them.

Mohanad M. Hilles is from Department of Information Technology, University College of Applied Science, Palestine.

Shadi M. S. Hilles has teaching and research experience in computer science and engineering, with a Ph.D. in Computer systems and Networks. Currently, is an associate Prof, in software Engineering Department, Faculty of engineering, Istanbul OKAN University, Turkey. in addition, has 10 years academic experience in computer Science department, faculty of computer & IT, in Al-Madinah International

University, Malaysia. Interested area image processing, machine learning and security, Has published several research papers in indexed journals such as ISI and Scopus also book chapters in Springer and IGI, and presented in several International conferences included IEEE and was one of track chair of IEEE conference. Has participated in numerous project of computer science in courses, workshop.

Nicola Del Sarto is a post-doctoral research fellow at Scuola Superiore Sant'Anna in Pisa. He received a Ph.D in Management of Innovation, sustainability and healthcare from Scuola Superiore Sant'Anna in 2019. Nicola's research interests focus on small businesses and start-ups and support mechanisms such as incubators, accelerators and corporate accelerator programs. Moreover, he is investigating the processes of business creation under the Open Innovation paradigm. Nicola's work has been published in high-quality peer reviewed journals and presented at international conferences.

Yousef A. Baker El-Ebiary holds a Ph.D. in MIS, two Masters in IT and Business administration, a high diploma in Executive Management, and Bachelor in Software engineering. Working at Faculty of Informatics and Computing (FIK), Universiti Sultan Zainal Abidin (UNISZA), Malaysia, as a senior lecturer and member of several committees that related to postgraduate studies, conferences coordination, designing and promoting programs, this role involved in writing, design, and validation of the programs and as they developed. As well as working as a part-time senior lecturer at (MEDIU) University and (SSM) collage, Switzerland. Also Senior Fellow Researcher at (AIU) University, Malaysia. Moreover, board member of Gyancity Research Lab for research and development, India. Over 11 years experience in teaching levels of degree and graduate studies. With good experience in administrative work in the education sector as I held many positions such as dean of student affairs for 3 years, faculty's deputy for postgraduate and scientific research for 2 years, and deputy for scientific research deanship for a year. In addition, extensive experience in managing and organizing international conferences. Also supervise both Ph.D.'s and Master students, alongside working as an editor in chief for research journal and reviewer in several indexed journals as well, with experience in scientific publication and international conferences participation more than 55 international conferences with good enough number of indexed research papers (WoS and Scopus) around 100 published and in press manuscripts in fields Information Systems, Enterprise Systems, Electronic Enterprise, Internet of Things, Theory of Computation and Contemporary Management, besides some research projects locally and internationally with governments and industry. Plus, one printed book with ISBN. With a good number of awards from international exhibitions and competitions and Intellectual property has been acquired. A member in many related associations such as IEEE, IAENG, ACSE, IACSIT.

Elizaveta Fainshtein is a PhD Student at the Department of Management at the Higher School of Economics, the National Research University (HSE), Russia, Saint Petersburg. Main areas of research interests include Strategic Marketing and Business Modelling.

Lisa Ferraz holds a Master's degree in Management from the University of Aveiro.

Nelson Ferreira graduated in Electronics & Telecommunications Engineering by the University of Aveiro and pos-graduate in Business Management by the Porto Business School. In September 1995, started his functions at Bosch Termotecnologia as a software engineer in the area of microcontrollers, ERP and database design. After 2000 changed his area to the coordinator of IT area responsible for Bosch

Aveiro plant (infrastructure, server farm & support services). In 2008 initiated an internationalization experience inside Bosch, sitting in Stuttgart-Feuerbach, as responsible for administration, sizing and architecture of SAP systems for Bosch Termotechnology division worldwide. Returned to Portugal in end 2010, integrating the R&D department, in the area of electric products & systems, having during that time developed connected solutions (ZigBee, Smart Energy), namely through the participation in consortium partnership projects. In end 2014, he was named advisor of Bosch Termotecnologia SA vice-president, a function that has accumulated with the coordination of industrialization projects for new products (PMO). Starting September 2018 he has the responsibility for the coordination of Manufacturing Digitalization (Industry 4.0) for all Bosch Thermotechnology plants worldwide.

Adelaide Freitas is an Associate Professor at Department of Mathematics. She has a MSc in Probability and Statistics from University of Lisbon (1991) and a PhD in Mathematics from University of Aveiro (1998). Her scientific activity has been mainly in the area of Multivariate Statistics, Probability and Statistics in Education, Extreme Value Theory, and Statistics application in several scientific areas (e.g., social, genomic, and health). Actually, her research interests include the development and applications of sparse principal components analysis and compositional data analysis.

Ana Freitas has a Bachelor Degree in Applied Mathematics and Statistics Degree from the University of Minho and a post-graduation in Business Intelligence and Analytics from Porto Business School. Her main interests are in customer insight forecasting, predictive models and customer behaviour segmentations in the retail space at SONAE MC.

Purificación Galindo-Villardón is Professor of Statistics of the University of Salamanca. Visiting Professor in 20 European and American universities, including Trinity College, University of Oxford, and the University of Reading (England), Stanford University of California (USA), UNIBE (Costa Rica), University of Algarve (Portugal), Veracruzana University (Mexico), University of Concepción, University of Temuco, and Bernardo O´Higgins (Chile), Central University of Venezuela and University of Oriente (Venezuela), University of Bariloche (Argentina), University of Panama, ESPOL University and UNEMI University in Ecuador. Former Chair of the international PhD program in Statistics and Former Head of the Department of Statistic. Vice-Rector for Health Sciences, Quality Management and Academic Policy. University of Salamanca. Spain. Director of 64 PhD theses. More than 100 papers published in high impact scientific journals. Awarded as the "Educator of the Year 2013" in Latin America, Brazil, Spain and Portugal by the "Juarez-Lincoln-Marti" Prize from USA. Maria de Maeztu Award for Scientific Excellence in 2016.

Julia Gallardo-Pérez is a professor in the Department of Financial Economics, Accounting and Operations Management, University of Huelva, Huelva, Spain.

Petia Georgieva is Professor in Machine Learning at the Department of Electronics Telecommunications and Informatics, University of Aveiro in Portugal and senior researcher at the Institute of Electronics Engineering and Telematics of Aveiro (IEETA). She holds a Master and PhD degrees in Control System Engineering from Technical University of Sofia and a PhD degree in Computer Science from Faculty of Engineering of University of Porto in Portugal. She has held several visiting positions. In particular, she was a visiting faculty at Carnegie Mellon University (CMU)-Silicon Valley CA in 2019 (Fall Semester), an invited professor at Rowan University, New Jersey, USA in 2016 (Spring Semester), a visiting faculty at CMU -Pittsburg, USA in 2012 (Fall Semester), an invited researcher at the University of Lancaster, UK in 2010 (Spring Semester). Dr. Georgieva is a Senior member of IEEE and a Senior Member of International Neural Network Society (INNS). Her research interests are in machine/deep learning and data mining with strong focus on computer vision, brain imaging, optical communications, wireless networks.

Petra Heck has been working in IT since 2002. She started as software engineer, then quality consultant and now lecturer Software Engineering. Petra has a PhD (quality of agile requirements) and started a research project on Applied Data Science and Software Engineering in February 2019. Petra holds talks on a regular basis and is author of several publications, amongst which the book (in Dutch) "Succes met de requirements".

Solène Le Bars holds PhD in cognitive neuroscience and neuropsychologist. Altran Lab, France.

Alfonso Infante Moro is a professor in the Department of Financial Economics, Accounting and Operations Management, University of Huelva, Huelva, Spain. Info: http://uajournals.com/alfonsoinfante/en/.

Juan Carlos Infante Moro is a professor in the Department of Financial Economics, Accounting and Operations Management, University of Huelva, Huelva, Spain. Info: http://uajournals.com/jcinfantemoro/en/.

Parth Patel is a ML enthusiast from the golden city of Ahmedabad. He wants to strive to make the world a better place by completing my endeavors. He has several machine learning projects that will tend towards the working of betterment of the world. One out of which is a chatbot that will make people's lives easier by having conversational command interfaces. The other is an illegal fish catching system to prevent the precious marine life of our oceans.

Riddhi Patel is a Software Engineer Intern at Gridscape Solutions, a Media Strategist at NinjaTalks, a Python Developer, a Machine Learning Enthusiast, and an Anchor.

Antoine Trad is a holder of a PhD in computer sciences degree and a DBA in business administration. He is a professor and a researcher at IBISTM in France. His research field's title is: "The Selection, Architecture, Decision Making, Controlling and Training Framework (STF) for Managers in Business Innovation and Transformation Projects"; where he published more than 60 articles on the subject. In this research project, he works on inspecting enterprise architecture solutions in business transformation projects; parallel to that he works as a consultant in enterprise architecture projects.

Alicia Izquierdo Yusta studied Economics and Business Administration in Valencia (Spain). She is assistant professor of Marketing at the University of Burgos. She received her PhD in Economics and Business Administration at the University of Burgos. She is director of the Degree in Tourism at the University of Burgos. Her research is published in international journals of business, management, and social issues such as Telematics and Informatics, Frontiers in Psychology, Service Business; European Journal of Marketing; Computers Human Behavior, Tourism Management, among others.

Norman Jacknis is currently a Senior Lecturer at Columbia University in the Technology Management Program where he teaches Machine Learning and Artificial Intelligence. He previously taught in and designed several courses for the Master's program in Applied Analytics. He is also a Senior Fellow at the Intelligent Community Forum Prior, Dr. Jacknis was Director of Cisco's IBSG Public Sector Group, where he worked with governments and businesses around the world on open innovation and technology-based strategies for marketing success. Before joining Cisco, he served more than ten years as CIO and Commissioner of Westchester County, New York government, where he was responsible for all technology and analytics, as well as technology-based economic development. Dr. Jacknis earned his BA, MA and PhD at Princeton University.

Mónica Jiménez-Hernández researcher at CIEMA (Research Center for Applied Multivariate Statistics of the University of Colima). Bachelor degree in Marketing at University of Colima and Master student in Analysis Advanced in Multivariate and Big Data at University of Salamanca, Spain. Experience in market research and digital marketing

Ana Jiménez-Zarco is Associate Professor of Innovation and Marketing Economics and Business Open University of Catalunya (UOC) and Part-Time professor at Marketing Department (ICADE-Pontificia of Comillas University). PhD in Economics and Business from the University of Castilla la Mancha and Graduate Building Models in Ecology and Natural Resource Management at the Polytechnic University of Catalonia. PhD thesis Award by the Institute of Economic Studies of Madrid. Evaluator at the European Union Programme (H2020-MSCA-ITN), is author of more than 70 articles in journals of national and international and serves as associate editor of Frontiers in Psychology Journal and Sustainability.

Özlem Karadağ Albayrak is married and has a son. She completed my primary, secondary and high school education in Istanbul. She then moved to Sakarya for university education. She graduated from Sakarya University, Department of Industrial Engineering in 1999. She worked in various companies in Istanbul for 12 years in quality, production planning, quality and production responsibility positions. She has been working as a lecturer at Kafkas University since 2013. She received her doctorate degree from Atatürk University, Department of Econometrics in 2019. She makes use of her experiences in the private sector in her lectures at the university. Later, along with my academic career, new research areas were directed to research. These areas are renewable energy sources, regional development, and logistics.

Marcel Kyas received his PhD from the University of Leiden in 2006. In his dissertation "Verifying OCL specifications of UML models", he developed compositional, computer-aided verification methods for object-oriented real-time systems. After that, he became a PostDoc at the University of Oslo. He researched type systems for dynamically evolving distributed systems. He became an assistant professor at the Freie Universität Berlin. He studied indoor positioning systems and their empirical validation. He published competitive positioning methods and an indoor positioning test-bed. Since 2015, he works at Reykjavik University. He extends his work on indoor positioning systems to distributed systems. Marcel studies statistical methods for the Internet of Things. In this context, he investigates telematics and computer security.

Markus Lamest is a PhD from Trinity College Dublin Ireland. He is interested in the area of enterprise risk management and AI governance.

Abdilahi Liban is the chief executive officer of QETC Education and Training Consultancy SDN. BHD – Malaysia, where he has been since 2018. From 2014 to 2018 he served as a part-time lecturer at Al-Madinah International University-Malaysia and Head of the Development and Training department. He received a B.IT (Hons) Information Systems Engineering. from Multimedia University - Malaysia in 2010, and a Master of Computer Science (Information Security) in 2012 from University Technology Malaysia. He received his Ph.D. in ICT from Al-Madinah International University in 2018. His research interests span both image processing and computer security. Dr. Abdilahi Liban served as an internal auditor of academic programs, university rankings and research.

Maria João Lopes is an Industry 4.0 Software Engineer at Bosch Thermotechnology, managing Industry 4.0 topics in several manufacturing plants across the world. She has a MSc in Physics Engineering with a specialization in Instrumentation from the University of Coimbra. Since 2019 she has been a student of the Doctorate in Business Innovation, a pioneer program from the University of Aveiro which aims to bring together professionals from the Industry and academia. The focus of this PhD is applying Machine Learning methods in a general way to be able to tackle different types of problems.

Sandra Maria Correia Loureiro's current research interests include relationship marketing and new technologies (VR, AR, AI), tourism marketing, and corporate social responsibility issues. She has published in top journals such as: Journal of retailing, Journal of business research, International journal of hospitality research, Journal of product and brand management, Journal of retailing and consumer services or International journal of tourism research. She recently won the 2012 Best Paper Premier Award presented by the Global Marketing Conference (comprised of EMAC, ANZMAC, KSMS, and the Japanese Association of Marketing). Highly Commended paper Award 2014 - 7th EuroMed Conference and EuroMed Research Business Institute (EMRBI), Highly Commended paper Award 2016 - 9th EuroMed Conference and EuroMed Research Business Institute (EMRBI), Best Paper Award 2016- IC-CMI 2016, Highly Commended paper in the 2017 Emerald Literati Network Awards for Excellence, Best Paper Award TomiWorld 2017 for Marketing, Promotion & Consumer Behavior and Highly Commended paper in the 2018 Emerald Literati Network Awards for Excellence and 2019. Best paper award at Global Management Conference 2019 GAMMA Paris.

Mara Teresa da Silva Madaleno has a Ph.D. in Economics from the University of Aveiro (UA) since 2011, under the subject "Essays on Energy Derivatives Pricing and Financial Risk Management". Is an effective member of the Research Unit on Governance, Competitiveness and Public Policies (GOVCOPP) and Vice-coordinator of the Research line Systems for Decision Support (SAD). Currently lectures Finance and Economics at the undergraduate, graduate MSc and Ph.D. levels as an Assistant Professor at the Department of Economics, Management, Industrial Engineering and Tourism (DEGEIT) at the UA.

María Pilar Martínez-Ruiz Cathedratic professor since 2018, 21 years of research, teaching, academic and management activity at the University, and more than 16 years since obtaining the PhD degree. 6 Doctoral Theses directed and presented between 2013 and 2019 (3 with International Doctorate Mention). 103 articles published in scientific journals, 95 of which have appeared in indexed journals of relative quality. More than 90 works presented in congresses, conferences and seminars.

João Lourenço Marques is assistant professor at the Department of Social, Political and Territorial Sciences of the University of Aveiro, lecturing courses in the areas of Urban and Regional Planning (in the field of quantitative methods and techniques to support decision making). PhD in Social Sciences by the University of Aveiro, he did a MsC in Innovation and Regional Development Policies, and his graduation studies in Urban and Regional Planning by the same university. Currently he is member of the research group on Planning and Innovation (GETIN_UA); and of the Research Unit in Governance, Competitiveness and Public Policies (GOVCOPP). He is currently coordinator of the Research Group of Systems for Decision Support – GOVCOPP; and director of the Master in Data Science for Social Sciences. His current area of interest is the development of tools and methodologies to support the decision in public policy. The application of these methodologies covers various issues (housing, demographics, mobility, planning, equipment and infrastructure, employment etc.) and various territorial levels (local to national scale).

M. Dolores Méndez Aparicio is a computer engineer and Marketing degree, PhD in Legal, Economic and Social Sciences. Since 2014, certification and active member in research at the Association for the Development of the Customer Experience, and in associations Interdisciplinary Research Group i2TIC, ACEDE and AEMARK organizations as a listener and participant in the research in the field of Customer Experience and digital behavior. Software development manager since 1982 in the Mutua Madrileña group, leader in the Spanish insurance sector. Collaborating professor at the Open University of Catalonia and reviewer of articles for prestigious magazines. As a researcher in digital client experience, she has published at various conferences, Congresses and reports. Last publication in Frontiers in Psychology.

Nigussie Mengesha is an Assistant Professor of Information Systems at the Goodman School of Business, Brock University in Canada. He teaches graduate and undergraduate courses such as Data Analysis and Business Modelling, Management of Information Systems and Technology, Database and Management of Information Systems and Technology. Prior to joining Brock University, Dr. Mengesha taught computer science and information systems courses at Ryerson University and Addis Ababa University. Dr. Nigussie Mengesha received his Ph.D. in Information Systems from the University of Oslo in Norway, and an MSc in Information Science from Addis Ababa University in Ethiopia. Dr. Mengesha's research areas include IT and Strategy, Data Analytics, Information Systems Implementation and Integration, Open Source Software, and ICT4D. He has published in Information Technologies and International Development (ITID), Electronic Journal of Information Systems in Developing Countries (EJISD), African Journal of Information Systems (AJIS), International Journal of Information Systems and Social Change (IJISSC), and major international conferences in information systems such as International Conference on Information Systems (ICIS) and International Federation of Information Processing (IFIP) WG9.4.

Filipe Miranda has a Master's Degree in Computer Degree from the University of Porto. His main areas of interest are machine learning research and data analysis. He is currently working as a data scientist on customer behaviour analysis and prediction in the retail sector.

Jorge Mora-Fernandez obtained his Ph.D. in Interactive Media, supervised by Lev Manovich and Sheldon Brown at CRCA and the VisArts Department, UCSan Diego, and by Isidro Moreno at Laboratory of Digital Culture, UCM-Spain, thanks to the European Union Social Funds and Community of Madrid

Grants. He obtained his M.F.A. in Interactive Media and Postdoctoral specialization at IMDivision, School of Cinematic Arts, University of Southern California- USC, with La Caixa and the Fulbright Commission Grants. Jorge Mora-Fernandez is a story-writer, director, line design producer and editor is supervisor specialized in avant garde narratives (parallel, interactive, multi-perspectives, transmedia circular...) for documentary and fictional projects (Fictions of Reality). He is currently post producing the documentary project DQR66, Don Quixotes in Route 66. A road movie documentary about the idealist people, from different cultures and origins, living in alternative ways along the Route 66 while keeping the history of the Mother Road and its principles alive. He is a Spanish-LatinAmerican initial-mid-career cinematic artist and researcher specialized in digital storytelling who is trying to develop his creative career between USA, Europe and Latin America. He did graduate studies in California, developing later on digital narratives & multicultural cooperation projects between Latin-America-USA-Europe, such as founding the first videoart/animation LatinAmerican Festival Video Babel http://www.festivalvideobabel.org/SobreElFestivalEng.htm or the Media Literacy Workshops https://www.youtube.com/user/multiculturalvideos/videos ; mostly focus on underrepresented communities, multiculturalism, independent perspectives and recovery from addictions. He has obtained several international awards, workshops scholarship and grants as screenwriter and director of shortfilms and researcher in the areas of cinema and new media narratives: Festival Internacional de Cine de Guadalajara FICG (Between Lives Script Selected by the Program Iberoamerican Films Crossing Borders, http://www.drjorgemora.com/wp-content/uploads/2015/05/DossierEntreVidasBetweenLivesDr.JorgeMora.compressed.pdf), Festival de Cannes (Inside Track Transmedia Short-Film Awarded by the Program European Films Crossing Borders Short Film Corners https://youtu.be/j8RR-rCq1jI), Imperial Beach International Film Festival (Avant-Garde Best Short Film for Inside Track, https://youtu.be/j8RR-rCq1jI), Harold Lloyd Foundation and Electronic Arts Foundation (for his project www.multiculturalvideos.org project https://vimeo.com/129149879), an online interactive museum based on short documentaries and artistic videos, advised by Marsha Kinder Steve Anderson. Best Audiovisual Project Award by Injuve (Institute of the Youth), Spanish Ministry of Social Affairs and MediaLabMadrid presented on traveling exhibitions in all Latin-America, Short Film Corner at Cannes Festival, Festival International de Cine de Guadalajara FICG, Seoul Interactive Film Festival, International Festival of Human Rights, etc. . Inside Track was broadcasted at Canal-Arte in Europe and on La2 Spanish National-Television (https://youtu.be/j8RR-rCq1jI/https://vimeo.com/127994381). Saint Mary of Europe Best Short Film Award for his short Film Nobody, https://youtu.be/aGUI3vnBH4U, and the Imperial Beach Film Festival Award for the Best Avant Garde Short Film. He has also received grants, collaborations and recognitions from the Fulbright Commission, Siggraph, United Nations, UNESCO, AECID Spanish Agency of International Cooperation, https://youtu.be/6GCd1fLMDZI, EAP UCSD (University of California San Diego), FPI CAM EU, La Caixa, Prometheus Program, etc. His transmedia scripts were selected at Iberoamerican-Films-Crossing-Borders Program, FICG, and at European-Films-Crossing-Borders, Cannes Festival.

José Moreira received his Ph.D. in Computer Science and Networks from the École Nationale Supérieure des Télécommunications de Paris (France) and the Faculdade de Engenharia da Universidade do Porto (Portugal) in 2001. He is currently an Assistant Professor at the Department of Electronics, Telecommunications and Informatics of the Universidade de Aveiro and a researcher at IEETA, a non-profit R&D institute affiliated to the same university. His background includes programming languages, data structures and databases. His main research interests cover spatiotemporal database systems and

Geographical Information Systems. He is also interested on spatiotemporal data analysis and knowledge engineering.

Elissa Moses is Founder & CEO, BrainGroup Global, Partner, HARK Connect and Bellwether Citizen Response, former CEO Ipsos Neuro & Behavioral Science, faculty at Columbia University on AI/ML, neuromarketing innovator, brand, advertising and technology expert. Marketing strategist with expertise in innovation, emotion and the consumer decision process . Published book, chapter and academic journal author; frequent global speaker. Advisor for boards and start-ups. Education: MS Technology Management, Columbia University and AB Human Behavior, University of Chicago.

Helena Nobre is an Assistant Professor at the Dept. of Economics, Management, Industrial Engineering and Tourism, and Researcher at the Research Unit of Governance, Competitiveness and Public Policy (GOVCOPP), at the University of Aveiro. She is an Associate Editor of the RBGN-Review of Business Management (indexed by SCOPUS Elsevier and Thomson Reuters: SSCI, JCR), and she is a member of the Editorial Board of the International Journal of Consumer Studies (Impact factor: 1.506 - ISI Journal Citation Reports © Ranking: 2018:112/147 (Business). Her main research topics are in Branding and Consumer Behavior, in particular, luxury brands, and consumer experience. Her work is published in reputable academic journals.

Rafal Ohme (PhD) is a psychologist, expert in emotions, communication and consumer neuroscience. He is a professor at WSB University in Torun and Stellenbosch University in South Africa. He held a Fulbright scholarship at Kellogg School of Management, at Stanford University he conducted research on unconscious emotions. Awarded by the President and the Prime Minister of Poland, a finalist of EY Entrepreneur of the Year 2015 program. Founder of NEUROHM, a smart tech company which licenses new research tools for HR, sales, marketing & PR. Author of articles, chapters and books including Mind Spa (2019), Emo Sapiens (2017), Unconscious Affect (2007), Subliminal Facial Information (2003), and trilogy on Automaticity (2001, 2003, 2003). Writes for Forbes.

Jan Tore Pedersen is Managing Director of Marlo a.s. He holds an MSc in Control engineering and a PhD in manufacturing from the Norwegian University of Science and Technology (NTNU) and an MSc in Computer Science from University of California at Santa Barbara. Since the early 1990ies, Dr Pedersen has been active in EU and national projects for development of innovative logistics solutions and related information technologies. Noticeable projects are e-Freight (DG MOVE) and iCargo (DG CONNECT). Since 2012, Marlo collaborated with 3M, DHL and Gebrüder Weiss to develop the Software-as-a-Service solution MixMoveMatch – aimed to ensure that transportation resources are utilised to their maximum capacity. In 2017, this development led to forming the company MIXMOVE, which is now further commercialising the MIXMOCE Solutions. Before founding Marlo, his experience includes business and technology development of advanced software systems (The Kongsberg Group), and business- and technology development in the maritime sector (The Kvaerner Group), including an integrated system for ships covering all on-board control and navigation capabilities. From 1995 to 1998, Dr Pedersen held a part-time position as professor at the Technical University of Norway in the field of mechatronics. From October 2009 until September 2011, he was an adjunct professor in logistics at the BI Norwegian Business School.

Andrea Piccaluga is Full Professor of Innovation management at the Institute of Management and delegate for Technology Transfer at Scuola Superiore Sant'Anna, Pisa. He has published several articles in leading management journals, including R&D Management Journal, Small Business Economics, California Management Review, Journal of Technology Transfer, Journal of Knowledge Management, Technology Analysis & Strategic Management, European Management Journal, and Creativity and Innovation Management. His research and teaching mainly deal with: R&D and innovation management; open innovation; and the collaboration between firms and research institutions in the innovation process.

Ilhem Quenel is in charge of the Applied AI research program at the Research and Innovation Department of Capgemini Engineering. During his PhD thesis, he worked on the application of metaheuristics (which are bio-inspired algorithms) to solve complex problems. Before joining ALTRAN 3 years ago, he was a lecturer at the University of Algiers for ten years.

Mrugendrasinh Rahevar is an Assistant professor in U &P U. Patel Department of Computer Engineering, CHARUSAT University, Gujarat, India. He received his B.E.C.E. from Gujarat University in 2006 and M.E.C.S.E. from Gujarat Technological University in 2014. Currently pursuing PhD in action recognition. His research interest includes Computer vision and deep learning.

Dorota Reykowska has over 14 years of experience in marketing research, helping build brands, generate insights, transform data into brand stories. Currently responsible for leading the R&D department in NEUROHM. Previously held the position of a Research Director in research and media agencies. Specializes in quantitative research. Expert in non-declarative studies, and application of innovative technologies to testing emotions and attitudes. Involved in the development of biometric methodology and creation of the first polish neuromarketing project. A participant and speaker on many conferences both scientific (e.g. ICORIA, NeuroPsychoEconomics), and industry (ARF, PTBRiO, Neuroconnections, etc.). A co-author of publications in polish and international journals/books.

Juan Rivera Medina has extensive work experience in the implementation of strategies and programs in public institutions linked to the Presidency of the PCM Council of Ministers; National Civil Service Authority SERVIR, National Fund for Compensation and Social Development FONCODES, Ministry of Tourism and Foreign Trade MINCETUR, Program National Agrarian Innovation PNIA, PRONAA-MIDIS National Food Assistance Program. More than 8 years of experience in advanced teaching in postgraduate degrees and three years in undergraduate degrees. Work experience with multidisciplinary, multicultural and multilingual teams in various rural regions of Peru and abroad on issues of public management, planning and foresight, strategic direction, leadership and social responsibility, conflict management and research project management in the field of social innovation.

Eugénio M. Rocha is professor of the department of mathematics and researcher at CIDMA, Univ. of Aveiro, with a PhD in Mathematics and a degree in Computer Science (artificial Intelligence), has more than 90 publications in theoretical mathematics (e.g., partial differential equations or hybrid systems) and applications into Biology, Civil Engineering, Chemistry, Econometrics, Education, and Industry. Coordinator of several projects with the Industry.

Mariana Rodrigues completed her Master in Marketing at ISCTE Business School, in Lisbon. After working as a copywriter for hospitality, sports and art brands, she recently focused her professional path on content marketing for a technology company.

Deepak Saxena is an Assistant Professor at the Department of Management at Birla Institute of Technology & Science Pilani (India). Prior to this, he worked as a Research Fellow at Trinity College Dublin and as an Assistant Lecturer at Dublin Institute of Technology. He has published with the journals such as Australasian Journal of Information Systems, Journal of Information Science, Irish Journal of Management, Electronic Journal of Business Research Methods, and Electronic Journal of Information Systems Evaluations.

Gerard Schouten is a professor at the School of ICT, Fontys University of Applied Science and research fellow at the Jheronimus Academy of Data Science, both situated in The Netherlands. He holds a master's degree in physics and has a PhD in the field of cognitive science. He is a self-made deep learning and machine learning practitioner and is experienced in large-scale software development in the healthcare industry. He is member of the Methodology Advisory Board of Statistics Netherlands and the AI Advisory Broad of the province of Noord-Brabant. He initiated a new educational program on AI engineering at Fontys UAS. His research covers a wide array of topics in the broad field of AI, with a special interest in solutions that benefit society and foster our natural environment.

Nandini Sen is an anthropologist who has done her PhD (social anthropology) from Goethe University, Frankfurt, Germany, and Masters from the University of St Andrews (Social Anthropology), Scotland, UK. Her anthropological experience with the waste pickers "Urban Marginalisation in South Asia: Waste Pickers in Calcutta" was published by Routledge in 2018. Now it has been turned into a paperback edition since August 2020 after being well acclaimed by academicians and peers. Nandini had published her paper "Women and Gender in Short Stories by Rabindranath Tagore, An Anthropological Introspection on Kinship and Family' in Anthropological Journal of European Cultures in 2016. Her book chapter, How Bollywood Filmdom Operates in India and the International Arena, Consumption of Bollywood, was published in Anthropological Approaches to Understanding Consumption Patterns and Consumer Behaviour published by IGI, Global, 2020. In 2021 she has co-authored 'Gender-based Violence in India in Covid-19 lockdown'. It is published in Journal of Comparative Literature and Aesthetics, 2021. In 2020, she has published an essay, 'Pandemics, Covid-19, and literary studies, past and present' in Covid-19 Perspectives, University of Edinburgh. She has also co-authored few essays on Indian situations in Covid-19 lockdown in different academic blogs, Department of Law and Anthropology, University of Edinburgh, 2020.

Elena Serova, Assoc Prof, Ph.D. in Economics, is working now in National Research University Higher School of Economics St. Petersburg Branch. Her role combines teaching and research in equal measure. Her research interests are related to Business Analysis, Strategic Management, Marketing, and Information Management. She has co-authored books and collections of essays, regular key presenter at national and international conferences. As a research-active academic with a number of Ph.D. Students under her supervision, Elena is focusing on Complex Information Systems Modeling and Business Models in Global Environment.

Özge Sığırcı is an Assistant Professor of Marketing at Kirklareli University, Turkey. She received her Ph.D. in Marketing from Marmara University, where she also worked as a research assistant. During her Ph.D. studies, she was awarded a scholarship from the Scientific and Technological Research Council of Turkey and spent a semester at the University of Texas at Dallas as a visiting scholar. Her research interests include consumer-artificial intelligence interaction, sustainable consumption, consumer food consumption, and behavioral pricing. Her publications appeared in the Journal of Marketing and Marketing Research, Bogazici Journal, and Journal of Global Fashion Marketing. She loves playing tennis and practicing yoga.

Dora Simões received her PhD in Informatics Engineering from University of Porto, Portugal, in 2008. Actually, she is an Assistant Professor in computer science area, at the Higher Institute of Accounting and Administration – University of Aveiro (ISCA-UA), Portugal. She is member of DigiMedia Research Centre. Her current research interests include data management, organizational information systems, relationship marketing and collaborative virtual networks, and information and communication technologies in education. She has two books by IGI Global and in various conferences and journals, nationals and internationals.

Joshua Springer is a PhD student in computer science at Reykjavik University. His primary focus is control methods for autonomous, multi-rotor drones.

Nathalia Tejedor Flores is a PhD in Applied Multivariate Statistics, a full-time researcher at the Hydraulic and Hydrotechnical Research Center, professor at the Civil Engineering Faculty of the Technological University of Panama and member of the National Research System of Panamá (SNI). She is an environmental engineer with more than 5 years of experience in teaching and research, a specialist in data analysis, R-Statistical-Package, Sustainable Development, Water-Energy-Food Nexus.

Elizabete Thomas is a specialist at the National Waterway Transportation Agency, Brazil.

Adalberto Tokarski is Director at the National Waterway Transportation Agency, Brazil

Ana Maria Tomé is an Associate Professor at the Department of Electronics, Telecommunications and Informatics of the University of Aveiro, Researcher at the Laboratory of Biomedical Systems and Technologies at the Institute of Electronic Engineering and Telematics of Aveiro (IEETA). Scientific activity in digital processing, pattern recognition and machine learning for biomedical applications. The application and development of unsupervised algebraic techniques for extraction of relevant information in biomedical signals has been the focus of his activity in recent years. She has participated in several projects under the responsibility of IEETA.

Muhammad Tufail has a Ph.D. Degree in Economics from the National University of Sciences and Technology (NUST), Pakistan (Specialization in the field of Environmental and Resource Economics), a master's degree in Economics (Specialization in Technological Innovation, Economic Growth) from NUST, and a Bachelor's degree in Economics from the University of Malakand. Dr. Tufail is an Exchange Researcher at the Institute of Agronomy, University of Lisbon, and an Associate Researcher in the group of Decision Support System in the unit of Governance Competitiveness and Public Policy,

University of Aveiro, Portugal. In his research, Dr. Tufail primarily focuses on coupling economic and ecological systems to evaluate natural resource (forest) degradation issues. While interested in many natural resources, part of his work focuses on the Himalayas and Hindu Kush conifer forest region and evaluating the economic and ecological implications of natural resources degradation to the region. He enjoys working with students and engaging students of all backgrounds and interests. He is an experienced researcher with a demonstrated history of working in the Research Industry Higher Education Commission (HEC) Pakistan, International organizations such as the International Union for Conservation of Nature (IUCN), Food and Agricultural Organization (FAO), Institute of Environmental Sciences and Engineering (IESE), National University of Sciences and Technology (NUST). Skilled in Econometric Software; (STATA, SPSS, Eviews, OxMetrics, MiniTab), Microsoft Excel, Microsoft Word, Data Analysis, Quantitative and Qualitative Research, Data Science, Report Writing, and Policy Analyst. Consultant on Assessment of Economic Valuation of Chilgoza Forest (IUCN, FAO). Consultant on Assessment of Economic Valuation of SMOGE Episodes in Pakistan (IESE, NUST, HEC).

Erika Velásquez Chacón is an economist, Master with a mention in Social Management and Sustainable Development, held positions in public and private entities for more than 20 years, an expert in development projects. Current adviser and consultant in government entities. Undergraduate teacher at the Universidad Católica San Pablo and Postgraduate at the Universidad Nacional de San Agustín de Arequipa. Speaker at conferences of the Latin American Council of Management Schools (CLADEA), in 2012 (Peru) 2013 (Brazil) 2018 (Costa Rica) 2019 (Peru) 2020 (Virtual). Speaker at the Peruvian Congress of Economic History (2019). Speaker at CAPIC (2020). Winner of the Pacific Alliance Grant - Mexico (2020). Acceptance of article and presentation at the Twentieth Ibero-American Conference on Systems, Cybernetics and Informatics CISCI (2021).

Purificación Vicente-Galindo is Professor of Statistics. Chair of the international PhD program in Statistics and Head of the Department of Statistic. University of Salamanca, Spain. Visiting Professor in European and American universities, including Trinity College, UNIBE (Costa Rica), University of Algarve (Portugal), Veracruzana University (Mexico), University of Panama, ESPOL University and UNEMI University in Ecuador. Director of 20 PhD theses. More than 40 papers published in high impact scientific journals.

Index

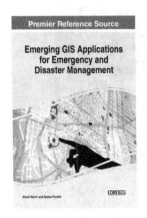
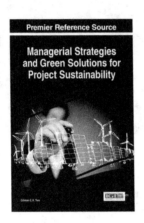

IGI Global Author Services

Providing a high-quality, affordable, and expeditious service, IGI Global's Author Services enable authors to streamline their publishing process, increase chance of acceptance, and adhere to IGI Global's publication standards.

Benefits of Author Services:

- **Professional Service:** All our editors, designers, and translators are experts in their field with years of experience and professional certifications.

- **Quality Guarantee & Certificate:** Each order is returned with a quality guarantee and certificate of professional completion.

- **Timeliness:** All editorial orders have a guaranteed return timeframe of 3-5 business days and translation orders are guaranteed in 7-10 business days.

- **Affordable Pricing:** IGI Global Author Services are competitively priced compared to other industry service providers.

- **APC Reimbursement:** IGI Global authors publishing Open Access (OA) will be able to deduct the cost of editing and other IGI Global author services from their OA APC publishing fee.

Author Services Offered:

English Language Copy Editing
Professional, native English language copy editors improve your manuscript's grammar, spelling, punctuation, terminology, semantics, consistency, flow, formatting, and more.

Scientific & Scholarly Editing
A Ph.D. level review for qualities such as originality and significance, interest to researchers, level of methodology and analysis, coverage of literature, organization, quality of writing, and strengths and weaknesses.

Figure, Table, Chart & Equation Conversions
Work with IGI Global's graphic designers before submission to enhance and design all figures and charts to IGI Global's specific standards for clarity.

Translation
Providing 70 language options, including Simplified and Traditional Chinese, Spanish, Arabic, German, French, and more.

Hear What the Experts Are Saying About IGI Global's Author Services

*"Publishing with IGI Global has been **an amazing experience** for me for sharing my research. The **strong academic production** support ensures quality and timely completion."* – **Prof. Margaret Niess, Oregon State University, USA**

*"The service was **very fast, very thorough, and very helpful** in ensuring our chapter meets the criteria and requirements of the book's editors. I was **quite impressed and happy** with your service."* – **Prof. Tom Brinthaupt, Middle Tennessee State University, USA**

Learn More or Get Started Here:

For Questions, Contact IGI Global's Customer Service Team at cust@igi-global.com or 717-533-8845

IGI Global
PUBLISHER of TIMELY KNOWLEDGE
www.igi-global.com

www.igi-global.com

Publisher of Peer-Reviewed, Timely, and
Innovative Academic Research Since 1988

IGI Global's Transformative Open Access (OA) Model:
How to Turn Your University Library's Database Acquisitions Into a Source of OA Funding

Well in advance of Plan S, IGI Global unveiled their OA Fee Waiver (Read & Publish) Initiative. Under this initiative, librarians who invest in IGI Global's InfoSci-Books and/or InfoSci-Journals databases will be able to subsidize their patrons' OA article processing charges (APCs) when their work is submitted and accepted (after the peer review process) into an IGI Global journal.

How Does it Work?

Step 1: **Library Invests in the InfoSci-Databases:** A library perpetually purchases or subscribes to the InfoSci-Books, InfoSci-Journals, or discipline/subject databases.

Step 2: **IGI Global Matches the Library Investment with OA Subsidies Fund:** IGI Global provides a fund to go towards subsidizing the OA APCs for the library's patrons.

Step 3: **Patron of the Library is Accepted into IGI Global Journal (After Peer Review):** When a patron's paper is accepted into an IGI Global journal, they option to have their paper published under a traditional publishing model or as OA.

Step 4: **IGI Global Will Deduct APC Cost from OA Subsidies Fund:** If the author decides to publish under OA, the OA APC fee will be deducted from the OA subsidies fund.

Step 5: **Author's Work Becomes Freely Available:** The patron's work will be freely available under CC BY copyright license, enabling them to share it freely with the academic community.

Note: This fund will be offered on an annual basis and will renew as the subscription is renewed for each year thereafter. IGI Global will manage the fund and award the APC waivers unless the librarian has a preference as to how the funds should be managed.

Hear From the Experts on This Initiative:

"I'm very happy to have been able to make one of my recent research contributions *freely available* along with having access to the *valuable resources* found within IGI Global's InfoSci-Journals database."

– **Prof. Stuart Palmer**,
Deakin University, Australia

"Receiving the support from IGI Global's OA Fee Waiver Initiative *encourages me to continue my research work without any hesitation*."

– **Prof. Wenlong Liu**, College of Economics and Management at Nanjing University of Aeronautics & Astronautics, China

For More Information, Scan the QR Code or Contact:
IGI Global's Digital Resources Team at eresources@igi-global.com.

Printed in the United States
by Baker & Taylor Publisher Services